Freedoms Delayed

According to diverse indices of political performance, the Middle East is the world's least free region. Some believe that it is Islam that hinders liberalization. Others retort that Islam cannot be a factor because the region is no longer governed under Islamic law. This book by Timur Kuran, author of the influential *Long Divergence*, explores the lasting political effects of the Middle East's lengthy exposure to Islamic law. It identifies several channels through which Islamic institutions, both defunct and still active, have limited the expansion of basic freedoms under political regimes of all stripes: secular dictatorships, electoral democracies, monarchies legitimated through Islam, and theocracies. Kuran suggests that Islam's rich history carries within it the seeds of liberalization on many fronts; and that the Middle East has already established certain prerequisites for a liberal order. But there is no quick fix for the region's prevailing record on human freedoms.

TIMUR KURAN is Professor of Economics and Political Science, and Gorter Family Professor of Islamic Studies at Duke University. His publications include *Private Truths, Public Lies: The Social Consequences of Preference Falsification* (1995) and *The Long Divergence: How Islamic Law Held Back the Middle East* (2011), each widely translated.

Freedoms Delayed

*Political Legacies of Islamic Law
in the Middle East*

TIMUR KURAN
Duke University

CAMBRIDGE
UNIVERSITY PRESS

CAMBRIDGE
UNIVERSITY PRESS

Shaftesbury Road, Cambridge CB2 8EA, United Kingdom

One Liberty Plaza, 20th Floor, New York, NY 10006, USA

477 Williamstown Road, Port Melbourne, VIC 3207, Australia

314–321, 3rd Floor, Plot 3, Splendor Forum, Jasola District Centre, New Delhi – 110025, India

103 Penang Road, #05–06/07, Visioncrest Commercial, Singapore 238467

Cambridge University Press is part of Cambridge University Press & Assessment, a department of the University of Cambridge.

We share the University's mission to contribute to society through the pursuit of education, learning and research at the highest international levels of excellence.

www.cambridge.org
Information on this title: www.cambridge.org/9781009320016
DOI: 10.1017/9781009320009

© Timur Kuran 2023

This publication is in copyright. Subject to statutory exception and to the provisions of relevant collective licensing agreements, no reproduction of any part may take place without the written permission of Cambridge University Press & Assessment.

First published 2023

Printed in the United Kingdom by TJ Books Limited, Padstow Cornwall

A catalogue record for this publication is available from the British Library.

Library of Congress Cataloging-in-Publication Data
NAMES: Kuran, Timur, author.
TITLE: Freedoms delayed : political legacies of Islamic Law in the Middle East / Timur Kuran, Duke University, North Carolina.
DESCRIPTION: Cambridge, United Kingdom ; New York, NY : Cambridge University Press, 2023. | Includes bibliographical references and index.
IDENTIFIERS: LCCN 2022057792 (print) | LCCN 2022057793 (ebook) | ISBN 9781009320016 (hardback) | ISBN 9781009320023 (paperback) | ISBN 9781009320009 (epub)
SUBJECTS: LCSH: Public law–Middle East. | Human rights–Middle East. | Middle East–Politics and government. | Law–Middle East–Islamic influences.
CLASSIFICATION: LCC KMC510 .K87 2023 (print) | LCC KMC510 (ebook) | DDC 340/.11–dc23/eng/20230208
LC record available at https://lccn.loc.gov/2022057792
LC ebook record available at https://lccn.loc.gov/2022057793

ISBN 978-1-009-32001-6 Hardback

Cambridge University Press & Assessment has no responsibility for the persistence or accuracy of URLs for external or third-party internet websites referred to in this publication and does not guarantee that any content on such websites is, or will remain, accurate or appropriate.

In memory of four teachers who inspired, encouraged, and
taught me to think across boundaries

Neriman Hızır (1908–1985)

Leon Gersten (1930–1986)

Grady Hobson (1926–2011)

Kenneth Arrow (1921–2017)

Contents

List of Figures	*page* ix
List of Tables	xi
Preface	xiii

PART I THE MODERN MIDDLE EAST'S AUTHORITARIAN FACE

1	Islam and Political Underdevelopment	3
2	Explaining Illiberalism, Identifying Opportunities for Liberalization	33

PART II PERSISTENT SOCIAL ATOMIZATION

3	Nongovernmental Organizations under Islamic Law	47
4	The Political Impotence of Islamic Waqfs	60
5	Waqf Corruption and Its Degradation of Civic Life	77
6	The Islamic Waqf's Long Civic Shadow	89

PART III RELIGIOUS REPRESSION

7	Religious Freedoms in Middle Eastern History	111
8	The Marginalization of Islam	133
9	The Resurgence of Assertive Islamism	147
10	Religious Diversification, in Fact and in Law	171
11	The Absence of Liberal Islamic Schisms	190

PART IV ECONOMIC HINDRANCES

12 Unshackled States, Shallow Economic Governance   213
13 Politically Powerless Entrepreneurs and Enterprises   232
14 Islamism's Missed Opportunities to Promote Liberalism 254

PART V CONCLUSION

15 Islamic Institutions and Muslim Freedoms   269

Notes   287
Bibliography 341
Index   411

Figures

1.1	The Middle East and the rest of the Organization of Islamic Cooperation	page 7
1.2	Periodization of Middle Eastern history and chronology of major political events	10
1.3	Desire to migrate: Middle East in global perspective	12
1.4	Civil liberties: Middle East in global perspective	12
1.5	Rule of law: Middle East in global perspective	13
1.6	Government cleanliness: Middle East in global perspective	13
3.1	Generalized trust: Middle East in global perspective	48
3.2	Typology of waqfs	56
4.1	Factors that limited the political power of waqfs	61
6.1	Number of new regular Islamic waqfs registered in Istanbul courts, 1453–1923	92
6.2	Political participation (percentage of population): Middle East in global perspective	98
6.3	Self-reported voting in last election (percentage of population): Middle East in global perspective	99
6.4	Trends in measures of political performance for Arab League, Iran, and Turkey: Freedom House Civil Liberty (1972–2020) and Polity (1946–2019)	102
6.5	Percentage of out-marriages: Middle East in global perspective	104
9.1	Freedom from government restrictions on religion: Middle East in global perspective	164
9.2	Freedom from government limitations on religious conversion: Middle East in global perspective	165
9.3	Government impartiality toward religion: Middle East in global perspective	165

9.4	Freedom from social regulation of religion: Middle East in global perspective	166
9.5	Freedom of the press: Middle East in global perspective	167
9.6	Internet freedoms: Middle East in global perspective	167
9.7	Where World Values Survey question on religiosity was not asked: Middle East in global perspective	168
9.8	Where World Values Survey question on belief in God was not asked: Middle East in global perspective	169
10.1	Two stylized schisms	
	(a) One religious community spawning a second and third	179
	(b) A single religious community splitting in two	179
10.2	Gender equality in global perspective: composite index	183
10.3	Gender equality in political empowerment: Middle East in global perspective	183
10.4	Gender equality in educational attainment: Middle East in global perspective	184

Tables

3.1 Waqf assets or revenues: estimates *page* 53
3.2 Restrictions on the two main investment instruments of classical Islamic law 57
6.1 Characteristics of Islamic and modern waqfs 95
6.2 Four indices of civic life: Middle East in global perspective 102

Preface

Not long ago I attended a conference on Islam and liberty. A participant confessed that he once decided to list everything that some authority considers un-Islamic. "A few hours later, the work was not yet finished," he said, with an air of desperation. Restrictions of the kind that entered his list are integral to Islam's current image. For many Muslims, but also huge numbers of others, they are among the features that have come to differentiate Islam from other religions. Examples of restrictions associated with Islam include constraints on female mobility, the prohibition of charging or paying interest, the shutting of restaurants during Ramadan fasting hours, and speech codes that inhibit honest discourse on Islamic practices.

One can also list what a religion enables. Islam is central to communal life in many places. It forges global bonds. In certain contexts, it builds interpersonal trust. For all such benefits, Islam does little to facilitate civic engagement. And, outside of explicitly religious domains, it hardly helps private groups organize to achieve common goals. The failure of the "Arab Spring" is among the manifestations of Islam's chronic links with weak private organization.

The euphoria that erupted in 2011 was misplaced, I suggested a few months after the unexpected Egyptian Revolution, in a *New York Times* op-ed, "The Weak Foundations of Arab Democracy." A sustainably liberal social order is impossible, I wrote, in a region lacking a tradition of "autonomous nongovernmental organizations serving as intermediaries between the individual and the state." More than a decade later, the preconditions of a liberal order are still lacking across the Middle East. A key reason is that Islam, the region's majority religion for a millennium, has failed to generate the organizational means for preventing arbitrary governance.

In parts of the Middle East, Islamic law was abrogated formally a century ago, as the region was modernizing hurriedly in response to existential fears. And in the rest, it continues to be enforced only on matters minimally relevant to political checks and balances. Nevertheless, Islamic law casts a dark shadow on social capabilities. Though the region has achieved vast transformations since the 1800s, insufficient experience holds back grassroots politics. That legacy is rooted in Islamic institutions. Meanwhile, personal freedoms remain limited because of inabilities, also grounded in legal history, to assert and defend individual rights. In a nutshell, that is this book's main message. With respect to the near future, it exudes pessimism on the grounds that liberalizers cannot organize effectively.

Reasons exist for optimism about the longer term. Precisely because Islamic law has generally been discarded, barriers to civic engagement have fallen. Though still weak, civil society is developing. The resonance of Islam's premodern interpretations is fading. By no means do all practicing Muslims accept all, or even most, prohibitions of the kind that made it into my colleague's list. Signs of growing resistance include the proliferation of hidden conversions out of Islam. It so happens that few of the troubling bans are grounded explicitly or unequivocally in Islam's most authoritative source, the Quran. In each case, alternative readings allow much discretion. For instance, the fasting requirement accommodates broad exceptions. Evidently, modernizing Islam's interpretation is by no means impossible.

Among my goals is to highlight the availability within Islam's rich heritage of resources for liberalizing how it is understood and practiced. If the history of Islam's apostasy rules were better understood, early Islamic policies commonly viewed as banning Muslim out-conversion would be treated as acts to build state capacity rather than restrict religious choice. If it were understood why zakat, now a form of charity of minor economic significance, ranks among Islam's canonical five pillars, the Quran could be read as promoting private property rights and constraining government. Islamic teachings harbor liberal principles antithetical to movements that treat Islam as a prohibition machine.

If many freedoms now taken for granted around the world are widely treated as un-Islamic, it is not because Muslims are inherently conservative. Contrary to claims of many Islamists, the "Islamic way of life" was never fixed or uniform. Only since the nineteenth century has Islam appeared out of tune with the prevailing global norms of liberty. Four centuries ago, Europe's Thirty Years War sowed devastation in the name of religious purity; and as recently as the nineteenth century, Christians were less free to debate their doctrinal differences, and Jews were relatively less welcome, in Christian-controlled Europe than in Muslim-governed lands. Such patterns make it particularly baffling that Europe took the lead in expanding various freedoms. Why has the Middle East *become* extraordinarily repressive?

The research in this book began as an effort to explain the economic and political underdevelopment of the Middle East through a unified theory. It quickly became obvious that the task would result in an overly thick tome liable to exhaust the patience of even a motivated reader. I decided then to split the project in two. The chapters focused on economic underdevelopment went into *The Long Divergence: How Islamic Law Held Back the Middle East* (2011). This sequel emphasizes political underdevelopment, which entails weak personal freedoms. The freedoms in question include those made possible through checks and balances, organized and persistent collective action, and belief systems. If autocracy is one manifestation of weak freedoms, others are feeble civil society, poor political accountability, religious repression, and politically marginalized entrepreneurs and enterprises. The complementarities between the two books will be apparent in overlaps among the structures to which they give center stage. Several institutions explored in the 2011 book for their economic effects – the Islamic waqf, the Islamic inheritance system, Islamic partnerships – reappear here with a focus on their political legacies. Additional Islamic institutions – the transfer system known as zakat, punishments for apostasy, blasphemy, and heresy – also play major roles. Their interactions with those in the first group will be of special interest to readers focused on the economic legacies of Islamic law.

Many people and organizations contributed to this endeavor. My deepest indebtedness is to my wife Wendy, who provided a supportive home environment and helped my ideas mature through probing questions and insightful feedback.

The book's initial draft was critiqued at a conference organized on 21–22 March 2019 by the Mercatus Center's F. A. Hayek Program for Advanced Study in Philosophy, Politics, and Economics. While I could not possibly address all the suggestions articulated there, many refinements and major extensions resulted from the rich conversation on the work's structure and themes. For taking time from their busy schedules to read and critique the draft, I am grateful to all the participants: Eva Bellin, Lisa Blaydes, discussion leader Peter Boettke, Mahmoud El-Gamal, Noel Johnson, Mark Koyama, Avital Livny, Jennifer Murtazashvili, and Jared Rubin. I owe a debt of gratitude also to the staff who handled the logistics: Giorgio Castiglia, Malia Delasandry, Steffanie Haeffele, and Haley Larsen.

Very few books benefit from even a single pre-publication conference. This one was fortunate enough to have two. The manuscript's second draft received rich feedback on 29–30 July 2021 at a conference organized over Zoom by the Religious Freedom Institute. The participants were Mustafa Akyol, Masooda Bano, Alexandra Blackman, Nathan Brown, Amaney Jamal, Mirjam Kuenkler, Ahmet Kuru, Richard Nielsen, John Owen, and moderator Timothy Shah. I thank all of them for abundant insights that took me a year to process and address. Suggestions on framing the argument and linking its components were especially valuable. Nathan Berkeley and Michaela Scott made the event run smoothly.

Scores of scholars contributed to the book's development, often unknowingly, by answering specific questions, correcting misperceptions, reacting to presentations, and discussing issues. Though I could not possibly name everyone who was helpful, I am particularly grateful, in addition to those already named, to Cihan Artunç, Chad Bauman, Fahad Bishara, Henry Hansmann, Murat Iyigun, Faisal Khan, Tine De Moor, Jean-Philippe Platteau, Jan Luiten Van Zanden, Taisu Zhang, and Jaco Zuijderduijn. Several scholars served as coauthor of one or more articles related to themes developed here. As with any tight collaboration, what I learned through these projects transcended the findings reported in our joint articles. For their collaborations, I am grateful to Serkant Adıgüzel, Aslı Cansunar, Murat Çokgezen, Nisan Görgülü, Scott Lustig, and again Jared Rubin. Special appreciation goes to participants at the annual and thematic conferences of AALIMS (Association for Analytic Learning about Islam and Muslim Societies), which I have attended regularly since its founding in 2010. I have come away from each AALIMS conference intellectually energized and bubbling with new ideas.

Over the years, numerous students and consultants assisted with tasks that contributed to this work. My greatest indebtedness is to two research assistants who came on board as I worked on draft 2. Mustafa Batman, visiting Yale's Macmillan Center during the spring 2020 semester when I held a visiting professorship at Yale Law School, started assisting my research then, and he continued to do so after his return to Boğaziçi University to complete his doctorate. He was a master at surveying broad literatures, identifying controversies, finding documentation, and critiquing my interpretations. I learned an immense amount from the sources he found, but also from our meetings, during which he shared his impressive knowledge of history. Harunobu Saijo, a doctoral student in Political Science at my home university, also surveyed literatures, mainly conceptual scholarship but also research focused on the Middle East. In addition he computed many of the statistics reported in tables and graphs. I benefited especially from our exchanges on broad trends in political economy and political science.

Three Istanbul-based consultants transliterated documents in Ottoman Turkish: Ömer Bahadur, Müslüm İstekli, and Faysal Murat Demir. Over the years, other research assistants gathered and analyzed data for related projects that preceded this book: Rong Chen, Gloria Cheung, Dean Dulay, Linh Nguyen, Hannah Ridge, and Diego Romero. In locating sources and obtaining data, I received help from several librarians: Julian Aiken, Jordan Jefferson, Maryellen Larkin, and Sean Swanick.

It was a pleasure working with Cambridge University Press as my project transitioned from manuscript to book. I thank Robert Dreesen for taking on the work and for his patience during the evaluation. His anonymous readers provided constructive comments that led to numerous improvements. Joan Dale Lace performed the copy-editing efficiently and meticulously. I also thank the rest of the production team: Sable Gravesandy, Robert Judkins, and Hemalatha Subramanian.

Work of this kind cannot be accomplished without financial support. My professional home, Duke University, provided an intellectually rich environment as well as financial support through various programs. I am also grateful to several other organizations that served as host during an extended visit, granted resources to release time for writing, or financed the gathering of data: the Religious Freedom Project of the Berkeley Center, Georgetown University; the Economic Policy Research Foundation of Turkey (TEPAV); the College of Administrative Sciences and Economics, Koç University; the Religious Freedom Institute; and Yale Law School.

Portions of some chapters draw on three published articles: "Political Consequences of Islam's Economic Legacy," *Philosophy and Social Criticism*, 39 (2013): 395–405; "Legal Roots of Authoritarian Rule in the Middle East: Civic Legacies of the Islamic Waqf," *American Journal of Comparative Law*, 64 (2016): 419–54; and "Zakat: Islam's Missed Opportunity to Limit Predatory Taxation," *Public Choice*, 182 (2020): 395–416. I thank their publishers for permission to use them here.

In a book about a region featuring several leading languages that have all undergone significant variations over time, full consistency on spelling is impossible. But I adhere to a few basic rules. Within notes and the bibliography, author names and titles are spelled as in the original. In the main text, Islamic concepts are rendered in their Anglicized forms (Quran rather than Qur'ān, waqfs instead of *awqāf*, Ghazali for al-Ghazālī) or, where no Anglicized standard exists, in the closest English equivalent (Islamic pilgrimage for *hajj*, caretaker for *mutawallī*). Wherever confusion is possible, at first usage the Islamic original is indicated either in the text or in a note. Foreign terms in Latin-alphabet languages, including modern Turkish, are rendered as in the original.

Gregorian dates are used throughout, with the year 0 dividing dates "Before the Common Era" (BCE) from those of the "Common Era" (CE). Quotations from the Quran are from N. J. Dawood's classic translation and biblical quotations from the New Revised Standard version.

PART I

THE MODERN MIDDLE EAST'S AUTHORITARIAN FACE

1

Islam and Political Underdevelopment

In 2011, as uprisings in Tunis and Cairo initiated the Arab Spring, a common interpretation was that long-submerged Arab yearnings for freedom were catapulting to the surface. The masses that toppled aging dictators united young and old, high professionals and illiterates, rich and poor, the pious and the secular, Muslims and Christians, economic conservatives and socialists. From this rich diversity, observers inferred that the overthrow of dictators would usher in a liberal order. Arabs would gain freedoms to pursue lifestyles of their choice, speak their minds, interpret religion on their own, even opt to remain irreligious. Moreover, in exercising freedoms themselves, they would respect those of others.[1]

This optimism was misplaced. What united these Arab demonstrators was not a commitment to freedoms, and certainly not a desire to institute a generally liberal new political order. Some were seeking dignity. Others were simply fed up with incompetent, corrupt, and oppressive governance. Every individual demonstrator wanted to be freer in some respect – to express dissent, call out nepotism, decline conservative attire. In the case of Mohamed Bouazizi, the fruit vendor whose self-immolation triggered fateful riots in Tunis, it was simply to do business without extortion from the police. But no grand vision united the protestors. Nowhere in the Arab world had a coherent liberal ideology emerged. The demonstrators formed no organized movement, let alone one aimed at general liberalization.

The absence of a systematic reform plan and lack of an organized movement were themselves consequences of the repression responsible for widespread discontent. Arabs are not free to conduct honest public discussions about the causes of social pathologies. They cannot explore, except superficially, how their institutional history, which was grounded in Islamic law for more than a millennium, limits present possibilities. They cannot contextualize how institutions absent from the original Islamic order came to be identified as Islamic without risking charges of sacrilege. No meaningful diagnosis can emerge in an intellectual vacuum. No movement can be organized without general agreement on objectives.

The jubilation of the Arab crowds that toppled dictators signaled a widespread desire for change. It pointed to a potential for basic reforms if ever a critical mass manages to unite in favor of a new social contract, a new form of governance, and a new set of common understandings. In 2011, though, few demonstrators had well-formed preferences as to what sustainable reforms would entail. That, too, reflected a history of systemic repression. When options cannot be debated freely, it is hard even to imagine future possibilities, to say nothing of evaluating their feasibility and identifying paths for reaching them. For this reason alone, the Arab Spring generated overly optimistic expectations.

Indeed, with the fleeting exception of Tunisia, the regimes that followed the toppling of widely despised dictators became at least as repressive as their predecessors. Egypt's experience is revealing. The first national election after Mubarak's fall brought to power the Muslim Brotherhood, Egypt's only nationally organized opposition movement, which stood on the sidelines until the uprising appeared certain to succeed. Terminating a brief "Spring," the Brotherhood took to forcing on Egyptians its own brand of cultural conservatism. Though it had won a basically fair election, crowds filled the streets again, this time to install a new dictatorship headed by Mubarak's cronies.[2] At no stage of these developments did liberalization dominate Egyptian discourses. Although advocacy of specific freedoms was not absent, the most salient themes involved the containment of feared groups.[3]

The Arab Spring was not the Middle East's first explosion of liberal optimism. Two centuries earlier, in 1839, the Ottoman Sultan's Gülhane Edict granted equal rights before the law to all his subjects, regardless of faith or social status; it also voided his longstanding right to confiscate property at will. Though details of the reforms remained to be specified, celebrations erupted across the empire. Ecstatic crowds had inferred that liberalization was afoot on multiple fronts. In fact, nobody understood what it would take to implement the new freedoms, make them sustainable, and fulfill the new expectations they unleashed.[4] Though the edict set a precedent for bold innovations, no subsequent modernization initiative – the Reform Edict of 1856, the constitutions of 1876 and 1908, the Kemalist reforms of the 1920s and 1930s – aimed at broadening individual freedoms generally. Extending Westernization into new domains from above, Kemalism quashed dissent and replaced one form of religious repression with another.

A century and a half later, in 1978–79, Iran experienced a moment of liberal optimism. The occasion was the toppling of the repressive Pahlavi monarchy. The demonstrators who vanquished the Pahlavis united socialists committed to radical redistribution with Islamists eager to make religion omnipresent. Neither side favored free speech for all or the freedom to choose a lifestyle.

After defeating their common enemy, they turned on each other. Winning quickly, the Islamists proceeded to force their own values on Iranian society. Again, the outcome was the replacement of one repressive regime with another – a brutal secularist monarchy with a brutal theocracy.

The Middle East has seen many successful attempts to end specific forms of repression. None has produced liberalization in general. Hence, the Middle East stands out as an unfree region. It is also an undemocratic region, which is no coincidence.[5] One virtue of democracy is that it tends to support civil liberties; another is that it enables broad political participation through institutionalized constraints on executives, legislatures, and courts. Political freedoms rest partly on checks and balances among branches of government. Private associations, which collectively form civil society, contribute to preserving democratic rule.

But democracy does not necessarily advance freedoms, and it may even help to extinguish them. Free and fair elections may empower groups prepared to restrict dissent and impose their values on citizens who reject them. Turkey's democratic era, which began in 1946, offers a poignant example. For several decades, secularist-dominated governments restricted public manifestations of Islam, most notoriously headscarves in official spaces. The conservative party that achieved power in 2002 initially advanced certain civil liberties. But it used its rising popularity to destroy political checks and balances; and thereafter it unleashed the worst repression of Turkey's Republican Era, which began in 1923.[6]

Regardless of religious beliefs and attitudes toward religion, every decision maker in the region operates within an institutional complex inherited from the past. Today's institutions obviously bear the influence of yesterday's institutions, which in turn rest on those of the day before. For more than a millennium, the entire Middle East was governed under Islamic law, known formally as Sharia and colloquially as Sharia law. Islamic institutions must matter, then, to present patterns. The channels of influence form the essence of our inquiry. Islamic law was abrogated in some places, and in others it has been superseded by essentially secular systems that retain few substantive connections to Islam. Nevertheless, Islamic law remains deeply rooted in the region's politics. Patterns of civic engagement, understandings of religious liberties, distributions of political power, and relative economic capabilities all bear influences of the Middle East's legal history.

THE MIDDLE EAST AND ITS HISTORY

Choosing a geographic scope would pose a challenge for any work focused on the long-term effects of an institutional complex as vast as a world religion. Limiting the analysis to the Middle East, rather than the broader Muslim world, avoids complexities stemming from interactions with Hinduism, Confucianism, Buddhism, and other religions outside the Abrahamic tradition.

It simplifies the task by narrowing the variations that must be considered. For instance, it avoids the need to address the effects of India's caste system, which predates Islam. The chosen regional emphasis is also advantageous because it focuses analysis on countries that fell under Islamic rule, largely if not fully, through conquest and within the first half-millennium of Islam's existence. Islam reached the territories of today's Muslim-majority countries outside the Middle East mostly through traders. Yet another rationale for highlighting the Middle East is that among all Muslim-majority regions it has had the longest and strictest exposure to Islamic law. Prior to the 1800s, the waqf – Islam's instrument for providing social services – saw much more use in the Middle East than elsewhere.

"The Middle East" is an elastic term. Ordinarily it includes Israel, but here it serves as a shorthand for an area that, in the early twenty-first century, spans the twenty-two members of the Arab League, including those in North Africa, plus Iran and Turkey. All twenty-four of these states belong to the Organization of Islamic Cooperation (OIC), founded in 1969 as the "collective voice of the Muslim World." The OIC has fifty-seven members – all the world's Muslim-majority countries, plus several with a large Muslim minority. Geographically, it also spans parts of Central, South, and East Asia, Sub-Saharan Africa, Eastern Europe, and South America (Figure 1.1). Territories under the control of Israel are considered part of the Middle East only until 1948. The analytic justification is that a substantial share of the Jewish immigrants to Palestine and then Israel originated in countries where Islam's historical influence was slim. Besides, at least until the late 1970s, Jews with European origins formed a highly disproportionate share of elites who shaped Israeli institutions. Indigenous Israelis, Jewish or Muslim, played minor roles.[7] Cyprus was part of the region until 1878, when it became a British Protectorate.

Turkey's inclusion in the Middle East may draw objections on the ground that it has belonged to pan-European organizations since the Congress of Paris in 1856. But until its modernizing reforms of the 1800s and 1900s, Turkey's basic institutions were all grounded in Islam, as they were in the Arab world and Iran. Besides, analogous modernization campaigns were launched elsewhere in the region, too. True, Turkey's repudiation of Islamic law under its first post-Ottoman leader, Kemal Atatürk (1881–1938), was the Muslim world's boldest attempt to break with the past. Nevertheless, Turkey's history of secular government provides a difference of degree rather than kind. Even the Islamic Republic of Iran refrains from enforcing certain Islamic prescriptions; and life in Saudi Arabia, whose constitution consists of the Quran and Muhammad's Sunna (his remembered words and deeds), departs from traditional Islamic norms in broad domains, in some cases more radically than generally appreciated. As the book's argument unfolds, we shall see that all Muslim-majority countries of the Middle East, including those with secular constitutions, share a common legal heritage. This heritage poses similar

Islam and Political Underdevelopment

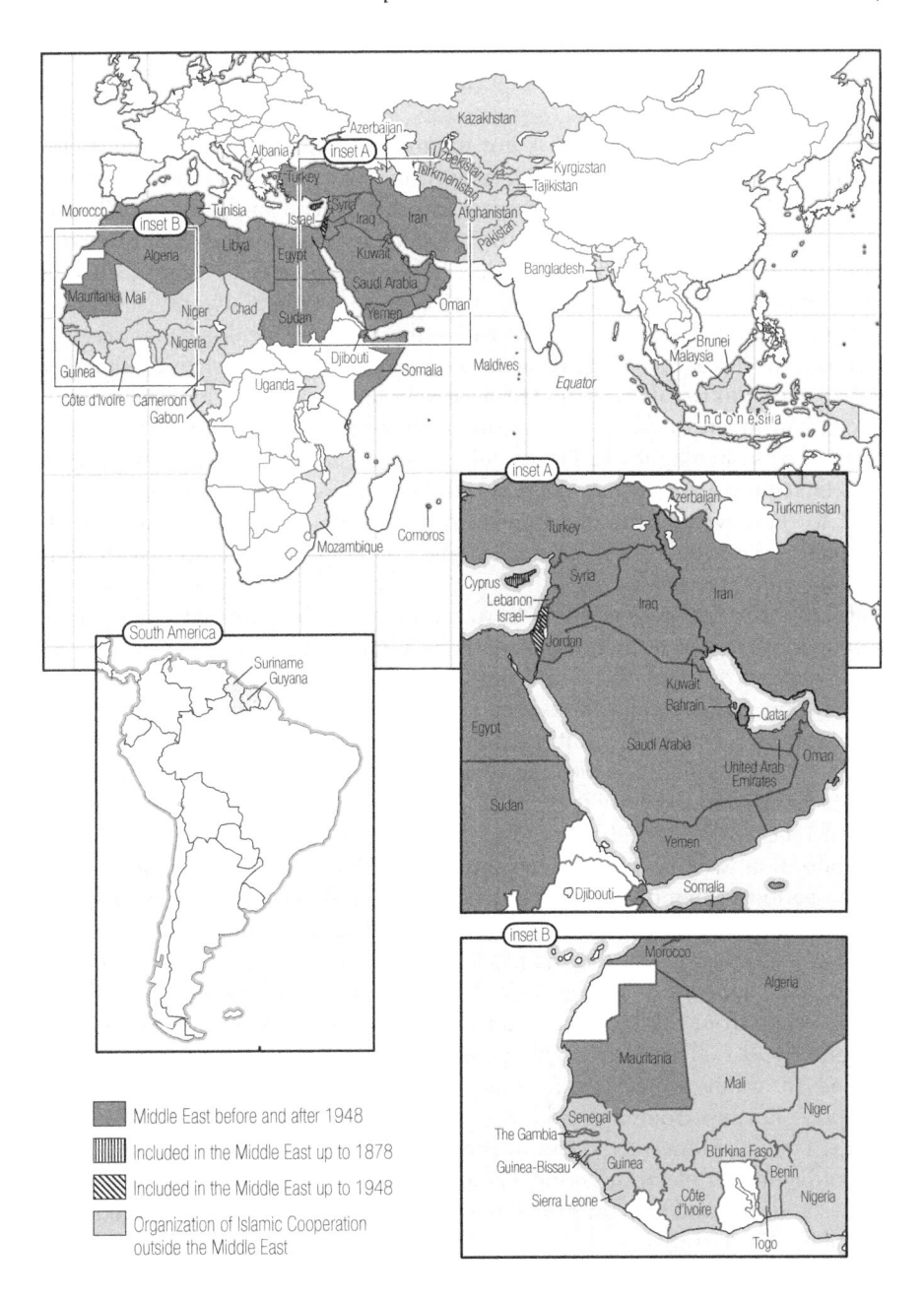

FIGURE 1.1 The Middle East and the rest of the Organization of Islamic Cooperation

challenges everywhere, with differences only in details and severity. There is an analytic rationale, then, for treating Turkey as Middle Eastern for the purpose at hand.

To pick a geographic focus is not to ignore developments and trends elsewhere. The Middle East has never existed in isolation. It has interacted with other Muslim-majority regions as well as other places. Impacting the flow of history in the Balkans, Iberia, East Africa, and elsewhere, it has itself reacted to external challenges and opportunities. Some phenomena of central concern here cannot be understood without reference to interactions among regions. Consider the rise of modern Islamism – the political ideology that seeks to reconstitute states according to what it considers authentic Islamic principles. Indians and Pakistanis contributed massively to its ideology, and their motivations had much to do with intercommunal conflicts and matters of identity without close analogues in the Middle East. In earlier times, caravan traders who linked the Middle East with Central Asia and Sub-Saharan Africa contributed to the development of supra-regional Islamic commercial practices. As necessary, the Middle East's historical and contemporary relations with other regions will make appearances.

Many historical works use a Euro-centric periodization that distinguishes among four eras: Antiquity to the fall of the Western Roman Empire in 476; the Middle Ages or Medieval Era from 476 to the fall of the Eastern Roman Empire, the Great Explorations, the Protestant Reformation, and the start of the Europe's Scientific Revolution around 1500; Early Modernity from around 1500 to the beginnings of the Industrial Revolution around 1750; and Modernity from 1750 to the present. This periodization will serve us well in referencing Western history. But for the Middle East itself, a different periodization will be more informative. We shall distinguish among three main periods: Premodernity, Modernization, and Modernity (Figure 1.2). Premodernity begins around 613 with the founding of the first Islamic community; it continues to the beginnings of state-directed Modernization around 1820. Two subperiods of the region's Premodernity will be invoked. "Early Islam" runs from the birth of Islam to the end of the Medina-based Islamic Empire in 661. The "Development of Classical Islamic Law" spanned the period to about 900. To turn now to the Middle East's "Modernization Period," it runs from around 1820 to the Ottoman Empire's collapse in 1922. Finally, Modernity refers to the period from 1922 onward. The lower left of Figure 1.2 illustrates critical country-specific periods within the Modern Era. The right-hand column provides a chronology of the major political events in the book's narrative.

MEASURING POLITICAL PERFORMANCE

By itself, the Middle East's distinct institutional heritage does not imply that as a region it must stand out in political performance. Institutional reforms could have voided the impact of its history. However, the Middle East *is* a poor political performer according to diverse basic indices. It underperforms relative to the rest of the world, but also relative to the rest of the OIC. Although these statistics say nothing about the *causes* of the Middle East's troubles, they provide an added reason to probe the legacies of the Middle East's distinct institutional history.

One indicator of political performance lies in global migration patterns. Far more people leave the Middle East to settle elsewhere – mainly Western Europe – than move into it. Middle Eastern emigration is driven partly by poverty. But economic deprivation depends, in turn, on political repression. In any case, political repression itself fuels departures. Between 1990 and 2018, Middle Easterners constituted 26.5 percent of the world's refugees, as against 7.6 percent of the world population; and from 2000 to 2018, 16.1 percent of asylum seekers originated in the Middle East.[8] Some Middle Eastern political refugees were escaping ethnic or religious persecution; others were displaced because of dissent. Almost 100 million more Middle Easterners would have emigrated for one reason or another if they had had the opportunity. According to a Gallup poll conducted in 2018 in 119 countries, Middle Easterners are twice as likely as others to want to emigrate (Figure 1.3).[9] As with all bar graphs in the book, figures for country groupings are weighted by population.

The region contains a few spots teeming with foreigners. In oil-rich monarchies of the Arab Gulf, nonnationals make up around half the population, and high-skilled foreigners constitute 17 percent of the labor force.[10] In contrast to Middle Eastern immigrants in the West, practically none want to stay permanently. Living mostly in expatriate enclaves, they are in the Gulf temporarily to work for multinational companies chasing oil wealth.[11]

There exist country-based global indices that enable quantification of the Middle East's political blemishes. One is the Civil Liberties Index of Freedom House, which is based on four factors: freedom of expression and belief; associational and organizational rights; rule of law; and personal autonomy and individual rights.[12] This index puts heavier weight on personal freedoms than on government functions through which people achieve joint objectives. Its 2019 figures show that civil liberties are much weaker in the Middle East than in the rest of the world (Figure 1.4).[13] The Middle East also performs poorly relative to OIC, which underscores the Middle East's exceptionalism within the Muslim world.

Abundant examples of restricted personal freedoms give credence to the Middle East's low Freedom House scores. Only in 2017 did Saudi Arabian women acquire the right to drive, and less than 2 percent are exercising this freedom.[14] Moreover, through arrests of women's rights activists, the Saudi regime has signaled that rights will be expanded only from above and only as much as the leadership wants.[15] In Egypt, a Coptic man may be forced to divorce his wife if she converts to Islam.[16] In Turkey, criticizing the president's policies is to risk being charged with belittling the state, insulting him personally, even abetting terrorism.[17]

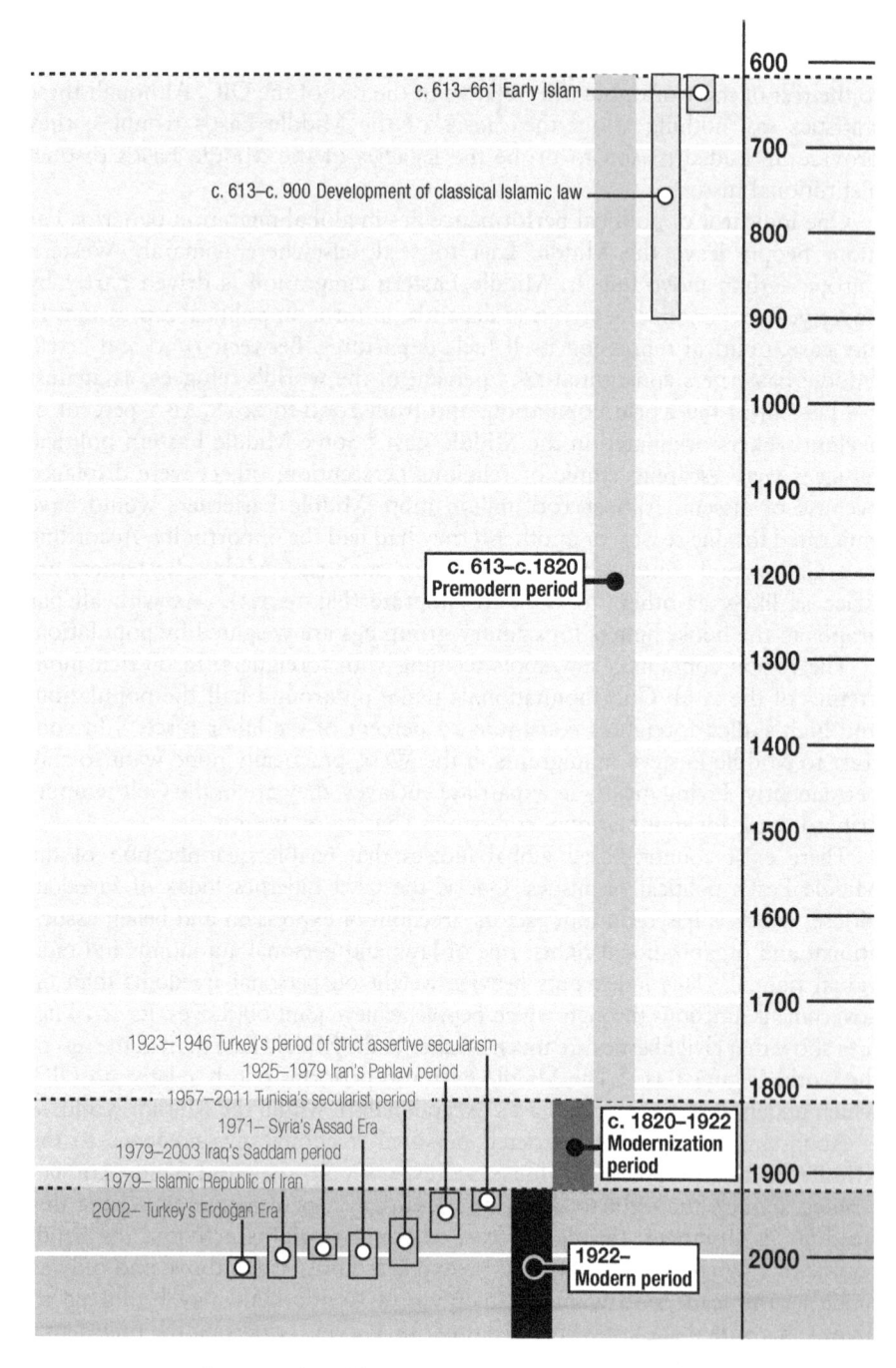

FIGURE 1.2 Periodization of Middle Eastern history and chronology of major political events

Islam and Political Underdevelopment

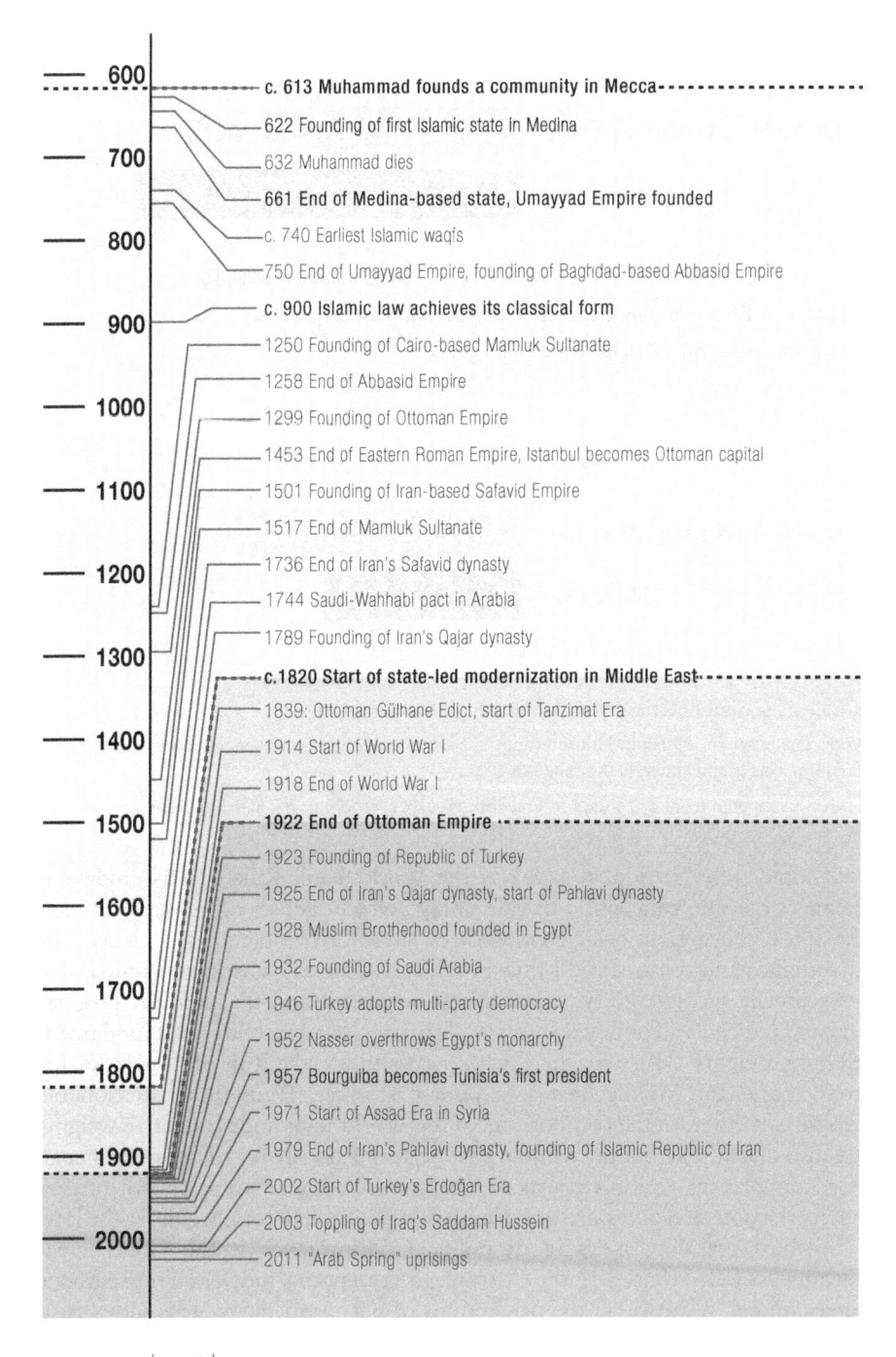

600	c. 613 Muhammad founds a community in Mecca
	622 Founding of first Islamic state in Medina
700	632 Muhammad dies
	661 End of Medina-based state, Umayyad Empire founded
800	c. 740 Earliest Islamic waqfs
	750 End of Umayyad Empire, founding of Baghdad-based Abbasid Empire
900	**c. 900 Islamic law achieves its classical form**
	1250 Founding of Cairo-based Mamluk Sultanate
1000	1258 End of Abbasid Empire
	1299 Founding of Ottoman Empire
1100	1453 End of Eastern Roman Empire, Istanbul becomes Ottoman capital
	1501 Founding of Iran-based Safavid Empire
1200	1517 End of Mamluk Sultanate
	1736 End of Iran's Safavid dynasty
	1744 Saudi-Wahhabi pact in Arabia
1300	1789 Founding of Iran's Qajar dynasty
	c.1820 Start of state-led modernization in Middle East
1400	1839: Ottoman Gülhane Edict, start of Tanzimat Era
	1914 Start of World War I
1500	1918 End of World War I
	1922 End of Ottoman Empire
	1923 Founding of Republic of Turkey
1600	1925 End of Iran's Qajar dynasty, start of Pahlavi dynasty
	1928 Muslim Brotherhood founded in Egypt
1700	1932 Founding of Saudi Arabia
	1946 Turkey adopts multi-party democracy
	1952 Nasser overthrows Egypt's monarchy
1800	**1957 Bourguiba becomes Tunisia's first president**
	1971 Start of Assad Era in Syria
1900	1979 End of Iran's Pahlavi dynasty, founding of Islamic Republic of Iran
	2002 Start of Turkey's Erdoğan Era
2000	2003 Toppling of Iraq's Saddam Hussein
	2011 "Arab Spring" uprisings

FIGURE 1.2 *(cont.)*

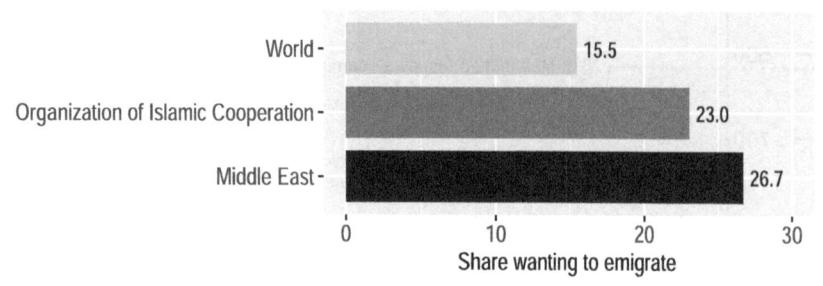

FIGURE 1.3 Desire to migrate: Middle East in global perspective
Source: Computed from Gallup World Poll, 2018.

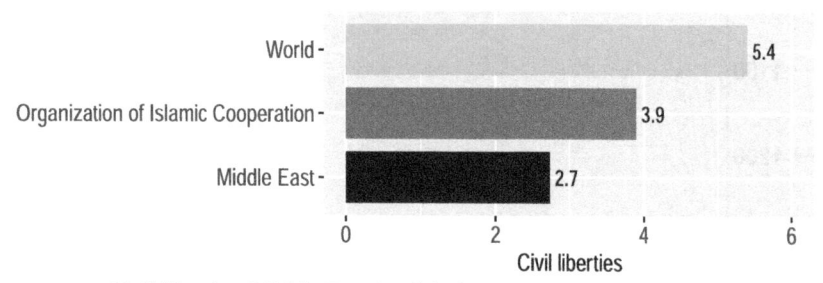

FIGURE 1.4 Civil liberties: Middle East in global perspective
Note: The range for Freedom House ratings is 0–100, with higher numbers referring to more freedom. This graph converts the range to 0–10.
Source: Computed from 2019 data in Freedom House, *Freedom in the World 2020*.

Another relevant global index is the World Bank Rule of Law Index. It balances the thin conception of rule of law, which focuses on procedures, and the thick conception, which emphasizes substantive outcomes such as self-governance and censorship. It thus provides a summary statistic encompassing government accountability, equal access to justice and the political process, efficient judicial and political systems, clear laws, legal stability, and fundamental human rights.[18] As with the Civil Liberties Index, the Rule of Law Index for 2019 marks the Middle East as a poor performer (Figure 1.5). Reasonable people can differ on the components of the World Bank index; relative weights are also disputable. But the Middle East performs poorly on all its components. For example, the region's courts are notoriously slow; and, as shown further on, its religious freedoms are quite limited in practice, if not also under the law.

A third revealing measure of political performance is the Government Cleanliness Index. Based on the Corruption Perceptions Index of Transparency International, it draws on the perceptions of businesspersons. This index is of interest for two reasons. First, obstacles to commerce limit various economic freedoms. Second, in corrupting government, economic roadblocks also tilt the

Islam and Political Underdevelopment

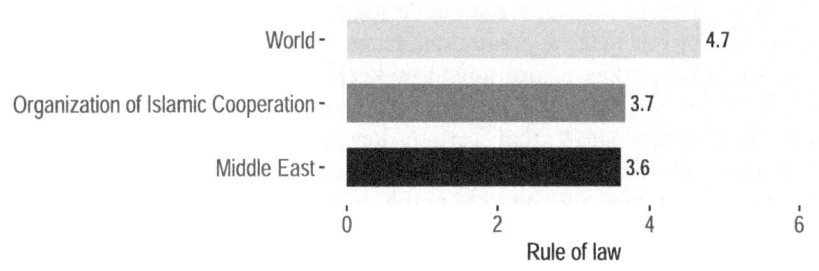

FIGURE 1.5 Rule of law: Middle East in global perspective

Note: This index gives country scores in units of a standard normal distribution, on a scale running from –2.5 to 2.5. This graph converts scores to a 0–10 range, with 5 corresponding to 0 on the World Bank's scale.

Source: World Bank Worldwide Governance Indicators, 2019.

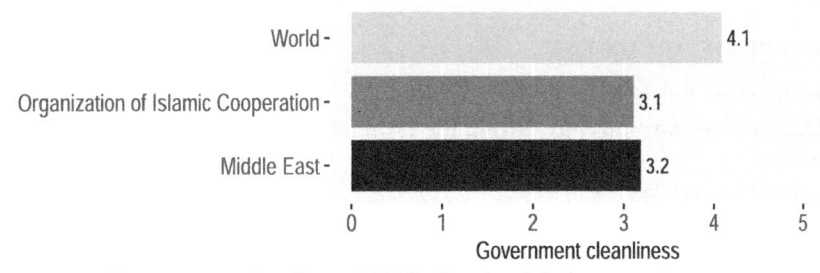

FIGURE 1.6 Government cleanliness: Middle East in global perspective

Note: The Government Cleanliness Index rates countries on a 0–100 scale, with higher numbers referring to less perceived corruption. This graph converts the range to 0–10.

Source: Computed from data in Transparency International's Corruption Perceptions Index 2020.

political playing field against the unconnected. According to the 2020 edition of the index, Middle Eastern governments are considerably less clean than those elsewhere (Figure 1.6).[19] The pervasiveness of Middle Eastern corruption is widely recognized even among people unfamiliar with formal indices. In 2011, Arab protestors complained bitterly about the bribes required for routine government procedures and cronyism in public hiring and contracting.

Tradeoffs may exist in the short run among elements of a liberal order. Certain civil and economic liberties may be curtailed during wartime or to respond effectively to a natural disaster. Over the long run, however, there are no basic conflicts. Political liberalization requires the strengthening of rule of law, the extension of a broad range of freedoms, and cleaner government.

Numerous indices prepared by different organizations, based on distinct methodologies, and varying in factor weightings all rank the Middle East as a poor performer. In fact, according to the indices used in Figures 1.4–1.6, it is the world's least free region.[20] But validating a pattern meriting explanation is the easy part of our task. A greater challenge is to identify the social mechanisms through which key institutions now keep the region relatively repressed. Another is to explain the origins of freedom-suppressing institutions. Following chapters show that certain key institutions of the premodern Middle East, all associated with Islam, kept civic engagement weak, government unrepresentative and unaccountable, corruption endemic, both expressive and religious freedoms highly restricted, and commercial enterprises politically uninfluential.

What Islam entails is open to reinterpretation. Certain elements of what became the Islamic institutional complex were absent from the Islamic order established in seventh-century Arabia. Controversies over what counts as Islamic will be covered extensively as the narrative unfolds. Suffice it to say here that our focus throughout will be on institutions shared widely and for centuries throughout the Middle East.

PREVIEW OF ARGUMENT

Until modern times, the Middle East was governed under Islamic law, which started taking shape already during the Prophet's lifetime. The effects were not necessarily negative; and even when they were, liberalization opportunities presented themselves.

During the rise of Islam, the Muslim community did not lack checks and balances. A verse of the Quran says that good believers conduct their affairs by "mutual consent."[21] Indeed, there are indications of broad participation in early Islamic governance.[22] At his deathbed, the second caliph Umar (served 634–44) had a consultative committee known as a *shura* select his successor, Uthman (644–56).[23] Yet Uthman was the only *shura*-selected Arabian caliph. Three different procedures were used to select the other caliphs who led the Muslim community from Muhammad's death in 632 to the traumatic Sunni–Shii schism in 661. These variations sowed confusion as to what qualifies as properly Islamic succession.

No political system is equally responsive to every constituency. This puts in perspective the political inconsistencies of Islam's inaugural decades. The new procedural precedent set at each new caliphal transition must have reflected changes in the relative strengths of Muslim factions, which multiplied as the community expanded through conversions.

Intra-communal tensions made it impossible to govern by consent even the Sunnis, whose doctrines kept it legitimate for believers to disagree on what God prescribes. After 661, Sunnis were governed autocratically, with power passing from father to son. True, the Damascus-based Umayyad caliphs, who ran the first Arab empire centered outside Arabia from 661 to 750, operated a *shura*. But the Umayyad *shura* did not broaden political participation. Composed of the caliph's cronies, it merely simulated power sharing.[24] Among the consequences was lower material security. Restraints grounded in balances among factions gave way to arbitrary dynastic rule. A century after Islam's emergence, high officials, who were paid mainly through conquered lands, responded by seeking a tax and wealth shelter. The outcome was the development of the waqf, which became a key Islamic institution.

The Waqf and Its Thwarting of Civic Engagement

An Islamic waqf was a trust established to finance designated services in perpetuity. The founder and his or her family could be among the named beneficiaries of its endowment's income. They could also benefit by serving as successive caretakers. What shielded waqf revenue from rulers was primarily the common belief that waqf assets are sacred. This belief made rulers reluctant to confiscate waqf assets, lest they lose legitimacy by appearing impious.

In allocating resources, caretakers were supposed to follow the founder's directives. In principle, their own preferences were immaterial, as were those of beneficiaries; Islamic courts made caretakers enforce waqf deeds. The waqf's emergence in the Middle East coincided with the spread in Western Europe of the corporation, which was used to provide analogous services. Whereas mosques and madrasas (Islamic colleges) were established as waqfs, churches and universities were founded increasingly as corporations. Unlike the Islamic waqf, the corporation is a self-governing organization.

Waqfs came to control vast resources. They could have used their financial base to constrain the state and advance their constituents' freedoms. The resulting decentralization of power might have placed the Middle East on the road to liberalization and perhaps also democratization. However, despite their immense wealth, waqfs remained politically powerless, glaringly so in relation to European corporations. Chapters 3 and 4 show that several factors kept them persistently weak. Above all, the requirement to follow the founder's instructions denied waqfs the flexibility to respond to the evolving needs of their beneficiaries. Second, waqfs lacked legal standing as organizations, which denied them a collective voice. Third, beneficiaries had no say over caretakers, who were accountable only to courts.

Organizations standing between the state and the individual serve as barriers to despotism. They ensure that if the state tramples on liberties, civil society will resist. Cognizant of the potential reactions, state officials show restraint in the first place. Classical Islamic law granted the freedom to found nongovernmental organizations (NGOs). A waqf could serve any function allowed under Islamic law, as interpreted by ruler-staffed courts. Yet engaging in politics was not among the permissible functions. The waqf's capacity for civic engagement was also weakened by its lack of organizational autonomy.

The Islamic waqf's organizational features constituted key reasons why, as the West developed political checks and balances, no such tendency emerged in the Middle East. The West liberalized and democratized through epic struggles driven partly by groups organized through universities, cities, religious orders, and guilds. Such groups demanded rights. Challenging power structures, they developed ideologies and institutions that extended both personal and associational rights. A virtuous circle thus emerged. As civil society strengthened, it took steps to facilitate the establishment, management, and security of private organizations. In the Middle East, by contrast, the waqf created a vicious circle. By keeping civil society weak, it limited freedoms and perpetuated autocracy. Strong NGOs could not exist, making it hard to challenge rulers through organized collective action from outside the state. Revealingly, over more than a millennium, waqfs fostered no political movements or ideologies.

Under changing conditions, every waqf that adhered to its deed eventually became dysfunctional. The consequent inefficiencies held back the region economically.[25] Along the way, though, the needs of beneficiaries incentivized the circumvention of deed stipulations, as did caretakers' interest in self-enrichment. Enterprising caretakers found ways to overcome inconvenient restrictions with the help of judges, who made their cooperation contingent on side payments. Chapter 5 shows that waqf rules, practically unchallengeable because of their benefits to clerics, contributed to a culture of corruption. As it became common knowledge that rigidly enforced waqf rules caused economic harm, they helped to make law breaking socially acceptable.

Islam has no priesthood, so the term "cleric" is used in a generic sense. A Muslim cleric is someone who exerts Islamic authority through generally recognized genres of Islamic leadership. Often, clerics have Islamic educational credentials and hold religious positions recognized by the state. But sometimes they derive authority simply from their reputation among the faithful.[26]

By the early 1900s, the provision of Middle Eastern urban services passed to municipalities and private companies formed under new local laws or foreign legal systems. The charities, professional societies, cultural organizations, and political associations established during this tumultuous transformation laid the foundations of today's civic life. To one extent or another, the Middle East's modern private organizations enjoy self-governance. Ordinarily, they are bound by the preferences of their founders only at a high level of generality. Meanwhile, the waqf was reborn as a fundamentally different organizational form. A modern waqf enjoys flexibilities that its premodern namesake lacked. Functionally, it resembles the West's charitable corporations.

Yet more than a century after the removal of legal obstacles to forming self-governing organizations, civic engagement remains weak. A proximate reason is that autocracies try systematically to undermine NGOs. But states succeed in keeping power centralized because NGOs are weak. That weakness is a legacy of the Islamic waqf, Chapter 6 proposes. Most protests of the Arab Spring brought together masses unaffiliated with any political organization. That, too, is among the manifestations of chronically weak civil society.

One century is a short time to learn how to form and collectively operate politically effective NGOs. Western Europeans have had a millennium and a

Islam and Political Underdevelopment 17

half to master these skills. For all their political ineffectiveness now, the Middle East's current NGOs, except those captured by the government, are serving as founts of civic education. Promoting a culture of bargaining and compromise, they are teaching how to communicate ideas and form coalitions. Although the region's path to a liberal order is long, at least it has already freed itself from the civically suffocating Islamic waqf.

Weak Religious Freedoms and Missing Schisms

Organizational weaknesses can hinder the production and spread of ideologies. But ideological change depends on individual creativity, which itself depends on interpersonal communication and cooperation. Although a radically new vision may emerge from a single mind, it will more easily be refined in environments where ideas are shared and critiqued. By this logic, the Islamic waqf would have hindered intellectual progress by limiting innovation. The waqf was designed to have a caretaker follow instructions blindly, not to facilitate the spotting of new opportunities. Rules that excluded beneficiaries from governance also restricted the caretaker's inventiveness by limiting feedback. True, every caretaker received complaints from beneficiaries. But beneficiaries lacked incentives to think deeply about the allocation of waqf resources. Waqf restrictions induced thinking about circumventing rules for marginal gain, not about redesigning organizations.

In the premodern Middle East, the Islamic education system was supported through waqfs, which kept curricula essentially fixed through specifications included in deeds. In a slowly changing world, the resulting brake on intellectual advances might have been insignificant. Under rapidly changing conditions, outdated curricula handicapped generations by making education irrelevant to real challenges. Madrasas thus hindered Muslim intellectual development both because of rigidities common to all waqfs and by failing to prepare students for addressing social problems.

Observers who treat Islam as an impediment to intellectual progress usually point not to the waqf, which emerged several generations after the birth of Islam, but instead to repressive institutions thought to have been present, if in rudimentary form, during Islam's inaugural decades. These institutions include punishments for apostasy, blasphemy, and heresy. The fear of being accused of such sins has impoverished intellectual discourses down to the present. The 1988 controversy over Salman Rushdie's *Satanic Verses* is a case in point. Many Muslim leaders accused Rushdie of blasphemy, and Iran's Ayatollah Khomeini ordered his execution. In response, Rushdie took to avoiding commentary on Islam. Nevertheless, he was gravely injured by an attacker convinced that he deserved execution.[27] Consider also the Egyptian blogger Abdel Karim Suleiman, who in 2005 criticized the teachings of al-Azhar, his former school, and decried attacks on Copts. He was sentenced to three years for blaspheming Islam.[28] Like Rushdie's ordeal, Suleiman's persecution impoverished discussions on policies somehow identified with Islam. As in the past, apostasy, blasphemy, and heresy charges are used to restrict various liberties. The fear of being accused of religious offense constrains political discourses, deflects attention from inequalities, preserves ethnic and/or sectarian dominance, protects monopolies, and prevents mass mobilization.

Contrary to a common view, Islam's fundamental sources do not unequivocally bar out-conversions or novel religious viewpoints. The Quran's relevant verses are subject to interpretation. Accordingly, Islamic apostasy, blasphemy, and heresy rules could have evolved in the direction of broadening tolerance and liberties. In fact, critical events during Islam's initial few decades diminished Muslim religious choices and restricted acceptable discourses. Chapter 7 covers the key episodes and consequent dynamics.

At Muhammad's death, certain Arabian tribes suspended tax payments to the Islamic state on the ground that they had agreed to pay tribute to him personally. Accusing these tribes of apostasy, the first caliph Abu Bakr (served 632–34) forced them to comply. Abu Bakr could make the episode a matter of religious loyalty because the tax in question, zakat, was a Quranic requirement. But his reaction may be likened to any state's enforcement of its tax laws. Hence, later interpreters could have treated his coercion as necessary for tax enforcement. Conventionally, though, the "Apostasy Wars" are viewed as a precedent for barring out-conversion. Opportunistic uses of Abu Bakr's apostasy charge, like other early episodes that cloaked political repression in religion, have harmed intellectual development.

Precedents do not necessarily carve patterns in stone. Christianity, too, has a history of punishing alleged sinners. The Spanish Inquisition is among the infamous attempts to squash religious freedoms. It restricted public discourse in various contexts, including science and dealings with non-Christians. Equally significant, most Christians now consider it a horrible aberration. In the same vein, Muslims could have reinterpreted the "Apostasy Wars" as an unfortunate episode driven by a young state's fiscal needs. However, for most Middle Eastern Muslims overt out-conversion requires emigration to freer lands.

In stages, Middle Eastern modernization drives have transferred power from clerics to secular officials. Turkey's secularization under Atatürk and İnönü (1923–50) is the boldest effort in this vein. Other ambitious campaigns occurred in Iran under the Pahlavis (1925–79), Egypt under Nasser (1954–70), and Tunisia under Bourguiba (1957–87). These regimes might have been expected to facilitate exit from Islam, radically reinterpret the Quran, and broaden religious freedoms generally. In fact, they simply made it easy to ignore Islam. Their ideal was to have citizens basically disconnect themselves from religion of any sort. Meanwhile, they treated certain Islamic practices as archaic. However, as Chapter 8 shows, their reinterpretations of Islam occurred through top-down commands, with minimal debate beyond the leadership. Just as reformers were once repressed as heretics, so now the pious were persecuted as obscurantists. In the process, modernizers constricted discourses on adapting Islam to the modern age.

Secularist repression caused widespread discontent, which then induced leaders of all stripes to broaden the rights of the pious. It also paved the way for regimes led by traditionalists or Islamists. Both groups have contributed to the aridity of discourses on Islam through selective secularization. A case in point is the corporation's presence in the region's modern legal systems. The corporation violates the Islamic principle of limiting legal standing to natural individuals. In failing to disclose that Islamic law fell behind the times with respect to legal personhood, traditionalists and Islamists alike have allowed secularization in disguise. In so doing, moreover, they have lightened pressures for comprehensive debate on the content of Islamic law. An unintended consequence is the domination of discourses on Islam's substance by Islamists, who espouse cultural isolationism.

Disagreements over a religion's interpretation can cause a schism – a formal division into variants with their own officials, doctrines, and rituals. Islam's main division, the Sunni–Shii split, came early in its history, over succession disputes. One might expect Muslim modernizers, or liberal Muslims, to have split Islam further. They have done so only informally, in that the global Muslim community is divided between practicing and nominal Muslims. For reasons developed in Chapter 10, one might expect nominal Muslims to have produced major movements espousing a radically new interpretation. But there is no Islamic counterpart to Protestantism or Reform Judaism. Ongoing religious tensions within the Middle East hint that such a break is in store. Chapter 11 attributes the absence of liberal schisms thus far partly to collective action difficulties rooted in the chronic weaknesses of civil society. A reinforcing factor is the potency of the apostasy charge, which preserves the appearance of a unified Muslim community. Potential members of a liberal Muslim denomination lack a comparably effective ideological instrument.

Economic Hindrances to Liberalization

The freedoms of a liberal order include the rights to produce at will, exchange on mutually agreed terms, own property, and accumulate wealth. These may be restricted where they clash with other freedoms or provide public goods. But any restrictions are transparent and applied uniformly. Tax obligations are predictable. People who prosper through hard work know that their assets will not be seized through arbitrary taxation or outright confiscation.

The Quran contains rules to regularize taxation. They involve zakat – one of Islam's canonical five pillars. As initially understood, Muslims of sufficient wealth and/or income paid zakat to the communal treasury. Dues were fixed in proportional terms to finance eight broadly defined functions, each of which corresponds to services that modern states generally supply themselves or else regulate. As its specifics unfolded, zakat also capped dues to the state. As discussed in Chapter 12, therein lies an additional reason behind zakat's status as a "pillar." In financing the state and stipulating public responsibilities, it also put Islam's weight behind private property rights.

Yet zakat's enforcement lasted just a few decades. It became an anachronism under the Arab empires that ruled for several centuries starting in 661; and, down to the modern era, it has remained an unenforced Islamic tax, except in scattered small localities where communal pressures ensure compliance. A consequence was the waqf's emergence as a core Islamic institution. In effect, the waqf was a creative response to zakat's abandonment as a state-enforced transfer system. As zakat gave way to arbitrary taxation, rich landowners yearned for a wealth shelter. The institution that met this need precluded the deployment of sheltered assets for political activity, which then inhibited the growth of civil society.

Zakat has survived widely only as a voluntary practice that follows no set template. Donors decide amounts and recipients themselves. The history of zakat's implementation will ring familiar to anyone acquainted with distributional politics. Powerful constituencies captured both sides of the transfer system. On the collection side, broad exemptions appeared; and the resulting revenue loss then induced the imposition of new taxes, all free of restrictions that had strengthened material security. On the disbursement side, the beneficiaries were mainly powerful constituencies. These developments diminished zakat's value to the poor and powerless.

As zakat lost economic significance and arbitrary taxation became the norm in Muslim-governed states, it practically disappeared from religious discourses. Limited and predictable taxation ceased to be viewed as a fundamental principle enshrined in a religious pillar. Scripture on zakat was not used to resist arbitrary fiscal policies as un-Islamic, or to hold rulers accountable for their policies.

Private economic players shape political outcomes through collective action of their own and financing broader civic activity. Chapter 13 shows that several elements of the Islamic institutional complex restricted the size and longevity of commercial enterprises. Some of these institutions were rooted in the Quran; others were transplanted from other civilizations and given an Islamic pedigree. As European merchants gained political influence during the half-millennium preceding Europe's Industrial Revolution, the Middle East's merchants were conspicuously weak. One manifestation is a delay in the emergence of formal business associations, which tiny and ephemeral enterprises could not have sustained.

Until the 1800s, when many European institutions were transplanted to the Middle East, even the largest indigenous enterprises were established for finite periods. One reason was that, as a matter of practice, ongoing Islamic commercial partnerships were easily terminated under the pretext of sickness or other hardship. Premature dissolution harmed partners who wished to continue. Another factor was the Islamic inheritance system, which by premodern standards was notably egalitarian. Because a sudden death could force remaining partners to deal with numerous heirs, partnerships were kept small and short-lived.

Islam and Political Underdevelopment

Had Islamic law allowed some form of corporation, handicaps rooted in Islam's inheritance and partnership rules could have been overcome. The corporation could have been used in business, as it was in Europe when the need emerged during the Great Explorations that presented lucrative investment opportunities in distant lands.[29] Every Middle Eastern country now recognizes both business corporations and charitable corporations. Evidently, there was no insurmountable obstacle to borrowing the corporate form from Europe. But this became a practical option only after the transplant, during the modernization wave of the 1800s, of other institutions that had failed to develop indigenously.

Islam's main political mission was to unite Arabia's feuding tribes. That is why the Quran recognizes no community between the individual and the full community of believers, the Muslim umma. Recognizing some form of the corporation would have given Arabia's tribes, and, within decades, also communities beyond Arabia, the organizational means for autonomy. But the corporation's exclusion from Islam's legal toolbox reduced the bargaining power of entrepreneurs. It thus compounded the political weaknesses of the Middle East's private enterprises and business communities.

The persistent handicaps of private companies stemmed from the simplicity of their operations. Because structurally simple enterprises do not face the coordination and communication problems that fuel institutional creativity, advanced organizational forms did not emerge indigenously. This stagnation handicapped the Middle East during the Industrial Revolution, when the efficient use of modern technologies required large and enduring companies. Small and transitory Middle Eastern businesses could not bargain collectively with the state, as their counterparts in Western Europe were doing long before the Industrial Revolution. Their impermanence also precluded business associations.

The private commercial sector's atomism was among the factors holding back civil society across the Middle East. Merchants organized into larger units could have worked with other constituencies to impose mutually beneficial restraints on rulers. True, they might have brandished power also to gain monopoly rights. But monopolization and the binding of rulers are mutually compatible processes. The history of English liberalization offers a case in point.[30]

Since its existential crisis that erupted in the 1800s, the Middle East has witnessed many campaigns for economic reform. Few have drawn inspiration from Islamic history. The main exception is Islamist movements of the twentieth century. Attributing Muslim failures to colonization and secularization, they have sought to restore selected Islamic institutions. Their main initiatives are critiqued in Chapter 14. Prioritizing symbolism over substance and conformism over liberalization, Islamism has missed opportunities to draw from Islam's rich history universal lessons for economic progress and rule of law. Its initiatives have reinforced the illiberal view, widespread among Muslims, that Islamists are unfit for governance.

Among the economic themes of Islamism is that Muslim-governed regimes are neglecting to enforce zakat. But the Islamist-initiated new zakat systems are vastly truncated versions of what they purport to be reviving. They are meant only to alleviate poverty and reinforce Muslim identity. None has dented inequality. More critical here is that none serves functions commensurate to its status as a religious pillar – strengthening property rights, constraining the state, and financing public goods. Nevertheless, in practically all Islamic education today, zakat is treated as a pillar of Islam. The dissonance between the reality of zakat's minor role in modern Muslim life and its persistent centrality in basic teachings is a manifestation of expressive taboos on Islam's social roles.

Much more salient than zakat initiatives have been efforts to purge interest from economic life through Islamic finance. Its various forms – banking, bonds, credit cards – avoid interest symbolically, through euphemisms and accounting gimmicks. Though Islamic finance holds about 1 percent of global financial assets, it has not contributed measurably to Muslim economic development. Its costs include lower financial transparency, the legitimation of obfuscation, and the neglect of major social problems. As with zakat, an opportunity is being wasted to demonstrate the relevance of early Islamic institutions to modern economic life. The Quran's interest ban that Islamists treat as a blanket prohibition of interest originally targeted a genuinely menacing practice, one that commonly led to enslavement.

A broader missed opportunity is the stimulation of discourses on Islam's possible roles in a liberal order. Deep cleavages exist on Islam's compatibility with various freedoms. Differences could be bridged through frank exchanges. They could help non-Islamists recognize that the Islamic heritage harbors lessons compatible with their own ideals.

Reasons for Guarded Optimism

If in the early 2000s the Middle East is extremely repressed, it is not destined to remain so. The book's core argument, developed in Chapters 3–14, gives reasons why speedy liberalization is impossible. However, in reviewing and linking the mechanisms at play, Chapter 15 also identifies grounds for optimism over the long run.

Certain elements of Islam's historical institutional complex have delayed the region's establishment of a liberal order, not blocked it permanently. The institutions primarily responsible for the Middle East's historical trajectory are either gone or, under new conditions, no longer inhibit liberalization. The region now possesses the institutional infrastructure for a stronger civil society. In addition to laws that support private associations, it includes networks of large and enduring firms that allow private capital accumulation and decentralize political power. Were their significance better understood, these developments of the past couple of centuries would foster hope that Middle Eastern liberalization is not an oxymoron. There is great discontent in the region, as evidenced by the emigration preferences shown in Figure 1.3. The wish to emigrate reflects a sense of hopelessness – a feeling that the Middle East cannot escape heavy repression for the foreseeable future. Yet such despair makes the region ready for a revolution from below. The East European revolutions of 1989 broke out at a time of immense pessimism about the future even among dissidents who held – correctly, it turned out – that their communist dictatorships would fall quickly if ever their vulnerability was exposed.[31] Indeed, just as self-propagating fear sustained hated communist regimes for decades, opposition to the regime, once it reached a critical mass, fed on itself. The mass mobilizations of the "Arab Spring" show that the Middle East, too, is capable of sudden political eruptions.

An institutional complex entails many mutually supporting institutions. So it is with the institutions responsible for repression in the Middle East. Religious illiberalism facilitates associational repression, and vice versa. The interlinkages among the region's various institutions provide ample grounds for hopelessness: change in any one context is difficult because its success depends on appropriate changes in many complementary institutions. But these interlinkages provide reasons for optimism, too. The very complementarities among Middle Eastern institutions imply that altering a single institution can destabilize others, possibly unleashing a cascade of mutually reinforcing reforms. The region is unlikely to transition within a generation or two to what one might characterize as a liberal order. However, successes in one place would energize reformists elsewhere.

Islam's fundamental sources have been reinterpreted repeatedly. Various reinterpretations coexist today. Insofar as the Middle East's political deficiencies are linked to religion, they involve Islamic institutions that took shape mostly after its canonical Golden Age. Besides, even those that rest on early precedents, such as the criminalization of apostasy, have alternative interpretations derived from readings of the Quran and contextual knowledge. Therein lies yet another reason for long-run optimism. No absolute barrier exists to religious freedoms in the Middle East. They can be activated by Muslims who believe sincerely that they are correcting misinterpretations.

LIBERAL ORDER

The foregoing preview has invoked the concept of a liberal order, which needs to be defined precisely. The word "liberal" connotes the protection of freedoms. As for "order," it connotes constraints. A liberal order is also known as an "open-access order," which Douglass North, John Wallis, and Barry Weingast define as a system in which enforceable laws protect a constellation of social, economic, and political freedoms.[32] Another equivalent is "open society," by which Karl Popper means a society whose members give one another freedoms out of awareness of their personal limitations, how often they err, and their dependence on others for knowing their shortcomings.[33] The antithesis of liberal order is "illiberal order," whose characteristics closely match those of a "closed society" and "limited-access order." For maximal clarity as well as brevity, we shall continue to use the liberal–illiberal distinction here.

Implicit in the notion of "order" is a state that taxes citizens through transparent, predictable, and broadly supported means. It supplies services that cannot be provided optimally through private initiatives. Maintaining a monopoly over instruments of mass violence, a liberal state defends society against external enemies and preserves internal peace, as necessary, by enforcing rules coercively. The rules of the state form its constitution. The officials who wield powers on its behalf are themselves subject to the constitution. The constitution contains procedures for sacking, and possibly punishing, any official who abuses the state's capacities.[34] A liberal order is protected from its own guardians partly through institutional checks and balances that empower branches of the state to keep each other in line.[35] Ordinary citizens assist the protection process through autonomous civic organizations that monitor official agencies and expose their abuses. A liberal order's checks and balances also protect civil liberties by keeping any person or clique from attaining absolute power.

The civic organizations that help to restrain the state and keep it from governing arbitrarily include, among others, professional societies, social clubs, neighborhood associations, ethnic assemblies, religious organizations, political lobbies, labor unions, and consumer cooperatives. Collectively such associations form "civil society."[36] Their common trait is de facto, if not also de jure, autonomy from the state. A robust civil society requires freedom of association. Individuals must be able to join organizations through which like-minded people pursue collective action. Like-mindedness need not entail a perfect coincidence of wants or visions. A civic association can be effective even if its members disagree on objectives, strategies, or tactics. Yet its influence requires a membership ready to compromise with each other in the interest of unity on core issues. Members must also be in broad agreement on procedures for admitting members, selecting officers, dividing tasks, and formulating policies. In a liberal order, the offenses that draw responses from civic organizations may involve any violation of the general rules within the constitution. They could mobilize to protect a minority's expressive rights or to end discrimination in government contracting. In either case, they might seek redress from the state's dispute-resolution institutions.

By itself, a strong civil society cannot protect, let alone advance, freedoms. Political checks and balances give civic organizations the capacity and security to be effective.[37] Conversely, a state's own checks and balances are insufficient to generate a sustainable liberal order. They could harmonize the powers of elites without extending freedoms to the masses. Despotic states of Antiquity balanced elite factions while denying their subjects associational rights.[38]

Islam and Political Underdevelopment

Civic organizations, or their members as individuals, do not necessarily respect liberal principles themselves. Groups need not feel bound by rules that they support in the abstract and find beneficial when enforced on others. A generic name for such discrepant behavior is free riding. Among its manifestations are efforts to divert resources to one's own group or cause even when the transfer results in a net loss to society.[39] Timeless and universal forms of privilege include trade restrictions detrimental to consumers, censorship that suppresses information on policy outcomes, regulations that block religious competition, subsidies favoring politically connected charities, licensing requirements unnecessary to professional efficacy, and regressive tax codes. Even in democracies that score high in indices of political performance, much legislation contains provisions that benefit narrow groups.

No society, past or present, has been governed strictly according to general rules, without special privileges for any persons or groups. But departures from liberal principles are matters of degree. Some societies have political institutions that make it difficult to obtain special privileges. Administrative transparency norms serve this purpose by facilitating countermobilization; so do judicial systems committed to impartial enforcement of the constitution. Throughout history, most constitutions, written or implicit, have been conspicuously illiberal; they have privileged certain groups, for instance a ruling family, a caste, an ethnicity, or a religious community. Illiberal constitutions typically criminalize organizing to equalize rights, and even speaking of equality. The liberality of a constitution may differ across contexts. Societies with religious outgroups vary in the forms and severity of sectarian discrimination. Besides, those that persecute outgroups may be quite liberal on, say, economic matters.

A liberal order's defenses against special interests include an ideology that venerates freedoms and impartial governance. Known generically as liberalism, it promotes confidence in markets and values free speech. It treats individuals as the best judges of their personal interests. A freedom may be restricted in a liberal order, but only to avoid undermining other general goals. Yelling "Fire!" in a mosque can be prohibited to prevent panic. Weapons transactions may be regulated for public safety. Building codes may be imposed to protect occupants from underestimated risks. Such constraints often enjoy broad acceptance as widely beneficial. By the same token, the acceptable constraints may change over time. As lifestyles evolve, certain building regulations may become anachronistic; and climate change may make others seem too permissive. Liberalism does not stand, then, for either unlimited or unchanging liberties. But it treats freedom as the default condition and imposes a high bar for restrictions. It stands out among rival ideologies as promoting skepticism toward rationales for regulation or coercion.

Supporters of liberalism in the abstract may inadvertently interpret rules self-servingly. It is routine to confuse one's personal interest with the common good.[40] Thus, the beneficiaries of privileges will often portray them as constitutional policies serving the common good.[41] Whatever their awareness of self-serving biases, state authorities inevitably face demands for special favors. They are asked to bend rules for a particular group or to allow discriminatory policies that are unconstitutional. A liberal state's officials are expected to avoid special favors. Insofar as members of society subscribe to liberalism, they will support the enforcement of general rules even when inconvenient to themselves. Liberalism uses both the state and civic organizations to align social norms with enforcement of the constitution.

Coercive religion is obviously incompatible with liberalism. Religion per se is not. Within established rules, people are free to form a religion, proselytize, worship as they please in spaces of their own, enjoy recognition as an autonomous social organization, display markings of their beliefs, and generally pursue the life they want. What liberalism disallows is religious compulsion and favoritism. Individuals must be as free to exit a religion as to enter it. Opportunities accorded to any one religion must extend equally to other religions as well as to the nonreligious. The state must not privilege a certain religion by using it for guidance, or allowing it to vet policies, or helping it financially.

In certain contexts, including contemporary politics in the United States, the term "liberalism" is associated with interventionist and heavily regulatory economic policies; considered the opposite of "conservative," it is about ends rather than means.[42] That is not what the term connotes here, so it will avoid confusion to elaborate on the economic dimensions of liberalism, in its sense adopted in this book. In line with its high trust in markets, liberalism entails skepticism of the capacity to correct for market failures through state intervention. Sensitized to state failures, it insists on weighing the tradeoffs between state and market inefficiencies. It also aims to keep the state as small as possible. Indeed, liberalism considers it healthy for economic activity to be carried out primarily by private enterprises within markets open to competition. As in other contexts, exceptions to these principles are allowed according to general rules, not ad hoc considerations tailored to narrow constituencies. Food processing may be regulated because consumers cannot judge food safety on their own. For legal efficiency, enterprise founders may be required to choose among a finite number of organizational templates.

The concept of a liberal order is not specific to any one region or civilization. It is used in this book as a reference point in interpreting the Middle East's historical political trajectory and evaluating its potential for further transformations. The dynamics just outlined, such as the struggle between enforcers of general rules and seekers of special treatment, have counterparts throughout Middle Eastern history. The Quran contains prescriptions that are reasonably construed as elements of a liberal order. The region's ruling elites have had many opportunities to deploy these as justifications for liberalization. As we shall see, Islam has expanded freedoms, sometimes dramatically. It has also been reinterpreted to legitimize practices once considered un-Islamic. Yet missed opportunities have also been plentiful. Facing a fork in the road, leaders have often favored coercive uniformity over negotiated pluralism, or the familiar over the new. The book's key challenge amounts to explaining why, thus far, the Middle East has failed to take advantage of its critical liberalization opportunities. In addressing this challenge, we shall gain an understanding of why the Middle East is now the world's most repressive region.

Countries that have come closest to attaining the ideals of a liberal order are generally in Western Europe and its cultural offshoots in the New World. That does not make Western politics an infallibly superior model universally. For one thing, even in modern times the West has produced destructive dictatorships, Nazi Germany being the most notorious example.[43] For another, the West's liberal institutions are not carved in stone. Since the 2010s, many Western countries have experienced "democratic backsliding" and "de-liberalization."[44] Two countries that have set standards of liberalism, France and the United States, are less liberal in the 2020s than they were in the 1990s.[45] In both countries, people feel less free to express their opinions publicly.[46] As of late 2021, 40 percent of Americans who identify as Republican support state censorship of disfavored media networks, as do 38 percent of Democrats. At least 4 percent of all Americans would support using violence if the other party wins the next presidential election.[47] In 2004, France banned "the wearing of signs or clothes through which pupils ostensibly express a religious allegiance."[48] Evidently, sustaining a liberal order is a constant struggle even in the West, its birthplace. To borrow a metaphor from Daron Acemoglu and James Robinson, the task requires running just to stay in place.[49] Whether Western countries will run fast enough to maintain even their diminished freedoms is by no means assured.

The terms democratic backsliding and de-liberalization often go together. But they are distinct. Whereas the former refers primarily to the weakening of political checks and balances, the latter emphasizes loss of liberties. The links between these processes go both ways. Greater concentration of power diminishes society's ability to preserve personal rights and freedoms. Conversely, weaker rights and freedoms pave the way for dictatorship. This book's focus on liberties rather than democracy has two pragmatic justifications. First, liberties mattered to development long before modern democracy. Second, democracy of any kind has never been common in the Middle East.

PRE-ISLAMIC, EXTERNAL, AND COLONIAL INFLUENCES

The Middle East has never existed in isolation from the rest of the world. Its peoples have had intercontinental commercial relations. Ideas have flowed between the Middle East and other regions, sometimes over fabled paths, such as the Silk Road, or through legendary intermediaries, such as Venetian merchants. The inspiration for the Islamic waqf and various tax policies came from institutions present in the Persian and Roman empires. Certain key themes of modern Islamism were hatched in India. Middle East-centered empires once controlled far-flung areas that are now self-ruling: the Caucasus, the Balkans, Iberia, and the Sahel. Developments in these regions affected trajectories of the Middle East.

Although the significance of external effects is uncontroversial, disagreements abound on specifics. Because of data limitations, debates are particularly heated on pre-Islamic influences. But even here scholars generally agree on the significance of conditions in Arabia during Muhammad's youth.[50] Insofar as early Islamic institutions had pre-Islamic roots, the Middle Eastern trajectory under Islamic rule is attributable to non-Islamic institutions. Indeed, by invoking pre-Islamic origins, some scholars absolve Islam of responsibility for undesirable historical patterns; and, using analogous logic, others deny Islam credit for commendable outcomes. This origin-focused logic is applicable, of course, to every civilization. All political analysis, not just research on the Middle East, can be deepened by stretching its temporal range further into the past. For instance, partisan polarization in the United States draws energy from parliamentary rules transplanted from England. Yet every social inquiry must start from an institutional complex in place at some point in history.

Patterns observed under Islamic rule do not become un-Islamic merely for having pre-Islamic roots. When an institution was borrowed from a non-Islamic source, it became Islamic; and insofar as it evolved under Muslim rule, it became a distinctly Islamic variant or descendant of the original. What justifies designating such an institution Islamic is its selection by Muslims from among all the available pre-Islamic options. When the caliph Umar convened an assembly to designate his successor, it was a *shura*, not a town council of the type used in the Mari Kingdom in Mesopotamia (2950–1760 BCE), or the Athenian *ekklesia*, which in the 650s BCE gave lower-class men a political voice, or the Persian Empire's assembly of elders (550 BCE–651 CE).[51] Islamic institutions also influenced the uses of Islamized pre-Islamic institutions. If no *shura* assembled to choose the successor of the *shura*-selected third caliph, and subsequent Umayyad caliphs turned the *shura* into a legitimation instrument, other institutions must have been at work. Even Islam's transplanted institutions are inexplicable, then, without reference to its broader institutional complex.

External political effects on a society can work through invasions. In the case at hand, the Mongol invasion of the thirteenth century – most notoriously, the sacking of Baghdad in 1258 – is often cited as the cause of sundry problems, including economic torpor, scientific stagnation, and persistent authoritarianism.[52] The Mongol raids did indeed devastate present-day Iran, Iraq, and parts of Syria and Turkey. But the long-term effects are vastly exaggerated.[53] Islamic law attained its classical form almost a quarter-millennium before the fall of Baghdad. By the time the Mongols reached the Middle East, key Islamic institutions that sustained autocracy were already in place; so were complementary institutions that kept merchants politically powerless, allowed arbitrary taxation, and limited religious and expressive freedoms. These institutions

Islam and Political Underdevelopment

outlasted the Mongols, without identifiable changes. They include, for instance, waqf law and the apostasy ban, both politically significant. In any case, when military occupation has lasting effects, they are not necessarily unfavorable. Defeat in World War II made the Japanese and Germans freer, not more repressed. Another reason for skepticism about lasting damage is that the ills attributed to Mongols transcend Mongol-ravaged areas. North Africa, which Mongol hordes did not reach, is no beacon of freedom.

European colonization is a more recent intervention that gets blamed for Middle Eastern authoritarianism.[54] The British and French grabbed resources, redrew borders without regard for communal links, stoked divisions, and destroyed traditional institutions. The interferences occurred in some places after annexation (for example, Algeria, as a French department); in others, under a partly autonomous colonial administration (French and British mandates in Syria, Lebanon, Palestine, Iraq); and in still others, through influences over independent regimes (Iran, Turkey). Whatever the form of interference, it is said, European misdeeds distorted economic and political development. Some authors stress that colonial powers sapped the region's capacity for collective action especially by keeping it from forming cohesive nations.[55]

Other scholars go so far as to claim that European colonizers actively undermined democratization drives. Ostensibly, one such drive was the power-sharing agreement between Syrian liberals and Islamists in 1920; had the French withdrawn from the region after the end of Ottoman rule, Syria would have evolved into a freer, more democratic society.[56] This argument presumes that neither party to the Syrian agreement would have tried, after a French departure, to gain advantage over the other. Yet similar alliances formed against a common enemy have collapsed after the enemy's defeat. People of diverse persuasions united during Turkey's War of Independence in 1919–22. After the coalition's victory, the modernizers lost no time in ejecting traditionalists from positions of power. They also took to secularizing the country aggressively.[57] In Pahlavi Iran, Islamists and communists formed an alliance to topple the monarchy. The shah ousted, they turned on each other, and Islamists decimated their former allies.[58]

Among the contributions of colonial rule was the establishment of modern schools that provided instruction in a foreign language. Variants teaching in local languages were quick to follow. Prominent families, which had been sending their children to Islamic schools, started favoring modern schools. One side effect was lower student quality at Islamic schools; another was a decline in the quality of Islamic scholarship.[59] It does not follow, though, that colonization of the Middle East led to de-liberalization through lower educational performance. The graduates of modern schools played leading roles in invigorating civic life. They contributed mightily to economic growth. They served as conduits for liberal philosophies. Insofar as Islamic schools lost appeal as vehicles of upward mobility, it is because of their lack of responsiveness to changes in labor demand and their adherence to outdated pedagogies.[60]

Other reasons exist for dismissing colonization as the main cause of the Middle East's poor record in advancing freedoms. Among formerly colonized peoples that won independence in the twentieth century (mostly after World War II), 89.5 percent of those in Latin America had an electoral democracy in 2020, as did 18.6 percent of those in non-Arab Africa; the corresponding figure for the Middle East was just 2.7 percent.[61] On the standardized 0–10 scale used in Figure 1.4, the corresponding population-weighted civil liberties ratings were 4.5 for the decolonized countries of non-Arab Africa and 6.5 for those of Latin America, as against 2.8 for those of the Middle East.[62] The reason for the Middle East's rock-bottom numbers is not that European colonizers treated it especially badly. Former colonies that are both freer and more democratic than the Middle East include ones that endured the worst abuses of colonization.[63] Evidently, colonial rule is not the key to understanding modern Middle Eastern politics.

Might proto-colonization stemming from patron to client relationships with a superpower explain the Middle East's political record? A prominent view is that alliances with the United States corrupted the region, tilting its political playing field in favor of pro-American groups, which happen to be antidemocratic.[64] True enough, ever since World War II, the policies of certain regimes have reflected the interests of American elites. But it does not follow that the United States has shaped, or could shape, the Middle East's institutions from scratch. American-influenced institutions have been superimposed on a vast preexisting institutional complex. It is the historical roots of that preexisting complex that is under investigation here. The effects are shared by longstanding American clients in the region – Saudi Arabia, Kuwait, Jordan, Egypt – but also nonclients – Baath Syria and Iraq, Islamic Iran, Libya, and Yemen. Evidently, American patronage is not a necessary condition for political repression.

Nevertheless, colonization *is* relevant to the task at hand. A more sophisticated class of explanations, initiated by Daron Acemoglu, Simon Johnson, and James Robinson, merits serious consideration.[65] This trio recognizes variations in how Europeans treated their colonies. In places where colonizers intended to resettle permanently, they established "inclusive institutions" – institutions favorable to broad-based growth with expanding personal freedoms. But in climatically hostile territories that interested colonizers only for their resources, they installed "extractive institutions."

In the Acemoglu–Johnson–Robinson framework, precolonial institutions are irrelevant to current patterns, presumably because they were superseded by whatever institutions colonizers chose. The literature based on this framework has pointedly avoided engaging with the Middle East, which is fortuitous.[66] French, British, and Italian institutions were superimposed on an institutional complex that could not possibly have been voided no matter how hard the colonists tried. When national regimes emerged, many precolonial institutions, or at least their legacies, were still influencing individual behaviors and social patterns. This point is substantiated in following chapters. In any case, the

Islam and Political Underdevelopment

Acemoglu–Johnson–Robinson logic suggests that European colonies would have established inclusive institutions at least where they settled in large numbers, for example in Algeria, Tunisia, eastern Libya, and Ottoman Istanbul.[67] And if they did not stay, it is because they were forced out – in Turkey after World War I and the War of Independence, in Egypt under Nasser, and in Algeria after its own War of Independence.[68] Hence, the legacies of European colonization should not have been uniformly negative across the region.

Indeed, certain colonial policies helped to overcome inefficiencies of Islamic institutions. In Algeria, for instance, France expropriated waqfs on a huge scale, both to expand its economic footprint and to release resources for development.[69] Hence, the net effects of these confiscations were not necessarily negative. That many native Algerians lost wealth is clear. However, as we shall see later on, there were also unmistakable gains from unlocking resources trapped in a dysfunctional institution. Besides, in Algeria and other Arab lands, the French followed a pattern already initiated by Ottoman, Egyptian, and Turkish leaders, who acted with broad local support.[70] Colonizers also founded modern courts, which displaced Islamic courts in expanding domains. Furthermore, they helped to establish municipalities, which took over many functions from waqfs. Such measures created markets, spawned opportunities, facilitated transactions, and expanded freedoms.

Even some explicitly extractive institutions of the European powers brought long-run benefits. The infrastructure of the Ottoman Public Debt Administration (OPDA), which creditors established to make their Ottoman debtor solvent, contributed to the fiscal capacity of Ottoman successor regimes.[71] Their modern tax systems all benefited from the OPDA's architecture. Although enhancing a regime's fiscal capacity does not necessarily improve economic freedoms, in this case there were obvious gains. For instance, taxation became more predictable and property rights stronger.

To sum up, whatever their benefits to foreigners, interventions did not necessarily diminish local political freedoms. Moreover, in certain contexts the effects were decidedly positive. The region's pre-Islamic heritage also affected its political trajectory. But the influences involved distinctly Islamic and sometimes also distinctly Middle Eastern interactions.

THE CENTRALITY OF ISLAMIC LAW

In sketching the book's architecture and highlighting its relevance to prominent controversies, this chapter has identified diverse mechanisms involving Islamic law. Some scholars confuse inquiries into the effects of legal institutions with "Islamic essentialism," an approach that treats early Islamic institutions, described in caricatured form, to have sealed the fate of Muslim societies.[72] In fact, there is no connection. We have already seen that Islamic law was reinterpreted in various contexts and periods. We know, too, that certain

Islamic institutions have been dismantled or drastically altered. In any case, no necessary link exists between an institution's fixity and its long-term consequences. Depending on specifics, lack of institutional stability can harm freedoms as surely as the fixity alleged by essentialists.

The multiplicity of the Islamic institutions that left imprints on the Middle East's political culture may raise additional qualms; so may the multiplicity of the mechanisms associated with each institution. Some readers may expect the book to identify a single Islamic institution that has made the Middle East score low on global freedom indices. Hence, it will help to review the book's analytic challenges early on, before delving into details. How does one select elements of Islamic law to focus on? What connections exist among the various mechanisms at play? There is nothing unusual, of course, about multiple institutions contributing to an observed outcome. Christianity affected European societies through myriads of factors: Church dogma, canon law, the Protestant Reformation, ecclesiastical governance, overtly political clerical initiatives, and more. Likewise, Islam has affected the Middle East's political performance through multiple channels.

2

Explaining Illiberalism, Identifying Opportunities for Liberalization

Many civilizations of Antiquity were ruled by coalitions that retained power through violence. Pharaonic Egypt, Sumer, and the Aztec Empire all enslaved people and committed genocide. They killed humans through rituals such as ripping hearts out of conscious victims and burying servants with their masters. In each case, the ruling coalition enjoyed rights that it denied to the masses, who were supposed to accept their inferiority. Organizing to pursue broader rights was risky, except insofar as it suited elites. Structural inequalities were rationalized through religion. Challenges to the ruling coalition usually came from within, or from rival coalitions. Wars were fought over territories and taxpaying inhabitants.[1]

Through epic struggles glorified in the histories of modern nation-states, elite privileges were tempered, powerless groups gained rights, and rule of law emerged in various forms. The requisite redistribution of power and restraints on rulers always involved organizations representing the oppressed. Over time, as legal systems developed, rules emerged to facilitate private collective action by new constituencies. General tax rules extended property rights to the masses. Religions legitimized these transformations and spurred them on.

The institutional creativity that accompanied the advent and spread of Islam was one manifestation of this civilizing process. The Quran's transfer system, zakat, limited taxation and provided general property rights, and its beneficiaries extended beyond elites. Serving all classes and creeds, Islamic courts enforced private contracts and resolved disputes. Though not impartial, they gave commoners of all faiths some protection against state-connected elites. The waqf created opportunities to serve large constituencies privately, outside direct state control.

From this long perspective, our master puzzle is that the political civilizing process has lagged in the Middle East relative to the global norm. The slowdown started before Modernity. Already in the Middle Ages, the Middle East was falling behind Western Europe in civic life, and the pattern then extended to personal freedoms and rule of law.[2] For a while, the gaps were not necessarily perceptible. There were variations across space and time; and, in some respects, such as cross-religious tolerance, the Middle East continued to perform well by the prevailing global standards. Its underperformance entered the strategic agenda of local leaders two centuries ago. As various comparative indices suggest, the process has been slower in the Middle East than in other lagging regions. The catch-up remains gravely incomplete, which is itself puzzling.

The purpose of this chapter is methodological. Since the book aims to assess the roles of Islamic institutions in suppressing freedoms and to identify past and present opportunities for liberalization, we must specify what makes an institution Islamic, as opposed to merely Middle Eastern. In probing specific institutions, we will encounter consequences that were intended. However, especially over long time periods, effects once unimaginable became critical. Insofar as a particular institution persisted, it did so by incentivizing relevant actors to perpetuate it. The mechanisms generating the incentives need to be uncovered.

We shall be seeking, then, self-enforcing equilibria that hindered institutional dynamism. A self-enforcing equilibrium may be self-undermining as well. Specifically, it may induce chains of individual responses that make it increasingly fragile, culminating in the demise of incentives essential to its reproduction. Interactions existed among institutions with disparate primary functions, such as partnership rules (which facilitated joint commercial ventures) and blasphemy rules (which protected Islam's dominant interpretation). In applying these concepts from the historical political economy literature to the Middle East, we shall uncover critical junctures at which the region might have started to liberalize. This methodology will form the basis of a prediction: plausible paths to liberalization are not entirely blocked.

POLITICALLY CRITICAL ISLAMIC INSTITUTIONS

Since the birth of Islam, innumerable social constructs have affected the Middle East's political trajectory. We need to identify those that affected freedoms central to a liberal order. A prerequisite is to specify what made an institution, perhaps temporarily, part of the Islamic institutional complex.

Quranic and Post-Quranic Islamic Institutions

After its chapters began to emerge in 610, the Quran served as a basic reference point in Muslim community- and state-building. Accordingly, certain institutions became part of the Islamic institutional complex by virtue of prescriptions in the Quran. The significance of Quranic institutions to early Muslims varied, and their roles evolved. Certain Quran-based regulations are generally enforced

Explaining Illiberalism, Identifying Opportunities 35

even today, in some cases with adjustments. For example, the Islamic inheritance system elicited broad, though never full, compliance from the start; and it has been transmitted across generations as a settled part of the Islamic institutional complex. Other Quranic institutions underwent huge transformations within decades. Zakat rules generated incentives to reinterpret, distort, and selectively ignore them. Though canonically zakat remains among Islam's pillars, as a matter of practice it metamorphosed quickly into a minor ritual of negligible economic, political, or social impact.

As the Muslim community grew and Islam's geographic domain expanded, the Islamic institutional complex acquired new elements, and generations of jurists and practitioners gave them increasing significance. Like Quranic institutions, post-Quranic Islamic institutions differed in their longevity. Certain innovations remained localized and short-lived. Moreover, those institutions that got absorbed into classical Islamic law – the compendium of durable laws in place by the 900s – differed in significance. The waqf remained a core Islamic institution right up to the 1800s, when elites realized that it impeded modernization and exacerbated existential threats from the West.

Retrospective insights can help to identify early Islamic institutions that gained political significance over the long run. They can also uncover missed opportunities for liberalization. Given what is known about pathways to expanding freedoms in the modern era, which Quranic and post-Quranic Islamic institutions have been agents of liberalization in one way or another? Which were designed to block liberties, or had that effect? Such questions are asked in trying to explain any region's political trajectory. They are not specific to the Middle East.

Institutions Vital to Liberalization

A liberal order is impossible without the capacity to form organizations that engage in collective action on behalf of private constituencies. Apart from providing shared goods, private organizations restrain the state as well as other private organizations capable of repression.[3] The size of the middle class and the urban population are other factors that shape political trajectories. As the middle class grows through commercial expansion or technologically induced resource reallocation, elites worried about political stability are incentivized to broaden rights and enhance social mobility. Urbanites are harder to repress than peasants because industrial and cerebral production are more difficult to measure than agricultural output, and because it is costlier to monitor factory workers and bureaucrats than to supervise farmers.[4] Evidently, factors of no consequence in any given period may subsequently gain enormous importance. Thus, in the Middle Ages, the egalitarianism of the Islamic inheritance system and the rigidity of the waqf did not stand out as obstacles to political development. However, they became handicaps as technological advances compounded the advantages of scaling up organizationally and made allocational flexibility critical to wealth creation. Accordingly, they now require attention in identifying obstacles to invigorating civil society, strengthening rule of law, and expanding economic opportunities.

Religious freedoms, including the right to remain irreligious, are essential to liberal governance. At the dawn of Islam, certain rules provided religious freedoms to both Muslims and non-Muslims. Controversies over their interpretation are salient in accounts of that period. But within decades, officials were ignoring these rules to preserve power and maximize revenue. Among the manifestations of religious repression was the concealment of discontent over state policies linked to Islam. Muslims withheld criticisms for fear of retaliation, as did non-Muslims afraid of a Muslim backlash.

Religious repression induces self-censorship even on issues remotely connected to religion. It makes people falsify their preferences and knowledge in broad domains, concealing doubts about policies promoted in the name of religion. Public discourses are distorted. Intellectual creativity wanes. For these reasons alone, it matters here that in the premodern Middle East practically all education was based on religion. Muslim education was carried out through Islamic schools that limited worldviews, curiosity, and analytic skills. Non-Muslims were also educated through religious schools, which created analogous handicaps.

The claim that religious restrictions sapped intellectual creativity bears the objection that brilliant minds can produce penetrating ideas even in an intellectual desert. Consider Ibn Khaldun (1332–1406), author of *Introduction to History*, which would have brought credit to any luminary of the Enlightenment – Europe's philosophical movement of the 1700s, which promoted rationalism. Writing alone, and shunning the ideology and rhetoric of Islamic scholarship, Ibn Khaldun anticipated concepts such as self-undermining institutions and unintended consequences, which are elements of this book's theoretical scaffolding. He even observed that ongoing Italian transformations were absent in his own milieu, North Africa.[5] For all his precocious insights, Ibn Khaldun had no significant followers. No Ibn Khaldunian school emerged. Unlike the treatises of Ghazali (died 1111) and Ibn Taymiyya (1263–1328), thinkers who operated self-consciously in an Islamic framework, his own masterwork did not inspire others to extend its insights. The intellectual climate remained hostile to his analytic mode even as the Middle East and the broader Muslim world fell on hard times. In the nineteenth century, *Introduction to History* did resonate with a few reformists. But they were unequipped intellectually to apply its methods to their own time.[6]

Like religious freedoms, economic freedoms are pivotal to a liberal order. Rights such as owning property securely and investing freely are critical to its reproduction. But the capacity to exercise economic freedoms depends on the available menu of economic organization. Thus, Islamic institutions responsible for the scale, longevity, and complexity of Middle Eastern profit-seeking enterprises determined what technologies they could exploit, their potential for wealth creation, and their global competitiveness. These institutions also determined the political reach of private economic actors. The Islamic inheritance system is another institution that blocked liberalization through multiple channels. Inhibiting private capital accumulation, it also fragmented successful enterprises and constrained the business community's civic capacity.

INTENDED AND UNINTENDED CONSEQUENCES

Social analyses that blame or credit a single factor find a receptive audience because they are easy to understand, but also because they minimize the required contextual knowledge. Popular arguments that link Middle Eastern authoritarianism to corrupt Umayyad caliphs or the Mongol invasion fit the pattern. It is easy to imagine the ravages of unscrupulous leaders or ruthless pillagers. Yet simple accounts can hide more than they reveal. Some societies overcome the harms of bad leaders and foreign invasions more easily than others; and differences in resilience are inexplicable through a single factor. Credible explanations of long-term social processes inevitably entail multiple institutions. As diverse examples in following chapters will show, interactions among institutions can generate unintended consequences. My interpretations involve two concepts central to analytic historical studies: self-enforcing equilibria and self-undermining equilibria.[7] Though these terms have a short history, the concepts are found in some of the most important social scientific works of the past millennium. Ibn Khaldun's *Introduction to History* is one. Adam Smith's 1776 classic, *The Wealth of Nations*, is another.[8]

Self-Enforcing and Self-Undermining Equilibria

In interacting with each other, the institutions that shaped the Middle East's political trajectory generated incentives to keep reproducing them. These regularities are called self-enforcing equilibria. Consider the Islamic apostasy ban. It induced fears that made Muslims withhold objections to religious coercion. The near-absence of open opposition then emboldened clerics to keep teaching that out-conversion is forbidden to Muslims. Overwhelmingly illiterate populations learned that Islam welcomes in-conversion but bars out-conversion.

Islam's illiberal religious policies were also self-*reinforcing* insofar as they bolstered conformism. A central theme of persecutions launched in the name of Islamic purity is that fear of punishment fed on itself. During the Kadızadeli oppression in seventeenth-century Istanbul, congregations turned on alleged sinners.[9] Individual Muslims thereby earned the right to be left alone. A byproduct of their conformism was a rise in the dangers endured by critics of the Kadızadelis. Iran experienced a similar process in the 1980s, as it became a brutal theocracy. Every Iranian who made involuntary displays of piety – donning a headscarf, becoming an "Islamic" intellectual – made it even harder for other dissenters to push back.[10]

Judaism and Christianity, too, have been interpreted as banning out-conversion. Medieval inquisitions executed Christians for blasphemy, heresy, or apostasy on the basis of biblical mandates such as: "A man or a woman who is a medium or a wizard shall be put to death" and "He who blasphemes the name of the Lord shall be put to death."[11] By the Modern Era, though, most branches of Christianity had liberalized their practices regarding apostasy.[12] Even as they continue to believe that their own form of Christianity provides the surest path to salvation, they allow out-conversion, whether to another branch of Christianity, another religion, or atheism. What would explain why the ban on out-conversion was self-undermining in Christianity but not in Middle Eastern Islam? A key difference lies in opportunities to form self-governing private organizations. By the second millennium, Western religious entities could become corporations. They were also common in other sectors of society, including education and crafts.[13] The civic activities of these autonomous organizations pressured churches to become more tolerant of dissent, apostasy, and other religions.[14] In the Middle East, by contrast, the absence of opportunities to form self-governing private organizations hindered collective action promoting religious tolerance. Evidently, the evolution of any given institution depends on other elements of the institutional complex within which it is embedded.

Middle Eastern history, too, features self-undermining institutions. Consider again the Quran's zakat rules. Absent from them are provisions for aligning state revenues and expenditures. Officials were impelled to impose other taxes, which then lowered zakat's significance and raised the state's willingness to grant payment exemptions. As exemptions broadened, zakat's perceived fairness would have fallen, along with confidence in the state's commitment to rule of law. In any event, zakat evasion became increasingly common. Zakat's centrality to the Islamic order thus dissipated as responses contrary to its original spirit fed on themselves.

Whether self-enforcing or self-undermining, an equilibrium can be unintended. Insofar as it produces good outcomes, the beneficiaries need not have anticipated them. Likewise, bad outcomes need not have been driven by villains who caused harm knowingly. Actors can come and go without ever understanding the effects of their actions. The Islamic jurists who constructed the rules of the waqf could not have known that their choices would contribute, a millennium later, to making the Middle East vulnerable to colonization. Had they foreseen how delayed institutional modernization would harm their descendants, they might have given waqf caretakers more discretion. Similarly, jurists of Islam's early centuries could not have foreseen the long-term effects of letting clerics supervise waqfs. One has been to implicate clerics in the Middle East's economic underperformance. As we shall see, many political shortcomings of the modern Middle East are unintended consequences of premodern institutional choices.

By no means are all policy outcomes unintended. The authorities who devised Islam's apostasy, blasphemy, and heresy rules included people who

Explaining Illiberalism, Identifying Opportunities 39

believed that benefits to the Muslim community outweighed costs to accused individuals, or simply that the rules fulfilled a sacred duty. Clerics were also motivated by maintaining influence. Often, then, they achieved precisely what they intended. But, over many centuries, their religious repression weakened the Middle East vis-à-vis global rivals. Intellectual life was impoverished. Creativity diminished. Institutional development slowed. And the region lost competitiveness in global markets. In the early centuries of Islam, these outcomes, which unfolded over more than a millennium, were probably not on the minds of clerics who promoted illiberal interpretations of Islam. There is nothing unusual here. On many matters, the horizons of modern democratic governments are tied to election cycles. Decisions geared to short-run goals yield unimaginable long-term results.

Unintended Consequences of Inaction

In historical research, there is a tendency to attribute observed patterns to salient actions. Many attributions in this vein have a solid empirical foundation. The claim that the waqf was created to benefit elites accords with centuries of data showing that the wealthy endowed most waqfs and that waqf benefits accrued substantially to founders and their descendants.[15] But important patterns can also be generated by doing nothing. Baffling outcomes can arise from failing to respond to an unanticipated outcome or delaying the transplant of a foreign innovation. In brief, inaction is a hidden source of social change.[16]

Indeed, inaction is vital to understanding how the Middle East, by no means unusually repressive in the Middle Ages, became conspicuously unfree. The Middle East could have avoided that fate by initiating Western-inspired structural reforms far earlier than the nineteenth century. To anyone intellectually equipped to connect observable dots, the flaws of the Islamic institutional complex were apparent well before the Industrial Revolution. By the mid-second millennium, the Great Explorations were revealing a dynamism absent in the Middle East; the Protestant Reformation was tempering religious corruption; and technological advances were now coming mainly from the West. The West was not developing uniformly; Iberia lacked England's institutional creativity.[17] Variations within the West provided clues to what an economic catch-up would require. But in the Middle East clues were noticed only after it fell prey to Western colonizers. At that point, it took to transplanting Western institutions. Centuries of inaction are responsible, in part, for these consequences as well as the dynamics they unleashed.

The inaction that delayed Middle Eastern responses did not reflect conscious choices to reject obviously beneficial innovations. Lack of attention was one factor at play. Muslims were accustomed to ignoring developments in the West, which they considered backward. They were also habituated to ignoring the evolution of Christianity, which Islam treats as a legitimate but superseded monotheism.[18] Furthermore, the region's Islamic education system and its public discourses long blinded Middle Easterners to the growing disadvantages of their traditional institutions. If before the 1800s anyone considered the waqf a source of interregional divergence, the insight left no record; nor is there evidence that anyone saw weak property rights as seeds of an existential crisis. Unnoticed problems do not spur thinking about potential reforms.

INTERACTIONS AMONG SPHERES OF FREEDOM

The foregoing methodological illustrations draw linkages among various liberties. Those connections justify studying them together, within a single historical inquiry. In political thought, the emphasis on the interdependence of freedoms has a long pedigree.

Political Checks and Balances

In dividing federal powers between three coequal branches of government, the framers of the US constitution reasoned that concentrating power in one body would breed corruption and threaten cherished rights.[19] Having branches of government constrain each other would keep political power fragmented, they thought, but also protect economic, organizational, expressive, and religious liberties. In the twentieth century, Friedrich Hayek considered personal economic liberties essential to preventing political despotism. People in control of the fruits of their labor would not allow dictatorship, he believed.[20] Indeed, economic liberties preserve political liberties through freely formed private organizations and freely articulated thoughts.[21]

Institutional Complementarities

Each category of freedoms considered in this work encompasses many specific rights that can be unbundled. In any given context, the effectiveness of a particular right may depend on the presence of others. If icons of liberalism favor a high bar for restricting *any* freedom, it is to preserve *all* freedoms.

The Quran and early Islamic norms accommodated the rights to own property, form commercial enterprises, and trade for profit. Yet the effectiveness of these economic freedoms depended on other freedoms. Consider commercial enterprises formed under Islamic law. Their profitability depended on the available organizational templates, which for a millennium remained essentially fixed. Various elements of Islamic law, including inheritance and waqf rules, kept the organizational options of entrepreneurs from broadening beyond those of the Middle Ages. Hence, as Western commercial organizations expanded in scale and scope, those of the Middle East neither grew nor gained complexity.[22] Islam's commerce-friendly institutions thus failed to keep Middle Easterners competitive against Westerners. But the harm that Middle Eastern merchants endured because of organizational handicaps transcended their loss of global economic competitiveness. The same handicaps also kept them politically powerless at home by curbing their civic capacity. In sum, numerous complementarities kept the Middle East's economic and political trajectories intertwined. The connections are central to explaining why a religion founded by a merchant and initially hospitable to private enterprise eventually weakened merchants both commercially and politically.

Complementarities have guided the selection of the institutions scrutinized. A rationale for starting with waqfs is their role in keeping civic engagement feeble in cities, where their services were concentrated. Their rigidities held back urbanization in the Middle East, which in the second millennium was slower than in Europe.[23] Cities play outsized roles in political development because their populations are more threatening to the sovereign's power. In the countryside, low population density hinders collective action by disaffected groups. By contrast, an urban mob can paralyze a capital overnight. Thus Ottoman rulers kept major cities well stocked with food even during rural famines.[24] Starting with the waqf will also lay the groundwork for exploring the trajectories of religious and intellectual freedoms. Through their organizational limitations, waqf-financed schools constrained public discourse. Structurally inflexible themselves, they also suppressed personal inquisitiveness and creativity.

Inseparability of Religious and Secular Life

The motives for forming an Islamic waqf included wealth-sheltering, philanthropy, and charity. Often all three were present, with resources directed mostly at self-serving asset protection.[25] However, even waqfs founded mainly for charity had long-run effects on wealth distribution, the production and dissemination of knowledge, economic development, and civic life.

The richness of the waqf's legacies puts in relief interactions between religion and spheres of activity now generally considered secular. In the Middle East, the treatment of religion and secular activities as separable pursuits entered political discourses in the 1800s, and the separation became formal under secular regimes of the 1900s.[26] Before reforms shrank the jurisdiction of Islamic courts, many activities now considered outside religion were subject, in principle but often in practice as well, to religious rules. Clerics ran all Muslim schools. Through their authority to declare ideas un-Islamic, they limited the content of intellectual life. Clerics were also deeply immersed in political and economic life. They legitimated state policies, ran the judiciary, collected economic data for the state, monitored waqfs, and enforced inheritance rules. Hence, the Middle East's trajectory of organizational, economic, and political freedoms cannot be understood without reference to the history of how Islam was interpreted and practiced.

Mention of economic life in the premodern Middle East evokes bustling bazaars and winding caravans. The types of contracts used by the participants in these exchange venues essentially stagnated for a millennium. That fixity limited the civic engagement of merchants. It also denied them a place at the region's "political bargaining table."[27] Inclusion in high-level policy making did not require the business corporation, which was invented during Europe's Global Explorations and gained much broader significance only during the Industrial Revolution.[28] However, given the stagnation of classical Islam's contractual options, the corporation's absence denied merchants an *alternative route* to acquiring political influence; and, in turn, their persistent political frailty bolstered Islamic rules harmful to economic development.

Interactions between economic and political life thus pointed in both directions – from political weakness to the corporation's absence, and vice versa. Bidirectional interactions were also present between the religious and economic spheres. A presence at the Middle East's bargaining table would have allowed merchants to counterbalance the economic conservatism of clerics. Tellingly, fundamental legal reforms started after clerics suffered substantial losses in wealth. At least on economic matters, reforms might have come earlier had Islamic law furnished a broader menu of wealth-creating institutions in the first place.

MANY POSSIBLE PATHWAYS TO A LIBERAL ORDER

A book exploring why many interconnected freedoms have been delayed in one region, or why they are relatively more constrained, must explain why potential pathways to liberalization stayed closed for centuries on end. This task is achieved partly by focusing on early Islamic institutions that could have served as plausible starting points, along with institutional roadblocks that kept liberalization from taking off. For pragmatic reasons, we shall start with the waqf, which stymied organizational capabilities essential to advancing any bottom-up reform process.

The existence of many potential pathways to an Islamic liberal order will not surprise readers familiar with comparative political development generally. Liberalization hardly followed a set template. In France, England, and Japan, for instance, checks and balances arose through distinct processes.[29]

This multiplicity confirms that no single institution, let alone a specific institutional complex, is vital to a self-reinforcing liberalization process. Nevertheless, successful transitions outside the Middle East matter to the task at hand. They furnish clues as to which Islamic institutions might have influenced political development. They point to linkages among specific freedoms. Moreover, they illuminate why the Middle East may not have replicated them.

A Europe-focused work by Noel Johnson and Mark Koyama argues that religious toleration advanced in tandem with the fiscal capacity of states. Stronger states found it increasingly advantageous to move from "conditional religious toleration" to full religious liberty. Under conditional toleration, dominant religious groups lacked the right to apostasy; full liberty was achieved through religiously neutral rule of law.[30] As later chapters show, this transition has far to go in the Middle East. Johnson and Koyama's logic suggests that a basic cause is the low fiscal capacity of the Middle East's preindustrial states.[31] Several Islamic institutions constrained this capacity, I propose. For one thing, weak property rights drove enormous wealth into tax-exempt waqfs. For another, a restricted menu of contracts limited taxable wealth.

Liberalization is often spearheaded by political elites who expect to gain from the resulting wealth creation and political stabilization. In Middle Eastern history, the emergence of the Islamic waqf fits this pattern; so does the formal initiation, a millennium later, of feverish Ottoman, Egyptian, and Iranian reforms.

When elites extend freedoms to new groups, the motivation is often to neutralize threats. They make concessions preemptively, to avert showdowns. Outsiders threaten incumbent elites insofar as they are organized. Among the vehicles of collective action by outgroups is the corporation, which in premodern Europe brought about a "silent revolution." Tine de Moor, who coined the term, observes that in Western Europe corporations broadened rights through civic engagement, ultimately laying the groundwork for rule of law and democracy.[32] Such transformations could not occur in the Middle East, where the functions of corporations were met through waqfs. On occasion, the constituents of waqfs let off steam participating in riots. But they could not count on waqfs for assistance in addressing the root causes of their grievances.

PART II

PERSISTENT SOCIAL ATOMIZATION

3

Nongovernmental Organizations under Islamic Law

The Middle East's secularists and Islamists, but also its Shiis and Sunnis who fall into neither camp, object vehemently to being governed by parties under the other's authority. That is because political checks and balances tend to be weak. People of all walks of life expect a state controlled by another group to treat them poorly. Moreover, there is a consensus that people enter government mainly to obtain privileges, fill their pockets, and help kin.

In line with these perceptions, trust in strangers, or generalized trust, is low by the standards of relatively liberal societies. Among the questions of the World Values Survey, one asks the following: "Generally speaking, would you say that most people can be trusted or that you need to be very careful in dealing with people?"[1] Outside the Middle East, more than one-third respond that most people can be trusted. In the Middle East, the share is just 19.4 percent (Figure 3.1). Answers to the question are sensitive to translation; the closest equivalent to "trust" may conjure different thoughts depending on the language; and for any given language, the word's meaning may differ across countries. But the relative orderings given here are consistent with both quantitative and qualitative data collected using other methodologies. In a study on trust in the Muslim world, Avital Livny finds, with special reference to Turkey, that mistrust of strangers makes it relatively difficult to mobilize people around a common cause.[2] Other work points to limited trust in communal and governmental organizations.[3] Mistrust of strangers and institutions typically complements fierce loyalty to kin. Indeed, nepotism, the tendency to favor family members, is also common in the Middle East.[4]

There exist valuable studies that focus on proximate factors.[5] Since the end of foreign rule or occupation, they observe, Middle Eastern monarchs and presidents have emasculated the news media, suppressed intellectual inquiry, restricted artistic expression, banned political parties, and coopted regional, ethnic, and religious organizations. With autonomous political advocacy by

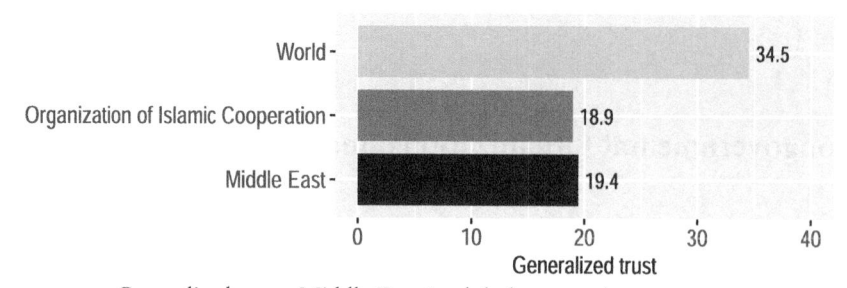

FIGURE 3.1 Generalized trust: Middle East in global perspective

Note: The figures refer to the percentage of people who "consider most people trustworthy."

Source: World Values Survey, Wave 6, 2010–14. The wave covered fifty-nine countries, of which thirteen are in the Middle East (twelve Arab League members plus Turkey) and twenty in OIC (including seven outside the Middle East).

nongovernmental organizations severely restricted, sustained collective action has been limited to extraordinary circumstances. Moreover, NGOs that overcome obstacles to political action remain unaccountable to their constituencies. But these patterns do not explain why the oppression in question has lasted for decades on end or why NGOs were frail at the founding of national regimes. They are present not only in the Arab world, which endured European colonization, but also in Iran and Turkey, which did not. And in colonized lands, the scantiness of organized civic engagement did not start with colonization. Their precolonial centuries featured few private organizations capable of restraining the state. Precolonial institutions would have affected colonial and postcolonial civic patterns.

This chapter and the next three suggest that the region's recent political trends, including the persistence of authoritarianism, political passivity of the masses, and weakness of civic engagement, are rooted in historical processes that predate European intrusions by a millennium. Colonial as well as postcolonial institutions were grafted onto social structures already unsuitable to autonomous civic engagement. Initially, the analytical focus is on a key element of the Islamic institutional complex: the Islamic waqf. Known in English as a "pious foundation" or "Islamic trust," the Islamic waqf is called *habous* in parts of North Africa and *bonyad* in Iran. It is a foundation established under Islamic law. Most comprehensively in Chapter 6, we shall see that the Islamic waqf differs fundamentally from a modern waqf. In certain countries, the latter has emerged under secular laws; in some others, it exists under radically modernized laws that a premodern Islamic jurist would barely recognize.

Within the premodern Islamic legal system, the Islamic waqf was the closest thing to an autonomous private organization. As such, it might have served as a vehicle for organized political participation, mass collective action, and political accountability, among other indicators of democratization. It might have generated a vibrant civil society able to constrain rulers and majorities. In fact, the

Islamic waqf kept civil society anemic, hindered democratization, and sustained various forms of repression.

The autonomous organizations that form civil society compete with the state as sources of information, vehicles of communication, interpreters of events, and agenda setters. Individually and jointly, they limit the state's capacity to control society. They restrict its ability to create and draw rents, direct economic resources, and regulate political life. They also resist state encroachment on personal freedoms.

In pursuing the interests of their members, civil organizations do not necessarily benefit society as a whole; their activities may have negative externalities. Advocates of urban development often work at cross-purposes with environmentalists. There also exist organizations that aim deliberately to harm certain groups. Examples include organizations committed to violence, racism, or political destabilization. Social networks composed of private clubs and associations aided the rise of Germany's Nazi Party by endorsing it and intimidating its opponents.[6] These organizations were exercising associational rights won during the uprisings against European monarchies between 1848 and 1850. Credited with helping to build and preserve Germany's first democracy, German civil society thus also contributed to its demise. For another poignant example, this one from our region of focus, the first and only democratically elected government in Egypt's history, the Muslim Brotherhood government headed by Mohamed Morsi between 2012 and 2013, was supported by thousands of Brotherhood-linked private organizations – suppressed for decades, but finally operating freely. With help from its affiliates, the Brotherhood tried to dismantle Egypt's newly installed political checks and balances.[7]

These examples call for caution in linking civil society to a liberal order. But they do not negate the importance of civic engagement to liberalization. Although civic organizations are susceptible to radicalization, no liberal order is possible without them. This is evident in trajectories of established liberal orders. Beginning their transformations at different times, they also experienced different social cleavages. Their democratic characteristics – enforced human rights, broad political participation through parties and lobbies, autonomous legislatures and judiciaries, and universal suffrage – did not develop in lockstep. Whereas some transitions involved epic violence, others were essentially peaceful.[8] Yet for all their differences, the European paths to democracy also share family resemblances. All involved protracted struggles by perpetual private associations. Through these struggles, impoverished and dominated groups learned to organize, challenge the status quo, and start participating in the determination of social priorities. Each national path produced bottom-up checks and balances of some sort – a civil society that placed power holders under rule of law.

The multiplicity of Western paths suggests that the Middle East could have followed a distinct path, or even several paths unique to subregions. Investigating the waqf's political consequences amounts, then, to asking why the Middle Eastern counterparts of European private organizations achieved less political influence. A fine-grained identification of the waqf's political functions will also illuminate critical obstacles to sustained democratization in the present.

To summarize the argument, I identify several mutually supportive mechanisms through which the waqf blocked the expansion of individual freedoms and restrained civic engagement. The waqf's operation was essentially set by its founder, which limited its capacity to meet new political challenges. In disregarding beneficiary preferences, it curbed political participation. It could not pool resources with other entities, which kept it from forming durable political coalitions. The waqf constrained political participation further by denying its beneficiaries formal rights in selecting officers. These constraints blocked many forms of civic engagement and diminished the effectiveness of others. Two further effects contributed to restraining individual freedoms. Circumventing stringent waqf rules required a court's permission. Together with lack of transparency in waqf management, this obligation fueled corruption. And the process of appointing successive officials promoted and legitimized nepotism. By supplying alternative means to address personal problems, both mechanisms dampened incentives for civic engagement.

In the modern Middle East, the corporation, a self-governing organization conducive to politics, has taken over many social functions of the Islamic waqf. Notwithstanding its name that harkens back to early Islam, even the modern waqf is a charitable corporation, which is an indefinitely existing and self-governing organization that does not distribute profits to stakeholders.[9] Islamic charities of the twenty-first century tend to be organized as modern waqfs, rather than as Islamic waqfs. In identifying the Islamic waqf's political consequences, this pattern makes it especially useful to keep an eye on corresponding developments in Western Europe, where sundry charitable corporations first contributed to broadening personal freedoms.

THE ISLAMIC WAQF AND ITS ECONOMIC SIGNIFICANCE

Under classical Islamic law, formed during Islam's first quarter-millennium, a waqf is a foundation that an individual establishes by turning privately held real estate into an endowment.[10] The endowment's revenue is to finance chosen services in perpetuity. A judge (*kāḍī*) must ratify the waqf's purpose. He records the endowed assets along with the founder's stipulations regarding goods, beneficiaries, maintenance, and expenditures.[11] The resulting deed (*waqfiyya*) is meant to govern the waqf forever. To minimize disputes over the founder's intentions, major waqfs had them carved into buildings. In certain places, it became customary to set a legal precedent for the deed's immutability by having the founder sue for modifications; the court's refusal would substantiate the inviolability of the deed's instructions.[12]

The service could be anything legitimate under Islamic law. Waqfs were established to support mosques, schools, Quran readings, fountains, hospitals, public kitchens, bathhouses, inns, families and their descendants, the founder him- or herself, and funerary complexes, among many other purposes. Whatever the chosen services, the endowment was supposed to support operational expenses, including staff remuneration and likely repairs.[13] Sometimes the deed explicitly named the beneficiaries.[14] When none was specified, the locational choice could privilege a particular community. For instance, the patients of a Damascus hospital would consist disproportionately of Damascenes. Ordinarily, the waqf's income was exempt from taxation, as were its payments to employees.[15]

Responsibility for managing the waqf's endowment and implementing its deed fell to a caretaker (*mutawalli*), who was typically a man.[16] The caretaker rented out properties, authorized repairs, hired and supervised employees, and delivered services. He performed these tasks as an agent of the founder, who might be dead. The caretaker's duty was to follow directives, not to pursue his own priorities or exercise judgment. The founder selected the initial caretaker and specified succession procedures. Sometimes he or she would name a sequence of successors, or alternatively, reserved the position for a specific office holder, such as a certain mosque's imam. Some founders simply included the succession decision among the caretaker's duties. Occasionally, they left the decision, at some point, to neighborhood residents, though without specifying procedures.

Ordinarily, the appointment was for life. When a caretaker died in office without a designated successor, the nearest judge made the new appointment. The local judge played other roles, too. His duties included enforcing the deeds of waqfs that delivered services or held properties in his area.[17] In this capacity, he could remove a caretaker for shirking or embezzlement. In principle, the local judge thus provided the waqf's main line of defense against mismanagement. But supervisory duties were commonly abused. Chapter 5 covers the means and consequences of waqf-related corruption.

Before modern times, the Middle East had weak property rights. Until 1839, the Ottoman sultan regularly exercised his imperial right to confiscate private property at will. But until at least the 1750s, waqfs enjoyed considerable immunity against expropriation. The source of this immunity was a belief in the sanctity of waqf property.[18] The belief essentially served as a credible commitment device. Knowing that a sultan who grabbed waqf assets would appear impious, people expected him to respect their inalienability. That made waqfs reliable tax and wealth shelters. The exceptions generally occurred during regime changes or major internal challenges. Sultans would declare a cluster of waqfs invalid, usually under the pretext that the endowed properties had not belonged to the founder, as waqf law required.

The origins of the sacredness belief probably lie in the Roman and Persian trusts that inspired the waqf concept. Both preexisting forms of trust were used to finance temples. Because temples served a religious purpose, their assets were considered intrinsically sacred. As the waqf rules were emerging, the principle of asset sacredness was extended to all waqfs, regardless of function; the reason must have been to make asset sheltering credible. A self-reinforcing equilibrium took hold, whereby sultans respected waqf inviolability, and elites put more assets into waqfs, in each case in the belief that waqf properties are sacred; and the longer the waqf enjoyed immunity, the more credible its sacredness principle became. Meanwhile, financially strapped sultans confiscated private properties even as they respected the inviolability of waqfs. In the process, they solidified the distinction between private and waqf property, making it even costlier for themselves or their successors to expropriate waqfs.

True, massive waqf confiscations occurred under Mamluk sultans facing a military threat (1400s–1517); when the Ottoman Sultan Mehmet II (reigned 1444–46, 1451–81) wiped out Anatolia's Turcoman elites during a struggle for control over his expanding realms; and following the Ottoman conquest of Syria and Egypt (1516–17). But even these exceptions prove the rule that lasted at least into the eighteenth century. The Mamluk sultans usually backed down in the face of resistance; the expropriations of Mehmet II sowed enough resentment to make his successor restore some of the destroyed waqfs; and, likewise, Egypt's Ottoman administrators reversed many waqf annulments.[19] Until the eve of the region's modernization drives, waqf assets were more secure than private property.

The relative security of waqf assets steered resources into waqfs. Although no comprehensive dataset exists, various indicators testify to the waqf's economic significance. Firstly, most monographs on a premodern Middle Eastern city or region devote at least a chapter to local waqfs; invariably, they convey the massive weight of waqfs in the local economy. Second, the available estimates of waqf assets and income involve huge figures (Table 3.1). The three studies using statistical sampling show that the share of tax revenue accruing to Anatolian waqfs was 27 percent in the 1530s, 26.8 percent in the 1600s, and 15.8 percent in the 1800s. The Ottoman treasury received about half of its tax revenue from real estate; poll taxes and opportunistic taxes (*avârız*) were the other major categories. Hence, until the start of fundamental institutional reforms, around half of all Ottoman taxes on land and buildings went to waqfs. The dip in the nineteenth century had two causes. Nationalizations accompanied the reforms that gradually replaced Islamic laws with secular laws. The reform period also saw an acceleration of privatizations, often with the connivance of clerics, who shared in the gains from illicitly liberating waqf assets. We shall return to these nationalizations and privatizations. A third indicator of the waqf's economic importance is that waqf-related cases appear very frequently in court records. Of 19,009 commercial cases in a judicial database of Istanbul for 1602 to 1836, 15.8 percent concerned a waqf matter. By contrast, a state official was a party to just 4.2 percent of all cases.[20] Finally, most surviving Middle Eastern buildings from before the 1800s were financed through a waqf. The main exceptions are palaces, fortresses, and harbors.[21]

TABLE 3.1 *Waqf assets or revenues: estimates*

Source	Place	Date	Share of total tax revenue collected by waqfs	Waqf assets	Estimation method
Behrens-Abouseif	Egypt	1517		Half of land	Ottoman land survey
Barkan and Ayverdi	Anatolia	1530	27%		Statistical sampling
Yediyıldız	Anatolia	1601–1700	26.8%		Statistical sampling
Ubicini	Turkey	1800		Three-quarters of landed property	Aggregation of official opinions, reports
Öztürk	Anatolia	1801–1900	15.8%		Statistical sampling
Berque	Algiers	1830		Half of buildings in city	French land survey
Deguilhem	Damascus and environs	1922		More than half of real estate	Impressions of historians

Sources: Behrens-Abouseif, "Waqf, in Egypt," pp. 64, 66; Barkan and Ayverdi, *İstanbul Vakıfları*, p. 17; Yediyıldız, "Vakıf," p. 161; Ubicini, *Lettres sur la Turquie*, p. 261; Öztürk, *Türk Yenileşme Tarihi Çerçevesinde Vakıf Müessesesi*, p. 54; Berque, *Maghreb*, p. 173; Deguilhem, "On the Nature of Waqf," pp. 395, 410.

Waqfs held abundant assets in both cities and the countryside. Their huge asset base made them potentially effective political players. In principle, they could have used their resources to constrain the state on behalf of groups that they were chartered to serve. Had they done so, the nucleus of a civil society capable of advancing liberal political objectives might have emerged. The resulting political decentralization could have placed the Middle East on the road to a liberal order.

Remember that a waqf caretaker's authority came from a court-certified deed that put him in charge of an organization commanding income-producing assets and usually also employees who served at his discretion. These factors alone gave the caretaker potential political clout.[22] The caretaker was also the natural leader of his waqf's constituency – the teachers of a school, the community living near a particular fountain. With each such constituency, the caretaker provided a focal point for coordinating demands. Hence, every set of waqf beneficiaries formed a community potentially capable of collective action. Insofar as waqf beneficiaries worked collectively to advance their joint interests, they might have developed the organizational and strategic skills to pursue collective action in other contexts. The waqf could have turned the Middle East into a region hospitable to organized bottom-up initiatives, and, hence, rich in social capital.[23] Alas, the waqf was designed to inhibit collective action by subcommunities, not to facilitate it.

ORIGINS OF THE WAQF'S POLITICAL FEATURES

Nothing is certain about the waqf's origins except that it was an addition to Islam's original institutional complex – the set of institutions shaped by Muhammad, his close companions, and the rest of the earliest Muslim community. The Quran does not mention the waqf, which suggests that it emerged after Muhammad's death in 632.[24] Although recollections recorded generations later have the earliest Muslims forming waqfs, these accounts are almost certainly apocryphal. They were probably concocted to give the waqf Islamic legitimacy.[25]

Institutions resembling the waqf were present in pre-Islamic civilizations of the Middle East. In the Sassanid and Byzantine empires, temples had long been financed through forms of the trust.[26] The concept of a permanent endowment to provide standing services was appropriated from these empires during Islam's expansion into Syria and Iraq. By 661, about half of Byzantine and most Sassanid territories were under Muslim rule. With conquests continuing, Muslim officials gained familiarity with Roman and Persian practices. The Umayyad Empire, which shifted the Islamic seat of power from Medina to Damascus, employed bureaucrats who had served preexisting states.[27] The Iraq-based Abbasid dynasty (750–1258), which superseded the Umayyads, employed foreign-trained bureaucrats even more liberally.[28]

Under both dynasties, the consolidation of power involved higher taxes on subjugated groups as well as expropriations. Tax exemptions were given selectively, to accommodate political pressures. These policies bred insecurity among administrators. A talented person could prosper by serving a caliph; he could obtain land grants and tax exemptions. But the danger of being fired, expropriated, and even executed was ever-present; a misjudgment or rumor could destroy a career. The motives for confiscation included balancing factions within the bureaucracy. Sultans routinely impoverished threatening coalitions.

Insecurity among elites always fuels a quest for risk-reducing institutions. The debated alternatives in Islam's formative period are evident in the earliest work aimed at standardizing waqf law, al-Khassaf's *Kitāb Aḥkām al-Awqāf*, which dates from the 800s.[29] According to al-Khassaf, the waqf entered the Islamic institutional complex about a century after Muhammad, and it represented compromises among elites. The negotiated rules were legitimized through hearsay recollections of Muhammad's life. Collectively, they gave powerful constituencies a stake in the waqf. All state officials – bureaucrats, soldiers, clerics – obtained material security through tax exemptions and the right to shelter wealth from unpredictable rulers. Clerics also gained rents through supervisory authority over waqfs. As for rulers, the ability to shelter wealth for their own families and descendants provided insurance against a palace coup. Besides, waqf-supplied social services helped keep their subjects content.

The centrality of the material security motive is evident in institutional transformations after the Umayyads and Abbasids. In the Cairo-based Mamluk Sultanate (1250–1517), successive dynasties relied on armies consisting of slave soldiers known as mamluks. The mamluks' lack of local roots was expected to keep them loyal to the sultan. Mamluks were typically remunerated through temporary, revocable, and nonhereditary land grants (*iqtaʿ*). Naturally, they feared state predation and wanted to pass wealth to their descendants. The waqf fulfilled these needs. Sultans allowed mamluks to endow land. This right gave mamluks considerable material security as well as the ability to pass privileges on to their sons.[30]

From the 800s onward, some of the largest waqfs were established by members of the ruling dynasty and their top officials. These may be called "state-connected Islamic waqfs," as distinct from "regular Islamic waqfs" – for simplicity, "state waqfs" and "regular waqfs."[31] Examples of state waqfs include the Complex of Sultan Barquq in Cairo (1384) and the Süleymaniye Complex in Istanbul (1557).[32] Serving dynastic objectives, state waqfs were concentrated in capitals, militarily strategic areas, newly conquered cities where sultans sought legitimacy, and trade routes. Top state officials and members of the ruling dynasty also formed state waqfs as insurance against loss of influence. For instance, the mother of a crown prince would endow land to form a private financial base in case, say, he died prematurely or was outsmarted by a rival claimant. Yet another function of a state waqf was to insure against

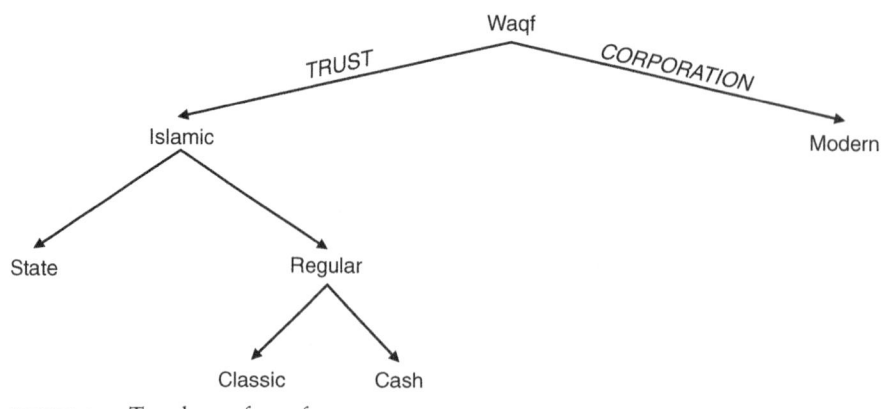

```
                        Waqf
          TRUST                  CORPORATION
        Islamic                            Modern
      /        \
   State      Regular
              /     \
          Classic   Cash
```

FIGURE 3.2 Typology of waqfs

Source: Adıgüzel and Kuran, "Inequality-Preserving Benevolence," fig. 1.

changes in state priorities. By virtue of its sacredness, a waqf built in the name of Sultan Süleyman II would endure even if his descendants spurned its documented objectives. It would give his rule visibility and cement his reputation as a generous monarch. No matter how strong or popular, every ruler had to worry about predation by future rulers and about being diminished in stature, even erased from history, by later chroniclers. In principle, and largely also in practice, state waqfs extended the reputations of sultans and their close circles. The top branches in Figure 3.2 separate the Islamic waqf, a form of trust, from the modern waqf, functionally a charitable corporation. The secondary branches on the left make the distinction just discussed.

Two waqf characteristics, both already mentioned, confirm that high state officials expected to capture most of the benefits to waqf founders. Because they were paid primarily through land grants, the immovability restriction suited them well. The restriction's burden fell on merchants whose wealth consisted of movable goods. Not until the 1500s did merchants secure the ability to shelter liquid wealth, and then essentially in an area comprising modern Turkey, northern Syria, and the Balkans.[33] A waqf that conformed to the immovability requirement is a classic waqf; and one whose endowment was at least partially liquid is a cash waqf. The tertiary branches in Figure 3.2 capture this distinction.

The requirement that only a Muslim could form a waqf at will also favored political elites, most of whom were Muslim by birth or conversion. Non-Muslims were allowed to found waqfs only by special permission, which must have required side payments to high officials.[34] Evidence of disproportionate benefits to Muslim elites challenges a huge romantic literature that treats the waqf mainly as an expression of pious charity.[35] But it accords with the lack of religious restrictions on *using* waqf services. Ordinarily, Christians and Jews were eligible to draw water from waqf-maintained fountains, stay in waqf-funded inns, and receive treatment from waqf-financed hospitals. True,

TABLE 3.2 *Restrictions on the two main investment instruments of classical Islamic law*

	Islamic waqf	Islamic partnership
Faith of founder	Ordinarily a Muslim; Christian or Jew at ruler's discretion	Unrestricted
Form of capital	Real estate (exceptions allowed after c. 1500)	Currency

non-Muslims were not welcome in mosques, unless they intended to convert. However, the resulting consumption exclusions did not stem from waqf law itself. They reflected sectarian prejudices that infused daily life. Just as Muslims could establish waqfs exclusively for Muslims, they could establish waqfs in predominantly Christian or Jewish neighborhoods.[36] Also telling is that non-Muslims freely used an institution that competed with the waqf for private capital: the Islamic partnership. An Islamic partnership's capital had to be liquid. Its returns were taxed. And it served short-lived ventures.[37] Its unsuitability for sheltering wealth explains why Christians and Jews, largely banned from founding waqfs, freely formed cooperative commercial ventures (Table 3.2).

Various details of Islamic law accord, then, with the waqf's emergence as a wealth and tax shelter for Muslim elites. Although some officials participated in commerce, their wealth was concentrated in real estate. In creatively adapting pre-Islamic variants of the trust, they gave themselves the lion's share of the resulting gains. It appears that they continued to benefit disproportionately right up to the Modern Era. In the 1700s, 68.5 percent of all Anatolian waqfs were founded by state officials, including clerics.[38] In Ottoman Istanbul, similarly, elites formed 73.7 percent of all regular waqfs founded between 1453 and 1923.[39] Because ruling families and top officials founded the largest waqfs, the disparity was even greater in relation to control of waqf assets.

The Umayyad and Abbasid rulers who consented to the waqf's inclusion in the Islamic institutional complex must have understood that aides with a secure financial base posed the greatest challenge to their rule. Waqf-based threats could be dampened by restricting the uses of waqf assets. Several rules discussed in the next chapter served that objective. They include the requirement to follow the founder's instructions in perpetuity, the judiciary's duty to monitor waqf operations, and obstacles to waqf mergers. Evidently, in giving their officials material security, rulers also avoided destabilizing their regimes. It mattered, too, that many high officials of Muslim-governed states were foreign-born slaves.[40] Their low legal status made it easier to neutralize and even execute those who became threatening.

This interpretation is consistent with recorded correlations between the modern Middle East's "democratic deficit" and the diffusion of the Islamic institutional complex. Highlighting the reliance of Muslim sultans on slave armies,

Lisa Blaydes and Eric Chaney find that this form of military recruitment caused Middle Eastern rulers to lag behind those of Western Europe in legitimacy.[41] Extending this argument, Chaney identifies a positive relationship between the share of a country's landmass that early Muslim armies conquered and its democratic deficit in the early twenty-first century.[42] Insofar as premodern military recruitment has a footprint in modern politics, influences must operate through the entire institutional complex associated with slave armies. As both works underscore, transplanted slave soldiers had difficulty forming coalitions with disgruntled local groups. However, slave soldiers and their descendants came to control enormous wealth. Besides, they were assimilated into local communities. Undermining the loyalty objective, these factors would have generated power centers beyond the ruler's control. The reliance on slave soldiers required, then, measures to weaken potential centers of opposition. Restricting the uses of waqf assets would have reduced the effectiveness of slave-driven challenges to the ruler's power. As we shall see, the adopted rules kept all waqf caretakers, including slaves, from using waqf assets to foment political opposition.

Waqf scholarship commonly distinguishes between the charitable waqf, whose stated objective is to serve a broad constituency such as a neighborhood or the poor, and the family waqf, which provides income to a family. In practice, these categories represented the extremes of a continuum. Many wealth-sheltering waqfs devoted some income to a public service.[43] As for substantially philanthropic or charitable waqfs, typically their benefits went disproportionately to the founder's family. A fountain built next to the founder's home allowed running water inside; other residents of the neighborhood had to carry water to their homes.[44] Besides, the caretaker often belonged to the founder's line.[45] For his services, the caretaker received a fixed salary, or a proportion of the waqf's revenue, or its residual revenue after deed-specified expenses were met; hybrid patterns were not uncommon.[46] Relative to major state waqfs, waqfs established primarily to secure wealth were minuscule. This accords with the goal of limiting autonomous power centers.

THE POSSIBILITY OF NONGOVERNMENTAL ORGANIZATIONS

Whatever the source of its endowment and intended beneficiaries, every waqf belonged to civil society. Regardless of its founder's identity, it controlled resources potentially available to restrain the state. Even a waqf established to support a family sheltered resources that might have been used to shape state policies. Policies of interest to waqfs included ones that complemented their chosen missions. Take a waqf-based hospital. The quality of its services depended on its water supply and local road network. It thus had incentives to lobby the state for improvements to the local infrastructure. Other waqfs serving the area shared those incentives. And collectively they had the financial capacity to influence local governance, if not also state administration generally. They might have fulfilled the functions of a healthy civil society comprising multitudes of NGOs established independently, in a decentralized manner, by individuals with diverse social objectives.

It merits emphasis that a waqf's founder selected its purpose, not the state. Hence, insofar as waqfs shaped state policies, a range of individual preferences would have determined the outcomes. If wealth holders valued education more than health, their waqfs would have given priority to schools over hospitals. Founders were also free to select their employees, including caretakers. Islamic law thus gave waqf founders some freedom of association. These privileges might have sufficed for the emergence of a politically influential NGO sector. Though it would have consisted disproportionately of Muslim-founded organizations, their goals would have covered a broad spectrum.

We have touched on three distinct freedoms: to establish a waqf, to choose waqf goals, and to deploy waqf resources. With respect to the first two goals, at least to Muslims waqf law provided broad options. In exploring the last freedom, we shall learn about civic life in the premodern Middle East.

4

The Political Impotence of Islamic Waqfs

In agreeing to the waqf's inclusion in the Islamic institutional complex, Arab caliphs of the 700s ceded fiscal capacity. Losing tax revenue on endowed properties, they also limited their expropriation options. They would not have consented to reduced fiscal capacity without commensurate gains.

One compensating benefit was relief from the costs of keeping cities and trade routes functional. Most schools, inns, mosques, fountains, and sundry other services would be financed by rich elites. Another benefit to rulers was that the suppliers of social services would not engage in politics at any level, on any issue. Waqfs would not constrain how rulers governed, or the state's alliances, or the taxation of non-endowed properties. In hindering the development of what we now call civil society, waqf law would thus contribute to political stability. Since the dawn of history, political regimes have sought to minimize civic engagement through a bewildering variety of institutions. In Middle Eastern states governed under Islamic law, the Islamic waqf was the chief instrument for keeping civil society toothless.

To limit the waqf's political potential, rulers constrained its autonomy, restricted participation in governance on the part of its beneficiaries, and essentially blocked cooperation among individual waqfs. Such measures denied waqfs capabilities critical to monitoring the state and holding officials accountable for their acts. They did so while preserving elite incentives to endow waqfs. An added benefit was that subjects enjoyed a vast array of services for free or else a nominal fee. Once the waqf entered the Islamic institutional complex, it thus became self-enforcing, because key players – rulers, wealthy property owners, and the ruled masses – had stakes in its preservation.

The channels through which the waqf failed to convert economic resources into political power operated directly through waqfs and indirectly through waqf beneficiaries. As a preview of the chapter, Figure 4.1 shows that restrictions on the use of waqf resources contributed directly to the political

The Political Impotence of Islamic Waqfs

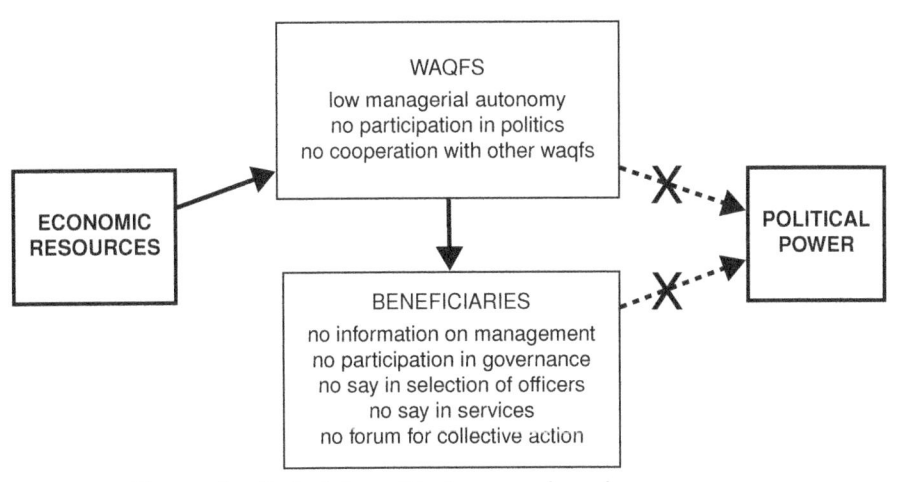

```
                    ┌─────────────────────────────────┐
                    │             WAQFS               │
                    │    low managerial autonomy      │
                    │    no participation in politics │
                    │  no cooperation with other waqfs│
                    └─────────────────────────────────┘
   ┌──────────┐      ↗              ⋮ X ⋱           ┌──────────┐
   │ ECONOMIC │─────                                  │POLITICAL │
   │RESOURCES │                  ↓                    │  POWER   │
   └──────────┘                                      └──────────┘
                    ┌─────────────────────────────────┐  ⋰ X ⋰
                    │         BENEFICIARIES           │
                    │  no information on management   │
                    │  no participation in governance │
                    │   no say in selection of officers│
                    │        no say in services       │
                    │   no forum for collective action │
                    └─────────────────────────────────┘
```

FIGURE 4.1 Factors that limited the political power of waqfs

impotence of waqfs by keeping them out of politics. The figure also identifies features that keep waqf beneficiaries powerless to shape waqf actions and incapable of acting collectively themselves. The figure's solid arrows represent actual flows or influences. The dashed arrows represent influences that waqf rules suppressed.

LIMITS ON MANAGERIAL AUTONOMY

By design, the Islamic waqf was a rigid organization. In its canonical form, its assets were inalienable. They would never be sold, bequeathed, pawned, or transferred. Endowed properties would finance designated services forever through steady rental income. The operational ideal presumed a complete contract. It also posited a static world with fixed relative prices and technologies. Four examples will illustrate these points.

The first is a Cairene waqf established in 1408 to deliver water from the Nile to a cistern. Its revenue is to finance two camels, several waterskins, some clay jars and mugs, and several workers. One of the workers is a cupbearer, whose job is to fill the vessels from which people drink, but also to protect the vessels from reptiles and insects.[1] The second waqf is a Damascus-based charitable complex, founded in 1595. Its deed lists the duties of 374 employees, each of whom will receive a nominally fixed salary. The deed also covers minute details about services and expenses. The specifications include the contents and costs of the meals to be served in various parts of the complex.[2] An Isfahan school dating from 1711 forms our next example. Its deed stipulates the salaries and duties of all personnel. The staff will include two lamp-men, who are to spend 29 tumans periodically to illuminate certain rooms.[3] The last waqf, registered in 1803, was to support an Istanbul neighborhood's mosque and school. Its cash endowment was to finance loans at 15 percent per annum. The school's teacher would receive twenty-two aspers per day and his assistant two aspers. Three aspers per day would be spent on candle wax to illuminate the mosque. The caretaker's daily pay was set at eight aspers.[4]

Each of these deeds considers revenue immune to shocks. Implicitly, it treats the waqf as eternally able to finance its stipulated services. It also supposes fixed prices. The Cairo deed assumes that two camels will always be affordable. The Istanbul deed treats as fixed both the price of candle wax and the going wages of teachers and teaching assistants. Moreover, in treating a 15 percent nominal return on the endowment as sufficient to cover designated expenses, it rules out inflation. All four deeds presume fixed technologies. Camels will always remain the most efficient way to transport water; cities will always rely on cisterns for water; and candles will always illuminate mosques. Other questionable assumptions involve management. The deeds presume that successive caretakers will all manage waqf assets competently, and that every supervising judge will perform his duties impeccably and honestly.

Lack of managerial discretion on budgetary matters could lower service quality drastically. In exploring the natural sciences in Istanbul between 1660 and 1772, Harun Küçük ascribes the observed decline in scholarship – evidenced, for instance, in the vanishing of contributions to theoretical astronomy, natural philosophy, and anatomy – to the plummeting of teacher salaries through sustained inflation. By this time, a professor's waqf-stipulated salary did not even cover subsistence. Professors tended to be destitute and increasingly lacked prestige. The erosion in the professoriate's living standards caused the smartest students to choose careers other than education. The professoriate was filled with ignoramuses. "As poor and ignorant people," observes Küçük, professors became "the target of insults and attacks as well as pity from those who could claim elite status." The semi-educated supplemented their income by moonlighting as private physicians. The luckiest managed to use teaching as a springboard for obtaining a judicial post.[5] Private medicine and the judiciary, each free of waqf-based restrictions, paid far better than the professoriate. Rulers regularly adjusted salaries within the judiciary, and market forces drove medical fees. In sum, the rigidity of nominal madrasa salaries enfeebled scholarship through several interrelated mechanisms: deskilling of the professoriate, impoverishment of professors, and professors' need for side jobs. Revealingly, professors did not respond collectively to their pauperization. Instead, they competed among themselves for more lucrative jobs, often by seeking patronage.[6]

Nothing here implies that the professoriate literally ceased to generate new ideas. Even as they fell into poverty, madrasa professors participated in religious discourses and helped to refine religious interpretations. Yet their innovations stayed within the bounds of traditional Islamic thinking. Although their teachings accommodated certain changes in daily life, they did not address the challenges or opportunities that global intellectual advances were presenting.

Madrasas did not produce new pedagogies to prepare students for an increasingly dynamic economy. They generated no notable ideas on reorganizing society to make it more innovative. They did not create new academic disciplines. All such manifestations of intellectual sclerosis were apparent to Middle Eastern leaders well before Europeans started colonizing parts of the region.[7] A broad literature within Islamic Studies blames European colonizers and their local allies for the degrading of madrasas.[8] This literature overstates the roles of colonial and postcolonial administrations. Even before colonization, a madrasa education was becoming inadequate even to become a bureaucrat or judge.[9]

The architects of waqf law understood that conditions relevant to the waqf's usefulness could change. To limit inefficiencies, they allowed founders to preauthorize specific modifications. Accordingly, a school's waqf deed could permit the caretaker to swap one revenue-producing asset for a more favorable one. It could also allow the construction of new classrooms in case of need. Occasionally, a judge would authorize an alteration during the founder's lifetime.[10] But legitimate changes were limited to those expressly permitted in the deed. If the deed allowed only the founder to make changes, none could be made after the founder's death.[11] If it permitted a single asset swap, once that option was exercised, the waqf's properties became strictly inalienable regardless of circumstances. Because managerial discretion was exhaustible, sooner or later every waqf became frozen, at least under the law.

Just as significant as the managerial restrictions is what caretakers were *not* required to deliver. They had no efficiency targets. Thus, a school caretaker was not expected to stay above some threshold of educational performance, such as reading proficiency by age eight. He did not have to please students or their parents. Likewise, the caretaker of a caravanserai did not need approvals from the merchants he served. His remuneration was independent of how well he fed them, cared for their animals, and protected their merchandise. A waqf caretaker was accountable to the founder alone, and courts, not beneficiaries, determined whether he met the founder's directives. The founder's preferences usually trumped those of end users. To a degree, state waqfs formed an exception. Insofar as they boosted the reigning sultan's legitimacy, he had an incentive to keep them useful. But even with state waqfs, maintaining efficiency would eventually become challenging. If only to earn the loyalty of its subjects, a new dynasty would favor state waqfs bearing the names of its own members over those of preceding dynasties. Its commitment to the services of a particular locality, or to a certain class of services, could wane for strategic reasons.

For their part, the intended beneficiaries of waqfs were not expected to participate in governance. They had no right to demand resource reallocations or changes in services. They were to consume passively, with gratitude toward founders for their generosity and caretakers for their efforts. These strictures accord with the norms of waqf founding. The immediate beneficiaries of new waqfs were not consulted about their priorities. In keeping with that pattern, later beneficiaries were never polled on possible managerial modifications.

Actual waqfs enjoyed greater managerial discretion than the waqf described in legal sources. Because a waqf deed, however long, could not cover every possible contingency, unavoidably it gave the caretaker some discretion. Adjustments made by the caretaker would not necessarily violate the spirit of the founder's objectives. But sometimes they rested on logic that the founder would have rejected, had he or she been able to imagine future circumstances. Through creative interpretations, a caretaker could make adjustments unimaginable at the time of the founding.[12]

CURBS ON POLITICAL PARTICIPATION

The many varieties of a liberal order share an emphasis on broad political participation. This is achieved through such means as town meetings, referenda, lobbies, protests, opinion polls, and elections. The masses participate in governance through choices at the ballot box, voicing preferences and ideas, and working within advocacy organizations toward common goals. Grassroots politics molds public discourse. It also aligns governance with the popular will. Transparency is another feature of liberal governance.

An additional characteristic is mandatory information sharing by official bodies. Although even the most transparent regimes conceal sensitive data such as defense policies and health records, in liberal countries officials must report periodically on their activities. Moreover, many government decisions, including budgets, are debated in public. Whether the typical citizen grasps the intricacies of policy options is beside the point.[13] It may suffice to have a representative subset of citizens follow any given issue.[14] A universal problem, mentioned earlier, is that political players distort information self-servingly. Information pollution is reduced by standardizing disclosure requirements.

The rules of the Islamic waqf promoted neither broad political participation nor transparency in governance. Authority to execute the waqf deed belonged to a single person, the caretaker. Apart from judges, no one was entitled to information about assets, income, expenses, or service quality. The caretaker was not accountable to beneficiaries specified in the deed. The consequent opacity facilitated whatever modifications the caretaker desired personally.[15]

Ordinarily, the waqf deed itself was public knowledge. The familiarity generated expectations concerning services. People living near a fountain counted on running water, because typically a plaque publicized its endowment. If the flow stopped, residents could sue the caretaker for negligence. Hence, it was risky for a caretaker to ignore the expectations of beneficiaries.[16] But to make a convincing legal case, aggrieved beneficiaries had to prove that the caretaker was violating the deed. In 1811, several beneficiaries of an Istanbul waqf serving the poor sued the caretaker for mismanagement, and the court replaced him. The new caretaker then had his deposed predecessor return what he embezzled, with interest.[17] However, because information on the waqf's management was confidential, beneficiary lawsuits against caretakers were rare. Out of 539 waqf-related trials in an Istanbul sample running from 1602 to 1836, only 20 entailed an accusation of caretaker mismanagement. In three-quarters of these trials, the plaintiff was an active or former waqf employee privy to inside information.[18]

In any case, the right to complain was no substitute for required periodic disclosures. It did not give beneficiaries the means to make the caretaker optimize resource use. By spending excessively on maintenance, a fountain's caretaker could harm its viability over the long term. Though he himself would escape charges of mismanagement, his successor would inherit an endowment so diminished as to preclude further maintenance. At that point, an honorable judge would have to dismiss complaints about service quality as frivolous.

Besides, not every judge was committed to deed enforcement. Some judges could be bribed to overlook improprieties. If the judge was colluding with the caretaker, knowledgeable beneficiaries could report both to higher authorities. But that would risk alienating officials capable of retaliation. Indeed, fear of reprisals made people refrain from suing state officials unless their case was exceptionally strong.[19] Court fees could also deter a lawsuit. For many reasons, then, waqf beneficiaries had limited sway over caretaker actions. Although capable of combating egregious mismanagement, they could not ensure a caretaker's good will or competence.

Every waqf's beneficiaries formed a potential political community. But they did not necessarily develop a communal identity. The users of a caravanserai could remain mutual strangers indefinitely. The waqf's centralized management prevented the forming of group consciousness among co-beneficiaries who lacked reasons to interact. Moreover, even when a group identity developed naturally, as with a fountain's co-users or a mosque congregation, the waqf did not foster a political community. By contrast, periodic elections nurture in modern urbanites an awareness that they form a community capable of shaping city governance. In a city served by waqfs rather than a municipality, a sense of powerlessness would have discouraged beneficiaries from seeking to influence policies. It would also have dissuaded them from exploring alternative means of supplying social services. Accepting what came their way, and withholding feedback to suppliers, they would have become accustomed to passive consumption.

Court records present cases of beneficiaries participating in the selection of a new caretaker. Most involve a vacancy that the deed requires a judge to fill.[20] A group of beneficiaries present to court a recommendation, and the judge then appoints the nominated person. Such cases are exceptions that prove the rule. A judge authorized to pick the replacement was not required to accept the community's recommendation. The decision was ultimately his alone. In any case, when it was known that the local judge wished to appoint a relative or friend, beneficiaries might not have even tried to exert influence. Under Islamic law, they had no legal standing as a group anyway.

Except the very poor, the urbanites of the premodern Middle East consumed waqf services throughout their lives. None of their providers was accountable to them as individuals. Consequently, rarely did they participate in the determination of how resources assigned to their benefit would be spent. They could not have resources shifted from, say, mosques to schools, or vice versa. No formal mechanism existed for aggregating the wants of any designated constituency. Hence, beneficiaries could not gauge the representativeness of their personal priorities or levels of satisfaction. These patterns would have promoted a culture of political passivity. People would have been acculturated to consider themselves powerless to improve the social services they consumed.

It was not uncommon for waqfs to deplete their assets and wither away.[21] Unanticipated expenses lowered the survival rate, as did weak incentives to manage the endowment effectively from the standpoint of beneficiaries. One indication lies in the tenure of caretakers. In the Anatolian town of Sivas, no less than 74 percent of the successions between 1700 and 1850 followed a death in office; typically, the successor was the retiring caretaker's son. A caretaker's performance had to slip severely for it to provoke a challenge, which made dismissal rare. One Sivas caretaker was replaced by his son when he became deaf. Another was fired when he could no longer recite the Quran, which was among his duties.[22] By itself, poor financial management rarely brought termination, despite its prevalence.[23]

The lack of beneficiary participation in waqf governance was compatible with the logic of the waqf rules instituted during Islam's initial quarter-millennium, which was to keep the masses apolitical. Predicated on the passivity of service recipients, they made no provision for feedback from residents. Consequently, there was no systematic way to know whether and when a reallocation of waqf resources became desirable; or why, when someone happened to notice potential benefits to modification, the prevailing rules dampened incentives to act. In a nutshell, freezing waqf functions reduced political awareness and engagement.

Nonetheless, the waqf has been characterized as the nucleus of a vibrant civil society. Observing that sultans often had to reissue orders repeatedly, some scholars infer the existence of a waqf-based civil society capable of resisting the state.[24] In fact, it shows that sultans lacked full control over waqf officials, many of whom were clerics. A related observation is that clerics spearheaded riots that toppled palace officials, even sultans.[25] Actually, except possibly for nineteenth-century Iran, the source of the resistance corroborates the weakness of civil society.[26] Outside of Iran, clerics belonged to the ruling coalition. That they led revolts points to intra-coalition showdowns rather than civic activism.[27] The showdowns occurred during crises, when it became relatively easy to mobilize angry subjects who lacked channels of peaceful political communication. Mass participation in cleric-led riots bears closer resemblance to the spontaneous Tahrir Square protests that toppled Mubarak than to the orderly voicing of opinions that characterizes a healthy civil society. Still another argument centers on waqf employees. They created piety-based networks, it says, and their moral influence helped to define religious legitimacy and

The Political Impotence of Islamic Waqfs 67

authority.²⁸ But the purported evidence pertains to the social status of pious dignitaries with waqf connections. It does not establish sustained influence over state policies or political trajectories.

Another possible objection to the foregoing "passive beneficiaries" claim is that regular waqfs sheltered family wealth. Their beneficiaries routinely influenced the caretaker's decisions, observe some scholars.²⁹ But this exception stemmed from a universal characteristic of the family – closeness and trust among relatives – rather than a property of the waqf itself. The beneficiaries of family-serving waqfs were primarily the caretaker's relatives. Those of primarily charitable waqfs need not have even known the caretaker; and, if they did, rarely did they have the clout to sway his decisions. The concept of civil society transcends intra-family bargaining. It involves political associations far larger than the biggest extended family.

EFFECTS OF BENEFICIARY PASSIVITY ON POLITICAL STABILITY

Each of the identified limitations on mass participation would have served the ruler's survival. Leaving his subjects ignorant about the management of waqfs promoted political stability by keeping waqfs from becoming foci of discontent. The absence of forums for discussing waqf preferences slashed the capacity for mass reactions to economic downturns and military defeats. Lacking preexisting consumer organizations and experiences with collective action, disgruntled subjects had to start organizing from scratch. As for the caretaker's lack of accountability to end users, it would have lowered expectations of official accountability in other domains, too.³⁰ Had the caretaker been required to deliver periodic public reports, precedents for inclusive governance would have been set, undermining the autocratic status quo. In sum, waqf rules perpetuated political centralization by keeping potentially subversive communities unorganized.³¹

Students of participatory politics distinguish between "tame" and "rebellious" organizations.³² In preventing the waqf's use for political advocacy, Islamic law barred the latter type.³³ It then reduced participation further by denying a hand in management even to the beneficiaries of tame waqfs. A byproduct was the impoverishment of public discourse on social services. Users also failed to develop the habits and skills needed to communicate thoughts, expectations, and grievances relevant to institutional efficiency.

All premodern Middle Eastern polities experienced rebellions targeted at the sultan or his administration. Tellingly, they tended to be led by already organized professions, which were supervised by the state, if not also part of it. The major roles of clerics have been mentioned. They led revolts as state officials and protectors of religious purity, not on behalf of any waqfs they managed.³⁴ In Ottoman realms, military units spearheaded many revolts, and they were at the forefront of others. On some occasions, urban craft guilds also joined rebellions. Neither in the Ottoman Empire nor elsewhere do waqf beneficiaries appear as coordinated groups in narratives of uprisings against the state or, in the 1800s or early 1900s, of resistance against a European power.[35] Evidently, rules instituted around 800 to keep waqfs apolitical succeeded for a millennium in blocking collective action on the part of beneficiaries. In the process, they kept civil society practically nonexistent.

The passivity of beneficiaries would have harmed creativity, too. The pace of innovation is correlated with the number of ideas in circulation.[36] That is why metropolises, where people of diverse backgrounds interact regularly, contribute to knowledge production highly disproportionately to their populations.[37] In excluding the masses from politics, waqf regulations diminished the production of new ideas, reduced awareness of shared problems, and discouraged institutional innovation across the social system.[38]

In *Rulers, Religion, and Riches*, Jared Rubin identifies two main strategies that rulers use to propagate their authority: legitimation and coercion.[39] And in *Bandits and Bureaucrats*, Karen Barkey shows how the Ottoman dynasty used these twin strategies to retain power for many centuries.[40] The Islamic waqf served both strategies at once. In curbing mass dissent, it fostered an appearance of good governance. Subjects remained ignorant of others' grievances, and they lacked awareness of potential institutional reforms. By keeping beneficiaries from organizing uprisings, waqf rules also facilitated the control of aggrieved groups. But these advantages harbored a hidden danger. In undermining creativity and innovation, they also limited economic growth, which gradually weakened incumbent rulers vis-à-vis outside challengers. Indeed, the waqf is among the institutions that, over a millennium, set the stage for the colonizations and territorial losses of modern times.

THE WAQF VS. ITS EUROPEAN COUNTERPARTS

The properties of the waqf may be contrasted with those of the charitable corporation, whose use spread in Western Europe as the waqf gained popularity in the Middle East. The comparison will be helpful because it is in Western Europe that rule by consent was scaled up to nation-states and that modern ideals of personal freedom emerged. The usefulness of the exercise is not diminished by the erosion of Western freedoms in the early 2000s through toxic mixes of low birth rates, xenophobia, hyper-nationalism, and virulent polarization.

Of the factors that fueled liberalization and democratization, one was that social services were delivered through a rich mix of organizations that allowed political decentralization, steady collective action by NGOs, and durable coalitions among interest groups. An indispensable part of the organizational mix was the charitable corporation, which is a nonprofit association that claims the collective authority of a set of individuals in some domain and under a certain legal system.[41] It has legal personhood and a perpetual existence independent of its membership. It differs from the business corporation in its basic goal:

The Political Impotence of Islamic Waqfs

providing services rather than earning profits. The distinction will be dropped wherever the type is clear from the context.

In the Middle Ages, thousands of European cities received a royal corporate charter or simply declared themselves a corporation and bargained with power holders for acceptance of their legal autonomy.[42] Universities, guilds, fraternities, women's associations, religious orders, and monasteries also achieved corporate status.[43] They participated in politics as entities with legal standing. For example, guilds sat on town councils as organizations. Autonomous cities and professional organizations became major drivers of European urban growth. To be sure, Europe's incorporation waves had downsides. Certain autonomous organizations formed monopolies and cartels, which then blocked innovations and restricted political rights. The net benefit of incorporation thus varied spatially and temporally.[44]

In historical accounts of Europe, the corporation tends to receive far less attention than uprisings and wars that brought immediate relief from crises. Yet Europe's incorporation waves produced enduring transformations that were essential to its subsequent political liberalization.[45] Enjoying indefinite lives, corporations were largely self-regulating. They adopted their own membership criteria and financial measures. Monarchs had to negotiate with them and often accommodate their demands. The consequent power sharing broadened human rights.[46]

In principle, the decisions of a charitable corporation may be determined by the entire membership. Usually, though, certain officials hold the reins, and most members participate in its management episodically. Ordinary members might have a voice through meetings where issues are debated and resolved by vote. On selecting officials, various options exist. The officials themselves may appoint their successors. Alternatively, the membership may participate in the selection. Precisely because a corporation enjoys managerial autonomy, it may modify its own rules. Hence, corporate management and succession patterns present huge variety.[47]

The default for a corporation is complete autonomy, within the law. But in practice it has a charter that defines a mission. If its purpose is limited to education, it does not provide poverty relief. If it is meant to raise domestic literacy, it does not build schools abroad. Its charter may also constrain the management of its assets. State-imposed covenants may add to the restrictions.[48] In general, though, premodern charitable corporations enjoyed more flexibility than corresponding Islamic waqfs. Consider higher education. In the Middle Ages, it was provided mainly through incorporated universities in Western Europe but waqf-financed madrasas in the Middle East.[49] A European university had greater managerial flexibility than a madrasa.[50] Whereas a university could change its curriculum, the madrasa was constrained by the founder's stipulations. The deeds of certain madrasas contained instructions on exactly what each professor would teach.[51] Others limited teaching to "revealed knowledge" and excluded the rational sciences. Some named the subjects to be taught, even the textbooks.[52] Iran's Madrasa-yi Sultani, founded in 1711 as a school of higher learning, was supposed to teach "religious sciences," including prophetic tradition, sayings of the imams, Quranic exegesis, Islamic jurisprudence, and theories of law. It was to avoid "philosophical and Sufi works."[53]

Madrasas and universities differed also in numbers of decision makers. At the typical European university, the curriculum was set by professors and administrators; students were not consulted. At a waqf-maintained school, even fewer people made the pertinent decisions. In principle and often in practice as well, the caretaker followed the founder's wishes. Not even faculty had authority over instructional content. Madrasa histories include examples of unauthorized books or subjects being taught.[54] But the exceptions were like ripples in a calm sea. They barely disturbed the fixity of a madrasa curriculum's content.

The difference in the managerial default conditions between the waqf and the corporation – no flexibility for the waqf, full flexibility for the corporation – need not have mattered at the outset. Waqf founders could have accommodated all imaginable contingencies simply by giving successive caretakers the necessary flexibility. But the difference at hand mattered massively as evolving conditions presented situations unimaginable at the founding.[55] A university exercised options that might have been barred if foreseen at its establishment. For its part, a madrasa could not even exercise options that, with the requisite foresight, the founder would have granted happily.

Whereas in the Middle East the waqf was the only organizational form suited to providing social services privately, in Europe there were alternatives to the corporation. From the early Middle Ages, some services were supplied through organizations resembling the waqf. Indeed, hospitals and public kitchens were often established as a trust, also known as a foundation. Like a waqf, a medieval European trust was designed as an inflexible organization with set rules. Uses of its revenues were predetermined, generally to prevent diversions to unintended uses. For all their similarities to waqfs, however, European trusts were relatively more pliable. They were less committed to the founder's wishes.[56] Provided cumbersome procedures were followed, the assets of a European trust could be augmented or directed to new uses. In 1526, for example, officials of a Dutch hospital established as a trust were able to take over a monastery's assets, though the transfer required a trip to Rome for the necessary permission.[57] By and large, a European trust also made decisions more democratically. It could be administered by a board of trustees rather than a single caretaker.[58]

Yet another European vehicle for providing social services was the entail. Like many regular Islamic waqfs, the entail sheltered wealth for a family and its descendants. Creditors could not touch entailed assets; ordinarily, nor could the state. This made it particularly popular whenever and wherever property rights weakened. As with waqf founders, those of entails could direct expenditures from their graves. They could also bar their descendants from alienating specific assets. Still, the entail was relatively less rigid. Depending on the region, the law limited the founder's authority to between two and four generations; eventually, therefore, its assets were liberated. An entail was also revocable through an agreement of its living beneficiaries. Moreover, beneficiaries regularly participated in its management.[59]

To recapitulate, two of the organizational options for providing social services in premodern Europe, the trust and the entail, had waqf-like features, but they were less rigid. In any case, the corporation offered a third option, which differed fundamentally from the waqf. The waqf bestowed governance privileges primarily on the founder, who continued to exercise powers posthumously. In contrast, the corporation allowed self-governance by at least some living beneficiaries. Thus, Europe provided social services through organizations that were relatively more adaptable as well as more democratic.

Notwithstanding the above interpretations, rules of the waqf also had positive effects on governance. Consider again political participation. Reducing the number of decision makers can accelerate decision making and avoid gridlock. Under certain circumstances, such benefits can swamp losses from obstacles to fine-tuning services. In principle, then, a single caretaker could provide a given service more efficiently than a committee. That is among the reasons for separating beneficiaries and management in modern charitable corporations. Consider Doctors Without Borders, the Swiss-based charity that assists victims of disasters and wars. Though its managerial team consists of dozens of executives, the team's size is vastly outnumbered by its benefactors and beneficiaries around the globe.[60]

But Doctors Without Borders differs critically from hospitals established as Islamic waqfs. It can shift its operations easily between regions and adapt its surgical teams and procedures to new technologies. Although its board of directors may disagree on details, widely favored modifications will be made. For their part, waqf hospitals did not need the agreement of even one beneficiary; if the caretaker needed to convince anyone, it was a single judge. By the same token, the deed limited his discretion. He could not relocate a hospital; nor could he adjust expenses in response to technological advances or price changes. Except with a judge's consent, he could not make such adjustments – at least not legally – even with broad support from intended beneficiaries.

For the reasons outlined, the West's organizational options were more conducive to civic participation in governance than the corresponding Middle Eastern menu, which was restricted to the Islamic waqf. The breadth of the West's options facilitated its democratization and liberalization.

OBSTACLES TO FORMING COALITIONS

Waqfs pursued activities in mutual isolation. In principle, though, they could have formed coalitions with an eye toward maximizing their combined influence. Just as industrial workers formed labor movements and European cities joined forces to limit royal taxes, so waqfs could have mobilized to advance common interests, preserve privileges, and address shared grievances. And just as urbanites produced rationales for local administration, and workers for collective bargaining, waqf coalitions might have generated ideologies partial to their beneficiaries. In the millennium preceding Europe's early democracies, diverse coalitions of corporations helped to constrain monarchs.[61]

The rigid managerial rules of waqfs kept them from using their resources for political purposes. In any case, they were envisaged as apolitical organizations. Whereas an incorporated European church was free to challenge state policies, a waqf-based mosque was not. And whereas European cities formed coalitions, waqfs within the same city did not join forces, to say nothing of forming intercity political blocs. Indeed, no federation of madrasas emerged, no association of fountain operators, and no confederation of waqf unions. The lack of ties among waqfs weakened their already compromised capacity to constrain sultans.

The inability to pool resources at will limited the political potential of waqfs also by generating waste. If a waqf's founder did not explicitly allow it to work with other organizations, achievable economies of scale or scope remained unexploited. Multiple small waqfs would provide services that a single large waqf could deliver more efficiently. Road maintenance and water supply provide examples. Founders were free to authorize transfers to a large waqf. But such resource pooling required an unlikely coincidence of goals between the donor waqf and the receiver.[62] Moreover, the coincidence had to be predictable. A fountain founder in the 1500s had to foresee the water distribution technologies of the Industrial Era to know that eventually efficiency would require the transfer of all fountain endowments to a single water supplier serving a broad territory. Resource sharing by functionally complementary waqfs did occur. For example, waqf-funded bathhouses drew water from the pipelines of preexisting waqfs.[63] But many such exceptions involved state waqfs created to provide urban infrastructure. Water pipelines were endowed explicitly to serve as conduits to the fountains of new waqf founders. Likewise, many mosques were built under the presumption that wealthy users would supply critical inputs, such as candle oil and employee housing.[64] Resource sharing also occurred when a road built to serve an endowed house came to benefit the users of a nearby fountain and the residents of another endowed house. Such sharing involved informal arrangements. Sometimes, judges facilitated resource sharing just by looking the other way.

Group-endowed waqfs need to be distinguished from the merger of waqfs established separately. The former usually entailed resource pooling within families, with one person serving as the founder before the law; pragmatic judges occasionally made exceptions for neighbors and co-workers.[65] As for waqf mergers, they were extremely rare. Moreover, when they occurred, the founders were typically relatives or else the same person.[66] Mergers of existing waqfs were discouraged because of obstacles to ascertaining whether the founders would have accepted the terms. Consider two adjacent schools. Merging them could economize on administrative overheads. But would the founders, both dead, have agreed to combine classes in one building and rent the other for additional income? If the schools were kept separate and administrative overheads shared, what if one needed relatively more costly repairs? Would the founder of the better-constructed school have endorsed the merger if he or she foresaw the other's maintenance needs? Because such questions were unanswerable, many potentially beneficial mergers were not even attempted. Consequently, when new technologies enabled previously unimaginable gains from a merger, preexisting waqfs continued to operate independently.

The inefficiencies in question need not have afflicted waqfs founded simultaneously. Suppose that three property owners decided to establish a school, each in his or her name. They could agree to future mergers under certain conditions and record specific contingencies in their respective deeds. Yet no examples of such synchronized founding exist. Merging resources at the start comes to mind as an alternative. But under the law, the founder had to be an individual, not a group.

The rationale for the latter requirement probably lay in sultans' aversion to autonomous private coalitions – the very consideration that excluded the corporation from Islamic law. The exclusion undermined the organizational capacity of potential separatists and rivals. Rulers must have understood that political opponents would benefit from operating through organizations able to reallocate resources and build coalitions. Trimming their organizational options to the waqf protected the political status quo by denying challengers opportunities to join forces within a flexible organization. In any event, restricting the number of founders set a pattern that lasted a millennium. Even after Egyptians obtained alternatives to the waqf, the modernizer Rifaah al-Tahtawi (1804–73) wrote that "associations for joint philanthropy are few in [Egypt], in contrast to individual charitable donations and family endowments, which are usually endowed by a single individual."[67]

The near absence of resource pooling opportunities kept waqfs with common needs from campaigning jointly for external resources. It blocked waqfs from participating in initiatives to address communal grievances. In 1792, a group of Muslim clerics in Istanbul's Kasımpaşa neighborhood sued the caretaker of a waqf-maintained public toilet complex for allowing sewage to drain into the street. Apparently, they had asked him to direct sewage elsewhere, to no avail. The lawsuit was ultimately withdrawn when the toilet caretaker redirected sewage into the drainage pipe of another waqf.[68] The case constitutes a rarely documented instance of two waqfs cooperating to remove a neighborhood nuisance.

But the case is significant especially for the clues it furnishes about Kasımpaşa's institutional deficiencies. Even though Kasımpaşa's dozens of waqfs faced many common challenges – roads, local security, flood prevention – they had no association to foster inter-waqf cooperation.[69] Faced with a lawsuit, one waqf caretaker found an ad hoc solution, which personal connections probably facilitated. No Kasımpaşa waqf was legally entitled to initiate a private association to address shared waqf problems. Waqf regulations prohibited caretakers from combining forces for sewage removal. Each caretaker was alone vis-à-vis the state, which decided on its own who merited help and who did not. In other words, Kasımpaşa's NGOs were powerless to respond jointly to common nuisances. A problem might fester even if a coordinated action by a group of waqfs could solve it easily.

Just as cooperation between waqfs was lacking within sectors, it was absent between those of any given locality. The caretakers and beneficiaries of waqfs serving a neighborhood – through a school, a hospital, a fountain – had a common interest in developing infrastructure. Nevertheless, they could not combine resources to campaign for, say, better roads. Because their deeds were interpreted as precluding collective action, they had to act independently. It is as if the residents of a modern apartment were precluded from running an apartment association, and towns from forming town councils. Modern neighborhoods are unimaginable without such geographically defined organizations situated between the individual and the state.

Nothing in Islamic law keeps the individual beneficiaries of waqfs from working together to address challenges. Parents from multiple neighborhoods could form a delegation to request better infrastructure from the state. However, this was unlikely without leadership from waqf caretakers, who tended to have high social status. Here, too, the hindrances to mass collective action would generally block cooperation. Isolated constituencies do not easily recognize the potential gains from intergroup collective action; nor do they develop a common political identity. In any case, beneficiaries somehow aware of the potential gains would lack the motivation to incur the setup costs.[70] For all these reasons, waqf-related petitions to sultans rarely requested help for multiple waqfs at once. Actions were initiated by either lone individuals or groups concerned about a single waqf.[71] After fires, Istanbul's courts received petitions from waqf caretakers demanding authorization to make repairs, sometimes with modifications.[72] If cases exist of a group of caretakers asking to work collectively on reconstruction, they must be rare exceptions. Under the circumstances, no city of the premodern Middle East had a master plan for development.[73]

Waqf law treated the founder as a principal and the caretaker as an agent hired to implement directives conservatively. Accordingly, they favored the status quo unless the deed explicitly stipulated flexibility.[74] Insofar as the founder's directives were incomplete and his intentions unknown, the caretaker lacked certainty as to how the founder would have wanted him to act. Nevertheless, he was to avoid substituting his own preferences for those of the founder. Absent evidence to the contrary, the presumption had to be that the founder separated the waqf's affairs from those of other entities. Hence, caretakers often disregarded opportunities for advancing beneficiary interests through cooperation with others.

THE SUPPRESSION OF SOCIAL CAPITAL

A wide array of genuinely free NGOs is essential for safeguarding personal liberties, rule of law, and meaningful elections. Accordingly, illiberal regimes discourage civic engagement to avoid constraints, but also for self-survival. In Middle Eastern states governed under Islamic law, the Islamic waqf was the chief instrument for accomplishing these ends. Its rules denied self-governance to the only legally autonomous institution that might have threatened autocratic rule. It served to depress mass political participation, dampen dissent, and hinder nonstate political coalitions.

Might all these political consequences have reflected deeper historical forces than the waqf itself? Trivially, the answer is yes, for two reasons. For one thing, the waqf was inspired by preexisting institutions. For another, the conditions that made Muslim landowners look for a credible wealth shelter about a century after the birth of Islam included perennially weak property rights. But analogous points can be made about any institution, past or present, anywhere in the world. None started from a blank slate. What matters here is that the waqf became a stable fixture of the Islamic institutional complex early on, and thereafter shaped the Middle East's political trajectory fundamentally, under the rubric of Islamic law. As we shall see in following chapters, although it has now been dismantled throughout the Muslim world, it continues to shape political patterns. From the eighth century to the present, Middle Eastern politics is incomprehensible without an understanding of how the Islamic waqf worked and what options it foreclosed.

Among the byproducts of the measures that kept the waqf politically feeble is that peoples of the region failed to develop the skills for sustaining a liberal order.[75] These skills include banding with others to tackle social problems, resolving inevitable conflicts efficiently, negotiating compromises, monitoring and enforcing group contacts, running organizations, funding collective campaigns, choosing leaders, and holding officers accountable for their performance. Members of liberal societies hone the requisite skills through interactions with associations and committees. They also develop capabilities through organized collective action. In denying individuals such opportunities to acquire social capital, waqfs habituated them to accept passively whatever services elites chose to provide. It even disincentivized thinking about improvements to existing services, the provision of new services, and how consumers could organize on their own to raise living standards.[76]

Regimes of the premodern Middle East did not find these patterns worrisome. On the contrary, they stoked the civic side effects of waqfs to promote political stability. But it is one thing to encourage mass passivity, another to accept waqf rules in toto. The very rules that suppressed social capital also blocked resource reallocations beneficial to elites and commoners alike. They depressed the quality of social services, causing many waqfs to become dysfunctional. Insofar as waqf deeds were enforced strictly, an eventual negative byproduct would have been widespread discontent. Irrespective of social status, people would have complained about repairs forgone because of insufficient maintenance budgets, opportunities bypassed for lack of foresight, and technologies ignored to satisfy the letter of the deed.

Rulers had much to gain from resource reallocations that improved services, mass satisfaction, economic productivity, and taxable capacity. Hence, they allowed rule bending, though on a selective basis and without enabling the ruled masses to acquire social capital. The compromise was to let waqf caretakers circumvent waqf deeds surreptitiously, under clerical supervision. This solution amounted to tolerance of institutionalized corruption, which itself hindered liberalization.

5

Waqf Corruption and Its Degradation of Civic Life

Throughout history, rulers of settled populations have sought to keep cities content. Knowing that a critical mass of disgruntled urbanites can trigger a ferocious mob, they have tried, especially in strategic centers, to secure urban peace through social services. By today's standards, the amenities did not necessarily go beyond basics. Those that would impress most residents of seventeenth-century Paris, Beijing, or Cairo would disappoint even their poorest descendants today. Nevertheless, it was challenging to keep neighborhoods supplied with potable water and, in lean years, to alleviate destitution.

In pacifying cities, premodern rulers of the Islamic Middle East were constrained by more than resources. As far back as Islam's second century, they were outsourcing urban services to waqfs. Regardless of the founder's identity and social status, the created organization was legally autonomous. Under a strict interpretation of waqf law, a ruler dissatisfied with a city's waqfs could not make them adjust their priorities.

To make matters worse, waqfs were designed as rigid organizations mandated to operate according to their deeds. Legally, it did not matter whether they remained functional, whether their resources were being used efficiently, whether technologies emerged that the founder could not have anticipated, or whether a crisis was brewing. There was no remedy for a founder's misjudgments. A natural disaster could shift the needs of a waqf's targeted constituency while also diminishing its income. Alas, if the founder had not planned for such an eventuality, its caretaker could not redirect expenditures.[1]

For all these difficulties, Middle Eastern cities looked rather functional until around 1800. Visitors from Western Europe did not consider them poorly serviced, as they commonly did after modern utilities became commonplace in their homelands.[2] Therein lies a puzzle. If Islamic law kept waqfs from adjusting to the times, how is it that, during their heyday, they did not make Middle Eastern cities look primitive?

The catch is that actual waqfs, whether of the regular or state variety, were not managed as rigidly as the law required. Permissive supervision enabled the caretakers of regular waqfs to depart, albeit in limited ways, from the founder's instructions. Besides, the judges monitoring regular waqfs could authorize broader departures in emergencies. Escape valves allowed some adaptations to changing conditions, unanticipated events, and misfortunes. State waqfs had even greater flexibility because ruling dynasties could effectively exempt them from inconvenient restrictions. Though rulers and their administrations sought to maintain an appearance of piety and respect for Islamic law, the civic weaknesses discussed in Chapter 4 gave them some cover against improprieties. Thus, many waqfs remained functional for centuries because in practice they departed from the fixity ideal enshrined in Islamic teachings.

Courts had the final say on whether a caretaker was complying with the deed and, insofar as he was not, whether his exceptions were justified. A judge could rule that the founder, were he or she alive, would have authorized certain changes that the deed did not explicitly allow. Alternatively, he could treat certain changes as incompatible with the waqf's spirit. He was thus the arbiter of what resource reallocations conformed to the law. Unsurprisingly, this privilege was abused. A judge could withhold permission for managerial adjustment until he was bribed. The waqf caretakers who paid bribes for, say, the permissions to make repairs, did not necessarily resent the payments. First, they understood the legal restrictions that their bribes would circumvent. Second, the social value of the permitted adjustments, even their value to the caretaker himself, could far exceed the demanded bribe.[3] Third, bribing state officials was generally considered understandable, if not essential, in view of the low salaries of government officials. Even in cases of well-paid judges, their staffs could include poorly paid clerks. Hence, judges would not be considered abusive for expecting their services to be remunerated; and bribe-paying waqf caretakers were not necessarily treated as depraved.[4] The acceptance of bribing as an imperative practice contributed to making the Islamic waqf a self-enforcing core institution of the Middle East's social order.[5]

The waqf was so central to the Middle East's premodern economy that its practices had region-wide implications. Indeed, efforts to transgress waqf rules promoted a culture of corruption, which infected social interactions unrelated to the waqf. Our primary interest here lies in the political consequences. Members of a society with rampant corruption tend to solve their problems with the state through bribery and reciprocal favors. They find personal solutions easier than trying to form coalitions with others facing similar challenges. One unintended effect is that civil society remains embryonic. Another is that individuals fail to cultivate the skills necessary for monitoring, controlling, and influencing state policies. Among the legacies of waqf-based corruption is that Middle Eastern societies combine high corruption with low civil engagement.

By no means was the waqf the only source of corruption in the Middle East. It became common for Ottoman sultans and their top aides to demand large gifts from those appointed to important positions, and the practice spread throughout the bureaucracy and the military.[6] Tax farming became another practice rife with corruption. Purchasers of the right to collect taxes from a particular area or sector for a specified period started passing the revenue streams on to their children, with officials in Istanbul looking the other way in return for shares of the appropriated income.[7] Clerics, the enforcers of Islamic law, participated in corruption themselves. Judges allowed overtaxation to share in the profits. For a fee, madrasa professors brought unqualified people into their profession.[8] Such forms of corruption all have analogues in contemporaneous states of Europe. What stands out in the premodern Middle East is not corruption per se but the prevalence of waqf-related corruption. The immensity of the waqf's asset base made this type of corruption a major driver of the interregional divergence in political trajectories. Insofar as waqfs met demands for adjustment through disguised corruption rather than transparent reforms, they reinforced the endemic weaknesses of civil society.

FORMS OF WAQF INFLEXIBILITY

To demonstrate how waqf rigidities fueled corruption, it will help to distinguish between restrictions on the choices of founders and those of their caretakers – "ex ante" and "ex post." Both foreclosed options.

Ex ante restrictions entail constraints on the founding of waqfs. Although the only formal substantive requirement was compatibility with Islamic law, in practice elites, especially those closest to the sultan, were expected to serve strategic constituencies. This policy is evident in the abundance of major endowed structures in places where rulers aimed to build legitimacy. No hard rule existed as to the discretion founders could give to caretakers. The decisions assignable to caretakers were restricted by judicial custom, with no discretion the default. Some deeds specified that certain revenue sources could be swapped with assets of at least equal value.

To turn now to ex post restrictions, these could involve mission or management. Mission restrictions concerned modifications to the waqf's intended purpose. The madrasas that Süleyman the Magnificent established in the 1550s taught revelation-based Islamic knowledge, along with medicine and mathematics. But they could not open an astronomy department even when later sultans needed astronomical expertise. When his grandson Murat III (reigned 1574–95) established an observatory, he deliberately kept it independent of madrasas.[9] The typical madrasa deed did not preclude professors from making marginal adjustments to the curriculum. However, the madrasa culture strongly discouraged innovation. As late as the 1700s, some Istanbul madrasas were not teaching anything about the Americas, which Columbus reached in 1492, or about the heliocentric theory of the universe, which Copernicus first presented publicly in 1543.[10]

Later chapters evaluate organizational and theological differences between Islam's two main denominations. Suffice it to say here that Sunni–Shii contrasts had no critical impact on the intellectual productivity of waqf-based madrasas. As Westerners were welcoming the printing press and discovering the New World, the madrasas of Shii-controlled Safavid Iran were just as hostile to innovation as those of Sunni-controlled Ottoman madrasas.[11] Critical thinking was not entirely absent in the Middle East. But it occurred outside madrasas. The most notable Iranian scholars of the age, Mir Damad (1543–1631) and Mulla Sadra (1571–1640) of the "Isfahan School" of philosophy, were independent scholars; so was Kâtip Çelebi (1609–57) of Istanbul, the most prolific Ottoman intellectual of his time. All three were born into wealth, which allowed them intellectual freedoms denied to madrasa professors.[12] Their productivity undoubtedly suffered from the intellectual conservatism of their societies generally and madrasas specifically. Intellectual creativity benefits from sophisticated feedback, which is rare in milieus that value conformist thought and punish heterodox speech.

Restrictions on intellectual discourse would have harmed educational quality. And the costs would have grown as global competitiveness came to depend on innovation and adaptability. The adverse effects were certainly unintentional. Had the founder of a madrasa with tight restrictions come alive several centuries later, he might have favored a broader curriculum. He might have wanted to reconcile religious training with up-to-date knowledge about the physical world. But a madrasa deed could not be amended lawfully, except if it explicitly granted the caretaker specific modification rights. A madrasa founder in, say, the 1300s, could not have anticipated the opportunities that mass printing or geographic discoveries would create.

In principle, inefficient uses of a madrasa's resources could be overcome if it ran out of students. At that point, the resources would pass to "the poor" – the ultimate recipients of every waqf's income. But in this context, jurists defined the poor to include clerics, regardless of their actual wealth.[13] Ex post restrictions on waqf missions thus benefited clerics financially. If for no other reason, clerics were generally content with waqf rules dating from early Islam.

Ex post managerial restrictions concern the caretaker's administration of waqf assets and disbursement of waqf revenue. Trying to empower their future caretakers on managerial matters, founders often pre-authorized certain operational changes, including asset swaps, reconstructions, and job reclassifications. Courts helped founders equip caretakers with operational discretion through formulaic escape clauses. But even with escape clauses, eventually deed restrictions became binding. The number of changes had to be finite, and the founder's initial choice was always the default. Sooner or later, as economic conditions evolved and maintenance was performed, keeping the waqf functional required extralegal measures. If upkeep slackened, service quality would fall, as would asset values. A school's leaky roof would hinder learning. A decaying shop would ultimately lose its tenants and stop producing income.

In a static world, the dangers in question would be moot. Nothing would alter the usefulness of established services; repairs would be unnecessary; satisfied tenants would remain happy indefinitely; and returns from assets would be stable. In fact, assorted processes threatened waqf performance. Though periodic roof repairs could be anticipated, natural disasters were unpredictable; so were price trends, demand patterns, and technological innovations.

Waqfs became even less viable in the era of modern economic growth, which began around 1750. That is when technological and institutional innovations took a quantum leap, inducing global adaptations that fed on themselves.[14] As the Industrial Era unfolded, waqfs faced even more pressing demands to reallocate resources and modernize their services. Meanwhile, Middle Easterners were drawn to other, and generally transplanted, organizational forms for delivering social services. In stages, waqfs were dismantled on a massive scale. With variations in timing across regions, their functions passed to more flexible organizations. But before modern economic growth discredited Islamic waqfs and eroded their significance, Middle Eastern policy makers had routine responses to waqf rigidities. Inefficiencies were dampened, and the lives of many waqfs lengthened, through several tools of questionable legality.

LEGAL RUSES TO SOFTEN WAQF RIGIDITIES

Countless waqfs fell on hard times because their caretakers lacked authorization to address financial issues pragmatically. Launching a public fundraising campaign was out of the question, as the endowment had to originate from a single person's property. But opportunities existed to alter operations without violating the letter of waqf law. The Islamic judicial system was accustomed to circumventing inconvenient laws through ruses (*hiyal*). Indeed, ruses existed to evade waqf restrictions.

The simplest ruse involved treating deed ambiguities as a license for pragmatism. Thus, the authority to make repairs was used to adapt buildings to emerging needs. Finding anything in disrepair – a chipped tile, a squeaky door – could suffice for a permit to convert a building's function.[15] By stretching the meaning of "repairs," the letter of the law was fulfilled, even as its spirit was violated deliberately. Such circumstances did not necessarily conflict with the founder's intentions. Conversions accorded with the deed's spirit when they benefited constituencies that the founder meant to serve.

A second form of adaptation exploited the authorization to conduct asset swaps beneficial to the waqf (*istibdāl*). Even if the deed was silent on swaps, in extenuating circumstances a judge could make exceptions on efficiency grounds alone.[16] Thus, in the 1700s, Aleppo courts permitted numerous local waqfs to give up rural farms for urban properties. Invariably, the logic was that urban caretakers would find the latter easier to manage. Monitoring assets did indeed become easier, as did the collection of payments. Asset swaps certainly enhanced the capacity to meet the founder's goals. On rare occasions, swaps were achieved by rewriting the deed. This option presented itself when one could reasonably consider the original deed damaged, stolen, lost, or illegally modified.[17]

Another form of adaptation met maintenance expenses. Because repair bills could exceed the deed allowance, caretakers often left maintenance to tenants, for subsequent reimbursement. Presumably because of mistrust, the repayment amounts were determined not by actual costs but by experts who estimated what repairs should have cost. The practice amounted to financing current expenses through borrowing against future income. A variant of this practice involved an out-of-pocket loan from the caretaker to the waqf. Thus, in 1696, a fire-destroyed Istanbul mosque was rebuilt by its caretaker, who then had a judge certify his due through an expert's estimation.[18] Although waqfs were not supposed to operate on credit, the practice was often allowed on the ground that no loan was negotiated, only a maintenance contract. This legal ruse, too, aided many waqfs. Most founders would have endorsed its use, provided their waqfs were spared undue risks.

Lengthening leases beyond the permissible was a fourth form of legally dubious adaptation. To help the caretaker keep control over the waqf's assets, classical Islamic law capped the lease period at one year, except for land, for which the maximum was three years. This provision discouraged the lessee from making long-term investments; it even deterred maintenance. A common practice that incentivized tenants to care for leased assets was to sign a long-term contract scheduled to lapse periodically for a few days and then be revalidated (*icâreteyn* in Ottoman usage). Although the practice obeyed the letter of the law, everyone understood that it extended effective agreements beyond the legal cap.[19] The lengthening of actual leasing periods kept many waqfs operational and extended their lives.

CORRUPTION THROUGH LEGAL RUSES

In societies governed under Islamic law, legal ruses saw use in diverse contexts to simplify life without having to reinterpret God's law, presumed fixed. Most prominently, they concealed the use of interest in credit contracts. The financial gimmicks of the Islamic Middle East had parallels in medieval Europe, where the Church treated usury as sinful.[20] As in the Christian context, interest-enabling ruses generally made financial markets more efficient. Today, they see use in Islamic finance. Ostensibly free of interest, the activities of Islamic banks, investment companies, and insurance agencies camouflage interest through modern variants of old ruses.[21]

Legal ruses often enriched waqf officials and supervising clerics in the guise of improving services or preserving financial sustainability. In treating a particular modification as legal because of necessity, a judge could simply generate concealed wealth that he and the caretaker would share. Consider unnecessary repairs authorized to provide employment to a caretaker's friend; and suppose that the repairman's "fee" is split between him, the caretaker, and the supervising judge. The waqf's beneficiaries need not lose anything immediately. But nor do they gain anything, and the waqf's finances worsen, endangering its future services. Officials responsible for enforcing the founder's goals end up diverting waqf assets to personal uses. Although the share of reimbursements that entered private pockets is unknown, court records suggest that embezzlement was common.[22]

Ambiguities in waqf deeds were also exploited to broaden classes of beneficiaries beyond the founder's intentions. A case in point is a sixteenth-century endowment established in Jerusalem for the benefit of "the poor and the humble, the weak and the needy, ... the true believers and the righteous who live near the holy places." Its deed was interpreted as encompassing all pious Muslims of the city, including top officials.[23] In the same vein, residences endowed for specific professionals, such as a local teacher, were frequently assigned to a friend of the caretaker.[24]

Property transactions, too, were subject to abuse. Commonly, they benefited officials at the expense of the waqf's designated constituency. Under one variant, a waqf asset would be swapped with a less productive asset whose value was inflated on paper; and the caretaker would share the disguised difference with the supervising judge. Another variant involved rentals to the caretaker's relatives at submarket prices. The records of an Istanbul waqf speak of farms rented to the caretaker's daughter and son-in-law at unusually low rates; with the connivance of judicial authorities, the caretaker had avoided seeking other bids.[25] Judges supervising waqfs were authorized to block asset swaps. Accordingly, often they acquiesced only in return for favors.

The practice of lengthening lease periods facilitated their privatization without compensation for the waqf. Lessees would refuse to return the properties, usually on the pretext that costly improvements accounted for most of their value. In the process, caretakers lost the ability to adjust contract terms, even to reclaim properties. Leases even became inheritable. A lessee's descendants would assert outright ownership by virtue of long hereditary tenure.[26] If in the meantime waqf documents disappeared through theft or a natural disaster, privatization became inevitable. Waqf properties changed status unless courts strongly resisted the misconduct, which often they did not.

If leased assets were the most productive properties in the waqf's portfolio – a common occurrence – the waqf would be left with only poorly performing assets, causing its demise. Lessees of the productive assets would then effectively be relieved from the obligation to pay rent. They would become owners of the leased properties. This outcome was often intended. The leases constituted a ruse that the caretaker and supervising judge used to strip the waqf of its valuable assets. They each took shares of the ensuing profits.

Though detrimental to certain constituencies, privatizations of waqf assets did not necessarily impose a net harm on society. Insofar as they freed misallocated assets, the social gains could have swamped the losses of the intended beneficiaries. In the eighteenth and nineteenth centuries, privatizations served to transfer resources from dysfunctional waqfs to dynamic equity markets.[27] Privatizations would also have augmented the resources available for civic engagement. But the latter effect must have been trivial, because up to the twentieth century lack of incorporation opportunities hindered sustained collective action by nonstate actors.

The logic of the outlined corrupt practices begs the question of why any waqf, or specifically any regular waqf, escaped full asset stripping. Countervailing incentives were present. Rulers relied on waqfs and their inviolability for both legitimacy and signaling piety. Hence, they had a stake in the preservation of waqfs that provided useful services, including wealth sheltering for elites. They would have had judges, who served at their pleasure, limit asset stripping to genuinely dysfunctional waqfs. The observed corruption would have represented an equilibrium between, on the one hand, the ruler's efforts to keep waqfs productive and financially healthy, and, on the other, appropriation initiatives by colluding entrepreneurs and judges.

HARMS TO CIVIL SOCIETY

The methods used to modify waqf services and reallocate their income-producing assets contributed to a culture of corruption. Indeed, buying off judges, exploiting textual ambiguities, and making authorities look the other way became not only common but acceptable throughout the region. Even respected people used legal ruses, which supported their legitimacy. Although corruption in Muslim-governed states predates the waqf and always transcended it, the waqf's economic centrality gave special salience to the forms it induced and enabled.

Tolerated law breaking is universal, of course. Even in societies that rank high in rule-of-law indices, jaywalking is common, and citizens do not necessarily frown upon it. However, in the premodern Middle East circumvention of the law took place in far more contexts than in today's advanced societies. Moreover, a greater share of resources was involved. It bears repeating that waqfs controlled abundant real estate and fulfilled functions that Western Europeans generally met through more flexible organizational forms. As the Middle East fell behind the West economically, the divergence was reflected in the extent of corruption. Though no standardized international corruption statistics were compiled before modern times, the Middle East was already developing a reputation for rampant corruption.[28] Prejudices undoubtedly contributed to perceptions. But the reported patterns were not simply imagined. The privatization and nationalization of waqf assets – colossal processes that the next chapter revisits – were neither orderly nor transparent. On the contrary, they involved sundry dishonest practices that enriched elites who pretended to be assisting waqfs, when in fact they were simply grabbing resources.

With any given waqf, individual beneficiaries may have lacked awareness of the resource transfers taking place. They could have noticed a decline in service quality without necessarily knowing the reasons. After all, waqf management was never transparent, and nor was judicial supervision. But reasonably alert people could see that charity was losing its importance as a function of the waqfs that touched their lives. They could see that even state waqfs no longer served their intended functions alone. They understood that waqf caretakers abused age-old waqf privileges, with judges looking the other way. The collective reputations of caretakers and judges were getting sullied, lowering their trustworthiness. The constituencies willing to defend the waqf as an institution would have shrunk.

Loss of legitimacy would also have sunk the waqf's already negligible capacity to galvanize collective action. As services diminished and lost reliability, the waqf's intended beneficiaries would be even less likely than before to consider themselves a collective constituency. Considering collective action futile, they would also be less likely to consider the waqf caretaker a natural leader for pursuing causes on their behalf. If they harbored thoughts of influencing state policies through inter-waqf cooperation, they would lose any slim hope of forming alliances across separate constituencies. In sum, the waqf's reduced significance as a source of charity diminished its already stunted contribution to civic life.

State officials never considered the waqf an instrument of civic engagement anyway. For more than a millennium, they had viewed it as a tax and wealth shelter for the rich and a convenient instrument for elite-chosen social services. At no point did sultans or their aides pursue initiatives to ascertain what the masses thought about waqfs ostensibly built for their benefit. If waqf law bothered them at all, it was because of the waste it generated and the economic opportunities it blocked. In the writings of reformist Ottoman, Arab, and Iranian statesmen of the 1700s and 1800s, nowhere does one encounter a call for revising waqf law to give beneficiaries a say in management. Just as the waqf's stultification of civic life never became an issue for elites during the waqf's heyday, after it passed its prime no concerns were voiced until the nineteenth century. The last theme will be developed in the next chapter.

WAQF CORRUPTION VS. CORPORATE CORRUPTION

The founders of charitable waqfs usually managed to deploy resources optimally to achieve immediate goals. In delivering health services, they typically prescribed resource uses consonant to available medical knowledge and local needs, as the founder perceived them. Waqf-financed hospitals were founded to have trained physicians deliver "humoral medicine," which aimed at balancing the four Hippocratic humors, along with "Prophetic medicine," which drew on Islamic traditions and folk medicine. These hospitals were also meant to enhance the founder's social status and reputation. A hospital packed with patients would keep alive its founder's memory better than an empty building. Patients were to be the "needy." As in contemporaneous Europe, wealthy patients had healers visit their homes; rarely did they use a hospital. When people of status checked into a hospital, as they might during a trip, they were segregated from ordinary patients, in luxurious wards.[29]

Some of the Middle East's traditionally trained physicians modified their remedies in the light of new medical knowledge, which increasingly came from Western Europe.[30] Yet, with advances in European medicine, the services of waqf-financed hospitals became outdated. Already in the 1700s, they were losing reputation, as practitioners of "new medicine" – disproportionately European immigrants and indigenous non-Muslims – outcompeted Middle Eastern physicians in the traditional mold. The early 1800s saw the opening of Ottoman medical schools teaching "new medicine"; their curricula followed European templates. Evidently, Ottoman elites were coming to appreciate the advantages of modern medicine.[31] Medical modernization in Iran, Egypt, and Tunisia matched the Ottoman pattern. European emigration, rising international commerce, and epidemics all stimulated medical reforms. Shifting confidence from Islamic to European medicine, they also enlarged constituencies for organizationally modern medical schools and hospitals.[32]

The growing inefficiencies of waqf-financed services, such as hospitals practicing traditional medicine, created incentives to circumvent their deeds through some form of corruption. The illegitimate modifications of waqfs included ones that would have been legitimate had the services been delivered instead through charitable corporations. For reasons already covered, the corporation has more managerial flexibility. Though its managers do not have boundless discretion, they are empowered to carry out adjustments on their own that functionally equivalent Islamic waqfs could make legally only with judicial permission.

Consider an Islamic waqf and a Western corporation, both founded in 1300 to provide health services. Centuries later, because of medical advances, it becomes inefficient to spend resources as their founders had envisioned. Now it makes sense to hire new physicians, use different remedies, deploy new equipment, and reallocate physical space. Such changes involve more discretion than the waqf's founder had authorized. Therefore, if implemented, they may well be perceived as corruption. Yet the same adaptations will be viewed as fully legal for the hospital organized as a corporation, which need not require permission from an outside authority. In other words, the waqf might appear more corrupt than the corporation simply for making adjustments that the latter can make at will. An unintended consequence of the waqf's legal restrictions was thus to broaden the range of its potential policies considered illegitimate.

How much discretion the boards of charitable corporations should enjoy has long been debated; so have institutions meant to secure corporate accountability. Among the themes of the pertinent literatures is that a charitable corporation's optimal structure varies greatly because of differences in complementary institutions and educational, scientific, and religious cultures. In fact, charitable corporations differ widely on such matters as information shared with constituents, how information is communicated, the monitoring of board members, the means for replacing board members, incentives of individual constituents to act in their own interest, ability to form coalitions pursuing common goals, the right to call board meetings, and powers to remove managers.[33] But even the best efforts to avoid corporate pathologies often fall short. Examples of disengaged and incompetent corporate boards are ubiquitous. Abundant cases exist of managerial malfeasance in charitable corporations. Typically, the underlying circumstances involve some combination of fiduciary negligence, poor organization, ignorance, and divergent interests on the part of beneficiaries.[34] In 1992, a notorious scandal befell United Way, a network of 2,100 charitable corporations. Its board was found to have overlooked or deliberately allowed huge misappropriations and extensive conflicts of interest.[35] Such major wrongdoings are followed by remedial legislation. But it has proven impossible to protect charitable corporations from all breaches of fiduciary responsibility.

An organization does not become immune to corruption, then, just by taking a corporate form. Yet this chapter's central point remains valid. For one thing, in keeping up with the times and even in trying to survive, Islamic waqfs were more likely than their corporate counterparts to violate laws. Hence, they fueled corruption on a greater scale. For another, the founders of waqfs had far less flexibility in stipulating managerial rules. Learning from the mistakes of previous waqf founders, they could restrict uses of their endowment; and, in anticipation of specific changes in conditions, they could give caretakers discretion in tightly defined areas. But the range of structural options available to waqf founders pales in comparison to those of corporate architects. They could not institute measures to empower beneficiaries or mandate performance disclosures. Accordingly, the pathologies of Islamic waqfs were generally far more serious. Besides, centuries of corrupt practices did not generate corrective measures to prevent their eventual demise. Whereas the Islamic waqf is now essentially defunct, the charitable corporation flourishes. The charitable corporation sector of the United States alone is so large that if it were a country, it would be the world's eighth largest, ahead of Italy and Brazil.[36] Countries of the Middle East have their own charitable corporation sectors, which are larger by orders of magnitude than any remnants of Islamic waqfs.

LASTING EFFECTS OF WAQF CORRUPTION

In the historical literature on classical Islamic institutions, evasions of waqf rules are sometimes treated as substitutes for legally granted flexibility.[37] Although evasions certainly made waqfs less rigid than if the law was interpreted strictly, the long-term effects were not benign. In overcoming immediate obstacles to resource reallocation, they also dampened pressures against law breakers in general. That made it harder to institute new rules and regulations, which is integral to modernization. In societies accustomed to obeying the law, new laws alter practices quickly, simply because lawfulness comes naturally. By contrast, in those accustomed to circumventing rules, new laws are not taken seriously. People socialized to view rule breaking as essential to survival expect compliance to be minimal. For this reason alone, they feel no compulsion to adjust their own behaviors. They also avoid inconveniencing themselves. Free riding remains common and tolerated, hindering socially beneficial cooperation.

Many influential historians consider Islamic waqfs to have remained efficient centuries after their founding.[38] Some also believe that the Islamic waqf's serious troubles began with European colonization.[39] European colonizers certainly contributed, wherever they could, to the nationalizations and privatizations of waqf assets. But the Islamic waqf's problems started long before the rise of Europe and its global expansion. Its corruption is among the manifestations of built-in rigidities that were bound to stimulate bypasses as conditions changed. Because of the waqf's enormous weight in the Middle East's economy, the evasions that became integral to its management were bound to color norms of decision making and resource allocation in a panoply of contexts.

We come finally to the lasting political effects of the mechanisms through which the Islamic waqf undermined the rule of law and limited political participation. The effects are not obvious, for the Islamic waqf's functions have passed to new institutions, including the modern waqf, which is basically a form of charitable corporation. Given the Middle East's poor record in expanding liberties, it is natural to wonder whether the Islamic waqf still casts a shadow on the region's political life. A related issue is whether the modern waqf's political effects differ from those of its historical namesake.

6

The Islamic Waqf's Long Civic Shadow

By the nineteenth century, social service suppliers unable to adapt to the Industrial Revolution's new technologies seemed glaringly inefficient. Water supply systems consisting of physically and financially disconnected fountains looked quaint to anyone familiar with the water delivery systems of London or Paris.[1] In principle, the hundreds of fountains that delivered water to Istanbul's neighborhoods could have contributed their resources to a city-wide water distribution network. However, as we know from Chapter 4, waqfs could not pool resources even among themselves, to say nothing of transferring assets to another type of organization. Hence, if piped water was to become a standard service to Istanbul's homes and businesses, the necessary planning and investment could not come from waqfs. Similar challenges existed with respect to electricity, natural gas, paving, sidewalks, street lighting, mass transportation, and sanitation. For each such amenity, abundant new capital had to be raised. In addition, organizations without local precedent had to be founded.

If any Middle Eastern locality tried to supply modern urban amenities through an Islamic waqf, it must have been a minor exception. Often, a foreign company was hired to construct and operate a new utility. Sometimes, a new government agency was established to function under ad hoc rules. Still other cases involved a joint venture with foreigners, under a foreign legal system. Eventually, municipalities were established under new local laws to supply many services in coordinated fashion. All were modeled after Western local governments.[2]

The needed capital was not readily available. Due largely to the rising cost of equipping standing militaries, but also to the expenses of building modern infrastructure quickly, the region's governments had no money.[3] Some capital was raised through borrowing. Foreign direct investment supplied additional resources. Rulers also raided Islamic waqfs, effectively competing for their assets with caretakers, judges, and private investors. Though they had been milking Islamic waqfs for decades through ostensible rescue operations, the remaining waqfs still controlled abundant productive assets. Expropriations accelerated with the formation of centralized waqf administrations. Absorbing vast assets, they freed most waqfs of founder-imposed constraints.[4] Nationalizations continued in waves into the 1900s, with cross-national variations in pace and scope. Through these processes, governments financed modernization drives. Across the Middle East, many mosques and a few odd charities still operate as Islamic waqfs. Otherwise, this venerated institution is defunct. Egypt's oldest higher education provider, the Al-Azhar Madrasa founded in 970, has been reorganized repeatedly since 1896. Today, it operates as Al-Azhar University. Formally it is no longer a waqf of any sort but a charitable corporation. Moreover, as a matter of practice, it operates as a semigovernmental agency.[5]

As the region's elites came to recognize the Islamic waqf's unsuitability to a dynamic economy, they developed new legal codes to support nascent organizational forms that lacked standing in a bona fide Islamic system. Beginning in 1908, these non-Islamic organizational forms included the charitable corporation and the business corporation. Eventually, variants of the former entered Middle Eastern legal systems under the name waqf. This modern construct, which we are calling the modern waqf, differs fundamentally from the Islamic waqf.

The Middle East's modern private organizations, including its modern waqfs, were born into societies with anemic civic lives. Their contributions to building civil society thus started from a low base. Under these circumstances, regimes bent on minimizing individual and organizational freedoms found it easy to quash democratization movements.

But why, in the first place, did it take so long to broaden the region's menu of legally recognized organizational forms? And why did the Islamic waqf not acquire capabilities found in alternative organizations? Addressing those questions will set the stage for analyzing modern institutional developments and their implications for civic life.

IMPRACTICALITY AND UNDESIRABILITY OF REFORMING THE ISLAMIC WAQF

As the Islamic waqf's organizational limitations became apparent, and Middle Eastern elites recognized its harm to urban prosperity and the state's fiscal capacity, traditional waqf rules might have been reinterpreted to suit a relatively dynamic social order. New waqf categories might have been created for sectors where relaxing restrictions on resource use was particularly desirable; urban water delivery is a case in point. But nowhere in the region did the waqf adapt. One obstacle to reform was the trait that made the Islamic waqf a credible wealth shelter: its sacredness. The sanctity of its assets meant that reform proposals could be treated as heresy. The danger of religious pushback would have made the potential beneficiaries of looser regulations refrain from criticizing the system or proposing modifications. Therein lay a key reason why the principle of static perpetuity – commitment to the fixity of waqf objectives, administration, and resource allocation – remained resistant to fundamental change.[6] Another obstacle to reform was that clerics, who tended to be conservative, controlled the lion's share of remaining Islamic waqf properties, largely because dysfunctional waqfs fell, at least initially, under their management. To avoid empowering clerics, reformers withheld from them greater flexibility in waqf administration.

The availability of opportunities to improve social services without taking on Islamic institutions also quashed the will to challenge the formal rigidity of waqfs. By the early 1900s, the corporation, a transplanted institution, became the basic delivery vehicle for various services long provided through Islamic waqfs.[7] In the preceding decades, the Middle Eastern economic infrastructure had expanded to include institutions that complement the corporation: standardized accounting, courts that recognize fictitious individuals, and stock markets. Hence, it was possible to form efficiently operating corporations. Even earlier, state agencies were forming organizations with corporate features, under special laws. The region's early municipalities offer examples.[8]

Although clerics had lost considerable power over the preceding centuries, they remained strong enough to incite serious protests, even rebellions. By welcoming new institutions *without* destroying the Islamic waqf, the reformers maintained some religious legitimacy. Even as they pleased modernizing communities – merchants and financiers, elites eager to shift resources from waqfs to new investment vehicles, military officers threatened existentially by European advances – they minimized the alienation of conservatives.[9]

Meanwhile, fewer new Islamic waqfs were being formed. At least in Istanbul, where foundings peaked around 1650, new waqfs were mostly cash waqfs established, in the absence of banks, to earn income through interest-bearing loans. By 1800, practically no real estate-owning classic Islamic waqfs were being formed (Figure 6.1). Among the motives for these transformations is the strengthening of property rights in response to pressures from European businesses as well as local beneficiaries of expanding trade with the West.[10] A related motive lies in European wars that ended in Ottoman defeat. In the late 1700s, they resulted in treaties that extended to European powers formal rights to protect Ottoman Christians – rights that they were already exercising, but informally. Russia acquired de jure protection rights over Eastern Christians (most of the total), France over Catholics, and Great Britain over Protestants. Critical here is that in the 1700s foreign-protected Christians started to acquire stronger property rights than other Ottoman subjects. These rights empowered Christians economically, enhancing their capacity to invest in emerging private sectors without fear of expropriation. Wealthy Muslims could not keep pace with Christians, partly because a

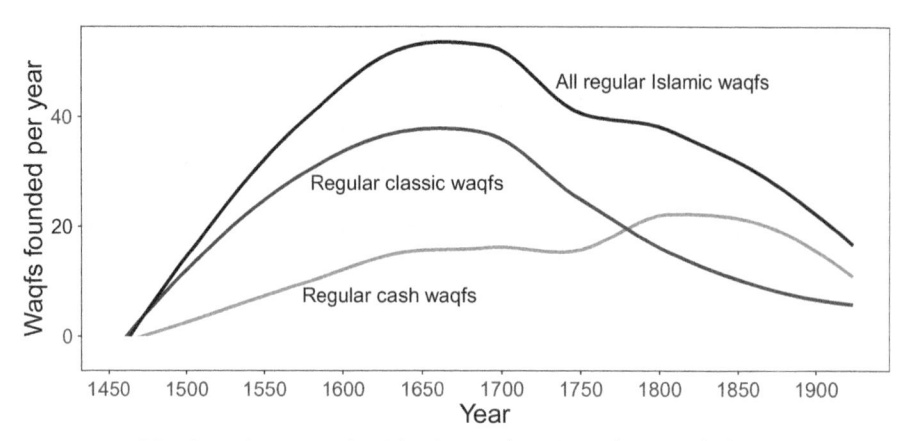

FIGURE 6.1 Number of new regular Islamic waqfs registered in Istanbul courts, 1453–1923

Source: Adıgüzel and Kuran, "Inequality-Preserving Benevolence," where the data sources and smoothing technique are described. In essence, for 1453–1599 the data come from the Istanbul waqf census of 1600, and for 1600–1923 from deeds located in surviving court registers.

disproportionate share of their assets was frozen in waqfs. They became increasingly prepared to swap wealth shelters, whose reliability was falling anyway, for general property rights. They began demanding stronger property rights for all Ottoman subjects. The process culminated in the Gülhane Edict of 1839. Among other momentous reforms, this edict abrogated the sultan's right to confiscate private property at will.[11] Falling expropriations further lowered incentives to channel private wealth into waqfs.[12]

As private investors lost interest in the Islamic waqf, new opportunities became available to all faith groups. In certain large cities, a new investment vehicle emerged in response to credit shortages: equities known as gediks. A gedik consisted of a fractionally tradable productive enterprise, such as a bakery. Gedik owners received commensurate shares of the profits.[13] Unlike a full-fledged stock market, the gedik market lacked a centralized registry. This complicated the tracking of ownership. Consequently, gediks were limited to sectors with small enterprises. Poorly suited to impersonal exchange, they were bound to fade away when stock markets emerged. In the meantime, though, gediks attracted massive domestic capital. In Istanbul, the region's leading commercial center, the gedik became by far the leading investment vehicle during the 1700s and early 1800s for Muslims and non-Muslims alike. The capital that fueled the explosion of gedik investments came substantially from waqf privatizations through the corrupt procedures reviewed in Chapter 5. Although the timing of the waqf's loss of popularity varied geographically, by the 1900s it was retreating everywhere.[14]

The Islamic waqf's displacement as a provider of charitable services was matched, then, by its eclipse as an investment instrument. Largely because of its

The Islamic Waqf's Long Civic Shadow 93

rigidity, statesmen and private investors alike considered it outdated. Reformist intellectuals commonly included the Islamic waqf among the institutions responsible for the Middle East's economic backwardness. Ziya Gökalp (1876–1924), the chief ideologist of Turkish nationalism, spoke for many modernizers through a poem entitled "Vakıf." One of its stanzas identifies inflexibility as the waqf's key flaw:

> Why, I don't know, the dead
> Control the reins of the living.
> Why a nation fond of running
> Has been ordered to stand still.[15]

Modernizers considered the belief in waqf sacredness a tale concocted by devious clerics seeking to control wealth. Here is the Iranian periodical *Rastakhiz*, addressing Reza Shah Pahlavi in 1925, as he acceded to the throne: "The root of our evil is ... the clergy. ... The best method of eradicating the clergy is to take away their means of livelihood. The waqf lands should be taken away and sold to poor peasants."[16] It helped the modernization cause that the Quran does not mention the waqf. Its post-Quranic status enabled reformers to desacralize, delegitimize, and discard the waqf without being stigmatized as anti-Islamic. [17]

EARLY ALTERNATIVES TO THE ISLAMIC WAQF

By the time Middle Eastern modernizers started to criticize the Islamic waqf overtly, as an autonomous institution, it was already a shadow of its former self. Not only were far fewer being formed but vast numbers of preexisting waqfs had seen their inalienable assets converted legally to freely tradable private property. States had also joined the plunder of waqf properties. On the pretext that waqfs were hopelessly corrupted and that governments could meet founders' wishes more reliably, they established waqf agencies to take over the duties of caretakers. Thus, a Ministry of Waqfs was established in Istanbul in 1826 and in Cairo shortly thereafter.[18] In principle, waqf ministries kept separate accounts for the thousands of waqfs under their control, including both state and regular waqfs. In practice, nationalized assets became part of a fungible investment portfolio.[19] Huge financial mergers effectively occurred through means antithetical to the spirit of the Islamic waqf.[20] The nationalization of waqfs was accompanied by transfers of their functions to Western-inspired service providers, such as municipalities and private utilities. Meanwhile, in Iran, where waqf nationalizations followed a distinct trajectory, the result was the same. By the twentieth century, the state had taken over the Islamic waqf's key social functions, and many waqf assets had passed to the state or individuals.[21] As France colonized Algeria, it moved quickly to open the most productive farmland to settlers. In 1843, the colonial "Land Department" seized waqf endowments and voided their inalienability.

Marketed as private property, most reclassified land passed to European immigrants.[22]

Outside of European-colonized territories, Ottoman and Egyptian reformers took the lead in laying the legal infrastructure for state agencies and private companies to provide urban amenities hitherto supplied through Islamic waqfs. In the mid-nineteenth century, it became possible to establish, under special laws, corporate-like entities to provide education, health care, and piped water, among other public services. Newly established municipalities took on certain functions of urban waqfs; and semi-official agencies, such as the Red Crescent, assumed responsibility for emergency aid and relief to the poor. Monarchs themselves started forming social and charitable organizations outside of waqf law. By the early twentieth century, legal transplants enabled the forming of nonprofit corporations through simple procedures. Private parties started establishing perpetual NGOs to deliver social services more flexibly than through waqfs.[23]

EMERGENCE OF THE MODERN WAQF

The Islamic waqf is now a relic. Nowhere does it survive in its classic form, as an autonomous organization using a fixed endowment to meet the founder's recorded stipulations. Waqfs with religious functions live on as semi-autonomous organizations within state-operated waqf agencies. The bureaucrats running these agencies keep some separation among mosque endowments. But routinely they reallocate revenues and override deeds.[24]

As the Islamic waqf entered the twilight of its existence, an institution sharing its name emerged in various parts of the Middle East. Certain promoters of the modern waqf claim that it has Islamic origins.[25] Yet in Turkey, Kuwait, the United Arab Emirates, and even in theocratic Iran, waqfs established in the twentieth and twenty-first centuries operate under rules fundamentally different from those of the premodern era. Legal texts call the new institution "new waqf" or "civil law waqf," to distinguish it from waqfs founded under Islamic law.[26]

Whatever its legal designation, a modern waqf can be formed by a consortium, which may include both natural persons and organizations. It can accept donations and run fundraising campaigns. It may invest in liquid assets, such as equities. It is directed by a board of trustees rather than a single caretaker. Whereas the Islamic waqf lacked standing before a court, the modern waqf enjoys legal personhood; as such, it can sue and be sued as a legal entity. Its administrators are supposed to be selected on merit, as judged by its board of trustees. A modern waqf must issue financial reports regularly. It has managerial flexibilities that the Islamic waqf lacked. Most importantly, it can dissolve itself or recast its objectives.[27] Table 6.1 summarizes the differences between Islamic and modern waqfs. Note that the modern waqf may engage in politics. Although it cannot endorse a political party, it may express opinions on policy matters. It can organize conferences, issue publications, give awards, and make

TABLE 6.1 *Characteristics of Islamic and modern waqfs*

Characteristics	Islamic waqf	Modern waqf
Founder	Single natural person	Any combination of natural persons and corporate entities
Manager	Single caretaker	Team working under board of trustees
Discretion	Very limited	Depends on charter
Political role	None	May be politically active
Longevity	Perpetual	Indefinite

grants, all to influence political opinions and outcomes. Moreover, it can pursue such endeavors in cooperation with other entities.[28] The modern waqf thus operates more like an American charitable corporation than like any Islamic waqf of premodern times.[29]

Just as an Islamic waqf's caretaker had to follow the founder's stipulations, so a modern waqf's trustees must abide by directives in its charter. But it is no longer presumed that the founding document constitutes a complete contract. A modern waqf's board is authorized to change services, procedures, and goals without outside interference. It is charged with maximizing the overall return on its total endowment, subject to intertemporal tradeoffs, risk preferences, and financial regulations. The permanence of any particular asset or expense is not itself an objective. The board may judge that the waqf's substantive goals require, say, a payroll cut to finance repairs. Another innovation is the board's integral role in determining how goals are served. It would not feel obliged to preserve an obsolete hospital out of deference to a founder's preferences. All these observations hold irrespective of the political or religious beliefs of founders. They apply as much to secular modern waqfs such as the Antalya Culture and Art Vakıf (AKSAV), whose activities include Turkish film festivals, as they do to Islamist modern waqfs such as the Fatih Youth Vakıf, which promotes Islamic education in Istanbul.[30]

As in the rest of the region, in Egypt entities called a waqf include both old and new organizations. But *all* are under tight state supervision; the country lacks modern waqfs of the Turkish variety. Whether inherited from before the nineteenth century or founded in recent decades, an Egyptian waqf is subordinate to bureaucrats. Accordingly, surviving Egyptian waqfs from before the twentieth century have metamorphosed into organizations that no longer merit the characterization "Islamic waqf." Because this loss of autonomy is well understood, no more than ten new Egyptian waqfs are formed each year. Typically, the objective is to support a mosque or burials.[31]

Egypt's lack of modern waqfs is not for absence of motivation to found functionally analogous organizations. Due to tight supervision, Egyptians wishing to supply nongovernmental social services in areas such as health care or education generally establish "foundations" (*mu'assasat*). These are charitable corporations governed under an NGO law adopted in 2002.[32] Although foundations are also subject to political pressures, at least they can move resources around and raise funds continuously from multiple sources, including both natural and legal persons.[33] Egypt has only a single modern NGO bearing the word "waqf" in its official name, under special permission. This is the Waqfeyat Al-Maadi Community Foundation, which funds development in poor Cairo neighborhoods and lobbies for public education. It was founded in 2007 to revive a tradition of social solidarity (*takāful*) through waqfs, under modernized rules.[34] Dozens of other foundations formed under the 2002 NGO law or a successor characterize themselves informally as a waqf. Examples include seven Cairo foundations of Mohamed Al Fangary, which help students at religious schools.[35]

In Iran, the waqf's rebirth as an autonomous organization followed the Islamic Revolution of 1978–79. The impetus was the reallocation of assets seized from foundations of the overthrown Pahlavi regime.[36] Nationalized assets were transferred to newly created *bonyad*s, which were billed as waqfs mandated to operate autonomously to fulfill, without transitory political considerations, Islamic goals such as social justice, poverty reduction, education, and youth development. Although officially these new organizations were grounded in Islamic law, in fact their structural features drew neither on traditional Islamic practices nor on Shii jurisprudence. They were designed as organizations that make their own budgets, raise funds continuously, create and operate profit-maximizing businesses, reallocate assets, and, subject to the theocracy's general objectives, even revise their missions. Thousands of modern *bonyad*s provide diverse services. Examples include the Farabi Bonyad, which promotes Iranian cinema, and Bonyad-e Resalat, which publishes a conservative newspaper. The largest modern bonyads, including the Bonyad for the Oppressed and Wounded Veterans (Bonyad-e Mostazafan va Janbazan), pursue policies that sometimes contravene government objectives. They have clashed with state agencies over such matters as marketing contraband American cigarettes and dealings with Iranian military proxies in Lebanon.[37]

In countries where the modern waqf exists, it carries much less importance in daily life than the Islamic waqf once did. It is not the primary vehicle for social services, which are supplied largely by state agencies and commercial enterprises organized as corporations. Consumers may favor certain suppliers over others, depending on price, quality, and location. In many sectors, market competition thus constrains the viable organizational options. Where markets are not competitive, elections may substitute for them. In places with some form of local democracy, consumers punish unsatisfactory public corporations at the ballot box. In the 1989 local elections in Izmir, voters replaced a mediocre mayor with a challenger who promised to improve and broaden municipal services.[38] The political ascent of Recep Tayyip Erdoğan, Turkey's most powerful official from 2002 onward, began with a stint as mayor of Istanbul.

The Islamic Waqf's Long Civic Shadow

Through a range of new initiatives, which charmed even voters apprehensive about his Islamist political roots, he became a viable candidate for national office.[39]

The presence of alternatives to the modern waqf motivates its officers to keep their organization flexible. Organizational competition also makes them cater to the needs of their constituents. Yet the modern waqf has not overcome all obstacles to organizational efficiency. As with the constituents of other organizational forms, those of a modern waqf may lack the incentives to educate themselves about the available choices. In any case, vested interests may render officials unresponsive to the expressed wishes of nonpaying beneficiaries. The threat of retaliation may silence potential critics. Nevertheless, there is a fundamental difference in accountability between, on the one hand, the caretakers of Islamic waqfs and, on the other, the officials of modern service providers. In the premodern Middle East, the consumers of social services were expected to be passive recipients. Now, to one degree or another, they are entitled to a voice. And, again in varying degrees, service providers are expected to please them.

There is a major exception to the rise in accountability on the part of modern suppliers characterized as some form of waqf. Iran's postrevolutionary bonyads have asserted a right to conceal their finances. Recipients of their services have called for financial transparency. Bonyad managers respond by invoking Iran's "traditional moral order." Before Iran fell under foreign influences, they hold, clerics like themselves had nonreciprocal rights to control charitable resources, and beneficiaries remained passive.[40] In fact, what bonyad managers call Iran's "traditional moral order" was central to the Islamic waqf's operation in both Iran and the rest of the Middle East. As previous chapters showed, the caretaker of an Islamic waqf was not required to publicize information about its resources or operations. With respect to managerial accountability, then, the modern waqf's Iranian equivalent lies closer to a classic Islamic waqf than to a modern charitable corporation.

PERSISTENCE OF ANEMIC CIVIC LIFE

It is the sharp differences between the waqf's modern variants and the Islamic waqf that are critical here, not the resemblances. One might expect the novelties to have led to a blossoming of civic life. In fact, though Middle Eastern civic activities have become much more sophisticated in an organizational sense, premodern civic routines live on. Limited organizational autonomy and low civic engagement endure even as the region's nation-states acquire the trappings of modern political life, such as parties, elections, and constitutions embodying basic human rights.

The literature on civil society in the modern Middle East abounds with observations that mirror the historical accounts above. For example, in a 2002 article Asef Bayat writes: "Many NGO advocates have complained about the absence of a spirit of participation in the NGOs.... Paternalistic NGOs

```
World -                                    59.9
Organization of Islamic Cooperation -      44.9
Middle East -                              37.2
         0         25        50        75
               Political participation
```

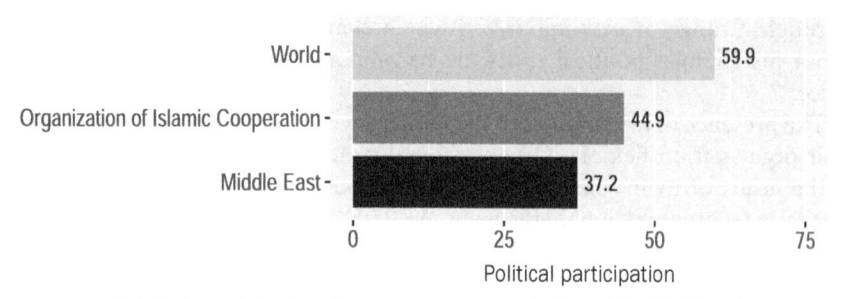

FIGURE 6.2 Political participation (percentage of population): Middle East in global perspective

Sources: Country-level data compiled by Avital Livny from the following surveys: for demonstrations, European Values Study (waves 1–4), World Values Survey (waves 1–6), Afrobarometer (waves 1, 2, 4, 5), Asian Barometer (wave 4), Latinobarómetro (1995–96, 1998, 2000, 2002–3, 2005–8, 2015), and AsiaBarometer (2004, 2006, 2007, dropping 2005 because of methodological flaws); for petitions, European Values Study (waves 1–4), World Values Survey (waves 1–6), Afrobarometer (waves 1, 2), Asian Barometer (wave 4), Latinobarómetro (2002, 2005–8, 2015), AsiaBarometer (2004, 2006, 2007); and for boycotts and participation, European Values Study (waves 1–4), World Values Survey (waves 1–6), Latinobarómetro (2008), AsiaBarometer (2004, 2006, 2007).

perceive their beneficiaries more as recipients of assistance than as participants in development. . . . It is not the place of beneficiaries to question the adequacy and quality of services or the accountability of NGOs."[41] These impressions are all the more significant because Bayat makes no reference to waqfs of any kind.[42] In another work unconcerned with waqfs, *Trust and the Islamic Advantage*, Avital Livny uses cross-national surveys to compare political participation across religious groups.[43] She finds that rates of political participation in the form of signing a petition, joining a boycott, or demonstrating is substantially lower in the Muslim world, defined as the aggregate of Muslim-plurality countries, than outside it. Livny's data allows us to put the Middle East in comparative perspective (Figure 6.2). In line with previous comparative indices, a lower percentage of respondents acknowledges participation or willingness to participate in at least one type of political activity: 23.9 percentage points less in Middle East than outside it.[44] Surveys thus validate the perception that Middle Easterners are substantially more likely to treat citizenship as a passive commitment than as a duty to be politically engaged.

The Middle East's low share could reflect fear of government retaliation, Livny observes. People dissatisfied with the political status quo might mislead pollsters for fear of government retribution.[45] The presence of social desirability bias is evident in the corresponding figures with respect to self-reports of having voted in the last election. The respondents who reported having done so were 20 percentage points lower for the Middle East than for the rest of the world (Figure 6.3).[46] This gap is narrower than the political participation gap because, in and of itself, voting does not reveal a particular political preference.

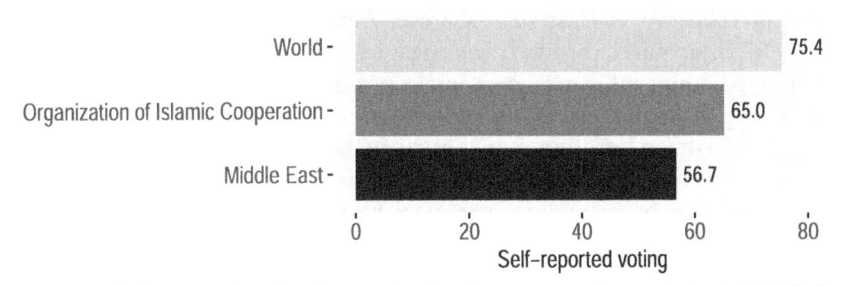

FIGURE 6.3 Self-reported voting in last election (percentage of population): Middle East in global perspective

Sources: Country-level data compiled by Avital Livny from the following surveys: World Values Survey (wave 5), Afrobarometer (waves 1, 2, 4, 5), East Asian Barometer (waves 1–4), Latinobarómetro (2000, 2002, 2005–6, 2008–9, 2013, 2015), Eurobarometer (1986, 2004), Caucasusbarometer (2008–13, 2015, 2017).

Rampant political preference falsification is not only a cause of the passive citizenship that Bayat and Livny observe independently. It is also an enduring consequence of weak civic society. Strong NGOs, by defending their members and sympathizers against retaliation from the state or vigilantes, give them the courage to convey preferences honestly. In contrast, weak NGOs fail to instill in individuals the confidence to speak honestly and openly.

A complementary drag on political participation is that state agencies have taken over many functions long performed by Islamic waqfs. Organized hierarchically, these agencies tend to execute orders from above. Consequently, they may be unresponsive to the citizenry, especially on matters that the leadership considers settled or sacrosanct. The modernizers responsible for reforming the state understood that satisfied subjects are easier to keep politically docile. But their overriding objective was to escape Western domination, not to satisfy bottom-up demands.[47] Hence, their reforms did not require democratic organizational governance or broader personal freedoms. In any case, a history of passivity with respect to the provision of social services tempered expectations. Weak civic engagement was thus transplanted from the region's premodern empires to its modern nation-states through a combination of inherited conditions and new political decisions.

Not all functions of the Islamic waqf passed to state agencies. Under new laws of association that Middle Eastern countries began to institute before World War I, modern NGOs took on expanding roles. These organizations have included charitable associations, trade unions, chambers of commerce, and professional associations, generally structured as some form of corporation.[48] Autonomous to one degree or another and empowered to change with the times, they began to instill in people self-governance skills that Islamic waqfs had failed to impart. The most critical are strategic planning, public relations, consensus building, coalition formation, and collective negotiation.

As we have known at least since Gabriel Almond and Sidney Verba's *Civic Culture*, skills acquired through civic engagement make citizens more confident in their capacity to influence government policies, more active in politics, and more willing to share their private political preferences with others.[49] The skills that citizens obtain through active participation in civic organizations thus provide channels of recruitment into politics from outside political structures. They ensure that political elites regularly face challenges from newcomers.[50] Civic participation empowers citizens also by embedding them in dense networks of social relations. A society replete with politically skilled people can be short of social capital if its members are isolated from one another. Insofar as they interact with each other in social associations, they will possess social capital that will translate into political influence.[51]

Starting from a very low base, the Middle East's modern NGOs are, then, contributing to building civil society. The learning in question may well overcome the Islamic waqf's adverse legacies, though the process is likely to span generations. After all, in Western Europe the same learning process has been underway for more than a millennium, with occasional setbacks, as in the early twentieth century, which was a time of generally declining organizational freedoms. Just as Western civic organizations faced opposition from constituencies with a stake in regulated civic life, so in the modern Middle East governing elites feel threatened by autonomous organizations with agendas of their own.

THE PREVALENCE OF GONGOS

Among the first Middle Eastern charitable organizations established outside the Islamic waqf sector, the largest were all initiated, directed, and managed with government involvement. Though formally autonomous, each was a GONGO – a *government-organized* nongovernmental organization. During the first decade of the Republic of Turkey (1923–33), the top three charitable organizations as measured by mass participation, fundraising, and branch offices were the Red Crescent Society, the Children's Protection Society, and the Turkish Aviation Society. Each pursued state goals without restraining the country's top leadership. Lack of accountability to the citizenry is another shared feature of these organizations. Just as an Islamic waqf served its founder's needs, so a GONGO measured its performance mainly in relation to state objectives.[52]

In Egypt, various NGOs were formed in the early twentieth century in reaction to foreign cultural influences. Eschewing a political identity, they tended to subordinate themselves to the government. They went so far as to invite members of the royal family to serve as honorary presidents. Over subsequent decades, governments encouraged the creation of NGOs, provided they remained apolitical and allowed state officials to control administration, including the selection of leaders, members, and activities. Under President Gamal Abdel-Nasser

(1956–70), Egyptian NGOs became appendages of the state bureaucracy. No fewer than 60,000 NGO employees received a government salary.[53] A 1964 law authorized the state to close any NGO that refused to cooperate with the regime.[54] An even harsher NGO law was adopted in 1999.[55]

In the early twenty-first century, Middle Eastern states by and large continue to control NGOs tightly. Organizations established privately without state guidance or support are susceptible to state capture. Consider again Egypt, where, by 2021, 52,000 officially registered domestic NGOs existed, along with 59 foreign NGOs, a few dozen domestic advocacy organizations disguised as law offices to minimize state interference, and hundreds of unregistered NGOs, many with Islamist agendas. As few as 2,500 of the registered NGOs were active. Moreover, some of those had been infiltrated by government agents, and others were being persecuted. No NGO could expose government corruption or mobilize public outrage against the perpetrators. Most had agreed implicitly to respect the government's red lines on criticism. Only superficially did they monitor the state.[56]

Egyptian NGOs played marginal roles in the uprisings of 2011–13. The revolution that ended Hosni Mubarak's thirty-year dictatorship was dominated by youths without any history of active opposition or cooperation with known dissidents. A few NGOs joined in only as Mubarak accepted defeat.[57] Although high youth participation was unprecedented in Egypt, the lack of NGO leadership was nothing new. NGOs had played no key role in prior regime changes. Political and military elites spearheaded Egypt's autonomy within the Ottoman Empire, and military officers overthrew the Egyptian monarchy in 1952.[58] Another shared civic characteristic of the Mubarak and post-Mubarak periods is lack of collaboration among NGOs. Just as Islamic waqfs were barred from forming coalitions, successive Egyptian regimes have generally discouraged cooperation among NGOs, doubtless to block avenues for mass mobilization. The exceptions have involved strictly economic or social projects with goals complementary to those of the incumbent government.[59]

Turkey has substantially more private organizations. This accords with its more democratic governance by Middle Eastern standards, and greater protection of civil liberties, for much of the post–World War II period; its huge setbacks since 2011 have ended Turkish exceptionalism (Figure 6.4). In 2005, early in the Erdoğan era, it had 71,240 active associations (94 per 100,000 people, as against 36 for Egypt) and 4,367 modern waqfs (6 per 100,000 people as against none for Egypt).[60] Nevertheless, participation in Turkish civic life is muted according to the standards of advanced democracies, as is support for NGO activities. The patterns are reflected in Table 6.2, which is based on data of the World Alliance for Citizen Participation (CIVICUS). In Turkey, the table shows, civic engagement matches the average for the rest of OECD. However, *political* participation is strikingly low, as is philanthropy – used here in the sense of *organized* philanthropy. Consequently, civil society is relatively ineffective.

TABLE 6.2 *Four indices of civic life: Middle East in global perspective*

Region or country	Participation in civic activities	Philanthropy	Policy dialogue	Political participation
Organization for Economic Co-operation and Development (except Turkey)	0.54	0.45	0.76	0.67
World	0.70	0.30	0.50	0.49
Organization of Islamic Cooperation	0.60	0.34	0.46	0.43
Turkey	0.55	0.20	0.67	0.39
Iran	–	0.28	0.22	0.28
Arab League	0.36	0.29	0.36	0.49
Middle East	0.42	0.27	0.40	0.42

Note: "Participation in civic activities" refers to the percentage of people who say they "have done" or "might do" any of three suggested activities: signing petitions, joining boycotts, attending peaceful demonstrations. "Philanthropy" captures the propensity of people to get involved in "formal charitable activities." Finally, "policy dialogue," a subdimension of the Enabling Environment Index's "governance environment" dimension, assesses the openness of institutional processes to civil society organization inputs. It is derived from variables such as the extent to which "there [is] a network of cooperative associations or interest groups to mediate between society and the political system" and the degree to which "the political leadership enable[s] the participation of civil society in the political process."

Source: CIVICUS Enabling Environment Index 2013. The Arab League and OECD indices are population-weighted averages of the member country figures.

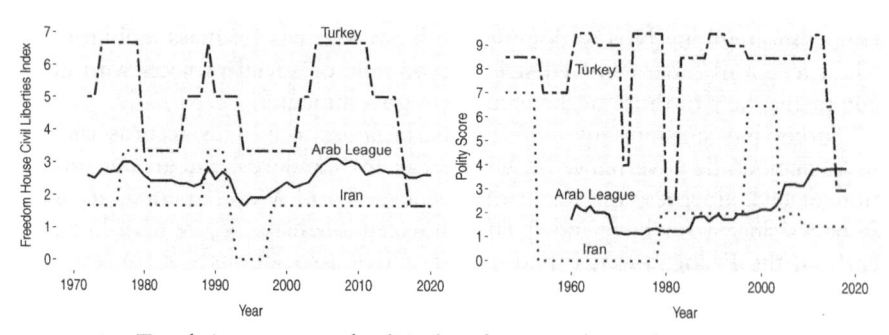

FIGURE 6.4 Trends in measures of political performance for Arab League, Iran, and Turkey: Freedom House Civil Liberty (1972–2020) and Polity (1946–2019)

Note: The Freedom House Civil Liberties Index is described in association with Figure 1.4; in this 0–10 conversion, higher numbers represent greater freedom. The Polity score measures regime authority score; in this 0–10 conversion, 0 represents hereditary monarchy and 10 consolidated democracy

Source: Computed from data in Teorell, Sundström, Holmberg, Rothstein, Pachon, and Dalli, "Quality of Government Standard Dataset." The Arab League series are based on annually moving country weights calculated from World Bank population figures included in this dataset.

Proximate reasons for Turkey's relatively poor civic performance include decades of restrictive legislation.[61] A deeper factor is the absence of a tradition of mass involvement in organized philanthropy. As in the past, most people assist close kin and neighbors. Few participate in, or financially support, organizations working toward shared social goals. Citizens exhibit a preference for individual-to-individual giving over organized collective giving.[62] The same preferences are observed in Arab countries.[63]

These patterns are legacies of the Middle East's premodern institutional history. When organized philanthropy was limited to Islamic waqfs, giving was necessarily individual-to-individual for all but the few people who were wealthy enough to found a waqf. Under the circumstances, the personal skills needed for a vigorous civil society failed to develop. This heritage has facilitated state capture of civic associations – in other words, their conversion from NGOs to GONGOs.[64]

CORRELATES OF STUNTED CIVIC LIFE

Among the functions of civil society is enhanced personal security. Autonomous organizations provide protection against arbitrary taxation, harassment by the police, religious or ideological persecution, discrimination in public services, and censorship, among other harms. One consequence is greater trust in strangers. Confident in being treated fairly, individuals interact readily with people previously unknown to them. They also deal routinely with organizations. However, where civic organizations are relatively weak, citizens interact mostly with kin and close acquaintances. Their exchanges are mostly personal rather than impersonal. They try to restrict business dealings to people they know well. In times of need, they turn to family, expecting little from public agencies. Primordial attachments based on ties of blood, race, language, region, or religion remain strong because they serve as sources of mutual insurance.

As discussed in Chapter 3, "generalized trust" represents the readiness to cooperate and engage in civic endeavors with fellow citizens. Relative to the rest of the world, the Middle East scores low in generalized trust (Figure 3.1). That pattern accords with the feebleness of the region's civic life, historically and now. Low generalized trust is among the persistent effects of the Middle East's civic history, which bears the influence of choices made during Islam's early institutionalization. One was the decision to keep the corporation outside the confines of Islamic law. Another was the creation of the Islamic waqf as Islam's main vehicle for providing social services. The very choices that kept the Middle East as a low-trust region should have made it stand out in other observable variables. Three of these are worth reviewing: persistently high rates of in-marriage, the prevalence of nepotism, and the acceptability of bribing.

In-Marriage

If dealing primarily with kin and acquaintances provides one defense mechanism in societies with low generalized trust, a second is in-marriage, known in genetics as consanguineous marriage and colloquially as cousin marriage. In-marriage is prevalent in countries where the fear of being swindled induces measures to keep wealth within the family. It is uncommon in societies with institutions that successfully protect the individual against lawlessness and misfortunes.

For various country groupings, Figure 6.5 provides a population-weighted percentage of out-marriages. If all marriages were between non-relatives, the share would be 100; and if all were between cousins, it would be 0. The figure indicates that the share of out-marriages is strikingly low in the Middle East compared to the rest of the world, which implies that in-marriage is more common.[65] The variations in out-marriage rates within the Middle East are instructive: 82 percent in Turkey, as against 67 percent in Iran and 68 percent in the Arab League. These differences are consistent with, on the one hand, the earlier start of institutional modernization in Turkey than in the rest of the region, and, on the other, Turkey's relatively stronger civil society. In the 2010s, Turkey's political system became as repressive as that of Iran and the Arab League taken as a whole (Figure 6.4). But marriage customs are slow-moving institutions.[66]

Contrary to common belief, the Quran does not promote in-marriage. It explicitly bans many consanguineous pairings. Although under certain interpretations it allows first-cousin marriages, the relevant verses probably made exceptions to limit social disruption at a time when supporting the widows of fallen Muslim soldiers posed an acute challenge.[67] Nonetheless, Islamic law allows in-marriage. One justification is that Muhammad married one of his daughters to his cousin Ali, the future caliph.[68] But far more important are the gender-egalitarian provisions of Islam's inheritance system, which incentivized fathers to marry their daughters to relatives. Because around one-third of

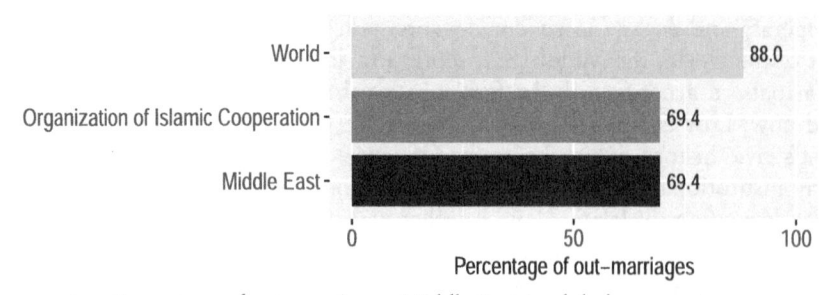

FIGURE 6.5 Percentage of out-marriages: Middle East in global perspective
Note: The population data used to weight countries are from World DataBank.
Source: "Global Prevalence of Consanguinity."

estates went to women, in-marriage served to keep daughters from carrying substantial wealth outside the family. Islamic family rules that denied women agency in choosing a husband effectively enabled families to preserve wealth.[69] In-marriage may have social advantages: stable marital relations, compatibility of in-laws, lower domestic violence, and capital preservation. On the downside, it poses health risks to offspring.[70] More significant from the standpoint of social welfare is its hindrance to developing impersonal relationships and generalized trust.

It is no coincidence that the corporation first spread in a part of the world where the dominant religion favored out-marriage.[71] Beginning in the 500s, Western Christianity prohibited cousin marriage, and restrictions on marrying relatives tightened over time. The corporation thus emerged in a setting where family bonds were attenuating, and individualism was gaining acceptance. Meanwhile, in the Middle East, the waqf became the dominant vehicle for supplying social services against the backdrop of a marriage regime that bolstered family loyalty and fueled mistrust among non-kin. Deepening cleavages among lineages, the marriage regime fragmented society.[72]

Nepotism

Yet another common defense against low trust is nepotism. Favoring kin enjoys fertile ground in societies that put a premium on family and close friends. In a traditional Muslim society where in-marriage is the norm, withholding priority from family and friends could result in ostracism from one's in-group. By analogous logic, arranged marriages have another socially critical effect. In keeping the family as the basic unit of cooperation and prioritizing personal relationships, they diminish the need for civic organizations. In the premodern Middle East, arranged marriages must have weakened pressures to reform the waqf. Flexibilities and capacities of the corporation would have seemed less valuable than in societies where out-marriage was the norm.

Earlier, we saw that the waqf itself fueled nepotism. Caretakers tended to appoint relatives as successors. During the nineteenth-century reforms, employees socialized to favor relatives and friends carried the pattern over to the organizations that supplanted Islamic waqfs. Today, nepotism remains both common and tolerated in professional life.[73] People in positions of power are expected to reward their relatives, provided the favors remain within bounds. Mubarak was widely resented for grooming his son Gamal as his successor at Egypt's helm. Likewise, even Erdoğan's base had qualms about the lionization (until a rift in the first-family) of his son-in-law Berat Albayrak as Turkey's strongman-in-waiting.[74] Lesser instances of nepotism do not necessarily draw objections. Among the reasons is the paucity of organizations that track and publicize procedural violations of public hiring. General anti-nepotism initiatives tend to fail because they conflict with entrenched norms that treat nepotism as integral to friendship and generosity.

Tolerance of Bribery

Government is strikingly unclean in the modern Middle East, as we saw in the book's introduction (Figure 1.6). In other words, it stands out as an especially corrupt region. As in the past, Middle Easterners widely hold corruption responsible for various social ills. They commonly attribute poverty, underdevelopment, and poor governance to embezzlement of state resources by unscrupulous officials and businesses. Meanwhile, petty corruption is widely viewed as just compensation for special services to low-paid officials. People who consider corruption a social cancer happily pay bribes themselves to expedite government procedures. As with nepotism, so with bribery, the process is viewed as improper mostly when the magnitude exceeds norms. Then it becomes extortion, as opposed to fair compensation for a valuable service. Rarely are citizens faulted for paying "reasonable" bribes.[75] This pattern harkens to the prevalence of side payments for keeping Islamic waqfs up to date. It relates also to the weaknesses of civic society, which are legacies of Islamic institutions. Alone or jointly, civic associations that monitor state agencies lack the clout to make governments pursue effective anticorruption measures.[76]

Bribery is a universal problem, which is ineradicable even in countries with strong democratic institutions. But its prevalence varies greatly across space, time, and contexts. Political checks and balances are among the determinants of its prevalence; they limit bribery by keeping power holders in check. Another determinant is the capacity of people to mobilize in pursuit of common goals. And still another consists of bribing norms.[77]

LEGACIES OF THE MIDDLE EAST'S CIVIC PAST

Theories of why the Middle East is the world's least free and least democratized region often point to coalitions among ruling families in control of critical resources, military officers who share in the spoils, and businesses sheltered from competition.[78] Well-organized vested interests do indeed suppress basic freedoms and rig elections. But by themselves these theories fail to make sense of why the Middle East's masses have endured oppression and dictatorship for so long. After all, other regions, including those now home to social orders providing broader freedoms and opportunities, have featured coalitions designed to monopolize political power.[79] Some societies have managed to limit this monopolization, transitioning to a liberal order. Staying there is an unending struggle, as Daron Acemoglu and James Robinson argue in the *Narrow Corridor*. Setbacks lasting decades are possible. Germany between World Wars I and II provides a notorious example. Its losses in World War I and the ensuing burdens brought to power an illiberal coalition that extinguished economic, social, and political rights once taken for granted.[80] This book's key question has been why the Middle East remains persistently weak at generating enforceable and sustainable rules to prevent extreme concentrations of power. None of the region's components – Arab countries, Iran, Turkey – has ever completed a transition to an essentially liberal order.

Reflecting on the question led inexorably to civil society. What does civil society lack in the Middle East that is present in liberal orders? NGOs exist in the tens of thousands. Current laws do not keep private organizations too small or too rigid. For more than a century, private corporations, which are among the linchpins of existing liberal orders, have been prominent in the Middle East, too. True, the region's authoritarian states keep NGOs from using their capabilities to the fullest. And the Middle East's private charitable corporations are not as free as their counterparts in, say, Scandinavia. But these observations return us to a general puzzle. If in some places NGOs have gained and extended legal rights, what blocks civic progress in the Middle East?

The Middle East's distinct institutional history keeps its NGOs persistently weak, curbing their ability to advance personal freedoms and restrain authoritarian rule. Although the region's prevailing legal systems support private corporations, the Islamic legal system – the foundation of its governance until modern times – had greatly restricted the organizational options of NGOs. Required to organize as Islamic waqfs, NGOs were barred from political advocacy. Their ability to broaden freedoms and opportunities was limited also by their rigidities, inability to form coalitions, and lack of accountability to their beneficiaries. Among the consequences was the impoverishment of civic life. Skills critical to effective civic engagement have remained undeveloped, as has the capacity to pursue collective action through private coalitions.

The twentieth century witnessed a remarkable expansion of civil society in the Middle East. In some places, it accompanied the waqf's rebirth as a modern organizational form akin to the charitable corporation. If the region has not transitioned quickly to a liberal order, a basic reason lies in its longstanding tradition of civic passivity. In limiting participation in civic life, this tradition hampers the political effectiveness of NGOs. It also facilitates their capture by the state.

The vicious circle that long kept Middle Eastern states authoritarian has mutated, then, but not snapped. Before the modern reforms that enabled flexible nongovernmental organizations, Islamic waqfs lacking autonomy kept civil society weak. In turn, the weakness of civil society hindered the development of alternatives to founder-controlled, rigid organizations. Thus, politically effective private organizations could not exist, absolutist rulers faced no serious challenges from below, ideologies supportive of structural reforms failed to emerge, and political checks and balances did not arise. Since the emergence of new organizational alternatives outside of government, these constraints have all weakened. But the transformations have not progressed enough for transition to a self-sustaining liberal order. The requisite organizational capabilities will take time to develop, as will complementary social norms.

The norms in question transcend NGOs and their regulations. Tolerance of corruption and nepotism, the prevalence of in-marriage, and a preference for dealing with kin and friends are other elements of the broader institutional complex that keeps civil society feeble. All the other elements, too, have deep roots in Islamic history. They are all mutually reinforcing. In other words, they are both causes of the others and among their effects.

There is still more to the institutional complex that keeps the Middle East the world's least free region. It also includes various obstacles to religious freedom as well as economic patterns that limit the political influence of businesses. Following chapters identify the legal roots, historical trajectories, and current dynamics of other institutions that impede liberalization.

PART III

RELIGIOUS REPRESSION

7

Religious Freedoms in Middle Eastern History

Like other religions, Islam defines right and wrong on many matters. Pronouncing principles to guide personal and collective choices, it prescribes certain behaviors and bans others. The Quran is Islam's most authoritative source; and, for most Muslims, the Sunna is an auxiliary source of guidance. But who interprets Islam's fundamental sources in specific contexts? Who enforces Islamic directives?

The Quran itself lacks clear answers. Eight of its verses call for "commanding right and forbidding wrong." In general, though, it does so without specifying who, or what group, is responsible for interpreting God's law and ensuring compliance. Only one verse, which follows a passage about keeping believers undivided, assigns these duties explicitly to the entire Muslim community.[1] The Quran is replete with additional verses that prescribe duties without stipulating means of enforcement. They cover matters such as performing prayer, paying taxes, believing in God, showing moderation, and accepting whatever unfolds.[2]

The Quran addresses readers as individuals. On that basis, certain interpreters hold that it encourages Muslims to take it upon themselves, alone or in groups, to enforce Islamic morality. They may wander through the streets and shame people dressed ostentatiously, monitor markets for unfair pricing, steer shoppers to mosque services, require rich-looking people to pay alms, and vet speech for signs of unorthodoxy. Concerned Muslims may try to mobilize the community to enforce Islamic morality collectively, as necessary by punishing fellow Muslims who refrain from participating. The Quran does not limit the measures permitted in commanding right and forbidding wrong. Suppose a man and a woman are walking in the park, holding hands. Convinced that Islam limits cross-sex affection to married couples, a Muslim vigilante could ask for proof of marriage; and, if the couple turns out unmarried, he may shame them as bad Muslims.

Inviting everyone to be an enforcer of debatable rules is a recipe for perpetual discord. Hence, as Islam expanded, Muslim elites quickly took charge of defining and enforcing Islamic morality. Their justification for centralized enforcement was that Islam is fully comprehensible only with deep knowledge of its fundamental sources and communal organization.[3] Various coalitions competed to become a self-perpetuating class of professional interpreters. Establishing criteria for joining their ranks, they founded study circles, mosque schools, and colleges known as madrasas to provide a standard education.[4] In need of legitimation, states have tried to control institutions of religious certification and opinion making.

For much of Islamic history, and in most places, Islam's professional interpreters have been known as *ulema* (plural for *'ālim*, literally, learned person). Serving as jurists, scholars, teachers, preachers, judges, and mosque administrators, most *ulema* have shared a commitment to monopolizing religious interpretation on personal piety, but also on economic relations, social interactions, political authority, and governance. For simplicity, I shall keep calling them clerics, in the generic sense. Insofar as clerics viewed personal freedoms or popular consent as worthy ideals, they subordinated them to Islam's requirements. "Democracy," as we now understand the term, was out of the question. They might reference uses of the *shura* in early Islam. But in interpreting the Quran the views of ordinary believers could not carry much weight. If a common interpretation conflicted with the dominant opinion among clerics, the latter had to prevail. Doctrinal correctness would always trump popularity. Though the Quran says nothing about privileged interpreters, the duties of commanding right and forbidding wrong were reserved for trained clerics.

The interpretations of Muslim clerics have always drawn objections. Areas of steady disagreement include credit practices and playing music. The Quran bans riba, a pre-Islamic financial practice that involved doubling the debt of a debtor who failed to repay on time. Many clerics inferred that all interest is un-Islamic, regardless of form or rate. Tending to disagree, lenders and borrowers kept alive an interest-based credit market that relied on legal ruses to make interest payments look like compensation for a good or service.[5] Unlike credit, music receives no mention in the Quran. But remembrances of Muhammad's life contain relevant materials in abundance, most of them apocryphal. The bulk of these remembrances treat music as a pagan practice that distracts from religious duties. It incites drinking, sorcery, gambling, immodesty, fornication, and sodomy, they say. Condemnations of music have never enjoyed full acceptance in any Muslim society. Muslim popular culture, the entertainment of Muslim elites, and Sufi rituals have all involved music, but also dancing – sinful, according to opponents of music, for similar reasons.[6]

The objectors of clerical teachings on interest and music do not necessarily question the institutions that authorize clerics to interpret Islam on behalf of all Muslims. But the promoted conformity has itself been controversial. Rejecting the monopolization of interpreting the Quran – often drawing on the Quran itself – independent-minded Muslims have asserted the right to interpret Islam for themselves. They have even formed distinct subcommunities with their own hierarchies and shared beliefs. Though these heterodox denominations and sects have been tolerated for strategic reasons, often they have suffered persecution and moved underground. Open opposition to orthodox Islam is uncommon.

This rarity poses a puzzle. Why did objections not broaden religious freedoms? The contrast with Western Europe is especially striking. There, too, clerics asserted the right to interpret the dominant religion. But they encountered strong resistance, and, with local variations, their power diminished. By no means is it obvious why Europe and the Middle East diverged with respect to religious freedoms. In what ways is this divergence related to the organizational divergence already interpreted? Have other elements of Islamic law played critical roles? We shall see that the lack of an Islamic concept of corporation – a self-governing organization that enjoys legal personhood – hindered collective action against orthodoxy. We shall see, too, that apostasy laws deterred open and honest discourses among groups opposed to clerical domination.

With this chapter, we move back in time, from the present to the inaugural Islamic state and later Muslim-governed empires. The history covered in this chapter is essential to understanding twenty-first-century obstacles to liberalization in various domains. It will also lay the groundwork for identifying potential pathways to Middle Eastern religious liberalization.

COMPARATIVE HISTORY OF RELIGIOUS REPRESSION

Until recent centuries, the religious repression now observed in the Middle East was the norm across the world. As Noel Johnson and Mark Koyama observe, states persecuted "religious deviants" because this provided a low-cost vehicle for legitimation. In the Middle Ages, both Islam and Christianity aggressively sought converts, punished critics, and banned apostasy. Religious freedom arose and spread in Western Europe as rulers, and eventually democratic governments, acquired alternative sources of legitimation, primarily nationalism and economic growth. The transition varied across countries. In England it was apparent by 1750, and in France after the revolution of 1789. Meanwhile, across the Atlantic, Americans instituted religious freedoms to protect competing churches from the state. For all this diversity of origins, the emergence of religious freedoms gave Europeans and North Americans the right to choose whether to practice a religion and, if so, which one. It also ensured that people's choices would not affect their dealings with the state.[7]

The new order, observe Johnson and Koyama, replaced identity-based rights with general rights that were independent of personal religious beliefs. A liberal order has thus depended critically, they say, on the separation of state affairs from religion.[8] In a liberal order, the state treats private individuals and organizations equally, irrespective of any religious affiliation. No actual state has met this criterion exactly. But, in one form or another, secularization has been central to all major political reforms associated with democratization and liberalization. The Protestant Reformation and the American Declaration of Independence are cases in point.[9]

States are not the only players with a stake in religious freedoms. Shopkeepers, artisans, and merchants of diverse services may develop a consensus that a "live and let live" attitude on religion will be mutually beneficial by enabling people of different faiths to interact with one another and capture gains from trade. A symbiotic relationship may develop between state officials and religious minorities, with both benefiting through commercial expansion. Such developments preceded the Union of Utrecht in 1579, which allowed each province of the Netherlands to regulate religious matters as it saw fit, prohibited the official establishment of religion, and banned persecution based on religious beliefs. The resulting economic prosperity inspired neighbors and eventually colonies in North America to promote religious freedoms as a matter of common interest in economic development.[10]

"Live and let live" entails a strategic retreat driven by a recognition of stalemate. Religions do not necessarily abandon their goals to convert individuals or to mold society's institutions according to their beliefs. Their adherents simply accept that, for the time being, religious strife would be counterproductive; in so doing, they do not necessarily abandon efforts to create conditions under which coercion would be more effective. An alternative path to religious freedoms, also starting from below, is a belief that religion is corrupted if it is interpreted by the state; thus, secularizing the state is packaged as divinely inspired restoration. Martin Luther's uprising against the Roman Church aimed to reduce corruption by truncating the temporal powers of clerics.[11]

Still another pathway to religious freedoms starts from a demonstration that it was implicit all along in the religion's original teachings; making it explicit just refines and develops original religious doctrine.[12] The Catholic Church took this route in 1965 through its Declaration of Religious Liberty. For more than a millennium, it had denounced "liberty of conscience" and legitimated coercion against its detractors. Nevertheless, it embraced religious liberty as an act of clarification rather than innovation. Thinkers of Christianity's first three centuries promoted religious freedoms as a basic human right, said the Declaration; and repressive interpretations reflected political exigencies.[13] Various Christian theologians have argued that the New Testament, unlike the Torah, never promotes coercion of heretics.[14]

The availability of multiple pathways to broadening religious freedoms casts doubt on the common claim that Islam is inherently incapable of meeting the religious requirements of a liberal order.[15] Islam's main instruments of religious repression, its apostasy, heresy, and blasphemy rules, could have evolved differently. Many precedents as well as Quranic verses allow the liberalization of these rules. Hence, liberal Muslims should have no trouble harmonizing the practice of Islam with advanced standards of religious freedom.

Commentators who portray Islam as unchangeable on basic freedoms consider the core problem to be that early Islamic jurists neglected to distinguish between a sphere of religion and spheres of secular life. At least formally, they sought to regulate the totality of the human experience – not only relations with God but also government, family life, commerce, and distribution.[16] On similar grounds, modern Islamists say that Islam defines a "complete way of life."[17] Indeed, the Arabic word for religion, *dīn*, traditionally encompasses not only beliefs and activities that anyone would associate with religion but also economics and politics.[18] Yet the goal of comprehensive religious regulation failed in seventh-century Arabia, at the birth of Islam. More critical, it is unachievable in the far more complex societies of the present. Hence, the perceived fixity of Islam with respect to freedoms is rooted in an illusion.

Of necessity, Islam's reach has always been bounded. Every Muslim-governed society has left a wide range of matters to individual discretion. As a matter of practice, then, Islam has provided room for individual freedoms. The precise mix varied in the past, and it need not remain fixed from now on. It is true, of course, that precedents and persistent understandings make religious freedoms harder to advance than other freedoms.

Reinterpreting Islam has been routine. Over the past two centuries, Middle Eastern societies have welcomed many new technologies and undertaken fundamental economic reforms. Pious Muslims have abandoned longstanding economic practices based on Islamic law and alternatives developed without any reference to Islam. Banks, corporations, municipalities, credit cards, and online shopping offer examples. For one reason or another, each of these innovations violates classical Islamic law. For instance, none accords with the classical Islamic law of sale (*muʿamalat*), which requires a face-to-face meeting before any exchange.[19] Today's practicing Muslims do not consider any of these innovations un-Islamic, which confirms the flexibility in interpreting what Islam allows.

Evidently, conservatism per se cannot explain the weakness of religious freedoms in Muslim societies. Cases of uncontroversial institutional borrowing also hint at what a satisfactory explanation requires. If the corporation was transplanted from the West with little resistance from clerics despite its obvious incompatibility with classical Islamic law, the reason is that government officials, investors, merchants, and service providers grasped its immense advantages. Moreover, the masses were quick to appreciate the benefits of certain corporate structures, such as the municipality, over the traditional institutions they replaced. If an attempt were made to close municipalities as un-Islamic, the beneficiaries of their services would rise in protest. Likewise, if one were to shut down the Muslim world's top private companies on the grounds that their modes of organization are un-Islamic, millions of employees, shareholders, suppliers, and consumers would object. Yet no notable constituencies openly champion broad religious freedoms. Muslims who consider them central to human rights opt to stay silent. Moreover, large constituencies oppose broader religious freedoms for fear of weakening Islam and harming Muslims as a community.

Our challenge amounts, then, to explaining the lack of sufficiently powerful Muslim constituencies that want to expand religious freedoms and are also prepared to fight for them. We shall start with two basic religious freedoms, the rights to join and to leave a religious community of one's choice.

ENTRY AND EXIT

Entry into Islam has always been easy. Initially, one needed merely to convey acceptance of God's oneness by reciting the declaration of faith, the shahada. About a century later, the shahada gave way to the double-shahada, which also required the acceptance of Muhammad as God's prophet.[20] There have been no restrictions based on income, reputation, gender, ethnicity, lineage, prior religious affiliation, character, or even criminal record. Islam welcomes all conversions, without exception. According to Islamic teachings, Islam is the last and only perfect monotheistic religion; Christianity and Judaism are compromised through corruption of their scriptures. If Islam is unsurpassable, it is obviously desirable to bring everyone into its fold, including the adherents of other monotheisms.

Keeping it simple to become a Muslim has always been central to Islamic teachings. The declaration of faith need not be based on knowledge of Islam. Other requirements, such as prayer and fasting, can be mastered after conversion. The ease of conversion is common knowledge, which makes it nearly impossible to close the Muslim community to outsiders.[21] The Dutch politician Joram van Klaveren was once a senior member of the virulently anti-immigrant Freedom Party (PVV). He had pleaded for a minaret ban and de-Islamization of the Netherlands. In October 2018, while working on an anti-Islamic book, he "suddenly felt more Muslim than Christian" and recognized Muhammad as Allah's last prophet.[22] Despite his infamous history, he was immediately welcomed into the fold. Around the world, Muslims view his conversion as evidence of God's grace.

By contrast, exit from Islam is generally considered prohibited.[23] Under traditional interpretations, a key source of this prohibition is an episode triggered by Muhammad's death in 632. Certain Arabian tribes refused to pay taxes to Abu Bakr, Muhammad's successor as the Muslim community's leader. Having submitted to Muhammad himself, they said, they were not obligated to Abu Bakr. Charging the withdrawing tribes with renouncing Islam, Abu Bakr launched the military campaigns known as the Apostasy Wars.[24] Through these campaigns, the rebellious Arabian tribes were defeated, and their members were forced to continue paying taxes to the Islamic state. For a while, the rebels were excluded from Muslim armies, which deprived them of war booty. Although Umar I, who succeeded Abu Bakr in 634, restored the rights of the defeated tribes, the precedent established an apostasy ban.[25] Whatever the circumstances that made a person Muslim – birth into a Muslim family, choice based on cross-religious comparison, coercion – a Muslim had to remain Muslim. The precedent also legitimized the punishment of leavers.

Whether Abu Bakr's policies conform to the Quran is unclear. In early Islam, apostasy meant more than out-conversion. In all its reliable usages, its meaning included using force against Muslims.[26] On out-conversion, the Quran presents conflicting positions. Some verses suggest that religious choices must be made freely. "There shall be no compulsion in religion," says one; "For you is your religion, and for me is my religion."[27] Other verses permit exit, adding that Muslims should respond to it with a warning, not temporal punishment. "To him who goes astray, say: 'I have warned you,'" is one such instruction. Another: "He that follows the right path shall follow it to his own advantage; and he that goes astray shall do so at his own peril. You are not accountable for them."[28] These verses seem to keep both entry and exit unrestricted. They also seem to allow, even encourage, diversity of religious interpretation. The absence in the Quran of any reference to apostasy (*ridda*, *irtidād*) supports these inferences. Yet the Quran also calls for the subjugation of "unbelievers" and the killing of those who resist subordination.[29] Thus, simply by choosing judiciously, the Quran may be used to either support or deny religious freedoms.

To make sense of the Quran's apparent contradictions on religious freedoms, it helps to know the chronology of its 114 chapters. Muhammad conveyed them over twenty-three years, from 609 to his death in 632. Most Quran specialists date verses calling for religious tolerance to Islam's earliest period, when Muhammad's followers, all Meccans, constituted a persecuted minority seeking recognition as a distinct religious community. The verses calling for compulsion, many experts believe, are from the period when Arabian tribes were accepting Muhammad's authority.[30] Such contextual details get lost in the Quran's canonical compilation, which orders chapters mostly by length rather than chronology.[31] Although certain scholars have claimed that later verses may annul an earlier one on the same subject, there is no consensus with respect to any specific case.[32] Under the circumstances, the dominant view on the Quran's authority is that all verses are equally binding eternally. This position gives interpreters wide latitude in picking verses without attention to the social context of their emergence.

As Chapter 12 will show, an analogous loss of liberty occurred on taxation. In Islam's earliest period, the new community financed social services through voluntary contributions.[33] After its move to Medina in 622, the swelling of its ranks through conversions precluded reliance on voluntary contributions alone. Hence, formal taxation was imposed. The Quranic requirement to pay zakat annually appears to date from Muhammad's Medina years, when the rapidly growing Muslim community established its first state.[34]

The transformation of zakat from charity to taxation contributed to the Islamic state's success by stabilizing its revenue. It apportioned the burden among select groups identified according to source of income or wealth. Payment had to be mandatory due to the universal human proclivity to free ride in large groups. Individuals who contribute readily to small groups will withhold contributions to large groups in the belief that the effects on the total collection would be negligible. Precisely because of the prevalence of free riding in large groups, modern governments finance their operations mainly through taxation. Correctly, they reason that their revenue would plummet if they relied on donations alone. The transformation of zakat is explicable, then, through the basic logic of public finance.

According to the Quran, revenues obtained under the rubric of zakat are to finance various state functions.[35] Exempting certain tribes from periodic zakat payments would have set a precedent for groups to withdraw from financing the new Islamic state. It would be like allowing Connecticut, which has the highest per capita income among the fifty states of the United States, to withdraw from paying federal taxes. Accepting that the rebellious tribes owed allegiance only to Muhammad as a person would have set still another troubling precedent. It would have permitted groups to condition their tax payments on the head of state's identity. Tax revenue would have become unpredictable, lowering state efficiency. Massive free riding would have been another result, because it is impossible to exclude subgroups from consuming public goods. If a Medina-based government is protecting Arabia's trade routes from marauders, all Arabians benefit, regardless of their participation in financing law enforcement.

The key lesson is that certain basic requirements of early Islam rested on universal principles of governance. They served functions that many states, past and present, have pursued for reasons that transcend religion. Although Abu Bakr's military campaigns against recalcitrant Arabian tribes are remembered as "Apostasy Wars," his primary goal was probably tax enforcement rather than religious conformity.

Another analogy with modern governance may help. To incentivize tax compliance, states of the twenty-first century commonly label tax evaders "unpatriotic." Yet evaders include citizens who love their country to the point of being willing to die for it. Similarly, the tribes that Abu Bakr's regime accused of apostasy might have been deeply committed to Islam's emerging principles. Hence, Abu Bakr's apostasy charges were dispensable. If an alternative compliance instrument existed, such as the accusation of unpatriotic behavior, the conflict could have been decoupled from the offenders' religious beliefs. The Islamic state could have enforced tax obligations without undermining the freedom to exit Islam. This observation accords with the Johnson–Koyama thesis on religious freedoms in Europe. European states restricted these freedoms until they could appeal to nonreligious sources of communal solidarity.

There is yet another reason to doubt that Abu Bakr's civil war was about religion in the narrow sense. In seventh-century Arabia, contracting was intensely personal; it involved commitments made between individuals known to one another. Not until many centuries later did Muslims begin treating their state as a legal person. Precisely because a real human being personified each Islamic state, the commercial privileges of foreign merchants had to be reconsidered at each sultanic succession. Mamluk rulers followed this pattern in the eleventh through fifteenth centuries, as did Ottoman rulers subsequently.[36] So the tribal leaders who had negotiated treaties with Muhammad were justified in expecting new negotiations at his death. In considering treaties with him to have lapsed, or in demanding modifications, they were not necessarily renouncing Islam. Likewise, Abu Bakr's military response may indicate that he wanted a quick settlement or that he pursued a reputation of toughness for the sake of bargaining power in other negotiations.

THE POSSIBILITY OF REINTERPRETATION

The ban on out-conversion during a period that most Muslims consider a "Golden Age" of Islam is widely accepted as proof of Islam's inherent repressiveness. But religions can change; historical understandings and even scriptures are reinterpreted. The Bible states that apostasy is punishable by death.[37] The Spanish Inquisition targeted people who appeared to have repudiated the Christian faith. Most of its victims were Jews who converted to Christianity in the 1300s and were suspected of reverting secretly to Judaism. They were executed as Christian sinners, not Jews.[38] Yet practically no Christian church now treats apostasy as a crime warranting earthly punishment.[39] A common justification for the switch is that punishment made sense only when church and state were fused, in other words, when apostasy could amount to political treason. Accordingly, in countries where church and state are separated in fact, if not also by law, Christians generally explain away scriptures that condone violence. The overriding message of Christianity, they reason, centers on inner conviction, peace, and tolerance. And, faced with discordant historical episodes such as the Spanish Inquisition, they disown them.

There are grounds for believing that Islam can undergo an analogous change with respect to apostasy. Even prescriptions of the Quran, which conventionally take priority over policy choices in the Golden Age, have been treated as obsolete. "Cling one and all to the Faith of God and never be divided," says verse 3:103, "Remember ... how, after your enmity, He united your hearts, so that you are now brothers through His grace." This is among the Quran's many attempts to replace the destructive tribalism of pre-Islamic Arabia with religious brotherhood. It can reasonably be interpreted as prohibiting the global Muslim community's fragmentation into nation-states with budgets of their own, citizenship rights, borders, and national goals. Until recently, Muslim statesmen interpreted it to mean that their courts could not apply different rules to the Muslims of other states, as they could to non-Muslims, whether domestic or foreign. They inferred also that a single trade regime must cover all Muslims, including the subjects of other states. Thus, Ottoman courts did not differentiate among Muslim litigants according to political allegiance; and all Muslim traders carrying goods across Ottoman borders, even those from states at war with the Ottomans, like Iran repeatedly between 1514 and 1823, faced the same tariff.[40] Nevertheless, there now exist fifty Muslim-majority countries that bestow upon their own citizens rights denied to the Muslim citizens of other states. The Kingdom of Saudi Arabia and the Islamic Republic of Iran, two states committed to upholding Islamic principles, regulate entry and employment by Pakistanis. Just as most modern Christians treat the Bible's out-conversion punishments as outdated, so most Muslims treat the Quran's calls for communal unity as specific to Islam's initial period.[41]

In modern times, Muslim-majority countries have revised other elements of the social system established in early Islam. The Quran denies explicit recognition to any entity between the individual and the full community of Muslims. It names no subcommunity, association, or organization. Nevertheless, all members of the Organization of the Islamic Conference recognize both profit-seeking and charitable corporations. The corporation plays an important role even in Saudi Arabia and Iran; and in neither country is it controversial.

In the early twentieth century, Muslim-governed countries welcomed the corporation as indispensable to exploiting technologies of mass production, finance, communication, and transportation.[42] Entities typically established as corporations include municipalities, government ministries, sports clubs, utilities, banks, and airlines. Islam was born a millennium before the emergence of modern technologies, which limited the immediate drawbacks of the corporation's exclusion from Islamic law. But since the Middle Ages the costs of shunning the corporation have surged. A state that prohibits an organizational form vital to economic development can hardly be viable in the modern world. It helps that the Quran, while not mentioning the corporation, does not ban it.

The adoption of the corporation and neglect of the Quran's prescriptions on Muslim unity reveal a capacity to update Muslim practices and modify understandings of proper Muslim behavior. Islam is routinely reinterpreted according to changing needs. Hence, Abu Bakr's response to the withholding of zakat payments might have undergone a fundamental reinterpretation. The restriction that he imposed on exiting Islam could well have been reinterpreted as a time-bound instrument for preserving the first Islamic state during its second decade of existence. Likewise, the "Apostasy Wars" could have been renamed, say, as the "Wars of State Preservation." The violent reactions of 632 could have been treated as context-specific responses without relevance to later conditions. In brief, Abu Bakr's military campaigns need not have set a precedent for Muslim attitudes toward religious freedoms today.

Had the main conflict after Muhammad's death been over religious freedoms, violent responses would have been out of character for the period. Under Muhammad and the early caliphs, murderers were put to death, as were people who took up arms against Muslims. However, evidence of capital punishment for apostasy dates from after the Golden Age. The practice began with the first

Religious Freedoms in Middle Eastern History

Umayyad caliph, Muawiya I (r. 661–80). Under the Umayyads, the accused were mostly political opponents. Apparently, the apostasy charge served to cloak personal vendettas in an aura of religious correctness. Maintaining the Umayyad pattern, Abbasid caliphs executed countless opponents for apostasy.[43] This record is consistent with the canonical view that the Umayyad and Abbasid regimes corrupted the social order of the "Golden Age." Hence, later Muslims might have treated the criminalization of apostasy as epitomizing the dangers of letting leaders judge people by their beliefs.[44]

But the strongest rationale for rejecting the punishment of apostates lies in the Quran. Although the Quran treats apostasy as punishable, it says that a penalty will be delivered by God on Judgment Day. Consider this verse: "Those who deny Allah after professing Islam and open their bosoms to unbelief shall incur the wrath of Allah and be sternly punished." It says nothing about temporal punishment. Like other such verses, it warns apostates of consequences, without specifying when or what. A subsequent verse adds specificity by indicating that they will go to Hell: "In the life to come they shall assuredly be lost."[45] Certain other verses invoked as justification for executing apostates concern people who use violence against Muslims. Here is an example: "The punishment of those that make war against God and His apostle and spread disorder in the land shall be to be slain or crucified." This verse is not about Muslims who lose faith in Islam or switch religions. It is about protecting the Muslim community against violence. Moreover, no verse of the Quran equates leaving Islam with harming Muslims.

A fuller exegesis would show that the Quran's relevant verses lend themselves to interpretations consistent with free exit. Abdullah Saeed and Hassan Saeed have performed the task in exhaustive detail.[46] They have sketched out a plausible liberal reading under which Muslims may renounce Islam with impunity.

DOCTRINAL OBSTACLES TO UNFETTERED
RELIGIOUS FREEDOMS

The foregoing reasonings will please readers committed to religious liberties. Suggesting that the Quran rejects religious coercion, they support the view that, in addition to free entry, Islam allows free exit. Yet Islam does not treat all its alternatives as interchangeable. The Quran's tolerance of other monotheisms and even of atheism does not extend to polytheism. Its uncompromising condemnation of polytheism undermines full freedom of religion. Explaining the difficulties requires a return to Islam's origins, with emphasis on the identity of its early adherents.

Muhammad's mission was not to add a Muslim God to Arabia's pantheon, Mecca's Kaaba. Islam would replace *all* tribal religions of Arabia, with Kaaba becoming the house of Allah, a single God. Polytheism was thus illegitimate from the start. Its idols were fit only for destruction, and its adherents were expected to convert. This hostility toward polytheism, and the rejection of coexistence between Islam's strict monotheism and Arabia's preexisting native religions limited the religious choices implied by Quranic calls for freedom of conscience.

The nomenclature that the Quran uses for the righteous is revealing. It addresses them as "Believers" (*mu'minūn*) on 567 occasions and Muslims (*muslimūn*, literally, "people who submit") 73 times.[47] Evidently, Muhammad and his followers considered themselves above all as believers in the oneness of God, as opposed to submitters to divine authority. Documentary evidence dating from after Muhammad's death supports this interpretation. For at least a half-century, outside observers, including the region's Christians, characterized the new community as a monotheist reform movement rather than a new religion. The Quran itself accepts righteous Christians and Jews ("People of the Book") as Believers:

There is among the People of the Book some upright men who all night long recite God's revelations and bow down in worship; who believe in God and the Last Day; who enjoin justice, and forbid the reprehensible, and strive to do good works. These are among the righteous; whatever good they do, its reward shall not be denied them. God well knows those that fear him.[48]

In line with this verse, some Christians and Jews were integrated, as such, into organs of the community of Believers. Muhammad's armies, like those of his early successors, included Christian tribesmen. For them, conversion would not have been an issue, because as monotheists they were already Believers.[49]

The Quran instructs Christians and Jews to follow their own institutions: "People of the Book, you shall not be guided until you observe the Torah and the Gospel and that which is revealed to you from your Lord."[50] By the same token, it criticizes Jews for disobeying the Torah and killing Jesus, who tried to improve their ways. It also criticizes Christians who believe in the Trinity: "Unbelievers are those that say: 'Allah is one of three.' There is but one God."[51] Most Christians of Arabia and the territories conquered immediately after Muhammad's death happened to be Monophysites, who considered Jesus to have a single nature.[52] This may explain the generally smooth relations between Muhammad's followers and their Christian neighbors. Indeed, the armies of Muhammad's first four successors faced amazingly sparse resistance in conquering Syria and Palestine. Though they taxed the Christians and Jews of these areas, they did not force conversions. Archeological research has uncovered scant evidence of towns or churches destroyed during Islam's early decades. The pattern accords with the generally peaceful relations between Arabian Believers and the native Believers of conquered realms.[53]

That Christians and Jews outside Arabia considered the conquerors unthreatening to their lifestyles is evident also from the lack of seventh-century Christian and Jewish polemics against conquering monotheists. The massacre of certain Medinese Jewish tribes during Muhammad's lifetime is an exception that proves the rule. Those same tribes had welcomed Muhammad to Medina in 622. They had also supported his campaigns against Arabia's pagans. Their fallout was political, not theological. Furthermore, Muhammad and his followers originally considered themselves part of a single monotheistic community that included Jews and Christians. Initially, Muslims turned in prayer toward Jerusalem rather than Mecca. A building between Jerusalem and Bethlehem functioned concurrently as a church and a mosque.[54]

Interreligious relations of the earliest Muslims conflict with the traditional narrative of Islam's emergence and expansion. According to the conventional account, Muhammad and his companions saw themselves, from the start, as a new religious community distinct from preexisting monotheists. Moreover, as the Quran's chapters started emerging, converts viewed them as the scriptures of a new religion that superseded older monotheisms. In fact, Islam's now-traditional origin narrative developed many decades after Muhammad's death in 632, through projections into the past of intercommunal distinctions that gained salience gradually.

The interpretation offered here is consistent with surviving Middle Eastern Christian and Jewish sources of the seventh century. These refer to Muhammad as the leader of an Arabian pietist movement, not the founder of a new religion. Only about a century after Muhammad's death, in the twilight of the Umayyad Empire, did Christian and Jewish sources start treating Islam as a new religion and Muslims as a distinct confessional community. By then, identification with Muhammad had emerged as central to the collective identity of the new Believers. From 685 onward Umayyad coins featured the double-shahada – "There is no god but God," plus "Muhammad is God's apostle" – as the key marker of the issuing authority. The increasing emphasis on Muhammad's status excluded Christians and Jews from the ranks of the Believers. During this transformation, Believers acquired a new collective identity. Specifically, "Muslim" and "Believer" became synonymous. To readers of the Quran, each term came to signify Muhammad's followers specifically.[55] Meanwhile, Christians and Jews were demoted from the community of Believers to the upper ranks of the "Unbelievers."

If the earliest understanding of Islam were to regain currency, Islam would become more ecumenical, at least more accepting of Christians and Jews. The monotheisms that preceded Islam would no longer be targets of jihadi ideology. Muslims who convert to Judaism or Christianity would not be considered apostates, for they would remain Believers in the original sense of the Quran. Still, Muslims would not gain unfettered freedom to exit Islam. The Quran repeatedly and unequivocally condemns polytheism (*shirk*).[56] The destruction of Kaaba's pagan idols symbolized the legitimacy of suppressing polytheism. The Quran's chapters that date from Muhammad's final years urge Believers to cleanse the world of corruption through jihad; the arrival of these chapters coincided with increasingly militant campaigns against Arabia's pagans.[57]

Hence, a return to the Quran's original interpretation would not lead to full freedom of conscience or exit. A Muslim would still be barred from converting to Hinduism, which is polytheistic. A strict interpretation of the Quran's monotheistic emphasis could also bar conversion to Christianity, which gives divine traits to its founder. To make Islam compatible with full religious freedom, the Quran's pronouncements on paganism and polytheism would have to be treated as specific to seventh-century Arabia.

Lest the required reinterpretation seems unrealistic, it is worth recalling that what passes now as the traditional understanding of Islam includes substantial revisions. One more example will suffice. Among the eight communal expense categories that the Quran lists, one is the emancipation of slaves. The illegality of slavery makes this category irrelevant to the modern age. No one proposes to relegalize slavery to fulfill the Quran's instructions on communal spending.

Thus far, we have seen that Islam's heritage poses no insurmountable obstacle to an expansion of Muslim religious freedoms. For one thing, Islam has undergone reinterpretations through changes in the significance attached to specific scriptural commands; like other major religions, it treats certain scriptures as irrelevant to modern conditions. For another, during its initial phase, which Muslims tend to revere, Islam promoted tolerance of other monotheisms.

ROUTINIZATION OF THE APOSTASY CHARGE

The existence of a potential for change does not mean that its realization would be easy. Revisions of Islam's content depend not only on the Quran's openness to reinterpretation but also on institutionalized practices considered Islamic. With this in mind, we can turn to the social forces that made apostasy a potent instrument of social control.

The Apostasy Wars constituted only the first of many episodes involving opportunistic uses of the apostasy charge. As the spread of Islam inevitably diversified Muslim worldviews, it became a recurring theme of political and intellectual rivalries. Shiis and Sunnis charged each other with abandoning the fundamental tenets of Islam. Various Muslim communities were accused of collective apostasy, and some of them responded in kind. The stage for the demonization of rival religious camps was set through literalist interpretations of texts. Shafii (767–820), founder of a canonical school of jurisprudence, wanted the law to be based primarily on the Quran and remembrances of the Prophet, and secondarily on clerical consensus and analogical interpretation; he ruled out reason, which earlier interpreters had included in their exegetical toolkit.[58] Ibn Hanbal (780–855), founder of another canonical school, rejected context-based interpretation of Islam's fundamental sources; their prescriptions are perpetually valid in a literal sense, he held, and regardless of circumstances.[59] Sunni Islam's even older major schools of law, the Hanafi and Maliki schools, had been more flexible. The Hanafis left room for reason and the Malikis for living tradition. But within a couple of centuries the uncompromising literalism of the Shafiis and Hanbalis took hold even among the Hanafis and Malikis. All four of Sunni Islam's major schools of jurisprudence agreed on text-based literalism as the proper method of Islamic interpretation.[60] As literalism gained prominence, two forms of religious offense became salient: blasphemy (*kufr*, *shirk*) and heresy (*bid'a*, *zandaqa*). These terms were often equated with apostasy. Thus, one could be accused of apostasy for criticizing a practice of Muhammad (such as polygamy). It became risky even to articulate polygamy's social dangers (such as the alienation of poor men whose marriage prospects fall when the wealthy take multiple wives).

This uncompromising approach is known as Sunni orthodoxy. In early centuries of the second millennium, Islamic thinkers hardened Sunni orthodoxy, partly through writings that have remained influential down to the present, but also by legitimizing the persecution of deviants. Ghazali (1058–1111) helped to establish the practice of treating heterodox Muslims as apostates who deserve execution. He urged the killing of independent-minded philosophers as well as Ismaili Shiis, insisting that rulers and their military had a duty to destroy heretics.[61] He even endorsed the execution of "secret apostates" – outwardly Muslim individuals suspected of heterodoxy or unbelief.[62] Two centuries later, Ibn Taymiyya (1263–1328) targeted other heterodox groups as apostates; these included Alawis (Nusayris), Batinis, Druzes, Ismailis, Karmatis, and Muslim Mongols.[63] One of his fatwas, or religious opinions, characterizes several of these groups as "more heretical than the Jews and the Christians and even more heretical than many of the polytheists." It goes on: "Their harm to Muhammad's community is greater than the harm of infidel fighters such as the Mongols, the Crusaders, and others." The fatwa then declares that these deviants should be hunted and killed.[64] Fatwas played important roles in shaping public opinion as well as the evolution of Islamic law. The fatwas of leading Islamic interpreters, such as Ghazali and Ibn Taymiyya, were collected in volumes for use by later interpreters, but also by statesmen and judges.[65]

The victims of the terror unleashed by such calls for Islamic purity included numerous towering Muslim thinkers.[66] Philosophers and scientists who developed stellar reputations well beyond the Muslim world suffered persecution, as did contributors to Islamic law and ideology who are still widely revered among Muslims, even by Islamists. The mystic philosopher Suhrawardi (1154–91) was accused of heresy and executed in Aleppo.[67] The political philosopher and scientist Ibn Rushd (1126–98), known also as Averroes, was tried for heresy and banished from his home in Cordoba.[68] As is common in witch hunts, some of the great thinkers persecuted, tortured, and killed in the name of Islamic purity had promoted coerced Islamic conformity themselves. Considered a heretic by Malikis, Shafii appears to have died in Egypt at the hands of a Maliki vigilante.[69] Ibn Hanbal was beaten, jailed in Baghdad, and tortured for heresy.[70] Ibn Taymiyya endured imprisonment for heresy in both Cairo and Damascus; eventually banned from issuing opinions and even writing, he died in jail.[71] The motivations behind these persecutions were complex. Political and intellectual rivalries played roles. Oppression also served to settle personal scores. However complex the rationales, though, such persecutions were rationalized through Islamic orthodoxy.

Non-Arab regimes, too, used the apostasy charge as a convenient tool against opponents as well as original thinkers. The Ottoman Empire, which grew out of a tiny principality (*beylik*) that promoted a variegated and particularly tolerant form of Islam,[72] took to enforcing an intolerant form of Sunni Islam as it became a global power. Thus, it began to accuse of apostasy people who appeared to reject the official imperial religion, or whose practices deviated from the norms of Ottoman clerics. Ottoman sultans between the mid-1400s and late 1500s presided over a gory religious homogenization drive that has been likened to the Spanish Inquisition.[73]

The juxtaposition may seem odd because the Ottomans had no autonomous Islamic organization resembling the Catholic Church. In the absence of centralized leadership, how could an inquisition have existed? In Ottoman governance, there was no separation of religion and state. Clerics monitored religious discourse and practices as state employees. In that capacity, they identified what constitutes blasphemy, heresy, and apostasy. Just as inquisitors targeted ostensibly deviant Christians who threatened the Spanish Crown, Church authority, or simply social harmony,[74] so Ottoman clerics were concerned primarily with Muslims who irritated the broader Ottoman establishment. Ottoman communities persecuted for apostasy include the Bektashis, Rafizis, Haydaris, Kizilbashs, Kalendaris, Abdals, Babais, Bedreddinis, and Ishiks.[75] The sufferings of these sects have left traces in residential patterns. Their Anatolian descendants tend to live at high altitudes, in areas that were inaccessible to Ottoman officials and distant to Sunni-dominated villages.[76]

The practices that Ottoman Sunni clerics treated as evidence of apostasy included not fasting during Ramadan, drinking wine, neglecting to pray five times a day, and skipping the congregational prayer on Friday. They also included expressions at odds with Sunni beliefs. Expecting the coming of a Messiah or doubting the existence of an afterlife was commonly equated with apostasy. Disapproval of the first three communal leaders after Muhammad, which is characteristic of Shiism, would also invite an apostasy charge. Activities deemed to distract from Sunni Islam could serve as evidence of apostasy; they included playing music, dancing, and celebrating an event other than the end of Ramadan or the Feast of Sacrifices. One could be labeled an apostate merely for questioning the basis for apostasy allegations, or even the punishments imposed on the accused.[77]

In the high period of the Ottoman Empire, huge numbers of Muslims perished for offending orthodox Sunni sensibilities. Under Selim I (r. 1512–20) around 40,000 Kizilbashs were executed for apostasy.[78] But even such brutality did not eliminate deviant practices in Anatolia or, for that matter, in other Ottoman realms. This is obvious from the frequency of edicts and fatwas aimed at eradicating heterodoxy and heteropraxy – deviant beliefs and deviant practices. The most famous of all Ottoman grand muftis (*şeyhülislam*s), who served as the empire's supreme judge and highest Muslim official, is Ebussuûd, whose tenure lasted thirty-seven years, much of it under Süleyman the Magnificent (r. 1520–66). Ebussuûd is celebrated for his lenient attitude toward commercial practices involving disguised interest and his endorsement of new tax reforms. Yet he also issued dozens of opinions legitimizing the persecution of nonconformist Muslims. Ebussuûd wrote that villages without a mosque should be forced to build one; that Muslims who refrain from praying or from fasting during Ramadan should be killed; and that Islam allows the raping of Kizilbash women.[79] He promoted Sunnitization as well as the homogenization of Sunni beliefs and lifestyles.

The harshness of Ebussuûd's fatwas on religious deviants, like those of other senior Ottoman jurists, can give the impression of uniformly brutal hostility toward Muslims who deviated from official Ottoman norms.[80] In fact, responses depended on whether Ottoman military, commercial, and financial interests were threatened.[81] Tolerating deviance that was harmless to their objectives, Ottoman rulers even formed pragmatic alliances with certain heterodox communities. The trajectory of Ottoman policies toward the Kizilbashs is apposite.[82] In the 1450s, the Ottomans assisted and protected Kizilbash communities. The formal reason was that Kizilbash leaders, ostensibly descendants of Prophet Muhammad, merited special respect. The actual motivation was to keep Kizilbashs loyal at a time of military expansion. By Selim I's ascension to the throne, the Sunni Ottoman dynasty was at war with Iran's Shii Safavid dynasty over lands inhabited, in varying concentrations, by Kizilbashs. Some Ottoman Kizilbashs had declared allegiance to the Safavid Shah Ismail I (r. 1501–24). Denying Ottoman sovereignty over their regions, they were paying taxes to Ismail I, endangering Ottoman merchants, and even aiding Safavid armies. Meanwhile, a nephew of Selim I had "turned Kizilbash" himself and assembled soldiers, aiming to split Ottoman realms. The Ottoman responses included not only heresy trials and public executions but also forced conversions to Sunnism and fines for men who failed to attend Sunni congregational prayers. Especially during periods of Ottoman–Safavid peace, Ottoman rulers preferred conversions and behavioral controls to executions and expulsions.[83]

The variations of policies toward Ottoman Kizilbashs were replicated in the Middle East's other imperial power of the period. Iran, a Sunni polity as late as the 1400s, had its own Kizilbash populations. Before founding an empire in 1501, the Safavid dynasty led a movement to make Twelver Shiism, the largest of Shiism's three main branches today, Iran's official religion.[84] Along the way, Safavids formed spiritual ties with Iranian Kizilbashs and used them to consolidate power at home, but also to weaken their Ottoman archrivals through cross-border Kizilbash cooperation. In return, Safavid rulers granted Kizilbashs a near-monopoly over top government and military positions. They also tolerated Kizilbash rituals offensive to the Twelver Shiism of urban Iran. Nevertheless, power sharing between the Safavid house and Kizilbash leaders was rife with tension. A showdown came under Abbas I (r. 1587–1629), when a Kizilbash rebellion triggered a ferocious campaign to annihilate the sect. As in

Ottoman realms, Kizilbash Islam went underground, and Twelver clerics obtained free rein to pursue puritanism with Safavid help. Thus, coffeehouses were banned; Islamic garb was made mandatory for Muslims; wine was prohibited; and art forms were limited to Twelver icons. In essence, the religious freedoms of Kizilbashs were withdrawn when they posed an existential threat to Safavid rule, and shahs felt strong enough to dispense with their support.[85]

Among the heterodox Ottoman communities whose religious freedoms waxed and waned, the Bektashis constitute another instructive case. Bektashi Islam gave priority to the individual, regardless of national origin or even religion. It also disregarded broad segments of the Sharia.[86] Bektashis suffered heightened persecution in 1826, following the dissolution of the Janissary Corps, composed of Christian-born soldiers who were separated from their families as boys and raised as Muslims. Once a fierce fighting force, the Janissaries lost effectiveness as advances in global military technology, combined with vested interests that blocked their modernization, turned them into an anachronism. By 1700 they were becoming a crime syndicate that threatened the sultan's legitimacy.[87] For this reason, many segments of Ottoman society welcomed the dissolution of the Janissary Corps as part of a military modernization drive. From the late 1400s onward, the Janissaries had links to the Bektashis.[88] These connections seem to have been tolerated in order to facilitate, on the one hand, the Islamization and Turkification of Janissary recruits, and, on the other hand, the monitoring of Janissaries, whose periodic mutinies threatened Ottoman elites.[89] The Janissary Corps was disbanded in 1826, when the sultan felt confident of winning a showdown. With the bloody dissolution, the Sunni establishment lost interest in the relaxed and ecumenical Islam of Bektashism. Leading Bektashis were hanged for apostasy. Many Bektashi lodges were destroyed, and numerous others were turned over to Sunni clerics.[90] The episode thus reveals that the Ottoman establishment tolerated the Bektashis only insofar as they served its core goals of military strength and political stability.

IRREPRESSIBLE AND INSTRUMENTALIZED
RELIGIOUS FREEDOMS

The bloody crackdown on the Bektashis provides yet another illustration of this chapter's major theme: Middle Eastern history features numerous cases of religious repression. But the tolerance that the Bektashis enjoyed until 1826 testifies also to the persistence of religious diversity even during drives to homogenize Islamic practices. So does the Bektashis' survival after the destruction of their physical infrastructure. For half a millennium, they had given cover to various persecuted heterodox sects, which influenced their own beliefs and practices.[91] After 1826, they themselves had to mask their identity; hiding among relatively tolerated heterodox sects, or among Freemasons, they survived as a religious community, influencing the communities that sheltered them from intolerant officials.[92] Moreover, they regained political clout within three decades, partly through alliances with anticlerical groups and Europhilic reformers.[93]

Even within specific Middle Eastern states, Islam has remained heterogeneous to one degree or another; and sometimes heterogeneity has enjoyed official approval, even support. Three factors have accounted for the endurance of religious diversity: limited state capacity, political opportunism, and the decentralized production of fatwas.

To start with limited capacity, no state, not even one with a ruthless leader, can fully control the behaviors of its subjects, to say nothing of regulating thoughts and preferences. The costs of gathering information about subjects' beliefs, intentions, and behaviors constrain the state's options. The difficulties of monitoring state agents – tax collectors, soldiers, judges, undercover informers – pose another obstacle to projecting state power.[94] Middle Eastern Islam has remained heterogeneous, then, only partly because the region was never fully unified politically. Also critical is that rulers and the clerics pursuing religious uniformity on their behalf could not track all Muslim practices or punish every departure from ruler-favored Islamic ideals.

Heterodox and heteroprax Islam thus emerged and spread for the same reason that taxes owed to Muslim rulers were commonly evaded or embezzled. The aftermath of the crackdown on Ottoman Bektashism illustrates the point. For the Ottoman state, substantial religious diversity was unavoidable. It could be contained but never eradicated; and the challenges varied. Under new circumstances, a significant share of the surviving Bektashis resurfaced as a modified heterodox sect. Safavid Iran, too, faced constraints in its Shiitization campaign. Although it managed to eradicate certain heterodox sects from Iran – Khalvatis, Nimatullahis, Naqshbandis – other Sufi sects gained popularity in the mid-1600s. Iranian Sunnism lived on for two centuries, usually in disguise. It even regained official tolerance on multiple occasions, though in each case violent reactions drove it back underground.[95]

Political opportunism was on display when Ottoman sultans saw the Bektashis as useful allies. Heterodox Bektashi practices provided instrumental value to the Ottoman dynasty not only in managing the Janissaries but also in countering nonconformist movements that posed threats transcending religious disobedience. During the Safavid conflicts, Bektashis helped Ottoman rulers identify Kızılbashs. Bektashism was tolerable also because it had no links to an Ottoman enemy. For their part, Ottoman clerics tolerated Bektashis as vehicles for stamping out mystical beliefs that they considered even more heretical than Bektashism. Several once-salient heterodox sects, including the Haydaris, Kalendaris, and Abdals, were absorbed into Bektashism by the early 1600s.[96] Like the Ottomans, the Safavids allowed exceptions to religious purity on a selective basis, when it contributed to centralization. Even as they strove to destroy organized forms of "folk Shiism," they encouraged individualized and ascetic "high Sufism." The underlying logic is clear. Whereas organized Sufi sects subverted Safavid authority, ascetic Sufis, being radically individualistic and apolitical, were unthreatening.[97] Even resident Hindus – under Twelver Shii doctrine, polytheists deserving death – were tolerated because, as traders and financiers, they served vital economic functions.[98]

Finally, the fatwa production process was neither controlled by states nor used solely, or even mainly, to serve the incumbent regime. Most fatwas were issued by jurisconsults in response to practical needs, such as resolving legal disputes among individuals, drawing commercial contracts, and responding to crimes. As a rule, a jurisconsult did not need anyone's permission to issue a fatwa. Over the ages, fatwas produced in an uncoordinated manner were incorporated into law books to provide legal guidance to both officials and ordinary people. Islam's schools of law each produced many such law books, whose substance evolved with changing needs.[99] Variations in needs affected the substance of law books. Hence, the legal guides available to judges varied over time, and, in any given period, across space. Inevitably, then, fatwas hindered Islamic homogenization. Following chapters address the implications for both persistent religious diversity and Muslim freedoms.

Even when Middle Eastern rulers were able to enforce religious orthodoxy, they would not necessarily have wanted to eliminate all heterogeneity. In seeking to remain in power, they had alternatives to repressing groups refusing to conform to an official religion. Potential challengers could be neutralized politically through economic incentives. They could also be tolerated in return for tributes. Both options contributed to keeping the Middle East multireligious after the rise of Islam, but also Islam itself heterogeneous even in polities committed to an orthodoxy.

Another phenomenon that helped keep the Middle East religiously heterogeneous was religious preference falsification – the misrepresentation of religious convictions and wants to accommodate perceived social pressures.[100] Previously discussed cases of forced and opportunistic conversion furnish evidence spanning many periods. Extreme forms have included crypto-conversions to Islam, such as the formal Islamization of non-Muslims who continued to practice Christianity covertly.[101] Within Islam, they have included crypto-switches across denominations. Formally Sunnitized Shiis have waited, sometimes for generations, for opportunities to resume professing Shiism openly. And outwardly Shiitized Sunnis have remained Sunni at heart.[102] Premodern Muslims of the Middle East probably also included people that modern scholarship would characterize as secular, irreligious, agnostic, or atheist. What is certain is that in Muslim-governed polities, understandings of Islam, interpretations of Islamic texts, and attitudes toward Islamic norms were all more diverse than orthodox religious leaders ever acknowledged. There is no way to gauge religious preference falsification in Middle Eastern history according to modern scientific standards. For example, Safavid specialists cannot quantify crypto-Sunnism in seventeenth-century Iran. But it is possible to identify sundry signs of substantial falsification of religious preferences.

Large numbers pretended to follow the letter of Islamic financial rules, and thus to pay lip service to orthodox Islamic principles, even as they knowingly violated them in spirit. At least with respect to finance, then, the Sharia was widely considered inconvenient or misconstrued.[103] For all the evidence of intra-Islamic diversity, departures from orthodoxy lacked legitimacy. In both Sunni- and Shii-ruled areas, diversity was equated with ignorance, if not with malicious heresy. Even rulers who followed heterodox practices themselves participated in propagating orthodoxy. They acted as though most of their Muslim subjects genuinely accepted the official religious orthodoxy and heeded its dictates.

Monotheistic non-Muslim minorities fared better than heterodox Muslims in terms of official recognition. They enjoyed legal status as non-Muslims. They could openly profess adherence to a different religion. They could worship in autonomous spaces of their own. They were exempt from Muslim rituals such as Ramadan fasting and Friday services. On the downside, they were second-class subjects expected to be submissive. They were forbidden to share their theologies with Muslims; and proselytization was out of the question. They had to live in homes no taller than those of nearby Muslims. Christians and Jews were also barred from building new houses of worship. Although such bans were not always enforced, they stood as steady markers of Christian and Jewish inferiority.[104] Non-Muslims were also barred from serving as legal witnesses against Muslims. Though entitled to sue a Muslim for a perceived wrong committed against themselves as individuals, their legal testimony was discounted.[105]

POSSIBILITIES OF RELIGIOUS LIBERALIZATION

Ottoman and Safavid treatments of their heterodox populations illustrate another theme of this chapter, which will be developed further. Just as the "Apostasy Wars" of seventh-century Arabia were motivated by more than enforcing religious conformism, the Ottoman Sunnitization and Safavid Shiitization campaigns reflected, in addition to religious intolerance per se, complex political and economic considerations. An important implication follows. Like the "Apostasy Wars," the religious persecutions of the Ottomans and Safavids lend themselves to interpretations centered on factors beyond Islamic purity. The alternative narratives presented here stress the contributions of religious repression to state development and preservation. However, along with evidence of coercion, they have highlighted indications of de facto heterogeneity in beliefs and practices.

Three pathways to religious freedom were identified early in the chapter, referencing historical patterns in Western Europe. All three were available to peoples of the Middle East, this chapter has shown. The persistent heterogeneity of Islamic interpretations might have motivated sultans to abandon coerced religious orthodoxy in favor of religious tolerance and coexistence. Collectively, heterodox Muslims represented a potential coalition for separating mosque and state as a means of instituting religious freedoms. Finally, early Islamic precedents often used to justify coerced Islamization also lend themselves to readings compatible with a liberal order. To date, these liberalization options have not been exercised. The task ahead is to explore why.

8

The Marginalization of Islam

For Middle Eastern elites, the nineteenth century was a time of mounting existential crisis. Muslim empires were losing territories to Europeans, who were building colonial empires. Ottoman defeats at the hands of Austrians and Russians (1787–92) and Napoleon's campaigns in Egypt and Syria (1798–1801) were inflaming awareness of military weakness. Government insolvency was a chronic problem, and its solution required borrowing from adversaries that used every opportunity to consolidate political gains. Budgetary crises were deepening. As if falling behind imperialistic Western Christians was not humiliating enough, local Christians and Jews, long treated as legally and socially inferior, and economically useful but not more competent, were now leading better lifestyles. All these developments induced soul searching and, in stages, diverse government reforms. Military reorganization came first, followed by new agencies that replaced clerics with experts trained outside the Islamic education system. Reconstituted bureaucracies, European-inspired schools, and nascent commercial courts employed professionals with credentials lacking in madrasa graduates. As modernization unfolded, clerics found themselves marginalized.

This story has been told aptly, from many angles.[1] Though insightful, the influential narratives underappreciate, if not miss altogether, the economic transformations that enabled once unimaginable social reforms. Over the previous century, clerics had weakened financially and politically. Waqf privatizations and nationalizations had reduced the wealth under their supervision, shrinking their capacity to resist modernization. Meanwhile, new wealth was being created in economic sectors outside clerical control.[2] Time and again, clerics had managed to block reforms they disliked, going so far as to dethrone sultans. Now, their ability to resist was falling. The new balance of power made many clerics cast their lot with modernizers.

The modernizers eager to weaken Islam's roles formed a heterogeneous bloc. In one way or another, most wanted to reinterpret Islam to suit the times. Certain modernizers wanted to shrink the scope of Islamic law and to minimize the functions of clerics. A smaller number wanted to go further and disestablish Islam. In historical narratives, these groups are commonly lumped together as precursors of the "secularists" who gained power across the region in the 1900s. Yet they differed enormously in terms of what religious freedoms they supported. Some modernizers sought to broaden Muslim freedoms as a means of allowing heterodox practices. Their goal was to develop relatively liberal forms of Islam without restricting the freedoms of genuine believers in the prevailing orthodoxy. Seeking to eradicate traditional Islam, which they held responsible for sundry ills, others sought to replace it with a variant suited to the times.

As a rule, with differences in timing and specifics, the latter group of reformers won the day. In Turkey, Iran, Egypt, Iraq, Syria, Algeria, Tunisia, and several other Arab countries, secular regimes opted to regulate Islam to their liking; they also persecuted dissenters. In effect, they replaced a premodern orthodoxy with a modernist orthodoxy, which they propagated through clerics who chose, sometimes out of conviction but often opportunistically, to accommodate the modernist social agendas. These cooperative clerics created structures that maintained the state–clergy alliance. They also retained another longstanding state practice: social and political control of what it means to be a good Muslim. Many devout Muslims went underground. Starting to hide their convictions, they made their religiosity less salient.

Through coercion, secularists gained freedoms to pursue reforms with minimal resistance from traditional Islamic communities. But the relief proved temporary. It set the conditions for a surge of assertive Islamism and the return of constraints on secular lifestyles.

ISLAM'S SHRINKING FUNCTIONS IN THE AGE OF MODERNIZATION

As the Middle East began to look increasingly underdeveloped economically and weak militarily, its Muslim populations contained numerous communities alienated from the prevailing Islamic orthodoxy – heterodox orders practicing their beliefs in hiding, or at least discreetly. In Iran, Sufism had regained a huge following among elites and Babism, a millenarian offshoot of Shiism, among poor peasants and workers. Both heterodoxies endured systematic repression from Twelver clerics allied with the state.[3] In Iraq, Ottoman governors were resisting the spread of Shiism, whose adherents they distrusted.[4] In Syria, the Ottomans were striving to strengthen Muslim defenses against Christian missionaries by indoctrinating "heretical" sects – mainly the Alawis – with orthodox Sunnism.[5] In Egypt, recognized Sufi orders were policing unrecognized orders, such as the Qayatiyya and the Arabiyya.[6] In Arabia, Indian immigrants were being jailed for contradicting Meccan clerics and disavowing Sunni Islam's canonical schools of law; and Rashidi Sufis were enduring persecution for heresy.[7]

The alienated population also included Muslims who, while sharing with heterodox Muslims a distaste for orthodox Islam, favored reforms that extended beyond Islam itself. Like heterodox Muslims, they rejected Islam's dominant interpretation, resented the powers of clerics, and considered various Islamic institutions outdated, if not inherently harmful. Unlike most heterodox Muslims, they sensed that overcoming the brewing crisis would require solutions outside the realm of religion. It was self-evident that local Christians and Jews, treated as followers of superseded monotheisms, were advancing economically and that their European connections mattered.[8] Reforms would entail sidelining clerics in a broad range of domains, transferring their functions to experts without religious training.[9]

The 1700s generated assorted responses showing foreign influences. From Qajar Iran in the east to pre-protectorate Morocco in the west, Muslim elites became increasingly open to emulating Christian Europeans, long considered culturally and religiously inferior. A printing press for publishing in Turkish and Arabic opened in 1727, almost three centuries after the Gutenberg Press and 234 years after Sephardic-Jewish refugees in Istanbul began printing books in Hebrew.[10] Starting in 1793, permanent Ottoman embassies were opened in Western capitals, partly to facilitate intelligence gathering; their reports reflected growing curiosity about emerging technologies and institutions.[11] Located in Istanbul, the region's first modern engineering school started classes in 1795; its curriculum, which included French-language instruction, resembled that of a European university.[12] Iran opened its first state-sponsored European-style secondary school in 1851, as part of a broader reform agenda.[13] Around the same time, it established permanent diplomatic missions in European capitals as well as in the Ottoman Empire, whose reforms it followed with growing fascination.[14] The region's militaries started to show Western influences in more than choice of weaponry; armies and navies were reorganized according to Western templates, often with assistance from Western advisors. Military symbols were also adapted to Western tastes.[15] All such transformations betray a sense of Western superiority in various domains.

As the region took its first Westernizing steps, it also began to dismantle core Islamic institutions. The nationalizations and privatizations of waqfs, discussed in Chapter 6, constituted a massive transformation that altered property rights, private investment, social services, charity, wealth distribution, and state–subject relations. For a millennium, the waqf had been a bedrock of the traditional Islamic order. Its downgrading by both private investors and state officials was a momentous turn that presaged the marginalization of Islam. The traditional Islamic order was losing its luster well before observers started to characterize it as dysfunctional.

Ideas leave no historical traces until expressed publicly and somehow recorded. They may circulate for generations within families, among trusted friends, and, covertly, in oral humor before becoming accessible to researchers. Fear of punishment by the guardians of orthodoxy would have kept the earliest de-Islamization plans from gaining publicity. They entered public discourse, and then started building on each other, only when conditions became sufficiently hospitable to reforms aimed at curtailing the role of Islam. In the early 1800s, that point had not yet been reached.

In Ottoman realms, the Gülhane Edict of 1839 marks the watershed.[16] That is when a broad coalition of elites, including the Ottoman Sultan's chief aides, sensed – correctly, it turned out – that an unarticulated private consensus had formed in favor of fundamental reforms. With the support of a coalition of Ottoman elites, Sultan Abdülmecid I (r. 1839–61) admitted publicly that the traditional Islamic order was unsustainable. His edict annulled Muslim privileges with roots in polities stretching back to the mid-600s. State officials, including clerics, lost tax exemptions. Christians and Jews obtained equality before the law. The scope of the changes was unprecedented in Islamic history.[17] To make them credible, Abdülmecid pledged his commitment to the new legal order before the dignitaries of a dozen cities. In the process, he legitimated a redistribution of power in favor of non-Muslims, under way de facto for decades.[18] He also encouraged open debates on further reforms. The reform package that followed, known as Tanzimat (literally, Reordering), transplanted Western institutions to Ottoman lands. Examples include schools with a mostly secular curriculum, including ones operated by Christian missionaries; secular commercial courts, which followed nonsectarian procedures and recognized contracts alien to Islamic law; and secular municipalities, which provided urban services without the supervision of Islamic courts. All these transplants shrank the role of Islam in everyday life. They also compounded the marginalization of clerics. Though clerics continued to conduct religious rituals, legal and educational reforms progressively excluded them from social functions they had long monopolized.

Three decades before the Gülhane Edict, Egypt had already started to modernize its public administration through new functional departments run by personnel with special secular training. The new offices created through successive reforms included a Department of Public Works, a Bureau of Statistics, a Railway Administration, and an Office of European Affairs. Each resembled a European bureaucracy. None had any use for clerics. The idealization of Europe peaked under Khedive Ismail (r. 1863–79), who aimed to restore Egypt's status as a center of civilization by accepting European culture and emulating European material development.[19] By Ismail's time, Egypt's elites considered Europeans superior to locals in most domains. Many Europeans were welcomed as agents of modernization: 80,000 by 1872 and 140,000 by 1907. Local Christians, too, saw their stock rise. Like foreigners, they served on the Mixed Courts established to take over commercial and financial matters from Islamic courts.[20] Speeches given at the opening of the Suez Canal in 1869 all but said that Muslims were looking to Christianity for deliverance from underdevelopment. Speaking on behalf of Egypt, a Muslim cleric lauded the Europeanization that the canal would facilitate. The French representative,

The Marginalization of Islam

a chaplain, also praised the participation of Christian dignitaries in the religious ceremonies that preceded the opening. He welcomed the opportunity for Europe to bestow, along with the "secrets of civilization," "spiritual light and religious guidance."[21] The chaplain's words drew no objection from Ismail or his assembled guests.

It is one thing to equalize religions before the law, another to implement religious equality. The Gülhane Edict did not specify the meaning of equalizing religions. In any case, it could not have equalized the social status of the empire's three monotheisms overnight. Still treated as socially inferior, non-Muslims continued to endure what Selim Deringil calls the "small insults of everyday life."[22] But the Ottoman sultan's vow to protect religious freedoms in a nonsectarian manner was no empty gesture. In 1860, following economically motivated anti-Christian riots in Damascus, the Ottoman government made forcibly converted Christians return to Christianity.[23] Christians and Jews expanded their practical freedoms also because of their economic successes. As they prospered and acquired education, they found it easier to defend their rights, including their formal religious freedoms. They gained influence over government bureaucracies.

Although certain Tanzimat interpreters make light of this period's achievements, in fact, it activated a new dynamic with huge consequences.[24] The century preceding the Gülhane Edict had seen the progressive weakening of a self-enforcing equilibrium under which Islamic law and clerics were central to the region's economic, social, intellectual, and religious life. That equilibrium had been in place since around the year 900. Though rulers habitually used clerics to legitimize their decisions through convenient interpretations, they did so within limits imposed by basic Islamic structures, which conditioned their visions and policies. Toward the end of the pre-Tanzimat period, it became increasingly common for rulers as well as their subjects to address problems outside the confines of Islamic formulations; and political elites started paying increasing attention to Western innovations. These developments were undermining the longstanding institutional equilibrium; they were making it increasingly vulnerable without destroying it – just as the shrinking habitat of a species lowers its numbers without erasing it. The Middle East's legal, educational, and economic systems remained mostly intact, as did its rules governing religion and interfaith relations. Rulers still sought fatwas to support their major decisions. People of all vocations pretended that the traditional order, however corrupted, lived on. They treated innovations such as the printing press and Western-inspired military units as adaptations that did not challenge the reigning Islamic orthodoxy, not as precursors of an impending social revolution.

The Gülhane Edict exposed changes that had been unfolding silently for decades, but without gaining recognition as radical reforms. It ushered in a period of explicit breaks with the past. Nevertheless, it was not a revolution that obliterated everything old to create a blank institutional slate. It preserved various components of the traditional Islamic order.[25] Islamic courts continued to function. For more than a decade, they remained the only venue for adjudication involving Muslims. The curricula of Islamic schools barely changed. In short, the Tanzimat initiated successive transformations that fostered new institutions without immediately discarding their old counterparts. It created a hybrid order in flux – still basically Islamic, but under modification and increasingly faulted for failures. New constituencies and coalitions were taking shape.

ATTEMPTS AT DISESTABLISHMENT

During this period of dizzying institutional modernization, growing numbers of foreign observers started to characterize Islam as a religion that is backward, rigid, and inherently incompatible with Modernity.[26] For decades, Muslims never went that far, at least not publicly. True, they kept welcoming initiatives that narrowed Islam's roles in daily life, established new institutions that competed with centers of Islamic authority, and reinterpreted Islamic precepts creatively. But they did not consider it necessary to disestablish Islam. The farthest they would go was to lambast dogma and superstition, or to refute Christianity as a means of signaling distaste of religion without mentioning Islam.[27]

In both Sunni-majority and Shii-majority lands, the boldest critics of orthodox Islam emerged as much of the region was falling under the control, economically but in many places also militarily, of European colonizers. They include Abdullah Cevdet (1869–1932), an Ottoman Kurd who became an ideologist of the Young Turks, Ali Abd Al-Raziq (1888–1966), an Egyptian cleric, and Iranian intellectuals who wrote, often anonymously, for anticlerical publications. Writing in the 1890s through the 1920s, Cevdet characterized Islam as a source of backwardness. Ottoman intellectuals should replace Islamic notions with "scientific" ones, but always using remembrances of the Prophet to hide their provenance. Islam's five canonical pillars – profession of faith, prayer, zakat, fasting, pilgrimage – needed to be replaced by a more useful trio, he wrote: "being rich, being powerful, and being knowledgeable."[28] Cevdet had a negligible impact on Ottoman public opinion, and his religious agenda received scant support even from the founders of the Turkish Republic, who were poised to abrogate Islamic law and include secularism among their guiding principles.[29] In a 1925 book, Abd al-Raziq argued that Islam provides spiritual guidance but nothing relevant to modern governance. He thus called openly for the disestablishment of Islam, which had happened already in administration, finance, and commerce.[30] In the same year, the Iranian periodical *Rastakhiz* argued that "there is much of great importance in today's society that is unmentioned in the Quran." Giving examples of economic and political institutions vital to modern life, it went on: "We must respectfully approach the house of the 'unclean and heathen' Westerners and implore them to save us from our ignorance and misery. . . . True Islam is not opposed to civilization."[31]

The Marginalization of Islam

None of these champions of disestablishing traditional Islam gained a mass following. But they facilitated attempts to marginalize it further through institutional reforms that trimmed the already diminished functions of clerics. Turkey went the farthest. In abolishing the Ottoman Caliphate and abrogating Islamic law in 1924, it denied clerics even a symbolic role in governance; it also devalued Islamic higher education. The adoption of secularism as a constitutional principle in 1937 was meant to erect an insurmountable barrier to the re-politicization of Islam. For Kemal Atatürk and his followers, turning to the West as a model would amount to a permanent rejection of Islam as a source of governance.[32]

Pahlavi Iran (1925–79) followed in Turkey's footsteps, though more cautiously and leaving room for ambiguity. Clerics could maintain their traditional hierarchy and, if they stayed clear of politics, their institutional autonomy.[33] As Turkey and Iran marginalized Islam on their own, in the most populous Arab countries European administrators pursued reforms inspired by their home institutions. They considered Islam an impediment to progress, yet also a force to be accommodated. They would weaken Islam by removing its financial sources wherever possible, but without turning it into a focal point for nationalist resistance. Independent nationalist regimes were less constrained. Various postcolonial regimes opted for softer versions of Kemalist Turkey's hostility to Islam. Tunisia under Bourguiba and Ben Ali (1957–2011), Nasserist Egypt (1952–70), Baathist Syria (1963–present), and Baathist Iraq (1968–2003) all defined themselves through Western visions.[34] "Arab socialism," the official ideology of most such regimes, blended Marxism and local versions of nationalism. Like Iran, the Arab world's secular regimes stopped short of disestablishing Islam formally. The most radical modernist Arab regime, Bourguiba's Tunisia, kept Islam as its official religion and required the president to be a Muslim. It also retained Islamic law in certain areas, including inheritance, in modified form.[35]

The public façade of oil-exporting Arab kingdoms gives an appearance of retaining Islam as the foundation of governance. From its founding in 1932, Saudi Arabia's royal family has legitimated its rule through an alliance with Wahhabi Islam, an ultra-puritanical branch of Sunnism. As part of the bargain, Wahhabi clerics enforce Islamic morality in public spaces.[36] Even in oil-rich kingdoms, though, clerics have lost most of their substantive functions. Their duties are limited essentially to performing religious rituals, policing morality, and operating religious courts dealing with matters of private status.[37] Officially, the Saudi monarchy treats all its Sunni subjects as Wahhabis, but it turns a blind eye to various practices at odds with austere Wahhabi teachings.[38] Although Saudi students of the 1970s received much more religious instruction than their Tunisian peers, secular subjects dominated even their curricula, and most of their teachers were trained outside religious seminaries.[39] Saudi government ministries, including the judiciary and the social welfare system through which citizens share in oil wealth, are run overwhelmingly by secular-educated civil servants. The same is true of Saudi Arabia's major private companies.[40] They use organizational forms transplanted from Europe, not ones derived from Islamic law. Saudi homes feature technologies that clerics initially opposed, including radio, television, illustrated books, and sound systems. Across the country, brand-name clothing, fragrances, and vehicles are marks of social status. Western fast-food outlets are ubiquitous, as are shopping malls packed with goods from around the world.[41] Ideology and symbolism aside, by the late 1960s, the rapidly expanding Saudi middle class already exhibited secularized lifestyles. With respect to the social roles of Islam, then, differences between "secular" and "conservative" Arab states are matters of degree rather than kind.

ASSERTIVE ISLAMIC SECULARISM

Secularism refers to a class of ideologies that aim to limit the role of religion. One of its basic types, "passive secularism," simply accepts the transfer to nonreligious professionals of functions once performed by clerics. It does nothing to shape unfolding processes. Respecting freedom of conscience, it treats all religions as well as nonreligious commitments evenhandedly. Without pursuing an agenda with respect to the place of religion in social life, it rationalizes the decline of religious activity that tends to accompany economic development. The decline need not involve the rejection of religion. Intensely religious people may lack the time to attend religious services; for instance, surgeons may find it difficult to attend Friday congregational prayers because of the vagaries of their operating schedules. The physical demands of certain jobs may create additional obstacles; professional athletes cannot perform the Ramadan fast without endangering their health and impairing their performance. At the other extreme, "nihilistic secularism" seeks to eradicate religion as a source of superstition, anxiety, and false hope. Working actively to undermine religious beliefs, it aims to sideline clerics.[42]

Other types, known collectively as "assertive secularism," seek to weaken and transform religion without destroying it. They do so by denigrating religiosity, restricting clerical communications, punishing religious acts, outlawing religious congregations, and regulating houses of worship, often to serve a temporal agenda.[43] Its Islamic variants invariably place mosques under government control. Some government agency restricts and monitors mosque activities; it also advances state objectives, say, by dictating the content of Friday sermons. Unlike passive secularism, assertive secularism tries to direct the transformation of religious life; and unlike nihilistic secularism, it aims to coexist with a subordinated and confined form of religion.

All three forms of secularism played prominent roles in the Western political cultures that inspired Middle Eastern secularizers. Freedom of conscience was an integral element of early modern European governance systems and their offshoots in certain European-settled territories, such as the United States.[44]

The Marginalization of Islam

Anticlericalism has been another salient European theme. The Protestant Reformation, which started in 1517, and the French Revolution of 1789 led to widespread dispossession of church properties. Both events weakened clerics politically.[45] During the half-millennium that began with the Reformation, many regimes separated church and state. Some of them also took to stigmatizing clerics eager to maintain salient political roles.[46]

The secularist campaigns of Middle Eastern modernizers drew on all these varieties of secularism. On the one hand, they embraced freedom of conscience, but in a limited form. Tolerating irreligiosity as well as forms of Islam compatible with their social visions, they persecuted dissenters. They also dispossessed clerics, largely by nationalizing remaining waqfs. On the other hand, the region's secularizers refrained from separating mosque and state. Establishing state agencies to tame Islam, they filled them with clerics willing to accommodate Westernizing reforms.[47] In brief, the region's modernizers pursued pragmatic policies designed to contain Islam but also to transform it into an instrument of modernization.

SECULARIST RELIGIOUS REPRESSION

As it became increasingly clear that traditional Islamic institutions are incompatible with modern economic life, the Middle East's secularists could have sought to live outside the confines of Islamic law without denying traditionalists the right to maintain lifestyles of their choice. Wherever they gained power, they could have extended to Muslims the choice of law that classical Islam always granted to Christians and Jews. "We are adapting to the times," they could have told traditionalists, and "if you wish, you can follow suit." Promoting unfettered religious freedoms, they could have withdrawn clerics' right to regulate social routines without denying the pious the use of their services on a voluntary basis. Conservative Muslims could still have had their children taught by clerics trained in traditional seminaries. They could have continued to take their conflicts among each other to Islamic courts. Clerics committed to traditional Islam could have kept preaching their ideals and interpreting events. In a nutshell, secularists could have promoted what one might call "libertarian secularism" – a form of secularism that combines the right to pursue new lifestyles with broad religious freedoms.

None of the Middle East's secular regimes provided religious freedoms to traditionalists. Support for comprehensive religious freedoms was absent in the nineteenth and early twentieth centuries. It remained highly uncommon even in later times. In the 1990s, a few Tunisian professors began campaigning openly for full separation of religion and state. The state would be neutral vis-à-vis religious choices, and individuals would have an unrestricted menu of options, from atheism to ultra-puritanical Islam. Intolerant secularism is as destructive as intolerant religion, argued Mohamed Talbi, one of these professors. Complete separation of religion from politics is unattainable, said Hmida

Ennaifer, another member of the group, but the state must respect and enforce religious liberties for everyone. Yadh Ben Achour demanded for Muslims, but also for atheists and polytheists, the freedom of belief accorded to Christians and Jews.[48]

These Tunisian professors understood that their proposals entailed radical departures from what passed as secularism across the region. Every secular regime of the Middle East had dismantled institutions central to Muslim life. Trying to make Islam invisible, and redefining the concept of "good Muslim," they had replaced one form of religious repression with another. Their modernization programs had not freed citizens from religious constraints.

Founded in 737, the Zaytouna Madrasa of Tunis became a highly prestigious center of Islamic learning. In French Tunisia (1881–1956), it billed itself as the world's oldest college. After independence, President Bourguiba shut it down as part of his campaign to secularize Tunisian life; the advanced study of religion was to be conducted at the Faculty of Religious Science and Theology, part of the University of Tunis.[49] Bourguiba's role model was Atatürk, who, in 1924, had dealt even bigger blows to Turkish Islam. Under Atatürk, Turkey abolished the Caliphate, entrusted the teaching of Islam to the Ministry of Education, and closed traditional Islamic colleges.[50] In both countries, the training of prayer leaders and preachers was transferred to agencies outside the control of traditional clerics; and the teaching of Islam disappeared from school curricula.[51]

In Egypt, too, secularists aimed to bring religious institutions under state control, though they could not go as far Tunisia or Turkey. In 1961, a decade after Nasser took power, the Egyptian government was administering just 17.5 percent of the country's mosques, though many private mosques were emulating the regulated ones to escape state takeover. But Nasser's regime succeeded in curbing Al-Azhar's conservative influence. It also enhanced Al-Azhar's ability to compete with the Muslim Brotherhood and other anti-regime Islamists. Nasser's team achieved the former objective by reassigning some of Al-Azhar's functions to government ministries, reorganizing it, controlling its appointments, and updating its curricula. The latter objective required giving Al-Azhar access to state resources.[52]

As secularist regimes dismantled the institutional bases of orthodox Islam, they also sought to curtail public displays of religiosity. Religious symbols were removed from public buildings, which were also cleared of prayer spaces. Government communications were freed of religious references. Throughout the region, the coverings (hijab) that women wore in the presence of male nonrelatives had kept Islam on steady display. Secularists encouraged women to unveil as a sign of liberation, and they passed laws requiring women to keep their hair uncovered in public spaces. In Iran, Reza Shah Pahlavi's "Unveiling Decree" of 1936 banned veils and chadors in all urban spaces, except at home. In various cities, police and municipal officials enforced the ban by forcibly removing piety-signaling female coverings in the streets. To win favor with the regime, shopkeepers erected signs denying entry to veiled women.[53]

The Marginalization of Islam

During Ramadan, fasting heightens Islam's salience by altering meal routines and increasing mosque attendance. In secular regimes, having lunch in public view became an unofficial, though widely understood, requirement for advancing in government. Bourguiba gave speeches characterizing fasting during workdays as harmful to development. Refusing to adjust work schedules during Ramadan, and making state-owned restaurants keep normal hours, he stigmatized fasters as backward. Further, trumpeting his disdain for fasting, he appeared on daytime television during Ramadan and drank a glass of orange juice.[54] In Turkey, zealous officials required underlings to snack during fasting hours, making the secretly pious break their fast.[55] The pilgrimage to Mecca was prohibited from 1924 to 1947 – formally for wasting foreign exchange and exposing Turks to exotic diseases.[56] In 1944, stores were prohibited from displaying Quran verses on their walls.[57]

The Baath regimes of Iraq and Syria kept mosques under surveillance, officially to prevent them from driving a wedge between citizens and the state. To that end, they incentivized clerics to become regime lackeys and ruthlessly punished troublemakers. Baath-dictated sermons highlighted mundane Muslim teachings, de-emphasizing spirituality. All Iraqi and Syrian religious officials were regularly evaluated for political leanings. Iraq executed at least forty-one clerics between 1970 and 1985, most for membership in the outlawed Islamic Dawa Party, the Iraqi counterpart of the Muslim Brotherhood. Syria's regime killed around 20,000 Hama residents in 1982 in retribution for an uprising led by the Muslim Brotherhood's Syrian branch. Prior to the Syrian civil war that broke out in 2011, this was the bloodiest response to Islamism anywhere in the region.[58]

Baath regimes, too, sought to reduce Islam's visibility. In Iraq, military officers were prohibited from praying or attending a mosque as a group, lest others feel pressured to join in. Private funeral processions were banned, as they involved religious recitations, weeping, and ululating – acts that publicized religiosity. Food was banned at religious ceremonies in order to decrease participation.[59] Meanwhile, tribal and familial conceptions of honor were manipulated to incentivize informing on violators of state norms. Also, policies were implemented to make Islam appear vanquished. The call to prayer was outlawed. Holy places were desecrated. And a statue of Abu Nuwas (756–814), an Arab poet who celebrated wine and hedonism, was erected at the heart of Baghdad.[60] In Syria, religion was removed as a subject from schools. Regardless of faith, citizens were discouraged from wearing religious symbols in public. They were also required to keep public discourse free of "superstition" and focused on "reason."[61] In 1976, Syria's intervention in Lebanon's civil war on the side of Maronite Christians reinforced the regime's anti-Islamic image in the eyes of its citizens.[62]

By no means were secularist regimes content to leave Islam unregulated even in private spaces. Thus, they outlawed polygyny, reduced male privileges within the family, and raised the age of marriage. Certain regimes also replaced Islam's male-favoring inheritance rules with a secular system that adjusted shares in favor of females.[63] Moreover, secular regimes molded teachings of what Islam requires. By overseeing mosques, if not also by appointing preachers and dictating sermons, they fed congregations their own views regarding family relations, philanthropy, hygiene, state services, and children's education. They used sermons to discredit superstitions, cultivate respect for science, bolster nationalist as opposed to sectarian solidarity, and alter work habits. Atatürk and his followers treated Friday services as instruments of cultural engineering.[64]

Few of the secularist leaders who regulated the public manifestations of Islam were practicing Muslims themselves. They did not study religion, or attend mosque services, or fast during Ramadan. Typically, their only religious experiences consisted of Muslim burials. They held a low opinion of clerics. Blaming them for many ills, including economic underdevelopment, they commonly treated them with contempt. Open resistance to modernization on the part of devout Muslims proved, they thought, that piety was a cover for obscurantism. Secular regimes used incidents of open resistance to secularization as pretexts for tighter religious regulation. Turkey's "Menemen incident" of 1930 and Egypt's "Military Academy attack" of 1974 are cases in point. The former refers to a messianic uprising led by seven illiterate men who proclaimed the restoration of Islamic law. When an unarmed reserve officer tried to intervene, the rebels beheaded him and, before a jubilant crowd, paraded his head on a pole. Military units sent to quell the rebellion killed three of the rebels on the spot; the rest were caught and tried, along with hundreds of onlookers; twenty-eight offenders were hanged, and dozens were sentenced to jail.[65] The Egyptian case was instigated by Hizb ut-Tahrir, an Islamist organization aiming to establish a global caliphate. About 100 of its militants stormed the armory of the Military Academy in Cairo and seized weapons and vehicles. They had planned to assassinate President Sadat and other top leaders at an event nearby, occupy radio and television headquarters, and restore Islamic rule. Guards confronted the militants before they left the school. Many militants died in the ensuing gunfight; thirty-one survivors were convicted of attempting to overthrow the government; two were executed.[66]

For decades after the Menemen incident, successive Turkish governments used it to keep alive the specter of a mass Islamist uprising. The fear induced in irreligious Turks served as a pretext for religious regulations such as excluding headscarf-wearing women from universities. In the same vein, Egyptian leaders used the 1974 attack and similar incidents to justify close surveillance of Islamist communities, censorship of Islamist publications, and restrictions of Islamist political rights. Islamists have been barred from forming philanthropic associations and organizing peaceful protests for reasons of state security. From 1981 to Mubarak's toppling in 2011, Egypt was continuously under emergency rule, which served to suppress dissent generally.[67]

The official historiography of the Menemen incident inflated the numbers involved. It also portrayed the bloody event as the work of a hidden network seeking opportunities to strike harder.[68] The exaggeration of such cases of resistance and the associated crackdowns made the pious downplay religiosity in public spaces, lest they arouse suspicion. It discouraged participation in Friday prayer services, though not necessarily mosque gatherings, for mosques served, as they had in Ottoman times, as sites of socialization and mutual assistance.[69] In Egypt's case, public spaces were already quite Islamized by the time of the 1974 attack. What was repressed was not piety per se but rather communal religious activities that threatened the state. Under secular regimes, the Middle East's religious landscape thus replicated a pattern with a long history: religious repression justified as a survival tool. Just as Ottoman and Safavid rulers persecuted heterodoxies to consolidate power and weaken political opponents, so the Middle East's secularists limited religious freedoms to protect modernization projects.

THE LOGIC OF SECULARIST REPRESSION

If they even recognized the historical continuity, ideologists of the reforms did not acknowledge it. On the contrary, they portrayed their initiatives as a rupture with the past. One big difference, they held, is that their policies served progress, liberation, and enlightenment. Excluding religion from public spaces made policy discussions more rational; unveiling women allowed their participation in social life as equals; and overseeing sermons protected congregations from superstition. Their predecessors had trapped people in a state of ignorance that left Muslim societies impoverished, powerless, and militarily outclassed.[70] It follows, held the reformists, that restricting religious freedoms would protect a more valuable freedom, namely the freedom to avoid religious harms.[71]

Insofar as they acknowledged that their reform policies entailed religious repression, modernizers added a strategic reason for restricting freedom of conscience. If given a chance, they imagined, obscurantists hiding within mosque congregations would force their religious preferences on everyone else. By implication, full freedom of conscience was not a sustainable option; complete mosque–state separation – the compact that some Tunisian academics would put forth in the 1990s – was self-defeating. A choice had to be made between two forms of repression: Islamic fanaticism and coerced modernization.

The freedom-for-all ideal could be implemented under one of two conditions. The first was a broadly shared respect for genuine freedom of belief. There was ample evidence, Middle Eastern secularist leaders believed, that this condition was absent. Although secularist leaders exaggerated the size of the constituency sympathetic to coerced religion, they were right that a critical mass of Islamists could instigate a self-reinforcing transformation of public opinion in favor of Islamist hegemony. As we shall see, following the relaxation of restrictions on Islamists, such a transformation unfolded in country after country. The other precondition of full religious liberty was political checks and balances. These would keep any one group from using the state to extinguish freedoms it deems offensive. No Middle Eastern state had the requisite institutions, which could not be created on short order.

Some secularists considered their illiberal measures transitional. In Western Europe, Christianity had weakened during modernization. Besides, as the Middle East developed economically, its people were also becoming less religious in two senses: decline in public worship and secularization of thought.[72] Insofar as trends continued, opposition to secularism would soften, reducing the need to protect it through force.[73] This logic harkens back to Friedrich Engels' prediction that under socialism the need for coercively enforced laws would dissipate, allowing the state to wither away.[74]

The variants of Islam that secularists repressed were not limited to the orthodoxy prevailing before their own ascent to power. In every secularist regime, the beliefs of pious Muslims spanned a wide range. Rejecting the official Islam of the prevailing secularist regimes, many belonged to formally unrecognized and often illegal sects that published clandestine literature, met secretly, and operated mutual help networks in the shadow of the law. Certain sects had millions of members, and some had revered spiritual leaders who issued instructions on how to vote.[75] Secularists saw well-organized sects as threats to their ideals. They reasoned that if these sects were given enough freedom and allowed to grow, economic progress would stall. Hence, the leaders of sundry sects were persecuted as deranged reactionaries. Their networks were infiltrated and broken up, and their followers were treated as criminals.[76]

Preemptive persecution of illiberal Islamists was compatible with maintaining the freedoms of devout Muslims who respected the freedoms of others. In practice, though, secular leaders conflated coercive Islamism with harmless piety.

9

The Resurgence of Assertive Islamism

In the Middle East's secularist regimes of the twentieth century, the exclusion of religion from public life sowed discontent, as did the regulation of private religious activity. Especially in rural areas, small towns, and poor urban neighborhoods, diverse believers found the constraints stultifying. Defiance of secular mandates became increasingly common. In response, secularist leaders followed the template of the Ottomans and Safavids. On the one hand, they intensified the repression of groups opposed to reforms. On the other, they made concessions to politically tame groups that seemed to want merely to lead openly religious lives. The compromises made Islam more visible to secularist constituencies. Secularists became more and more accustomed to public acts of religiosity. In Iran and Turkey, for instance, women wearing headscarves became a familiar sight in commercial areas that were once fully secularized.

The resurfacing of religiosity induced adjustments in the public persona of elites themselves. Politicians, entertainers, and journalists started pandering to the pious by feigning piety themselves. Religious preference falsification thus reversed direction. Now it exaggerated not genuine irreligiosity but genuine piety. Secularist regimes also adopted policies pleasing to pious constituencies. They metamorphosed into religiously hybrid regimes that, to one degree or another, drew legitimacy from Islam. This transformation did not restore the status quo ante. Religious life could not possibly have returned to the days before assertive secularists achieved power. In the interim, apart from rituals such as praying and fasting, the substance of Islamic religiosity had changed radically. Certain domains that were once integral to living a properly Islamic life were now severed from religion even in the eyes of the most pious. For example, commerce, municipal services, and medicine were basically free of religious supervision.

Nevertheless, it remained possible to force Islamic orthodoxy onto the masses. As in the period before secularist regimes took root, Muslims could be compelled to perform Islamic rituals. Religious officials could treat emerging technologies as un-Islamic. Heterodox religious communities could be denied autonomous organizations of their own. As secularist regimes softened, bona fide Islamists achieved power in one form or another. Repression of secularists and heterodox believers intensified. The breadth and severity of the ensuing religious repression is evident, we shall see, in various global indices. But for insights into why religious freedoms in the Middle East are sparse by today's standards, we must review the processes by which Islamism reestablished itself in countries with experience of secularist rule.

As with secularism, Islamism has basic varieties according to whether it is coercive and, if so, the extent of its ambitions. "Passive Islamism," generally observed in settings hostile to Islam, seeks to Islamize the lifestyles of willing persons or communities without forcing religiosity onto others. "Assertive Islamism" strives to homogenize society according to a religious blueprint, if necessary through coercion. The modern Middle East has witnessed both forms of Islamism, and each has treated assertive secularism as its main political enemy. The most extreme form of assertive Islamism is "nihilistic Islamism," which aims to destroy anything its leaders deem non-Islamic. Although it has achieved power in the modern Middle East, with few exceptions its influence has been ephemeral.

Modern Islamist movements of all forms have been studied extensively from sundry perspectives. What follows in this chapter is not a comprehensive overview of their emergence or advancement. The goal is twofold. First, the chapter highlights how assertive Islamism and its reliance on longstanding Islamic instruments of repression transformed religious freedoms, with some groups becoming freer and others less so. Islamism first destabilized the equilibria reproducing secularist repression, then replaced them with new equilibria involving a different form of preference falsification – in favor of signaling piety rather than irreligiosity. Second, this chapter provides additional contextual background for the next two chapters, which explore the institutional factors, and specifically Islamic law, that have blocked the development of organized liberal variants of Islam.

RESISTANCE TO ASSERTIVE SECULARISM

As secularist regimes endeavored to make Islam invisible, a common response on the part of the pious was to accept the restrictions and practice Islam quietly, outside the public eye. They sent their children surreptitiously to unregistered Quran schools. They also joined secret religious brotherhoods, seeking guidance from spiritual leaders in private houses. In the 1930s, as Turkey's regime was becoming increasingly hostile to public displays of religiosity, Quran schools multiplied outside the gaze of the state.[1] Meanwhile, pious Iranian women were circumventing their own religious restrictions whenever they could do so safely. Reluctantly abiding by the Unveiling Decree in

The Resurgence of Assertive Islamism

secularized spaces, they would re-veil in areas free of state surveillance.[2] Turks and Iranians who practiced Islam clandestinely did not necessarily oppose the right to remain irreligious or even antireligious. Some of them wanted religious freedoms for themselves without denying them to others.

In varying degrees, though, the region's pious masses resented the coercion that fostered a bifurcated existence: indifferent to religion in public settings, devout among family and trusted friends. They wanted to be themselves consistently, to share their religious views freely, to dress according to their own understandings of Islam, to join a religious brotherhood openly, and to have the state treat sects as legitimate associations pursuing respectable goals. In a nutshell, they wanted political elites to respect public religiosity and legitimize religious associations.

As secularist restrictions tightened, some devout people found living in truth, with all its reprisals, preferable to hiding in a religious closet. Veils began appearing in neighborhoods that were once fully secularized. Beards signaling piety gained visibility on university campuses. In conservative neighborhoods, restaurants began closing during fasting hours. The chronology of such initial acts of defiance varied across countries. But they formed a common pattern. Invariably, the first acts of insubordination consisted of self-initiated moves decoupled from any political agenda. They had the effect, though, of encouraging other pious individuals to begin self-identifying as religious. They also led associations pursuing a religious cause – mosque construction, religious charity, aiding Quran schools – to operate openly and seek a legal identity. In getting established, such associations typically conveyed narrow goals that respected the prevailing principles of secularism.

Where there is hidden discontent, aspiring leaders will sense opportunities to form organizations that publicize, if not also address, the underlying problems. So it was in this case. Ambitious conservatives, often people with a traditional education and a modest upbringing, started openly to criticize official religious controls and to demand tolerance of unofficial interpretations. Going further, some objected to the coerced privatization of religion. Rising numbers took to equating secularism with Godlessness. Charismatic religious leaders started to denigrate secularism. They also took the lead in bringing Islam back into public life. The most prominent include Hasan al-Banna (1906–49), the teacher who founded Egypt's Muslim Brotherhood in 1928; Said Nursi (1877–1960), the Kurdish theologian who inspired an anti-secularist Islamic revival movement in Republican Turkey; and Ruhollah Khomeini (1902–89), the Iranian cleric who resisted the Pahlavi monarchy's Westernizing reforms and led the revolution that toppled it in 1979.[3] Each of these dissidents became far more popular than the typical cleric, who took orders from secular governments without a fuss. One reason lies in their outspokenness. People flocked to them because they articulated grievances and visions that millions shared privately. Dissenting clerics developed huge followings also because, unlike secularist leaders who treated them as backward, they dignified the religious masses.

DYNAMICS OF ANTI-SECULARISM

Every social movement relies on interconnected individual decisions that incentivize others to join in. Once it achieves a critical mass, each new supporter reduces the risk of punishment for other joiners. In spreading awareness of certain preferences, it also awakens people to new political possibilities, enlarging the constituency that supports the cause at least privately. Some acts are especially influential because of the courage they convey and the virtuosity of the performance. Such was the case when Hind Chelbi, a renowned conservative professor, appeared, in 1975, at a televised Ramadan evening talk organized, ironically, to portray Bourguiba as a tolerant leader. Wearing a veil, Chelbi criticized Tunisians who aped other societies. She also asserted that dress is as fundamental to a nation's identity as its language. If her challenge to Tunisian secularism was shocking, so was her refusal, before a national audience, to shake Bourguiba's hand. Her audacity, the lively debate that ensued in the Tunisian press, and the regime's decision to let her go unpunished all signaled to alienated Tunisians that their struggle against secularism had reached a milestone. They inferred that the regime felt vulnerable. The founders of Ennahda, the Islamist movement that was established in 1981 and won the first Tunisian election of 2011, cite Chelbi's talk as an electrifying moment that gave them the self-confidence to go on record as dissidents. A "big wave of women" began to veil themselves, recalls an early Islamist.[4]

Ennahda's initial demands included withdrawal of the veiling ban and propagation of religious values to fight corruption and decadence. A decade after its founding, it asserted a right to participate in politics, openly stating that it aimed to restore Islam's role as a guidepost in policy making.[5] Neither Ennahda nor the region's other anti-secularist organizations wanted to revive a premodern orthodoxy. Just as the Bektashis became less mystical while in hiding, so under assertive secularism the aspirations of the pious changed enormously. For one thing, they and especially their children internalized many secularist reforms, including the transfer of various social functions from clerics to modern professionals. For another, they made peace with transplanted institutions at odds with Islamic law, such as the corporation, the stock market, and, to a degree, impersonal exchange. They also accepted modern institutions of governance, including parliaments, ministries, and municipalities. When Islamists talked about restoring the supremacy of Islamic law, they tended to mean it in a limited sense, to apply mainly to family matters and gender relations. The boldest Islamists demanded the re-legalization of polygyny and child marriage. But even they considered most major reforms of the preceding century both essential and irreversible.

Organized anti-secularist movements included political parties and civic associations that wanted Muslims to live according to an austere interpretation of Islam. Though some were based in socially conservative Arab kingdoms, others were active in secularist regimes. Still others, including assorted networks based outside the Middle East, operated globally.[6] The major Islamist movements, all more moderate, gave secular audiences reasons to confuse them with militant organizations. One consisted of slogans that inflated the practical impact of their agendas, such as "Islam is a way of life" and "Sovereignty belongs to Allah, not the people." The other source of confusion was their characterization of secular Muslims as traitors, agents of the West, sometimes even apostates. Such rhetoric gave secular Muslims reason to treat Islamists as enemies of cherished reforms. Convinced that Islamists sought to reinstate a social order responsible for backwardness, secularist leaders kept excluding them from governing bodies. They also punished influential Islamists who questioned the legitimacy of their regimes. Examples include the jailing and banishment of Said Nursi by Turkey's leaders from the 1930s through the 1950s, Nasser's execution of Sayyid Qutb in 1961, and Khomeini's exile by the Pahlavis from 1964 to 1979.

Every crackdown by a secularist regime softened Islamist demands, but only temporarily. It also deterred sympathizers of Islamist movements from openly joining their ranks. Reluctantly, many sympathizers continued to support the secularist agenda, including its repressive policies. At the same time, persecutions of prominent Islamists signaled growing organized resistance to the political status quo. They also made believers passing as irreligious realize that their fellow dissimulators were beginning to drop their masks and assert broader religious freedoms. They awakened hope that the openly pious could gain legitimacy in the eyes of elites, eventually even a seat at the political bargaining table. Although some Islamist leaders were pressured into withdrawing from politics, others kept struggling even in the face of harassment and imprisonment. Their recorded and widely circulated ordeals gave them moral stature. Even if they had few open followers initially, their movement was poised to explode if ever circumstances allowed them to operate openly.

In every secularist country of the region, a single organization became the primary voice of Islamists. With variations in timing and specifics, the sequence of events was the same. Through persistent agitation in the streets, on campuses, and in professional associations, the organization gains grudging recognition as a player to be reckoned with. Initially, it stays out of national politics. However, as its popularity grows, it begins fielding candidates. Against great odds, under rules designed to minimize the electoral success of Islamists, they advance politically. They broaden their demands, and the secularist establishment responds with a crackdown. Leaders are rounded up. Censorship tightens. Vilification intensifies. The movement reduces its visibility. Before long, assorted acts of defiance make secularist officials view the status quo ante as infeasible. Divided on how to counter Islamism, they let the movement return to formal politics. Islamist candidates win even more support. Once again, the establishment manages to push the movement back underground. This seesaw continues until Islamists, growing in numbers, make it into a coalition government, or they gain the right to govern on their own. This progression of events horrifies the secularist intelligentsia even as it starts making compromises. Convinced that it was an epic mistake to legitimize Islamist politics, it portrays the ongoing trajectory as a step back to the Middle Ages. Secularists start treating Islamist moves as evidence of unfolding tyranny.

In Egypt, it was the Muslim Brotherhood that became the flagship of the Islamist resistance. Attracting members through outreach, the Brotherhood began to lambast the prevailing constitutional monarchy as corrupt and to promote Islam as "the solution." Initially, it shunned political power itself. By 1941, though, the Brotherhood felt strong enough to field candidates in parliamentary elections. Alarmed by its claim to authority over what counts as Islamic, and sensing its electoral potential, the regime made sure all Brotherhood candidates failed. Yet with religious repression continuing, the Brotherhood kept growing. It tried to flex its muscles after Nasser came to power through a coup in 1952. Considering it a formidable rival, Nasser dissolved the Brotherhood in 1954 and, up to his death in 1970, persecuted its leaders ferociously. Though forced to operate secretively, the Brotherhood remained the focus of anti-regime resistance. When Nasser's successor, Anwar Sadat (president, 1970–81), tried to boost his popularity by branding himself the "Believer-President" and releasing jailed Brotherhood members as a counterweight to his leftist opponents, Brotherhood-affiliated candidates again tried to enter parliament, several successfully.[7] Meanwhile, the Brotherhood came to dominate many faculty, student, and professional organizations. Still formally illegal, it became the most influential segment of Egypt's historically anemic civil society. Under Sadat and his successor Hosni Mubarak, the Brotherhood endured alternating periods of repression and tolerance. Though barred from forming a party, its representation in parliament increased. At Mubarak's toppling in 2011, it remained Egypt's strongest nongovernmental organization by far. In 2012, the Brotherhood's candidate became the first Islamist to win an Arab presidency.[8]

In Turkey, Islamists were entirely absent from national politics during the Republic's first quarter-century. With the start of multiparty competition in 1946, brotherhoods serving the pious covertly – most importantly, branches of the Naqshbandi sect and the communities of Nursi's followers – entered politics indirectly. Initially, they urged their members to support relatively conservative parties that promised to soften secularist regulations. Some of their constituents found these parties too timid. The religious void that the population felt is evident in the explosion of associations to fund mosque building after this became legal in the 1950s. The share of such associations among all Turkish NGOs jumped from 1.3 percent in 1946 to 28.4 percent in 1968.[9] The members of religious associations acquired a bold spokesman with the founding, in 1970, of an Islamist party led by Necmettin Erbakan (1926–2011). His movement acquired a growing base among professionals, producers, storekeepers, farmers, and students who felt slighted because of their religiosity. Mirroring the Muslim Brotherhood's undulating fortunes in

Egypt, Erbakan's party was shut down four times as a threat to core republican principles. In each case, the party reemerged under a new name as soon as the establishment lowered its guard.[10]

Along the way, Erbakan's party served in several coalition governments without forsaking its polarizing rhetoric. Though its support increased, even many religious Turks considered it a menace. Sensing that political Islamism could never achieve full power without rebranding itself, a group of his protégés broke away from Erbakan in 2001 to form a new party, the Justice and Development Party, best known through its Turkish acronym, AKP. AKP billed itself as democratic, non-confessional, and committed to depoliticizing religion. Winning the 2002 parliamentary elections outright, it has governed Turkey ever since. Moving cautiously at first, in stages it ground down political checks and balances. And as democracy weakened, it became increasingly aggressive in expanding Islam's role in Turkish public life.[11]

In destroying the institutions of Turkey's democracy, AKP benefited from partnerships with two major branches of Turkish Sunnism, the Nurju movement and Naqshbandism, each of which has many subbranches.[12] The most influential Nurju subbranch, Gülenism, was led by the Pennsylvania-based imam Fethullah Gülen.[13] Gülenists established a major presence in the state bureaucracy, the judiciary, police forces, the military, and the private sector. They played a leading role in orchestrating vindictive show trials against Erdoğan rivals (mostly secularist journalists, academics, generals, and police officers), based largely, if not entirely, on fabricated evidence. Behind the scenes, AKP and the Gülenists clashed with each other over, on the one hand, dividing the spoils of their cooperation and, on the other, leading the contemplated dictatorship. The clashes became public in 2013 and they culminated, three years later, in a decisive break during a murky military coup against Erdoğan, which failed. A ferocious witch hunt against Gülenists followed, in Turkey and around the world. Tens of thousands of alleged Gülenists became victims of the very climate of fear their movement had helped to create.[14]

RETREAT OF ASSERTIVE SECULARISM

One difference between Islamism's political trajectories in Turkey and Egypt is that, unlike AKP, the Muslim Brotherhood failed to hold power for long. Dominated by politicians without managerial experience, the Brotherhood government openly tried to Islamize Egypt, and in a hurry. Its many radical moves catalyzed a mass reaction that toppled it just one year after its election victory. The general who took the reins in 2014, Abdel Fattah al-Sisi, decimated the Brotherhood, killing thousands. Yet under Sisi's leadership religion remains a salient feature of public life. There has been no return to the era when, at least in elite circles, religion became progressively less visible.[15]

Looking at the region's history from the rise of assertive secularism to the present, one sees that, in the face of growing Islamist resistance, secularists took measures to alleviate religious discontent. One common measure, which accounts for political advances of the Muslim Brotherhood, Erbakan's movement, and AKP, was to allow Islamists some political participation. A complementary measure was to soften secularism by letting religion return to public life, removing restrictions on private religious practices, and elevating the social status of clerics. Vote-seeking politicians took to signaling religiosity, promoting public religious activity, and forming alliances with secretive religious sects. The result was the same across the region, regardless of the type of regime. Islam's growing visibility fed on itself. There were also cross-national demonstration effects. Relaxations in one country emboldened dissenters elsewhere to demand further concessions.

The transformation was especially striking in Turkey, where assertive secularism had taken its most radical form. As it embraced electoral democracy in the late 1940s, conservative parties began to campaign, initially through coded language, for schools to train clerics and for the softening of restrictions on religious activity. The evident popularity of these measures induced the incumbent secularist government to implement them preemptively in the hope of retaining the support of pious voters. Conservative electoral successes allowed various formally banned religious groups to operate more openly. In stages, unofficial Islam reentered public life. Statesmen started to attend congregational Friday prayers, support mosque-building initiatives, and even insinuate membership in a brotherhood – often just to appear pious. Where in the 1930s Turkish state officials refrained from fasting during Ramadan, by the 1990s fasting (or at least pretending to do so) became the norm; and iftar (fast-breaking) dinners became commonplace even in secularist circles.[16] In the course of these developments, the tone of political discourse became increasingly religious. Even secularists abandoned their longstanding commitment to keeping policy discourses free of religious references.[17]

Meanwhile, in religious circles veiling among women became a symbol of liberation from coerced Godlessness. Growing numbers started wearing a headscarf. Although it became more common for women to be barred from public buildings for their attire, enforcing the veiling ban became increasingly difficult. By the time the AKP government lifted the ban in 2013, few universities, courts, or government offices were still enforcing it.[18] Other behavioral changes, too, raised Islam's salience in daily life. Alcohol-free zones and Islamic hotels proliferated, as did Islamic bookstores, "green" pop stars, Islamic fashion shows, Islamic dating sites, Islamic travel agencies, and gender-segregated entertainment venues.[19] The rise in public religiosity was driven partly by the surfacing of long-submerged spirituality. But it also reflected conformist pressures from Islamists. Women who preferred to remain uncovered were veiling for self-protection, to avoid harassment. With fear switching sides, preference falsification was now working in reverse, exaggerating piety rather than keeping it invisible.

That conformist pressures were now coming from the opposite side was evident even at the highest levels of government. From 1924 onward, Turkey's

Religious Affairs Directorate had portrayed Islam as compatible with Westernization, and pious critics generally kept their reservations to themselves. Under AKP, the Directorate routinely issued fatwas to legitimize policies that alarmed secularists, such as restrictions on LGBTQ+ activities and religious family counseling through state-paid imams. Its Friday sermons have heightened the emphasis on "shared Sunni identity" and decreased references to Turkishness, except in promoting discriminatory policies toward ethnic Kurds. In boosting Islam's visibility, the Directorate has also broadened its duties to include performing weddings, caring for refugees, issuing halal certificates, operating a twenty-four-hour television channel, running childcare centers, and treating drug addicts.[20] Some of its fatwas are eventually removed from its website without warning or explanation, either to appease critics or because they no longer serve AKP needs.[21] To forestall accusations of animosity to Islam, most secularist politicians turn a blind eye to the Directorate's Islamization initiatives.

Sisi's policies offer another illustration of secularism's retreat. He won the presidential election that followed the Muslim Brotherhood's brief and chaotic rule by positioning himself as the surest alternative to Islamist dictatorship. Yet in governing with an iron fist, he has legitimated his own dictatorship through religion. Outlawing the Muslim Brotherhood, he prohibited its apolitical activities as well. He also equated all dissent with treason, including reservations about his repression of the Brotherhood. By the same token, he refrained from privatizing Islam. On the contrary, by deferring to conservative Muslim sensibilities on cultural matters, he emulated his immediate predecessors, Sadat and Mubarak. Though the Egyptian Constitution allows atheism, his regime jailed Karim al-Banna, a twenty-one-year-old student, for self-identifying as an atheist on Facebook. As pro-government media erupted in outrage and reviled atheism as a threat to national security, Banna was found guilty of insulting Islam.[22] The goal of the Sisi regime's orchestrated war on atheism was to match conservative Muslims in appearing to guard public morality and honor religious values. Just as Turkish Islamism Islamized even the discourses of secular Turkish politicians, so the Muslim Brotherhood's religious illiberalism became the norm across much of the Egyptian political spectrum.

Because Karim al-Banna was Muslim by birth, his embrace of atheism amounted to renouncing Islam. It might look like progress that he was jailed and not executed. Yet exit from Islam is still punishable in Egypt, which accounts for its rarity as a public act. Moreover, public discussion on whether the Quran gives Muslims choice of religion remains anomalous.

The case of Tunisia displays the retreat of assertive secularism through the career of its chief architect. As Bourguiba excluded Islam from official public spaces, its visibility increased in conservative neighborhoods and relatively underdeveloped regions. Also, Islamist sheiks and imams gained popularity. With discontent rising, Bourguiba reversed religious policies that he once defended as essential to Modernity. School hours devoted to religion rose.

Working hours were now adjusted during Ramadan. State-controlled media started treating Islam as central to Tunisian identity.[23] As in Egypt and Turkey, piety signaling became customary among secularist politicians, even as they denied power to Islamists. Bourguiba's successor, Ben Ali, reaffirmed Tunisia's Islamic identity, made state television start broadcasting the call to prayer, and released from jail thousands of Islamists. He also performed a lavishly choreographed and highly publicized pilgrimage to Mecca. Such moves did not appease Tunisia's Islamists, who, by then, were a well-organized force. Secularists were feeling pressured to appear pious.[24] It is against this background that several Tunisian professors demanded full separation of mosque and state. They saw that secularists and Islamists were repressing each other and that religious preference falsification was rife in both directions.

For all their brutality, Syria and Iraq failed to keep Islam from encroaching into historically secular spaces. As Islamism started spreading in the broader Arab world and the Muslim world generally, Islam gained visibility in their Baath regimes, too. In neighborhoods around major mosques, Islamists managed to ban music and the sale of alcohol. It became common for veiled women to harass the unveiled. Both Baath regimes routinely allowed various coercive forms of Islamization, provided no weakness was signaled vis-à-vis an arch foe – in Iraq's case, Iran.[25] Even as they persecuted militant Islamists, they tried to ingratiate themselves with the pious.

In the 1990s, Iraq's Saddam Hussein launched a "Faith Campaign." It entailed building more mosques, repairing shrines, religious programming on state media, the closure of government cafeterias during Ramadan fasting hours, expanded religious education in public schools, periodic religious exams for Baath Party members, alliances with selected Islamic centers of learning, a "Saddam Institute for the Study of the Holy Quran," and adding the inscription "God is Great" to the Iraqi flag.[26] Saddam's Syrian counterpart, Hafez al-Assad (1930–2000), had already initiated a "Corrective Movement" to slow and soften secularization. A clause was added to the Syrian Constitution, which previously made no mention of religion or God, that the president must be a Muslim. Official media launched programs that promoted apolitical personal religiosity. A new edition of the Quran was published; known as the "Assad Quran," it had Assad on the cover. State media started characterizing massacres of Islamists as "God siding with the Baath." The state stopped preventing girls from veiling in school. It became legal to celebrate the Prophet's birthday. Personal Status Law was transferred to clerics, allowing the restoration of male biases in Muslim marriage and inheritance practices.[27]

Across the Middle East, Islamists consider the retrenchment of assertive secularism as a triumph for religious liberty. What they mean is that pious women can now veil freely, sermon givers no longer demean the lifestyles of believers, barriers to Ramadan fasting have fallen, and public religiosity no longer impedes professional advancement. No politician would dare mock Islamic institutions as Bourguiba did in a 1965 speech, during which he asserted that the French mismanaged their campaign to attract Tunisians to French citizenship. The French needed only to set up offices near Sharia courts, he quipped. Applications would roll in from Tunisians exasperated with Islamic law and its enforcers.[28] Yet Muslims outside the mainstream are not necessarily freer than in the heyday of assertive secularism; and nonpracticing Muslims are widely repressed. Millions are now veiling, fasting, and going to the mosque in response to pressures rather than because they genuinely want to. People praise Islamic institutions to pander to powerful Islamists. The state still promotes its favored variant of Islam. Only the mission of religious regulation has changed.

The timing of all these cases of secularist retreat is by no means mysterious. For one thing, because of civic weaknesses, it took decades for pious masses to find focal points for their grievances, for new leaders to emerge, and for forms of public resistance suited to the new political realities to develop. For another, rural–urban migration re-Islamized urban public spaces that were central to secularization. It brought to cities constituencies that had maintained religious lifestyles. In fact, the peasants who flowed into cities often became more religious in the process of adjusting to an alien environment. With secularists belittling them as uncultured and backward, many found comfort in religious associations that gave them dignity as well as social support. As migrant communities swelled, and they organized, appeasing them became a matter of political survival for all power holders.[29]

SUBORDINATE BUT RELIGIOUSLY FREER NON-MUSLIMS

The foregoing interpretation leaves out the region's non-Muslim communities. That is not an oversight. An unwritten rule of the Islamic Middle East is that local non-Muslims keep out of intra-Muslim affairs. They do not comment on controversies over Islam, at least not publicly. They do not interpret the Quran or Islam's trajectory as a religion. They do not question Islamic regulations, the content of government-directed sermons, or government funding for administering, teaching, and propagating Islam. Christians and Jews know that any pronouncement on such matters may be construed as evidence of disloyalty, ingratitude, and even hostility to Islam. The customary silence of local non-Muslims is especially striking because foreign non-Muslims – French Jews, American Protestants, German atheists – routinely contribute to discourses on every facet of Islam. Their works are translated into Middle Eastern vernaculars, sold freely in many places, debated, and cited. Because of their life experiences, Middle Eastern Christians and Jews are bound to have unique perspectives on this chapter's themes.

Except in Lebanon, which has the largest non-Muslim share of any Arab country, minorities are expected to accept a subordinate status. Most senior government positions are reserved for Muslims. A Christian or Jewish president is unthinkable, and many constitutions rule it out formally. In the minds of most of the region's residents, a "real Iranian," "real Turk," or "real Arab" is at least nominally Muslim.[30] Non-Muslim citizens are allowed to complain about the specifics of their rights. For instance, they may contest the treatment of minority schools and foundations. But the second-class status itself is off-limits to discussion, and subordination requires leaving intra-Muslim affairs to Muslims. There is nothing natural about these exclusions. In many Christian-majority countries, Muslims and Jews participate freely in discourses about the political influence of evangelicals, scandals of the Catholic Church, subsidies to religious schools, and interpretations of the Bible.

Along with faith-based political and expressive restrictions, the region's non-Muslims endure professional and social discrimination. Their military advancement opportunities are limited, or they are excluded from the military altogether.[31] In many Muslim-majority states, there are gender-asymmetric restrictions on interfaith marriages. A Muslim man may marry a non-Muslim woman, who would be expected to convert to her husband's religion. But a non-Muslim man may not marry a Muslim woman, lest she have difficulty raising her children as Muslims.[32]

For all their faith-based institutional handicaps, the region's non-Muslims are relatively freer in several important respects: interpreting their own religion, practicing religion in private, and conversion. In contrast to heterodox Muslims, Christians and Jews freely debate the requirements of their faith. Provided activities stay out of Muslim view, no one interferes with liturgical adjustments in churches or synagogues. Non-Muslims are free to move across denominations (for instance, between Armenian Apostolic Orthodoxy and Armenian Catholicism), convert to another religion, or abandon organized religion altogether. They can alter their religious life as individuals, unilaterally. But they can also make communal adjustments under the umbrella of a legally recognized organization. As of 2017, there were fourteen distinct Christian denominations with at least one active and legally recognized church in Cairo[33] and, as of 2018, there were fifteen in Istanbul.[34] Evidently, Protestant Turks are less constrained on how they practice religion than the 12.5 million Turkish adherents of Alevi Islam, a relatively permissive and liberal branch of Shiism. Despite their far greater numbers, Alevis lack state recognition. With some exceptions, they are barred from operating their own houses of worship. The Directorate of Religious Affairs expects them to follow Sunni rites. The European Human Rights Court ruled in 2016 that Turkey's second largest religious group after Sunnis is subjected to a "difference in treatment" without "objective and reasonable justification." As of 2023, though, the government has not budged.[35]

Historically, too, the Middle East's non-Muslims were relatively free to debate and reinterpret the specifics of their religion. In fact, during Europe's Wars of Religion, Christians were freer to discuss their theological controversies in the Islamic Middle East than in Christian Europe. That is one reason why, as Bernard Lewis observes, the flow of refugees was overwhelmingly from Europe to the Middle East – not, as in the present, solely in the opposite direction.[36] The region's attractiveness to Christians in the past is consistent with the choice of law that Islam, early in its legal development, granted to followers of other Abrahamic religions. Under the Pact of Umar (c. 718), a legal framework that regulated majority–minority relations in Muslim-governed lands, Christians and Jews were free to contract among themselves according to laws of their choice.[37] Like Muslims, they could do business under Islamic law and take civil disputes to Islamic courts. Unlike Muslims, though, they could choose to operate under an alternative legal system, for instance that of their own religion.[38] The logic of the Pact of Umar allowed individual Christians and Jews to reinterpret their religion without state interference and to move across denominations and religions.[39] A millennium later, it played a role in the successes of European missionaries in converting Middle Eastern Christians. Catholic and Protestant churches serving today's Middle Easterners are vestiges of the religious privileges that Middle Eastern Christians enjoyed in the early modern era. At a time when Bektashi Muslims could practice their rituals only covertly, the region's Western Christians were worshiping in state-recognized churches.

The share of Christians in the Islamic Middle East fell from 9 percent in 1914 to 2.7 percent in 2010; and that of Jews from 0.9 percent to 0.01 percent.[40] These declines resulted partly from emigration to countries with better economic opportunities, such as the Americas. Other factors include the exodus of Jews from Arab lands following the creation of Israel in 1948; the Christian–Muslim population exchange negotiated between Greece and Turkey in 1922; and the Ottoman massacres and deportations of Armenians during World War I.[41] But a deeper cause, which contributed to the latter set of factors, lies in Islam's denial of choice of law to Muslims. As the modern global economy took shape, the Middle East's Christians and Jews gained economic competitiveness by partnering with Westerners, often under Western rules. Muslims could not join the new economy until they undertook major structural reforms, collectively, through their elites. In the meantime, they fell behind in capital accumulation.[42] The ensuing resentments fueled policies to reverse the positional losses of Muslims. In Turkey, sectarian cleansing of Christians and a wealth tax targeted at non-Muslims helped Muslim Turks gain a foothold in lucrative economic sectors that non-Muslims had overwhelmingly dominated.[43] Jewish departures from Arab lands also created advancement opportunities for Muslim entrepreneurs.[44] Without the legal options that Islam denied to Muslims, non-Muslims could not have leapt ahead in the first place.

Policies to overcome the relatively poorer economic performance of Muslims thus played an important role in decimating the Middle East's non-Muslim population. The source of Muslim underperformance was a legal system that is now defunct. Islamic law has been abrogated in practically every sphere of life, and asymmetric choice of law is no longer an issue. Nevertheless, the region's legal history has shaped its interreligious policies through the economic dominance it conferred to non-Muslims. Precisely because of that dominance, secularist Muslims have been as eager as Islamists to oppress and drive away economically successful Christians and Jews. Turkey's wealth tax was imposed in 1942, at the height of its secularist period.[45] If religion per se was the main motive for discrimination against non-Muslims, it would have lightened under secularist regimes.

While state regulation of Christianity and Judaism is minimal in the Middle East, social regulation is not. The restrictions rooted in their subordinate status have been mentioned. Non-Muslims also endure conformist pressures within their own communities. Coptic Christians expect their fellow Copts to attend church on Sundays, and they turn on critics of Coptic Church leadership.[46] In Lebanon, communities pressure youths to marry within the faith.[47] In Turkey, the Armenian Patriarchate stopped sanctioning interfaith marriages in 2000, to preserve Turkish-Armenian culture.[48]

RELIGIOUS PREFERENCE FALSIFICATION

The Middle East's ongoing religious repression is often attributed to religious leaders trying to retain authority and block exits from their flocks. Al-Azhar sheikhs pressure the Egyptian government to disallow out-conversions and punish atheists. Coptic popes encourage their congregations to keep each other in line. But the policies of religious officials do not explain fully why the region is religiously repressed. The victims of such policies shape the religious climate through their own responses. Though our focus now returns to Muslims and Islam, the underlying mechanisms also apply, with institutional variations, to the internal dynamics of non-Muslim communities.

Secular Muslims contribute to their own victimization insofar as they refrain from articulating objections to Islamic orthodoxies, pretend to approve repressive policies, participate in vilifying the proponents of religious liberties, and feign religiosity – all to be left alone, or to gain social status, political advancement, or economic advantage. Such acts maintain an equilibrium whereby the proponents of coerced Islamization retain power. Victims of religious repression, even if more numerous than its perpetrators, refrain from articulating objections in the absence of a critical mass of fellow protestors. With millions of other victims behaving insincerely for the same reasons, freedom-promoting reforms fail for lack of overt support.

Religious repression is starkest when individuals are forced to perform public religious acts against their will, as when a Saudi religious policeman forces a retailer to close shop and head to the mosque. But most forms of preference falsification are invisible. For every Saudi shopkeeper openly compelled to attend Friday prayers, multitudes of others do so preemptively, to avoid harassment. Much of the pertinent evidence on coerced religious performances consists of private information exchanged confidentially within families or among friends. It becomes accessible to scholars only through ethnographic studies and anonymous surveys that require permission from

The Resurgence of Assertive Islamism

authorities with a stake in continued repression. Under the circumstances, no precise measures exist of religious preference falsification among Middle Easterners. Inquiries likely to challenge official narratives are not pursued. But some revealing statistics will be presented shortly.

Nowhere in the region do secularists hold powers akin to those they exercised in early decades of the independent states established between World War I and the withdrawal of European colonizers. When in power, they repressed Islam, forcing millions of genuine believers to practice religion privately and to pass as irreligious in public settings. Insofar as secularist regimes allowed Islamic rituals, they sought to homogenize them, empty them of spiritual content, and adapt them to their own goals. Persecuting traditional Muslims, they blocked open-ended discussion on religion, partly to avoid getting bogged down in controversies harmful to economic development and nation building. They presumed that religious conservatives would use expressive freedoms to resist modernization. Besides, opposition to modernist reforms would be transitory. It would dampen as new generations internalized a tamed variant of Islam.

Secularists could have used their time in power to broaden religious freedoms. They might have legitimized selected Islamic practices that they considered backward. They avoided that path largely in the belief that religious liberalism was unsustainable under the prevailing conditions. Indeed, Atatürk, Bourguiba, Nasser, and other secularist leaders all had opponents eager to reinstitute a coercive form of Islam. The Anatolian Şeyh Said rebellion of 1925, Islamist violence at Tunisian hotels and campuses, and assassination attempts on Nasser all testify to the potential for coercive counter-reforms.[49] Yet assertive secularism furnished reasons itself for considering full religious liberty unattainable. It gave pious Muslims excuses for restoring assertive Islamism, if ever they returned to power. Simply to protect the right to be religious, they would constrain the expressive rights of secularists and force them to participate in religious rituals. From the perspective of Islamists, denying the right to freedom from religion would be a price worth paying for guarding their own religious freedoms.

Institutions that secularists created for control and indoctrination have turned into instruments of their own oppression. Turkey's Religious Affairs Directorate (*Diyanet İşleri Başkanlığı*, Diyanet for short) is a case in point. From its beginnings in the 1920s, conservative Muslims despised it. They objected to the regulation of mosques by irreligious elites who disparaged piety. In treating pre-Republican religious teachings as sources of backwardness, Diyanet did not aim to cultivate tolerance for Islamic diversity. On the contrary, in mosques across Turkey, it promoted a single variant of Islam that was unobtrusive, apolitical, and barely visible in the public domain. A century later, secularists were the primary opponents of Diyanet's intolerant pursuit of religious uniformity. In 2014, a quarter of all Turks considered Diyanet a harmful political instrument of Islamism.[50] Often forgotten is that secularist modernizers founded Diyanet, following the norm, established in the early Islamic centuries, of accepting only state-approved forms of Islam.

Another perennial pattern is the weakness of civic resistance. Specifically, there is negligible pushback from groups that Diyanet spurns. Turkey's largest officially unrecognized Muslim community, Alevis, resent the sustained campaign to homogenize Turkish Islam. Although they have formed NGOs, none is powerful enough to end state regulation of their houses of worship, free the management of Alevism from Sunni oversight, or take over the formal religious instruction of their children.[51] Liberal Alevis may have been relatively less alienated under assertive secularism. But then, too, they lacked official recognition.

THE LIMITS OF RELIGIOUS HOMOGENIZATION

Regulators of Islam have never achieved all they wanted. Though Abu Bakr subdued the tribes that denied him allegiance, their Quran-based tax revenues quickly fell anyway, through emerging exemptions. Neither the Ottomans nor the Safavids managed to eradicate heterodox Islamic practices. Secularist leaders of the modern Middle East failed to keep Islam marginalized. Under Erdoğan's leadership, Turkish Sunnism has become markedly more visible; at the same time, religiosity among Turks has fallen, especially among the young, who were targeted to form a "pious generation."[52] Although about 1 percent of all Turks are formally non-Muslim, no less than 14 percent classify themselves as deist or atheist according to a 2017 poll whose subjects enjoyed anonymity.[53] A year later, another survey discovered that youths who consider themselves "religious and conservative" fell in one decade from 25 percent to 15 percent.[54] Most strikingly, participants in a 2018 workshop for teachers of religion spoke of "devotional confusion" among their students; outwardly conservative youths were converting in droves from Islam to deism or atheism, they observed.[55]

These findings on beliefs and self-identification accord with evidence of declining religious practices. Between 2006 and 2012, the Open Society Foundation found, the share of Turks fasting throughout Ramadan fell from 60 percent to 53 percent; and over the same period, the share praying five times a day dropped from 34 percent to 28 percent.[56] In the same vein, the World Values Survey's Turkish data show that between 2001 and 2018 mosque attendance fell for men, who are required, at least in Sunni Islam, to attend congregational prayers on Friday. The decline in mosque attendance went hand in hand with a lower share of the population believing in God, less importance accorded to religion, and decreased trust in clerics.[57]

In Iran and Saudi Arabia, too, state-organized religious coercion has lowered religiosity, but also satisfaction with Islamic institutions, or at least with those under government control.[58] Egyptians tend to be more religious than Iranians or Saudi Arabians, almost certainly because no religious police control their daily routines. But other forms of state-sponsored religious coercion seem to be causing disillusionment with Islam, as it is currently practiced. One indication lies in growing anxiety among Egyptian clerics over the spread of atheism. Of 87 million Egyptians, exactly 866 are atheist, says Al-Azhar. But a former Grand Mufti leaked that a 6,000-subject Al-Azhar youth survey revealed the atheist share to be 12.5 percent; and another sheikh estimates the number to be 3.7 million.[59] In line with these figures, the Arab Barometer found in 2018 that 10.4 percent of all Egyptians self-identify as "not religious."[60]

One cause of concern to the Egyptian government is the common view that atheists organized the demonstrations that toppled Mubarak. Another is the proliferation of atheist Arab magazines, online discussion groups, video channels, and resource sites. Egyptians are prominent in these corners of social media.[61] A reflection of such trends is the doubling, in the decade after 2011, of blasphemy cases taken up by Egyptian courts.[62] The Sisi regime considers "defamers of Islam" to be as threatening to political stability as militant Islamism. Committed to "battling atheism," it tries actively to prevent interactions among atheists. In December 2014, a Cairo café was closed following complaints that it was popular among atheists.[63] The state's hostility to atheism makes it impossible to measure Egypt's atheist population with precision. Many closeted Egyptian atheists act as "negligent Muslims." Others observe certain Muslim rituals, such as Friday prayers, simply to avoid persecution.[64]

Evidently, the ruled masses of the modern Middle East are resisting religious homogenization. Whatever the prevailing orthodoxy of their milieu – Sunnism, Twelver Shiism, secularism, modern Islamism – some are sustaining alternative beliefs, if not also alternative practices. While submitting to conformist pressures, substantial numbers are preserving convictions anathema to their rulers. Meanwhile, a concealed de-Islamization process is under way throughout the region. The Middle East has substantially fewer sincere adherents of Islam than official statistics suggest. Following chapters explore the implications for reform movements within Islam.

RELIGIOUS FREEDOMS IN THE MODERN MIDDLE EAST

All but six states of the contemporary Middle East grant citizens freedom of conscience through a constitution.[65] We have seen, though, that they all regulate every religion, including Islam. Government officials who privilege a particular interpretation of Islam typically vet, or even write, sermons delivered to Friday congregations. Non-Muslims are generally barred from proselytizing, and they face obstacles to building new spaces for their activities. Most Muslim minorities lack even official recognition. Interfaith marriages are constrained, if allowed at all. Governments also regulate the religious interpretations that may be discussed, defended, and disseminated. State regulation of religion is present outside the Middle East, too. However, the Middle East is an outlier. A standardized international index for 2014 shows that with respect to freedom

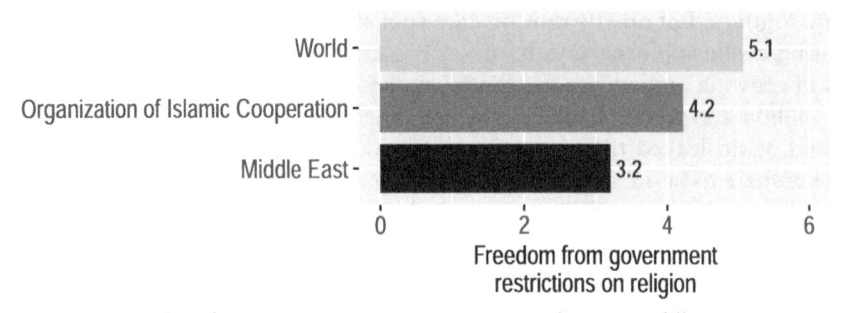

FIGURE 9.1 Freedom from government restrictions on religion: Middle East in global perspective
Scale: 0 (fully regulated) to 10 (unregulated).
Source: Derived from country data in Pew Research Center Government Restrictions Index for 2014, and, for population, World DataBank.

from government restrictions on religion, the Middle East scores well below the global average (Figure 9.1).[66]

Just one state in the region is formally secular: Turkey. Two others privilege Islam as a source of legislative guidance: Syria and Tunisia. Most treat Islam as the main source of legislation.[67] But regardless of whether and how they privilege Islam, all states of the Middle East pursue policies partial to it. Across the region, public schools mandate courses in Islam without providing opportunities to learn about other religions. Insofar as states finance houses of worship, only their preferred branch of Islam benefits; disfavored religious communities must fund themselves, and they endure bureaucratic obstruction. States pay the salaries of Muslim clerics but not those of other religious officials. They subsidize publications that promote their favored interpretation of Islam and debase other religions, including disfavored branches of Islam. In 2020, Diyanet had a budget twice as large as Turkey's Ministry of Culture and Tourism.[68] It propagated a variant of Sunni Islam favored by President Erdoğan, adjusting it according to his political needs.[69] For this reason alone, the secularism provision of Turkey's constitution serves only as a reminder that the Republic once tried to marginalize Islam. For all practical purposes, Turkey has a state religion.

A restriction of particular interest is the freedom to convert from one religion to another. The Middle East stands out as especially restrictive on apostasy, even in relation to the Organization of Islamic Cooperation (Figure 9.2). Almost all countries of the region have regulations that limit this freedom.[70] In Egypt, the state officially grants its citizens "freedom of belief" but not "freedom of expressing non-belief." Like many Egyptian citizens, Egypt's government equates apostasy with rebellion against public order.[71]

Nowhere in the world is government fully impartial across religions. To make Christmas a national holiday is a form of partiality. However, the

The Resurgence of Assertive Islamism

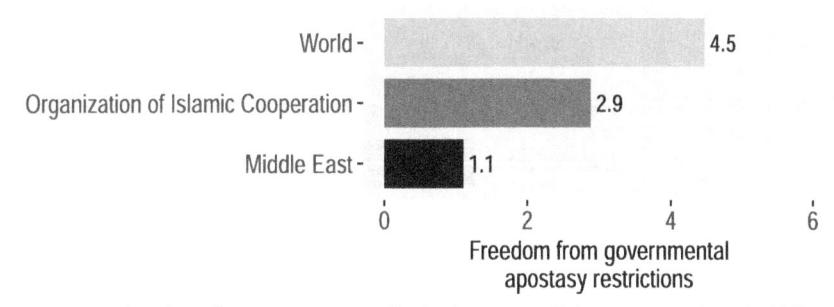

FIGURE 9.2 Freedom from government limitations on religious conversion: Middle East in global perspective

Scale: 0 (conversion forbidden) to 10 (conversion unregulated). The raw data are based on answers, for each country, to the binary question "Is converting from one religion to another limited by any level of government?."

Source: Derived from country data in Pew Research Center Government Restrictions Index for 2014 (GRI.Q.7), and, for population, World DataBank.

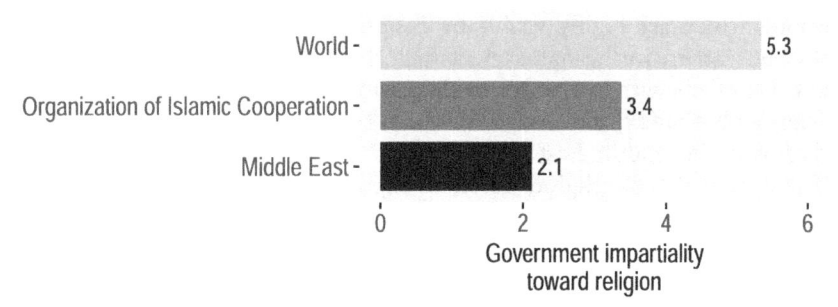

FIGURE 9.3 Government impartiality toward religion: Middle East in global perspective

Scale: 0 (fully partial) to 10 (completely impartial).

Source: Derived from Harris, Martin, and Finke, *International Religious Freedom Data, 2008*, and, for population, World DataBank.

Middle East's detachment from the impartiality ideal is particularly striking (Figure 9.3).

Formally legal practices may pose risks to individuals because of social regulation. The Ramadan fast is a case in point. Islam's fundamental sources make exemptions to the fasting requirement. Accordingly, no country requires individuals to fast. Nonetheless, in many communities eating in public during fasting hours brings scorn, harassment, and possibly also economic sanctions. In such contexts, people who opt not to fast for one reason or another – belonging to a different religion, irreligiosity, strenuous job, diabetes – consume food in private. Non-fasters are often numerous enough to justify keeping some restaurants open. Still, restaurant owners are pressured to suspend service

```
                World -  ████████████  3.6
Organization of Islamic Cooperation - ████████  2.4
           Middle East - ██████  1.7
                        0    1    2    3    4
                            Freedom from social
                            regulation of religion
```

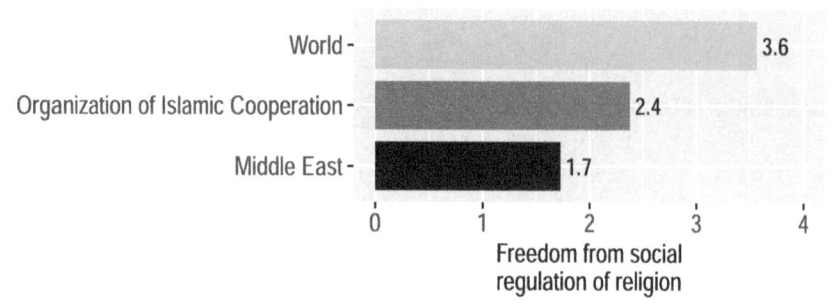

FIGURE 9.4 Freedom from social regulation of religion: Middle East in global perspective
Scale: 0 (full social regulation) to 10 (socially unregulated).
Sources: Derived from Harris, Martin, and Finke, *International Religious Freedom Data, 2008*, and, for population, World DataBank.

during fasting hours; or they close preemptively. Social regulation may also result in the concealment of religious activity. In some Middle Eastern cities, churches are hidden from public view behind high walls, in contrast to mosques, which are highly visible by design. The reason lies not in building codes but, rather, in the harassment that churchgoers face, especially during political conflicts with interreligious dimensions. According to the only directly relevant global index, freedom from social regulation of religion, too, is relatively low in the Middle East (Figure 9.4).

The dimensions of religious freedom captured through Figures 9.1–9.4 are not mutually independent.[72] In favoring a certain religion, if not also specific religious interpretations, states inspire and encourage social regulations. Conversely, social regulations embolden or impel states to control religious practices. In recent years, various parts of the Middle East have seen prominent persecutions for apostasy or blasphemy, and even assassinations. There have also been attacks on houses of worship offensive to dominant sectarian constituencies.[73] In some of these cases, the alleged religious offenses violated state laws; in others, only the sensibilities of religious zealots were at stake. Invariably, the state supported intolerant interpretations of Islam. It also facilitated social restrictions by failing to uphold the rights of victims.

The Middle East also ranks low with respect to expressive freedoms generally, including freedom of the press and internet freedoms (Figures 9.5 and 9.6). Religious speech tends to be among the leading targets of censorship. In various other domains, including gender, family, dress, international relations, education, and health, censorship aims partly, if not largely, at regulating religious expression. And religious functionaries are among the prime agents of censorship. Hence, Islamic institutions are involved in much Middle Eastern censorship even on matters widely considered unrelated to religion.

Discourses in the region are not equally restricted in every domain. On some subjects, censorship is uncommon, even nonexistent. For instance,

The Resurgence of Assertive Islamism

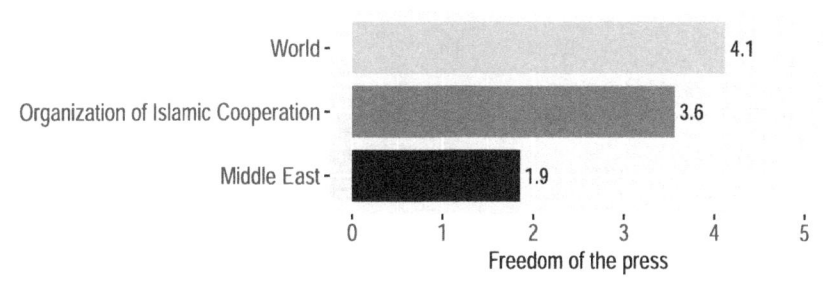

FIGURE 9.5 Freedom of the press: Middle East in global perspective
Scale: 0 (press fully controlled) to 10 (press totally free).
Source: Freedom House, *Freedom in the World 2020*. The data are for 2019.

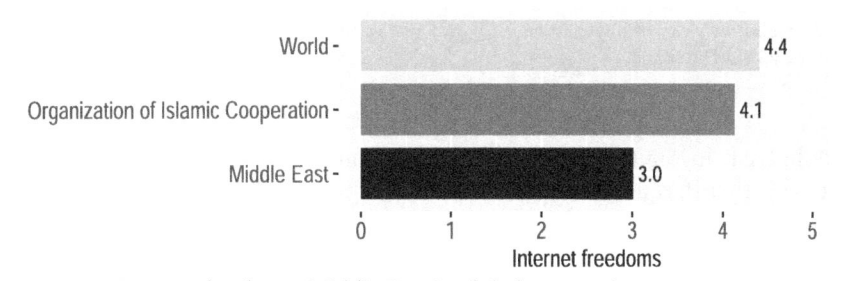

FIGURE 9.6 Internet freedoms: Middle East in global perspective
Scale: 0 (internet fully controlled) to 10 (internet unrestricted).
Source: Freedom House, *Freedom on the Net 2019*. The data are for the period from June 2018 to May 2019.

communications on chemistry and mathematics are essentially unconstrained. Scholars specializing in sea levels, for example, need not worry about religious taboos.[74] Domains differ in sensitivity because of their roles in legitimating power relations. Discourses on family structure are riddled with religious taboos because, from the beginning, Islam's content has involved prescriptions concerning such matters as marriage and inheritance. Besides, ruling coalitions have enforced these prescriptions for the sake of their own legitimacy. Like Islam's content, historical precedents constrain the regulation of public discourse. Today's regulation depends partly on regulatory patterns of the past.

HIDDEN IRRELIGIOSITY

For all the observed religious repression, the available scientific surveys indicate that, at least in terms of beliefs, regimes of the Middle East are not achieving the religious homogeneity to which they aspire. Of the sixty countries where the 2010–14 wave of the World Values Survey was conducted, thirteen are in the

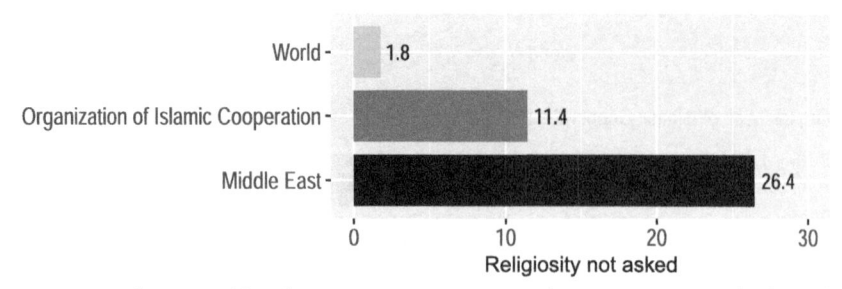

FIGURE 9.7 Where World Values Survey question on religiosity was not asked: Middle East in global perspective

Note: Each bar represents the share of the total population not asked, omitting countries where the survey was not conducted at all. The question asks whether the respondent is a "religious person," "not a religious person," or "an atheist"; "don't know" was also an option, as was declining to answer.

Source: Question V147 of Inglehart et al., *World Values Survey, Round Six*. The population data are from World DataBank.

Middle East. In the twelve Middle Eastern countries where respondents were asked whether they are a "religious person," 15.2 percent revealed that they are irreligious or atheist. And in the seven countries where people were asked whether they "believe in God," 0.5 percent replied that they do not.[75]

As striking as these figures – which exceed those one might glean from official data – is that in certain Middle Eastern countries the World Values Survey omitted one or both questions. The world's only country whose respondents were not asked the religiosity question is Egypt – on a population-weighted basis, about one-quarter of the surveyed Middle Easterners (Figure 9.7). And only eight countries were not asked the "belief in God" question, all in the Middle East: Algeria, Bahrain, Egypt, Jordan, Kuwait, Qatar, Tunisia, and Yemen; among the Middle Eastern countries surveyed, they hold around two-fifths of the total population (Figure 9.8). Tellingly, both questions were asked in all non-Middle Eastern OIC members included in the 2010–14 wave. These patterns accord with Figures 9.1–9.4, which depict Middle Eastern religious freedoms as conspicuously weak even within the broader Muslim world.

THE POSSIBILITY OF A HISTORIC SHIFT

Religious patterns in the contemporary Middle East may appear stable to casual observers. But they hide diverse strands of discontent. Public religious discourses and performances disguise rising irreligiosity, deism, and atheism. There are also practicing constituencies that feel oppressed by orthodoxies to which they are expected to conform. Individually and jointly, these dissatisfied constituencies harbor a potential for religious transformations. Should a critical

The Resurgence of Assertive Islamism

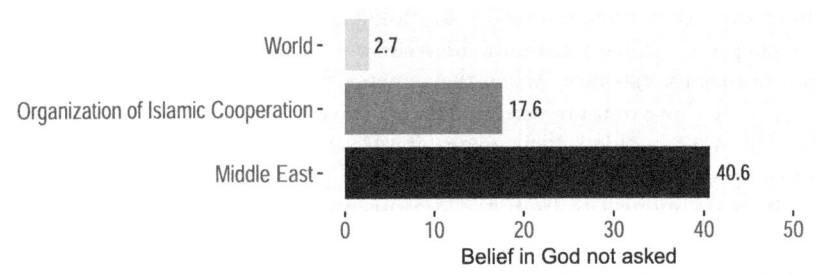

FIGURE 9.8 Where World Values Survey question on belief in God was not asked: Middle East in global perspective

Note: Each bar represents the share of the total population not asked, omitting countries where the survey was not conducted at all. The question asks whether the respondent believes in God. The possible answers are "yes," "no," and "don't know." Declining to answer was an option.

Source: Question V148 of Inglehart et al., *World Values Survey, Round Six*. The population data come from World DataBank.

mass of hidden opponents of the ongoing religious repression burst out into the open in some part of the Middle East, a movement for change could erupt through a self-augmenting process. And that explosion could trigger a domino effect whereby masses start challenging the local orthodoxy in many places at once. These processes could affect private religious preferences as well. Middle Eastern Muslims without well-formed opinions about the range of possible reinterpretations could find some heterodox alternative quite sensible once it enters public discourse. Meanwhile, other individuals may admit to themselves that they favor religious reforms. Spillovers from religion to other sources of discontent are also possible. For example, human rights and corruption generally could become targets of reform.

Under circumstances such as those unfolding in the Middle East, earth-shaking social transformations can occur at great speed, catching the world by surprise. Until the Berlin Wall fell, practically everyone considered communism invincible. Yet when a critical mass of disillusioned East Germans honestly poured out their grievances, the East German regime collapsed within days, triggering unanticipated uprisings in other Soviet satellites. Within the Middle East itself, the toppling of the Pahlavi monarchy and the "Arab Spring" stunned observers far and wide.[76]

Mass explosions do not necessarily result in major liberalization. Besides, gains may disappear quickly, as they did in Arab countries after 2011. The civic weaknesses that led to backsliding in politically shaken Arab countries have not been overcome. But the presence of hidden religious dissent points to a potential for mass public opposition to coerced religion. Any liberalization process is bound to be bumpy. Moreover, as with revolts that topple regimes, the timing of a shock to the religious status quo is inherently unpredictable.[77]

Religious communities forced into hiding usually lose members. But some members preserve their rituals and lifestyles out of the limelight, as they wait for opportunities to resurface. When they emerge from hiding, their practices will not replicate those that once defined them. The compromises of leading double lives will have molded their expectations and aspirations. Thus, modern Islamism promotes highly updated variants of premodern Islamic understandings. It bears influences from the reforms that conservative Muslims once resented intensely. Islamists are now comfortable with financial institutions, pedagogical methods, educational subjects, and governance practices introduced through Western-inspired reforms. Tellingly, the massive Islamist emphasis on veiling as the sine qua non of female piety camouflages more than female bodies. It also obscures the fact that the lifestyles of practicing Muslims have changed beyond recognition relative to those stigmatized by modernizers of the 1800s and 1900s. Heterodoxies of earlier times furnished precedents for such renewals. When the Bektashis fell out of favor in 1826, they were known for a mystical understanding of the Quran. By the time they resurfaced in the 1860s, they had a more worldly outlook.

Terms such as "Islamic revival," "Islamic resurgence," and "return of Islam" are often understood to mean that secularists battled with Islamists and lost. The story is more complex, if only because all parties have metamorphosed. Islamist women who don headscarves as a political statement differ in worldviews from their grandmothers who removed headscarves to accommodate secularist repression. Secularists have changed, too. Some of today's Middle Eastern secularists happily accommodate choices that their grandparents equated with obscurantism. For all this dynamism, though, Muslim religious freedoms remain limited. One indicator lies in range of Islam's variants. This range is considerably more restricted in Islam than in Christianity, the only other monotheism that rivals Islam in numbers and geographic spread.

10

Religious Diversification, in Fact and in Law

About 90 percent of the world's 1.6 billion Muslims are Sunni, and most of the rest are Shii.[1] The Sunni–Shii schism occurred just three decades after Muhammad's death, over the ensuing succession disputes. Each denomination has several schools of law (*madhab*s), which are living traditions initiated during Islam's formative period at prominent seats of learning.[2] Within each denomination, schools recognize each other, and their jurists study one another's rulings and reasonings as part of their legal training. Over the ages, schools have competed with one another for positions and influence, usually in a spirit of coexistence.

To outside observers, the doctrinal differences between the two denominations seem mostly minor.[3] But Sunnism and Shiism consider each other illegitimate. There is a long history of Shii persecution in Sunni-dominated states, and vice versa. Despite their formal collaboration in certain global bodies – most importantly, the Organization of Islamic Cooperation – there have been no notable efforts either to resolve doctrinal differences or to end centuries of enmity. There is no Islamic equivalent of the World Council of Churches, which has 350 members representing half a billion Christians around the world.[4] This council tries to bridge differences among Christian communities, some of which have fought extended wars with each other. It also runs interchurch aid, study, and promotion programs.

Each of Islam's two main denominations has spawned sects, most of which are geographically concentrated.[5] Examples already encountered include Alawi Shiism, whose 3.5 million adherents are centered in Syria, and Wahhabi Sunnism, the dominant creed in Saudi Arabia.[6] Such sects accept the core beliefs of their denomination but differ in rites and customs, often appreciably. Turkey's Alevi Shiis, who number around 12 million, do not observe the five daily prayers or the pilgrimage to Mecca. "The Quran does not require these rites," they say.[7] Sufism complicates this typology. Focused on purifying the inner self, it consists of loosely connected sects that may welcome both Sunnis and Shiis; several have non-Muslim members as well.[8]

The Sunni–Shii schism of 661 was not Islam's first. A schism in 650 had produced Ibadi Islam. Always a minor denomination, its adherents now number 2.7 million; most live in Oman, where they form a majority, and the rest are in East Africa.[9] Tolerated by both major denominations, they play a negligible role even in regional Islamic politics. A denomination of recent vintage is Ahmadi Islam, founded in 1889 in the Punjab. It has 5–15 million members, with the largest concentration in Pakistan. Ahmadism holds that Islam's "Rightly Guided Caliphate" was reestablished with the appearance of Mirza Ghulam Ahmad, the Messiah. Treated as infidels by both Sunni and Shii clerics, Ahmadis are persecuted in Muslim-majority countries; the severity generally rises with their share. For security, they moved their headquarters to London in 1984.[10] Apart from Sufism, which owes its survival partly to avoidance of politics, Ahmadism stands out as the only sustained post-661 challenge to the parceling of the world's Muslims between Sunnism and Shiism.

Given the Muslim world's massive traumas of the last two centuries, the paucity of new Islamic denominations is puzzling. Successive defeats at the hands of Westerners, territorial losses, occupations, civil wars, revolutions, economic underperformance, and marginalization in science might have galvanized far-reaching discussions about the shortcomings of Islam's prevailing interpretations. Were the ordeals limited to a certain region, there could be reasons to blame nonreligious factors. But strains and disappointments have been very widely shared. They have also been persistent. The Muslim world was visibly impoverished by 1800, and it remains economically underdeveloped in the 2020s.[11] Earlier chapters have shown that Islam's geographic core, the Middle East, is an especially repressed region.

MORE DIVERSITY IN FACT THAN IN LAW

The rarity of new alternatives to Sunnism and Shiism is remarkable particularly in view of the Muslim world's political divisions. From time to time, OIC members break diplomatic relations with one another. Feuds have lasted decades. Under Nasser, Egypt had notoriously bad relations with Saudi Arabia. When Iraq and Syria were both Baath-controlled, they were enemies. As regional rivals, Saudi Arabia and Iran have fought proxy wars. A Saudi-led Arab coalition tried to strangle Qatar.[12] Though most OIC members are republics, some are monarchies. Yet another political complexity lies in divisions within the Muslim-governed states that have meaningful elections. The electoral regimes of the Muslim-majority Middle East all have numerous political parties representing diverse philosophies. As of February 2015, Turkey had forty-four political parties, including nine with seats in parliament. Those without seats included fifteen left-wing, five conservative, six liberal, seven nationalist, and two green parties. Tunisia had fifty-four parties, of which fifteen had members in the legislature. Iraq had fifty-eight legal parties, plus two that were banned; eleven parties held seats in parliament. Evidently, Muslims are not immune to fragmentation. Significantly, the matters that divide Turks, Tunisians, and Iraqis into numerous political parties include the social role of religion. Each country has secular parties as well as ones with an Islamic identity.

In all three countries, multiple parties claim to represent the properly Islamic approach to governance. But they differ in policies and specific goals. That Islam has sundry interpretations is a theme developed by many prominent scholars, including Shahab Ahmed in *What Is Islam?* Ahmed points to contradictory claims by Muslims about the normative constitution of Islam not only on the margins of their religious discourses but also at the social, intellectual, and political centers of their arguments. Moreover, the contradictions lose visibility when Islam is conceptualized as spheres – religious and cultural, or religious and secular, as though there are self-evidently religious, cultural, and secular objects.[13] Ahmed's most poignant illustration concerns wine consumption. Based on a verse of the Quran, legal discourses prohibit it. But various nonlegal discourses laud it, especially ones among political elites. "Begin your drinking after the mid-afternoon prayers," advises an eleventh-century ruler of Iran. Through the ages, poets have routinely intimated that drinking wine deepens religious experiences.[14] Although countless Muslims have treated Islamic drinking traditions as perversions, Muslim wine lovers and prohibitionists view themselves as belonging to the same religious brotherhood. Why has the de facto diversity of what passes as genuine Islam not produced de jure diversity? To use Ahmed's example, why is there no branch of Sunnism, or of Islam itself, that openly and explicitly treats wine drinking as permissible? And, more generally, why have intra-communal tensions associated with the contradictions of Islamic teachings not generated formal religious disunions?

Compounding the conundrum is that Muslims have managed to live in peace with communities that Islam formally considers beyond the pale. Earlier, we saw that Safavid Iran welcomed Hindus, whose texts combine polytheism with a broader belief in divine unity.[15] Faced with far more polytheists, the Mughals of India (1526–1857) also opted for tolerance. While encouraging conversions, they did not force Islam onto polytheists who served important economic functions. In the interest of both revenue generation and political stability, they promoted trade across religious boundaries.[16] Though known for their tolerance toward polytheists, the Mughals did not extend choice of religion to Muslims. For fear of stoking Mughal disunity, they retained Islam's exit ban. In any case, no powerful force stood for the ban's abolition.

If Muslims can learn to live with polytheism, why, since 661, have we not seen any comparably large and durable monotheistic alternative to Sunnism or Shiism? Why is the richness of Muslim political organizations absent from Islam's main varieties? A related puzzle lies in an asymmetry in the major modern attempts to capture Sunnism and Shiism from within. Invariably, they have come from groups favoring a highly illiberal and uncompromising interpretation of Islam. Al-Qaeda, ISIS (Islamic State of Iraq and the Levant), Taliban, and Boko Haram are cases in point.[17] No liberal challenger to the dominant interpretations has achieved even remotely comparable influence. Previous chapters have furnished relevant clues. Drawing on them, this chapter and the next explain this pronounced asymmetry.

Boko Haram's base is West Africa, and most Ahmadis live in the Indian subcontinent or Sub-Saharan Africa. Although our focus remains the Middle East, we must now also pay attention to global trends. Just as the religion that helped to define European civilization was founded in the Middle East, so a movement that revolutionizes Middle Eastern Islam could originate elsewhere. South and Southeast Asia, jointly home to 45.6 percent of the world's Muslims, are obvious candidates. Europe, which has 52.0 million Muslims, is another. And still others are North America, Australia, and New Zealand, collectively home to 4.4 million Muslims.[18] Because they allow greater religious freedoms, Western countries could exert a disproportionate influence on Islam's trajectory.

The terms religion, denomination, and sect are used in many different senses, and there is no universally accepted classification system that relates them to one another. For our purposes here, a religion's branches are denominations, and branches of denominations are sects. Sects may have branches themselves: subsects, subsubsects, and so on. This criterion for subordinate relationships among religious communities is organizational. It sidesteps factors such as intensity of belief, time commitment, and rites, except insofar as they define co-religiosity among community members.[19] The cause of religious disunion could be a doctrinal difference that looks trivial to outsiders. If the subcommunities themselves consider it serious enough to hinder coexistence, they may reorganize as separate religious entities.

SCHISMS IN ABRAHAMIC RELIGIONS

When a religious community splits into two distinct communities, one religious brand gives rise to two. One new brand is created; and the preexisting brand may itself be transformed. A schism is not, then, the switch of a community between existing brands. In addition to organizational separation, it can involve innovations in rites, doctrines, and allegiances. The term "schism" presupposes some initial unity over matters that become increasingly contentious over time, culminating in organizational rupture.[20] Disagreements within a religious community do not automatically generate a split; every faith community harbors variation in tastes and beliefs. Dissatisfied members may seek change internally as an alternative to going their own way, or they may quietly acquiesce to the status quo. Differences cause a schism when matters important to sufficient members become openly contentious, and subcommunities that once considered themselves a single faith community start treating one another as outsiders. To an individual, switching religions can substitute for a schism. So can moving from one denomination or sect to another, or becoming agnostic, unaffiliated, or irreligious.[21]

Births of Christianity and Islam

A schism may unfold over generations. The birth of Christianity is a case in point. Early Christians were Jews who worshiped in synagogues, often with non-Christian Jews. Jesus was crucified as "King of the Jews." As late as 70 CE, most Christian communities considered themselves a Jewish denomination and were also treated as such.[22] But Christian practices and teachings were becoming increasingly distinct. The voiding of the circumcision requirement and new scriptures are among the manifestations of irreconcilable differences. As the differentiation progressed, Judaism's Christian denomination turned into a rival religion with its own organization.[23]

We already know that Islam emerged as a new interpretation of Abrahamic monotheism. Muhammad and his followers believed in the same God as other monotheists. They recognized Judaism and Christianity as legitimate but distorted variants of their own belief system. For their part, Jews and Christians initially treated Muslims as a syncretic Abrahamic sect that blended Judaism and Christianity. Meanwhile, the growing new community was sharpening its own identity. The decision to turn in prayer toward Mecca rather than Jerusalem symbolized radical novelty. As the differentiation proceeded, Islam became a new religion with partly hostile inter-Abrahamic relations. One cannot time the transition precisely. Perceptions as to when differentiation crossed a "red line" must have differed across regions and even within congregations.

Christianity's Great Schism and the Protestant Reformation

Another momentous religious schism is the split of Christianity in 1054 into two churches, one Rome-based and Latin-speaking, the other Constantinople-based and Greek-speaking. This "Great Schism," as it came to be known, followed centuries of differentiation in rites, doctrine, and organization. By the 600s, "catholic" and "orthodox," once used interchangeably, no longer had the same meaning. They defined two distinct, if formally still unified, families of churches.[24] The official rationale for the mutual excommunications by the Pope and the Patriarch was disagreement over the nature of the Holy Spirit. In fact, the two sides had grown apart also because of jurisdictional conflicts, procedural differences, legal divergence, and poor communication.[25]

Half a millennium after the Great Schism, the Protestant Reformation split Western Christianity. The Reformation's leading causes included both ideological innovation and distributional conflict. One basic cause was the swelling of payments that the laity had to make for eternal salvation. Another was scientific discoveries at odds with Church teachings. Still another was the invention of printing, which stimulated collective action against Church power by facilitating the dissemination of texts and images.[26] All reform movements were crushed brutally until 1517, when Martin Luther initiated the Protestant Reformation through his *Ninety-Five Theses*.[27] "Protestantism" is an umbrella term for various churches. Lutheranism and Anglicanism are examples. What united the early variants is twofold. Each offered a less hierarchical alternative to Roman Catholicism. And, unlike Catholicism, it enabled adherents to reach salvation without clerical intermediation. Protestant churches produced a burgeoning variety of subunits, offshoots that shared a mother church.[28]

Modern Schisms in Judaism

Judaism experienced two schisms in nineteenth-century Europe. They offer clues as to why modern Islam has seen many illiberal schisms but none providing a more permissive variant.

Across Central and Eastern Europe, the age of economic modernization and intellectual enlightenment brought greater acceptance of Jewish participation in mainstream society. In Germany, Reform Judaism emerged as a permissive denomination that facilitated Jewish participation in Christian-controlled milieus. In dress and diet, Jews would follow other Germans. Business on the Sabbath would be permitted. Prayers and sermons would be in the vernacular rather than in Hebrew. And the liturgy would avoid mention of returning to Zion. Concurrently with the rise of Reform Judaism, Orthodox Judaism emerged as a stricter alternative to traditional Judaism. Innovating in the opposite direction, it accentuated Jewish prohibitions and strengthened their enforcement. A Jew had to wear distinctive clothing, rigorously observe dietary laws, speak a language incomprehensible to Gentiles, keep the sexes socially segregated, and ignore "alien wisdom." Orthodox Jews viewed Reform Jews as heretics, even apostates. They also condemned the modest concessions that traditional Judaism made to Modernity. They held that cultural integration would extinguish Judaism.[29]

Jean-Paul Carvalho and Mark Koyama attribute both schisms to economic opportunities. Eastern and Central European Jews embraced Reform Judaism, they suggest, in places where economic development and religious tolerance enabled prosperity through integration. In return for increased financial contributions to the Jewish community, Reform Judaism relaxed Jewish life and reduced the time commitment for religious duties. It allowed Jews to accumulate wealth without shedding their Jewish identity – fully assimilating, as some Jews already had. For its part, Orthodox Judaism reduced conversions by minimizing cross-religious interactions as well as access to economic opportunities. Geographic variations in support for Reform, traditional, and Orthodox Judaism reflected prospects for enrichment. Where economic opportunities were ample, as in Germany, a lax denomination became dominant. By contrast, where they were scarce, as in northeastern Hungary, the tighter communal life achieved through strict religiosity outweighed the expected financial returns from social integration.[30]

As European Judaism split into three differentiated components, Middle Eastern Judaism experienced only minor splits. Moreover, the drivers of communal reconstruction were mainly foreign. One reason is that Middle Eastern Jews were more integrated into local life to begin with. Generally living near Muslims and often Christians as well, they were accustomed to adapting Judaism to changing social circumstances. Rabbinic teachings had absorbed diverse Islamic rules. Another difference is that economic modernization lagged in the Middle East, delaying sharp conflicts between religious duties and economic advancement. Notable attempts to form a legally autonomous subcommunity came from rich Jews with Western roots. In Ottoman realms, Jewish immigrants from Italy split from the Sephardi majority, as did those with roots in Central or Eastern Europe. Each community became an early reformer because of both professional needs and connections to European Jewry. A stimulus to broader-based Jewish modernization was the Paris-based Alliance Israélite Universelle (AIU), which, at a time when the Ottoman Empire was modernizing its economy and broadening non-Muslim rights, promoted Jewish empowerment through modern education. The AIU's success is evident in the proliferation of modern Jewish schools and dwindling enrollments at the preeminent yeshivas of Aleppo, Baghdad, and Tunis. By and large, rabbis made the accommodations required for successful modernization. Their flexibility limited pressures for a major schism within Sephardic Jewry.[31]

Beginnings of Mormonism

A recent Christian schism consists of the rise of Mormonism. At its birth in western New York, its adherents saw themselves as a vehicle for restoring genuine Christianity, which generations of Christians had corrupted. Yet they used an augmented scripture, including the Book of Mormon, considered as authoritative as the Bible. Persecuted, they fled in stages to the western United States. Some Christians consider Mormonism a new religion rather than a branch of Christianity. It departs, they say, from core beliefs common to Catholicism, Eastern Orthodoxy, and Protestantism.[32]

Commonalities

The reviewed schisms have three common elements.[33] First, breakaway communities consider the loyalists to have wrong or intolerably inconvenient norms. The loyalists often hold similarly adverse views of the leavers. Second, the leavers, and often the loyalists as well, consider it impossible to continue worshiping together. The disunited groups thus start conducting separate religious ceremonies, in spaces of their own. Third, the groups display mutual hostility. At least for a while, they deny one another legal rights, creating pretexts for violence. All three factors were present in the Protestant Reformation. Protestants and Catholics considered one another to have transgressed essential Christian principles. Protestants built churches of their own and developed new rites. And the centuries following 1517 saw long religious wars, most destructively the Thirty Years' War of 1618–48.[34]

A schism need not be permanent. Perceptions of distinctness and separation may soften through economic convergence, the appearance of a common enemy, or efforts at reconciliation. Moreover, rapprochement need not be uninterrupted or homogeneous. Tensions may subside in some places as they persist, or even rise, elsewhere. Christianity's Great Schism fostered numerous efforts at reconciliation, for nine centuries, all fruitless. At last, a Joint Catholic–Orthodox Declaration came in 1965. Deploring the "troublesome precedents" that caused a "rupture of ecclesiastical communion," it annulled the mutual excommunications of 1054.[35] Many high-level meetings followed, including joint prayer services that circumvented theological flashpoints.[36] In some places, rising intermarriage, which increases cross-participation in services, has made the reconciliation visible in daily life. Elsewhere, though, there are signs of resistance. Attitudinal surveys of Catholic and Orthodox Christians reveal wide variations in rapprochement. In Central and Eastern Europe, the share of Christians who view the other side as part of their religious family ranges, depending on the country, from one-third to above 90 percent.[37]

THE POLITICAL ECONOMY OF SCHISM

Although specific schisms have been studied extensively, no general theory exists on the determinants of religious ruptures. Useful insights can be drawn, though, from a heuristic device of Randolph Beard, Robert Ekelund, George Ford, and Robert Tollison (hereafter, BEFT).[38] The choice of whether to establish a new religious community is analogous to deciding whether to enter a "product space" through a new firm, they say. Accordingly, they reason that a schism's success depends on the selection of a "religious location" that allows enough converts to sustain operations. It also depends on the locations of preexisting religious communities and the distribution of religious preferences within the full population.

Consider the unidimensional example in Figure 10.1, focusing initially on panel (a). The continuum represents the possible options of a key religious trait. Adherents of the religion have ideal options distributed across this continuum. If the characteristic is strictness in observing Jewish requirements, R_m would represent traditional East European Judaism, R_l Reform Judaism, and R_r Orthodox Judaism. The schisms entailed exits from R_m to establish R_l and R_r. What determines the locations of R_l and R_r? A basic factor is the distribution of individual Jews' ideal points along the continuum. Insofar as maximizing community size was their goal, the founders of Reform Judaism would have

Religious Diversification, in Fact and in Law

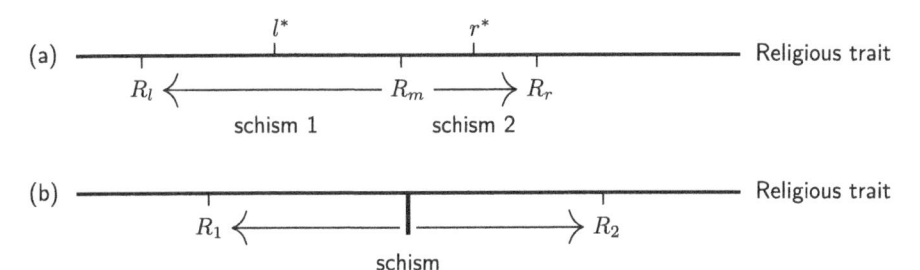

(a)

$R_l \longleftarrow \qquad l^* \qquad r^* \qquad$ Religious trait
$\qquad R_m \longrightarrow R_r$
schism 1 $\qquad$ schism 2

(b)

$R_1 \longleftarrow \qquad \longrightarrow R_2 \qquad$ Religious trait
schism

FIGURE 10.1 Two stylized schisms: (a) One religious community spawning a second and third, (b) A single religious community splitting in two

picked a spot that balanced the needs of Jews wanting radically relaxed rules and those seeking slight relaxation. R_l is the spot where the pressures from these subgroups balance out. Provided the distribution of religious preferences stayed fixed, this location would be stable. Analogous logic would have driven the location of R_r. In equilibrium, every Jew with an ideal point to the right of r^* would be Orthodox; those with an ideal to the left of l^* would be Reformist; and the domain of traditionalists would have shrunk to the space in between.[39]

The Great Schism followed a different path, which is depicted in panel (b) of Figure 10.1. Even prior to the division of the Roman Empire in 395, Christians of the Mediterranean were drifting apart, with no root community left behind. In 1054 the differences in rites and doctrines crossed a threshold that triggered the formal Catholic–Orthodox split. At that point, both sides formally recognized the vanishing of a geographically inclusive, trans-Mediterranean church. Their differentiation continued after the Great Schism.

CLASSIFYING ISLAMIC COMMUNITIES

All theorizing entails classification. In developing his theory of evolution, Charles Darwin used a widely accepted zoological classification developed by earlier biologists. Interpreters of religious schisms need an analogous classification. Alas, no consensus exists on what constitutes a religion, let alone religious branches. The sociology of religion presents myriad classification methods: functional, geographic, ethnographic, morphological, attitudinal, normative, philosophical, pedagogical, psychological, political, and more.[40] Hybrid variants add to the choices. This methodological chaos is reflected in the conceptualization of religious divisions. The most popular variant is the "religion–church–sect–cult" hierarchy. Developed to explain divisions within Christianity, it is problematic with respect to other religions.[41]

Either because they consider the controversies in the sociology of religion unresolvable, or simply for lack of interest in theorizing outside their expertise,

Islamologists have tended to limit themselves to concepts with an Islamic pedigree. A tradition based in classical Islamic thought starts from an apocryphal saying of Muhammad: "After my death, Islam will split into seventy-three *firqa*s." A contributor to this tradition typically opines that one *firqa* – his own – will go to Heaven and the remaining seventy-two to Hell.[42] This fanciful tradition is of no interest here. Within modern Islamic Studies, the literature aimed at systematizing Islam's divisions runs into the same dead-end as the Christian-centric religious classification. Overdoing parsimony, it loses generalizability. Despite its valuable insights, Fuad Khuri's work on Sunni subdivisions illustrates the problem. For Khuri, Sunni sects (*taifa*s) are religious protest movements that control territory.[43] By this criterion, Egypt's Muslim Brotherhood ceased being a subdivision of Sunnism at its ouster from power in 2013. Its members now tend to hide their affiliation. Besides, they lack political control even where the Brotherhood enjoys considerable sympathy.[44]

Taking a pragmatic approach here, I define a "religious community" as any organized group with a shared sense of spiritual fellowship and distinct religious rules and rites. The group need not enjoy outside acceptance. It could be illegal. Its members could be invisible to outsiders, as Bektashis were after Ottoman rulers took to persecuting them. Though the community will have rules of entry and exit, as well as a mode of organization, these, too, could be secret. A "religion" is a spiritual community of the highest order. When a religion subdivides, each branch is a denomination. The branches of a denomination are sects. Those of Sunni Islam include Wahhabism, the Muslim Brotherhood, and ISIS. By my definition, there are many others, such as Al-Azhar-centered Islam (official Egyptian Sunnism), and the Islam of Turkey's Diyanet (official Turkish Sunnism). Each Sunni sect is organized separately and has its own rhythms. But they all share a Sunni identity, which makes them subunits of the same denomination. Sunni sects typically have subsects. A subsect is often a community that follows a particular imam or charismatic interpreter, not necessarily living. Subsects may have subsubsects.

Each of the mentioned subdivisions has a geographic base. But its members are not tied to a single region, or even a single state. The Muslim Brotherhood is pan-regional. Diyanet contributes to the operation, or directly runs, mosques and other Islamic institutions in thirty-six countries. It also distributes publications in twenty-six languages.[45] New forms of Islam need not be centered in any one area or state. They could have global footprints and draw members from existing Muslim communities at multiple organizational levels. If a liberal variant of Islam emerged as a global branch of Sunnism, it might fill a spiritual space that is currently void in Shiism as well.

ORGANIZATIONAL DETERMINANTS OF SCHISMS

The reviewed schisms have hinted at the determinants of whether a schism emerges.[46] One is the evolution of religious preferences. Reform Judaism drew converts who came to consider traditional Judaism an obstacle to economic advancement. Another factor is the cost of founding a schismatic community. The higher the cost, the less likely it is to succeed and, hence, to be attempted in the first place. The ferocious punishments that the Roman Church meted out to potential schism leaders delayed Protestantism. When the Council of Constance declared the reformist leader Jan Hus (1370–1415) a heretic and had him burned at the stake, it was a massive blow to the Hussite movement.[47] For centuries, the Church blocked disunion by demonstrating to alienated masses the huge risks of attempting out-conversion. Repeatedly it signaled a commitment to protecting its religious monopoly and preserving its rents. Church violence against disillusioned Christians made many withhold dissent out of fear.

In contrast to Protestantism, whose spread was notoriously bloody, Reform Judaism emerged peacefully in nineteenth-century Europe. The placidity of this process reflected the inability of incumbent Jewish leaders to deter schisms through coercion. They had to rely on communal pressures alone. And the potency of pro-traditional pressures weakened as Reform and Orthodox Judaism expanded. With the shrinking of traditional Judaism, the cost of alienating it fell accordingly. In brief, obstacles to a Jewish schism were relatively small.

The cost of establishing a new religious community includes more than danger to life and limb. Worship facilities and revenue-yielding assets may have to be left behind. Insofar as the leavers cannot take with them the parent community's properties, the cost of separation will include property to be replaced. Further losses can come from denial of access to social and commercial networks. These additional costs were not prohibitive for Reform Jews or Orthodox Jews. Each group took with it a valuable subnetwork, and no state guarded physical assets on behalf of the Traditionalists.

BEFT tested a variant of the foregoing logic with respect to Protestant disunion in the United States. Some American churches, which they categorize as "congregational," have a bottom-up organizational structure, in that members select church leaders. Others, which they call "episcopal," have a hierarchical administration that makes decisions on doctrine, staffing, and activities. It is easier for a breakaway Protestant sect to extricate resources from a congregational church than from an episcopal church. Likewise, it is easier within a congregational church to achieve the collective action needed for a split. In fact, American sectional splits are more common in the family of congregational churches than in its episcopal counterpart.[48]

Schisms within Christianity sometimes reflect power struggles. But many others are triggered by social or political controversies that transcend religion. In the eighteenth and nineteenth centuries, slavery was just such a controversy. From its founding in 1739 in England, the Methodist Church debated slavery. In 1845, before the American Civil War, its American branch, the Methodist Episcopal Church, broke apart because of irreconcilable differences.[49] The two successor churches reunited in 1939, when the issue of slavery was settled. In the early twenty-first century, same-sex marriage has fractured Methodism again.

Officially, the United Methodist Church defines marriage as the union of a man and a woman. It also prohibits same-sex unions. But "Progressive United Methodist" clergy defied traditional United Methodist principles on this matter.[50] Conflict over same-sex marriage ultimately led to a "Protocol of Reconciliation and Grace through Separation," which initiated a formal schism in 2020.[51]

DIVISIVE ISSUES IN ISLAM

Controversies of the type that divide Christians exist in Islam, too. Areas of potent disagreement include economics, education, interactions with outsiders, and violence. However, it will suffice to survey just three substantive categories: gender matters, rituals, and politics. The accounts that follow are purely descriptive of the potential for a liberal split. They are not meant to endorse or denigrate any specific position.

Gender Matters

Women's rights and gender equality are sources of discord throughout the Middle East, as in the rest of the Muslim world. Flashpoints include norms that require women to dress modestly, rules against mixed-gender gatherings outside the family, restrictions on female mobility (such as norms against women traveling without a male chaperone), arranged-marriage customs, child marriage, gender discrimination in employment, and inheritance systems that give female relatives half as much as corresponding males.[52]

Each controversy pits supporters of male entitlement against rivals committed to improving women's lives. Most of the disputes have parallels elsewhere, including Western Europe and North America. But the polarities are especially intense in the Middle East. This is evident in global indices of gender equality for 2019. Based on data of the World Economic Forum, Figure 10.2 shows that the Middle East is generally low in gender equality. Using components of the same data, Figure 10.3 indicates that the Middle East lags behind in female political empowerment. The region's deficit practically disappears on educational attainment (Figure 10.4), though the displayed comparison conceals the relative prevalence in the Middle East of gender segregation in schooling. Jointly, the data reveal that gender-related Middle Eastern controversies concern more than symbolism. They reflect wide gender differences.

Gender inequalities on inheritance have a scriptural basis. The one-half ratio is a Quranic mandate.[53] On other gender inequalities, no scriptural foundation exists, at least nothing unambiguous. No Quran chapter calls for restricting female mobility, or gender segregation in schools, or denying women positions of political influence. In these contexts, female handicaps are rooted in pre-Islamic customs of Arabia and other lands that early Muslims conquered. Some such customs, including educational gender discrimination, were once shared by many non-Muslims both within and outside the Middle East. In medieval

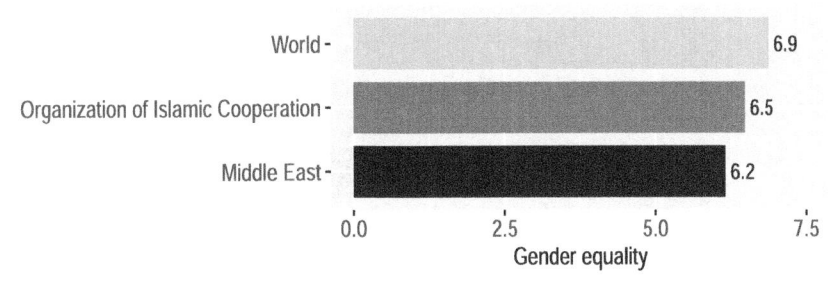

Religious Diversification, in Fact and in Law 183

FIGURE 10.2 Gender equality in global perspective: composite index

Note: The scale runs from 0 (maximum male–female gap) to 10 (females represented at least as much as men). The index averages four indices: economic participation and opportunity, educational attainment (Figure 10.4), health and survival, and political empowerment (Figure 10.3).

Sources: Computed from data in World Economic Forum, *Gender Gap Report 2020*.

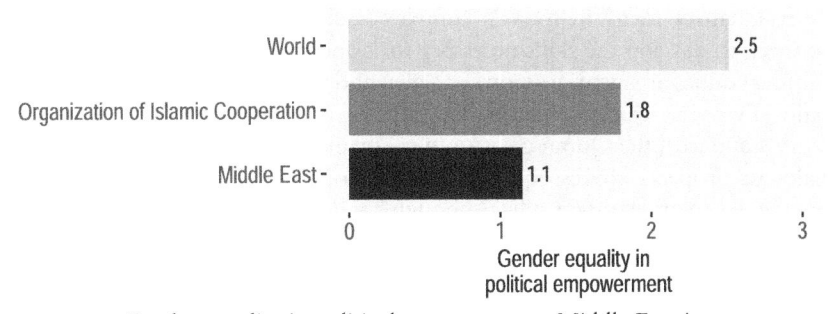

FIGURE 10.3 Gender equality in political empowerment: Middle East in global perspective

Note: The scale runs from 0 (maximum male–female gap) to 10 (females at least as numerous as men). The measure is a composite of gender gaps in parliamentary seats, cabinet ministers, and number of years with a female head of state.

Sources: As in Figure 10.2.

England and France, for instance, girls received less education than boys. Gender discrimination is now especially severe in the Middle East (and almost as bad in the Indian subcontinent, where Hinduism and Islam promote similar gender roles), because over the past two centuries other regions of the world went farther in reducing gender gaps, even reversing them in certain domains.[54] Educational gender discrimination is also associated with Islam because, along with Hinduism, it is the religion invoked most commonly by advocates of tilting educational opportunities in favor of males.[55]

Islam's fundamental sources and Islamic practices allow the reinterpretation of traditional Islamic prescriptions on gender matters. Consider the gender gap in education. The Quran holds individuals, regardless of sex, responsible for doing

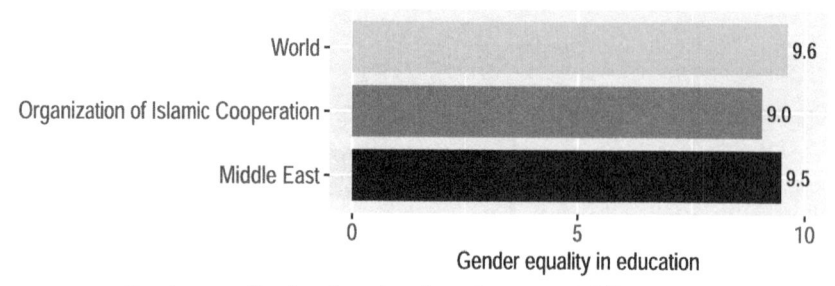

FIGURE 10.4 Gender equality in educational attainment: Middle East in global perspective

Note: The scale runs from 0 (maximum male–female gap) to 10 (females at least as successful as men). The measure is a composite of gender gaps in literacy and in school enrolment rates at all levels.

Sources: As in Figure 10.2.

good and preventing harm. These duties require literacy, if only to read the Quran and explanatory texts. In today's complex societies, they also require lengthy education, to develop the skills necessary for applying Islamic principles wisely. If communal duties are incumbent on both men and women, they should be educated equally. Even the Quran's inheritance rules admit reinterpretation. By seventh-century standards, the Quran gave women advanced economic rights. In entitling females to property shares equal to one-half of the equivalent male shares, it strengthened them economically. Although the letter of the Quran's inheritance system appears discriminatory to modern eyes, its advancement of women's rights in Islam's birthplace may be invoked to justify gender-neutral inheritance shares now.[56]

On the dress controversy, both sides offer justifications that speak to women's welfare. Opponents of veiling consider it an instrument of women's oppression. Ending the practice would give women benefits already available to men, such as comfort on warm days and a visible public identity beyond face, eyes, or body shape. It would also reduce bone diseases caused by inadequate exposure to sunlight.[57] For their part, the proponents of female veiling consider it an instrument of liberation from base drives. It enables men and women to interact without the distortions of sexual attraction, they say. It also prevents commodification of the female body.[58] On social gender segregation, too, rival arguments share a concern with women's welfare. It holds women back by limiting their professional contacts and advancement opportunities, say critics. Advocates counter that, by simplifying women's social lives, it helps them excel at being wives and mothers.[59]

Rituals

Over and beyond the rationales of its promoters, female veiling enjoys support as a communal or sub-communal ritual. Veiling styles vary across and within countries of the Middle East. In addition to defining piety differently, each style enacts a distinct custom. Many other Islamic rituals are also contentious. Alevis object to the Ramadan fasting requirement. Scientific discoveries, the realities of modern life, and demands to personalize religious obligations are all sources of tension. Surveys and interviews conducted in Turkey by Bahattin Akşit, Recep Şentürk, Önder Küçükural, and Kurtuluş Cengiz show that Sunni Muslims from diverse walks of life consider various Islamic rituals outdated, unnecessarily burdensome, even harmful. The religious attitudes of Turkish Muslims are far more varied, the team finds, than one might infer from the orderliness of a mosque service or the joyfulness of an iftar dinner on a Ramadan night.[60]

In an age when anyone can get prayer-time alerts from a cell phone app, why should the call to prayer blare from minaret loudspeakers, wonder some Muslims.[61] Others consider prayer meaningful only when performed in private; otherwise, they say, the performer obtains side benefits through piety signaling.[62] At the other extreme are advocates of mandatory prayers. To belong to a religion requires obeying all its dictates, they reason, however inconvenient; and Islamic prayers provide useful exercise and moments of reflection. The main purpose of the call to prayer, they add, was always to mark a territory as Muslim-governed and promote awareness of the dominant culture; its time-marking function has been secondary.[63] Granting the physical and mental benefits of periodic breaks during the day, some say that yoga and meditation serve the same functions better than ritualized prayers based on pre-Islamic Arabian customs.[64] In the 1920s, reforming the Sunni Islamic liturgy entered the agenda of Turkey's secularist leaders. A plan was developed to put chairs in mosques and have prayers recited in the vernacular as opposed to Arabic, which few Turks speak. Though sympathetic to the project, Atatürk had it shelved for fear of endangering reforms of higher priority.[65] One century after Turkish liturgical reform was stillborn, no movement exists anywhere to alter Islamic services nearly as radically as Atatürk's aides envisioned. By no means is the reason lack of imagination or want.

Only 23.4 percent of the world's Muslims and 71.7 percent of Middle Eastern Muslims reside in Arabic-speaking countries. In the rest of the world, including Iran and Turkey, few people understand Quran recitations in Arabic. For centuries, efforts to translate the Quran into vernaculars have met with resistance.[66] As with European priests before 1517, the opposition reflects the challenges clerics would face if laypeople started interpreting the Quran themselves. But the formal justification is that any translation will distort God's message. Whatever the true motives for the resistance, even Arabic speakers have trouble understanding the Quran, because classical Arabic, its original language, differs greatly from modern dialects.[67]

Ramadan fasting has already received attention as a battleground between assertive secularists and assertive Islamists. The main reason for its prominence as a flashpoint has been the visibility it brings to Islamic life.[68] Recent scientific research raises new reasons to either promote Ramadan fasting or discourage it. On the one hand, the fast is associated with increases in happiness and optimism. On the other hand, it has adverse health effects, most importantly, brain damage in the unborn children of mothers fasting during pregnancy. According to analyses based on variations in the length of the daily dawn-to-dusk fast, people whose mothers fasted while they were in utero have shorter lives, worse health, inferior mental acuity, lower educational achievement, and less successful careers. The harms are substantial. Mental disabilities stemming from exposure to fasting during month one in utero account for 15 percent of all mental disabilities among Muslims. Fasting also harms people with preexisting conditions. On long summer days, even healthy people may suffer, mainly through dehydration and lower drug compliance. The evidence is overwhelming that the fasting ritual, as currently practiced, depresses the economic competitiveness of Muslim-majority societies.[69] The identified harms furnish medical and economic justifications for allowing public eating and drinking during fasting periods.

Ritual slaughter is an Islamic custom that some Muslims consider out-of-date, unethical, and cruel. Like kosher slaughter in Judaism, halal slaughter is carried out by having blood drain out of the animal's slit throat. Because the procedure is performed without anesthetic, the animal suffers during the period between the cut and its loss of consciousness. For cattle and sheep, this period lasts up to fifteen minutes, because the vessel that transports blood to the brain remains intact. Some Muslim authorities allow prior stunning on the ground that the Quran requires only that the animal be alive, not conscious. Nevertheless, slaughter without anesthetic remains common. Animal rights activists, including Muslims, have pursued legal bans on the practice.[70] Sacrificial animals also suffer while being raised, transported to market, and held for slaughter.[71] Meanwhile, medical researchers raise concerns about zoonotic diseases spread through killings performed by untrained butchers.[72]

Politics

An overarching source of division among Middle Eastern Muslims of the twenty-first century stems from the weaponization of Islam against groups that states want to weaken, dominate, or silence. As in the past, the underlying motives need not be integral to Islam.[73] The Ottomans and Safavids decimated selected heterodoxies to advance state building. Secularist regimes of the twentieth century redefined Islam for the convenience of equating religion-based anti-modernization with obscurantism. Following myriads of such precedents, today's kingdoms, populist dictatorships, and Iran's theocracy make clerics serve as agents of social conservatism.

There is nothing surprising here, according to Wael Hallaq, who considers the essence of Islamic politics the unification of powers. Under Islamic law, a Muslim community does not possess sovereignty, which belongs to God alone. Qualified community members may interpret God's law but never make

Religious Diversification, in Fact and in Law 187

changes or additions themselves. Islamic law is thus in conflict, Hallaq infers, with a central tenet of the modern state, the separation of powers.[74] A broader implication is that Islamic liberalization requires reformulation of the traditional understanding that God meant to deny legislative rights to Muslims forever, and even to communities living in circumstances vastly different from those of seventh-century Arabia. In practice, as we have seen in diverse contexts, the governing elites of Muslim-dominated states have interpreted the law self-servingly, to enrich themselves, keep power, and tarnish rivals as enemies of Islam. "God's sovereignty" has never been more than an ideal.

Groups charged with religious crimes resent the use of Islam for defamation and discrimination. They consider it improper, if not also irreverent, to make clerics take sides on issues beyond their expertise. Thus, they object to fatwas meant to legitimize policies that Islamic scriptures leave unaddressed. Consider a Saudi fatwa issued during a controversy over satellite TV channels. The chairman of the Saudi Supreme Council of the Judiciary opined that, because these channels contain unregulated content, their owners should be tried and executed.[75] Even many puritanical citizens were outraged. Other Saudi fatwas by top clerics incite discrimination, even violence, against Shiis.[76] A fatwa of Egypt's highest religious authority banned a Turkish Netflix series popular among Arab audiences. It called the series a "Trojan Horse to revive the Ottoman Empire."[77]

Fatwas are often used to legitimize priorities popular among secularists. Examples include energy conservation, antiterrorism, vaccination, and disability rights. But they are used also to make religion more salient in daily life or to discourage popular activities. Examples include bans on remarrying after a divorce, yoga (lest it tempt conversion to Hinduism), building a snowman (because it might be worshiped as an idol), using cryptocurrency (to hinder money laundering), running an online business (because the internet is morally suspect), feeding a dog at home (on the ground that dogs are dirty), consuming imported medicine capsules (in case the shells contain pig fat), wearing evil-eye amulets (because causality should be attributed to nothing but God), and celebrating the Gregorian calendar's new year (to escape de facto conversion to Christianity).[78] A common objective of fatwas is to undermine widely accepted laws or subordinate them to religion. Another is to vilify a rival; during the Iran–Iraq war of 1980–88, each side produced fatwas accusing rival leaders of heresy.[79] Some fatwas are issued to foster society's Islamic identity by reversing the rulings of secular regimes or reducing contacts with non-Muslims. To move Iranians from global social media to local substitutes, Iran's Supreme Leader has issued fatwas against using Facebook and Twitter.[80]

Middle Eastern states have agencies whose tasks include issuing official fatwas – rulings meant to take precedence over all other opinions, ostensibly because they reflect the views of scholars with unsurpassed credentials. In Egypt, Al-Azhar issues official rulings in concert with the Grand Mufti. In Saudi Arabia, a Council of Senior Scholars headed by the Grand Mufti performs the same role. And in nominally secular Turkey, Diyanet serves as the official voice of Turkish Sunnism.[81] In practice, though, any Muslim adult can issue a fatwa, regardless of credentials. The discontent with state-directed fatwas is evident in the proliferation of relatively permissive private fatwa services, including many online.[82] Online services have formed searchable fatwa cyberbanks, which allow people to access and compare opinions anonymously. Official fatwa agencies treat these private sites as illegal, but internet traffic patterns indicate that they are far more popular.[83] This is among the reasons why Middle Eastern states feel threatened by unfettered access to the internet.[84]

Competing with state-affiliated muftis, but also with one another, cyber-muftis give moral guidance and comfort to clients on work, migration, cultural integration, social interactions, family, sex, mixing between men and women, and more. Known also as "media clerics," they are ridiculed as "Google sheiks" or "YouTube scholars," implying that they are impostors lacking proper credentials.[85] Many of the most frequently viewed fatwas in cyberbanks give opinions related to sex.[86] Sexual matters are very common among the questions directed at cyber-muftis, male and female.[87] One such issue is the permissibility of hymenoplasty, the cosmetic reconstruction of a woman's hymen, typically performed to restore the appearance of virginity. Many state-affiliated muftis, for example those of Saudi Arabia, consider virginity restoration a form of fraud and thus un-Islamic. But numerous cyber-muftis disagree. Hymenoplasty is religiously permissible, they opine, and it need not be disclosed to a future spouse. Sins committed in the past can remain between Allah and the repentant sinner, they rule.[88] Some of the clerics working for transnational fatwa services based in Europe, North America, and Australia are Western-born and educated. In the eyes of Muslims eager to integrate into their host societies, this is an advantage.[89] But the users of transnational services also include residents of Muslim-majority states. Through Western-based cyber-muftis, they overcome qualms rooted in the inconvenient rulings of local muftis.

A common source of political discord is the support that clerics give to oppressive and corrupt regimes. Critics of such support want clerics, and Islamic officials generally, to stay out of politics; and insofar as clerics do take political positions, they want them to oppose all violations of basic moral principles, regardless of the perpetrator or the prevailing state priorities. China's campaign to destroy Uyghur culture and identity offers a case in point. Opponents of state–cleric alliances are appalled by the steady refusal of practically all Islamic bodies, even the Organization of Islamic Cooperation, to denounce China's persecution of its largest Muslim minority.[90] Even more outrageous, say the opponents of alliances between clerics and oppressive states, are endorsements of China's policies and the extradition of Uyghur exiles at the request of Chinese authorities.[91] For their part, the defenders of acquiescence to China's Uyghur policies hold that it is the prerogative of Muslim political leaders to make tradeoffs between taking a moral stand and managing international relations. Or they assert that, given the West's animosity to Islam, the Muslim world cannot afford to alienate China.[92]

PRECONDITIONS OF ISLAMIC SCHISMS

More controversies could be added, but the point has been made. Today's Muslims are sufficiently divided on enough matters to justify exploring why modern Islam has seen few schisms. Polarizations of the type now common in Middle Eastern societies produced two new Jewish sects in nineteenth-century Europe. Endemic corruption and moral hypocrisy, highly prevalent in today's Middle East, begot the Protestant Reformation. Nowhere in the region is there a lack of discontent with existing, state-promoted interpretations of Islam, as evident in the enormous popularity of unregulated fatwa services. Large constituencies consider rituals outdated, clerics unprincipled, and gender discrimination unacceptable.

But widespread discontent is never sufficient to bring about mobilization aimed at reform. If the risk of supporting reform is grave enough, passivity will always appear as a more attractive option. Yet achieving a successful schism requires, at some stage, open collective action on the part of a constituency with a shared religious vision, possibly under leaders able to strategize, speak on behalf of members, and coordinate moves. Also necessary is that supporters of the religious status quo lack the organizational capacity to erect roadblocks. In nineteenth-century Europe, Jews dissatisfied with traditional Judaism found these preconditions in place. Hence, Reform Judaism and Orthodox Judaism both organized peacefully. By contrast, the Protestant Reformation entailed bloody struggles that lasted centuries. Before 1517, but also until the Peace of Westphalia in 1648, the Roman Church responded to reform movements with massive violence.[93] Neither case corresponds precisely to the conditions facing potential schism organizers in the modern Middle East. Nevertheless, for reasons already hinted at, any group trying to develop an alternative to Sunnism or Shiism is likely to face immense resistance.

The challenges would vary, depending on the substance of the alternative interpretations. Our next task is to identify these variations and explain their sources.

11

The Absence of Liberal Islamic Schisms

Discontent about existing interpretations of Islam stem partly from an ever-changing set of prohibitions imposed in the name of Islam. These prohibitions do not reflect the spirit of the Prophet's Islam, many Muslims believe, and they lack a scriptural basis. They also take the fun out of life. Often they represent automated rejection of innovation. The perception that Islamic conservatism hinders progress, broadly conceived, is not new. In the nineteenth and early twentieth centuries, it drove modernist efforts to marginalize Islam.

Regardless of whether objections to dominant interpretations are sound, they raise the question of why more permissive variants of Islam have not emerged as organized branches. The structures of authority within the two main denominations come to mind as fundamental obstacles. If anything, though, they should both have facilitated liberal Islamic schisms. With the partial exception of Iran after 1979, the Middle East has lacked a centralized religious body that wields power comparable to that of the Roman Catholic Church before 1517.

One liberal handicap in the region lies in the historical weakness of civic life – a legacy of the two core features of Islamic institutional history, the Islamic waqf and the absence of an Islamic concept of corporation. The Middle East has a long tradition of forming secret religious communities. However, liberalization inherently requires open dialogue. Under the circumstances, Muslims partial to a liberal interpretation of Islam refrain even from attempting to organize a new brand. Resigning themselves to ostensible religious deviance, they just keep quiet, or they disengage from religion and pursue a "secular lifestyle."

By itself, though, this explanation is incomplete because there have been momentous illiberal schisms. Why this asymmetry? Whereas Islam's apostasy and blasphemy rules fit naturally into the tool kits of illiberal challengers, they are anathema to the liberal mindset, which prizes tolerance, resolving conflicts

The Absence of Liberal Islamic Schisms

through dialogue, and coexistence of lifestyles. These profound differences disadvantage Muslims inclined to organize a liberal community. They also make elites in power, even secularists, prefer an Islam under their control to one that could turn against them or their policies.

Although Sunnis and Shiis are both spread across many nation-states, a much larger share of the world's Shii population is concentrated in a single country. The largest concentration of Sunnis, those of Indonesia, form 14 percent of the global Sunni population. By contrast, more than one-third of all Shiis live in Iran, a theocracy with a hierarchical clergy.[1] On this basis, it may seem that Shiism is less conducive to splintering. In fact, across the two denominations, the organizational differences relevant to fragmentation are less significant than the governance of Iranian Shiism might suggest. Besides, the centralization of Iranian Shiism is a recent phenomenon, and its present institutional structure lacks coherence. Hence, in seeking organizational clues to our puzzle, we must investigate both major denominations.

ORGANIZATION OF SUNNISM AND SHIISM

Starting with Sunnism, the larger denomination, we shall see that factors other than centralization are critical to whether liberal-minded Muslims can form their own variants of Islam.

Sunnism

Sunni Islam lacks a hierarchical structure conducive to internal unity. Since Turkey's abrogation of the Caliphate in 1924, no entity has come close to representing the entire community of Sunnis. Sunnis split among many nation-states are all regulated separately. Hence, they are free to develop their own interpretations of Islam. In principle, Egypt's Sunnis could develop a liberal variant of Islam without the acquiescence of Turkish Sunnis, and vice versa. But within each country, Sunnism lacks an autonomous communal status. It has no self-directing administration for managing mosques, Quran schools, fatwas, or other religious services. By themselves, these factors should lend themselves to diversity in values, rule enforcement, adaptability in scriptural interpretation, openness to learning from others, and attitudes toward cultural globalization. Indeed, the previous chapter highlighted a range of specific controversies that might fuel disunion.

The leadership for galvanizing a new Islamic denomination or sect could come from any quarter of society. A media star or famous philanthropist could fill the role. But independent-minded clerics are particularly well-suited to the task because of their relative immunity to the charge of lacking proper qualifications. Clerics have played vital roles in intra-Christian splits serving constituencies with distinct religious tastes. The initiator of the Protestant Reformation, Martin Luther, was a priest, monk, and professor of theology.

Schisms per se are not rare in modern Sunni Islam. Just as Orthodox Judaism was founded to meet the needs of Jews who wanted stricter enforcement of Jewish rules, so the Muslim Brotherhood was founded as a stricter alternative to the prevailing form of Egyptian Sunnism. Its ideologues depicted the lifestyles of Egypt's ruling elites as too lax, perverted by an illusion of Western superiority, and incompatible with Islamic morality.[2] Almost a century later, elsewhere in the Arab world and under different circumstances, ISIS emerged as an ultra-puritanical, anti-modern, highly intolerant, and selectively literalist variant of Sunni Islam.[3]

Each of these schisms encountered resistance from incumbent states, which responded to violence with violence of their own. A deterrent to peaceful schisms is that neither mosques nor their congregations are self-governing. Typically, as Chapters 8 and 9 discussed, state officials keep a watchful eye on Friday sermons. Commonly, they even dictate the content. Hence, despite Sunni Islam's fractured governance, Sunni-managed mosques are poorly suited to spearheading a reinterpretation of Islam on their own initiative. No matter how liberal their congregation or social milieu, they cannot adapt teachings to local preferences. Moreover, state control hampers local authority over staff appointments, outreach activities, and even uses of physical space.

When Islamic waqfs operated mosques, not even caretakers had a legal right to modify routines. Regardless of their preferences, congregations were supposed to accept the stipulations in the founder's deed. As with waqfs in general, deed ambiguities allowed many adjustments in practice, as did cooperative clerics willing to ignore specific instructions. Nevertheless, this organizational mode's overall effect was to hinder adaptation. Since the 1800s, state agencies have been monitoring most mosques, if not running them directly. Hence, altering a mosque's activities may now require taking on the state. This has compounded the obstacles to collective action aimed at modifying Sunnism or initiating a Sunni subdivision.

Where mosques are state-owned, an additional difficulty is that a breakaway Sunni constituency could not leave with property. The state would step in to prevent the splitting of assets. If surviving Islamic waqfs administered the disputed assets, there would be another problem. The remaining constituents could sue to keep all assets on the ground that waqf property is impartible.

Sunni Islam's organization bears little resemblance, then, to that of schism-prone congregational Protestant churches. Sects that enjoy monopoly power through state protection allow their members less say over governance than even episcopal Protestant churches, where feedback from members influences local appointments and activities.[4] Hence, the immersion of Middle Eastern states in Sunni religious affairs appears to undermine formal religious diversity. This inference would not have surprised Adam Smith, who held that state control of religion impoverishes religious life.[5] Smith's insight furnishes a clue as to why a liberal schism of the form that Judaism experienced in nineteenth-century Europe has eluded Islam. Central and Eastern European Jews were second-class citizens with limited political and economic rights. Traditional rabbis lacked the leverage to make states block Judaism's fragmentation.[6] In any case, European states did not want to intervene in the first place. In the Middle East, by contrast, undemocratic states without legitimacy fear the political destabilization that a liberal Sunni schism might cause. They discourage liberal Islamic causes as a matter of self-survival.

Shiism

The vast majority of the world's Shiis are divided into six sects: Twelver (80 percent of the total), Ismaili, Zaidi, Druze, Alawi, and Alevi. They form a religious majority in Iran, Iraq, Azerbaijan, and Bahrain. In Iran, home to the largest concentration, around 90 percent of the population is at least nominally Shii, almost all Twelver.[7] Since the Iranian Revolution of 1978–79, Iran has been ruled according to Khomeini's "clerical governance" (*wilayat-i faqih*) doctrine.[8] Under this doctrine, Islam provides all the necessary guidance to lead a righteous life; clerics enforce Islamic law, resisting foreign influences and keeping politicians from circumventing rules for expediency. In congruence with the clerical governance doctrine, Iran's 1979 constitution posits a cleric as the country's Supreme Leader, along with a Council of Guardians composed entirely of clerics, half of whom are appointed by the Supreme Leader. This council appoints an Assembly of Experts, whose duties include choosing the next Supreme Leader. The Council of Guardians vetoes un-Islamic legislation. It also screens candidates for elected office, including the Presidency.[9]

Starting under Khomeini, and continuing under his long-serving successor Ali Khamenei, clerics have sought to control every facet of Iranian life – bureaucracy, politics, economy, family, education, military, diplomacy, sports, arts, health, and more. This Islamization is reflected in the explosion of Iran's clergy from 20,000 in 1979 to 350,000 in 2008. The nearly twenty-fold rise reversed the long secularization process launched in the 1800s. A vast new administration guides the re-Islamization of Iran's labor market through strict rules on admission to the clerical corps, advancement through its ranks, and even clerical garb. Many top government positions are reserved for clerics. Vast funds flow to cleric-managed modern waqfs. Certification as a cleric provides entry to professionally lucrative networks. More than 100,000 students are enrolled at Iran's Shii seminaries. A small share will make it into the clergy. But in Iran's present political order even the unselected stand to benefit professionally from connections formed in school.[10]

This expansion of Iran's clerical footprint is not a return to some pre-Pahlavi past. Prior to the Islamic Republic of Iran, no centrally administered certificate was required to become an Iranian cleric. Khomeini's main teachers were four relatives. He gained recognition as a man of religious erudition (*mujtahid*) without completing the higher levels of religious education or receiving a certificate.[11] The process of becoming a teacher of Shiism was highly decentralized. A Shii became a cleric by taking self-selected courses and achieving recognition for religious expertise from someone already considered a cleric. Moreover, rising in the clerical hierarchy depended on acquiring many followers – much like becoming a YouTube celebrity requires developing a fan base.[12] Also unprecedented in Iranian history is the systematization of the clerical hierarchy. Although the Safavids made Shiism Iran's state religion, neither they nor their successors created a corporate body to regulate the clergy. Before the mid-1900s, Shii legal thought focused on civil and private matters, avoiding engagement with the practical aspects of governance. Under the Pahlavis, the clerics of Qom, Iran's most prestigious Shii center, enjoyed some autonomy. But they could not form a cartel to block competition. Hence, the organization of Shiism was quite conducive to splintering. In sum, Iran's theocracy is a massive Shii innovation, as are many of the duties it now assigns to clerics and its elaborate hierarchy.[13] The institutions that regulate Shiism in the Islamic Republic of Iran resemble synods that define truth and inquisitions that pronounce error – lapsed structures of Christianity without equivalents in Islamic history.

Even since 1979, though, Shiism has not been as tightly regulated as the clerical governance doctrine prescribes. Prominent clerics resisted Khomeini's centralization agenda, and the theocracy's repression and failed policies have divided the clergy further.[14] Besides, institutions such as Supreme Leader and the Guardian Council are embedded in an incoherent constitutional order. No clear demarcation exists between the Supreme Leader's constitutional authority and that of the legislature. A result is chronic legal ambiguity and social confusion. Prominent fatwas contradict state laws on the appointment of women as judges. Whereas the decisions of an Islamic judge are final under Islamic law, the Iranian constitution allows appeals. Shii institutions treat Shiis as privileged, but under the constitution all citizens are equal. The Council of Guardians considers un-Islamic the United Nations Convention Against Torture and Other Cruel, Inhuman, and Degrading Treatment or Punishment, which the Iranian legislature has ratified. And so on.[15] Evidently, the institutional earthquake of 1979 has not voided the conditions for an Iran-based liberal schism.

Shared Asymmetry

Tensions within Iran do not exhaust the motivations for Shii disunion. Shii populations elsewhere furnish additional possibilities. Iranian proxies control only a few communities outside of Iran. As with Sunnism, the variety of regimes under which Shiis live and the diversity of their conditions broaden the opportunities for a liberal schism.

The controversies discussed in the previous chapter make one expect modern Islam to be rife with schisms serving Muslims somehow disillusioned by Islam's prevailing variants. In fact, the twentieth and twenty-first centuries have seen

The Absence of Liberal Islamic Schisms

many globally salient Islamic schisms. Already mentioned cases include the emergence of the Muslim Brotherhood and the meteoric rise of ISIS.[16] All such widely known schisms share two critical characteristics. Promoting a strict variant of Islam, each considers violence a justified instrument for reaching its goals. Abundant visions of a liberal form of Islam appear in extensively read books. But none has generated an organized mass movement that claims a distinct Islamic identity. It is as though the Industrial Revolution instigated Orthodox Judaism but not Reform Judaism, leaving unmet the needs of Jews seeking a more accommodating religion. For insights into this striking asymmetry, we must delve deeper into the commonalities of illiberal Islamic schisms, then do the same for liberal responses rooted in religious disillusionment.

ILLIBERAL SCHISMS

The past century has produced many Sunni movements that aim to purify Islam by clearing it of ostensibly deviant values and practices brought into Islam after a brief "Golden Age" – usually the period up to the death of the fourth caliph. Known generically as Islamists (or Islamic fundamentalists), these purists include apolitical groups, such as a branch of Jordan's Salafis; politically active groups that wish to advance their goals peacefully, such as the dominant wing of Tunisia's Ennahda after the Jasmine Revolution of 2010–11; and groups prepared to use violence, as they deem necessary. It is the last category, dubbed "jihadis," that is of interest here. Determined to exterminate Shiism, secularism, and Western civilization, jihadi Sunnis treat most incumbent Muslim leaders, even most practicing Muslims, as brainwashed infidels. Their visibility is highly disproportionate to the size of their genuine constituency. They gain immense salience from media coverage of their repression and destruction. ISIS-staged public beheadings produced notorious images that went viral. But few people know of quietist Islamists who try, wishing to be left alone, to imitate Muhammad's lifestyle, going so far as to brush their teeth, as he reputedly did, with a miswak twig.[17] In justifying their killings, jihadis invoke premodern advocates of violence against heterodox Muslims; the works of Ibn Taymiyya and Ghazali are highly popular. They also draw on the eighteenth-century ideology behind bloody Wahhabi campaigns against idolatry.[18]

Pan-Islamic militant organizations such as Al-Qaeda, Egypt's Islamic Jihad, and ISIS espouse puritanical forms of Islam. They seek to replace the world's existing Muslim-governed states with a single caliphate modeled after Islam's earliest polity. Differing only in strategy and tactics, they share an ideology that justifies butchery, destruction, and mayhem in pursuit of this supreme goal. Middle Eastern states have joined international alliances aimed at eradicating jihadism. Since the 1970s, defeating jihadism has been a leading goal of OIC members, the United States, the European Union, the USSR, and Russia. True, jihadi-fearing states selectively arm jihadis themselves for use as mercenaries against rivals.[19] But that only confirms the distinctiveness of jihadis. Although jihadis lack international legitimacy, they are powerful global players. They negotiate with nuclear-armed governments as though they were states or global NGOs.

The lines between peaceful and jihadi Islamism are blurry as well as shifting. At its founding in 1928, the Muslim Brotherhood was quietist, but of necessity; its military capabilities were minimal. As its membership expanded through persuasion and charitable activities, some of its factions sought to accelerate Islamization through violence.[20] The ensuing threat to political stability triggered periodic government crackdowns, during which the Brotherhood lowered its profile, only to restore its visibility when repression eased. Before the 2011 revolution, Brotherhood leaders were divided on the best strategy for achieving political control of Egypt, then other Arab countries and the wider Muslim world. During their brief period in power under Mohamed Morsi, they disagreed on the pace of Islamization and the balance between force and persuasion. After Morsi's overthrow in 2013, members who escaped arrest went back into hiding. Following innumerable precedents of persecuted Islamic heterodoxies, the Brotherhood has fragmented into secretive subsects. Some favor gradual advancement through peaceful means. Others are defiant and violent.[21]

Violent Sunni sects may accept restraints in exchange for privileges. Arabian Wahhabism fits this pattern. After Muhammad ibn Abd al-Wahhab founded it in the 1700s, it expanded through conquests of Ottoman- or tribal-controlled lands. It forcibly purged areas of "idolatrous" practices such as saint veneration and restored "purely Islamic" practices, such as Sharia-based taxation. Along the way, the Wahhabis formed an alliance with Muhammad ibn Saud, whose descendants proclaimed the Saudi state in 1932. The House of Saud agreed to propagate Wahhabism and, in return, the Wahhabis accepted Saudi sovereignty. In the Kingdom's early years, Wahhabi scholars administered education, social life, and religious practices, and the Sauds were in charge of economic affairs, military protection, and foreign affairs. With inevitable tensions and adjustments, the alliance persists. Among its effects has been a moderation of Wahhabism. It has metamorphosed from a genocidal sect to one that keeps violence within state-agreed bounds.[22]

Resistance to jihadi Islamism has driven some of its variants underground and confined others geographically. These setbacks of jihadis should not surprise. Because they aim to restrict freedoms further in already repressed societies, they are widely hated.

LIBERAL REACTIONS

If Salafists find current religious practices too lax, liberal critics of mainstream, state-approved Islam consider Muslim freedoms too limited. Some of these liberals are known as modernists, though the terms are not synonymous. One can update a religion to suit modern conditions while insisting on coercive enforcement of its revised requirements. Assertive secularism is modernist but also illiberal.

Among the globally influential liberal modernists, one is Fazlur Rahman (1919–88), a Pakistani scholar who sought to revive independent Islamic reasoning (*ijtihād*) and reform education with an emphasis on critical thinking. His *Islam and Modernity* offers a Quran-focused blueprint for adapting Islam's intellectual and social development to the modern age. Another Muslim liberal is Abdullahi An-Na'im, a Sudanese-American legal scholar. In *Islam and the Secular State*, he contends that modern notions of human rights and citizenship dovetail with core principles of the Quran, but not with a coercive Islamic state. Practicing Islam *sincerely* is easier outside the Muslim world than within, he says; only in the absence of compulsion can choices reflect free will, which is essential to genuine religiosity. The Turkish writer Mustafa Akyol's *Islam without Extremes* builds a similar case that Islam is compatible with basic human liberties. Echoing Rahman, it adds that every new generation may amend and re-amend Islamic law, which is a human construct, in accordance with evolving needs. Another Akyol book, *Reopening Muslim Minds*, stresses that many issues now considered closed were debated freely in the early Islamic decades, before powerful states truncated discourses for political control. Invoking the "universalism" of early Islamic civilization as well as its overlooked contributions to the European Enlightenment, Akyol holds that a liberal interpretation of Islam can be derived from norms of "reason, freedom, and tolerance," for which abundant Islamic precedents already exist.

The three professors mentioned in discussing Bourguiba's coerced secularism – Talbi, Ennaifer, and Ben Achour – have made waves in liberal Middle Eastern circles beyond Tunisia. It will suffice to mention three more Middle Eastern or Middle East-rooted liberal thinkers with global reputations: Mohamed Arkoun (1928–2010), an Algerian scholar who spent his professional career mostly in France; Sadiq al-Azm (1934–2016), a Syrian philosopher; and Abdul-Karim Soroush, an Iranian philosopher.[23] Though differing in emphases, all have promoted Islamic liberalization. Their works seek to harmonize the Quran and Islamic customs with universal standards of free expression, religious pluralism, and human rights.

Liberal Islamic modernizers are distinct from liberal Islamic reconstructionists, known also as historicists or rationalists. Whatever their preferred self-identification, they aim to reinterpret the Quran as God's universal and timeless message that was expressed in terms comprehensible to the peoples of seventh-century Arabia. A modern interpreter's challenge, they say, is to decipher the historical context in which the Quran was revealed, winnow context-specific details from its basic principles, and reconstruct Islam as a religion suited to the present. The Egyptian literary scholar Nasr Hamid Abu Zayd (1943–2010) is the best known Arab reconstructionist of the early twenty-first century. There is no absolute interpretation of the Quran, say his works; and Islam must be freed from accumulated meanings and norms that reflect the priorities, challenges, and power struggles of generations long gone. Muhammad was Islam's first interpreter, Abu Zayd and his fellow reconstructionists hold. Nowhere does the Quran say, nor did Muhammad himself claim, that his words or deeds set timeless examples of virtuous conduct. Rather, Muhammad launched a perpetual process of rational interpretation and reinterpretation.[24]

Turkey has its own liberal Islamic reconstructionists. Sharing Abu Zayd's views, they go further in rejecting both Sunnism and Shiism overtly. Although they have produced 200 books collectively, they are barely known outside of Turkey, partly because they write mostly in Turkish, but also because scholarship on Turkish Islam focuses disproportionately on opinions favored by politically powerful religious players, who tend to share Diyanet-endorsed interpretations. Turkish reconstructionists view the Sharia as a legal structure suited to the Arab societies that produced it; in today's world, its requirements and prohibitions crush individuality, bolster autocracy, and legitimize corruption. An Islamic alternative to Sunnism and Shiism, say Turkey's reconstructionists, must be based on the primacy of reason in interpreting the Quran and the works of Muslim luminaries. It must treat the Quran not as a monologue but, rather, as the starting point for dialogue. Any institution that promotes a just and moral order is Islamic, they stress, regardless of whether it originated in a Muslim-majority country.[25]

None of these assorted liberal revisionists receive much attention from nonpracticing Muslims, who avoid thinking about Islam so long as they themselves are left alone. But in intellectual circles, they have been controversial. A common criticism is that they are insufficiently liberal in one respect or another. Far more often, however, they are pilloried for perverting Islam through alien notions of liberty. The participants in the relevant intellectual debates include European and American Muslims. They also include non-Muslims who consider the liberalization of Islam essential to easing global tensions and raising Muslim economic performance. Certain leading modernist liberals – Rahman, An-Naim, Arkoun, and Akyol – moved abroad permanently, giving up some political influence in their homelands. Many vocal modernists have faced persecution. As with European anti-clericalists before 1517, their lives were turned upside down when they started to develop a following. The cases of Rahman, Al-Azm, and Soroush are especially instructive.

Rahman became a target of conservative Pakistani clerics after his appointment, in 1961, as director of a new institute established to apply Islam's teachings to modern life. His use of modern methods of analysis caused an uproar, as did his dismissal of various traditional interpretations. Facing death threats, he left Pakistan to become a University of Chicago professor. His academic reputation then soared, even as his influence in the Muslim world sank.[26] To turn now to Al-Azm, early in his academic career he wrote biting essays that exposed how Arab governments use religion to deflect attention from failures. "Focus instead on Arab and Islamic practices that are keeping the Arab world weak, demoralized, and poor," he urged. When a collection of his reformist essays, *Critique of Religious Thought*, appeared in 1969, sustained protests prompted the Lebanese and Syrian governments to jail him. Though he was accused of belittling Islam and inciting sectarian conflict, actually he was targeted simply to appease his conservative critics.[27] Soroush provides our final case of persecution aimed at silencing. After the Iranian Revolution, he gained influence in cultural agencies of the theocracy. Before long, he was demonized for undermining the theocracy's "Islamization of knowledge" project, eased out of official positions, and marginalized politically. Continuing to promote intellectual freedoms, religious pluralism, tolerance, and decentralized governance, he co-founded a magazine featuring relatively free intellectual debate. Within a few years, Soroush's network became the nucleus of an anticlerical movement with general appeal. At that point, the regime started harassing Soroush and shut down his magazine. He relocated his work mostly to American and European universities, where the theocracy considers him less threatening.[28]

ASYMMETRIES BETWEEN ILLIBERAL AND LIBERAL ACTIVISM

None of these renowned proponents of Islamic liberalization led or leads a major movement for religious reform. Though they all have admirers and followers in educated circles, none is considered the founder of an organized school of thought. Moreover, not even among broader liberal Muslim constituencies does one find anyone with influence remotely comparable to Hasan al-Banna, founder of the Muslim Brotherhood, or Abu Bakr al-Baghdadi (1971–2019), the first caliph of ISIS. This void is emblematic of the asymmetries between liberal and illiberal reactions to the prevailing interpretations of Islam. Illiberal responses have spawned well-organized subcommunities with millions of members capable of projecting political and even military power. Liberal reactions have been limited essentially to uncoordinated intellectual agendas. They have not created a mass movement. No major entity collects funds or strategizes on their behalf.

Within the Middle East and in Muslim-majority countries of its periphery, the resonance of liberal voices does not vary with the incumbent regime's religious agenda. Even more or less secular regimes have been inhospitable to Islamic liberalization. The Lebanese and Syrian governments that jailed al-Azm were no friends of Islamists. Ayoub Khan's Pakistani regime (1960–69) that witnessed Rahman's persecution had pushed through a constitution that barred the use of Islam in politics, outlawed polygamy, and expanded women's rights – all against conservative opposition. Evidently, there was a line that even a reformist Pakistani government would not cross. It had to avoid the appearance of pursuing a break with mainstream Islam. To appease the conservatives who branded Rahman a heretic, Ayoub Khan's government pulled the rug from under him.

In denying support to a liberal Muslim it admired, the Ayoub Khan government followed a playbook used by generations of earlier modernizers. Iran's Pahlavis, Turkey's Kemalists, Egypt's nationalists, the Baathists of Syria and Iraq, and Tunisian secularists all considered traditional Islam a drag on modernization. Yet none separated itself formally from the religious interpretations they considered outdated. They did not encourage liberal Muslim thinkers to put their analytical constructs into practice. Under their regimes, liberal thinkers formed no organized religious movement, let alone a formal sect or denomination.

Instead of splitting from whatever qualified as mainstream Islam in their own milieu, the Middle East's modernizers all sought to control and suppress it. Coopting clerics as necessary, they remained indifferent to thinkers eager to overthrow traditional practices. Whenever a bold religious reformer drew angry objections, they either stayed on the sidelines or caved in to conservative demands. Insofar as they succeeded in purging Islam from the public sphere, they pursued political, educational, cultural, and economic reforms within religion-free zones. At least nominally, then, modernizers remained part of the religious community they were marginalizing.

Remember why modernizers showed restraint in forming a new denomination or sect. They tried to deny religious conservatives an excuse for mobilizing an anti-reformist opposition. Education and urbanization would weaken traditional Islam's appeal, they thought, and Islam would be reformed anyway, as a byproduct of modernization. In time, the masses would become more amenable to updating Islam, or they would become irreligious, allaying the need for reform. For all these reasons, modernizers chose to avoid a confrontation with religious conservatives.

History has been unkind to thinkers who expected modernization to liberalize Islam. Almost two centuries after the initial modernization campaigns based in Istanbul and Cairo, lifestyles have changed massively even in the poorest Muslim countries. Literacy has risen more than tenfold in the region at large, lifespans have doubled, the nonagricultural share of the labor force has quadrupled, and the urbanization rate has risen sixfold.[29] The internet and the cell phone alone have revolutionized lifestyles by expanding information access to a degree unimaginable until recently. Yet nowhere in the region have such developments galvanized a liberal Islamic interpretation with mass appeal. Liberalization efforts are confined to small circles. Academics treat liberal Muslims as forming a distinct tradition within Islamic thought.[30] But liberal writers themselves remain unorganized.

Three other potential sources of a liberal schism merit attention: Sufism, the Muslim diaspora in the West, and Indonesia's Nahdlatul Ulama. Sufis tend to preach religious tolerance, respect differences in interpretation, and follow distinct rites. Their members include Muslims who combine mysticism with affiliations opposed to core Sufi practices. An Iraqi might identify as both an orthodox Sunni and a member of the Jaysh Rijal branch of Sufism.[31] There are

The Absence of Liberal Islamic Schisms

Sufi sects that welcome literally anyone. A poem commonly attributed to the Persian luminary known popularly as Rumi (1207–73), but actually by a Central Asian mystic, embraces even idolaters and atheists:

> Come! Come! Whoever, whatever you may be, come!
> Heathen, idolatrous or fire worshipper, come!
> Even if you have broken an oath a hundred times, come!
> Our door is the door of hope, come! Come as you are![32]

Since its emergence in the eighth century, Sufism has gone so far as to legitimize learning from other religions; and most of its variants reject the possibility of omniscience.[33] During Sufism's formative period, various other groups began to advocate taking people at their word when they self-identify as Muslim. Only God knows, they held, people's true beliefs.[34] But such movements created only pockets of resistance to prevailing orthodoxies. They remained politically marginal.

Sufism is ideologically conducive, then, to initiating a liberal Islamic movement. Yet it is intrinsically quietist and apolitical. Emphasizing self-improvement and the cultivation of a personal relationship with God, it is indifferent to reforming social institutions. That is mainly why, following the precedents of the Ottomans and Safavids, modern Middle Eastern regimes have tended to tolerate, even support, Sufis. Both secular and religiously conservative regimes have promoted politically passive Sufi sects as a counterweight to Islamist opposition.[35] If a liberal Islamic movement somehow gets started, Sufis are unlikely to stand in its way. Until such a movement forms, though, they crowd out liberal Islam. Disillusioned Muslims who would readily join a liberal Muslim community are drawn to Sufism as an alternative.

The second possible source of Islamic liberalism is the Muslim diaspora in Western democracies. Taking advantage of relatively broad organizational and religious freedoms, Western Muslims have formed organizations that are extremely diverse in orientation. Along with organizations catering to militant or political Islamists of various shades, one finds organizations of secular Muslims (who are Muslim only in name), nominal Muslims (whose Islamic practices are limited to major life passages, such as circumcision parties, funerals, and religious holidays), and reformists. The last group forms a diverse lot. It contains subgroups that emphasize feminist causes, LGBTQ+ rights, or political freedoms. Some are attracted to economically illiberal doctrines, such as socialism. Still others, drawn to trends such as anticolonialism and postmodernism, find Western thought oppressive.[36] However, for all their differences, the reformists share a commitment to religious pluralism and a disdain for religious coercion. Accordingly, they reject Islam's apostasy and blasphemy rules.[37]

Like Western-based liberal Muslims writing as individuals, Western-based liberal Muslim communities have had minimal influence on religious discourses in the Middle East. The same is true of Western Islamic organizations.

Examples include the Zaytuna College in San Francisco, which promotes Sufism; Rumi's Circle in the United Kingdom, which brings together people of all backgrounds who are inspired by the teachings of Rumi; the American-based Sufi Order International, which blends mystical Islam with Buddhism and Hinduism; the Minaret of Freedom Institute, a libertarian outfit in Chevy Chase, Maryland; and the Canadian Council of Muslim Women, which advocates gender equality among Muslims, but also the integration of Canadian Muslims into broader Canadian society.[38] Eventually, such groups could provide Muslim-developed reference points for latent liberal movements in Muslim-majority regions.

To turn now to the third potential source of a liberal schism, certain Islamic organizations in Indonesia have been trying, for a century, to reconcile Islam with religious tolerance. Particularly relevant for our purposes here is Nahdlatul Ulama (literally, Rise of the Islamic Leaders), which has around 65 million members and followers, more than one-fifth of Indonesia's population. Nahdlatul Ulama was founded in 1926, during Dutch colonial rule, to defend traditional Indonesian Islamic practices from reformist Muslims. Because it was centered in a part of Indonesia with few Dutch missionaries, its leaders did not feel threatened by Christianity.[39] Perhaps as a result, its relations with native and European Christians were respectful. Unlike other Indonesian religious groups, Nahdlatul Ulama did not issue polemics against Christianity or mobilize against Christianization. While instructing its members to minimize interactions with Christians, it also preached tolerance of conversion to Christianity. Converts should not be killed or exiled, it instructed, or even treated as inferior to Muslims. It insisted only that out-converts be dissociated from Muslim affairs. Nahdlatul Ulama's tolerance toward Christians, and toward non-Muslims generally, has distinguished its worldview to the present.[40]

By itself, this interreligious tolerance makes Nahdlatul Ulama a possible model for Islamic liberalism in the Middle East. It could serve as a model of civic activism, too. In 1973, the government fused all Muslim parties, including the party that Nahdlatul Ulama had founded in 1952, into a single Muslim party. This turned out to be a step toward subordinating Islam to secular national goals under the guise of Muslim political unity. Within Nahdlatul Ulama, it led to massive soul-searching. A decade of internal debates culminated, in 1984, in Nahdlatul Ulama's withdrawal from formal politics and return to its 1926 emphasis on defending traditional Islam. The exact meaning of this momentous move has been debated ever since. The dominant view is that Nahdlatul Ulama rejected both political Islam and assertive secularism. From 1984 to 1999, when Nahdlatul Ulama kept out of formal politics, it ran a range of social programs and promoted contextualized interpretations of Islamic scriptures. As a nongovernmental organization belonging to Indonesian civil society, it also monitored the state.[41] Nahdlatul Ulama returned to formal politics in 1999, during the turmoil that followed the toppling of Suharto, Indonesia's dictator from 1968 to 1998.[42] Whatever Nahdlatul Ulama's motives for its policies of 1984–99, they constituted an exemplary attempt to use Islam as the basis for instituting political checks and balances and strengthening civil society.

For all its tolerance of non-Muslims, Nahdlatul Ulama is intolerant of Islamic heterodoxies that it finds threatening. From the 1930s onward, it has participated in campaigns that denigrate Ahmadi Islam as a perversion and an imperialist tool to divide Muslims. There are limits on how Islam may be interpreted, holds Nahdlatul Ulama. Specifically, interpretations at odds with Islam's basic teachings should be banned. Ahmadis cross a red line, says Nahdlatul Ulama, in treating their founder, rather than Muhammad, as the last prophet. And they cross another red line in rejecting the Sunni Muslim doctrine that "Prophet Jesus" was executed and will return to earth on Judgment Day. Ahmadis preach that Jesus died naturally and will not return.[43] Nahdlatul Ulama also limits political freedoms, in some contexts violently. In the 1960s, it participated in the massacres of at least a half-million Indonesian leftists.[44] These examples indicate that Nahdlatul Ulama is not a liberal organization in the sense of recognizing immutable individual freedoms. Its tolerance is best characterized as "pragmatic group tolerance," which is akin to the tolerance the Ottomans and Safavids displayed toward unthreatening heterodox sects. Nahdlatul Ulama denies the right of existence to communities that somehow endanger it. Besides, it gives group rights precedence over individual rights. It says that an ordinary Muslim may not challenge interpretations on which properly trained exegetes agree.

On religious and political freedoms, opinion surveys suggest, Nahdlatul Ulama members are no more liberal than the typical Indonesian.[45] This pattern is consistent with the selectivity of its leadership's tolerance toward other religious and political communities. But its leaders have always been divided on matters of freedom. Nahdlatul Ulama contains factions committed to broadening its notions of tolerance and individual rights. If for nothing else, it stands out as a possible starting point for Islamic liberalization.

ROOTS OF ASYMMETRIES

If no liberal Islamic denomination or sect exists anywhere, the reason could lie in the paucity of liberal Muslims who want to organize themselves as a distinct community. Because the opinion surveys of governments and international organizations do not ask the relevant questions, there is no way to estimate closely the demand for a liberal disunion in the Middle East. But the intra-Muslim controversies discussed in the last chapter furnish reasons to expect the potential constituency for a liberal Muslim community to number in the millions. It is certainly much larger than what is needed for a viable organization. In any case, the mystery is not the lack of a liberal branch with a membership rivaling, say, Twelver Shiism. It is why the world's second largest religion lacks *any* vocally liberal denomination, sect, subsect, or even subsubsect.

Two mutually complementary reasons may be distinguished, both rooted in Islamic laws already discussed. First, relative to illiberal Muslims, liberals suffer from an ideological asymmetry on the use of violence. Whereas illiberals readily use apostasy, blasphemy, and heresy charges as pretexts for suppressing heterodoxies, liberals are intrinsically reticent to settle disagreements by force. And second, if only for self-survival, political regimes pander to existing organizations, especially to ones capable of sowing trouble. Thus, all else being equal, they are likelier to accommodate an already existing religious community than one in formation. The organizational status quo is a product, of course, of Islamic history. For centuries, institutions that restrict organizational capabilities, impoverish public discourse, and constrain religious choices have denied Islam a liberal tradition.

Ideological Handicaps of Liberals

The headline-grabbing Islamic schisms of modern times have involved proclamations that uncooperative Muslims merit grave earthly punishment. Indeed, ISIS used hair-raising violence against Muslim resistors. Subduing around 10 million Iraqis and Syrians through terror, it justified its brutality as essential to combating apostasy, blasphemy, and heresy. It took a coalition of mighty professional armies to defeat ISIS.[46] A liberal Islamic organization, precisely because of its respect for individual freedoms, would espouse nonviolence. In the process, it would make itself vulnerable to persecution, whether by states or by rival communities. Its members could face fatwas declaring them infidels. Such dangers would harm the liberal organization's recruitment prospects.

Liberals are not ideologically defenseless against stigmatization. As we already know, the Quran contains verses supportive of religious freedoms. The recollections of Muhammad's life, too, feature motifs favorable to liberalism. In both Sunnism and Shiism, the canonical account of Islam's birth holds that before issuing commands Muhammad sought advice and weighed diverse opinions.[47] Relatedly, he is reputed to have said: "Disagreements within my community are acts of divine mercy."[48] The authenticity of these reports is beside the point. What matters is that many Muslims, including religious illiberals, consider the reports authoritative. They could be used pragmatically, then, to spur reconsideration of Islam's established interpretations.

In our own time, we saw earlier, certain liberal intellectuals of the Middle East have already paved the way through works that rely partly, if not largely, on Islamic sources to justify religious freedoms. Their rationales were not developed from scratch. Various early Islamic writers had defended freedom of thought and belief. They included freethinkers who, while accepting the existence of God, rejected the Abrahamic notion of communication between God and people through Prophets. These freethinkers also identified inner contradictions in the prevailing monotheisms, questioned claims of benign divine design, rebelled against the emerging specifics of Islamic law, treated skepticism as a virtue, and even held the human intellect as a sufficient source of knowledge. Though all these positions induced charges of religious offense, in some intellectual milieus they fell within the bounds of acceptable discourse.[49]

Islamic law allows original interpretations on issues that scriptures do not cover precisely or had not presented themselves in the early Islamic centuries (*ijtihād*). Technically, a new interpretation must be produced by a person with proper legal training (*mujtahid*); people without the requisite education must simply recognize their limitations and follow expert opinions.[50] For all the restrictions on original interpretation, its availability as a legal instrument provides a possible channel for liberalizing Islam. Treating the modern era as a context for which Islamic scriptures do not offer precise guidance, scholars steeped in Islamic law can effectively reinterpret traditional understandings of Islam on, say, apostasy. The qualifications for becoming an original interpreter are also open to challenge, as they themselves are based on the consensus of experts in Islamic law.

Yet again, the right to innovation and the existence of Islamic rationales for religious liberty are not enough to start a liberal Islamic movement that transcends intellectuals. In criticizing orthodox Islamic beliefs and policies, liberal Muslims open themselves to charges of rejecting Islam itself. And if, for fear of reactions, they cannot make their cases freely, and to broad audiences, a successful disunion becomes that much harder. It is a handicap to lack the right to critique and contextualize, openly and in forums accessible to the masses, what makes a tradition Islamic. But outside of academic settings, it is dangerous to say explicitly that one may live as a good Muslim without emulating the specifics of Muhammad's life. Even more risky is to say that being a good Muslim is compatible with rejecting, even condemning, specific lifestyle choices of the Prophet. We saw earlier that when liberal religious interpreters start developing a mass following, states make them retreat to highbrow discourses. Spectacles of their humiliation send warning signals to other promoters of Islamic liberalism, actual and potential: "While we may let you communicate with intellectuals through scholarly works, you must not agitate the masses. If you destabilize popular Islamic discourses, you will be punished ferociously."

There is no way to know whether liberal Muslim writings reflect all that the authors would have said if they felt completely free. At the very least, they must have avoided making some thoughts and observations explicitly. The technique of "writing between the lines," popular among heterodox philosophers in medieval Europe and the Middle East, is a timeless method of preference and knowledge falsification.[51] Cognizant of the personal calculations at work, defenders of the religious status quo make a point of highlighting the risks of being charged with apostasy, blasphemy, or heresy through lists of punishable offenses. These lists include uncontroversial manifestations of renouncing Islam, such as denying the existence of Allah. But the alleged offenses also include beliefs and behaviors that, while strictly un-Islamic by certain criteria, are common across the Middle East. A list from the 1990s, by Saudi Arabia's Grand Mufti, considers evidence of apostasy believing that Islamic law is unsuitable to modern life, following human-made laws, and disliking anything the Prophet treated as lawful. By these criteria, a Muslim becomes an apostate by objecting to slavery, which was lawful in seventh-century Arabia; or stopping at a red light, which is a human prohibition; or observing that the contracting rules of classical Islamic law disallow stock markets. In fact, the list's scope is broad enough to make every living Muslim – even Saudi Arabia's Grand Mufti himself – an apostate. It also gives Saudi clerics veto rights over almost anything they dislike, for whatever reason. Other lists in circulation include similar criteria that make every Muslim vulnerable to being charged with a religious crime. According to one list, failing to study Islam is tantamount to apostasy. This list could justify executing a Muslim unaware of some scriptural subtlety.[52] Lists of punishable offenses are inherently disadvantageous for liberals, as they generally violate the very freedoms that liberalism promotes.

There are health reasons, Chapter 10 showed, to keep restaurants open during Ramadan fasting hours. Other reasons involve religious liberty. Some Muslims do not consider the fast a requirement of Islam. Others wish to follow requirements selectively. Besides, Muslim-majority societies include non-Muslims who are not obligated to live by Islamic rules. Only the last of these latter considerations is discussed openly and frankly. Outside of select scholarly circles, articulating the full package is to risk accusations of maligning Islam. Illiberal viewpoints regarding the fast – that Islam requires restaurants to close during fasting hours, that Muslims have an obligation to ensure each other's compliance – are expressed and taught freely. But the medical, cognitive, and economic advantages of making the fast genuinely voluntary remain confined to high academic discourses.

Political Handicaps of Liberals

The constitutions of most predominantly Muslim countries provide freedom of religion. Many have also ratified the United Nations Covenant on Civil and Political Rights, which provides the freedom to practice a religion of one's choice, but also to be irreligious. Yet the meaning of these religious rights remains controversial throughout the Muslim world. Many Muslim leaders define them narrowly. Religious freedoms are all subordinate to a religion's own limits, they say; as such, these freedoms may exclude religious conversion. This qualification effectively denies Muslims the right to renounce Islam. It also allows spokespersons for Islam to treat vast classes of opinions as unspeakably repugnant.[53] It gives Muslim-governed states license to persecute groups for their religious beliefs without admitting any violation of a basic liberty.

The Absence of Liberal Islamic Schisms

Regardless of its orientation toward religion, every polity seeks self-survival. In the Middle East, this objective incentivizes states to get along with established religious communities, control them, and, in any way possible, use them for their broad agendas. They find safety in monopolizing the interpretation of Islam. Whether Salafi or liberal, a new variant of Islam could sow doubts about their policies, goals, and even legitimacy.

A liberal variant of Islam would be especially threatening if it aimed to restrain the state. It could pursue limits on state control over mosque activities. It could also cast doubt on religious rationales for state expenditures, media censorship, military ventures, and the persecution of minorities, among other contexts. It could challenge the legitimacy of state-run fatwa agencies. These are among the reasons why liberal Islam bothers both Islamists and assertive secularists, galvanizing an implicit antiliberal alliance. A liberal variant of Islam would give individual Muslims options that are anathema to Islamists. By the same token, it would permit public religious practices that assertive secularism either bans or relegates to private spaces.

Many religious leaders tolerate liberal thought so long as the target audience consists of already liberal and basically nonpracticing constituencies. Consider the works of the liberal icon Friedrich Hayek. These are freely available in Middle Eastern vernaculars. Though read by highbrow intellectuals, they do not resonate with ordinary mosque congregations. Hence, governments treat them as harmless. At the same time, they discourage discussion on concrete initiatives to liberalize religion. In line with the objective of keeping the masses from contemplating liberalization, mainstream public discourses respect long-standing taboos regarding religious freedoms. No public debate occurs on the pros and cons of allowing free exit from Islam. There is no discussion on the freedom to reinterpret Islam's canonical requirements.

In other Abrahamic religions, liberal schisms tend to occur in states subject to political checks and balances. As a case in point, the United States has seen innumerable liberal schisms – in the sense of generating "less restrictive" religious options, which may or may not align with priorities of the political Left.[54] Any given liberal American sect might hold positions in conflict with policies of the incumbent government. However, due to the multiplicity of veto players in American politics, politicians cannot shut down law-abiding religious sects they dislike. Liberal schisms occur, alternatively, in contexts where neither states nor politically dominant elites have a reason to oppose disunion. Reform Judaism's quick spread is a case in point. The states of Central and Eastern Europe, all Christian-dominated, considered the fragmentation of Judaism beneficial, as it made Jews less threatening politically.[55]

Ahmet Kuru attributes the Muslim world's authoritarianism and chronically low religious freedoms to a longstanding alliance between traditionalist clerics and the state. The state allowed traditionalist clerics to monopolize the official interpretation of Islam, he says, in return for clerics using their religious authority to legitimize state policies.[56] This alliance, which was solidified a millennium ago, does shed light on the absence of liberal Islamic branches. Indeed, states have used religion for legitimation, and clerics have done the state's bidding for security and advancement. But these observations do not explain fully why, to this day, Islam has lacked liberal variants. One also needs to make sense of why groups excluded from the alliance endured the state–clergy alliance for centuries. Why, for generations, did professionals excluded from the dominant alliance remain too weak politically to get themselves included in the ruling coalition?

A basic reason lies in the ideological and political asymmetries just outlined. A complementary reason consists of the institutional obstacle discussed in Chapters 3–6: the absence in Islamic law of instruments for forming autonomous private organizations. Groups outside the state–cleric alliance could not organize within professional or regional associations, except with the permission of the state, which would monitor them. And still another factor reinforcing the mutual dependence of the state and clerics is analyzed in Chapter 13. It involves legal hindrances to private capital accumulation. In weakening the global competitiveness of Middle Eastern entrepreneurs, these obstacles reduced their usefulness to ruling elites. The consequent vicious circle prevented entrepreneurs from obtaining a seat at the political bargaining table.

LATENT LIBERAL SCHISMS

Were the world's Muslims given a choice between several alternative Islamic ways of life, including one modeled after the works of Rahman, An-Na'im, and Akyol, substantial numbers would pick the liberal option. The numbers cannot be estimated with any precision, if only because most states of the region prohibit relevant investigations. Under the circumstances, one must rely on signs of religious alienation and tolerance to identify the potential constituency for liberal Islam.[57]

Starting in September 2022, Iran saw months of protests that challenged the theocracy's hijab requirement and even its very existence.[58] But well before those protests, many Iranian women were obeying the requirement just partially. Random photographs taken at a busy location on a typical Iranian university campus or at a bustling street in a middle-class Iranian neighborhood would show women wearing mini-headscarves covering just some hair – enough to pass as veiled and avoid the wrath of the religious police and puritanical vigilantes. This type of veiling, which has many variants, is generically known as "bad hijab" or "slutty hijab."[59] Elections for Iran's president, who reports to the Supreme Leader, feature candidates vetted by conservative clerics. In 2013 and again in 2017, the approved candidate with the most moderate platform won decisively. These elections revealed high demand for weakening the clergy's hold on daily life.[60] In Turkey, as Chapter 9 documented, religiosity fell even as the Erdoğan regime strove to make Turks more pious. Evidently, school curricula and lifestyle restrictions designed to strengthen religious beliefs and boost religious participation have backfired.

As in Iran, forced religion has expanded the potential constituency for a liberal variant of Islam.

Not all Middle Easterners exasperated with forced Islamization are liberal. Some, perhaps a majority, would want to reinstate assertive secularism, if only to keep illiberal Islamists out of power permanently. Insofar as considerable constituencies do indeed exist for forms of Islam harmonized with modern principles of human liberty, it is puzzling that no liberal variant of Islam exists anywhere as an alternative to orthodoxy. The proximate reason is that the potential beneficiaries of a liberal variant of Islam are unorganized. This lack of organization is due partly to exits from Islam, open or hidden. But exits are unlikely to be a leading factor because in anonymous surveys the share of the nonreligious and atheists among Middle Easterners is only 15.2 percent – higher than in the past, but far lower than the shares who favor reinterpretations concerning women's rights, family relations, dress codes, and the role of clerics.[61] In all likelihood, then, if a liberal Islamic sect or denomination were to emerge, it would attract people who consider themselves within the Sunni or Shii fold.

Once formed, a liberal movement could grow rapidly through conversions from repressive sects. If this sounds implausible, keep in mind that since the beginnings of the Middle East's modernization in the 1800s, many once unthinkable institutional transformations have run their course within decades, even years. The corporate form of business, which conflicts with premodern understandings of Islam, spread quickly wherever introduced, and without religious opposition.[62]

To qualify as a liberal Muslim, a person need not embrace every dimension of religious freedom. A Muslim may object to Islamic dress regulations and to using fatwas as a governance instrument but also endorse restrictions on Ramadan restaurant hours. The members of a liberal community would certainly differ in specifics. What they would share is a preference for a form of Islam that is less intrusive than prevailing variants, but also open to further reinterpretations. One element of the reinterpretation could be some compromise concerning the theological status of the caliphal successions between 632 and 656. Burying fourteen centuries of animosity between Sunnis and Shiis, it could welcome into the fold liberals from both sides.

Again, the conditions under which a liberal movement's growth would turn into a cascade is unpredictable. Clearly, though, the emergence of a broad demand for liberalization is insufficient. Even a huge majority may fail to assert itself if the expected personal risks of stepping forward seem high enough. To lower the perceived risks, something would have to split or weaken a religiously illiberal ruling coalition. A combination of political impasses, economic failures, and social disruptions could bring a society to a tipping point, reducing fear sufficiently to initiate a liberal mobilization process.[63]

Middle Eastern states have formed, and still form, alliances with clerics for legitimation. An alternative source of legitimation is economic development. The state gains legitimacy in the eyes of the masses by helping to achieve prosperity. Insofar as the region's states tried to promote investment, production, and exchange, they failed to keep their economies from slipping into underdevelopment. Uncovering the reasons requires exploring how Islamic law stimulated economic development in the Middle East's centuries of global economic prominence but also how, under different global conditions, it hindered economic modernization. We shall see next that, in weakening private merchants and investors, certain elements of Islamic law reinforced patterns identified in previous chapters: persistently weak civil society and chronic religious repression.

PART IV

ECONOMIC HINDRANCES

12

Unshackled States, Shallow Economic Governance

The Islamic Middle East is widely thought to have a long tradition of powerful and intrusive states.[1] This conception is based partly on projecting current realities onto the past. There are indeed similarities between premodern and modern political patterns. Like the region's present autocracies, the Arab caliphates and the Ottoman and Safavid empires had rulers who were unconstrained by assemblies of the ruled, such as parliaments.[2] They stifled dissent, denied religious freedoms, repressed civic life, and tried, subject to technological limitations, to centralize political power.

In documenting enduring political patterns, previous chapters also identified major reforms. Though still constrained, civic organizations have greater autonomy now than they did before the region's states adopted laws of corporations and associations. Another big change concerns state participation in producing goods and services. Modern Middle Eastern governance includes, for instance, mineral extraction, the production of consumer goods, and urban services. Government size in the Middle East now equals the world average.[3] Public employment as a share of total employment exceeds the average for the rest of the world: 18.4 percent versus 13 percent.[4] On both counts, the Middle East has changed hugely since it started to modernize. Prior to the nineteenth century, its states left production mostly to nonstate entities, including individuals, households, Islamic partnerships, and waqfs. In this sense alone, their economic governance was shallow.

It mattered to their economic output that the Middle East's empires were not shackled by institutional checks and balances. Precisely because they were unshackled, they controlled prices, blocked technological innovations that threatened political balances, protected friendly private monopolies, and ran courts tilted in favor of elites, men, and Muslims.[5] At the same time, they managed to avoid many responsibilities of modern states. After classical Islamic law took shape, Muslim rulers showed little interest in developing new organizational forms for private entrepreneurs, building new types of markets, standardizing weights and measures, or developing the economic infrastructure to exploit new investment opportunities. They also did little to assist private initiatives. Such forms of economic passivity are apparent in the region's lack of participation in the global explorations launched in the late 1400s.[6] Evidently, the region's shallow economic governance involved, along with meager state production, minimal state participation in expanding economic capacity.

The existential threat posed by Western Europe's ascent induced the region's states to become more active in economic management. The wholesale transplant of Western economic institutions was among the manifestations. So, too, was the founding of state-owned banks, manufacturing plants, transportation companies, and communication services.[7] This transition from shallow to deep economic governance entailed the discarding of core Islamic institutions. On that basis, one might infer that Islam, or the Islamic legal system specifically, was incapable of self-generating the modern economy. That would be correct only in part. Certain early Islamic institutions did indeed block economic opportunities. Some cases have already been discussed, and following chapters will build on these insights to link economic underdevelopment to political and social repression. We shall also explore how, in turning the Middle East into an economically underdeveloped region, Islamic laws that regulated commerce and finance contributed also to illiberalism.

Yet it is a misconception that all key elements of the modern economy, such as state-enforced private property rights and predictable taxation, had no indigenous roots and had to be transplanted to the Middle East from abroad. In fact, many of the functions that states took on were among the intended functions of an institution that was central to governance in seventh-century Arabia. The same is true of various economic rights that individuals obtained through economic modernization. This institution is zakat, the lynchpin of the inaugural Islamic state's fiscal system. So critical was zakat to the institutional complex established under Muhammad's leadership that it became one of Islam's five canonical pillars. At Islam's birth, zakat was meant to bind the Islamic state and regulate its taxation without committing it to shallow economic governance.

Zakat could have formed the doctrinal basis for both predictable taxation and limited but effective government. It could have secured property rights and hindered arbitrary taxation. Instead, within a generation it turned into a vehicle for almsgiving. Its eclipse helped to put the Middle East on an institutional trajectory that led to the economic underdevelopment and political repression observed today. Various later additions to the Islamic institutional complex were assigned functions fulfilled initially by zakat. Therein lies a reason for subjecting zakat to a deep analysis that, for this book's purposes, is unnecessary for other Middle Eastern instruments of taxation.

ISLAM'S INITIAL TRANSFER SYSTEM

Islam has five canonical requirements, all mentioned in the Quran with varying frequency. By the time Muslim children are old enough to learn about religion, they are familiar with three of them: the daily confession of faith; prayer performed five times a day; and fasting during the month of Ramadan. Children born into wealth may also know of a fourth requirement: the duty, incumbent on believers who can afford it, to make at least one pilgrimage to Mecca. The last requirement is one that Muslims typically learn through religious education rather than acculturation: for Muslims of sufficient means, the duty to pay zakat.

Like many other institutions that came to be known as "Islamic," zakat emerged from the ideals and practices of Middle Eastern communities around the time that Muhammad began spreading his message.[8] The Quran uses "zakat" thirty-two times to designate a transfer system under which donors periodically purify their property by giving away a small portion.[9] The contributions are to finance eight broadly defined constituencies: the poor, the needy, zakat administrators, potential and recent converts, freed slaves, debtors, God's servants, and travelers.[10] The earliest converts to Islam came from communities familiar with the concept of parting with some of one's resources in order to cleanse the rest. That awareness probably helped to legitimize the zakat duty. On the expenditure side, too, the categories must have struck a familiar chord. Assisting the poor and the needy are major themes of Judaism and Christianity. The region's older polities periodically alleviated debt burdens as a means of limiting discontent.[11]

The Quran neither quantifies zakat payments nor specifies who counts as well-off. Likewise, the frequency of payments is unspecified. Such practical details emerged as Muhammad founded his community in Mecca. Zakat dues were fixed in proportionate terms as a flat tax. They were payable in kind on the most common sources of income in ancient Arabia, such as farming, and the basic forms of wealth, such as precious metals and animal herds. Payments were due once every lunar year. Exemption thresholds were defined on both income and wealth categories. Farmers producing at subsistence levels were deemed too poor to pay zakat, as were camel herders with tiny flocks.

With the Muslim community's move from Mecca to Medina in 622, the Islamic wars of expansion made booty an additional, and possibly much larger, source of communal revenue.[12] Until then, zakat contributions had determined the resources available to finance the eight missions listed in the Quran. They went into the community's treasury (*bayt al-māl*).[13]

The collection side of this transfer system was designed to make taxes predictable. Rates would stay fixed over time. Prosperous Muslims would know what they owed on their assets and incomes. Once their zakat was paid, they would not be taxed again until the next year. Nothing here should be taken lightly, for opportunistic taxation, rather than fixed and predictable taxation, was the global norm at Islam's birth. Even today, many countries suffer from capricious and erratic taxation, which hinders planning and discourages investment. Remarkably, the tax side of the zakat system contained elements of what modern public finance considers an optimal tax system. Specifically, in producing revenue for the government, the system guarded private incentives to produce and accumulate. It taxed final goods uniformly and predictably. Though it also taxed wealth, the rates were set low.[14]

Exempting the poorest Muslims from the payment duty made zakat's tax system mildly progressive. But it is the levels that are particularly striking. Although Islam's schools of law disagree on many specifics, the rates on wealth amounted to around 2.5 percent. For example, the owner of thirty-six to forty-five camels paid one two-year-old female camel, and the rate on both gold and silver was exactly 2.5 percent beyond the metal-specific exemption (*nisāb*). An exception was made for "found treasure," such as coins that an unidentifiable person left buried; for such lucky finds, the rate was 20 percent.[15] As for income, the maximum tax rate was 10 percent, on the output of naturally irrigated land. These rates are amazingly low by the standards of Antiquity. In Mesopotamian kingdoms, prior to the Roman conquest in 115, between one-third and one-half of a merchant's earnings went to taxes, as did between one-fifth and one-half of a peasant's crops. Rates of 20–30 percent were also common in Ptolemaic Egypt (330–305 BCE). The kings of Mauryan India (322–187 BCE) claimed one-quarter of each harvest.[16] Medieval Europe would see some similar rates. Around 1400, England's export duty for wool was 25 percent, and in northern Italy direct taxes on certain goods exceeded 50 percent.[17]

As significant as the low rates were the exemptions. People with sufficiently limited earnings and assets paid no zakat at all. In many other places, by contrast, the destitute were subject to the corvée – forced labor exacted in lieu of taxation in kind or coin. Many great monuments of Antiquity were built by corvée teams numbering in the hundreds of thousands. They include the Egyptian pyramids (between 2670 and 664 BCE), the palaces and temples of Palestine under Kings David and Solomon (1000–931 BCE), the fortifications of Persepolis (550–330 BCE), and the Great Wall of China (220–206 BCE, reconstructed repeatedly).[18] At Islam's birth, forced labor saw regular use throughout the Roman Empire.[19] But it is not among the forms of paying zakat. Moreover, people too poor to pay taxes in any given year did not have to pay double the following year.[20]

In earmarking the contributions of well-off Muslims to communal governance, the zakat system also capped their obligations. In doing so, it restricted the emerging Islamic state's fiscal capacity, but without keeping people from paying more, if they so desired, to causes of their choice. It put a ceiling on what the state could exact from individuals for collective purposes, not on what individuals themselves could spend on social initiatives. Hence, zakat might have provided the doctrinal foundation of a social contract involving predictability and equity in taxation, limited government, and vibrant civic life. Such a social contract appears to have governed relations among Muslims during Islam's initial Mecca period (613–22) and even, to a degree, during the decade when Muhammad governed a state (622–32). Soon after, though, that notional social contract collapsed under the weight of exceptions for certain powerful groups. Specifically, as Islam became a world religion, zakat turned into a far more limited personal duty to give charity. Though remaining a "pillar" in Islamic doctrine, it lost relevance to Islamic rule. Among the byproducts of that transformation was the fall of a barrier to arbitrary government takings. From the 660s to modern times, Islamic tax practices evolved without reference to the Quran's transfer system.

EROSION OF FISCAL CONSTRAINTS

At the rise of Islam, Western Arabia lagged other parts of the Middle East in technologies such as metallurgy and tool making. Its products were also limited, though it participated in global trade as a minor commercial outpost on the margins of a prosperous region.[21] As Islam spread in all directions, its economic base diversified. Consequently, the Muslim community had to decide whether and how new sources of income and wealth would be taxed. Although the sequence of steps is unidentifiable, the surviving recollections of Islam's first century provide a general idea. Influential groups, many located outside of Arabia, demanded exemptions for numerous categories of wealth. Backed by jurists, caliphs granted requests to preserve alliances. Consequently, the tax code of the zakat system began to look like the present American tax code: riddled with loopholes and regressive at the upper end of the wealth scale.

Having curtailed zakat's coverage, influential groups then began to treat as sacred and thus unmodifiable the specifics of the restricted tax code, rather than the principles of predictable taxation, taxpayer equity, limited government, and civic freedoms inherent in its initial design. In the process, they curbed the state's capacity to finance the expenses that it had been covering through zakat. Hence, a few decades after the birth of Islam, Muslim-governed states were collecting taxes unknown to Muhammad's generation. Taxes were no longer capped or predictable, and they varied substantially across time and space.[22]

It is not obvious why major zakat exemptions were granted even as new taxes were imposed. If Arab caliphs could tax broadly, why did they so readily allow zakat exemptions? They might have gone in the opposite direction, interpreting zakat expansively, to cover forms of income and wealth particular to conquered lands. Invoking Abu Bakr's bloody enforcement drive, they might have signaled that they would follow his precedent in dealing with zakat evaders. But the Quran does not explicitly rule out other taxes from Muslims. Besides, interpreting the zakat duty narrowly gave Arab caliphs something they valued more, the capacity to raise more tax revenue than possible under zakat, however strictly interpreted. According to the calculations of David Stasavage,

Abbasid Iraq extracted about 7 percent of production around 850 CE, more than double the English crown's extraction in 1215. Though relatively low for the time, England's rate of extraction provoked a constitutional crisis, making English monarchs return to their norm of taxing about 1 percent of production. Not until 1542 did England return to the 3 percent level.[23] Stasavage attributes the interregional difference to checks and balances that emerged in Western Europe but not in the Middle East.[24] Previous chapters identified several institutions responsible for keeping rule of law weak in states governed under Islamic law. Our explanation will broaden as additional elements of the Islamic institutional complex come into focus.

One might expect the beneficiaries of zakat-financed expenditures to have defended the Quran's stipulations. But that would have been complicated, because on fiscal matters the Quran is subject to multiple interpretations. The principles of limited and predictable taxation are hardly self-evident; they require interpreting each verse within its original context.[25] Consider the verses that discourage stinginess and hoarding.[26] Isolated from the zakat verses, they can be used to justify arbitrary taxation. Another source of ambiguity is the Quran's inconsistency in treating zakat as obligatory; certain verses say that payment is voluntary.[27] Such apparent contradictions reflect intertemporal changes in the challenges the Muslim community faced. Verses that treat zakat as a tax appear to date from a period when the Muslim community was growing explosively through conquests. In contrast, the depictions as charity are from Islam's earliest years, when the Muslim community numbered at most in the hundreds.[28] Only in small and intimate communities might one realistically expect to finance communal expenses through voluntary donations.[29]

The logic of the switch from charity to tax cannot be gleaned from canonical compilations of the Quran, which order chapters from longest to shortest rather than chronologically.[30] The length-based ordering detaches chapter contents from their historical context. As a result, the Quran's typical reader overlooks its principles of limited, fixed, and predictable taxation.

Within the span of a few decades, then, zakat ceased to constrain Muslim rulers on taxation. Before long, Islamic taxation turned out to be whatever the state could get away with, and property rights weakened. Rulers derived immediate benefits from the ineffectiveness of the Quran's constraints on predation. They gained the ability to resolve crises through new taxes and arbitrary confiscations. This is evident in the high rate of resource extraction by contemporaneous global standards. Over the long run, however, the rapaciousness of rulers harmed the region. The permissiveness of the Islamic institutional complex on predation contributed to keeping states untrustworthy in the eyes of the ruled. Consequently, Muslim-governed states failed to acquire a capacity to borrow internally, as European states eventually did, partly through constitutions that tied their hands.[31] That unintended drawback is analogous to the waqf's crushing of incentives to seek general material security through stronger private property rights.

The Umayyad caliphs who governed from Damascus continued to collect zakat for a while, if irregularly. So did the Baghdad-based Abbasid caliphs who followed. Abu Ubayd (770–838), who wrote about almsgiving and taxation during the early Abbasid era, reports that enforcement of the zakat duty was patchy. Moreover, some zakat payers were choosing recipients on their own.[32] Collections were no less decentralized a century later, in the age of Mawardi (974–1058), who lived in Basra. Refusal to pay zakat to Abbasid officials was common, he writes.[33] Revealingly, even though his work was almost certainly commissioned by the Abbasid dynasty, he refrains from condemning zakat evasion.

The Umayyads and Abbasids both collected other taxes, too. In general, they kept in place pre-Islamic local levies.[34] Under their watch, zakat turned into a fungible component of a broader revenue stream. Having gone outside the Quran's fiscal system once, caliphs found it easy to add new taxes as well as to adjust and readjust rates. Net taxation became whatever rulers could get away with. The pattern continued in later regimes. In Umayyad Spain (711–1031) and Fatimid Egypt (909–1171), zakat was regarded as a matter of personal conscience for each believer. Sultans raised revenue almost entirely through other taxes.[35]

State collection of zakat resumed under the Ayyubid rulers of Egypt, Syria, and Western Arabia (1171–1260), but as a cover for rapacious taxation and with the flimsiest connection to early zakat practices. A pauper selling salt from a basket on his head was forced to pay zakat; under early practices, he would have been a recipient. Zakat proceeds were used to pay clerics, and the poor received nothing. Widespread aversion to paying zakat to Ayyubid officials is evident from an administrative manual on punishments for "misers" refusing to pay. In violation of early Islamic practices, "zakat" was collected from traveling pilgrims, who were body-searched to keep them from concealing money. The consequent resentment must have contributed to the fall of the Ayyubids. The Cairo-based Mamluks who followed (1250–1517) restored the pre-Ayyubid policy of letting subjects pay zakat as individuals, however they wanted.[36]

The concept of imposing fiscal constraints on rulers was not, then, an innovation when it became a feature of the Middle East's modernization drive. Ironically, although the modernizers did not think of themselves as restoring a religious principle, the fiscal constraints that they instituted were embodied in one of Islam's five pillars. In principle, that pillar, zakat, remains the most important of all the economic elements of Islamic law. In practice, even before the seventh century was out, it had turned into an economic ritual of little relevance to the state. As it lost significance, property rights weakened, sowing material insecurity. And the unshackling of the state generated new needs, some of which were met by adding the waqf to the Islamic institutional complex. The institutional developments under analysis are vital, then, for a deep appreciation of the political legacies of Islamic law.

ROLE OF COERCION IN ENFORCEMENT

Prior to 622, as the number of Muslims reached a few hundred, the community faced growing persecution. In hostile environments, small communities tend to develop sharing norms for survival. In this context, members were already familiar with them. Arabia's pre-Islamic tribal customs required everyone of means to assist orphans, widows, the infirm, and the hungry. They also made tribe members participate in communal defense. Under the circumstances, zakat could have been enforced reasonably well through multilateral social pressures.[37] As in all primitive face-to-face societies, wealthy individuals could have been induced to obey generosity norms through threats of ostracism.[38] Tellingly, in this period the term "zakat" was used interchangeably with sadaqa, which referred, and still refers, to voluntary almsgiving.

With the community's relocation to Medina in 622 and the establishment of an Islamic state governing a rapidly growing population of converts and other monotheists, zakat became a compulsory transfer system. The Quran's chapters thought to date from Muhammad's Medina period contain repeated admonitions to pay zakat. Evidently, some converts were resisting or neglecting this duty.[39] The same chapters also condemn hoarding and greed, presumably to make the delinquent feel guilty.[40]

Mandatory zakat payments to Islam's communal fund helped to finance the new state's activities. Meanwhile, Islam took to distinguishing between the zakat duty and voluntary almsgiving. To that end, a Quran verse that specifies zakat beneficiaries was reinterpreted to mean that the right to disburse zakat revenue belongs to the state rather than the individual.[41] The terminological ambiguities in question testify to the political transformation that unfolded during the Prophet's own lifetime – the emergence of a hierarchical and coercive Islamic state from a loosely administered face-to-face community regulated by social norms. If one characteristic of a state is monopoly over violence, another is the right to tax.[42] In a liberal order with checks and balances, the tax burden is distributed widely, according to transparent rules. In illiberal orders, the ruling coalition gives itself exemptions, and the ruled may pay unevenly according to opaque and volatile rules.

Not all converts to Islam accepted the emergence of an increasingly powerful Islamic state. The ensuing discontent may be gleaned from a Quran verse believed to date from the end of the Prophet's life. It threatens hypocritical payers of zakat with divine retribution: "Some desert Arabs regard what they give for the cause of Allah as a compulsory fine and wait for some misfortune to befall [the Prophet]. May ill-fortune befall them! Allah hears all and knows all."[43] Apparently, certain tribes were paying grudgingly, to avoid punishment. Treating zakat as burdensome, they were signaling that they would suspend payments if ever they could do so with impunity.

Organized challenges were not long in coming. As soon as the Prophet died, large groups refused to make payments to his successor at the community's helm, Abu Bakr. As we saw in Chapter 7, the caliph waged war against the rebels on the pretext that the refusal amounted to apostasy. This response underscored zakat's transformation from charity to a coerced transfer system. As far as state officials were concerned, zakat had become a fundamental Islamic duty, one on a par with professing belief in God's unity. In making rebellious tribes pay zakat to the Islamic state, Abu Bakr also affirmed the state's obligation to fulfill the Quran's eight service instructions.

The Quran is silent on the means for enforcing the zakat duty. And on disbursement of zakat revenue, it simply enumerates recipient categories. Taken as a whole, then, it rules out neither the voluntary and decentralized transfer system of the earliest Islamic years nor the obligatory and centralized system of the Prophet's final decade. The lack of specificity precluded the resolution of disputes simply by consulting the Quran. During the "Apostasy Wars," neither side could refute the rival case unequivocally through scripture. Each position was grounded in historical precedent.

THE END OF FIXED, LIMITED, AND PREDICTABLE TAXATION

The seventh-century disagreements over zakat were not limited to collection method and collector identity. We saw that controversies arose over specifics of the individual Muslim's obligation. Economically, the most significant exemption, enacted by the third caliph Uthman (governed 644–56), abolished the zakat duty on "hidden" (*bāṭin*) wealth. Thenceforth, dues would be limited to assessments on "apparent" (*ẓāhir*) wealth alone.[44] Hiddenness had a special meaning in this context. Uthman's administration took hidden wealth to include, in addition to easily concealed precious stones, ordinarily visible assets such as housing and slaves. Meanwhile, it considered as "apparent" concealable assets, such as gold jewelry. These mismatches indicate that the new collection policy reflected expedience rather than a coherent refinement.[45]

In later years, disagreements broke out among Islam's emerging schools of law as to what crops are subject to zakat. The Hanafi school of law included all products of the soil. The Shafiis and Malikis imposed zakat on foods stored as staples, exempting vegetables, spices, and condiments. The Hanbalis, like the Twelver Shiis, imposed zakat on crops that are stored but also measured by volume.[46] These variations must have reflected geographic differences in the relative strengths of narrow pressure groups.[47] Differences aside, all these variants of agricultural zakat collection amounted to an income tax.

Conflicts over the zakat duty thus raised fundamental issues that transcended the specifics of individual commodities. They put in doubt the very basics of the duty. Must well-to-do Muslims pay zakat on income, wealth, or both? The disarray is evident even in modern reference works. The *Encyclopedia of Islam* defines zakat as an "obligatory payment" on "lawful property." But it also says, in contradiction, that zakat is due additionally on certain forms of income, including agricultural output.[48]

Another nagging confusion concerns whether the annual Islamic duty ends with zakat payments. Certain Quran verses intimate that all additional donations count as sadaqa, earning divine favor for generosity. But other verses suggest that eternal punishment awaits accumulators. An example is: "Proclaim a woeful punishment to those that hoard up gold and silver and do not spend it in Allah's cause."[49] Readers of this verse might wonder whether being a good Muslim requires regular transfers beyond those paid as zakat. Like the Christian ascetics of medieval Europe, they could think that renouncing worldly comforts is necessary to avoiding hellfire.[50]

To add to these complications, the meaning of zakat itself narrowed over time. Under the Prophet and the first two caliphs (613–44), all taxes appear to have been called zakat, including the 2.5 percent customs duty imposed on Muslim traders. Subsequently, other taxes acquired distinct names.[51] Meanwhile, the Quran's fiscal nomenclature continued to sow confusion. In a treatise on taxation by Abu Yusuf, counsel to the caliph Harun al-Rashid (763–809) and co-founder of the Hanafi school of law, livestock taxes are called sadaqa; and sadaqa itself signifies not voluntary charity but the individual Muslim's obligatory payment to the state.[52]

Why might a renowned jurist of Islam appear, to modern eyes, to have confused zakat with sadaqa, in other words, tax with charity? That the confusion occurs in a treatise on taxation only compounds the mystery. Conceivably, by the time Abu Yusuf was writing, zakat was no longer a state-enforced tax but a form of charity. That would explain why a man steeped in Islamic law and familiar with economic principles used zakat and sadaqa interchangeably. If the Umayyad and Abbasid caliphates both taxed subjects under names absent from the Quran, and individual Muslims paid zakat dues mainly outside the state's purview, Abu Yusuf was probably referring to the voluntary transfers prevalent in his own milieu.[53]

Whether collected as zakat or as some other due, the tax on agricultural output was normally 10 percent or 5 percent, depending on whether irrigation was natural or artificial. The differentiation rested on the principle, followed widely at the time, that a farmer using artificial irrigation exerted more effort than if his crops were fed by rainfall alone.[54] Whatever the motivations for these rate choices during Islam's first century, the effort-based scale was not followed consistently. Sharp variations existed.[55] Rules also emerged for taxing livestock. Animals in a person's possession for an entire year were taxed according to their kind, provided they had not been put to work. Exemptions reflected animal values in the desert economy of seventh-century Arabia: five camels, or twenty cattle, or forty smaller animals. Evidently, equity across payers was a key objective.[56]

But it is the rates rather than the underlying equity objective that captivated Islam's later interpreters. Gaining precedence over the initial principles of the zakat tax itself, the rates acquired sacredness. Had the Quran's zakat duty generated widely accepted redistribution principles, rates could have been adjusted subsequently according to variations in income distribution and communal spending priorities.

Keeping rates fixed and coverage restricted to a few commodities made it infeasible to keep zakat as the main, let alone sole, source of tax revenue. Among the consequences was the ebb of zakat as a topic in Islamic discourses on public finance. Leading economic histories of the Middle East do not even mention zakat, except perhaps if they stretch back to the seventh century.[57] The zakat entry in the *Encyclopaedia of Islam* reports that "virtually nothing is known about the details of the official collection ... throughout most of [zakat's] history."[58] That is not through negligence. Unlike other taxes, which left written records, zakat is essentially invisible to economic historians working in archives and libraries. Indeed, after Islam's first century zakat stopped playing a major role in public finance. By then it was merely a personal ritual without the broader social purpose of Islam's initial decades. Nothing is said on zakat in the treatises that high officials wrote to advise rulers on governance.[59] No new public controversies on zakat emerged, because the state had left payment to the individual's own discretion.

An unfortunate byproduct of zakat's disappearance from policy discussions is that the goals inherent in its design ceased to command attention. Had zakat retained significance as a governance instrument, later interpreters might have used its early history as a basis for stabilizing and limiting taxes. They might have considered institutions to stimulate civic initiatives. They might also have pondered about making taxes predictable. It could have seemed obvious that both opportunistic taxation and expropriation are un-Islamic. Whether such thoughts would have affected policies is another matter. Fearing hostile reactions from rulers with a stake in the status quo, proponents of shackling rulers might have kept quiet. At the very least, though, a potential would have remained for rediscovering the core principles of zakat. In times of financial crisis, when a ruler is exceptionally open to change, they might have served as a reservoir of sacred wisdom against state predation.

DISBURSEMENT OF ZAKAT REVENUE

The eight canonical categories of zakat disbursement correspond to basic functions of any social system. These encompass services now generally regulated or directly supplied by states.[60] In modern societies, the poor and the needy are within the purview of private philanthropies as well as welfare and health ministries. "Servants of God" form hierarchical staffs reporting to a ruler or a defense department. The zakat administration's job belongs to a ministry of finance. And so on. Moreover, even in the poorest modern country specialization goes much farther than in Muhammad's era. Every modern society allocates resources to mass communication, the environment, and climate – concerns without salience in Antiquity. Because governance has broadened, most modern governments have more than eight ministries. For the Middle East's most populous states the average number is twenty.[61] Particularly relevant is that the multiplicity of the Quran's spending categories poses tradeoffs. Revenue spent on poverty alleviation reduces what is available for health services.

Zakat budgeting may well have proceeded smoothly during the earliest years of the Medina-based Islamic state. It was possible then to pass controversies to Muhammad. Yet his rulings were not necessarily accepted by all Muslims. Verse 9:60, believed to date from around 630, reiterates the rule that revenue is for eight specific constituencies, probably because some groups needed reassurance. Ambiguities on the composition of these categories guaranteed disagreements after Muhammad died. In fact, the distinction between "poor" and "needy" quickly sowed friction.[62] Can the needy include people living opulently? Are all poor needy? What defines "poor"? Certain jurists drew the line at the exemption limits; the poor consisted of people who could not pay zakat themselves.

Other jurists considered this approach flawed. For Shafii, founder of the law school bearing his name, the key factor was community standards of wealth. The goal was to raise the victims of misfortune back to their stations in life; redistribution had to restore the status quo ante. In the case of victims accustomed to consuming more than the exemption limits, zakat transfers would prevent loss of status. Opponents of this status-based definition of zakat assistance complained that it legitimized perverse redistribution. Zakat recipients could be wealthier, they said, than payers.[63] Indeed, the status-based definition tended to favor the rich facing temporary difficulties. Turning zakat into an instrument of consumption smoothing, it permitted the poor to remain stuck in poverty without any communal assistance. Whether they used a status- or poverty-based definition of entitlement, discourses on state-mediated zakat lacked a concept of budget constraint. In divorcing transfer decisions from resource availability, they left unaddressed tradeoffs among the eight categories. The Quran says nothing specific on the eight-way division. Hence, a single narrow constituency could claim the bulk of the zakat budget. Unsurprisingly, allocations fostered disputes from the start.[64]

In Antiquity, a common concern of rulers was to dampen the fluctuations of food supplies for themselves, the armies that defended them, and the remaining population. One purpose was thus to accumulate food surpluses in periods of plenty and draw them down in years of bad harvest.[65] Therefore, the classical literature on zakat is striking for its lack of intertemporal concerns.

A disbursement rule that emerged under the fourth caliph Ali (served 656–61) required the use of zakat revenue in the year of collection. And, according to a view that also gained currency, each year's zakat fund was to be divided equally among the eight categories. The equal-disbursement rule emerged to alleviate discontent over the perception that Uthman's administration had abused its discretion.[66] Like the same-year spending rule, it aimed at binding state officials. It is unclear to what extent such rules were enforced.

But no one familiar with the politics of redistribution in large societies will find surprising the implied mistrust or, for that matter, the enduring conflicts over zakat disbursement. Although generosity is a universal human trait, nepotism is also common. The tribes that defied Abu Bakr's zakat collectors were not necessarily uncharitable. They may simply have preferred local redistribution without intervention from distant authorities.

These interpretations negate historical accounts that portray the early Islamic community as a paragon of compassion. That early Muslims were highly motivated to assist the disadvantaged is plausible. But it is unlikely that treating all fellow Muslims equally was the norm. If nothing else, evenhandedness would have required the shedding of all tribal attachments at conversion. The bloody conflicts of early Islam testify to the internal divisions that plagued the Muslim community as it became increasingly heterogeneous in terms of prior loyalties. Further evidence of enduring tribalism and regionalism is that the first Islamic state's officials, including caliphs, were often accused of favoritism.

Three of the disbursement categories – zakat administrators, potential and recent converts, and servants of God – transferred zakat revenue to state officials and clerics. Initially, zakat shares formed the bulk of their personal earnings. However, booty and taxes on non-Muslim subjects quickly eclipsed zakat. Meanwhile, caliphs took to treating zakat as a fungible component of a broader revenue stream. Insofar as they collected zakat at all, caliphs seem to have spent the revenue as they chose, without feeling constrained by the Quran. No chronicles or recollections have survived to suggest that they worried about budgeting according to guidelines of the Quran. Leading jurists of the early Abbasid era believed that caliphs routinely spent communal funds illicitly.[67] At the time, this was nothing unusual. The medieval European Church enriched the clergy through tithes ostensibly collected for the poor.[68]

POVERTY ALLEVIATION

During the period when the Islamic state used zakat revenue to finance public goods, including social welfare, the poor were not ignored. Inasmuch as they received transfers, zakat would have contributed to poverty reduction. Indeed, economists Ahmad Oran and Salim Rashid claim that the formal zakat system of the first Islamic century was progressive. Its burden fell disproportionately on the rich, they suggest, and its benefits accrued primarily to the poor.[69] The polemical Islamist literature goes much further. "For about a thousand years," says a promoter of Islamic economics, "there was no accumulation of wealth in a few hands, no hoarding and no profiteering, as these had been tabooed in Islam ... the state was responsible for providing a living wage or relief to every inhabitant ... there were neither slums nor multi-millionaires."[70] These vast exaggerations rest on narratives developed in Islam's formative centuries. The early period produced many popular stories of compassionate rulers. One has the second caliph making the rounds of Mecca every night with a sack of flour, to ensure that everyone had enough to eat.

In the early Islamic centuries, the poor as a whole may well have been among the net gainers of transfers made under the rubric of zakat. However, for lack of documents recording disbursements, there is no way to verify that conjecture.[71] Beyond doubt is that radical equalization is a myth. We saw how, in Uthman's time, broad exemptions protected the wealthy. The same period also saw the defeat of equalization campaigns. They include a movement that pursued near-equality and considered zakat a barrier to meaningful redistribution. Uthman's administration silenced its members.[72] In later times, complaints about zakat evasion were commonplace. Ghazali listed ruses that enabled believers to fulfill the letter of the zakat duty while violating its original spirit. For example, a man would make a gift to his wife at the end of the year and take it back through an offsetting gift a few days later.[73]

THE WAQF AS ALTERNATIVE TO ZAKAT

In accounts of Islam's distributional roles, zakat and waqf are often invoked as complementary institutions serving the poor.[74] In fact, each served far broader roles than poverty relief alone. More critically, by the time the waqf entered the Islamic institutional complex, Arab caliphates were no longer enforcing the zakat duty. As instruments of governance, then, zakat and waqf were never complements. Rather, the waqf substituted selectively for certain features of the initial zakat system, and only after zakat was already voluntary. In enabling services that the Quran's zakat rules assigned to the state, it negated some of zakat's original functions. But it also switched the method of delivery from direct provision to outsourcing. Hence, it was central to the institutionalization of shallow economic governance. Like zakat, it shackled the state and promoted individual material security. Unlike zakat in its initial form, the waqf was partial to wealthy property owners. It sheltered real estate rather than all assets. Still another difference concerns civic life. Although zakat did nothing to boost civic life, nor did it hinder its development. By contrast, and as Chapter 4 showed, waqf law impoverished civic life through multiple channels.

We know already that waqf law reflected an implicit bargain among landowners (who attained material security), rulers (who incentivized their wealthy subjects to provide services vital to political stability), clerics (who earned rents from supervising waqfs), and the broader population (which obtained diverse social services, if not for free then at subsidized prices). Now we may add that the waqf absorbed social functions that one of Islam's five pillars had assigned to the state. By 1000 CE, privately endowed public kitchens, hospitals, hostels, inns, fountains, and schools had a far greater economic impact than zakat ever did. The poor were among the beneficiaries. But substantial waqf revenue accrued to clerics. One contributing factor is that clerics redefined the concept of "the poor" (*fuqarā*) to include themselves. Another is that waqfs supporting mosque employees, religious lodges, or schools put resources directly in the hands of clerics.[75] Waqf-funded services could also target other well-off groups. The beneficiaries of inns built on commercial routes were mainly merchants and commercial investors.

On poor relief, the waqf did indeed substitute for zakat. However, just as poverty relief was not zakat's primary function, so it was never the waqf's main function. Another commonality is that neither institution was designed to eliminate poverty. Both were predicated on the existence of poverty as an unalterable fact of life, like mountains and the sea. Accordingly, in no premodern city of the Muslim world did officials feel obliged to maintain a social safety net – to say nothing of performing that task through zakat transfers or waqfs. And nowhere did voluntary assistance end poverty. In the 1700s, Abraham Marcus writes, "Aleppo had no state-organized social security system that automatically took care of those unable to support themselves."[76] The poor turned to their families or to voluntary communal charity. Public kitchens and shelters attached to mosques assisted the needy. However, as in other premodern societies, Aleppo featured a large and seemingly irreducible underclass.[77] The same pattern has been documented also for Fatimid Cairo, Mamluk Egypt, and Ottoman Algiers, Istanbul, and Salonica.[78]

Transferring the task of poverty alleviation from zakat to waqfs promoted shallow economic governance. Limiting the resources at the disposal of state officials, it also secured a class of assets against expropriation. On the downside, the rules of the waqf did nothing to protect ordinary property rights – the security of assets that their owners had not placed in a waqf's endowment. Worse, in enabling wealth sheltering, it limited incentives to join coalitions working to bind the grabbing hand of rulers. Put differently, it delayed the promulgation of *general* property rights.[79] Rich Muslims of the seventh and eighth centuries sought wealth shelters precisely because zakat had ceased to constrain rulers as intended. Hence, a lasting consequence of sidelining zakat was the unshackling of the state. As we already know, for all the resources they controlled, waqfs were politically powerless. They did not constrain the ruler's capacity to tax or expropriate, as zakat might have done.

PERSONAL PURIFICATION AND FREEDOM
FROM SOCIAL RESPONSIBILITY

A charitable practice followed widely has been the transfer to the poor made on the last day of Ramadan. Known as zakat al-fitr or zakat Ramadan, it does not appear in the Quran and is distinct from zakat proper. Its purpose is, on the one hand, to absolve donors of their sins and, on the other, to relieve the poor from having to beg for food during the feast that marks the end of Ramadan.[80] Over the ages, zakat al-fitr has supplied poor relief, but on just one day of the year. It has never been a major source of redistribution. And, in contrast to zakat and waqf, no one claims otherwise.

The end of state-enforced zakat rendered moot the apportionment of zakat revenue among the eight canonical categories. No Islamic state attempted to coordinate the zakat transfers of its subjects.[81] Yet from the fact that decentralized zakat transfers left practically no historical traces, one may infer that they financed current consumption as opposed to perpetual public goods. In principle, a wealthy person could have used 2.5 percent of his or her wealth to build, say, a water fountain serving "the needy," one of the eight zakat categories. If any such zakat-financed structure exists, it must be a very rare exception.

Zakat-al-fitr's purifying function raises a question about zakat proper. Was equity among zakat payers or efficiency of redistribution ever zakat's dominant purpose? Non-Arabic cognates of zakat suggest that, from the beginning, its purposes included the cleansing of donor wealth. The Aramaic *zakūt* originally conveyed "purity," and Arabian Jews and Christians used it to mean "virtuous conduct." Early Muslims used zakat in a sense consistent with these two usages.[82] Evidently, by relinquishing some of their possessions, Muslims purified and legitimated the vast majority that they kept.[83] This interpretation draws additional support from two sayings attributed to the Prophet: "Goods on which one has paid zakat cease being part of one's treasure"; and "Allah instituted zakat so that you can enjoy the rest of your wealth with a clear conscience."[84]

Zakat thus released individual donors and the full community from the burden of monitoring the social consequences of zakat transfers – their effects, say, on inequality, poverty, or unemployment. It also absolved donors of reacting to zakat's effects. They did not have to worry about solving social problems. So long as donors gave out of the goodness of their hearts, it hardly mattered whether the recipients were rich or poor, good or bad Muslims, honest workers or lazy cheats.

Classical Islamic teachings addressed the definition of poverty, who qualifies as needy, and the specifics of a poor person's entitlement. But they did not forge a consensus capable of channeling zakat resources primarily toward the poor; nor did they generate a widely felt obligation for the wealthy to seek out the neediest people. In practice, as the Marcus study of Aleppo shows, voluntary zakat transfers flowed toward the most visible poor rather than the neediest.[85] The rich typically assisted their servants and the beggars in their neighborhoods. Without giving thought to overcoming the causes of need, they considered their zakat duty met.

That is a reason why, prior to the Westernizing reforms of the nineteenth century, the Islamic world produced no major organized movement aimed at eliminating poverty. Although countless constituencies demanded more of the economic pie, none took on poverty as a problem to be tackled across a region, an empire, or the Muslim world. Another reason lies in the frailties of civic organizational instruments – a theme covered earlier.

According to the Quran, though, the impoverished are entitled to zakat aid. While they should not expect to turn rich, they need not worry that their more fortunate brethren will keep their wealth entirely to themselves.[86] Framing zakat assistance as a poor person's entitlement also legitimizes the Islamic order in the eyes of the underprivileged. "You might feel exploited," it says to the downtrodden, "but know that your community will never forget you."[87] It reduces the likelihood of the poor viewing the social order as hopelessly rigged against them. In its state-enforced form, then, zakat performed a political role along with an economic function. Through its effects on attitudes, it served as a social stabilizer. On the one hand, it counseled the rich to avoid feeling obligated to eradicate poverty. On the other, it dampened resentments of the poor and moderated their demands. After the end of state enforcement, zakat continued to serve as a stabilizer for the same reasons, but to a lesser extent. The poor were conditioned to expect modest aid from the wealthy people with whom they interacted.

In line with these observations, pessimism on eliminating poverty was commonplace in Islamic discourses before the 1950s. And it was expressed without apology. In a 1921 treatise, Jamal al-Din al-Qasimi, a leader of a Syrian-led Islamic reform movement that evolved into modern Islamism, promoted a zakat system supported by obligatory payments from the rich. But he could not even imagine a society without widespread poverty. His ideal system would simply meet basic needs and overcome envy.[88]

Middle Eastern states formed after Islam's initial few decades were not indifferent to poverty. For political stability, they tried to keep it within bounds. But they did so through means other than zakat, principally by encouraging the wealthy to establish waqfs benefiting the poor. In a spirit akin to *noblesse oblige* (nobility obligates), a principle of the European aristocracy, they expected wealthy Muslims, especially the reigning dynasty and their high officials, to give back to the community something permanent. Yet the wealthy were not required to address the root causes of hunger or poverty. Rich Muslims have never been asked to coordinate their philanthropic activities so that every poor person in their own locality is fed. To do well on Judgment Day, so went the belief, the wealthy needed only to avoid being excessively closefisted.

These patterns align with Islam's stance on slavery. The Quran promotes the freeing of slaves.[89] But it does not insist on a slave-free society. On the contrary, it treats the free–slave dichotomy as part of the natural order.[90] In some verses, freeing a slave appears, like helping the poor, as a vehicle for atoning sins, as opposed to an intrinsically good deed.[91] Accordingly, up to modern times Islam was generally interpreted as allowing slavery. True, the actual rights of slaves and their masters, like restrictions on who may be enslaved, have varied greatly.[92] However, until reforms initiated in the 1800s, Muslims who met the zakat duty by freeing a slave had no obligation to investigate the causes of slavery or even oppose the practice.[93] They could win moral credit for freeing slaves even as they profited from the slave trade.

BROKEN SHACKLES, RESTORATION OF ARBITRARY RULE

Every polity must collect taxes to fund its services. The state that emerged under Muhammad's leadership was no exception. It could have taxed as it found necessary. Instead, it instituted zakat, a predictable, fixed, and mildly progressive transfer system designed to finance specific causes. In capping state size, it allowed private groups to expand and enrich social services through initiatives of their own. At its birth, Islam's formal transfer system was sufficiently important for inclusion among its canonical five pillars.

Implicit in zakat were personal property rights as well as constraints on government – two key elements of a liberal order. They could have provided the starting point for a political system conducive to broadening freedoms under a state with explicitly restricted functions. The principles of the zakat system might have fueled discourses on religious, intellectual, expressive, and organizational liberties, also perhaps on private philanthropy. Gaining sophistication over time, these discourses might have articulated justifications for institutionalized checks and balances. They might have weighed competing ideas on accountability, centralized provision of social services, and implementing zakat.

By itself, the retention of zakat would not have turned the Middle East into a paragon of liberalism. Apostasy and blasphemy accusations could have been used to constrain discourses. Just as the waqf was given features that allowed the circumvention of Quranic inheritance principles, new institutions could have been developed to undermine zakat. Tellingly, its successor as a vehicle for supplying public goods, the waqf itself, lacked the potentially liberalizing features of zakat. Limiting political participation, accountability, and resource reallocation, it also kept civil society anemic.

The Quran contains no theory of government predation. After all, it is not a treatise on political economy. But early interpreters of Islam might have identified the drawbacks of empowering rulers to choose social services themselves and of allowing them to spend without constraints. If any did so, their thoughts were not passed on. Later Muslims did not learn about timeless and universal general principles of limited government. For generations on end, the specifics of the initial zakat system applied in mid-seventh-century Western Arabia have been memorized and recited, even referenced in Quranic exegeses. Schoolchildren still learn about the Quran's eight zakat constituencies without being asked to reflect on their relevance to Islamic history or their own society, or on why zakat became a pillar of Islam, or on its loss of relevance to Islamic governance.

The specifics of the zakat system reflected the milieu in which Islam emerged. They related to the major taxable sources of wealth and income known to Muhammad's generation and to the basic functions of what leading minds of Antiquity considered effective state institutions. As Islam expanded to areas with different economic bases, zakat became increasingly unsuited to progressive and equitable taxation. To tax professions such as urban artisans, rulers inevitably went outside the zakat system. The stage was set for opportunistic taxes that could vary by region, over time, and across demographic groups.

At its emergence, Islam's main political mission was to weaken Arabian tribalism and replace it with religious brotherhood. Zakat was predicated on that mission's success. Transfers would be targeted at designated constituencies without regard to geographic origins or tribal descent. Even non-Muslims were eligible for certain transfers. In practice, though, the officials who disbursed zakat revenue did not treat all Muslims equally, let alone the whole population. By and large, donors cared relatively more about the poor of their own localities. Nepotism and corruption posed additional problems. Irregularities on the collection side delegitimized centralized zakat, as did favoritism in disbursements.

In one sense, the sidelining of zakat made individuals freer. They could provide as much, or as little, assistance as they wanted. However, this freedom came at the expense of a more consequential freedom, protection from arbitrary taxation and expropriation. State-enforced zakat might have safeguarded individual property rights by binding the state. Instead, barely a few decades after Muhammad's death, Muslim rulers were taxing their subjects without reference to Islam's distinct transfer system. Zakat had become an anachronism – an institution considered central to Islam but disregarded by policy makers ostensibly governing under Islamic law. Islamic states that came after Muhammad's Medina-based state were all unshackled states.

Zakat returned to Islamic discourses in the mid-twentieth century, with the rise of Islamism. But the renewed attention to zakat has sidestepped the seventh-century goals of limiting taxation, cementing private property rights, and binding the state. The new conception of zakat is addressed, and related to themes already developed, in Chapter 14. But first we must explore the role of merchants and financiers in the trajectories discussed. After all, where political freedoms and economic opportunities expanded, private businesses played a big role. In Europe, where liberal orders emerged first, they were central to the emergence of essential checks and balances.

13

Politically Powerless Entrepreneurs and Enterprises

Of all major religions, Islam is the only one founded by a merchant. Sensitivities characteristic of Muhammad's profession find expression in the Quran. They include property rights and predictable taxation, which are key ingredients of commercial productivity. Commercial partnerships through which Arabian merchants pooled labor and capital received Islamic legitimacy during Muhammad's lifetime, as did instruments they used to transfer money across long distances. Refined and developed under Islamic regimes, these institutions helped Muslim merchants dominate several of the world's leading commercial emporia from the 700s to the 1400s. They were central to the Middle East's internal trade, but also to its transactions with India and China. In some trading zones, such as the commercial routes linking the Middle East and East Africa, Muslim dominance lasted several centuries longer.[1]

The professional achievements of Muslim merchants might have brought them political influence. Seated at the political bargaining table, they could have ensured tight enforcement of property rights and tax rules. In certain premodern societies, rich merchants were using their economic clout to secure commercial wealth and improve business opportunities through political checks and balances. Thus, in the twelfth century Venetian traders managed to constrain the Doge's authority and to obtain regulations that strengthened their already powerful commercial capabilities.[2] Likewise, half a millennium later, rapidly prospering English merchants boosted Parliament's authority vis-à-vis the Crown.[3] In these cases, mercantile successes and democratization became mutually reinforcing. Curiously, the legendary successes of Middle Eastern merchants did not trigger analogous dynamics. For almost a millennium, Islamic commercial institutions precluded scaling up, and merchants lacked political power.

When profit-making merchants and financiers flourish, they do not necessarily use their wealth to improve the business climate. They may find it more profitable to form cartels, restrict competition, and resist technological innovation. Successful entrepreneurs may also be coopted by the state to help it extort wealth in return for commercial and financial privileges.[4] By no means, then, does the existence of productive commercial and financial sectors translate automatically into self-reinforcing political transformations. Yet successful businesses can initiate a path to political liberalization. An explanation is needed for why the Middle East did not move down such a path.

The European pattern could not be replicated in the Middle East because, for much of the second millennium, Middle Eastern enterprises remained atomistic and ephemeral. Among the consequences is that, except for artisans who formed state-supervised guilds, entrepreneurs established no organizations to pursue common objectives. Right up to the 1800s, the European growth in business scale and longevity had no analogue in the Middle East; nor did Middle Eastern businesses form associations. Indigenous changes did occur in the institutional framework within which the region's entrepreneurs operated. But none led to long-lasting giant enterprises capable of exerting political power, or to private organizations able to negotiate with the state as impersonal organizations. These are the main reasons why private economic sectors of the Middle East, advanced by global standards of the early second millennium, failed to track the innovations of their Western counterparts.

The economic mechanisms that made the Middle East fall behind Western Europe are laid out in one of my earlier books, the *Long Divergence*. Our focus here is on the political consequences of this institutional stagnation. We shall start by reviewing the relevant institutions of classical Islamic law, then summarize why these institutions changed minimally for almost a millennium. The account will prepare us for exploring how Middle Eastern private enterprises contributed to the political and religious patterns identified in preceding chapters: low organizational capacity for private constituencies, civic sclerosis, persistent religious repression, and both sluggish and limited democratization.

COMMERCIAL AND FINANCIAL INSTITUTIONS OF CLASSICAL ISLAM

Economic activity involves contracts that specify terms of exchange. Terms can be misunderstood, negligence is possible, and fraud is an ever-present danger. Hence, contract enforcement instruments are essential, and their reliability affects the volume of trade. Every enforcement system relies, to some degree, on social sanctions. Dishonest parties are punished through loss of repeat business and, more significantly, bad publicity of their performance. Already in Antiquity, formal courts emerged as complementary enforcement instruments. Communities recognized that bilateral monitoring and multilateral sanctioning are inadequate, particularly in dealings with strangers. To facilitate such exchanges, they established bodies experienced in dispute resolution. These were the precursors of courts staffed by professional judges.[5]

The generation of contracting templates for specific exchange categories – employment, credit, joint production – was another step that diverse civilizations took to minimize conflict and facilitate enforcement. Yet another was the standardization of measures, often in the face of resistance from local power holders with a stake in keeping markets fragmented.[6] Even in the global economy of the Digital Era, contract enforcement depends on a combination of bilateral monitoring, multilateral sanctioning, and arbitration or adjudication through formal organizations. New rules are emerging for the enforcement of virtual contracts. Rating applications are emerging for multilateral sanctioning on a global scale. Legal systems are evolving to accommodate the explosion of online trade.

Contracting forms were central to the development of Islamic law. Jurists transplanted into Islamic law, but also refined and standardized, partnership types used across the Mediterranean and Central Asia. These allowed the pooling of labor and capital for joint ventures in production, retail trade, and long-distance commerce. They enabled capital owners to participate in joint ventures without liability beyond their own financial investment. The profit shares of partners were negotiated freely in advance. And these could be contingent on the choices that the active partners made during execution, for example, on the mix of goods brought back from India by a Basra-based trader. Islamic partnerships were enforceable wherever Islamic courts existed. Although there are differences of interpretation among Islam's schools of law, the spread of Islam created a vast commercial zone supporting an essentially uniform set of contractual templates over three continents. This was a monumental achievement that contributed to the prosperity of Muslim-governed territories but also to the spread of Islam. Mass conversions in India, East Asia, and Sub-Saharan Africa were often a consequence of trade with Muslims, whose institutions diverse communities found advantageous. At the start of the second millennium, Islamic partnerships represented the state of the art. Nowhere, not even in Europe or China, were joint commercial ventures being organized and operated through clearly more sophisticated institutions.[7]

The lack of an Islamic concept of corporation would eventually become a handicap for the Middle East. The business corporation, which was a profit-maximizing venture, turned out to be the most efficient form of organization for economic activities requiring abundant capital. Thus, the overseas trade companies that Europeans started creating in the late 1500s were organized as some form of the business corporation.[8] The same is true of the most capital-intensive companies of the Industrial Revolution.[9] But at the start of the second millennium, no commercial enterprise anywhere came close in capital, workforce, number of shareholders, or longevity to the Dutch East India Company, founded in 1602.[10] What business historians call "super-companies of the Middle Ages," the leading family-dominated Florentine companies of the 1300s, had just dozens of shareholders each. None lasted more than a century.

These super-companies made structural improvements to increase their scope and life span. And in the process, they laid the groundwork for revolutionary organizational innovations. The web of partnerships formed by the Florence-based Medici family provides an example.[11] However, before 1600, Europe's advances in commercial organization did not catch attention as the groundwork of an institutional revolution. Accordingly, the Middle East did not yet look economically underdeveloped.

The Quran bans riba, a pre-Arabian credit instrument that doubled the debt of a defaulter and redoubled it in the event of another default. As with similar financial instruments of Antiquity, riba regularly turned delinquent borrowers into slaves. On that basis, the Quran's prohibition could have been interpreted as a measure attenuating the risk of enslavement. Instead, it was commonly treated as a ban on all forms of interest, including the commissions lenders charged to commercial and personal borrowers. Legal treatises and courts considered interest categorically un-Islamic.

A widely held modern view of the premodern Middle East is that Islam's ban on interest kept Muslims from participating in credit markets as suppliers. In fact, Muslim Middle Easterners participated heavily in interest-based finance as both suppliers and borrowers.[12] They did so with the connivance of Islamic jurists who, like medieval Christian theologians in relation to the biblical usury ban, developed legal ruses to legitimize interest-based transactions without formally violating the prohibition. What is notable about financial markets of the premodern Middle East is not, then, a reluctance to use interest for financial compensation. Rather, it is the absence of banks – organizations that pooled deposits from many sources to make numerous loans simultaneously. The Middle East's earliest successful banks were founded in the 1860s by Europeans, through European capital.[13] Iran's first bank was established even later, in 1889, by British investors.[14]

The banks of the modern Middle East are profit-making enterprises that specialize in financial intermediation. In the Middle Ages, though, financial intermediation was not yet a specialized pursuit. It was conducted by merchants, as a side service. Merchants put their idle capital to work through loans. They also transferred money over long distances – not by carrying coins but by paying someone's debt in one location and then getting repaid in another. The initiator of the currency transfer gave the intermediating merchant a note stating who would reimburse him and how much he would receive for the service. The transfer was legal under Islamic law, provided it was conducted in a single currency. Using multiple currencies was illegal, to prevent fluctuations in exchange rates from producing an unearned gain for one party and an undeserved loss for another. This currency restriction made the Middle Eastern bill of trade (*suftaja*) more restrictive than the bill of exchange, a European money transfer instrument that allowed the initial payment's currency to differ from that of the reimbursement.[15] Financial arbitrage opportunities lured European merchants to open branches in multiple cities. It also incentivized them to find organizational innovations that would expand the durability of their partnerships. In brief, it paved the way for banks.[16]

Banks are large organizations. In their absence, the Middle East's credit markets were served by small-scale money suppliers, mostly individuals seeking a return on their savings or merchants trying to keep capital lucrative. Borrowers, too, were typically individuals. The atomism of the region's credit markets was no anomaly. Its trade was conducted by atomistic producers and suppliers. In both commerce and finance, another common feature was that businesses were short-lived. Typically, a partnership lasted no more than a few months, though it was renewable as a contract independent of the one completed. Proprietary businesses ended with the retirement or death of the founder. In the Middle Ages, atomistic and ephemeral businesses were the norm everywhere, not only in the Middle East. Critical here is that in the Middle East, with a few partial exceptions, the pattern of Islam's early centuries lasted until reforms of the 1800s. Small and ephemeral businesses deprived the Middle East of the organizational innovations essential to exploiting opportunities of the Industrial Revolution. Concomitantly, they deprived the region of developments that might have induced political liberalization. The mechanisms keeping merchants and financiers politically powerless were intimately connected to those that prevented their businesses from growing and gaining longevity. To make sense of the political consequences, our primary concern here, we must first explore the underlying economic mechanisms.

INSTITUTIONAL STAGNATION OF COMMERCE AND FINANCE

In exploring why Islam lacks a concept of corporation, we saw that confining legal standing to natural individuals denied Arabian tribes formal recognition, thereby elevating the significance of a pan-tribal Muslim brotherhood. The primacy of the individual appeared also in Islamic partnership law, which required the contracting parties to be flesh-and-blood individuals.

The Islamic Partnership

An Islamic partnership had legal status only as a contract enforceable under the law. It was not an entity that could sue or be sued. Individual partners could pull out at will, forcing the liquidation and division of joint assets. These characteristics incentivized investors and merchants to reduce the chances of a premature liquidation. They achieved these objectives by working with no more than a few partners at any one time and limiting the expected duration of their joint mission. Islam's Quran-based inheritance system reinforced the incentives in question. In assigning mandatory shares to all surviving children and parents of both sexes, it lowered the probability of maintaining a successful enterprise across generations. As individuals, all heirs were free to walk away with their shares of the estate. Yet another reason to keep enterprises small and ephemeral lay in Islam's marriage rules. Precisely because of their successes, prominent businessmen often had multiple wives. Accordingly, they tended to leave behind many heirs. Unsurprisingly, the Middle East's premodern economies produced no legendary business dynasties. One searches in vain for families that kept major businesses going for generations.[17]

In the Middle Ages, the technologies of production, transportation, exchange, finance, and communication gave no major cost advantages to large or long-living companies. No region of the world bucked this pattern. Textiles were produced by households and small partnerships everywhere. Only with the Industrial Revolution did economies of scale and scope make it profitable to produce through heavily capitalized, perpetual, and profit-seeking enterprises with legal personhood. By the time the technologies of mass production emerged, Western Europe had already generated the organizational means for exploiting them efficiently. Specifically, it had developed business corporations of various types, along with banks, stock markets, insurance companies, business presses, and legal systems supportive of impersonal economic exchange. These prior developments, which spanned many centuries, were critical to Europe's ensuing global economic domination.[18]

In sharp contrast to Western Europe, the Middle East was unprepared institutionally for the Industrial Revolution. In the mid-1800s, when Europe was industrializing feverishly and financing giant economic ventures around the globe, the Middle East's private economic sectors were still limited to atomistic and ephemeral enterprises. Europeans established the Middle East's first perpetual enterprises. Locals began forming companies commensurate in size and longevity only after far-reaching reforms transplanted modern economic institutions in a hurry. The institutional transformations effectively scrapped the commercial and financial elements of Islamic law. Even in places where, in principle, the Sharia remains the law of the land – Iran after 1979, Saudi Arabia – as a practical matter transplanted institutions govern economic life.

Why did the institutional complex that accounted for the Middle East's economic successes during Islam's early centuries stagnate while its Western counterparts generated countless innovations that created the modern economy? Since the *Long Divergence* contains a detailed answer, a few highlights will suffice here.[19] Once in place, the Islamic inheritance system gave large constituencies a stake in its perpetuation. In addition to women, generally these included second and later sons. For its part, the waqf gave elites a vehicle for circumventing egalitarian inheritance provisions. In the face of weak general property rights, the waqf also served as a wealth shelter.[20] But in economic sectors requiring flexibility in capital use, its restrictions on resource allocation harmed investors. Moreover, its very existence sucked capital out of commerce and production, making it especially difficult for profit-seeking companies to grow in scale and scope. The small and ephemeral character of indigenous Middle Eastern enterprises virtually eliminated the need for institutional innovations that might have propelled the region's transition to impersonal exchange through indigenous means. Two-person partnerships expected to last a few months do not face the coordination and communication challenges of a twenty-person partnership expected to function, with intergenerational replacements, for decades.

The Middle East's merchants and investors did not feel pressed, then, to invent a basic analogue of the European joint-stock company, a simple business corporation. They certainly had no need for a full-blown business corporation, the type of enterprise known in modern economics as the firm. A firm can add shareholders and undertake long-term investments due to entity shielding – protection against liquidation demands from shareholders. Shareholders are free to trade their shares but, except as a majority, not to dictate firm policies.[21]

Capitulations

Prior to the 1800s, when Europe's economic ascent posed an existential crisis for Middle Eastern dynasties, European institutional advances served, paradoxically, to delay reforms that might have moderated the divergence. The Middle East gave European traders commercial privileges. Known as capitulations, these privileges allowed interactions between the two regions to proceed under increasingly sophisticated European institutions. Thus, they enabled the Middle East to benefit from European institutional advances through more efficient interregional trade without discarding outdated Islamic institutions and risking resistance from vested interests. In the 1600s and 1700s, even minor reform attempts by Ottoman sultans triggered revolts led by disaffected clerics and military units. One sultan was executed, four were deposed, and several others kept their throne only by scapegoating top aides.[22] Successful institutional reforms were launched only after constituencies anchored in the old order were severely weakened.

The Cash Waqf

The Middle Eastern institutional complex was never entirely stagnant. Rules were bent to overcome glaring inefficiencies, sometimes with the acquiescence of judges who could have enforced the spirit of the law. As with the waqf, judges often charged for their cooperation. In addition to practical changes accomplished through corruption, there were institutional innovations initiated by investors and accepted, if not also formally legitimized, by clerics. All reflected the basic limitations of Islamic law. Although they met important needs, none did so in a way that enabled large and perpetual companies with tradable shares. When in the 1800s Western equivalents were transplanted to the Middle East, innovations achieved within the confines of Islamic law just withered away.

The most significant financial innovations illustrate these points. In Anatolia and the Balkans, the 1500s saw the emergence of the "cash waqf." This was a form of waqf that earned returns by using a liquid endowment to make loans at interest. The cash waqf blatantly violated two principles of Islamic law: the ban on interest and the immovability requirement for waqf assets. Nevertheless, a compromise between conservative and pragmatic jurists legitimized it on the grounds that, by alleviating credit shortages, it benefited Muslims. The cash waqf could have initiated an indigenous path to modern banking. Alas, like a classic waqf, it lacked the right to pool capital across waqfs. This restriction limited its growth potential. The compromise that led to its inclusion in the Islamic institutional complex contained provisions that kept it as a variant of the waqf. Innovating within the bounds of Islamic law thus turned out to be a handicap. Never more than a minor supplier of credit, the cash waqf faded with the arrival of modern finance.[23]

The Gedik

The other indigenous innovation was the gedik, a freely transferable enterprise share that emerged from guilds. Initially, it involved court-registered transfers of physical capital and market privileges from fathers to sons. In the 1500s, cash shortages induced guilds to allow sales of these shares to outsiders. Within a century, even people unconnected to a guild were exchanging shares of productive enterprises. The gedik market grew massively starting around 1750, and by the early 1800s, three-quarters of all commercial cases in Istanbul's Islamic courts involved gediks.[24] This market for enterprise shares was the Middle Eastern counterpart of Europe's stock markets that emerged around 1600, starting with those of Amsterdam and London.[25] These stock markets recorded all transactions centrally. Gradually they instituted disclosure rules that made company shares attractive even to strangers.[26] Lacking a central registry, the gedik was poorly suited to large companies of the Industrial Era. Unsurprisingly, the gedik market vanished with the founding of formal Middle Eastern stock markets, all modeled after those of Europe. As publicly traded modern companies appeared in the Middle East, starting with exchanges in Istanbul, Cairo, and Alexandria, they issued stocks rather than gediks.[27]

Why might the Middle East have failed to generate an indigenous stock exchange, or even uniform equity trading and information disclosure regulations? A major obstacle was that companies securitized through gediks lacked legal personhood, which was a concept alien to Islamic law. Their shares represented ownership rights to enterprises subject to dissolution at will. If buyers valued them, it was because of private information about the enterprises generating profits on their behalf. Without such information, buying gediks would have carried risks that, generally, the purchasers of European stocks could avoid. Some fraud is unavoidable even in a well-functioning financial market. But the dangers of getting swindled would have been substantially greater with gediks issued in the thousands for a single enterprise. In fact, enterprises issued them in single digits or low double digits. Evidently, the gedik was a financial instrument suited specifically to an economy based on personal exchange.

As the gedik market opened to people without a guild affiliation, it came to be dominated by local Christians. Gediks were highly profitable because the securitized enterprises tended to enjoy protections against competition. Their liquidity proved to be another advantage. It enabled holders to transfer wealth into rising sectors. Muslim underrepresentation in the gedik market stemmed from the concentration of Muslim capital in waqfs, whose rules precluded resource reallocations unauthorized in the deed. A millennium later, the eighth-century decision to limit waqf formation at will to Muslims thus had the unintended result of restraining their descendants' participation in the most profitable investment markets of the day. Christians also benefited from international treaties that gave foreign powers, most importantly Russia, the right to protect local Christians. These treaties strengthened Christian property rights even as Jewish private assets remained vulnerable to expropriation, until rulers agreed to respect the property rights of all their subjects, irrespective of faith.

Choice of Law for Non-Muslims

As Western Europe developed the institutions of the modern economy, Middle Eastern Christians and Jews benefited from the choice of law that Islam gave to non-Muslim subjects. That privilege had been denied to Muslims, who were supposed to obey Islamic law in all domains of life. Lacking choice of law posed no serious economic disadvantage in Europe's Middle Ages, when Islamic commercial and financial institutions were at least as efficient as their counterparts elsewhere. But it became a growing handicap as Western legal systems started to provide a competitive advantage.

When mass production, banking, and insurance appeared in the Middle East, these new sectors came to be dominated by foreigners who chose their local partners, brokers, and increasingly also their mid-level and even top managers, from local minorities. Exercising choice of law, some Christians took to doing business under Western legal systems, sometimes simply by transacting with foreign companies, including those doing business locally; any dispute would be adjudicated under some foreign law rather than Islamic law. Through their dealings with Western Europeans, religious minorities acquired valuable know-how. By the time top-down reforms allowed Muslims to participate in the rapidly evolving industrial economy, non-Muslim minorities had already pulled ahead of Muslims economically. Disproportionately active in the most lucrative economic sectors, they were also leading conspicuously more affluent lifestyles.[28]

POLITICAL WEAKNESS OF MERCHANTS

The rising economic fortunes of the Middle East's religious minorities brought about a sectarian redistribution of power. Treated as second-class subjects from the seventh-century onward, non-Muslims demanded legal and political equality. Starting with the Ottoman Gülhane Edict of 1839, rulers and their governing coalitions responded through reforms that granted all subjects equality under the law. Although religious discrimination continued in various domains, Christians and, to a lesser extent, Jews rose to positions in high levels of government. They assumed ambassadorships, ministerial positions, and directorships of state agencies.[29] The region's first parliaments included non-Muslims.[30] As Christians and, generally with a lag, Jews continued to advance economically, they became more assertive politically. Their rising clout is evident not only at the highest levels of government but also in local politics across the region.[31]

Meanwhile, as the region's modernization unfolded, Muslim merchants and financiers were essentially absent from major decisions. The coalitions that tried to empower them through reforms consisted mostly of ruling families, high government officials, and military commanders. Specifically, the Muslims who spearheaded institutions that enhanced the capabilities of local economic players – banks, insurance markets, new organizational forms, stock markets, secular commercial courts, uniform measurements – consisted of elites whose professional expertise lay outside of commerce or finance. Sensing that their own survival was at stake, the region's ruling elites now recognized that state strength and private wealth are complementary rather than rivalrous. Abandoning their traditional indifference to structures of the private economy, they started pursuing initiatives designed to enhance opportunities to compete in the emerging global economy. Given the political weakness of Muslim merchants, producers, and financiers, the support they received from political elites was critical to initiating the process of restoring their competitiveness in domestic markets.

The commitment of ruling coalitions to improving the infrastructure of the private economy was facilitated by the steady reduction in clerical power during the 1700s and, in most of the region, at an accelerating pace in the 1800s. As discussed in Chapter 6, waqf privatizations and nationalizations eroded the economic base of clerics, as did the related fall in the founding of new waqfs. A cumulative effect of all these developments was the weakening of clerical resistance to reforms that shrunk the economic role of Islamic law.

The Middle East's Muslim merchants were not always politically weak. Remember that Islam's founder was a merchant and that its initial institutional complex included commercially useful elements. Most of the jurists who developed what became classical Islamic law were somehow involved with commerce themselves. Unlike post-1200 jurists, who lived mostly on waqf-generated rents, many earned substantial income from business.[32] In Islam's early centuries, then, merchants held prominent places at the region's political bargaining table. Their political leverage manifested itself through more than legal prominence. They also led diplomatic negotiations connected to trade and the purchase of captives.[33] Their political influence is evident in certain institutional choices relevant to commercial and financial efficiency. Fairs and market days were adjusted to coincide with Islamic celebrations and Friday prayers. Congregational mosques were located near major shopping centers. Mosques became depositories of official weights and measures. In early-Abbasid Iraq, when the political power of merchants appears to have peaked, trade taxes generally fell and stabilized.[34]

The waqf's growing importance was not the only reason why the private economic sector's political influence waned. Another was that the persistent atomism and evanescence of Islamic partnerships kept profit-seeking entrepreneurs from resisting rules harmful to their competitiveness. Tellingly, as capitulations were given to European merchants, Middle Eastern merchants did not insist on sharing the same privileges. French and English monarchs negotiated capitulations to help their subjects trading in Ottoman realms. Ottoman sultans were not pressured by the Ottoman business community for comparable privileges.

We already know that waqf law kept civic society anemic. Now we see that a byproduct of laws that kept Islamic partnerships small and short-lived was the private commercial sector's political weakness. Precisely because of their large numbers and fleeting existence, Islamic partnerships could not unite to advance their professional interests. They could not communicate to sultans their common needs. Worst of all, in the absence of professional organizations, they could not meet to strategize on improvements to prevailing institutions. Not until the late 1500s did their counterparts in Western Europe start incorporating businesses, and only in the 1800s did the corporation begin to see wide use. However, even in the Middle Ages, European entrepreneurs operating in the Middle East acted collectively through organizations with at least de facto legal personhood. They were represented by consuls. By contrast, the locals with whom they interacted lacked organizations of their own, except for guilds, which brought together artisans doing business in proximity to one another. The exception proves the rule. By facilitating monitoring as well as taxation, locational concentration served state interests. For their part, guildsmen benefited from their organization through protections against competition.[35] Rulers saw no need to organize mobile merchants who, precisely because of the smallness and impermanence of their businesses, had neither the incentives nor the capacity to form lasting lobbies promoting their shared interests.

The inability of Middle Eastern merchants to get organized is evident in tax farming, a method of taxation used since Antiquity in contexts where the state could not tax directly. It entailed auctioning off the right to "farm" a community's tax dues. Typically, the winner was an investor with deep knowledge about the community's wealth distribution, sources of income, and methods of evading taxation. In the late 1700s, the Ottoman Empire had between 6,000 and 12,000 tax farmers with lifetime rights to collect taxes. There were thousands of others with shorter terms. By contrast, France had just 88 tax farmers. The difference in order of magnitude reflects variations in ability to pool capital. A French tax farmer was a large enterprise that pooled the capital of hundreds, if not thousands, of investors. An Ottoman tax farmer was often a solo operation and sometimes a partnership pooling the capital of a few investors. This difference in numbers had profound political implications. Ottoman sultans changed the rules of tax farming repeatedly, even reneged on the commitments they made to incentivize high bids. Due to their high numbers, Ottoman tax farmers could not defend themselves against arbitrary state decisions.[36] For their part, French tax farmers became powerful players in French politics. A basic reason is that they could form a united front. Fewer than 100 tax farmers could manage types of collective action that eluded many thousands.[37]

The lifetime tax farmers of the Ottoman Empire included members of powerful families known generically as "provincial notables" (âyanlar). They signed a "Deed of Alliance" (Sened-i İttifak) with the Ottoman sultan in 1808, which may seem to undermine my claim that tax farmers were politically powerless. In fact, the Deed of Alliance is an exception that proves the rule. The provincial notables who participated in the negotiations formed a tiny share of all Ottoman tax farmers, and they represented only themselves, as regional strongmen. Neither individually nor collectively did they represent tax farmers as a profession, to say nothing of speaking for private entrepreneurs. Their goals were to maintain local privileges and make them heritable. Through the Deed of Alliance, they achieved this objective on paper, in return for declaring loyalty to the state and endorsing its ongoing financial and military reforms. But their goals did not include improving the empire's commercial or financial institutions. Equally significant, the Deed of Alliance did not constrain the Ottoman state in practice. Ignoring their power-sharing arrangement, successive sultans eroded the powers of notables wherever they could.[38] In brief, the provincial notables failed to bind the Ottoman state's decisions, whether on tax farming or other matters relevant to private wealth creation.

The absence of Middle Eastern parliaments until the late 1800s is yet another manifestation of the political weakness of the region's merchants. The West's royal councils and parliaments, such as those of Venice, France, and England, were established, in part, as forums where tax-collecting political authorities bargained with representatives of the private sector.[39] Typically, major challenges to the arbitrary use of state power came from parliamentary coalitions in which private entrepreneurs played leading roles. Differences in the size and longevity of businesses are key factors behind interregional variations in political representation. Had Middle Eastern private enterprises grown in scale and gained durability, they would have found it easier to project power collectively. They might have forced sultans to negotiate with them, possibly through parliaments.

MERCHANTS AND THE PERSISTENCE OF RELIGIOUS REPRESSION

Middle Eastern entrepreneurs undoubtedly understood the roles that religion played in their economic fortunes. They were responsive to the incentives that the inheritance system created to keep their enterprises small and short-lived. Insofar as they channeled capital into waqfs, they saw that clerical supervision prevented them from managing endowed assets efficiently and from adapting services to changing needs. Handicaps rooted in Islamic rules would have become increasingly obvious as their economic interactions with Westerners expanded. They would have noticed that Western companies were larger and that they could outlive their founders. In brief, Middle Eastern entrepreneurs would have seen connections between Islamic law and the ongoing economic divergence.

No record exists of Muslim entrepreneurs identifying Islamic law specifically as a source of their declining competitiveness. That itself is telling. Prior to the nineteenth century, nowhere did they have a forum to discuss their commercial and financial handicaps, let alone to develop a consensus on policy demands, put their agreements into writing, and appeal to state authorities. Thoughts in a merchant's head will not leave historical traces unless recorded. In an overwhelmingly illiterate society lacking a tradition of keeping a diary, this was extremely unlikely. Not even the most successful entrepreneurs of the premodern Middle East left behind accounts of their activities. Business historians of Western Europe can track the agendas of entrepreneurs through parliamentary votes of their representatives, but also through company archives, patent records, and the repositories of professional organizations.[40] Eventually, by 1599, chambers of commerce started giving voice to the concerns of business communities and engaging in organized networking.[41] The absence of indigenous Middle Eastern equivalents until 1882 is itself a result of the Middle Eastern economy's institutional stagnation from the early second millennium to the region's existential crisis in the 1800s.[42]

For a lone Muslim merchant, opposing Islamic law openly carried the risk of triggering charges of apostasy. Depending on his social visibility, the religious establishment would have condemned him, both to protect its rents from enforcing Islamic regulations and to avoid precedents for debating established religious teachings. By the same token, clerics were ready to assist with the circumvention of inconvenient Islamic laws, usually for a fee. They would do so through ruses designed to skirt rules without violating their letter. Thus, a judge would knowingly allow breaches of a waqf deed's stipulations, feigning meticulous enforcement. The commonness of waqf corruption, discussed in Chapter 5, was a byproduct of the punishments that awaited people who openly challenged Islamic laws.

When a formal reinterpretation of the law occurred, it was in response to widespread demand that split clerics themselves. Support from within the religious establishment gave the advocates of change cover against the charge of apostasy. The cash waqf controversy is a case in point. In the decades preceding the 1570s, it divided Ottoman clerics into conservative and pragmatic camps. The latter won with the support of the Ottoman Empire's chief mufti. The pragmatic side also drew strength from thousands of cash waqf founders and caretakers, plus everyone who benefited from them as borrowers.

The pragmatist argument was that an institution benefiting Muslim masses could not be un-Islamic. Among the conservative objections to the cash waqf was that it earned income through interest-bearing loans. The pragmatists could have argued that interest itself was justified because it permitted transactions beneficial to Muslim masses. But they did not go that far. Pretending that the loans were interest-free, they continued to disguise the truth through euphemisms. Throughout the dispute, no one addressed the broader question of whether the Quran truly bans all forms of interest, to say nothing of whether clerics ought to have jurisdiction over freely negotiated financial transactions. The contrast with Western Europe is striking here, too. The medieval Church considered interest sinful on the pretext that the Bible bans usury. For centuries, therefore, Christian financiers charged interest through ruses equivalent to those of the Islamic Middle East. As European financial markets gained complexity, Christian capital holders found it increasingly burdensome to perform obfuscations that fooled few. To simplify financial transactions, a distinction was drawn between interest, considered reasonable and legitimate, and usury, deemed excessive and forbidden. Not until the 1840s was that distinction officially made in the Middle East. Revealingly, the initiative came from statesmen collaborating with the forerunners of bankers, all European expatriates.[43] Indigenous financiers played no conspicuous role; nor did the masses of commercial and personal borrowers. Interest became an openly recorded financial transfer as high political elites recognized the benefits of transplanting Western financial institutions in toto.[44]

The architects of the Islamic institutional complex aimed to give Muslims advantages in their dealings with non-Muslims. To that end, they privileged Muslim testimony and banned non-Muslim testimony against Muslims. In Islamic courts, Muslim litigants also benefited from in-group bias – the universal tendency to find members of one's own group more credible than outsiders. In-group bias was inevitable because the Islamic judicial system, the mandatory venue for all adjudication between Muslims and non-Muslims, was staffed entirely by Muslims. An unintended byproduct of the pro-Muslim bias of Islamic courts was higher interest rates for Muslim borrowers. Because of this bias, it was harder to prevail in court against a delinquent borrower who was Muslim. Hence, even Muslim lenders charged Muslim borrowers more than they charged equally qualified non-Muslims.[45] The resulting handicap to Muslim merchants worsened as credit became increasingly important to business success.

One might expect the Middle East's Muslim business communities to have pressured clerics to end sectarian discrimination in the courts. But steps in that direction came only in the mid-1800s. The Ottoman Gülhane Edict granted non-Muslims equality before the law. Once again, ordinary Muslim merchants and investors played no apparent role in bringing about the key initiatives. Non-Muslim merchants were more active than their Muslim counterparts in the founding of secular commercial courts as alternatives to Islamic courts. Their main motivation was the advantage of adopting modern contractual forms without relying on a European legal system.[46]

MERCHANTS AND CIVIC SCLEROSIS

In today's economically advanced societies, sundry professional organizations take positions on matters directly relevant to their material interests.[47] These organizations also promote their views on broader policy questions. Even though an organization's members need not be united on matters of shared concern, ordinarily it speaks for most of those who are politically active. The organization also helps to shape discourses, worldviews, beliefs, and preferences. For these reasons, professional organizations exert influence over individuals, including politicians. The world's most successful entrepreneurs exercise political power as individuals, too. Leading American investors such as Bill Gates, Charles and David Koch, and George Soros use multiple levers to shape politics. They promote their causes through targeted donations, but also public pronouncements that surrogates and various media amplify.[48]

The atomism and impermanence of premodern Middle Eastern businesses kept merchants and investors from defending their interests, formulating policies, and disseminating their preferences. Entrepreneurs were absent from discourses on technological innovation, the content of education, the rights of foreigners, and religious assimilation campaigns, among other matters that affected the region's economic and political trajectories. There were no individual businessmen with enough clout to influence public opinion. The contrast with clerics is striking. As teachers at various levels, preachers, judges, and interpreters of religion, clerics shaped values, perceptions, and expectations. They kept people of all walks of life from questioning state policies. On occasion, they also helped to mobilize mutinies against the ruling sultan, by both propagating grievances and coordinating responses. The business community possessed none of the tools at the disposal of clerics.

We know already that across the Middle East the waqf kept civil society feeble. Not all private capital was frozen within waqfs. Profit-making private enterprises were free of the restrictions that kept waqfs from advocating on behalf of the constituencies they were established to serve. Long-distance merchants could express political views. And they could discuss economic policies with fellow merchants. But the smallness and evanescence of their operations stunted the impact of their views. Worse, the absence of means to join forces with like-minded entrepreneurs deprived civil society of their collective experiences. Their insights and perspectives did not enter public discourses. Outsiders to the business community did not come to appreciate how certain elements of Islamic law – inheritance system, partnership law, choice of law limited to non-Muslims – were turning the Middle East into a commercially and financially backward region. In other words, the very elements of Islamic law that kept Middle Eastern businesses atomistic and short-lived also bred ignorance of their unfolding long-term effects. They contributed to the civic sclerosis that allowed sultans to keep governing without accountability to organizations formed from below.

Modernization entails a transition from one institutional complex to another. But it never discards the old complex entirely. Parts of the old complex get carried into the new one, usually with adaptations. The transition's pace and trajectory depend on the set of decision makers. In the modernization of Western Europe, many innovations came from merchants and financiers, who refined organizational forms and developed new markets organically. Their motivations were to trim costs, alleviate risks, facilitate transactions, improve communication, collect information, and broaden coordination. Entrepreneurs seeking to gain competitiveness by such means were integral to the process at every stage.[49] Their roles in economic modernization required more than concocting new ways of deploying capital. They had to keep clerics from blocking their reforms.[50] They needed to make states support their innovations through complementary institutions, such as impartial courts and treaties opening foreign markets. They required organizations of their own, a presence in civil society, and representation in political bodies. As Europe developed the modern global economy, civic and political engagement gave its businessmen the space to make innovations with the cooperation of other constituencies. Innovations did not result simply from a profit motive that impelled merchants and financiers to alter their business methods. Their civic and political capacities were essential to the institutional transformations they brought about.

It was not enough, of course, for private economic actors to deliberate together, reach joint decisions, act as a unit, and make states hear their voices. States had to be equipped to overcome resistance from vested interests and deliver the desired innovations. In other words, states themselves had to have developed certain capabilities. In the present context, the emergence of impartial courts required more than a demand from users. At a minimum, the state had to be able to change the madrasa curriculum and legal procedures, but also to enforce these modifications. That would have been impossible without reforming waqf law drastically, against opposition from groups with a stake in its inviolability. For many centuries, then, state incapacity was a contributor to the Middle East's institutional rigidities.[51] But lethargy of the state can itself be a function of conservatism on the part of private entrepreneurs. State officials can learn from private actors. And in defeating resistance within the state itself, alliances involving nonstate actors can play crucial roles.

In the Middle East, merchants and investors had incentives to innovate in fewer areas than in Western Europe. Besides, over the long run, their institutional innovations were less consequential. The cash waqf and the gedik each became an anachronism with the transplant of Western-generated alternatives, which were better suited to the evolving impersonal economy. In sharp contrast to major European innovations, which spread globally, neither was transplanted beyond the Middle East. In any case, more ambitious institutional innovations were unthinkable, because they would have drawn opposition from clerics, if not also from rulers. The Muslim business community's lack of institutional creativity eventually came to be perceived, we already know, as an existential problem. But the diagnosis of systemic dysfunction did not come from Muslim merchants and investors, who found themselves outcompeted in international markets. It came in the 1800s from high-level statesmen, who proceeded to institute far-reaching reforms from above. The paucity of reformist demands from below stemmed largely from the atomism and transience of enterprises formed under Islamic law. These factors curtailed demand for structural change through two channels. On the one hand, they limited the need for new economic institutions. On the other, they kept the business community civically feeble and denied it a place in the ruling coalition.

THE POLITICAL ASCENDANCY OF NON-MUSLIMS

If what kept Middle Eastern entrepreneurs politically powerless was ultimately the simplicity of their enterprises and their inability to deploy capital efficiently, groups able to transcend these limitations would have acquired political influence accordingly. Indeed, beginning in the eighteenth century, the Middle East's non-Muslims, especially its Christians, became progressively more assertive. The political empowerment of non-Muslims reflected economic transformations that benefited Muslims only with significant lags. Specifically, in an era of expanding investment opportunities, it was advantageous to have formed few waqfs. Because classical waqf law denied non-Muslims the right to form waqfs at will, in the 1700s only a tiny fraction of all Middle Eastern waqfs had a Christian or Jewish founder. An unintended long-term benefit to non-Muslims is that a relatively much smaller share of their capital was frozen in waqfs. Hence, a correspondingly much larger share was available for investment in flexible financial markets. That is one factor behind the disproportionate participation of Christians in the highly profitable gedik market. With less property tied up in waqfs, they had minimal needs to engage in costly asset stripping, which, because of its illegality, required compensating clerics.

A complementary factor was the stronger property rights that non-Muslims received through international treaties. Meanwhile, by purchasing diplomatic protection from foreign consulates, some non-Muslim entrepreneurs acquired the ability to do business under a foreign legal system. But a much weightier contributor to the economic ascent of non-Muslims was their highly disproportionate representation among the local partners, agents, and employees of foreign companies. And another was that non-Muslims took the lead in modernizing business practices. Their leadership in the gedik market was just one manifestation. They also led in the establishment of "merchant houses" – European-inspired and -connected partnerships intended to have long lives.[52] In sum, for more than a century before the region's ruling elites embarked on ambitious modernization projects, their non-Muslim populations were already transforming their business practices and prospering as a result. Through all these means, indigenous non-Muslims became wealthier.[53]

The growing political influence associated with this enrichment is evident in the increasing frequency with which prominent non-Muslim families appear in accounts of Middle Eastern political history.[54] By the second half of the century, Christians and Jews were present not only at high levels of government but also prominently in intellectual life, publishing, modern education, and civic organizations.[55]

In the eighteenth century, before the arrival of formal banking in the 1850s, the scale of lending increased. Whereas the typical lender had run a tiny operation with few borrowers at any one time, lenders now extended credit on a large scale and to many borrowers simultaneously. The biggest lenders served as personal moneylenders to high elites, even to members of the ruling family. These professional moneylenders (*sarraf*s) consisted disproportionately of local non-Muslims or European expatriates. Without exception, those serving top Ottoman officials were Armenian, Greek, Jewish, or ex-European (Levantine), in that order.[56] In the first half of the nineteenth century, a share of these financiers, mostly Greeks, took to intermediating between Western banks and local borrowers, including the state. With access to the Palace, they exercised substantial political power. Organized as European-based merchant houses, they profited from interregional interest rate differentials. Financing trade, they also exchanged currencies. In the 1850s, some of these professional financiers established the very first banks of the Middle East. Though unsuccessful, they laid the groundwork for the durable financial intermediaries that followed, with Western financial consortia in the lead.[57] In Egypt, meanwhile, mass finance was controlled almost entirely by expatriates until the end of World War I.[58]

The economic ascent of the Middle East's non-Muslims galvanized initiatives that expanded the economic freedoms of all religious communities. They did so by broadening organizational menus, investment options, financial services, and consumption choices. The earliest municipalities were founded in disproportionately non-Muslim urban neighborhoods. New consumption forms – newspapers, art collecting, philanthropy through social clubs, public balls, theater, piano, modern residential amenities – were generally embraced by non-Muslims first, or at least disproportionately.[59] The key roles of non-Muslims are overlooked in histories of the region's modernization, which tend to focus on the actions of Muslim pioneers, or else on very high state officials, mostly Muslim, who are unrepresentative of the population at large. Also underappreciated is the role non-Muslims played in secularizing daily life.

Non-Muslim advances energized nationalist movements within the largest non-Muslim communities living under Muslim rule, including Greeks, Serbs, Bulgarians, and Armenians. Fueled by commercial wealth, Greeks sought independence in several areas where they were concentrated. Following a decade-long uprising, they managed to form a Peloponnese-centered state in 1832.[60] Tellingly, both merchants and intellectuals played critical roles in the parliamentary and executive councils that Greeks formed at the start of their struggle. Between 1822 and 1827, around 18 percent of their members were merchants, and 11 percent were intellectuals.[61]

The Greek secession and hopes that it generated in other Christian communities served as a wake-up call to Muslim bureaucrats, military officers, and educators. It expanded the ranks of reform-minded Muslims committed to stemming territorial losses. They began to view clerics – the custodians of the Islamic institutional complex – as an impediment to catching up with non-Muslims. Curtailing the jurisdiction of clerics became central to all reform agendas, as did resistance to various aspects of Islamic law.[62] In a nutshell, the advances of non-Muslims helped to jump-start the secularization drives that, in fits and starts, have shaped Middle Eastern politics down to the present.[63] Thus, the motivation for secularization was not simply the existential threat of the West, though growing cooperation between European powers and local non-Muslims made some interpreters treat the Western threat as paramount.

The first secularist reforms broadened Muslim economic options without restricting those of traditionalists. Longstanding institutions such as the Islamic waqf and Islamic partnership continued to see use. But over a period stretching into the 1900s, these initial secularizing transformations metamorphosed into assertive secularism. The shrinking of Islamic law's economic domain was broadly welcomed. But secularist repression fueled widespread resentment. The discontent would spawn assorted Islamist movements that, in the 2020s, exercise coercive political power across the region.

REVIVAL OF MUSLIM COMMERCE

The economic modernization drives of the region's Muslim elites thoroughly transformed its economic life, and within a few decades Muslim entrepreneurs were among the main beneficiaries. Starting well behind non-Muslims in liquid capital, international connections, and modern commercial know-how, they entered sectors dominated by foreigners and local non-Muslims. Banking and insurance are cases in point. In much of the region, Muslims had a minimal presence in either sector until at least the 1890s, and in some places until the 1920s. But by the mid-twentieth century they had established major footholds, if not dominance, in areas where non-Muslims had been prominent. Banks and insurance companies founded through Muslim capital and managed mostly, even exclusively, by Muslim executives were common.[64]

In terms of organization, these companies violated basic principles of Islamic law. Enjoying legal personhood, many issued freely traded stock. They also separated ownership from management. In terms of shareholder numbers and volume of business, they were incomparably larger than any premodern enterprise formed under Islamic law. Another novelty is that perpetual enterprises had become commonplace. These institutional transplants, which liberated the Middle East from premodern economic templates, took place at a moment of panic, but also clerical weakness. However un-Islamic they are from a legal standpoint, none was treated as alien by any significant constituency, not even by clerics.

The reforms allowed people to form businesses, invest, borrow, and transact without contact with clerics. Yet clerics did not mobilize against the secularization of economic relations. There were no objections akin to those against the cash waqf a few centuries earlier. Why the difference? In the mid-1500s, clerics could annul commercial contracts and interfere with waqf management. As institutions that gave them economic power lost significance, their political influence shrank. More important, though, is that the transplanted economic institutions were enormously useful to people of all walks of life. And none of the eclipsed Islamic institutions had non-clerical constituencies committed to keeping them alive. With the founding of banks, the pious might have objected to their reliance on interest. But nowhere was interest a novelty, except in name. Besides, rates were now much lower.[65]

As they introduced modern institutions, states were hardly indifferent to the sectarian distribution of gains. With variations in timing and intensity, they pursued policies of supporting Muslim entrepreneurs. The goal was to enable Muslims to capture major shares of strategically important sectors: finance, foreign trade, and mass manufacturing. Insofar as Muslims advanced in these sectors, Muslim wealth would grow, increasing opportunities for the region's states to borrow from subjects belonging to the dominant religious group. To that end, Muslims received priority in state contracts. They were also favored in state hiring, partly to give them skills transferable to business.[66] The policy of reversing Muslim positional losses did not necessarily stem from religious animus. In supporting Muslim-owned businesses, the assertive secularists of the 1900s acted in the name of nationalism rather than religious solidarity. In 1942, at the peak of its assertively secularist period, Turkey enacted a special wealth tax whose burden fell overwhelmingly on Jews and Christians. The architects of this policy singled out non-Muslims not out of sectarianism – some were Muslim only in name. Rather, they considered Muslim Turks more reliably "Turkish."[67] In the rest of the region, the economic policies of secular regimes were markedly less partial to Muslims. Nevertheless, the secular regimes of Iran and the Arab world also treated Muslim citizens as relatively more patriotic; and, as in Turkey, non-Muslims were subject to glass ceilings at the highest echelons of government.[68]

No state of the modern Middle East treats all Muslims equally. Religious discrimination extends to divisions within Islam. This is done openly under regimes that explicitly define themselves as "Islamic." Depending on their definition of "true Islam," they single out some Muslims for economic protection and others for severe discrimination. In Saudi Arabia, state employment is tilted in favor of Sunnis and against Shiis, especially in high-ranking posts.[69] In Iran, it is the other way around.[70] But no Islamic regime requires its favored businesses to operate under classical Islamic law. For all their rhetoric about promoting Islamic values, they take it as given that the economy's basic building blocks will remain those transplanted from Europe in the 1800s and 1900s. Neither Iran nor Saudi Arabia require modern enterprises to use Islamic partnerships, shun the corporate form, or take their commercial disputes to courts that enforce some form of Islamic law.

GIANT MODERN ENTERPRISES

Giant private companies now exist throughout the Middle East. True, they are not common by modern global standards. As of 2021, just two of the Fortune 500 companies (0.4 percent) and only forty-eight of the Forbes Global 2000 companies (2.4 percent) were based in the Middle East.[71] These shares pale in relation to the region's share of humanity, 7.7 percent. But they represent a huge advance relative to even the 1850s, when the region lacked a single indigenous enterprise comparable in employment or capitalization to the world's top companies. The Middle East now boasts private banks, airlines, and manufacturers with a global footprint. This, too, represents massive progress relative to the 1800s. It also resurrects an ancient pattern. A millennium ago, Middle East-based merchants were conspicuous in all the leading commercial emporia of the old world.

The Middle East's large firms now lobby local and national governments for various needs: physical infrastructure, pricing restrictions, employment regulations, export opportunities, the quality of courts, foreign competition, and more. They belong to business associations that represent them before authorities. They also organize trade shows, coordinate interfirm relations, negotiate production standards and protocols, and promote a climate favorable to business generally.[72] Individually and collectively, they exercise far more political power than the atomistic commercial sectors of the premodern Middle East.

Some firms and business associations support political organizations committed to advancing freedoms generally. For example, banks finance publishers whose lists include works that break taboos, challenge official interpretations of history, and give oppressed groups a voice. Companies also support civil society through grants to private organizations focused on such causes as education, environmental justice, legal defense, and prison conditions.[73] But successful private companies do not use their influence to advance freedoms or expand opportunities generally. On the contrary, most assist repressive governments as part of an implicit bargain whereby they accommodate the political status quo and the government protects them against competition, favors them in state contracting, or simply leaves them alone.[74] Mass media companies starkly illustrate the quid pro quo. They give the incumbent regime favorable coverage, rationalize its repression, whitewash its failures, and demonize its opponents. In return, the government supports them through advertising and by privileging their non-media affiliates in state procurement. The media arms of many Turkish and Egyptian conglomerates serve as mouthpieces of oppressive regimes as a survival strategy, but also a source of enrichment.[75]

In the Middle East today, large modern firms and leading entrepreneurs could strengthen civil society, if they tried to do so collectively. But bold attempts are uncommon. The exceptions explain why. Entrepreneurs who object publicly to government repression risk harsh retaliation. The Turkish businessman and civic activist Osman Kavala is an example. He has spent years in jail for challenging repressive policies of the Erdoğan regime.[76] In the three decades before the start of Erdoğan's national leadership in 2002, Islamist businessmen resisted policies of secularist repression. However, to avoid reprisals, they had to move cautiously. Initially, they just projected a religious identity. As their numbers grew and their side made electoral gains, they grew bolder. For instance, they made a point of employing women wearing headscarves and adjusting work hours to Friday prayer times. And they formed business associations and labor unions of their own.[77] Through such measures, they advanced their own religious freedoms. They also helped to reshape public opinion on anti-religious policies. On making Islam more public, secularists split into two camps, known colloquially as "mild secularists" and "authoritarian secularists."[78] The latter remain committed to making Islam invisible.

Turkish Islamists came on the scene with a broader economic agenda than simply increasing Islam's visibility in the workplace. Like Islamists across the Middle East, they aimed to re-Islamize the economy in its entirety. They would restore what they considered early Islam's just economic order and revive institutions whose virtues they imagined to be unsurpassed. What elements of the Islamic heritage have they attempted to restore, and to what extent have they succeeded? As we shall see next, Islamist regimes have taken mostly symbolic steps toward economic re-Islamization. Revealingly, the most important substantive initiative involves a ban that is routinely circumvented through legal ruses. Yet economic re-Islamization could have involved Quran-inspired initiatives that promote rule of law and individual freedoms.

14

Islamism's Missed Opportunities to Promote Liberalism

When in the eighteenth century Middle Eastern leaders started viewing their societies as underdeveloped, their first response was to equip their militaries with up-to-date weaponry.[1] In time, they identified a more serious problem: lack of know-how to produce the next generation of arms on their own. Unless they learned how to advance technology, every new round in the global arms race would be lost. Participating in technological development required new ways to classify facts, interpret observations, and manipulate objects. Fresh thinking was also essential for producing the new goods and services of the emerging modern economy. The region's feverish reforms of the 1800s reflected an understanding that religion-based traditional schooling was unsuitable to the challenges at hand.[2]

What unfolded has already been described. In steps, the Islamic educational and legal systems were sidelined. In some places and contexts, they were eventually abrogated. As Islamic institutions lost significance, their functions passed to Western-inspired secular organizations, including modern schools and regulation agencies.[3] Mass production thus emerged essentially outside of Islamic control systems. Islamic courts, which had overseen craft guilds, were practically irrelevant to modern industries. Meanwhile, municipalities, which were absent from the Islamic legal order, started to supply the urban services that symbolize a modern city. The contracts that the region's nascent municipalities and private utilities made with suppliers and customers bore little resemblance to familiar market arrangements. Consider illumination. Whereas candle producers sold their products at irregular intervals to households with which they had informal relationships, electricity suppliers used formal long-term contracts involving periodic payments tied to usage.

In keeping with such fundamental differences, the Middle East's new secular courts, not its shrinking Islamic courts, handled disputes concerning electricity transactions.[4] This was inevitable, because utility companies lacked standing under Islamic law. The Belgian-owned Bender-Ereğli United Coal Corporation could not have sued a delinquent customer in an Islamic court, which recognized only natural persons.[5] Public health is another area where the function of Islamic officials passed to new professionals. Modern hospitals, physicians, and pharmaceuticals, all based on medicine taught at new medical schools, eclipsed the health facilities managed by madrasa graduates.[6]

The Middle East's alarmed leaders of the 1800s felt that Islam needed to be preserved, even reinvigorated. It still served as a moral anchor, a source of identity and communal solidarity, and an instrument of cultural cohesion. By the same token, leaders believed that few indigenous commercial or educational institutions were worth preserving in any form. At one level, this attitude is surprising. The Islamic Middle East had long periods of economic prominence. Surely the region's successes provide useful lessons, as do its subsequent failures. Avoiding reflection on deep causes of the region's troubles, reformers simply transplanted institutions developed in the West.

Islamic history provides universal lessons for economic modernization. Openness to outside innovations is an early Islamic trait that the Middle East's reformers shared, but without necessarily appreciating how intercivilizational fertilization once contributed to their region's economic successes. Another valuable lesson is that the Middle East flourished economically when its judicial system accommodated refinements in business practices. For a third example, the history of zakat furnishes clues about links between fiscal constraints and commercial expansion.

Leveraging Islam or Islamic history for inspiration on reforms remained a fringe pursuit until the 1940s, when colonial and indigenous secular regimes triggered the rise of defensive Islamist movements. One grievance was the repression of practicing Muslims. Earlier chapters covered Islamist reactions to secularization, with an emphasis on efforts to make Islam more public. Islamists might also have initiated discussions on the roles of Islamic institutions in economic and political development. Instead, blaming every Muslim failure on colonization and secularization, they set out to Islamize public life and restore Islamic institutions, but selectively. Among the institutions Islamists singled out for revival was zakat, which they interpreted narrowly, as an instrument of poverty alleviation. They made hardly any effort to understand the principles that zakat originally promoted, or to adapt its specifics to a modern economy, or to identify why, more than a millennium ago, early Muslim leaders stopped enforcing it. Another early institution that Islamists opted to restore was the interest ban of classical Islamic law. As with zakat, this ban became a political symbol and a marker of religious identity. To Islamists, whether it would improve the lives of Muslims was at best a secondary matter.

Had they avoided an obsession with symbolism and instead sought to understand the sources of early Islamic economic performance, Islamists could have encouraged creativity within Islamic thought. They could have made Muslims treat Islamic history as a laboratory for exploring ways to advance

Muslim economic performance. Islamists could also have advanced religious freedoms for everyone. In defending their own right to interpret Islam, they could have granted that right to others as well. Further, they might have asserted the right to reject Islamic teachings altogether. A hefty broadening of religious freedoms could have set a model for expanding civil liberties generally, including organizational freedoms. Political checks and balances would have been bolstered, strengthening rule of law.

Islamism missed these opportunities. It remains an instrument for advancing a particular vision of Islam coercively. By and large, it stands for banning a wide variety of practices as un-Islamic and suppressing the rights of anyone who objects.

THE NARROWING OF ISLAM'S SOCIAL ROLES

In Middle Eastern historiography, a common claim is that transformations of the nineteenth and early twentieth centuries were superficial.[7] There are grains of truth here. Few of the region's early modernizers could have explained how intellectual, social, economic, associational, and religious freedoms contributed to the West's advances. Most were just dimly aware of connections between such freedoms and, say, industrial creativity. However, many individual reformers came to realize, some sooner and more fully than others, that Europe's rise depended on an institutional complex that embodied sundry freedoms and rights. Precisely because that linkage gained recognition, the most memorable reforms of the 1800s promulgated various individual rights and abolished certain identity-based privileges. The Ottoman Tanzimat Era (1839–56) extended legal rights to non-Muslims as well as Muslim commoners. It also enhanced material security by voiding the sultan's right to expropriate at will.[8] Under Mehmed Ali, Egypt undertook similar reforms that gave commoners and non-Muslims certain rights previously limited to Muslim elites.[9] Collectively, these reforms turned subjects into citizens. At least on paper, the ruled gained inalienable rights.

The Muslim elites who led the early reforms generally remained practicing Muslims. They attended Friday prayers, fasted at Ramadan, and celebrated Islamic holidays. In addressing personal dilemmas, they sought advice from muftis. They built mosques and other structures of religious significance. Moreover, they sought to boost Muslim solidarity, such as targeted assistance to Muslim disaster victims and Islamic appeals to motivate soldiers.[10] Partly because of secessionist movements by Christian minorities, they also considered Muslim citizens inherently more patriotic than non-Muslims. Only much later, beginning in the late 1800s, did Muslim leaders with secular lifestyles emerge. They were essentially irreligious leaders who identified with Islam culturally, or with a specific Muslim nation communally. The typical Turkish or Egyptian reformer of the time had some Islamic education as well as familiarity with

Islamic history. But for all their exposure to the region's Islamic heritage, their reforms were nearly devoid of Islamic content.

As the only pillar of Islam with explicitly economic content, zakat might have supplied insights into the region's challenges. It might have inspired ideas on optimal taxation, binding the state, or enforcing property rights. It might have spurred debates about the proper role of government. As far as is known, though, no Middle Eastern reformer of the 1800s saw connections between ongoing challenges and the abandonment, a millennium earlier, of the governance principles implicit in zakat. With a single exception, economic and political reforms were negotiated and executed without reference to zakat.[11]

The precedent-breaking codification of Islamic law under the Ottoman statesman Cevdet Pasha (1822–95) might have addressed the zakat requirement. Produced in 1869–76 and known as the *Mecelle*, it resulted from efforts to keep local institutions distinctly Islamic. The pious modernizers who prepared the *Mecelle* considered it possible to draw an up-to-date legal code from Islamic sources exclusively, without relying on European laws. The *Mecelle*'s content emerged as Cevdet Pasha's team sifted through a millennium of Sharia rulings, ignoring what seemed obsolete, picking whatever seemed useful, and reinterpreting liberally. It consisted of sixteen books, twelve on the substance of commerce and four on legal procedure.[12] Whether the resulting code is "Islamic" remains controversial. Yet selections and innovations were guided undeniably by the exigencies of modern economic life. Remarkably, the *Mecelle* excludes taxation and does not even mention zakat. No *Mecelle*-like effort has been made to modernize Islamic law in relation to public finance. At least implicitly, then, even traditionalist modernizers have treated public finance as a secular matter. Modern Middle Eastern officials have been devising tax policies without trying to harmonize them with Islamic principles or precedents.

The one notable exception is the Arabian movement that resulted in the Kingdom of Saudi Arabia. In the 1800s, as it spearheaded an anti-Ottoman resistance movement, the Al Saud family derived much of its revenue from the zakat dues of Bedouin tribes under its control. In alliance with Wahhabis, it treated strict enforcement of the zakat duty as well as the fiscal centrality of zakat as manifestations of returning to the authentic Islam of Muhammad's time.[13] Just as Abu Bakr made payment of zakat to the Medina-based Islamic state a litmus test of submission to Islam, so the Saudi leadership made fulfillment of the zakat duty an indicator of allegiance to its authority and a precondition for protection. Tellingly, Saudi rulers extended their revenues beyond zakat, imposing "voluntary taxes" on both sedentary and nomadic populations.[14] Here, too, they followed early Islamic precedents. Like the Umayyad caliphs, who imposed supplementary taxes lacking a Quranic basis, the Saudis imposed additional taxes pragmatically. Yet another precedent-based practice was the exemption of selected tribes or settlements from certain tax requirements, even from zakat. As the House of Saud consolidated its rule over the lands that formed Saudi Arabia, it relaxed the zakat duty. A 1951 decree kept the overall contribution at 2.5 percent of wealth or income but allowed individual subjects to disburse half the amount on their own.[15] As Saudi oil income skyrocketed, enforcement of the zakat duty loosened further. Even before the 1951 decree, zakat had ceased to be an instrument of state subjugation.

THE EXUBERANT REDISCOVERY OF ZAKAT

As Middle Eastern governments reacted to military defeats, territorial losses, and colonization with secular reforms, the masses did not necessarily endorse the responses. Various constituencies attributed the reversal of fortune vis-à-vis the West to a weakening of religion. Muslims lost competitiveness, they reckoned, by ceasing to live according to the dictates of Islam. Their humiliations stemmed from negligence in enforcing Islamic practices that had once worked wonders. Initially, this reactionary discourse consisted of diffuse and uncoordinated counter-interpretations. But by the 1930s, it had spawned a class of organized movements known collectively as Islamism.[16] Two founders of Islamism counted zakat's abandonment among the most unfortunate decisions of Islamic history. It contributed mightily, in their view, to the subjection of Muslims to European rule. However, the virtues that early Islamists attributed to zakat were not those identified in Chapter 12. Concepts central to that chapter's narrative – credible state commitments, predictability in taxation, property rights, economic freedoms – entered their thinking tangentially, if at all. As they saw it, zakat promoted psychological harmony, social peace, and economic equality, all at once. It provided an easy palliative to modern inequalities.

One Islamist leader who resurrected zakat as a major policy tool was Abul Ala Mawdudi (1903–79), an Indian (and after 1947 Pakistani) who popularized the term "Islamic economics." Mawdudi proposed reestablishing a state-operated obligatory zakat system. He was convinced that such an initiative would improve morality, lower poverty, raise productivity, and depress unemployment.[17] The other Islamist leader who sought to revive zakat was Sayyid Qutb (1906–66). Though agreeing with Mawdudi that zakat is a powerful economic instrument, he also favored additional taxes to reduce inequalities further.[18]

Subsequent proponents of economic Islamization have varied in their characterization of zakat's potential effects. Some see zakat as a cure-all for sundry social ills – in the most optimistic accounts, even the prevention of "famines and floods."[19] Others portray it as the linchpin of a comprehensive development strategy that maintains "justice and balance in every aspect of life."[20] Less sweepingly, many other Islamists hold that zakat's benefits are maximized within a fully Islamic socioeconomic order – a system that motivates generosity generally and rewards zakat payers specifically through inner peace.[21] Beyond dispute in Islamist circles is that zakat is Islam's key redistribution instrument.

Moreover, Islamists consider it self-evident that zakat-based redistribution necessarily transfers wealth from rich to poor.

Islamists who came of age in the shadows of Mawdudi and Qutb saw themselves surrounded by poverty and misery. It did not occur to them that this might have been an unchanging condition, that the Middle East and South Asia never lacked people at the margins of existence. For much of Islamic history, they believed, zakat served as a powerful equalizer that eliminated destitution. The weakening of religion and forced Westernization made this sacred institution degenerate and fall into disuse. Here is a 1995 passage in this vein:

Zakat was formerly applied in all Muslim territories and respected as an Islamic obligation. Because the general populace viewed zakat as a religious and moral duty, Muslim authorities had no problems in collecting it. With the advent of colonialism and the introduction of systems of government that excluded religious doctrine, authorities in most Muslim states largely abjured Islamic codes of law, including zakat.[22]

According to Islamists who share this understanding, massive advantages will flow from restoring zakat in its initial form. Their leading tracts provide a long list of rates and exemptions thought to have been enforced during Islam's initial few decades.[23] Here are two examples. A person who owns up to twenty-four camels is to pay one goat for every five camels. And the rate on gold and silver holdings is 2.5 percent of any amount beyond the corresponding exemption that the Prophet stipulated: for gold, 7.5 tolas (3 ounces), and for silver, 52.5 tolas (21 ounces).[24] The weight differences must have reflected the relative prices of these precious metals in Muhammad's own milieu. As of 2023, the exemptions amount to about US$5,800-worth of gold but only $500-worth of silver.

The original rates and exemptions supposedly demonstrate zakat's power as a timeless antipoverty instrument. Yet writings avoid references to certain major forms of contemporary wealth and income. Although no Islamist considers new categories of wealth zakat-exempt, the typical tract neglects to discuss, let alone specify rates for, stocks, bonds, vacation homes, collectibles, and retirement savings, to mention some of the most important. For all the specifics they provide regarding agricultural income, they ignore income from industry and services, both huge in the modern era. And while they explain how dues on gold and silver are to be calculated, they say nothing about cryptocurrencies. Clearly, the reference economy of Islamists is that of seventh-century Arabia, not one familiar to living generations. Their exemption limits, too, are anachronistic. Why should the zakat duty of a silver holder differ from that of a gold holder? And what are the exemption limits on platinum stocks, copper futures, and mortgage-backed securities?

Nevertheless, Islamic economists routinely exude great optimism regarding zakat's capacity to exterminate Muslim poverty. A 2015 paper coauthored by Monzer Kahf, a highly influential Islamic economist, claims that zakat is a more potent instrument of equalization than any known social security system.[25] Whereas social security systems serve "groups beyond those of the poor and the needy," zakat is "a religious duty involving direct transfer of wealth from the rich to the poor."[26] Moreover, unlike social security, whose ideological premises are "vague," zakat rests on clear theoretical foundations and moral principles.[27] This understanding of zakat's purpose happens to conflict fundamentally with the Quran.[28] It also overlooks fourteen centuries of Islamic history.

The Islamist engagement with zakat was an opportunity to open a dialogue with secularists who consider Islam a threat to economic development, political liberties, and secular lifestyles. It created an opening for demonstrating that zakat provides an untapped inspiration for solving entrenched social problems. More broadly, it provided a sound basis for drawing secularists into discourses on Islam's early contributions to rule of law. The inclusion of binding the state among the objectives of Islam's original political system might have become the starting point for discussions on instituting checks and balances to protect sundry liberties. The discourses would have educated the Islamist rank-and-file as well. Islamists would have learned about the freedoms that the Quran grants to individuals and the restrictions it imposes on states.

Instead, the fathers of modern Islamism were caught up in the symbolism of reviving a Quran-based institution. They promoted zakat, first and foremost, as a source of Muslim identity. Just as the mosque differentiates Muslims from other communities on worship, so zakat would differentiate them on fiscal management.[29] Every society has had institutions, if only informal, to care for the poor and the infirm. Zakat, Islamists held, was Islam's uniquely powerful formal institution. Restoring it now would remove modern inequalities rooted in un-Islamic institutions. It would also distinguish the Muslim world as uniquely compassionate. In two respects, this Islamist agenda undermined the cause of making Islam relevant to modern economic governance. First, in turning zakat into a caricature of its original function as a pillar of Islam, it reinforced perceptions of an outdated religion that is disconnected from prevailing social problems. Second, in trying to make zakat mandatory, Islamists compounded the perception that they aim to curtail freedoms.

ISLAM AS A PROHIBITION MACHINE

Islamists have sowed fears by promoting assorted prohibitions meant to prevent behaviors they consider un-Islamic. Restaurant closures during Ramadan, music bans, and gender segregation in public spaces are among the examples already encountered. In the economic sphere, a highly salient ban has been the prohibition of interest. It is doubtful whether interest can be purged from economic life. No example exists of a large polity, within or outside the Muslim world, that has done away with interest. It has been universal since time immemorial to incentivize investing, lending, and saving – all basic economic functions. Nevertheless, Islamists have been trying quixotically to make

Muslims avoid transactions that are critical to economic relations. In the process, they have missed another opportunity to advance freedoms of their own without alarming others. If Islamic finance were optional, it would be unproblematic. Just as no one objects to environment-friendly "green mutual funds," so only extreme secularists would fret about the presence of Islamic banks, bonds, mutual funds, credit cards, or cryptocurrencies. By trying to make interest categorically illegal, Islamists set off alarms. They provide pretexts for restricting Islamist political freedoms as a means of protecting widely cherished economic freedoms.

As a matter of practice, Islamic finance differs from conventional finance only cosmetically. Like the cash waqf, which used legal ruses to make its interest revenue seem like profit from commodity sales, Islamic finance uses gimmicks to disguise interest.[30] Another parallel with the cash waqf is that Islamic scholars declare every financial innovation strictly un-Islamic before objections from the devout make them reconsider, finding it acceptable after all. Consequently, Islamic financial practices follow conventional practices with a delay. At the emergence of a financial innovation, Sharia experts reflexively label it un-Islamic. Insofar as the practice is useful, conventional financial firms adopt it, which then pressures their Islamic competitors to follow suit. Thus, Sharia experts routinely produce Islamic rationalizations for practices they themselves condemned just a few years earlier.

The evolution of the Islamic credit card sector illustrates this religious legitimation process, which Mahmoud El-Gamal dubs "halalization."[31] When conventional banks of the Middle East – those that give and take interest openly – began issuing credit cards, Sharia experts denounced the cards as un-Islamic. Within a decade, though, Islamic banks were issuing functionally identical credit cards of their own to remain competitive with their rivals. The main difference between the two types is that Islamic credit cards use a euphemism such as "service charge" or "transaction fee" for payments that conventional credit cards call interest. Islamic credit cards also distinguish themselves through religious branding. Among the rules of Islamic cards is that they should not be used to pay for alcohol or pork. Certain Islamic cards contain chips that point to Mecca. Some card issuers allow paying for pilgrimage expenses in thirty-six "interest free" installments.[32]

In reinforcing its image as a prohibition machine, Islamism's preoccupation with disguising interest has kept it out of discourses on the history of Muslim financial practices. Islamists are absent from genuine scholarship on the contributions of Islamic financial practices to the Middle East's economic development during Islam's early centuries or on how these shaped the ensuing European–Middle Eastern divergence.[33] An obstacle is Islamism's attachment to the myth that, in the precolonial Middle East, finance avoided interest. This myth conceals the creative methods that lenders and borrowers used to circumvent the Islamic interest ban. It also blocks communication on how the pretense of enforcing the ban hindered economic development.

Among the other institutions that would distinguish a properly Islamic economy, say Islamists, are behavioral norms based on the Quran and Islamic traditions. In line with every major religion and diverse secular moralities, these norms require honesty and trustworthiness in economic dealings.[34] Now, complain Islamists, these norms have weakened due to inadequate piety. In fact, although the relationship between Islamic religiosity and either honesty or trustworthiness has been difficult to pin down, generalized trust is relatively low among Muslims.[35] Islamists believe that inculcating people with a puritanical interpretation of Islam would improve economic efficiency.[36] But prohibitions themselves can breed dishonesty, low trust, corruption, and lawlessness. The restrictions of Islamic waqf law promoted corruption on a large scale. For more than a millennium, the ban on interest routinized dishonesty, and now Islamic finance is replicating that pattern. Clearly, it serves rule of law better to get institutions right than to issue impractical religious prohibitions.

MODERN ZAKAT PRACTICES

Starting in the late nineteenth century, well before Islamists sought to revive zakat as an instrument of Islamic identity and poverty reduction, charitable organizations founded outside of Islamic law took to invoking Islam's zakat duty in their fundraising campaigns. In Turkey, for example, the Red Crescent (founded 1868), the Children's Protection Society (1921), and the Turkish Aviation Society (1925) collected donations under the rubric of zakat, as did religious associations pursuing causes such as mosque construction and Quran study. In the Palestinian Territories, zakat-funded charitable organizations have provided schooling, health insurance, and medical services since the 1970s. The Nablus Zakat Committee (1977) and Hebron's Al-Ihsan Charitable Society (1983) are prominent examples. In the West Bank and Gaza, such organizations have tended to enjoy high confidence. The main reason is that independence from local and foreign governments gives them wide latitude in prioritizing needs and in accommodating beneficiary preferences.[37] Other examples of zakat-collecting charitable organizations include the Rabaa al-Adawiya Medical Center (1993), Misr El-Kheir (2007), and the Egyptian Food Bank (2006), all in Egypt, and Jordan's King Hussein Cancer Foundation (1997).[38] As in Turkey, in Arab countries innumerable mosque- or community-based zakat committees also raise funds. Some of them operate clandestinely.[39]

Evidently, substantial numbers of Muslims pay zakat to private organizations, generally without state guidance. By supporting bottom-up political activities, some of these donations help to build civil society. One might expect the supporters of mandatory and centralized zakat to have investigated whether their projects would crowd out private zakat donations. If any Islamist has done so, the work has not been noticed.

Meanwhile, larger-scale zakat campaigns to fund political and military agendas have also been commonplace. In 1968, the Grand Mufti of Saudi Arabia opined that zakat collections could fund the Palestinian resistance to Israel, which he considered a holy war. The Quran lists people serving God among the beneficiaries of zakat, he explained.[40] Since its founding in 1928, Egypt's Muslim Brotherhood has funded its multifaceted activities partly through zakat committees.[41] For a final example, consider ISIS. In territories that it held for several years starting in 2014, it collected 2.5 percent as zakat on all commercial revenue. The collections financed its military operations, religious repression, and social engineering.[42]

In the 1900s, about a dozen governments, a quarter of the OIC's members, instituted an official zakat system of some kind. As of 2018, six countries had a mandatory zakat system and eleven others had an official agency facilitating zakat collection and disbursement.[43] All these systems are based, in one respect or another, on the Prophet's original zakat system. Nevertheless, they exhibit huge differences in terms of payers and beneficiaries. One system charges farmers while exempting industrialists; another makes automatic deductions, during Ramadan, from bank accounts. The beneficiaries vary, though rarely are the destitute included. Critically, none serves zakat's broader original goals. Government zakat agencies pursue just one objective of the original system: alleviating poverty.[44] None links its efforts with those of charitable organizations collecting zakat to finance other objectives of the seventh-century system. None contributes to protecting private property rights. Rampant corruption in their administrations undermines rule of law, which the original zakat system was designed to strengthen.

THE POLITICAL FALLOUT OF ISLAMIC FINANCE

As of 2021, the Islamic finance market holds assets of around \$2.2 trillion. The figure represents about 1 percent of the global financial market of around \$250 trillion.[45] The global share of Islamic finance is minuscule in relation to the 24 percent share of Muslims within the global population, or even the OIC's 14 percent share of global GDP.[46] Evidently, only a small share of the financial transactions by or among Muslims follows a self-consciously Islamic template. Nevertheless, in the Muslim world and even beyond, Islamic finance represents a challenge to conventional finance.

The ruses that Islamic finance uses to differentiate its products are not costless. Just as processing the operation "$(-0.7+1.7)^2+(3/3)=4^{1/2}$" takes more time than computing "$1+1=2$," so burying an interest payment in a double sale is more cumbersome than processing the payment transparently. The lawyers who seek acceptance from regulators do not work for free, nor do the Islamic specialists who issue halal certificates. The public relations officials burdened with differentiating Islamic goods absorb additional resources. More important, reducing financial transparency clouds the pricing of risk and facilitates corruption. In complicating financial transactions deliberately, Islamic finance opens itself to money laundering and financial fraud. Indeed, Islamic banks are more costly to operate than conventional banks.[47]

A 2015 study showed that on average OIC countries exhibit about 425 fewer financial accounts per 1,000 adults relative to the global average, 12 fewer financial branches per 100,000 adults, and about 20 percentage points lower credit use by firms.[48] The added costs of Islamic finance could be justifiable if they raised financial inclusion among Muslims. However, no association exists between financial inclusion and access to Islamic banking.[49]

But judging Islamic finance requires going beyond easily quantified metrics such as operational costs and financial inclusion. Also important are its effects on public discourse concerning Islam's past and future. Lack of transparency weakens generalized trust, which in the Middle East is already low. It creates a habit of addressing perceived problems through obfuscation rather than open discourse. Attention gets diverted from real economic challenges to phony issues. Moreover, when educators, journalists, and politicians get ahead by touting the virtues of Islamic finance, a byproduct is to convey that empty rhetoric can bring personal success.

Because Islamic finance is associated with religion, criticizing it is to risk accusations of blasphemy. The danger discourages many knowledgeable observers from speaking frankly about its inefficiencies. To avoid charges of prejudice, even secularists falsify their knowledge, or, more commonly, just avoid the subject. Insofar as Islamic finance is a religious practice, these forms of reticence feed into the religious preference falsification that suppresses liberal strands of Islam. They reinforce the norm of holding Islamist initiatives to a relatively low standard, implicitly on the pretext that their sacredness compensates for any practical shortcomings. It is thus a contributor to persistently low religious freedoms.

The premise that interest is categorically evil accounts for the alleged moral superiority of Islamic finance. Yet the Quran bans only an extreme form that in pre-Islamic Arabia commonly led to enslavement. Nowhere does it say anything relevant to forms of interest that benefit lender and borrower alike. Islamism might have used the Quran's prohibition of riba as the springboard for a drive against genuine poverty traps and ethnic discrimination within the Muslim world. In the mid-1900s, as Islamism became a global movement, severe group-based discrimination existed in many Muslim countries, and often the victims included a Muslim minority.[50] As late as 1950, the literacy rate in countries that now belong to OIC was 16.3 percent, as against a world rate of 51 percent.[51] Using the Quran as the basis for improving Muslim lives could have disarmed secularists conditioned to equating Islam with obscurantism. It could have stimulated conversations among religious and secular groups on alternative ways to address entrenched problems. In sum, by turning the riba ban into an empty ritual, the founders of Islamism missed yet another golden opportunity to modernize Islam, lessen its threats to secularists, carry its teachings into discourses on development strategies, and encourage civilized debates on the implications of Islamic scripture.

THE ILLIBERALISM OF ISLAMISM

The term "Islamism" evokes a global movement that seeks to force on masses a lifestyle ostensibly based on scripture and the examples of Muhammad and his companions. Most of its many variants are unabashedly illiberal. However, its sources of inspiration could have served a liberal agenda. The Quran and recollections of the Prophet's life contain many teachings compatible with broadening freedoms and strengthening rule of law. Yet Islamic economics, which encapsulates the economic agenda of Islamism, has promoted highly illiberal interpretations of Islamic institutions that, ironically, once served liberal ends.

Islamic economics justifies its main concrete initiatives – the building of a global Islamic finance sector and the reestablishment of mandatory zakat systems – through selected Quran verses. The original functions of those verses would appeal to sundry modern constituencies. One need not be an Islamist, or even a Muslim, to oppose contracts that result in enslavement. Likewise, predictable taxation and limited government are goals with universal appeal. Hence, the Quran's commandments that Islamic economics treats as foundational might have formed the basis for cooperation between Islamists and secularists. Alas, through campaigns that enhance Islam's visibility without solving real social problems, Islamic economics has merely discredited itself among constituencies it ostensibly seeks to enlighten. Nearly a century after its initiation, it lacks credibility among secular Muslims, who treat it as evidence of Islam's rigidity.

Islam was born in a commercial town. Early on, it developed a legal infrastructure supportive of trade, wealth creation, and material security. Islamism might have treated this record as the basis for economic initiatives favorable to a commercial renaissance. Squandering that opportunity, Islamists focus on contractual forms from a millennium ago, such as Islamic partnerships.[52] Except for camouflaging the interest charges and payments of Islamic banks, the practical effects of Islamic economics have been negligible.[53] At the same time, this obsession with form over substance has contributed to giving Islamism an archaic feel and to its exclusion from fruitful discussions on the Middle East's economic and political challenges.

PART V

CONCLUSION

15

Islamic Institutions and Muslim Freedoms

In the mid-twentieth century, as Islamism became a global political movement, its proponents insisted that Islam is much more than a form of worship. It is a complete way of life, they claimed. They meant that Islam regulates every domain of human existence, without separating the religious from the mundane. This imagined comprehensiveness makes Islam seem antithetical to individual freedoms. If in fact Islam regulated entire social orders, it would leave no room for human discretion. Believers would never need to think for themselves or weigh options. They would simply follow rules.

As a practical matter, no religion provides, or can provide, an all-encompassing blueprint that turns people into automatons. The limitations of human cognition and communication alone make human agency inevitable in vast domains. And every religion provides broad discretion in many areas, subject only to general principles. Indeed, even in highly pious Muslim communities, diverse issues are decided without reference to Islam on specifics. Examples include construction regulations, mathematics requirements, traffic lighting, and urban sanitation. Evidently, the "Islamic way of life" is less controlling than Islamists tend to imagine. By the same token, distinctly Islamic institutions have constrained Muslim liberties in diverse domains.

The Islamic institutional complex shaped the Middle East's political development most fundamentally through five channels: rules for providing social services, which kept civil society weak; the Quran's tax rules, which, though designed to strengthen property rights, set the stage for arbitrary taxation; the Islamic inheritance system and partnership rules, which kept commercial enterprises small and short-lived; strict legal individualism, which, by denying legal standing to organizations, hindered the emergence of political checks and balances; and blasphemy and apostasy rules, which restricted discussion on the content of Islam and denied Muslims religious choice. Thwarting liberal variants of Islam, the Islamic institutional complex has also convinced secular Muslims that to protect their own freedoms they must restrict open piety.

Among the consequences of the Islamic institutional complex is that the Muslim world's Middle Eastern core is the globe's least democratic and least free region. Its private constituencies have unusual difficulty engaging in organized collective action. Their religious freedoms are highly limited. And they belong to states where autocratic rule is the norm. No single element of Islamic law is responsible for these patterns. Various mechanisms have contributed to making the Middle East an especially repressive region by global standards of the 2020s.

POLITICAL LEGACIES OF ISLAMIC LAW

Around the time that Islam emerged as a world religion, no society provided anywhere near the range of freedoms that modern liberal societies have taken for granted. Nowhere were individuals free to form organizations dedicated to countering their ruler's policies. Nowhere was the law protective of political dissenters or religious nonconformists. Nowhere did people enjoy formally secure private property rights. Nowhere could private groups organize politically or pool resources through perpetual organizations. To signal submission to the ruling elite, individuals were expected to practice their religion visibly, through periodic rituals. The organizational, expressive, economic, intellectual, and religious freedoms of liberal orders all developed gradually, through processes involving epic struggles.

Legacies of the Islamic Waqf

Among the capabilities essential to a liberal order is the ability to pursue collective goals through perpetual private organizations. Such organizations constrain the state by limiting its ability to harm the governed. The resulting political checks and balances sustain individual freedoms that were once granted only insofar as the state expected to benefit. In the Islamic Middle East, a possible starting point for autonomous nonstate organizations was the Islamic waqf, a trust that an individual formed under Islamic law to provide designated social services in perpetuity. Massive resources flowed into waqfs. In some locations, waqfs controlled more real estate than the state. Because waqf assets were off-limits to the state, and because they were managed according to the founder's wishes, they could have formed the basis for freedom-enhancing political checks and balances. Waqfs might have used their vast resources to build a civil society akin to the legendary institutional complex that Alexis De Tocqueville identified as the fount of American liberties and creativity.[1]

Yet Islamic waqfs did not produce a vigorous civil society. On the contrary, they suppressed it by inhibiting mass political participation and mass collective action. Because a waqf's activities were essentially set by its founder, its

Islamic Institutions and Muslim Freedoms

capacity to fulfill emerging social needs was limited. Its beneficiaries had no say over its activities. Designed to provide services on its own, it could not participate in lasting political coalitions. The waqf's beneficiaries played no formal role in appointing its officers. For all these reasons, it did not become a counterweight to the state, and it obstructed the advancement of personal freedoms. Although it allowed wealthy individuals to provide services of their own choice, neither they nor other beneficiaries could use endowed resources to influence state policies.

The waqf formed under Islamic law is gone, but many countries of the Middle East feature modern organizations known, confusingly, also as waqfs. The modern waqf is the Muslim world's analogue of the charitable corporation. Self-governing at least in principle, it has a perpetual existence. Along with other formally autonomous nongovernmental organizations known under other names, the modern waqf has furnished the institutional infrastructure for a vigorous civil society. But it takes time to develop the civic skills that the Islamic waqf left uncultivated for a millennium. For that reason alone, civil society remains weak across the Middle East. Additionally, though, the very weakness of the region's civic legacy furnished fertile ground for the repressive regimes formed since the Islamic waqf lost political relevance. By and large, the Middle East's autocracies strive to keep civil society politically weak. Through two basic channels, then, the legacy of the Islamic waqf still constrains the Middle East's liberalization.

The Persistence of Religious Repression

Among the elements of a liberal order are religious freedoms. These include the right to disobey religious commandments, reject religious principles, change religion, and be irreligious. Because Islam's domain is formally unbounded, the range of its prescriptions, templates, and bans is remarkably broad. In practice, though, living Muslims, like their forebears, violate Islamic law routinely and with impunity. Consider an online purchase from a self-consciously Islamic company using an Islamic credit card. The act violates the Islamic law of transactions (which requires a joint examination of the goods exchanged through a face-to-face meeting between the two sides), the Islamic principle of legal status (which denies legal standing to companies), and the presumed Islamic ban on interest (which the issuers of Islamic credit cards obey just symbolically). Even Muslims familiar with the Sharia tacitly reinterpret Islamic rules to accommodate modern economic practices. Evidently, when a sufficiently powerful constituency openly objects to Islamic restrictions, accommodations will follow. It does not follow that all widely disliked rules get dropped. People do not necessarily publicize their discontent, let alone form organizations to eliminate the underlying problems.

The premodern Middle East featured many heterodox sects. Accused of heresy or apostasy, many were persecuted severely by the dominant Sunni or

Shii regime. If their members survived, it was often by going into hiding and practicing their favored rites secretly, or in inhospitable places that regime officials could not reach. But not all premodern heterodoxies faced hostility. Those perceived as unthreatening to the ruler, if not also as somehow useful, were tolerated, sometimes for centuries. Sufis, who pursued ascetic lifestyles and abjured temporal power, were often left alone as harmless.

Although entry into Islam is costless, exit was banned almost from the beginning. Now, a constituency exists for allowing free exit. It includes Muslims who find various Islamic restrictions intolerable as well as others who think that broadening religious freedoms would stimulate useful reinterpretations. Currently unorganized, this constituency already has Islamic justifications for annulling harsh rules against apostasy, upheld since the seventh century. Those rules built on a precedent set through state-consolidation efforts during Islam's formative period. While the precedent is widely viewed as banning out-conversion, in fact it signaled that tax rules would be enforced. To modern ears, the tax requirement sounds familiar and reasonable. Alas, recasting this detail of early Islamic history would not necessarily settle the controversy over Muslim religious freedoms. Certain Quran verses speak of retribution against nonbelievers. Although the verses do not say that punishments must be earthly, they lend themselves to illiberal readings. But other verses rule out compulsion, effectively establishing a right to leave Islam.

Insofar as textual inconsistencies are apparent, for interpreters the challenge boils down to prioritizing liberal verses over illiberal ones. A shift in the dominant interpretation, which currently privileges the illiberal verses, is not unthinkable. For one thing, analogous transformations have occurred in other religions, including Christianity. For another, Islam has been reinterpreted repeatedly since its emergence, radically so in modern times. Innovations include Islamic banks, which are business corporations, and various Islamic NGOs, which are organized as nonprofit corporations. Evidently, no absolute barrier exists to broadening Islamic religious freedoms.

As a strict monotheism, Islam has always divided other religions into two categories: older monotheistic religions, which it considers legitimate but superseded, and polytheistic religions, which are damnable. Under its canonical interpretation, the Quran requires the conversion of polytheists to Islam, if necessary by force. Thus, the religious tolerance enunciated in the Quran is limited. Achieving widespread acceptance of broader religious freedoms requires another distinction, one between parts of the Quran specific to seventh-century Arabia and those meant to be timeless and universal. Polytheism impeded Arabia's political unification. Beyond Arabia, though, Muslims have coexisted with polytheists. In India, Muslim administrations granted rights to Hindus and Buddhists.

Various popular discourses make it seem that objections to religious liberalization come mainly from clerics and their pious followers. In fact, secular constituencies have been among the enforcers of apostasy and blasphemy rules against nonconformist Muslims. Secular leaders participate in religious policing opportunistically, to pacify conservative opponents by outbidding them in religious intolerance. Likewise, ordinary secular individuals allow the enforcement of illiberal religious rules by withholding their objections. Secular Middle Easterners share responsibility, then, for the region's current religious illiberalism.

"Secular Muslims" include people who would become "practicing Muslims" if there existed a liberal variant of Islam. None exists, but the reason is not that Islam is monolithic. As with other religions, it admits diverse interpretations on many fronts. Amazingly, though, over fourteen centuries, these differences have produced only one major schism, the Sunni–Shii split of 661, and neither side formally recognizes even that. Since the history of Christianity is replete with schisms, one might expect many in Islamic history as well. To give one possibility, Turkish and Arab liberals might have established a modern form of Islam in the early 1920s – one that would broaden women's rights, modernize teaching practices, and adapt rituals to the rhythms of modern life.

For nonconformist Muslims, that was an opportune moment. Their conservative opponents were weakened and widely blamed for defeats at the hands of Europeans. The educated considered conservative understandings backward. If the collective action needed for a liberal schism failed to materialize, a basic factor was the inability to conduct honest and open discussions on religion. Anyone who set out to initiate a schism would face persecution, which would then discourage other reform-minded Muslims from lending support. Conservatives would treat the case as collective apostasy. Statements on the merits of establishing a breakaway denomination would be treated as blasphemous. Simply to avoid persecution themselves, potential joiners would participate in the persecution of schism supporters. Indeed, the founders of the Turkish Republic shelved a plan for a modern branch simply to avoid endangering reforms that were underway. Some nonconformist Turks expected liberal forms of Islam to emerge organically, as modernization unfolded.

Liberal Muslims are intrinsically opposed to settling conflicts through violence, which puts them at a disadvantage vis-à-vis groups prepared to charge ideological opponents with physically punishable religious offenses. Easily victimized, liberals cannot fight back as effectively. Thus, apostasy and blasphemy laws, the two most lethal weapons of Islamic illiberalism, represent a self-enforcing equilibrium. Their very existence reproduces the fears that allow their preservation. To avoid personal trouble, liberal Muslims, nonbelievers, non-Muslim believers, and assorted other dissenters all avoid taking a stand against Islam's apostasy and blasphemy laws.

Religious freedoms could have triggered liberalization across the board. In the Muslim world, the capacity to criticize Islam has been closely linked to the capacity to challenge ruling elites, the law, the courts, the educational system, investment rules, and more. After all, until modern times major social institutions were justified largely through religion. But these institutions were closed to honest debate because of the risk of giving religious offence. Nonstate entities supplying social services could have provided an alternative starting point for liberalization. They could have helped their constituencies acquire collective power. Personal freedoms would have broadened through political checks and balances grounded in organizations pursuing competing interests. But the waqf denied beneficiaries the necessary collective power.

Sluggish Economic Institutions

As the Middle East transitioned from an economically advanced region of the early second millennium to an underdeveloped region of the Modern Era, its merchants and investors did not form movements to constrain either rulers or clerics. They did not bring about liberalization through organizational innovations that strengthened them politically. A basic reason is that, until the transplant of modern economic institutions from Europe, the Middle East's profit-making private enterprises remained small and ephemeral. The smallness and rapid turnover of private commercial enterprises hindered sustained coalitions representing business interests. Under these circumstances, private enterprises did not generate political checks and balances of the type that made European rulers submit to rule of law.

Several elements of the Islamic institutional complex contributed to keeping Middle Eastern enterprises structurally stagnant until the modernization drive of the 1800s. One was Islam's partnership law, which dissolved enterprises at the incapacitation or death of even a single member. Another was Islam's inheritance system, which voided a deceased person's partnerships. A partnership's termination required the liquidation of its assets, which hindered capital accumulation. Rarely did a highly successful enterprise survive across generations. No major business dynasties formed. Thus, enterprises did not experience operational challenges of the type that would have stimulated organizational innovations. Among the innovations that did not emerge indigenously are banks, chambers of commerce, business publications, stock exchanges, and formal insurance markets. Such institutions were hastily transplanted from Europe when global economic modernization made structural reforms essential to regaining competitiveness.

The Middle East's modernization drives of the 1800s were initiated by high officials who considered economic underdevelopment an existential threat. In Western Europe, by contrast, modern institutions all emerged organically over centuries, through innumerable adaptations and refinements, and generally to facilitate communication, enable coordination, allocate risks, and reduce information asymmetries. As European economic life gained complexity, private businesses and individual entrepreneurs acquired political power. They used their growing clout to limit taxation, make obligations predictable, strengthen property rights, and obtain secular social services supportive of private economic activity. As wealthy businesses contributed to sundry private causes, civil society strengthened. In the Middle East, by contrast, the institutional sluggishness of the private economy kept private economic actors politically weak. It also compounded the endemic weaknesses of civil society.

The path to a liberal order could follow a dynamic distinct from that of Europe. In the Middle East, another possible starting point for broad liberalization was zakat, Islam's only pillar with an explicitly economic function. It appears in the Quran as a system that finances designated state expenses, including transfers to the poor, through a tax on wealth and income. By the standards of Antiquity, the rates were low. They were also fixed. Especially significant is that the Quran legitimates wealth and income on which zakat is paid. Zakat could have served, then, as a foundation for political checks and balances based on secure private ownership. It might have stiffened the backbone of wealthy producers, facilitating the binding of rulers. If such developments did not occur, one reason is that the specifics of the zakat system were tailored to Arabia. They left out major sources of income and wealth in the broader Middle East. Zakat also failed to produce checks and balances because powerful groups narrowed its scope through various exemptions.

Given these circumstances, rulers had to impose extra-Islamic taxes simply to survive. Having set precedents for arbitrary taxation, they then stopped enforcing zakat. A fundamental Islamic tool for empowering the individual against the state was thus transformed into a minor device for local poor relief. The waqf's emergence as a core Islamic institution was a creative response to zakat's abandonment as a state-enforced policy tool. With zakat driven to insignificance, arbitrary expropriation and taxation threatened wealthy high officials, who went looking for a wealth shelter. The waqf met this need. In return for the privilege of sheltering wealth, though, the wealthy agreed to use some of their sheltered assets to provide social services. They also agreed to keep waqfs out of politics. The persistent weakness of the Middle East's civil society is among the unintended outcomes, then, of zakat's declining relevance to Islamic governance.

Zakat returned to Middle Eastern political discourses in the 1930s, through modern Islamism. It became one of two concrete initiatives distinguishing a properly Islamic economy from economies ostensibly corrupted by secularists and colonialists. The other was Islamic finance. In both cases, the focus was more on the symbolism of Islamizing a secularized domain than on solving actual problems. Islamism tacitly stripped zakat of all but one of its many original functions: poverty alleviation. While failing to put a dent in poverty, it also sidelined zakat's roles in enforcing rule of law, protecting property rights, and public finance. In the process, Islamism has missed an opportunity to make Islamic institutions seem relevant to solving major contemporary problems in complex societies. Focusing on the broad functions that made zakat a pillar of Islam could have initiated a dialogue with secularists inclined to dismiss Islam as a fount of backwardness.

A similar scenario has played out in relation to Islamic finance. The Quran's ban on riba, which Islamists treat as a blanket ban on all interest, was directed at a form of interest that, in pre-Islamic Arabia, pushed vulnerable people into enslavement. A comprehensive ban has never been enforced anywhere. In every Muslim-governed polity of the past, interest-based credit was widely available, though the interest was often disguised through euphemisms or accounting tricks. In any case, an interest-free economy is a fantasy. In pretending that Islamic finance is interest-free, Islamism legitimizes dishonesty. Weakening rule of law, it also compounds mistrust between Islamists and secularists.

MUTUAL REINFORCEMENT OF ILLIBERAL INSTITUTIONS

The foregoing summary has related how, over more than a millennium, various Islamic institutions restricted freedoms in the Middle East and created an illiberal political legacy. Because of the Islamic waqf, the region entered the modern era with few civic organizations and weak civic skills. Meanwhile, the Islamic inheritance system contributed to low private capital accumulation. These institutions belong to what I have been calling the "Islamic institutional complex". This term is not simply a shorthand for a set of institutions that coexisted for centuries. Elements of an institutional complex complement one another. Often, they are mutually reinforcing. The Islamic inheritance system incentivized the founding of waqfs; and the existence of waqfs dampened incentives to revise the Islamic inheritance system. Complementarities within an institutional complex make it difficult to change, let alone remove, individual elements. By the same token, if one element is somehow removed, the rest will weaken, precipitating a chain of institutional changes.[2] It is no coincidence that in the Middle East the nineteenth century saw cascading institutional reforms. Each reform facilitated those that followed. Reviewing the key interactions will illuminate the stability of the institutional complex until the rise of the West. It will also set the stage for discussing why reforms have not yet run their course.

Provision of Social Services

The crimping of civil society through the waqf stabilized all other elements of the Islamic institutional complex by hindering the formation of reformist movements. Consider waqf-financed madrasas, which provided training in Islamic law. During their education, madrasa students learned that apostasy is punishable by death. They learned that only natural persons have standing before the law and that non-Muslim testimony is suspect. They learned to treat commercial partnerships as terminable at will by any party to the contract. And they learned to consider interest sinful. Parents had no way to form organizations tasked with reviewing the curriculum or pushing for change. They could not propagate alternative interpretations of the Quran, such as a narrow reading of the riba ban or an understanding that elevates the significance of verses favorable to religious freedoms.

In suppressing opportunities for civic action, the waqf thus reinforced religious prohibitions that were central to the Islamic institutional complex. It also helped to sustain economic institutions that bred corruption, hindered clear thinking about economic challenges, and made it impossible even to imagine modern banking. As the waqf lost popularity in the 1700s, and states started to nationalize them under the pretense of assistance, alternatives to the madrasa emerged. Modern schools provided fertile ground for new ideas. Previously unthinkable reforms became possible. They included the secularization of economic cooperation, the transplant of advanced financial institutions, the establishment of secular commercial courts, the extension of equal legal rights to non-Muslims, and the passing of laws of corporations. The shrinking of the waqf's economic footprint facilitated all such reforms by narrowing the economic base of clerics, a conservative constituency.

Many developments of the twentieth century became possible only after the Islamic waqf lost significance. Take the granting of labor rights. Across the region, a milestone in this process is the formation of labor unions. Unionization began after the Islamic waqf became an anachronism, a variant of the corporation became the organizational form of choice for social services, and private collective action became legal, albeit within bounds. Employers crushed many of the region's diffuse labor movements, often with government complicity. But enough survived to make labor a political player.[3] Unions obtained various rights precisely because they were perpetual associations. Had the waqf remained the only organizational form available for providing social services privately, the Middle East would have lacked labor unions. Although labor movements remain substantially weaker in the Middle East than in politically freer places, in premodern Middle Eastern history labor organizations with members drawn from innumerable enterprises were unimaginable. Guilds brought together producers or traders, not laborers who worked for others.

Religious Restrictions

In premodern Islamic courts, religion was a fundamental identifier of every party to a dispute, because it signaled legal rights. A Muslim had superior rights than a non-Muslim. Hence, it was far more consequential in the premodern Middle East than in a legally secularized modern society to be known as a Muslim in good standing. A "bad Muslim" reputation could jeopardize privileges and trigger punishments. These risks had implications for institutional stability.

The waqf's status as an Islamic institution protected against challenges. None of its drawbacks discussed in earlier chapters could have been articulated with impunity while clerics were economically powerful. Ziya Gökalp wrote his famous poem about the waqf's harms to Muslims at a time when it had already lost significance. In the heyday of the Islamic waqf, to characterize it as somehow inefficient might have brought accusations of heresy. Revealingly, Middle Eastern records from before the 1800s lack commentary concerning the institutions that Europeans used to provide social services. Muslims with European connections must have noticed the differences. But knowledge may never surface if its disclosure seems risky. Anyone who publicized the advantages of educating through corporations would have angered clerics. Religious repression was a factor, then, in the Islamic waqf's persistence as a core Islamic institution. Prior to the reforms of the 1800s, it helped to shape education and other social services.

Merchants who did business with Western Europe must have known that their Western competitors formed more durable companies and kept wealth undivided across generations. After the establishment of the English Levant Company, they would have seen, too, that Westerners were forming organizations that outlasted their individual members. As indigenous Middle Eastern merchants saw Western competitors prosper in the Middle East itself, they might have criticized Islamic law as outdated with respect to the commercial opportunities it supports. Conceivably, they could have asked Islamic scholars to study Western commercial institutions with an eye toward Islamic legal reforms. Such initiatives could have been interpreted as attacks on Islam. If any such requests were made, they have not come to light. Insofar as local merchants grasped the advantages of institutional borrowing, fears of adverse reactions from clerics would have made them withhold demands. Revealingly, critical discourses on Islamic economic institutions started after clerics lost much of their power and an existential threat from the West made ruling elites articulate problems themselves, collectively. It is significant that, unlike Muslims, non-Muslims could switch practices as individuals, by exercising choice of law in favor of Western institutions, or by partnering with Westerners, or simply by imitating Western practices within globally connected non-Muslim networks. As the West advanced economically, lacking choice of law became a growing handicap for Muslims. Unable to alter business practices as individuals, they had to wait until their troubles induced reforms from above, by ruling elites.

It has mattered to the Middle East's economic trajectory and its civic history that the freedom to interpret Islam was bounded, that institutions considered Islamic could not be debated freely, that religious affiliation affected organizational and commercial opportunities, and that, for more than a millennium, religious officials controlled substantial wealth. The region's civic and economic institutions have depended on how Islam was interpreted, who spoke for Islam, and the personal risks of demanding Islamic reforms.

Economic Organization

During Islam's initial centuries, many of the jurists who shaped Islamic law were active in commerce, which made them attuned to the needs of merchants. By virtue of their travels and cross-communal dealings, merchants were particularly familiar with foreign institutions. Revealingly, Islamic law was most dynamic precisely when the influence of merchants over clerics was at its peak. Those centuries saw the waqf's development as an Islamic institution based on Roman and Persian templates. Among the waqf's early uses was the financing of secure inns for merchants along the old world's main commercial caravan routes, those connecting the Mediterranean with China and India. The period also saw the refinement of commercial rules to lower the risks of doing business. Commercial advances and mercantile political influence thus kept religion innovative. But Islam's religious dynamism went beyond commercial contexts. Waqfs could finance any function considered legitimate under Islamic law. They supported the precursors of the madrasa, law colleges attached to mosques.[4]

The additions to the Islamic institutional complex during the centuries of mercantile political strength had unintended consequences for the power of merchants. In creating a dependable source of income for clerics, the waqf reduced clerical participation in commerce. And in securing wealth, it drew capital out of commerce. The resulting weaknesses of merchants diminished their capacity to induce adjustments in the commercially and financially relevant segments of Islamic law. Tellingly, the special legal rights that European merchants acquired through the capitulations were denied to domestic merchants. This asymmetry reflects at once their shrinking political influence and their contributions to the Middle East's continuing loss of global competitiveness.

The privileges that the capitulations granted to foreign merchants included exemptions from Islamic laws responsible for the smallness and evanescence of Middle Eastern enterprises. Among them was the Islamic inheritance law, which hindered capital accumulation and the preservation of enterprises across generations. With the sort of power they enjoyed in the 800s, Muslim merchants might have made clerics devise ways to circumvent the Islamic inheritance rules wherever a successful business was at stake. Another privilege that foreigners won through the capitulations was protection against undocumented financial claims. Starting in the late 1400s, this protection lowered the cost of doing business by blocking frivolous lawsuits. Extending the documentation requirement to all lawsuits, including those limited to local litigants, would have been easy to justify, for the Quran explicitly requires the documentation of long-term contracts.[5] Again, though, by that time Middle Eastern merchants were too weak politically to press for such a change in court practices. Unlike their Western competitors, they were unorganized. Lone individuals cannot identify social gains or lobby for a cause as well as an organized group.

Beginning in the 1700s, private merchants and investors participated in the dismantling of established waqfs. They operated as individuals, stripping waqfs of assets through corrupt procedures, always with the cooperation of judges who shared in the gains. Critically, waqfs were privatized without collective action. Had the task required merchants to get organized, privatizations would have been delayed indefinitely. The privatizations were financed disproportionately by non-Muslim merchants, whose wealth tended to be more liquid than that of Muslims. Therein lies another unintended long-term consequence of rules that made it far easier for a Muslim to establish a waqf.[6] By shrinking the economic base and political influence of clerics, the privatizations paved the way for reforms that narrowed the jurisdiction of Islamic law. Profit-driven commercial transactions thus resulted in broader religious freedoms. Over the long run, organizational freedoms also expanded, as the dismantling of waqfs accentuated the need for providing social services through alternative institutions.

FALLACIES OF ISLAM'S IRRELEVANCE

At the end of a study on how Islamic law has affected a range of freedoms, it will be instructive to revisit three classes of arguments that are commonly advanced as proof that Islam, or specifically Islamic institutions, do not account for present political patterns.

Secular Authoritarianism

A common objection to the existence of links between Islam and Middle Eastern repression is that secular Middle Eastern regimes have been as repressive as regimes that draw legitimacy explicitly from Islam. This objection appeals especially to Islamists. It absolves Islamic institutions of responsibility, they say, and discredits reforms that marginalized Islam in public life. Though this logic is flawed, the objection itself merits consideration.

As measured by human rights, the political performance of Iran's secular monarchy was no better than that of the Islamic Republic of Iran. During his thirty-eight-year reign to 1979, Mohammad Reza Pahlavi dealt harshly with dissenters, including both socialists and Islamists. In Turkey, the secular regimes that held power from 1923 to 2002 all persecuted Islamists, though decreasingly after 1950. The repression that gathered steam in 2011, when Erdoğan's Islamist party won a third election in a row, has topped anything the country saw during the presidencies of Atatürk and İnönü (1923–50).[7] To turn to the Arab world, modern dictators at war with Islamists have had terrible human rights records themselves, as measured by political and religious freedoms. Repressing opponents of all stripes, they have run highly corrupt regimes for decades on end. At the time of their ouster in 2011, Tunisia's Ben Ali, Egypt's Mubarak, and Libya's Gaddafi had held office for a total of ninety-six years, or thirty-two years per dictator on average. They all kept Islamists outside their governing coalition and repressed them to one degree or another. In the 2020s, Syria's Bashar al-Assad tolerates no dissent. In battling

Islamic Institutions and Muslim Freedoms 281

notoriously brutal Islamists, his forces, too, resort to extreme measures against both fighters and civilians.[8]

According to many Islamists, but also certain other observers, such patterns clear Islam, and by implication Islamic institutions, of responsibility for the pervasiveness of political repression in the Middle East.[9] Ostensibly they indicate that the prevailing political patterns stem from policies championed by secular leaders and their foreign sponsors. Some commentators, including scholars, go further in claiming that the repressiveness of the culturally conservative Arab kingdoms and emirates serves their "global masters," mainly the United States, their chief military protector.[10] Implicit in such reasoning is that institutions undergirding political performance are changeable at will. When Islamists gain power and reject military cooperation with the West, it is their needs that dictate political patterns; but Western clients are governed according to Western priorities.

In fact, the repressive policies of secular and Western-backed regimes establish only that religious movements have no monopoly on repression or poor governance. By themselves, they do not illuminate the institutions responsible for the observed political repression. No political actor, secular or religious, Christian or Muslim, can alter at will the institutions under which a government operates. Just as the tripartite division of powers of the United States constrains all American political actors, so Middle Eastern regimes of all stripes operate in an opportunity space constrained by the region's own preexisting institutions. The latter include weak checks and balances within the state itself as well as feeble civic organizations. Middle Eastern societies lack reliable ways of holding governments accountable for their misdeeds.

If the basic institutions of a country or region rest at some deep level on the institutions associated with a religion, characteristics of even an impeccably secular regime will reflect those institutions. The secular regime might have done away with all sectarian symbols, and it might be trying to overcome perceived weaknesses rooted in its religious heritage. But the religion that it is suppressing will have bequeathed certain institutions that are unchangeable on demand. The policies that it pursues in trying to secularize society will reflect its religion-influenced history.

Colonial Harm

Foreign interference in the region has gone beyond the manipulation of local leaders. Various places have experienced colonialism of one form or another, including direct rule and European settlement. A massive literature holds European colonialism responsible for exploitation and corruption.[11] It is fashionable to treat the British–French partition of the Middle East through the Sykes–Picot agreement of 1916 as a source of insurmountable distortions in governance. The machinations of the French and British ostensibly shifted the political priorities of Arab elites from building systems of liberal constitutional governance to ousting colonizers through assertive nationalism. Those intrigues gave rise to military regimes that have dominated Arab politics.[12] Going further, some authors hold that colonialism absolves everything connected to Islam of responsibility for the modern Middle East's political patterns.[13]

Several grounds for skepticism were covered in Chapter 1. Now that we have analyzed the Middle East's institutional trajectory, it is worth revisiting the main point. Islamic institutions created governance problems that made the whole region vulnerable to colonization. Therefore, the reality of colonization does not extinguish the need to study connections between Islam and the Middle East's political evolution. Two additional points may be added to those offered early on. Splitting ethnic, linguistic, or sectarian groups between multiple nation-states, as Sykes–Picot unavoidably did, is not necessarily a recipe for perpetual authoritarianism. The OIC countries that rank well above the Middle East in the political indices of Figures 1.3–1.6 include several with high fractionalization according to ethnicity, language, or religion, in some cases all three.[14] Second, colonizer-generated political distortions, which are real, need to be weighed against colonial contributions to institutional modernization and the liberalization of political thought. In Turkey, Lebanon, and Egypt, among other places, colonizers established the first schools providing a liberal education, often through missionaries.[15] Though the founders of these schools were motivated by more than political development, their graduates have played highly disproportionate roles in liberalization and democratization movements.[16]

Islam's Dynamism

Past chapters have featured changes to the Islamic institutional complex. One is the transformation of zakat from a state-enforced transfer system to voluntary charity. Another is the development of the waqf, at the end of Islam's first century, as a vehicle for securing property and providing social services. Seven centuries later, the rules for forming waqfs were broadened to allow liquid endowments. For a final example, Islamic waqfs were ultimately nationalized on a huge scale. All such cases have been treated as proof that Islam is an optimally dynamic religion.[17] This is fallacious for several reasons.

Firstly, cases of adaptation are compatible with desired or potentially beneficial transformations that fail to materialize. Blasphemy and apostasy rules have survived largely because Muslims who favor their revocation are afraid to speak their minds. The rarity of open and honest discourse on these rules precludes coalitions to advance the necessary rethinking. Among the consequences is the perennial absence of liberal variants of Islam. The Islamic partnership and inheritance laws offer another example. In keeping enterprises small and ephemeral, they prevented an indigenous institutional transformation that might have avoided the need for momentous legal transplants in the 1800s.

Islamic Institutions and Muslim Freedoms 283

A second reason why cases of adaptation do not prove optimality is that they could have come too late. The cash waqf emerged in an economy stifled by sky-high interest rates. Had this type of waqf been invented a century earlier, the supply of credit would have been greater, and more borrowers would have had their needs met. In the same vein, the liquidation of waqf assets came way too late to avoid costly institutional borrowing from the West. Had it gained steam earlier, municipalities could have been founded sooner. Urban administration might have modernized through indigenous processes rather than institutional transplants.

Finally, even a useful reform may be too timid. The cash waqf raised the supply of credit. But the compromise behind its legalization retained hazardous features of the classic waqf. These include denying beneficiaries a voice and obstacles to waqf mergers. Stalling the development of civic life, they also blocked a possible indigenous path to banking.

The evolution of the Islamic institutional complex hardly shows, then, that observed changes were optimal in any specific sense. Islamic institutions were not necessarily responsive to social demands. They did not always solve prevailing problems, or even address them. They also failed to keep the Middle East from becoming economically uncompetitive and politically very repressive. The record shows merely that a Muslim-governed society has a capacity for creating, modifying, and eradicating institutions. It is capable of successive reforms.

The transplant of the corporation and associated changes in legal procedures are apposite. Islamic law does not recognize fictitious persons. But when, in the early twentieth century, states of the Middle East instituted a law of corporations, religious resistance was negligible. Pious officials accepted this borrowing from the West as an organizational form essential to competing in the global marketplace, running cities efficiently, and enabling bottom-up initiatives for various social needs. State agencies unconnected to religion have been monitoring corporations founded under the revised legal order. Disputes involving corporations are now adjudicated in secular courts. Where they still exist, Islamic courts need not handle cases involving corporations, and madrasas do not have to make room in their legal curricula for the corporation. Clerics could be objecting to the transplant of the corporation on the grounds that it secularizes vast domains of activity. They are not.

THE FUTURE OF ISLAMIC ILLIBERALISM

Though in the early twenty-first century the Middle East stands out as illiberal by global standards, over the past two centuries it has made substantial progress in advancing human liberties. Even in its most repressed countries, personal property rights have become more secure. There is far more organized collective action by nonstate groups. Unless they want to, citizens need not follow Islamic templates in their economic affairs. Charitable corporations enable sustained collective action through perpetual autonomous organizations. And business corporations enable capital accumulation within perpetual enterprises. A side benefit of the business corporation's availability is that the Islamic inheritance system no longer hinders enterprise growth and survival. When a company's ownership is separated from its management, its shares can be subdivided without harming the business itself. Shares may change hands without affecting operations. Indeed, even though Islamic inheritance rules are still enforced in much of the Middle East, the region now has private companies of a scale unimaginable in premodern times.

These achievements give hope for continued liberalization. Wealthy families, even ones currently allied with oppressive dictators, have the means to carry liberalization further. Someday, they might finance initiatives to institute checks and balances, possibly because of an existential threat akin to that faced by Middle Eastern elites of the nineteenth century. Should rich elites decide to spearhead liberalizing reforms, they would have use of organizational forms unavailable to them before the 1800s. They already belong to various legally autonomous and self-governing professional organizations without analogues in premodern times. Also at work are sundry civic organizations favoring liberalization of one type or another. Liberalization in one domain can start chain reactions that trigger liberalization in others.

But there is no quick fix to the prevailing political illiberalism. For the Middle East to reach advanced standards of personal liberty, many patterns of behavior must change. Though changes can stimulate one another, each involves adjustments to interpersonal norms, organizational rules, and state laws. Some modifications would upset longstanding status rankings and hierarchies. Learning civic skills requires communal practice. Resistance is likely. Groups with stakes in repression are organized themselves. They, too, include powerful individuals, both civilian and military. Hence, even in the best scenario, comprehensive liberalization would span multiple generations.

This pessimism regarding the near term mirrors a central prediction of the *Long Divergence*, which focuses on the legal roots of economic underperformance. There, I show that economic institutions of the modern Middle East are much better suited to the present than their discarded Islamic counterparts. Nonetheless, I suggest, skills in building large organizations in finance and commerce, trust in institutions, and comfort with impersonal exchange all take time to develop. Nowhere do they mature within a few years. It is one thing to pass a law of corporations, quite another for citizens to warm up to transacting with impersonal business corporations, as opposed to flesh-and-blood people. The learning required for success in an impersonal economy overlaps with that necessary for establishing sustained mass movements and political checks and balances. In both its economic and political dimensions, achieving a liberal order involves acculturation to massive organizations operating according to impersonal rules.

Additional grounds for pessimism are that two illiberal elements of Islam's institutional complex remain in force, if not formally then at least in practice.

Its blasphemy and apostasy rules are used to block open and honest debate on any matter pertaining to religion. By giving issues a religious dimension and drawing religious red lines, states and private groups protect vested interests. The fear of being accused of religious offense keeps individuals from joining organizations that pursue widely shared goals. Hence, although the basic institutional ingredients of civil society are in place, civic life is particularly impoverished on matters to which some constituency has given a religious spin. Yet reinterpreting Islam's rules against out-conversion and religious criticism requires collective action itself, and successful reforms have made that simpler. Achieving the necessary rethinking and mobilization is easier now than it was before modern organizational forms entered the region's legal systems.

Islamic law delayed various economic and organizational freedoms that peoples of the Middle East now take for granted. It did not deny or block them. The delay is lasting longer for key religious freedoms. Many vestiges of political repression and economic privilege remain in place. But by no means has the Middle East's liberalization process reached a dead end.

Notes

CHAPTER 1

1 Examples: Slackman and El-Naggar, "Radical Revolution" (*New York Times*); Kaminski, "Arab Spring Is Still Alive" (*Wall Street Journal*); Malik, Shenker, and Gabbatt, "Arab Spring Anniversary" (*Guardian*).
2 Bassiouni, *Chronicles of the Egyptian Revolution*; Ketchley, *Egypt in a Time of Revolution*.
3 Boduszyñski, Fabbe, and Lamont, "After the Arab Spring"; Cook, *False Dawn*, chaps. 1–3; Fahmy and Faruqi, eds., *Egypt and the Contradictions of Liberalism*; Hamid, *Temptations of Power*, chap. 7; Seghal and Grim, "Egypt's Restrictions on Religion."
4 Cansunar and Kuran, "Economic Harbingers of Political Modernization."
5 On a population-weighted basis, just 2 percent of the Middle East's regimes were a flawed or full democracy in 2020 (Economist Intelligence Unit, *Democracy Index 2020*). The corresponding share was 9.5 percent in Sub-Saharan Africa, 11 percent in East Asia, 75.5 percent in South Asia, and 81 percent in Latin America.
6 Cagaptay, *New Sultan*, chaps. 8–10.
7 Mahler, *Politics in Israel*, chaps. 2, 5–7; Smooha, "Is Israel Western?"
8 Computed from records of the United Nations High Commissioner for Refugees and the United Nations Department of Economic and Social Affairs. In 2007, the term "refugee" expanded to include "persons who are outside their country or territory of origin and who face protection risks similar to those of refugees, but for whom refugee status has, for practical or other reasons, not been ascertained." Over 2000–18, the region's average population share was 8.2 percent. Before 2000, the United Nations kept no standardized records of asylum seekers.
9 Gallup's question: "Ideally, if you had the opportunity, would you like to move PERMANENTLY to another country, or would you prefer to continue living in this country?"
10 The figures are for 2018, and they cover five monarchies: Bahrain, Oman, Qatar, Saudi Arabia, and the United Arab Emirates. Sources: Statistics on "Gulf Labour Markets"; Khadri, "Professionals in GCC," table 5.2.

11 Jackson and Manderscheid, "Western Expatriates' Adjustment."
12 Freedom House, *Freedom in the World 2020*, 33.
13 The gaps narrowed in 2020, due to restrictions associated with the Covid-19 pandemic. From top to bottom, the indices in Figure 1.4 became 5.0, 3.9, and 2.7 (Freedom House, *Freedom in the World 2021*).
14 As of March 2020, 174,000 of the roughly 12 million women of driving age had a driving license (*Saudi Gazette*, "Driving Licenses").
15 Saab, "Can Mohamed bin Salman"; Al-Rasheed, "Women Are Still Not"; Boghani, "Paradox of Saudi Arabia's Reforms."
16 Immigration and Refugee Board of Canada, *Egypt*. Marriage rules of the Coptic Church reinforce those of Islam. See "Prohibition of Interfaith Marriage."
17 Cagaptay and Aktas, "How Erdoganism."
18 For fuller definitions see Agrast, Botero, Ponce-Rodríguez, and Dumas, "World Justice Project Rule of Law Index," pp. 6–7.
19 The indices are nearly identical for 2019, the last year before the Covid-19 pandemic. Only OIC differs: 3.2, instead of 3.1.
20 On a standardized 0–10 scale, the average of these indices is 3.2 for the Middle East, as against 3.7 for Sub-Saharan Africa, 4.2 for East Asia, 4.8 for South Asia, 5.0 for Latin America, and 7.3 for the Organisation for Economic Co-operation and Development (excluding Turkey, to avoid double counting).
21 Quran 42:38, 3:159.
22 For works that depict early Islam as a period when consultation was the norm, see Khatab and Bouma, *Democracy in Islam*, pp. 16–23; and Al-Raysuni, *Al-Shūrā*, pp. 1–40, 93–109, especially p. 58.
23 Shaban, *Islamic History*, vol. 1, pp. 61–63; Rahman, "Principle of *Shura*," p. 4.
24 Rahman, "Principle of *Shura*," p. 5; Crone and Hinds, *God's Caliph*, pp. 63, 65, 68, 127–28. For an overview of the Umayyad era, see Shaban, *Islamic History*, vol. 1, chaps. 5–10.
25 Kuran, *Long Divergence*, chaps. 6–7.
26 This follows the definition of Nielsen, "Changing Face of Islamic Authority," pp. 2–4 and n. 7. There is also a restrictive definition that excludes authorities that lack formal scholarly credentials.
27 Fatwa and its aftermath: Appignanesi and Maitland, *Rushdie File*. Narratives: Pipes, *Rushdie Affair*; Malik, *From Fatwa to Jihad*, chaps. 1–3. Attack: Root, "Salman Rushdie Is Attacked."
28 Radsch, "First Egyptian Blogger"; Uddin, "Blasphemy Laws," p. 51.
29 Hunt and Murray, *History of Business*, chaps. 6–10; Baskin and Miranti, *History of Corporate Finance*, chap. 2.
30 Cox, *Marketing Sovereign Promises*, documents how the monopolization of selling debt to the English state limited executive discretion over repayment.
31 Kuran, *Private Truths, Public Lies*, chap. 16.
32 North, Wallis, and Weingast, *Violence and Social Orders*, chap. 4.
33 Popper, *Open Society*, chap. 24.
34 Hayek, *Law, Legislation and Liberty*, vol. 3, chap. 14.
35 Hamilton, Madison, and Jay, *Federalist Papers*, nos. 10, 47, 51; Samuels, "Separation of Powers"; Persson, Roland, and Tabellini, "Separation of Powers."
36 This definition differs from influential alternatives in its inclusion of associations and lobbies serving profit-driven entrepreneurs. They have both played critical roles

in liberalization processes. For narrower conceptualizations, see Putnam, *Making Democracy Work*, chap. 4; and Habermas, *Between Facts and Norms*, chaps. 7–8. For Habermas, the "institutional core" of civil society consists of "nongovernmental and noneconomic connections and voluntary associations that anchor the communication structures of the public sphere in the society component of the lifeworld" (pp. 366–67). But he acknowledges that "economic" and "noneconomic" associations often work in concert. Associations with noneconomic goals depend on "the support of 'sponsors' who supply the necessary resources of money, organization, knowledge, and social capital" (p. 375).

37 Encarnación, *Myth of Civil Society*, also observes that a robust civil society is neither a prerequisite nor a precondition for the consolidation of democracy. Going further, though, Encarnación holds that state structures do the necessary work. As Hilbink, "Review of *Myth of Civil Society*," notes, Encarnación overlooks the roles of civic associations in generating and sustaining democratic institutions.

38 North, Wallis, and Weingast, *Violence and Social Orders*, pp. 49–54.

39 Olson, *Logic of Collective Action*, chaps. 1–2, 6.

40 Deffains, Espinosa, and Thöni, "Political Self-Serving Bias"; Mezulis, Abramson, Hyde, and Hankin, "Universal Positivity Bias in Attributions."

41 Hayek, *Law, Legislation and Liberty*, vol. 3, chap. 14; Baumgartner, Berry, Hojnaki, Kimball, and Leech, *Lobbying and Policy Change*, chap. 7; Klüver, Mahoney, and Opper, "Framing in Context."

42 Rosenblatt, *Lost History of Liberalism*, pp. 260–64.

43 Gellately, *Backing Hitler*, chaps. 2–3, 5–9.

44 On the concept, with data to 2010, see Bermeo, "Democratic Backsliding." Foa and Mounk, "Deconsolidation," cover the period up to 2014, with a focus on falling interest in living in a democracy and growing demand for a strong leader. In 2017, the Economist Intelligence Unit downgraded the United States from "full democracy" to "flawed democracy." Since 2015, the European Union has had more flawed than full democracies; and two-thirds were flawed in 2020 (computed from 2015–20 editions of Economist Intelligence Unit, *Democracy Index*).

45 France: Vauchez, "French *Laïcité*"; Bartolucci, "French Approach to Counterterrorism." United States: Neal, *Politics of Counter-Terrorism*, chaps. 5–6; Lukianoff and Haidt, *Coddling of American Mind*.

46 According to a Pew survey of 2020, 52 percent of French adults and 57 percent of Americans agreed that "people today are too easily offended by what others say" (Silver, Fagan, Connaughton, and Mordecai, "Political Correctness"). In the same year, according to a Cato survey, 62 percent of American adults reported that the political climate prevents them "from saying things they believe because others might find them offensive" (Ekins, "Poll"). According to a Jean Jaurès Foundation poll of 2021, 49 percent of French teachers self-censor on religious matters, a rise of 13 percentage points since 2018 (Radio France International, "Deflection").

47 Bright Line Watch, "Tempered Expectations."

48 Korteweg and Yurdakul, *Headscarf Debates*, chap. 2, quote at p. 15.

49 Acemoglu and Robinson, *Narrow Corridor*, chaps. 2 and 6, argue that good government requires "both state and society running together and neither getting the upper hand" (quote at p. 40).

50 Donner, *Muhammad and Believers*, chap. 2; Rodinson, *Muḥammad*, chap. 3; Blaydes, "State Building," pp. 489–93.
51 On these ancient assemblies, see Stasavage, *Decline and Rise*, pp. 30–36.
52 For a critical review of this literature, see Kuru, *Islam, Authoritarianism, and Underdevelopment*, pp. 123–27.
53 Jackson, *Mongols and Islamic World*.
54 Said, *Orientalism*; Alkadry, "Reciting Colonial Scripts"; Mir, "Colonialism, Arab Culture," especially p. 35.
55 Fildis, "Roots of Alawite–Sunni Rivalry"; Hinnebusch, "Historical Sociology."
56 Thompson, *West Stole Democracy*.
57 Berkes, *Development of Secularism*, chaps. 15–16.
58 Amanat, *Iran*, chaps. 13–15.
59 Pierret, *Religion and State*, chap. 1.
60 Pierret, *Religion and State*, p. 31.
61 Figures are weighted by population. The Middle East had just one electoral democracy according to the Freedom House definition: Tunisia, which has since reverted to dictatorship. Freedom House defines electoral democracy as a political order that meets "certain minimum standards for political rights and civil liberties." A liberal democracy observes a broader range of democratic ideals and enforces a wider array of civil liberties. Figures based on Freedom House, *Freedom in World 2021* and "Freedom in World Methodology."
62 Computed from data in Freedom House, *Freedom in World 2021*.
63 Examples: Ghana, Benin, Peru, and Indonesia. Each of these countries is an electoral democracy and has a civil liberties score higher than the Middle Eastern average.
64 Jamal, *Empires and Citizens*, especially chap. 5.
65 The seminal paper is Acemoglu, Johnson, and Robinson, "Colonial Origins of Development." Its influential critiques include Albouy, "Colonial Origins of Development." Acemoglu and Robinson, *Why Nations Fail*, chap. 9, generalizes the argument. On geographic and precolonial legacies, see Easterly and Levine, "Tropics, Germs, and Crops"; and Michalopoulos and Papaioannou, "Pre-Colonial Ethnic Institutions."
66 Acemoglu and Robinson, *Why Nations Fail*, makes passing references to Egypt (pp. 2–3, 395–98) and the Ottoman Empire (pp. 120–21, 213–16). But it does not cover the region in depth.
67 In Algeria, 16.6 percent of the population was European in 1926 (Epstein, *Statesman's Year-book*, p. 880); in Tunisia, 8.6 percent in 1936 (Clarke, "Population Policies," p. 47); in eastern Libya (Cyrenaica), 12 percent in 1939 (Hourani, *History of Arab Peoples*, p. 323); and in Istanbul, 14.8 percent in 1885 (Karpat, *Ottoman Population*, p. 103). As relevant as these numbers are the intentions of European powers. They wanted the settlers to live under European institutions (Balch, "French Colonization in North Africa").
68 Turkey: Pallis, "Population of Turkey," pp. 441–44. Egypt: Tignor, "Economic Activities of Foreigners in Egypt," p. 417. Algeria: Choi, *Decolonization*, pp. 52–62.
69 Powers, "Orientalism, Colonialism," sect. 2; Abi-Mershed, *Apostles of Modernity*, pp. 96–100; Khalfoune, "*Habous*," pp. 461–63. See also Kogelmann, "Legal Regulation of Moroccan Habous," pp. 212–13, 219–24; Blackman, "Ideological Responses to Settler Colonialism."

Notes to pages 31–38

70 Egypt: Baer, *History of Landownership in Modern Egypt*, chap. 5. Ottoman Empire: Cansunar and Kuran, "Economic Harbingers of Political Modernization." Turkey: Öztürk, *Türk Yenileşme Tarihi Çerçevesinde Vakıf Müessesesi*, pp. 63–167, 379–471.
71 Birdal, *Ottoman Public Debt*, chaps. 3–4, 6.
72 The most influential critique of Islamic essentialism is Said, *Orientalism*, especially pp. 70, 141–42, 255–56, 259. For a restatement, see Hamdi, "Edward Said."

CHAPTER 2

1 Finer, *History of Government*, vol. 1, pp. 126–27, 203–5, 235–37; Wittfogel, *Oriental Despotism*, chaps. 1–2. See also North, Wallis, and Weingast, *Violence and Social Orders*, chap. 2.
2 The rich civic life in medieval Europe, which is described in Berman, *Law and Revolution*, and Moor, "Silent Revolution," was absent in places under Islamic rule.
3 Schumpeter, *Capitalism, Socialism, and Democracy*, chap. 22.
4 Acemoglu and Robinson, *Economic Origins of Dictatorship*, pp. 32–40.
5 Ibn Khaldun, *Muqaddimah*, especially vol. 1, pp. 311–55; vol. 2, pp. 89–91, 93–96, 137–56, 340–42; vol. 3, pp. 1117–18.
6 On his limited influence, see Hourani, *Arabic Thought*, pp. 52, 72, 326, 328; and Lewis, "Ibn Khaldūn in Turkey." Neumann, *Araç Tarih, Amaç Tanzimat*, pp. 168–73, shows that conservative Ottoman thinkers of the 1800s used Ibn Khaldun's masterpiece to legitimize goals clashing with its core ideas.
7 The concepts of self-enforcing and self-undermining equilibria lie at the heart of institution-centered analytic political economy. Pioneering contributions include Platteau, *Institutions*; and Greif, *Institutions*. The economic counterpart of this book, Kuran, *Long Divergence*, also applies institutional political economy to the Middle East, as does Rubin, *Rulers, Religion, and Riches*. Another Islam-focused work that uses the framework is Kuru, *Islam, Authoritarianism, and Underdevelopment*, though in this case the methodological affinities are only implicit. Johnson and Koyama, *Persecution and Toleration*, apply the methodology to Europe, with global comparisons.
8 Smith, *Wealth of Nations*, bks. 1 and 4, treats the market as a self-correcting system. Fiori, "Smith and Unintended Consequences," shows that unintended consequences are pervasive throughout the treatise.
9 Zilfi, *Politics of Piety*, chap. 4.
10 Saghafi, "Crossing the Desert"; Tabari, "Enigma of Veiled Iranian Women," pp. 19, 28.
11 Leviticus, 20:27, 24:16. On Christian inquisitions, see Ames, *Righteous Persecution*.
12 Mantsinen and Tervo-Niemelä, "Leaving Christianity."
13 Makdisi, *Rise of Colleges*, pp. 224–25, 229–37; Berman, *Law and Revolution*, pp. 390–92.
14 Johnson and Koyama, *Persecution and Toleration*, chap. 15, stress that civil society produced these effects while simultaneously limiting state authority. Both a strong civil society and rule of law are essential to advancing religious freedoms. Acemoglu and Robinson, *Narrow Corridor*, chap. 6, shows that in Western Europe advancing

liberties required shackling the state through both civil society and constitutional checks and balances.
15 Adıgüzel and Kuran, "Inequality-Preserving Benevolence."
16 Hacker, "Policy Drift," especially pp. 43–57.
17 Acemoglu, Johnson, and Robinson, "Rise of Europe."
18 Lewis, *Muslim Discovery of Europe*, chap. 2.
19 The case for checks and balances appears in Hamilton, Madison, and Jay, *Federalist Papers*, primarily in nos. 10, 47, and 51, and secondarily in no. 78.
20 Hayek, *Road to Serfdom*, chaps. 5–7. Hayek was writing during World War II, when collectivists on both left and right were strengthening the state. Communism and fascism were not aberrations caused by madmen, he argued. Rather, they resulted from expecting government to engineer utopia through centralized economic decision making.
21 Boettke and Candella, "Liberty of Progress"; Boettke, *Hayek*, chap. 8.
22 Kuran, *Long Divergence*, chaps. 4–5, 7–8; Cansunar and Kuran, "Economic Harbingers of Political Modernization."
23 Bosker, Buringh, and van Zanden, "From Baghdad to London."
24 Genç, *Osmanlı İmparatorluğunda Devlet ve Ekonomi*, chap. 3.
25 Adıgüzel and Kuran, "Inequality-Preserving Benevolence."
26 On the ideological origins of secularism in the Middle East, see Mardin, *Genesis of Young Ottoman Thought*, chap. 9; Hanioğlu, *Young Turks in Opposition*, chap. 1; Al-Azmeh, *Secularism in Arab World*, pp. 85–126, 153–80; and Banai, *Hidden Liberalism*, chaps. 2–3.
27 The observation drives the argument of Rubin, *Rulers, Religion, and Riches*.
28 Harris, *Going the Distance*, chaps. 9–12; Lamoreaux and Rosenthal, "Legal Regime and Contractual Flexibility," sect. 2.
29 Moore, *Social Origins of Dictatorship and Democracy*, chaps. 1–2; Ward, "Political Modernization"; Rustow, "Transitions to Democracy."
30 Johnson and Koyama, *Persecution and Toleration*, chaps. 1–3, 13–14.
31 For the Ottoman Empire, see Karaman and Pamuk, "Ottoman State Finances."
32 Moor, "Silent Revolution." The seminal argument was developed by Tocqueville, *Democracy in America*. For another extension, see Putnam, *Making Democracy Work*.

CHAPTER 3

1 Question 24, Wave 6, World Values Survey of 2010–14. This question is part of the World Values Survey and the General Social Survey. Trust can also be measured through incentivized games. Measures obtained through trust games tend to correlate positively with survey-based measures (Johnson and Mislin, "How Much Should We Trust").
2 Livny, *Trust and the Islamic Advantage*, especially chaps. 4–5. For general insights, see Fukuyama, *Trust*; Stolle, "Trusting Strangers"; Putnam, *Making Democracy Work*.
3 Bohnet, Herrmann, and Zeckhauser, "Trust and Reference Points."
4 Cunningham and Sarayrah, *Wasta*, chaps. 1, 3–11; Sidani and Thornberry, "Nepotism in Arab World," pp. 72–77.
5 Browers, *Democracy and Civil Society*; Yom, "Civil Society and Democratization in Arab World"; Langohr, "Too Much Civil Society"; Bellin, "Robustness of

Authoritarianism"; Bayat, "Activism and Social Development"; Wiktorowicz, "Civil Society."
6 Satyanath, Voigtländer, and Voth, "Bowling for Fascism."
7 Osman, *Egypt on Brink*, chap. 7; Wickham, *Muslim Brotherhood*, chap. 9.
8 The roles of peasants, cities, and merchants in constraining the monarch varied across contexts. England's relatively peaceful Glorious Revolution (1688) and the notoriously violent French Revolution (1789) both instituted checks and balances, but through different coalitions. See Ziblatt, "How Did Europe Democratize?"; Tilly, *Contention and Democracy*; and Moore, *Social Origins of Dictatorship and Democracy*.
9 On the rise of charitable corporations, see Soskis, "History of Associational Life"; and Bromley, "Organizational Transformation."
10 For general accounts of waqf rules and practices, see Barnes, *Introduction to Religious Foundations*; Schoenblum, "Role of Legal Doctrine"; and Kuran, "Provision of Public Goods."
11 There existed waqfs founded by an oral declaration before witnesses (Beldiceanu, "Recherches," p. 29). At least in Ottoman realms, these were rare exceptions.
12 Examples from Istanbul: Galata 24 (1602), 11a/2; Istanbul 2 (1615), 14b/1; Istanbul 9 (1662), 191a/1; Istanbul 22 (1695), 27a/1; Bab 89 (1708), 5b/2; Bab 122 (1719), 21b/1; Galata 266 (1726), 2b/1; Bab 154 (1731), 48a/3; Galata 308 (1745), 45a/1; Istanbul 70 (1799), 97b/1; Galata 410 (1771), 62a/1; Galata 526 (1795), 84a/2.
13 Certain modest waqfs had no dedicated physical structure. Examples include waqfs established to assist widows, liberate indebted prisoners, or conduct prayers for the dead.
14 Among Istanbul's waqf deeds registered between 1453 and 1923, 64.6 percent of those established by someone outside the sultan's close circle named the founder and/or founder's family among the primary beneficiaries; 6.2 percent named the poor (Adıgüzel and Kuran, "Inequality-Preserving Benevolence").
15 Barnes, *Introduction to Religious Foundations*, pp. 38–40; Leeuwen, *Waqfs and Urban Structures*, pp. 53–54.
16 Although women could establish a waqf and serve as its caretaker, most founders and caretakers were men. The use of the male pronoun is for expedience.
17 The geographic contours of a judge's jurisdiction were diffusely defined. Two or more judges could oversee any given waqf. Custom often dictated which court had jurisdiction.
18 The sacredness belief was reinforced through waqf deeds, which typically stated that anyone harming a waqf would suffer both on earth and in the afterlife (Öztürk, *Türk Yenileşme Tarihi Çerçevesinde Vakıf Müessesesi*, p. 23). Early jurists based the waqf's sacredness on charitable functions (Gil, "Earliest *Waqf* Foundations," pp. 125, 128).
19 Oğuzoğlu, *Osmanlı Devlet Anlayışı*, pp. 37–38; Winter, *Egyptian Society*, p. 11; Lev, *Charity, Endowments*, p. 155; Leeuwen, *Waqfs and Urban Structures*, pp. 88–89, 96; Barnes, *Introduction to Religious Foundations*, p. 38; Behrens-Abouseif, "Waqf, In Egypt," pp. 64–66; Irwin, *Middle East*, pp. 96, 141; Yediyıldız, "Vakıf," p. 161.
20 The seventeenth-century cases are reproduced in Kuran, *Social and Economic Life*, vols. 5–8. Pro-state biases of the judges, which Kuran and Lustig, "Judicial Biases," identifies empirically, may have limited the latter number.

21 Petry, "Waqf as an Instrument of Investment"; Leeuwen, *Waqfs and Urban Structures*, chap. 6; Sanders, *Creating Medieval Cairo*, pp. 29–61; Behrens-Abouseif, *Egypt's Adjustment*, chaps. 8–9; Altınyıldız, "Architectural Heritage of Istanbul," pp. 282–93.
22 A common theme in histories of Middle Eastern cities is that waqf caretakers enjoyed high esteem (Behar, *Neighborhood in Ottoman Istanbul*, pp. 65–83; Leeuwen, *Waqfs and Urban Structures*, chap. 4).
23 On the role of social capital in economic development, see Coleman, *Foundations*, chap. 12; Fukuyama, *Trust*, pp. 3–57; Putnam, *Making Democracy Work*; and Guiso, Sapienza, and Zingales, "Social Capital." On the Middle East specifically, see Jamal, *Barriers to Democracy*, chap. 6.
24 Oberauer, *Early Doctrines on Waqf*.
25 Hâtemî, *Önceki ve Bugünkü Türk Hukuku'nda Vakıf Kurma Muamelesi*, pp. 29–38. During Islam's first few centuries, leading scholars dismissed hundreds of thousands of recollections as inauthentic. Modern investigators consider most of the remainder fabricated. See Kamali, *Textbook of Ḥadīth Studies*, chaps. 1, 9–11; Brown, "Even If It's Not True"; and Motzki, ed., *Ḥadīth*.
26 Thomas, *Private Religious Foundations*; Arjomand, "Philanthropy," pp. 110–11.
27 Köprülü, "Bizans Müesseselerinin Osmanlı Müesseselerine Tesiri." Providing a more nuanced interpretation, Yıldırım, "Pious Foundations," shows that the waqf and the Byzantine "pious foundation" developed in parallel, influencing one another.
28 On the Middle East's political evolution during this period, see Lapidus, *History*, chaps. 3–8. Crone, *God's Rule*, chaps. 17–22 surveys the associated evolution of political thought.
29 English translation: Verbit, *Ninth Century Treatise*.
30 Blaydes, "Mamluks, Property Rights," pp. 400–403; Haarmann, "Joseph's Law," pp. 70–77.
31 For details, see Adıgüzel and Kuran, "Inequality-Preserving Benevolence." In the literature, state waqfs are often called "imperial waqfs" or "sultanic waqfs" (Orbay, "Imperial Waqfs," pp. 138–39). Both are misnomers, because their founders were not limited to the ruling dynasty, and the dynasty did not necessarily rule an empire.
32 A waqf complex typically included a mosque plus several charities.
33 Mandaville, "Usurious Piety."
34 Between 1453 and 1923, only 0.7 percent of Istanbul's regular waqfs had a Christian or Jewish founder (based on dataset of Adıgüzel and Kuran, "Inequality-Preserving Benevolence"). During this period, more than 40 percent of the city's population was Christian or Jewish.
35 Examples include Laluddin, Haneef, Sabit, and Rahman, "Revisiting the Concept of Waqf"; Lev, *Charity, Endowments*; and Singer, *Constructing Ottoman Beneficence*.
36 Focusing on waqf-financed fountains in Ottoman Istanbul, Cansunar, "Distributional Consequences of Philanthropic Contributions," pp. 894–904, shows that they were spread across the whole city, including predominantly non-Muslim neighborhoods. But they served heavily Muslim neighborhoods disproportionately.
37 Kuran, *Long Divergence*, pp. 48–52, 59–68.
38 Yediyıldız, *Institution du Vakf*, pp. 121–22.

39 Adıgüzel and Kuran, "Inequality-Preserving Benevolence." In deeds, elites are distinguishable through their honorific titles.
40 Goodwin, *Janissaries*; Pipes, *Slave Soldiers*; and Uzunçarşılı, *Osmanlı Devleti*.
41 Blaydes and Chaney, "Feudal Revolution." See also Blaydes, "State Building," pp. 493–95.
42 Chaney, "Democratic Change," measures democratic deficit according to polity scores of the Polity IV Project. See also Blaydes, "Comment on Chaney," which shows that Arab League membership today and early conquest by Muslim armies are comparably sized predictors of contemporary authoritarianism.
43 When Istanbul's regular waqfs are classified by function, the share adds to 155 percent even with the coarsest classification, because many waqfs had multiple primary purposes. Though a large majority provided benefits to the founder and/or his or her family, 20.1 percent of these financed one or more social services unconditionally, and an additional 3.6 percent did so conditionally (based on dataset of Adıgüzel and Kuran, "Inequality-Preserving Benevolence").
44 Cansunar, "Distributional Consequences of Philanthropic Contributions," pp. 898–99.
45 Local social norms determined the dividing lines between family waqfs and charitable waqfs.
46 For deeds involving a fixed salary, see, in Kuran, *Social and Economic Life*, vols. 5–7, Istanbul 3 (1618), 31b/4, 85b/1, 62a/2; Istanbul 9 (1662), 167b/1; and for a stipulation of residual income, Galata 41 (1617), 36b/3. Baer, *Studies in the Social History of Modern Egypt*, p. 80, refers to salaries proportional to the endowment. For examples of all payment patterns, see Öcalan, Sezai, and Yavaş, *Bursa Vakfiyeleri* (fixed p. 361; proportional, pp. 190, 378, 388, 415, 556; residual, pp. 397, 550; hybrid, pp. 455, 479).

CHAPTER 4

1 Berkel, "Waqf Documents," pp. 238–41.
2 Pascual, *Damas*, pp. 39–64.
3 Moazzen, "Leading Religious College," pp. 481, 485.
4 Ahi Çelebi 335 (1803), 16a/b. For other deeds containing highly specific stipulations, see Istanbul 4 (1619), 54b/1, in Kuran, *Social and Economic Life*, vol. 6; Leeuwen, *Waqfs and Urban Structures*, pp. 128–30; Öcalan, Sevim, and Yavaş, *Bursa Vakfiyeleri*, pp. 360–63, 406–7, 550–51; and Behrens-Abouseif, "Waqf of Cairene Notable," pp. 126–27.
5 Küçük, *Science without Leisure*, pp. 39–40, 56–57, 63, 88–92, quote at p. 84. A madrasa education was fully subsidized through waqf resources. As the purchasing power of student stipends fell, the average quality of madrasa students would have declined in tandem.
6 Zilfi, *Politics of Piety*, pp. 82–84, 96–101; Küçük, *Science without Leisure*, pp. 261–62, n. 6.
7 Spannaus, "History and Continuity," pp. 83–91. As Eldem, "Amerika'yı Keşfetme(me)nin Yolları," points out, the critics themselves were ignorant of many global developments.
8 Bano, *Revival of Islamic Rationalism*, pp. 94–100.
9 Kütükoğlu, *XX. Asra Erişen Osmanlı Medreseleri*, pp. 10–14; Findley, *Ottoman Civil Officialdom*, pp. 132–39.

10 Ahi Çelebi 214 (1759), 80b, 81a; Pascual, *Damas*, p. 57.
11 For waqf deeds that authorized the founder to make unlimited changes, see Istanbul 4 (1619) 31b/3; 23 (1696), 51 b/2; and Galata 224 (1713), 82a/1, all recorded in Kuran, *Social and Economic Life*, vols. 5–8. Example from Syria: Leeuwen, *Waqfs and Urban Structures*, p. 145.
12 If a mosque's founder had not designated maintenance staff, a caretaker might appoint supplementary personnel under the pretext that relevant decisions were left to him. And if a school's founder had not chosen books to be taught, the caretaker could alter the curriculum through innovative readings.
13 On voter ignorance, see Caplan, *Myth of the Rational Voter*; Zaller, *Nature and Origins of Mass Opinion*; and Bowler and Nicholson, "Information Cues and Rational Ignorance."
14 Hirschman, *Exit, Voice, and Loyalty*, chap. 7; Dahl, *Democracy and Its Critics*, chap. 16.
15 A tradeoff between governance quality and decision making costs exists whenever there are multiple stakeholders (Buchanan and Tullock, *Calculus of Consent*, chap. 8).
16 For examples of lawsuits against caretakers, see Marcus, *Middle East*, pp. 303–4; Hoexter, *Endowments*, chap. 5; Gerber, *Economy and Society*, pp. 166–69; and Leeuwen, *Waqfs and Urban Structures*, p. 159.
17 Istanbul 105 (1811), 10b/1. For a similar case, see Galata 587 (1809), 92b/2.
18 See the following trials in Kuran, *Social and Economic Life*, vols. 5–8: Istanbul 3 (1618), 7b/4, 84a/1; Istanbul 4 (1619), 40b/2; Istanbul 9 (1662), 228a/1, 244b/3, 250b/2; Galata 130 (1683), 55a/5; Istanbul 22 (1695), 80b/2, 95a/2, 98a/2; Istanbul 3 (1696), 32b/1. The exception is Istanbul 3 (1618), 7b/4. The cases from the period 1700–1836 come from an unpublished database of the author: Galata 224 (1714), 58a; Galata 224 (1714), 105a/1; Galata 224 (1714), 107a/1; Bab 122 (1719), 46b/3; Bab 154 (1731), 63a/3; Galata 410 (1770) 7b/2; Galata 541 (1798), 59a/1; Galata 587 (1808), 25b/3; İstanbul 105 (1811), 10b/1. Trials with beneficiary-plaintiffs: Galata 224 (1714), 58a1; Galata 224 (1714),107a1; Bab 154 (1731), 63a/3; Galata 541 (1798), 59a1; Galata 587 (1808), 25b/3.
19 Kuran and Lustig, "Judicial Biases," pp. 649–52, 659.
20 Examples from Istanbul: Istanbul 3 (1618), 34a/4; Istanbul 16 (1665), 52b/2; Galata 130 (1683), 16a/4; Istanbul 23 (1696), 24a/3; Bab 122 (1719), 44b/1; Galata 266 (1726), 41a/1; Galata 360 (1760), 38b/3; Galata 541 (1798), 83a/1; Galata 567 (1803), 88a/3; Galata 587 (1808), 10b/4.
21 For cases of waqfs in financial distress, see Galata 41 (1616), 7a/4; Istanbul 23 (1696), 3b/1, in Kuran, *Social and Economic Life*, vols. 5, 8. On waqfs destroyed through corruption or mismanagement, see Yediyıldız, *Institution du Vaqf*, pp. 160–62; and Cansunar and Kuran, "Economic Harbingers of Political Modernization."
22 Demirel, *Sivas Şehir Hayatında Vakıfların Rolü*, pp. 127–31.
23 Leeuwen, *Waqfs and Urban Structures*, p. 135, reports cases from eighteenth-century Damascus. Each involved a prominent waqf with a huge budget.
24 Gerber, "Public Sphere," p. 78.
25 Hoexter, "Waqf and the Public Sphere," p. 133.
26 In Qajar Iran, waqfs provided an independent power base, especially because many were in Iraq, beyond the shah's reach. In resisting rulers, Iran's clerics sought mainly

to preserve their own power. Sometimes their interests coincided with those of the lower classes (Keddie, "Roots of the Ulama's Power," pp. 43 and 48–51).
27 Barkey, *Empire of Difference*, pp. 205–25; Abou-El-Haj, *1703 Rebellion*, pp. 91–92; Hatina, *'Ulama', Politics, and the Public Sphere*, pp. 19–62; Zilfi, *Politics of Piety*, chaps. 3–5.
28 Gürbüzel, "Citizens of Piety."
29 Doumani, *Family Life*, chaps. 4–5; Meier, "Waqf Only in Name," pp. 208–10.
30 Experimental researchers find that even when subjects may apply distinct strategies to each of many games, strategies used in one game bleed into those used in others (Vesterlund, "Using Experimental Methods," pp. 123–26; Kagel, "Auctions," pp. 503–35). A driver of behavioral spillovers is cognitive limitations, which render people susceptible to framing and learning transfer effects (Bednar, Chen, Liu, and Page, "Behavioral Spillovers"; Cason and Gangadharan, "Cooperation Spillovers"; Dolan and Galizzi, "Like Ripples on a Pond").
31 For complementary observations, see Zencirci, "Civil Society's History," pp. 1, 3–4.
32 Fung, "Associations and Democracy," pp. 515, 534–36.
33 The prevention was achieved through the deed registration process. A waqf's functions could include anything compatible with Islamic law. Forming an autonomous political association was excluded, as it could lead to sedition.
34 In accounts of Ottoman rebellions, participating clerics never appear as representatives of waqf constituencies, even though many served as waqf caretakers or, as judges, supervised waqfs.
35 Yıldız, *Crisis and Rebellion*, chaps. 5–6; Tezcan, *Second Ottoman Empire*, pp. 213–25; Arjomand, *Shadow of God*, chaps. 4, 8.
36 Mokyr, *Culture of Growth*, especially chaps. 11–12.
37 Glaeser, *Triumph of the City*, chaps. 1, 9.
38 This accords with slower urban growth in the Middle East than in Western Europe between 800 and 1800 (Bosker, Buringh, and van Zanden, "From Baghdad to London").
39 Rubin, *Rulers, Religion, and Riches*, chaps. 1–3.
40 Barkey, *Bandits and Bureaucrats*. See also Barkey, *Empire of Difference*, chap. 3.
41 The tax status of charitable corporations can vary across sectors, jurisdictions, and time (Silber, *Corporate Form of Freedom*, pp. 15–17).
42 Berman, *Law and Revolution*, chap. 12.
43 Greif, *Institutions*, chaps. 4, 10; Ogilvie, "Guilds, Efficiency"; Prak, "Corporate Politics"; Reynolds, *Kingdoms and Communities*, chaps. 3–6; Berman, *Law and Revolution*, chaps. 5, 11–12.
44 Stasavage, "Was Weber Right?"; Wahl, "Political Participation and Economic Development"; Bosker, Buringh, and van Zanden, "From Baghdad to London."
45 Moor, "Silent Revolution."
46 Greif, "Family Structure, Institutions"; Greif and Tabellini, "Clan and the Corporation."
47 Anheier, Lang, and Toepler, "Comparative Nonprofit Sector Research."
48 Hansmann, "Reforming Nonprofit Corporation Law."
49 In Europe, scholastic schools operated by churches and monastic orders coexisted with universities (Overfield, *Humanism and Scholasticism*; Greatrex, "Scope of Learning"). In the Middle East, subjects excluded from the madrasa curriculum could be studied in private homes (Makdisi, *Rise of Colleges*, pp. 75–78, 281–82; Moazzen, "Leading Religious College," p. 489).

50 Makdisi, *Rise of Colleges*; Huff, *Rise of Early Modern Science*, chaps. 4–6.
51 Memiş, "Osmanlı Dönemi Urfa Vakıfları," pp. 519–22.
52 Moazzen, *Formation of a Religious Landscape*, pp. 130–32; Nagata, *Tarihte Âyânlar*, pp. 147–50; İzgi, *Osmanlı Medreselerinde İlim*, vol. 1, pp. 117–18; Makdisi, *Rise of Colleges*, pp. 76–78.
53 Moazzen, "Leading Religious College," pp. 488–89.
54 Zorlu, "Klasik Osmanlı Eğitim Sistemi," p. 614; Nakissa, "Epistemic Shift," pp. 214–15, 232–35; Moazzen, "Leading Religious College," p. 489.
55 On the roles of organizational adaptability in Europe's economic ascent, see van Zanden, *Long Road*, chap. 2; Moor, "Silent Revolution"; and Greif, *Institutions*, chaps. 3, 10.
56 Rijpma, "Funding Public Services," chap. 2, p. 54.
57 Regional archive of Leiden 503, no. 212 (based on communications with Auke Rijpma). The hospital was itself established by a religious order.
58 In the Middle Ages, the trust and the corporation were not sharply differentiated. Because their characteristics could be combined, differences were of degree rather than kind. For hybrid organizations, the terminology was somewhat arbitrary (Rijpma, "Funding Public Services," pp. 30–33).
59 Zuijderduijn, "Grave Concerns," p. 343.
60 In 2021, the work of Doctors Without Borders was conducted by around 63,000 administrators, physicians, and staff. The organization provided over 12 million outpatient consultations and 1,044,000 patient admissions, among other health services. 97 percent of its activities were financed by 7 million individual donors along with dozens of governments and international organizations. See Médecins Sans Frontières, *Activity Report 2021*, pp. 8, 13, 76.
61 Berman, *Law and Revolution*, chap. 12; Reynolds, *Kingdoms and Communities*, chaps. 2, 9; Ogilvie, *State Corporatism*, chaps. 5, 9–10.
62 Çizakça, *History of Philanthropic Foundations*, p. 48. Vanity must also have limited resource pooling. A founder eager to be remembered would have kept his or her waqf from being absorbed into a larger waqf.
63 Cansunar, "Distributional Consequences of Philanthropic Contributions." Feeding water to multiple fountains and bathhouses through a single pipe lowered the cost of urban water supply.
64 Indeed, 11.4 percent of Istanbul's regular waqfs founded between 1453 and 1923 stipulated unconditional yearly expenses for mosque supplies and 21.5 percent unconditionally assigned revenue to mosque employees (based on dataset of Adıgüzel and Kuran, "Inequality-Preserving Benevolence").
65 Doumani, "Endowing Family," p. 38. In the Istanbul dataset mentioned in the previous note, 1.6 percent of all waqfs had multiple founders, always close associates; and in two-thirds of these cases, the founders were a married couple.
66 Among the 3,108 waqf-related cases in a court database running from 1602 to 1836, only one concerns a merger between two or more waqfs: Istanbul 142 (1824), 61a/1. It involves a founder augmenting the capital and broadening the purposes of a waqf that he himself had founded. The deed of his first waqf authorized him to make modifications. 1,544 of the cases are from the 1600s. These are recorded in Kuran, *Social and Economic Life*, vols. 5–8. The rest come from a private database based on twenty-nine registers of Istanbul's Bab, Galata, Central Istanbul courts.
67 As quoted by Cole, "Al-Tahtawi," p. 229.

68 Islamic court archive of Istanbul, Galata 515 (1792), 33a/3.
69 My Istanbul court database contains twenty-one registers of the Bab, Galata, and Central Istanbul courts from the 1700s. These alone refer to sixty-six distinct waqfs serving Kasımpaşa.
70 Olson, *Logic of Collective Action*, chaps. 1–3, 5.
71 Such cases were rare anyway. Out of 3,108 waqf-related court cases in an Istanbul database from 1602 to 1836, 35 involve charges of caretaker mismanagement. In most, the plaintiff is a subsequent caretaker or a beneficiary named in the deed. In only eight cases is the plaintiff a group of beneficiaries. Two of them [Istanbul 9 (1662), 274b/2; Istanbul 22 (1695), A4b/2] are recorded in Kuran, *Social and Economic Life*; the rest [Galata 224 (1714), 58a1; Galata 224 (1714),107a1; Bab 154 (1731), 63a/3; Galata 360 (1760), 17a/2; Galata 541 (1798), 59a1); Istanbul 105 (1811), 10b/1] come from an unpublished database of the author.
72 Examples: Istanbul 3 (1618), 93a/1; Istanbul 9 (1661), 9a/4; Istanbul 9 (1661), 61b/1; Istanbul 22 (1695), 23b/1; Galata 197 (1705), 104b/2; Bab 122 (1719), 33b/3; Galata 266 (1726), 48a/2; Bab 173 (1740), 1b/1; Istanbul 70 (1797), 13b/2; Galata 587 (1808), 15b/1; Istanbul 142 (1824), 48a/2.
73 Middle Eastern states launched urban renewal projects in the early 1800s, with Egypt in the lead. But major transformations started in the early 1900s. See Arnaud, "Modernization of the Cities"; Gül, *Emergence of Modern Istanbul*, chaps. 1–4; and Grigor, "Tehran."
74 Agency problems arise in many contexts. Recognizing the prevalence of opportunism and informational asymmetries, policy makers develop second-best contracts that incentivize the agent to comply with the principal's directives (Mirrlees, "Optimal Structure of Incentives," pp. 105–31; Platteau, *Institutions*, pp. 10–17).
75 Coleman, *Foundations of Social Theory*, chaps. 5, 8, 12; Putnam, *Making Democracy Work*; Fukuyama, *Trust*; Zak and Knack, "Trust and Growth."
76 These unintended political drawbacks of the Islamic waqf are broader than those stemming from making clerics state employees. Feldman, *Fall and Rise*, observes that in the early Islamic centuries self-financing clerics counterbalanced the ruler's powers. As they became employees, their capacity to restrain the ruler weakened. Checks and balances involving autonomous civic associations have a wider social base than clerics.

CHAPTER 5

1 Kuran, "Provision of Public Goods," pp. 861–69; Kuran, *Long Divergence*, chap. 6.
2 Brentjes, *Travellers from Europe*, pp. I:437, II:135; MacLean, *Rise of Oriental Travel*, pp. 155–56; Davis, *Aleppo*, pp. 3–6; Campbell, *Travels through Egypt*, pp. 149–50.
3 Shleifer and Vishny, *Grabbing Hand*, chap. 5.
4 With a focus on early Islam, Rosenthal, "Gifts and Bribes," documents that jurists distinguished between gifts and bribes; the boundary was fuzzy in practice, and judicial corruption was common. Kırlı, "Yolsuzluğun İcadı," pp. 45–63, develops a complementary argument concerning transfers between Ottoman subjects and officials. Only with the Ottoman Penal Code of 1840, he adds, did transfers from Ottoman subjects to officials start being classified categorically as corruption. Until

then, certain transfers were legal. Ashraf, "Politics of Gift Exchange," shows that in premodern Iran, too, no clear line existed between bribes and gifts.
5 Mumcu, *Osmanlı Devletinde Rüşvet*, surveys views toward bribing in the Ottoman Empire. Focusing on eighteenth-century Bursa, Düzbakar, "Bribery in Islam," documents widespread bribing as well as anti-bribing campaigns. Shafir, "Moral Revolutions," does the same for the Ottoman Empire in the sixteenth century; Miura, *Dynamism in the Urban Society of Damascus*, chap. 4, for Syria and Egypt under late Mamluk rule; Herzog, "Corruption and Limits of the State," for Baghdad in the early 1800s; and Bakhash, "Evolution of Qajar Bureaucracy," for Qajar Iran up to the late nineteenth century.
6 Shaw, *History of the Ottoman Empire*, vol. 1, pp. 170–71.
7 Darling, *Revenue-Raising*, chap. 8.
8 Zilfi, *Politics of Piety*, pp. 29–30.
9 Atay, "Fatih-Süleymaniye Medreseleri," p. 180.
10 İzgi, *Osmanlı Medreselerinde İlim*, vol. 2, pp. 231–45; Küçük, *Science without Leisure*, pp. 26–27.
11 Moazzen, *Formation of a Religious Landscape*, p. 76.
12 Kuru, *Islam, Authoritarianism, and Underdevelopment*, pp. 175–77. See also Dabashi, "Mīr Dāmād"; and Hagen, "Kātib Çelebī." Kâtip Çelebi is known also as Haji Khalifa.
13 For evidence from various places and times, see Kuran, "Zakat," sect. 7.
14 Easterlin, *Growth Triumphant*.
15 For examples from seventeenth-century Istanbul, see Istanbul 3 (1618) 13b/3; Istanbul 9 (1661), 243a/1; Istanbul 16 (1665), 22b/1; and Istanbul 16 (1665), 98a/2, all recorded in Kuran, *Social and Economic Life*.
16 For examples, see Hoexter, *Endowments*, chap. 5; Jennings, "Pious Foundations," pp. 279–80, 286; Marcus, *Middle East*, p. 311. All involved judicial approval. See also, in Kuran, *Social and Economic Life*: Galata 42 (1617), 76b/1; Istanbul 9 (1661), 32b/1, 37a/1, 54a/1, 147a/2; Istanbul 22 (1695), A18b/1; Istanbul 23 (1696–97), 69b/1, EK-13b/1.
17 Example of a rewrite: Nobuaki, "Waqf of Ustad 'Abbas."
18 Istanbul 22 (1696) 118b/1, recorded in Kuran, *Social and Economic Life*. Similar cases: Istanbul 4 (1619), 40b/1; Istanbul 16 (1665), 57a/2.
19 Gerber, *Economy and Society*, pp. 170–78; Gerber, *State, Society, and Law*, pp. 108–10; Yediyıldız, *Institution du Vaqf*, pp. 113–18.
20 Rubin, "Institutions, the Rise of Commerce"; Kuran, *Long Divergence*, chap. 8.
21 El-Gamal, *Islamic Finance*; Kuran, *Islam and Mammon*; Kuran, "Islam and Economic Performance," pp. 1307–11.
22 Most reimbursements left no historical trace. But the numbers recorded in court registers are not negligible. Between 1602 and 1836, 116 of 3,108 waqf-related cases (3.7 percent) involved reimbursements for repairs. The cases to 1700 are in Kuran, *Social and Economic Life*, vols. 5–8. The rest are in the author's digitized database.
23 Peri, "Waqf and Ottoman Welfare," pp. 172–74.
24 Leeuwen, *Waqfs and Urban Structures*, p. 83. See also, in Kuran, *Social and Economic Life*, cases Istanbul 9 (1661) 51b/4, 102b/3, 167b/1.
25 Behar, *Neighborhood in Ottoman Istanbul*, pp. 74–75.
26 Gibb and Bowen, *Islamic Society*, pt. 2, p. 177; Behrens-Abouseif, "Waqf, in Egypt," p. 67; Deguilhem-Schoem, "Loan of Mursad," pp. 74–75; Behar,

Neighborhood in Ottoman Istanbul, pp. 78–83. The extent of privatizations through illegitimate leasing is controversial (Gerber, *Economy and Society*, p. 174). Measurement is complicated because some privatized assets were reconverted into waqf property.

27 The equities were known as gediks. See Cansunar and Kuran, "Economic Harbingers of Political Modernization."
28 MacFarlane, *Constantinople in 1828*, pp. I:318, II:22; Warburton, *Crescent and the Cross*, pp. 38–39, 175; Hogarth, *Wandering Scholar in Levant*, pp. 95–97.
29 Shefer-Mossensohn, *Ottoman Medicine*, pp. 111, 117–21, 187–91; Ebrahimnejad, *Medicine, Public Health*, chap. 1; Gadelrab, "Medical Healers in Ottoman Egypt"; Gallagher, *Medicine and Power in Tunisia*, chap. 1.
30 İzgi, *Osmanlı Medreselerinde İlim*, vol. 2, pp. 41–42.
31 Zorlu, "Süleymaniye Tıp Medresesi," pp. 74–78, 90–97. Boyar, "Medicine in Practice," shows that as early as the 1400s European medicine was influencing Ottoman medical practices. On the modernization of medicine, generally, see Porter, *Health, Civilization, and the State*, chaps. 4–12.
32 Ebrahimnejad, *Medicine, Public Health*, chap. 2; Moulin, "Révolutions Médicales"; Gallagher, *Medicine and Power in Tunisia*, chaps. 3–4.
33 Arom, "Members as Monitors"; Schizer, "Enhancing Efficiency at Nonprofits."
34 For European and American examples from the Middle Ages to the present, see Fishman, *Faithless Fiduciary*. This work highlights sundry obstacles to effective accountability.
35 Fishman, *Faithless Fiduciary*, chap. 2.
36 Schizer, "Enhancing Efficiency at Nonprofits," p. 78. The comparison is for 2018.
37 Gerber, *Islamic Law and Culture*, especially pp. 85–86, 102–3; Deguilhem-Schoen, "Loan of Mursad," pp. 69–74.
38 Deguilhem, "Waqf in the City"; Dallal, "Islamic Institution of Waqf"; Shechter, "Market Welfare."
39 Baqutayan, Ariffin, Mohsin, and Mahdzir, "Waqf between the Past and Present"; Çizakça, "From Destruction to Restoration," pp. 86–90.

CHAPTER 6

1 Olsen, *City*; Dinçkal, "Reluctant Modernization"; Hegazi, "Authoritarian Governance," pp. 44–46; Cansunar, "Distributional Consequences of Philanthropic Contributions," pp. 894–96; Hanssen, *Fin de Siècle Beirut*, chap. 4.
2 Rosenthal, "Foreigners and Municipal Reform"; Reimer, "Urban Government and Administration in Egypt"; Cleveland, "Municipal Council of Tunis"; Zad, "Spatial Discrimination."
3 Rising military costs: Hoffman, *Why Did Europe*, chaps. 2–4. Ottoman indebtedness: Birdal, *Political Economy of Ottoman Public Debt*, chap. 2. Egyptian indebtedness: Issawi, "Egypt since 1800," p. 10.
4 The major exception was the assets of mosque waqfs.
5 Eccel, *Egypt, Islam and Social Change*, chaps. 3–8; Zeghal, "Religion and Politics"; Bano, "At the Tipping Point?"
6 Rubin, "Institutions, the Rise of Commerce," develops this argument with respect to Islamic institutions generally.

7 Hâtemî, *Medenî Hukuk Tüzelkişileri*, vol. 1, pp. 58–318; El-Daly, *Philanthropy in Egypt*, p. 119.
8 Kuran, *Long Divergence*, chap. 7.
9 On the tradeoffs between various forms of state legitimacy, see Rubin, *Rulers, Religion, and Riches*.
10 Kuran, *Long Divergence*, chaps. 10–12.
11 In the Ottoman Empire, the practice of arbitrary expropriation (*müsadere*) was abolished in 1839 (Findley, *Bureaucratic Reform*, pp. 145–46). Thereafter, property rights were strengthened. In Egypt, the process was more rapid (Baer, *History of Landownership*, pp. 1–70; Baer, *Studies in the Social History of Modern Egypt*, pp. 62–74).
12 Cansunar and Kuran, "Economic Harbingers of Political Modernization."
13 On the gedik markets of Istanbul, see Ağır, "Rise and Demise of *Gedik* Markets." Gedik markets emerged also in Cairo, urban Syria, and Salonika: Chalcraft, *Striking Cabbies*, pp. 19–22; Faroqhi, *Artisans of Empire*, pp. 139–41; Rafeq, "Craft Organization," pp. 502–4; Srougo, "Professional Characteristics," pp. 118–21.
14 Kuran, *Long Divergence*, pp. 161–64, 251–53.
15 Gökalp, *Yeni Hayat, Doğru Yol*, p. 35 (my translation).
16 Banani, *Modernization of Iran*, pp. 50–51. See also Mohseni-Cheraghlou, Marvi, and Kazemzadeh, "Waqf in Iran," pp. 193–95.
17 For accounts of nineteenth- and early twentieth-century thinking on the waqf, see Öztürk, *Menşe'i ve Tarihi Gelişimi Açısından Vakıflar*, pp. 140–41 (for Turkey); Sékaly, *Problème des Wakfs*, pp. 402–54, 601–59 (for Egypt); Powers, "Orientalism, Colonialism," sect. 2 (for Algeria); and Werner, Vaqf *en Iran*, pp. 136–43.
18 In several Arab countries, including Egypt, a Waqf Ministry remains in operation. In Turkey, waqf administration was downgraded to a general directorate in 1924, as part of efforts to drive Islam out of public life.
19 On the Ottoman transformation, see Öztürk, *Türk Yenileşme Tarihi Çerçevesinde Vakıf Müessesesi*, pp. 63–107, 379–471. Turkish waqf assets became even more fungible in 2012 with the transfer to the Treasury of the directorate's majority share in VakıfBank (Özsaraç, "Vakıflarda Anakronizm," p. 218). On Egypt's reforms, including legal changes that authorized the state to modify the expenditures of surviving waqfs, see Baer, *History of Landownership in Modern Egypt*, pp. 79–92; and Melčák, "Development of *Dīwān al-awqāf* in Egypt." On the Syrian transformation, see Meier, "*Waqf* Only in Name."
20 Turkey practically completed the process in the 1930s, under Atatürk (Dönmez, *Cumhuriyet Devrinde Vakıflar*, pp. 30–61; Hâtemî, "Vakıf Kurumuna Hukuk Tarihi Açısından Genel Bir Bakış," pp. 120–22). In Egypt, the last major nationalization wave was in the 1950s, under Nasser (Moustafa, "Conflict and Cooperation," p. 5). Finishing a process initiated during the French Protectorate, Tunisia's independent government nationalized or privatized nearly all remaining waqfs by 1957 (Duwaji, "Land Ownership in Tunisia," p. 130; Tessler, "Political Change," p. 10). In Iran, some Islamic waqfs remained autonomous even through Pahlavi rule. But the state had turned a blind eye to the pillaging of their assets; those that had escaped nationalization were commonly privatized (Fischer, *Iran*, pp. 117–19). In some cities, mosques and religious schools are still operated through Islamic waqfs (Bonine, "Islam and Commerce").

21 In Iran, privatizations and nationalizations usually involved forged documents or forced sales. A state-led waqf administration was established in 1964. See Çizakça, *History of Philanthropic Foundations*, pp. 141–57; and Mohseni-Cheraghlou, Marvi, and Kazemzadeh, "Waqf in Iran," pp. 193–95.
22 Abun-Nasr, *History of the Maghrib*, pp. 261–62.
23 Focusing on 1876–1914, Özbek, *Osmanlı İmparatorluğu'nda Sosyal Devlet*, documents the institutional transformation of charity in Turkey. On Egypt, see Ener, *Managing Egypt's Poor*, pp. 1–25; Baron, "Islam, Philanthropy"; Sullivan, *Private Voluntary Organizations in Egypt*; and Abdelrahman, *Civil Society Exposed*, chaps. 4–6.
24 Moustafa, "Conflict and Cooperation"; Onay, "Osmanlı'dan Cumhuriyet'e Camilerin Finansmanı," pp. 59–71.
25 Examples: Kala, "Mazbut Vakıfların Günümüz Hayır Hizmetleri"; Ertem, "Osmanlıdan Günümüze Vakıflar," pp. 59–60; Raissouni, *Islamic "Waqf Endowment*,*"* pp. 27–42; Deligöz, "Legacy of Waqf Institutions"; Aliyu, "Treatise on the Socioeconomic Roles of Waqf." The former two authors consider the structural similarities between premodern and modern waqfs to outweigh the differences. The latter three consider the differences symbolic.
26 Turkish law refers to "waqfs formed according to Turkish civil law" (Demir, *Yeni Vakıfların Temel Kitabı*, p. 89; my translation). The Iranian Constitution of 1911 incorporated waqf law into the civil code, with relaxed requirements. Iran's Civil Code of 1928 made the waqf a legal entity, specifying that its management may be left to the caretaker's discretion (*Qanuni Madani 1928*, art. 87). A new waqf law expanded its corporate powers in 1975, toward the end of the monarchy. And in 1984 the Islamic Republic reconfirmed that the waqf has legal personhood and may be represented by another organization (Werner, *Vaqf en Iran*, pp. 38–45). For more on novel applications, see Çizakça, *History of Philanthropic Foundations*, pp. 149–52, 157–68.
27 For relevant Turkish statutes, see Demir, *Yeni Vakıfların Temel Kitabı*, stat. 60–65, 67–68, 76–77, 79–80, 119–21, 128–37, 159.
28 On such reforms, see Çizakça, *History of Philanthropic Foundations*, chap. 4; and Pioppi, "Privatization of Social Services."
29 On American charitable corporations, see Dirusso, "American Nonprofit Law." American laws regulate relationships between nonprofit organizations and their funders. They also prevent abuses of tax-exempt status. Both functions are central to modern waqf laws.
30 AKSAV, *Antalya Altın Portakal Kültür ve Sanat Vakfı Resmi Senedi*; http://fgv.org.tr/.
31 Atia, *Building a House in Heaven*, p. 86.
32 This law recognizes two types of NGOs: community development associations and civic foundations. The difference is that the former type must have at least ten founders. See Law No. 84, *al-Jarīdah al-Rasmīyah*, 5 June 2002, no. 22 ter (A), translation at www.icnl.org/research/library/files/Egypt/law84-2002-En.pdf. It makes no reference to the waqf.
33 Herrold, *Delta Democracy*, pp. 29–38. In terms of financing, structure, and objectives, Herrold stresses, Egypt's private foundations resemble American-based charitable organizations more than Islamic waqfs.
34 Khallaf, "Community Foundations," p. 124; Atia, *Building a House in Heaven*, pp. 89–90.

35 El Daly, *Philanthropy in Egypt*, pp. 73–74. On Egypt's NGOs, see also Atia, *Building a House in Heaven*, chap. 4.
36 Some of these foundations were known as a bonyad. Explicitly secular, they all served Pahlavi goals. None was autonomous (Maloney, "Agents or Obstacles?" pp. 150–51).
37 Saeidi, "Accountability of Para-Governmental Organizations," pp. 483–98; Maloney, "Islamism and Iran's Postrevolutionary Economy," pp. 192, 195–98, 205, 207; Jenkins, "*Bonyads*"; Mohseni-Cheraghlou, Marvi, and Kazemzadeh, "Waqf in Iran," pp. 195–204.
38 Yalansız, "İzmir'de 1989 Yerel Seçimleri," pp. 578–83.
39 Heper and Toktaş, "Islam, Modernity, and Democracy in Contemporary Turkey"; Cagaptay, *New Sultan*, chaps. 5, 7.
40 Saeidi, "Accountability of Para-Governmental Organizations," pp. 494–97.
41 Bayat, "Activism and Social Development," pp. 17–18.
42 Neither waqf nor *awqāf*, its Arabic plural, appears in the text.
43 Surveys used: various waves of Afrobarometer, Arab Barometer, AsiaBarometer, Caucasusbarometer, Asian Barometer, Eurobarometer, European Values Study, Latinobarómetro, and World Values Survey.
44 Computed from data that Livny compiled for use in *Trust and the Islamic Advantage*, chap. 4. Outside the Middle East, the share is 61.1 percent.
45 On the prevalence and drivers of preference falsification, see Kuran, *Private Truths, Public Lies*, chaps. 1–5.
46 Calculated from data collected for work reported in Livny, *Trust and the Islamic Advantage*, chap. 4.
47 Zürcher, *Turkey*, chaps. 10–11; Marsot, *Egypt in the Reign of Muhammad Ali*, chaps. 7–8.
48 Hâtemî, *Medenî Hukuk Tüzelkişileri*, vol. 1, pp. 58–318; Yener, *Dernekler ve Vakıflar Kanunu*, pp. 9–49; El Daly, *Philanthropy in Egypt*, p. 119.
49 Almond and Verba, *Civic Culture*, chap. 11. See also Putnam, *Making Democracy Work*, pp. 99–116.
50 Almond and Verba, *Civic Culture*, pp. 310–19.
51 Putnam, *Bowling Alone*, pp. 18–24.
52 Çapa, *Kızılay*, pp. 52–59; Sarıkaya, *Türkiye Himaye-i Etfal Cemiyeti*, pp. 58–67; Baytal, *Atatürk Döneminde Sosyal Yardım*, pp. 6–69.
53 Abdelrahman, *Civil Society Exposed*, p. 128.
54 Law No. 32 of 1964 (Law of Associations), *al-Jarīdah al-Rasmīyah*, 12 February 1964, no. 37, cited in Abdelrahman, *Civil Society Exposed*, p. 129.
55 Law No. 153 of 1999 (Law Regulating Civil Associations and Institutions), *al-Jarīdah al-Rasmīyah*, 27 May 1999, no. 21. Although the Constitutional Court voided this law within a few months, its critical clauses were included in Law no. 84 of 2002 (On Nongovernmental Organizations), *al-Jarīdah al-Rasmīyah*, 5 June 2002, no. 22 ter (A), translated at www.icnl.org/research/library/files/Egypt/law84-2002-En.pdf. See Abdelrahman, *Civil Society Exposed*, pp. 131–32.
56 *Egypt Today* staff, "Egypt's Solidarity Ministry"; International Center for Not-for-Profit-Law, Civic Freedom Monitor: Egypt (www.icnl.org/research/monitor/egypt.html). The figure was about 31,000 in 2006 (Abdou, Atia, Hussein, Kharas, and Maaty, "How Can the U.S. and International Finance Institutions," p. 3) and almost 13,000 in 1991 (Al-Sayyid, "Civil Society in Egypt?" p. 231).

57 For an interview-based account, see Ghabra, "Egyptian Revolution." Complementary insights: Carapico, "Egypt's Civic Revolution"; Acemoglu, Hassan, and Tahoun, "Power of the Street."
58 Mestyan, *Arab Patriotism*; Marsot, *History of Egypt*, chaps. 4–6.
59 Yom, "Civil Society and Democratization in the Arab World"; Herrold and Atia, "Competing Rather than Collaborating."
60 Bikmen, *Landscape of Philanthropy*, p. 14.
61 Doyle, "State Control," pp. 252–56.
62 Çarkoğlu, *Trends in Individual Giving*, pp. 98–108; Tiltay and Torlak, "Similarities and Differences."
63 El Daly, *Philanthropy in Egypt*, pp. 158–67, observes the same pattern in Egypt, where a perception of corrupt NGO officers supports a preference for giving directly to individuals of one's choice. Matic and AlFaisal, "Empowering the Saudi Social Development Sector," p. 14, note that in Saudi Arabia "only a fraction of the philanthropic money is institutionalized ... with the remainder often given through informal channels or hand-to-hand."
64 For state control of civic associations, see also Khatib, "Syria's Civil Society"; Josua, "Co-optation Reconsidered," pp. 38–56 (on Jordan); Rivetti, "Co-opting Civil Society Activism in Iran"; and Durac and Cavatorta, *Politics and Governance in the Middle East*, pp. 173–76 (on Middle East generally).
65 See also Tadmouri et al., "Consanguinity"; Kaplan et al., "Consanguineous Marriages in Turkey"; Akrami, Montazeri, Shomali, Heshmat, and Larijani, "Is There a Significant Trend"; and Meriwether, *Kin Who Count*, pp. 132–40.
66 On the concept and its implications, see Roland. "Understanding Institutional Change," pp. 116–25.
67 Quran 4:23, 33:50.
68 Hodgson, *Venture of Islam*, vol. I, p. 168.
69 Goody, *Development of the Family and Marriage*, pp. 31–32; Edlund, "Cousin Marriage"; Do, Iyer, and Joshi, "Economics of Consanguineous Marriages."
70 Bittles and Black, "Consanguinity, Human Evolution," pp. 1781–84.
71 Goody, *Development of the Family and Marriage*, pp. 35–39, 50–59; Henrich, *Weirdest People*, chaps. 5–6.
72 Akbari, Bahrami-Rad, and Kimbrough, "Kinship, Fractionalization and Corruption," sects. 1–2.
73 Sidani and Thornberry, "Nepotism in the Arab World"; Sapsford, Tsourapas, Abbott, and Teti, "Corruption"; Chekir and Diwan, "Crony Capitalism in Egypt"; Rahman, "Overview of Corruption," pp. 7–9; Kilani and Sakijha, *Wasta*, chap. 1; Zonis, *Political Elite of Iran*, pp. 22, 142–44; Behravesh, "Corruption"; Mohamadi, Rafiey, Mousavi, and Hosseinzadeh, "Which Institutions Are Most Corrupt?"; Rakel, *Power, Islam, and Political Elite in Iran*, sects. 1.4, 2.3–2.6; Cengiz, Dilek, Özdemir, Özhabeş, Tarhan, Yırcalı, and Zeytinoğlu, *Yolsuzluk Türkiye Raporu*, chaps. 1, 5. See also Gürakar, *Politics of Favoritism*, chap. 4; though focused on favoritism in public procurement generally, she shows that the families of top officials have been among the beneficiaries.
74 On Mubarak: Arafat, *Rise of Islamism*, pp. 9–11. On Albayrak: "Erdoğan, Albayrak."
75 On the acceptance of nepotism and bribery as essential to daily life in the modern Arab world, see Cunningham and Sarayrah, *Wasta*; Tlaiss and Kauser,

"Importance of Wasta"; Khalaily and Navot, "Hamulas and Structural Corruption in the Middle East"; and Al-Mutairi, Connerton, and Dingwall, "Understanding 'Corruption'." For Turkey, see Giannakopoulos, "Yunanistan ve Türkiye'deki Yolsuzluk Algıları."

76 Anti-corruption campaigns: Gillespie and Okruhlik, "Cleaning up Corruption." Turkey: Tarhan, Gençkaya, Ergül, Özsemerci, and Özbaran, *Bir Olgu Olarak Yolsuzluk*, pp. 40–55, 77–87; Kimya, "Political Economy of Corruption in Turkey," pp. 354–66. Iran: Salihu and Jafari, "Corruption and Anti-Corruption." Egypt: Fayed, "Current Status of Corruption in Egypt." Morocco: Suárez-Collado and García-Rendón, "Sweeping under the Rug."

77 Fighting bribery as a collective action problem: Mungiu-Pippidi, "Controlling Corruption"; Persson, Rothstein, and Teorell, "Why Anticorruption Reforms Fail." Variations in acceptability of bribing: Anand, Ashforth, and Joshi, "Business as Usual"; Cameron, Chaudhuri, Erkal, and Gangadharan, "Propensities."

78 Two variants: Cammett, Diwan, Richards, and Waterbury, *Political Economy of the Middle East*, chaps. 3, 8, 11; Rivlin, *Arab Economies*.

79 North, Wallis, and Weingast, *Violence and Social Orders*, shows that every liberal order emerged from a system whose ruling clique suppressed freedoms.

80 Acemoglu and Robinson, *Narrow Corridor*, chaps. 2, 13.

CHAPTER 7

1 Cook, *Commanding Right and Forbidding Wrong*, chap. 2. The verses are 3:104, 3:110, 3:114, 7:157, 9:71, 9:112, 22:41, and 31:17. Only the first specifies responsibility.
2 Cook, *Commanding Right and Forbidding Wrong*, p. 15, which lists the relevant verses.
3 Dabashi, *Authority in Islam*, chaps. 5–7; Crone and Hinds, *God's Caliph*, chaps. 3–4.
4 Makdisi, *Rise of Colleges*, chap. 2.
5 Kuran, *Long Divergence*, chap. 8.
6 Shiloah, "Music and Religion in Islam"; Otterbeck, "Battling over the Public Sphere."
7 Johnson and Koyama, *Persecution and Toleration*, sects. 9.2–9.3, 13.2, 13.4, 14.3.
8 Johnson and Koyama, *Persecution and Toleration*, pp. 15–19.
9 Cantoni, Dittmar, and Yuchtman, "Religious Competition and Reallocation"; Dittmar and Meisenzahl, "Public Goods Institutions"; Hamburger, *Separation of Church and State*, chaps. 4–6.
10 Gill and Owen, "Religious Liberty," pp. 119–25.
11 Owen and Owen, "Concluding Thoughts," pp. 269–70.
12 Owen and Owen, "Concluding Thoughts," pp. 270–71.
13 Philpott, *Religious Freedom in Islam*, pp. 209–26. Shah, "Roots of Religious Freedom," identifies support for religious liberties in early Christian writings.
14 Zagorin, *How the Idea of Religious Toleration*.
15 Philpott, *Religious Freedom in Islam*, chaps. 6–8, argues that pathways analogous to those used by Christian thinkers are available to modern interpreters of Islam.
16 Macdonald, *Religious Attitude*; Grunebaum, *Medieval Islam*, chap. 5.

17 Mawdudi, *Let Us Be Muslims*; Mawdudi, *Islamic Way of Life*; and Qutb, *Milestones*, chaps. 5–7, offer modern variants of this view. All three are popular among Islamists throughout the Middle East.
18 Gardet, "Dīn."
19 The objective was to minimize frictions by familiarizing all sides with everything reasonably knowable about the quid and the quo (Udovitch, "Islamic Law").
20 Donner, *Muhammad and the Believers*, pp. 111–12, 205–6.
21 A notable exception occurred when a governor of eighth-century Iraq discouraged new conversions to preserve tax revenue. Non-Muslims paid higher taxes than Muslims, which was the main motivation for conversion. See Dennett, *Conversion and the Poll Tax*, pp. 40, 87, 114–15; Løkkegaard, *Islamic Taxation*, pp. 128–29; and Abu Yusuf, *Taxation in Islam*, pp. 82–83.
22 Cole, "Why I Left."
23 Peters and De Vries, "Apostasy in Islam"; Schirrmacher, "Leaving Islam."
24 Berkey, *Formation of Islam*, p. 71.
25 A fatwa of Ibn Taymiyya, a towering Sunni scholar, is a prominent statement of the ban (Friedman, "Ibn Taymiyya's Fatāwā"). The modern Islamist Ya-sin, *Book of Eemaan*, pp. 231–32, relies on this fatwa in justifying the killing of apostates. For historical context, see Masud, "Reading Ibn Taymiyya's *al-Ṣārim*."
26 Kadivar, "Toward Removing the Punishment of Apostasy," pp. 214–19.
27 Quran, 2:256, 109:6.
28 Quran 27:92, 39:41. Another verse in the same vein is 10:109.
29 Quran 9:4–5.
30 Compare 7:199 and 109:6, probably both from Muhammad's Mecca years, with 4:89, 4:115, 8:39, and 9:73, from his Medina years. The Medina verses include one that warns renouncers of divine punishment: 4:137.
31 On the arrangement of the Quran's chapters and the disconnectedness of its narratives, see Esack, *Qur'an*, pp. 64–66; Öztürk, *Surelerin İniş Sırası*; and Watt, *Bell's Introduction to the Qur'ān*, pp. 108–20. Watt suggests that a chapter's verses did not necessarily come all together. Many chronologists hold that "Meccan chapters" include a few verses from Muhammad's Medina years, and vice versa.
32 Powers, "On the Abrogation of the Bequest Verses"; Burton, *Sources of Islamic Law*; İltaş, "Kur'an Araştırmalarında Nesih Meselesi."
33 In pre-Islamic Mecca, it was customary to tax as necessary, for specific purposes (Ibrahim, "Social and Economic Conditions," pp. 343–44).
34 Quran 2:177, 2:215, 4:8, 9:60, 24:22.
35 They include redistribution, social welfare, defense, public works, and social stability. For a mapping between the Quran's expenditure categories and the functions of a modern state, see Rahman, "Islam and Problem of Economic Justice," p. 33; and Kuran, "Zakat," pp. 401–3.
36 On the history and functions of the capitulations, see Liebesny, "Development of Western Judicial Privileges"; and Kuran, *Long Divergence*, chaps. 11–12.
37 For instance, Deuteronomy 13:6–9: "If your brother, the son of your mother, or your son, or your daughter, or the wife of your bosom, or your friend who is as your own soul, entices you secretly, saying, 'Let us go and serve other gods,' which neither you nor your fathers have known, some of the gods of the peoples that are round about you, whether near you or far off from you, from the one end of the earth to the other, you shall not yield to him or listen to him, nor shall your eye pity him, nor shall you

spare him, nor shall you conceal him; but you shall kill him; your hand shall be the first against him to put him to death, and afterwards the hand of all the people."
38 The Spanish Inquisition was most active between 1480 and 1600. Rarely did it target the Jewish- or Muslim-born, who were expelled. See Netanyahu, *Origins of the Inquisition*, book 2.
39 Mantsinen and Tervo-Niemelä, "Leaving Christianity," pp. 68–74.
40 Kütükoğlu, "Osmanlılar'da Gümrük," p. 264; Darling, "Ottoman Customs Registers," pp. 5–7, 12. Rates varied according to type of good and the merchant's identity. The overriding identity of a Muslim trader was his religion.
41 Brown, "Citizenship, Religious Rights," shows that the division of Muslim-governed lands into independent territorial states got formalized with written constitutions, beginning with that of Tunisia in 1861.
42 Kuran, *Long Divergence*, chaps. 6–7.
43 Saeed and Saeed, *Freedom of Religion*, pp. 66–68.
44 For complementary insights focused on blasphemy, see Saeed, "Blasphemy Laws in Islam."
45 Quran 16:109. Other verses cited as justification for executing apostates are 5:54, 9:11–12, and 22:11. None specifies a temporal punishment.
46 Saeed and Saeed, *Freedom of Religion*, chap. 5.
47 Searches done through Kassis, *Concordance of the Qur'an*.
48 Quran 16:106, 3:113–15. Verse 3:199 delivers the same message.
49 Donner, *Muhammad and the Believers*, pp. 114, 124; Hallaq, *Origins and Evolution of Islamic Law*, pp. 19–25.
50 Quran 5:68.
51 Quran 5:73.
52 Frend, *Rise of the Monophysite Movement*, chap. 8.
53 Donner, *Muhammad and the Believers*, pp. 107-10, 114–15.
54 Donner, *Muhammad and the Believers*, pp. 107–8, 115.
55 Donner, *Muhammad and the Believers*, pp. 111–12, 205–6.
56 Polytheism appears in the Quran forty-nine times and unbelief fifty-six times (counts based on Kassis, *Concordance of the Qur'an*).
57 Donner, *Muhammad and the Believers*, pp. 87–88.
58 Chaumont, "al-Shāfiʿī," sect. 2.
59 Laoust, "Aḥmad b. Hanbal," sect. 2.
60 On this timeline, see Kuru, *Islam, Authoritarianism, and Underdevelopment*, pp. 94–96; and Melchert, *Formation of the Sunni Schools of Law*.
61 Griffel, *Al-Ghazālī's Philosophical Theology*, pp. 103–5. Jackson, *On the Boundaries of Theological Tolerance*, pp. 55–59, shows that Ghazali was less concerned with avowed atheists than with crypto-infidels, who, while rejecting Muhammad's prophethood in their hearts, pretended that their beliefs accorded with Islam.
62 Griffel, "Toleration and Exclusion," pp. 350–54.
63 Laoust, *Essai sur les Doctrines*, pp. 58–65, 117–25.
64 Talhamy, "*Fatwa*s and the Nusayri/Alawis," pp. 178–80; Friedman, "Ibn Taymiyya's Fatāwā."
65 Hallaq, "From Fatwās to Furūʿ," describes their characteristics (pp. 32–38) and illustrates how some turned into canonical laws (pp. 39–61).

66 Saeed and Saeed, *Freedom of Religion*, chap. 2, provides more details.
67 Marcotte, "Suhrawardi," sect. 1.1.
68 Fakhry, *Averroes*, pp. 166–67.
69 Chaumont, "Al-Shāfiʿī," sect. 1.
70 Laoust, "Aḥmad b. Hanbal," sect. 1.
71 Laoust, *Essai sur les Doctrines*, pp. 132–39, 145–50.
72 Kafadar, *Between Two Worlds*; Yıldırım, *Aleviliğin Doğuşu*, pp. 82–89; Varol, *Islahat Siyaset Tarikat*, pp. 24–28.
73 Yıldırım, *Osmanlı Engizisyonu*. The subsequent two centuries also saw religious repression directed by high-ranking clerics. See Zilfi, *Politics of Piety*, chaps. 4–5; and Terzioğlu, "How to Conceptualize Ottoman Sunnitization."
74 Rawlings, *Spanish Inquisition*, chap. 5; Kamen, *Spanish Inquisition*, chaps. 8–10.
75 On the doctrines of these groups, see Eyuboğlu, *Günün Işığında Tasavvuf*. Karamustafa, *God's Unruly Friends*, interprets their beliefs and reviews their practices.
76 Shankland, "Maps and the Alevis," pp. 231–38; Çakmak, "Richard Leonhard'ın Değerlendirmeleri," p. 64. Yıldırım, *Aleviliğin Doğuşu*, pp. 299–303, adds that Ottoman armies relocated heterodox groups, sometimes to inhospitable places far from Istanbul.
77 Yıldırım, *Osmanlı Engizisyonu*; Dressler, "Inventing Orthodoxy," pp. 154–56, 163–64.
78 Savory, "Consolidation of Safavid Power," pp. 86–87; Zarinebaf-Shahr, "Qizilbash 'Heresy' and Rebellion."
79 For texts of the opinions, see Yıldırım, *Osmanlı Engizisyonu*, pp. 122, 160–63; and Düzdağ, *Şeyhülislâm Ebussuûd Efendi Fetvaları*, pp. 109–18.
80 Atçıl, "Safavid Threat," compares the pertinent fatwas of three leading Ottoman jurists, Sarıgörez (d. 1522), Kemalpaşazade (1469–1534), and Ebussuûd (1490–1574). They agreed that Kızılbashs were apostates who deserved death.
81 Winter, *Shiites of Lebanon*, shows that Ottoman policies toward deviant Muslims were not uniformly hostile. In Lebanon, revenue considerations induced a pragmatic approach.
82 The term "Kizilbash" came into use in the 1460s. Until then, Kizilbashs were known to Ottomans as the Safaviyya order. See Baltacıoğlu-Brammer, "Formation of Kızılbaş Communities," pp. 28–32.
83 Baltacıoğlu-Brammer, "Formation of Kızılbaş Communities," pp. 23–24, 29–46.
84 Twelver Shiism is also known as Imamate Shiism.
85 Babayan, "Safavid Synthesis"; Arjomand, "Religious Extremism," pp. 3–10; and Abisaab, *Converting Persia*, pp. 31–32, 45–49, 54–55. For a general history of Iran's Safavid Era and the tenets of Twelver Shiism, see Amanat, *Iran*, chaps. 1–3; and Arjomand, *Shadow of God*, chaps. 4–8. On Twelver tenets and objections to Sunnism, see also Majlisi, *Haqqul Yaqeen*.
86 Faroqhi, *Anadolu'da Bektaşilik*, pp. 11–46.
87 On the Janissaries, see Aksan, *Ottoman Wars, 1700–1870*, pp. 48–53; Uzunçarşılı, *Osmanlı Devleti*, chap. 3.
88 Uzunçarşılı, *Osmanlı Devleti*, pp. 147–50; Faroqhi, *Anadolu'da Bektaşilik*, pp. 190–91.
89 Doja, "Political History of Bektashism," pp. 429–30; Yıldırım, *Aleviliğin Doğuşu*, pp. 343–47. On Janissary-led Ottoman rebellions, see Yıldız, *Crisis and Rebellion*,

chap. 1. On the use of Bektashism for political control, see Varol, *Islahat Siyaset Tarikat*, pp. 28–38.
90 Aksan, *Ottoman Wars, 1700–1870*, pp. 313–17; Doja, "Political History of Bektashism," pp. 440–45; Yıldız, *Neferin Adı Yok*, pp. 115–30.
91 Varol, *Islahat Siyaset Tarikat*, p. 28; Karamustafa, "Ḳalenders, Abdâls, Ḥayderîs."
92 All lowered their social profile. See Doja, "Political History of Bektashism," p. 443; Varol, *Islahat Siyaset Tarikat*, pp. 61–79.
93 Doja, "Political History of Bektashism," p. 443.
94 The generic name for these difficulties is the "principal–agent problem." On limits to state capacity, see Scott, *Art of Not Being Governed*; Lee and Zhang, "Legibility and State Capacity"; Levi, *Of Rule and Revenue*.
95 Johnson, "Sunni Survival"; Arjomand, *Shadow of God*, pp. 112–13, 116–18; Babayan, *Mystics, Monarchs, and Messiahs*, chaps. 11–12.
96 Yıldırım, *Aleviliğin Doğuşu*, pp. 345–46.
97 Arjomand, *Shadow of God*, pp. 118–19.
98 Moreen, "Status of Religious Minorities," p. 134.
99 Hallaq, "From Fatwās to Furū'."
100 On preference falsification generally and religious preference falsification specifically, see Kuran, *Private Truths, Public Lies*, especially pp. 3–9.
101 Reinkowski, "Hidden Believers, Hidden Apostates"; Deringil, *Conversion and Apostasy*, chap. 3; Nissimi, *Crypto-Jewish Mashadis*, chaps. 3–5.
102 Mariuma, "Taqiyya as Polemic, Law," pp. 89–97; Kohlberg, "Taqiyya in Shī'ī Theology"; Bateson, "This Figure of Tinsel"; Baltacıoğlu-Brammer, "Those Heretics Gathering Secretly," pp. 45–46, 55–56; Abisaab, *Converting Persia*, pp. 26–40.
103 Kuran, *Long Divergence*, chap. 8.
104 Barkey, *Empire of Difference*, chap. 4.
105 On the biases of Islamic courts, see Kuran and Lustig, "Judicial Biases."

CHAPTER 8

1 Lewis, *Muslim Discovery of Europe*; Ahmad, *Making of Modern Turkey*; Hourani, *History of the Arab Peoples*, chaps. 15–16, 18, 20; Brown, *Tunisia of Ahmad Bey*.
2 Cansunar and Kuran, "Economic Harbingers of Political Modernization."
3 Founded in 1844, Babism gave rise to Bahaism, a new Abrahamic religion, in 1863. It, too, was repressed. On Iranian heterodoxies of the Qajar era, see Algar, *Religion and State in Iran*, chap. 8; Arjomand, *Shadow of God*, pp. 242–57; and Moaddel, "Shi'i Ulama," pp. 519–33.
4 Çetinsaya, *Ottoman Administration of Iraq*, chap. 5.
5 Alkan, "Fighting for the Nuṣayrī Soul."
6 De Jong, "Ṣūfī Orders in Egypt," pp. 131–36.
7 Ochsenwald, *Religion, Society*, pp. 41–50.
8 Kuran, *Long Divergence*, chaps. 9–10.
9 The boldest writings in this vein include reports by Ottoman emissaries to European capitals (Şakul, "Nizâm-ı Cedid Düşüncesinde Batılılaşma"), witnesses of military defeat (Menchinger, *First of the Modern Ottomans*, chap. 3), and Arab officials in contact with French civilization (Hourani, *Arabic Thought*, chap. 3).

Notes to pages 135–39

10 Sabev, *İbrahim Müteferrika*, sect. 3; Meral, "Osmanlı Yahudi Matbaası," pp. 456–60.
11 E. Kuran, *Avrupa'da İkamet Elçilikleri*.
12 Kenan, "III. Selim Dönemi Eğitim Anlayışı," pp. 137–45.
13 Ringer, *Education, Religion*, chap. 3.
14 Marashi, *Nationalizing Iran*, p. 20. In the 1800s, Iran's transformation was slower than that of the Ottoman Empire. Its reforms were also less centralized, and they faced greater resistance from better-organized clerics (Sohrabi, *Revolution and Constitutionalism*, chap. 6).
15 Shaw, "Origins of Ottoman Military Reform"; Cronin, "Importing Modernity"; Yapp, "Modernization of Middle Eastern Armies."
16 Translation of edict: Liebesny, *Law of the Near and Middle East*, pp. 46–49.
17 For further details and a fuller interpretation of the Gülhane Edict, see Cansunar and Kuran, "Economic Harbingers of Political Modernization."
18 Cansunar and Kuran, "Economic Harbingers of Political Modernization."
19 Asad, *Formations of the Secular*, chap. 7; Hunter, *Egypt under the Khedives*, pp. 41–54, 80–99; Mestyan, *Arab Patriotism*, chaps. 2, 4.
20 Toledano, "Social and Economic Change," p. 254; Kenny, "Khedive Isma'il's Dream," p. 149.
21 Kenny, "Khedive Isma'il's Dream," pp. 154–55.
22 Deringil, "There Is No Compulsion in Religion," surveys the transformation in Ottoman religious freedoms; quote at p. 547.
23 Fawaz, *Occasion for War*, p. 152. For earlier cases of resistance to forced conversions, see Deringil, "There Is No Compulsion in Religion," pp. 556–59.
24 Çakır, "Türk Aydınının Tanzimat'la İmtihanı," surveys the interpretations articulated over the 165 years following the edict. Variants that consider the reforms superficial were popularized by later reformers to aggrandize their own achievements.
25 The edict contains many references to Islamic law. See Liebesny, *Law of the Near and Middle East*, pp. 46–49. Eldem, "L'Édit des *Tanzimat*," notes that the religious references served as window dressing.
26 They include Renan, *L'Islamisme et la Science*; and Cromer, *Modern Egypt*, vol. 2, pp. 228–29.
27 Hanioğlu, "Garbcılar," pp. 137, 146.
28 Hanioğlu, "Garbcılar," p. 141.
29 Hanioğlu, "Garbcılar," p. 145.
30 Translated as Razek, *Islam and the Foundations of Political Power*. On al-Raziq's impact on the politics of Islam, see Ali, *Religion, Not a State*, chaps. 4, 7–8.
31 Quoted in Banani, *Modernization of Iran*, pp. 23–24.
32 Mango, *Atatürk*, chap. 20.
33 On Iranian Westernization, Banani, *Modernization of Iran*, chaps. 3–7; Amanat, *Iran*, pp. 479–93.
34 General overviews: Azak, *Islam and Secularization in Turkey*; Amanat, *Iran*, chaps. 7–12; Masri, *Tunisia*, chaps. 12–13, 15; Warburg, "Islam and Politics in Egypt"; Hinnebusch, *Syria*, chaps. 3, 5; Baram, *Saddam Husayn and Islam*, chaps. 2, 6–7.
35 McCarthy, "Re-Thinking Secularism," p. 736.
36 On the logic of religious legitimation in the region, see Rubin, *Rulers, Religion, and Riches*; and Platteau, *Islam Instrumentalized*.

37 Saudi clerics participate in politics, but their influence is minimal. Their objections to innovations have been overruled repeatedly. See Bligh, "Saudi Religious Elite."
38 Yamani, "Two Faces of Saudi Arabia," pp. 143–47.
39 As of 1950, in elementary education 82 percent of class instruction focused on religion, and even in secondary education more time was spent on religion than on the natural sciences (Trial and Winder, "Modern Education," pp. 123, 129–30). Subsequently, time for religion plummeted (Rugh, "Education in Saudi Arabia"; Nevo, "Religion in Saudi Arabia," p. 36).
40 Hertog, "Shaping the Saudi State"; Rugh, "Emergence of a New Middle Class."
41 Assad, "Rise of Consumerism."
42 David Hume (1711–76) and Karl Marx (1818–83) developed rationales for extinguishing religion. Hume, *Enquiries Concerning the Human Understanding*, chaps. 10–11, considered religion a manifestation of ignorance. Marx, "Contribution," added that it camouflages exploitation.
43 McCleary and Barro, *Wealth of Religions*, chap. 2, analyze secularism and secularization with attention to finer gradations. Kuru, "Passive and Assertive Secularism," discusses the varieties of secularism, specifying why only passive secularism serves democratic ideals. See also Taylor, "How to Define Secularism."
44 Zagorin, *How the Idea of Religious Toleration*; Johnson and Koyama, *Persecution and Toleration*, chaps. 9–10, 13.
45 Cantoni, Dittmar, and Yuchtman, "Religious Competition and Reallocation"; Bodinier, Teyssier, and Antoine, "L'Évenement."
46 Hamburger, *Separation of Church and State*, examines the case of the United States. On anticlericalism in the early United States, see also Luebke, "Origins of Thomas Jefferson's Anti-Clericalism."
47 The agencies established to control and mold Islam included Turkey's Religious Affairs Directorate founded in 1924 (Gözaydın, *Diyanet*, chaps. 1–2; Kara, *Cumhuriyet Türkiyesi'nde İslâm*, vol. 1, pp. 53–92), Algeria's Ministry of Traditional Education and Religious Affairs, which became its Ministry of Waqfs and Religious Affairs (Bormans, "Ministère"), Syria's "Ministry of Waqfs" (Böttcher, "Ministère des Waqfs"), and Iraq's Ministry of Waqfs, which became the Ministry of Waqfs and Religious Affairs in 1985 (Baram, *Saddam Husayn and Islam*, pp. 76, 187–88). Tunisia started with a Directorate of Religious Affairs, which was elevated to a ministry in 1992 (Bras, "L'Islam Administré"). Egypt established private fatwa bodies and reorganized Al-Azhar as both a school and an interpreter of Islam. Its Ministry of Waqfs has regulated mosques (Skovgaard-Petersen, *Defining Islam*, chaps. 5–6; Gaffney, "Changing Voices of Islam").
48 Lee, "Tunisian Intellectuals," pp. 161–70, surveys this group's writings.
49 Shahin, *Political Ascent*, p. 39.
50 Berkes, *Development of Secularism in Turkey*, pp. 457–60, 483–90; Clayer, "Imposed or a Negotiated *Laiklik*?" pp. 100–101.
51 In Turkey, religion classes were eliminated between 1927 and 1937 (Kara, *Cumhuriyet Türkiyesi'nde İslâm*, vol. 2, chap. 5, pp. 209, 225; Paçacı and Aktay, "75 Years of Higher Religious Education"); and mosque sermons came to be regulated formally starting in 1927 (Kılıç, "Cumhuriyetin İlk Yıllarında Devlet İle Vatandaş Arasında Bir İletişim Aracı Olarak Hutbeler"). In Tunisia, certain Zaytouna graduates served as religion teachers in secondary schools. Most were

eventually laid off (Shahin, *Political Ascent*, p. 39). By 1958, the teaching of Islam had fallen to one hour a week (Kinsey, "Education," p. 23). Officials of the Directorate of Religious Affairs were writing the sermons delivered in mosques (Wolf, *Political Islam in Tunisia*, p. 111).
52 Zeghal, "Religion and Politics in Egypt"; Skovgaard-Petersen, *Defining Islam*, chaps. 5–6; Gaffney, "Changing Voices of Islam."
53 Chavoshian, "Secular Atmospheres," sects. 1, 4. For broader accounts of Pahlavi policies toward Islam, see Amanat, *Iran*, pp. 486–93; and Abrahamian, *History of Modern Iran*, pp. 93–95.
54 McCarthy, "Re-Thinking Secularism," p. 737.
55 Clayer, "Imposed or a Negotiated *Laiklik*?" p. 105.
56 Kara, *Cumhuriyet Türkiyesi'nde İslâm*, vol. 2, pp. 35, 73.
57 Kara, *Cumhuriyet Türkiyesi'nde İslâm*, vol. 2, p. 108.
58 Iraq: Blaydes, *State of Repression*, pp. 238–55. Syria: Pierret, *Religion and State in Syria*, chaps. 2–3.
59 Sassoon, *Saddam Hussein's Ba'th Party*, pp. 259–64.
60 Faust, *Ba'thification of Iraq*, pp. 9, 129–30.
61 Khatib, "More Religious, Yet Still Secular?" pp. 44–51.
62 Khatib, *Islamic Revivalism in Syria*, p. 72.
63 Turkey's reforms were radical even by Western standards of the time (White, "State Feminism"). Tunisia and Algeria: Charrad, *State and Women's Rights*, chaps. 8–9. Iraq: Anderson, "Law of Personal Status." Syria: Berger, "Legal System of Family Law in Syria." Egypt: Abu-Odeh, "Modernizing Muslim Family Law."
64 Bein, *Ottoman Ulema, Turkish Republic*, chaps. 6–7; Kara, *Cumhuriyet Türkiyesi'nde İslâm*, vol. 1, pp. 107–77.
65 Azak, *Islam and Secularism in Turkey*, pp. 21–38.
66 Kepel, *Muslim Extremism in Egypt*, pp. 93–94. On the origins of Islamist violence in Egypt, see Musallam, *Secularism to Jihad*.
67 Reza, "Endless Emergency."
68 Azak, *Islam and Secularism in Turkey*, pp. 31–38.
69 Metinsoy, *Power of the People*, pp. 206–9.
70 Berkes, *Development of Secularism in Turkey*, chaps. 12, 16–17, surveys the variants of this view among late Ottoman and early Republican thinkers. See also Hanioğlu, "Blueprints for a Future Society," pp. 65–69. Tunisia: Shahin, *Political Ascent*, pp. 35–36. Iraq: Torrey, "The Ba'th," pp. 449–50. Syria: Talhami and Al-Azm, "Interview with Sadik Al-Azm," p. 114. Egypt: Hourani, *Arabic Thought*, chaps. 6–7.
71 See speeches in the Turkish parliament, 1 January 1931 (Türkiye Büyük Millet Meclisi, "On Yedinci İn'ikat," pp. 3–9); and Bozarslan, *Histoire de la Turquie*, pp. 301–3.
72 Lerner, *Passing of Traditional Society*, pp. 162–63, 234, 277, 370, 408–9; Brown, "Role of Islam," pp. 97–98, 107–12.
73 For variants of this thinking among Turkish secularists, see Kara, *Cumhuriyet Türkiyesi'nde İslâm*, vol. 2, pp. 59, 86. Bora, *Cereyanlar*, p. 148.
74 Engels, *Anti-Dühring*, pt. 3, chap. 2.
75 Yavuz, *Islamic Political Identity in Turkey*, pp. 141–44, 173–76.
76 Yavuz, *Islamic Political Identity in Turkey*, pp. 139–40, 145–46.

CHAPTER 9

1. Clayer, "Imposed or a Negotiated *Laiklik*?" pp. 113–14; Meeker, *Nation of Empire*, pp. 55–76; Metinsoy, *Power of the People*, chap. 13.
2. Chavoshian, "Secular Atmospheres," pp. 192–98.
3. Krämer, *Hasan al-Banna*; Mardin, *Religion and Social Change*; Algar, *Imam Khomeini*.
4. McCarthy, "Re-Thinking Secularism," p. 739; Wolf, *Political Islam in Tunisia*, p. 51.
5. Boulby, "Islamic Challenge," pp. 599–614; Wolf, *Political Islam in Tunisia*, chaps. 1–2.
6. Syria: Lefèvre, *Ashes of Hama*, chaps. 5–6. Iraq: Cline, "Prospects of the Shia Insurgency." Egypt: Kepel, *Muslim Extremism in Egypt*. Tunisia: Boulby, "Islamic Challenge," p. 602. Algeria: Celso, "Al Qaeda in the Maghreb." Global Islamic terrorism: Cook, *Understanding Jihad*, chaps. 5–6; Gerges, *Far Enemy*.
7. Wickham, *Muslim Brotherhood*, chaps. 1–2.
8. Wickham, *Muslim Brotherhood*, chaps. 3, 6, 9.
9. Yücekök, *Türkiye'de Örgütlenmiş Dinin Tabanı*, pp. 136, 140–41.
10. White, *Islamist Mobilization in Turkey*, chap. 3.
11. Axiarlis, *Political Islam*, chaps. 3–7; Baykan, *Justice and Development Party*; Bermek, *Rise of Hybrid Political Islam in Turkey*, chaps. 3–6.
12. On these subdvisions, see Dogan, *Political Islamists in Turkey*; Gaborieau, Popovic, and Zarkone, *Naqshbandis*, chap. 3; Bacık, *Contemporary Rationalist Islam in Turkey*, chaps. 4–5; and [Diyanet İşleri Başkanlığı], *Dinî-Sosyal Teşekküller*, pp. 128–202. The last source is a leaked classified report of the Religious Affairs Directorate, which has not dissociated itself from the work. It provides a fine-grained schema of Turkish Sunnism.
13. Its adherents call Gülenism the "Hizmet Movement."
14. Bora, *Cereyanlar*, pp. 508–13; Dogan, *Political Islamists in Turkey*, chaps. 2–3; Cagaptay, *Erdogan's Empire*, pp. 91–92, 218, 231–34.
15. Brown, "Transition"; Sobhy, "Secular Façade, Neoliberal Islamisation"; Bano and Benadi, "Regulating Religious Authority."
16. Erkilet-Başer, "Sağ Siyasetin Payandası." See also Akşit, Şentürk, Küçükural, and Cengiz, *Türkiye'de Dindarlık*, pp. 337–53, who show that political Islamization enjoys substantial support.
17. Şen and Yenigün Altın, "Sosyal Demokrasiden Yeni Sağa CHP'nin Söylemsel Dönüşümü," pp. 453–55, show that leader speeches and election declarations of the main secular party became more religious between 1990 and 2018. Dündar and Taylan, "İki Laiklik Modeli," provide supportive evidence for the 2010s.
18. White, *Muslim Nationalism*, chaps. 4, 6, Afterword; Özcan, *Mainstreaming the Headscarf*, chaps. 2–4.
19. Aygül and Öztürk, "Dini Çoğulculuk"; Demirezen, *Tüketim Toplumu ve Din*, chap. 3. Akşit, Şentürk, Küçükural, and Cengiz, *Türkiye'de Dindarlık*, chaps. 4–5, highlight Islam's growing visibility in economics, politics, and social interactions.
20. Lord, *Religious Politics in Turkey*, pp. 111–21; Öztürk, "Turkey's Diyanet under AKP Rule," pp. 8–14; Kocamaner, "Regulating the Family through Religion"; Ongur, "Performing through Friday *Khutbas*"; Gözaydın, *Diyanet*, pp. 339–47, 352–64.

21 Öztürk, "Diyanet Fetvaları."
22 Nader, "Egyptian Court"; Human Rights Watch, "Egypt: 3-Year Sentence for Atheist".
23 Tessler, "Political Change," p. 12; McCarthy, "Re-Thinking Secularism," pp. 739–41.
24 Allani, "Islamists in Tunisia"; Gasiorowski, "Failure of Reform in Tunisia," pp. 86–91.
25 Khatib, "Islamic Revival," p. 45; Faust, *Ba'thification of Iraq*, pp. 140–41.
26 Blaydes, *State of Repression*, pp. 255–63; Sassoon, *Saddam Hussein's Ba'th Party*, pp. 266–68; Helfont, *Compulsion in Religion*, chap. 8; Faust, *Ba'thification of Iraq*, pp. 130–41; Bengio, *Saddam's Word*, chap. 13.
27 Khatib, "More Religious, yet Still Secular?" pp. 48–53; Khatib, *Islamic Revivalism in Syria*, pp. 85–94, 114–19; Pierret, "Syrian Baath Party," pp. 3–4; Kelidar, "Religion and State in Syria," p. 18.
28 Brown, "Role of Islam," p. 111.
29 On the political effects of migration to Middle Eastern cities, see Dorman, "Informal Cairo," pp. 424–36; Karpat, *Gecekondu*, pp. 31–34, 45–47; and Denoeux, *Urban Unrest*, chap. 11.
30 Turkey: Ünlü, *Türklük Sözleşmesi*, pp. 231–53. Iran: Elling, *Minorities in Iran*, chap. 5. Entire region, focusing on Arab countries: Haider, *Persecution of Christians in the Middle East*.
31 In Egypt, Christian advancement within the military is generally limited to the lower ranks (Hussein and De Martino, "Egypt's Military Post-2011," pp. 57, 60). In Turkey, informal discrimination against non-Muslim soldiers is widespread; sometimes they serve in separate units (Bali, *Gayrimüslim Mehmetçikler*). During their respective civil wars, Syria and Iraq were exceptions. Christians played major military roles in areas where they predominate. Another exception is Lebanon, where the national army's sectarian composition rests on negotiated quotas (Eleftheriadou, "Christian Militias").
32 Algeria, Egypt, Kuwait, Syria, and the United Arab Emirates all formally restrict the marriage options of women. Saudi Arabia and Qatar leave the matter to local courts, which enforce strict regulations. For details, see An-Na'im, *Islamic Family Law*. Where legally allowed, interfaith marriages are widely frowned upon; attitudes are more negative toward marriage of one's daughter compared to one's son (Niekerk and Verkuyten, "Interfaith Marriage Attitudes"). Mahmood, "Sectarian Conflict and Family Law," shows that religion-based family laws make marriage a matter of communal preservation. They also heighten sectarian tensions. "A vast number of sectarian incidents are set off," observes Mahmood (p. 55), "by rumors about an interfaith romance." On interfaith marriages in Turkey, where they are legal but widely reprehended, see Adar, "Religious Difference."
33 Ordered by approximate national membership: Coptic Orthodox, Greek Orthodox, Evangelical Church of Egypt, Coptic Catholic, Roman Catholic, Armenian Apostolic, Assyrian Orthodox, Maronite, Episcopal, Armenian Catholic, Melkite Greek, Baptist, Presbyterian, Seventh-Day Adventist. At least as many small Christian communities held services in legally unrecognized churches. They included the Mormons, Jehovah's Witnesses, Gospel Missionaries, and Christian Modelists. Sources: United States Embassy in Egypt, "International Religious Freedom Report," websites of Egyptian churches, and *Europa World Year Book*, pp. 1497–98.

34 Ordered by number of active churches with majority-national members: Greek Orthodox, Armenian Apostolic, Armenian Catholic, Roman Catholic, Protestant, Turkish Orthodox, Armenian Protestant, Russian Orthodox, Turkish Protestant, Assyrian Orthodox, Bulgarian Orthodox, Chaldean Orthodox, Independent Protestant, Presbyterian, Seventh-Day Adventist. Along with other churches serving primarily foreign communities, there also exist numerous "private churches," which are listed in church directories but lack legal personhood. Sources: Karaca, *İstanbul'da Osmanlı Dönemi Rum Kiliseleri*, p. 39; Yılmaz, *2012 Declaration*, p. 187; Malkoç, *İstanbul'daki Protestan Kiliseler*, pp. 33–140, 198–99; Baş, *Türk Ortodoks Patrikhanesi*, pp. 152–54.

35 Mazlumder, *Türkiye'de Dini Ayrımcılık Raporu*, pp. 315–74; Bardakci, Freyberg-Inan, Giesel, and Leisse, *Religious Minorities in Turkey*, chap. 4.

36 Lewis, *What Went Wrong?* pp. 33–34.

37 It is unknown whether the Pact was codified by the second caliph Umar I (r. 634–44) or the Umayyad caliph Umar II (r. 717–20). The latter is more plausible, because in Islam's early decades Muslims and non-Muslims were not yet sharply differentiated. See Cohen, "What Was the Pact of 'Umar."

38 Kuran, *Long Divergence*, chap. 9.

39 On tolerance toward non-Muslims generally and the limits of non-Muslim freedoms, see Barkey, *Empire of Difference*, chap. 4.

40 The 1914 figures are computed from Karpat, *Ottoman Population, 1830–1914*, table I.17.B; Courbage and Fargues, *Christians and Jews*, tables 6.1, 8.2; Clarke, "Population Policies and Dynamics in Tunisia," tables 1–2; Bharier, "Note on the Population of Iran"; Bohdanowicz, "Truth about the Armenian Question," p. 185; Prothero, *Arabia*, pp. 10–11; Prothero, *French Morocco*, p. 13; Schanzer, "Italian Colonial Policy," p. 446; Evans-Pritchard, "Arab Status in Cyrenaica," p. 4; Harrison, "Migrants in the City of Tripoli," table 1; "Fezzan," p. 308; and Oppenheim, *Jewish Year Book*, pp. 339–42. For Christians, the 2010 figure is computed from Hackett and Grim, "Global Christianity," pp. 71–77; and for Jews, from DellaPergola, *World Jewish Population, 2010*, pp. 61–62.

41 On the Jewish exodus from Arab lands, see Bensoussan, *Jews in Arab Countries*, chaps. 10–13. Three complementary accounts on the Armenian tragedy: Akçam, *From Empire to Republic*, chaps. 4–5; McCarthy, *Muslims and Minorities*, chaps. 3, 6–7; Çiçek, *Ermenilerin Zorunlu Göçü*. The population exchange between Greece and Turkey is formally known as the "Greek–Turkish exchange." This is a misnomer. Turkish-speaking Christians were shipped to Greece and Greek-speaking Muslims to Turkey, often against their will. See Yıldırım, *Diplomacy and Displacement*, pp. 105–6.

42 Kuran, *Long Divergence*, chap. 10. For further evidence, see chap. 13 of this work.

43 Üngör and Polatel, *Confiscation and Destruction*, chaps. 2, 4; Onaran, *Cumhuriyet'te Ermeni ve Rum Malları*, chaps. 2–6; Aktar, *Varlık Vergisi*, chap. 5; Bali, *"Varlık Vergisi" Affair*, chap. 1.

44 Prior to 1948, during World War II, Jews in pro-Nazi Arab states endured anti-Jewish policies. Between 1948 and 1970, 800,000 Jewish citizens of the Arab world emigrated, most to Israel. The circumstances varied greatly across states, by social class, and over time. Though some Jews left property behind, others transferred capital abroad in an orderly manner. Zionists encouraged departures to increase Jewish capital and labor in Israel. Certain Arab governments imposed economic

restrictions on their Jewish citizens in the belief that every Jew was Zionist or in retaliation for Israeli expropriation of Palestinians (Fischbach, *Jewish Property Claims*, chap. 1).
45 On the impact of this tax, see Ağır and Artunç, "Wealth Tax of 1942."
46 Tadros, *Copts at Crossroads*, chaps. 3, 8.
47 Thomas, *Women in Lebanon*, chap. 3.
48 Güreh, "Karma Evliliğe Takdis Yok."
49 Violent opposition to Atatürk's reforms: Bruinessen, *Agha, Shaikh, and State*, chap. 5. Islamist violence in Tunisia: Shahin, *Political Ascent*, pp. 96–99. Attempts to kill Nasser: Wickham, *Muslim Brotherhood*, pp. 27–28.
50 Konda Araştırma, "Diyanet İşleri Başkanlığı Araştırması," pp. 109–19. A classified but leaked 2017 report of Diyanet ([Diyanet İşleri Başkanlığı], *Dinî-Sosyal Teşekküller*) reinforced these perceptions. Diyanet's critics consider the report's "religious map" of Turkey evidence of the AKP government's religious homogenization campaign (Çelik, "'Dini Oluşumlar' Raporu").
51 Lord, *Religious Politics in Turkey*, pp. 151–56; Bardakci, Freyberg-Inan, Giesel, and Leisse, *Religious Minorities in Turkey*, pp. 121–27.
52 Eroler, *Dindar Nesil Yetiştirmek*, pp. 240–302; Koyuncu, "Benim Milletim," pp. 64–77, 164–205.
53 A consulting firm tied to Erdoğan conducted the survey. See Kulat, *Türkiye'de Toplumun Dine Bakışı*, p. 4
54 Konda Araştırma, "10 Yılda Gençlerde Ne Değişti?" slide 4.
55 İKDAM Eğitim Derneği ve Uluslararası Öncü Eğitimciler Derneği, "'Gençlik ve İnanç' Çalıştayı." This report was read at the workshop but not made public. Leaked to the media, it has been discussed widely.
56 Ertit, "God is Dying," pp. 195–96.
57 Çokgezen, "Can the State Make You More Religious?," pp. 355–65.
58 Kazemipour and Rezaei, "Religious Life under Theocracy," shows that between 1975 and 2001, faith in Iran shifted from "organized" to a more "personalized" Islam. Based on values surveys conducted in 2001–3, Moaddel, "Saudi Public Speaks," finds that, by several measures, Saudis are less religious than Egyptians or Jordanians, two religiously freer Arab nations. Tezcür and Azadarmaki, "Religiosity and Islamic Rule in Iran," report that in Tehran going to the mosque has turned from an act of piety to an act of political performance by people who are not necessarily religious.
59 Van Nieuwkerk, "Religious Skepticism and Nonbelieving in Egypt," pp. 309–10.
60 Arab Barometer Wave 5, question on "level of religiosity." An additional 2.5 percent refused to answer the question or chose the "don't know" option.
61 Al-Soukkary, *Becoming and Being*, pp. 3–6; Al Hariri, Magdy, and Wolters, "Arabs and Atheism," pp. 18–20; Van Nieuwkerk, "Atheist Spring," p. 1044.
62 Al-Soukkary, *Becoming and Being*, pp. 9–10.
63 Al-Soukkary, *Becoming and Being*, p. 5.
64 Al-Soukkary, *Becoming and Being*, especially chap. 4.
65 Exceptions: Comoros, Iran, Mauritania, Morocco, Saudi Arabia, and Yemen (Fox, "Religion and State Constitutions Dataset," 12 February 2019).
66 For country reports on religious freedoms, see Boyle and Sheen, *Freedom of Religion*.
67 Exceptions: Algeria, Comoros, Djibouti, Jordan, Lebanon, Libya, Morocco, Tunisia, Turkey (Fox, "Religion and State Constitutions Dataset").

68 Türkiye Cumhuriyeti Cumhurbaşkanlığı, *2020 Yılı Merkezi Yönetim Bütçe Kanun Teklifi*, p. 33. Tourism is a huge source of revenue in Turkey, the world's sixth-largest tourist destination (World Bank, "International Tourism").
69 Öztürk, "Turkey's Diyanet under AKP Rule," pp. 8–10; Lord, *Religious Politics in Turkey*, pp. 111–23; Gözaydın, *Diyanet*, pp. 311–75.
70 Exceptions: Algeria, Djibouti, Libya, and Somalia.
71 Van Nieuwkerk, "Atheist Spring," pp. 1040–41.
72 For a complementary categorization of religious freedoms in the Muslim world, along with additional observations, see Kuru, *Islam, Authoritarianism, and Development*, pp. 34–42.
73 Egypt: Rowe, "Christian–Muslim Relations"; El Fegiery, "Guarding the Mainstream." Iran: Mostafaei, "Crimes of Blasphemy and Apostasy in Iran"; Vahman, *175 Years of Persecution*, especially chaps. 14, 17. Iraq: Al-Khalidi and Tanner, "Sectarian Violence." Syria: Phillips, "Sectarianism and Conflict."
74 Censorship and self-censorship have always been present in scholarship, including the natural sciences. As with religion, repression of scholarship varies across topics, space, and time. For historical examples and insights into the underlying mechanisms, see Kuhn, *Structure of Scientific Revolutions*, chaps. 7–8. Modern examples: Pinker, *Blank Slate*, chaps. 6–7.
75 *Source*: Questions V147 and V148 of Inglehart et al., *World Values Survey, Round Six*. Countries where V147 was asked: Algeria, Bahrain, Iraq, Jordan, Kuwait, Lebanon, Libya, Morocco, Qatar, Tunisia, Turkey, Yemen. Countries where V148 was asked: Algeria, Iraq, Jordan, Lebanon, Libya, Morocco, Turkey.
76 East European and Iranian revolutions: Kuran, *Private Truths, Public Lies*, chap. 16. Arab uprisings: Brown, "Constitutional Revolutions."
77 Kuran, *Private Truths, Public Lies*, chaps. 17–19.

CHAPTER 10

1 Few Muslim-majority countries distinguish officially between denominations. This 2009 estimate belongs to the Pew Research Center, "Mapping the Global Muslim Population."
2 There are four major Sunni and three major Shii schools of law. See Schacht, *Introduction to Islamic Law*, chaps. 6–9; Melchert, *Formation of the Sunni Schools of Law*; and Stewart, *Islamic Legal Orthodoxy*.
3 Most outsiders notice only two differences. One concerns the legitimacy of Islam's first three caliphs and the other the Muslim community's leadership. Others receive attention mainly from exegetes. See Haider, *Shī'ī Islam*, chaps. 1–2; and Stewart, *Islamic Legal Orthodoxy*, pp. 53–59, 209–39.
4 The members include most Protestant and Eastern Orthodox churches, but not the Roman Catholic Church or the Southern Baptists of the United States.
5 The conceptual literature on classifying religions lacks coherence. For sophisticated approaches, see Stark and Bainbridge, "Of Churches, Sects, and Cults"; and Roberts and Yamane, *Religion in Sociological Perspective*, chap. 8.
6 Alawis: Goldsmith, "Alawi Diversity." Wahhabis: Commins, *Wahhabi Mission*, chap. 6 and pp. 207–9; and Lacroix, *Awakening Islam*, chap. 2. According to the last two sources, the number of sincere Wahhabis is much lower than the number

Notes to pages 171–76 319

of apparent Wahhabis. Besides, non-Wahhabi Sunnis generally comply with Wahhabi norms, preserving a façade of Sunni religious uniformity.

7 Bardakci, Freyberg-Inan, Giesel, and Leisse, *Religious Minorities in Turkey*, p. 99; Üçer, "Geleneksel Alevîlikte İbadet Hayatı," sect. 2.
8 Knysh, *Sufism*; Bos, *Mystic Regimes*, chap. 7; Weismann, *Naqshbandiyya*, chap. 9.
9 Hoffman, *Essentials of Ibādī Islam*, pp. 3–53.
10 Friedmann, *Prophecy Continuous*, chaps. 1, 8; Valentine, *Islam and the Ahmadiyya Jama'at*, chaps. 3, 11–12. Estimates vary widely because of persecution as well as restrictions on data collection.
11 On shifts in the global economic standing of Muslims, see works surveyed in Kuran, "Islam and Economic Performance." For comparative evidence and causal analysis focused on the Middle East, see Kuran, *Long Divergence*; and Rubin, *Rulers, Religion, and Riches*.
12 Kienle, *Ba'th v Ba'th*; Roy, *Politics of Chaos*, chap. 2; Hiro, *Cold War*; Monshipouri, *Middle East Politics*, chaps. 1–2, 4–5.
13 Ahmed, *What Is Islam?*, pp. 71–73.
14 Ahmed, *What Is Islam?*, pp. 57–71, 417–24; specific examples at pp. 62, 65.
15 Doniger, *On Hinduism*, pp. 10–17. The latter feature supported the rationalization that Hinduism was progressing toward Islam's unitary conception of God.
16 Prior to the Mughals, some Muslim rulers of India had destroyed temples and run massive conversion campaigns. Most Mughal emperors tolerated India's other religions, including Hinduism, the faith of the majority. For an overview, see Alam, "Competition and Co-existence." Jha, "Trade, Institutions," shows that commercial complementarities between Hindus and Muslims contributed to Mughal tolerance.
17 Byman, "Understanding the Islamic State"; Gerges, *Rise and Fall of Al-Qaeda*; Rashid, *Taliban*; Thurston, *Boko Haram*.
18 The figure for Europe excludes Turkey. Computed from Muslim population shares in Pew Research Center, "Mapping the Global Muslim Population" and 2020 population data in World DataBank.
19 Iannaccone, "Formal Model of Church and Sect," provides an alternative general system.
20 Beard, Ekelund, Ford, and Tollison, "Economics of Religious Schism," pp. 439–40.
21 Geographic separation alone does not amount to a schism. Moroccan and Iraqi Sunnis treat each other as members of the same Islamic denomination. Likewise, a split motivated by congestion concerns is not necessarily a schism. There is no schism if a congregation splits only because of growing membership.
22 Marcus, "Jewish Christianity"; Fredriksen, *When Christians Were Jews*.
23 Johnson, *History of Christianity*, pp. 1–43; Lieu, "Self-Definition"; Lupovitch, *Jews and Judaism*, pp. 44–48.
24 Chadwick, *East and West*, chaps. 24, 33; Cougar, *After Nine Hundred Years*.
25 What sparked the formal break is the "*filioque* controversy." See Siecienski, *Filioque*, chaps. 5–6.
26 For a survey of relevant research, see Becker, Pfaff, and Rubin, "Causes and Consequences." Cameron, *European Reformation*, narrates the key events. On the role of the Roman Catholic Church's monopolistic practices, see Ekelund, Hébert, and Tollison, "Economic Analysis of the Protestant Reformation"; and on that of printing, Rubin, *Rulers, Religion, and Riches*, chap. 6.

27 For pre-Lutheran opposition movements, see Deane, *History of Medieval Heresy and Inquisition*. Some of them were connected to struggles between the Church and scientists (White, *History of the Warfare of Science with Theology*). On Luther's rebellion, see MacCulloch, *Reformation*, chap. 3.
28 MacCulloch, *Reformation*, chaps. 3–12, surveys Protestant movements and reactions within Catholicism. On post-1517 transformations of Christian religious life and social relations, see Collinson, "Late Medieval Church."
29 Carvalho and Koyama, "Jewish Emancipation and Schism," sects. 1–2; and Lupovitch, *Jews and Judaism*, pp. 145–69, give broad accounts. See also Steinberg, "Reform Judaism"; and Lupovitch, "Between Orthodox Judaism and Neology."
30 Carvalho and Koyama, "Jewish Emancipation and Schism," sects. 3–4.
31 Shaw, *Jews of the Ottoman Empire*, pp. 128, 170–75; Zohar, "Religion: Rabbinic Tradition," pp. 66–78; Lewis, *Jews of Islam*, pp. 175–80.
32 Shipps, *Mormonism*.
33 Maloney, Civan, and Maloney, "Model of Religious Schism," pp. 443–45.
34 Wilson, *Europe's Tragedy*. The Catholic–Protestant conflict eased in 1521–66, when the Ottoman threat to Central Europe peaked. Ottoman expansionism thus allowed Protestants to spread and strengthen before the escalation of intra-Christian hostilities (Iyigun, *War, Peace, and Prosperity*, chap. 6).
35 For a documentary history, see Stormon, *Towards the Healing of Schism*. Quote at p. 127.
36 Siecienski, *Filioque*, chap. 10.
37 Pew Research Center, "Religious Beliefs." The survey was conducted in 2017.
38 Beard, Ekelund, Ford, and Tollison, "Economics of Religious Schism," pp. 441–46. My terminology differs, as do my illustrative cases.
39 This stylized example follows spatial voting theory, which posits that in multiparty elections voters pick the party closest to their own ideal. More complex variants account for intensity of voter preferences, heterogeneity in the likelihood of voting, and bargaining dynamics within parties, among other factors. See Iversen, "Logics of Electoral Politics"; and Ceron, "Politics of Fission."
40 Dawson, "Church–Sect–Cult."
41 An insightful Christian-centric analysis: Iannaccone, "Sacrifice and Stigma."
42 Sedgwick, "Sects in the Islamic World," p. 195. The remembrance has variants (Goldziher, "Dénombrement des Sectes Mohammétanes"; Eren, "İslam Toplumunda Ayrıştırıcı/Ötekileştirici Söylemin Oluşumunda İftirâk (73 Fırka) Hadisinin Rolü").
43 Khuri, *Imams and Emirs*, chap. 5.
44 Al-Anani, "Rethinking the Repression–Dissent Nexus." Another oddity of Khuri's classification pertains to the colonial period. Wherever the colonial power controlled Arab religious life, Islamic sects would have disappeared.
45 Öztürk and Sözeri, "Diyanet," pp. 632–33. On the Directorate's foreign activities, see also Bruce, *Governing Islam Abroad*, pp. 81–92, 186–212; and Öztürk, *Religion, Identity and Power*, chaps. 6–9.
46 Beard, Ekelund, Ford, and Tollison, "Economics of Religious Schism," pp. 441–46, identify both.
47 Haberkern, *Patron Saint*, pp. 1–103.
48 Beard, Ekelund, Ford, and Tollison, "Economics of Religious Schism," table 23.1. The figures are suggestive, though the authors do not check whether the differences hold up in controlled regressions.

49 Mathews, *Slavery and Methodism*.
50 Tooley, *Taking back the United Methodist Church*.
51 Watson, "Methodism Dividing"; Fowler, "Why Congregations Aren't Waiting."
52 Moghadam, *Modernizing Women*, chaps. 2–4, 6; Mernissi, *Beyond the Veil*; Kocamaner, "Regulating Family through Religion"; Stowasser, *Women in the Qur'an*, chap. 10; Bacık, *Contemporary Rationalist Islam in Turkey*, pp. 74–88.
53 Quran 4:11–12, 4:176.
54 Goldin, Katz, and Kuziemko, "Homecoming of American College Women"; Klesment and van Bavel, "Reversal of Gender Gap."
55 Using a global dataset for 1991–2006, Cooray and Potrafke, "Gender Inequality in Education," find that educational discrimination against girls is especially pronounced in Muslim-majority countries. In the same vein, McClendon, Hackett, Potančoková, Stonawski, and Skirbekk, "Women's Education," find wider gender gaps for Muslims than for other religious groups, except Hindus. Gender inequality in education has fallen over time, they report, and advances correlate positively with income.
56 Turkey equalized inheritance rights in 1926, but it justified the reform in secular terms, as integral to civilizational progress (Arat, "Women's Rights," pp. 237–38). In 1959, Tunisia increased actual female inheritance shares through a new law that favors members of the nuclear family of both sexes over other kin (Charrad, *State and Women's Rights*, pp. 228–31). Iraq equalized shares in 1959, then restored Islamic principles in 1963 (Efrati, "Negotiating Rights in Iraq"). For a Quran-based argument in favor of gender-neutral shares, see Öztürk, "Toplumsal Cinsiyet Meselesi," pp. 168–70, 178–80, 190–91. Hanafi and Tomeh, "Gender Equality in the Inheritance Debate in Tunisia," sects. 5–6, interprets the Tunisian debate over inheritance rights.
57 Gülalp, "Religion, Law and Politics," sects. 3–7; Shirazi, *Veil Unveiled*, chaps. 2, 4–5; Elsammak, Alwosaibi, Al-Howeish, and Alsaeed, "Vitamin D Deficiency"; Tanyeri-Erdemir, Çıtak, Weitzhofer, and Erdem, "Religion and Discrimination"; Bottoni, "Headscarf Issue."
58 Sullivan, "Eluding the Feminist"; Macleod, *Accommodating Protest*, chaps. 5–6; Göle, *Forbidden Modern*, chap. 4; Posner, *Sex and Reason*, pp. 158, 246–47; Carvalho, "Veiling."
59 Ahmed, *Women and Gender in Islam*.
60 Akşit, Şentürk, Küçükural, and Cengiz, *Türkiye'de Dindarlık*, pp. 232–79. A related survey, conducted in 2005 by Coşkun, *Sosyal Değişme ve Dini Normlar*, p. 189, finds that most Muslims favor the reinterpretation of Islam to suit modern life; though its sample is small, practicing Muslims are represented disproportionately.
61 Akşit, Şentürk, Küçükural, and Cengiz, *Türkiye'de Dindarlık*, p. 252; Arab, "Minaret of Light," p. 140. The latter source discusses alternatives based on modern technologies.
62 Akşit, Şentürk, Küçükural, and Cengiz, *Türkiye'de Dindarlık*, pp. 238–39, 246–47.
63 Aydar and Atalay, "Issue of Chanting the *Adhan*," pp. 46–49; Günaydın, "Din Hizmetlerinde Teknolojinin Kullanılması," pp. 32–35.
64 Akşit, Şentürk, Küçükural, and Cengiz, *Türkiye'de Dindarlık*, p. 256.
65 Azak, *Islam and Secularism in Turkey*, p. 53; Kara, *Cumhuriyet Türkiyesi'nde İslâm*, vol. 2, pp. 130–36, 150–53.

66 Kuru, *Islam, Authoritarianism, and Underdevelopment*, pp. 210–12; Wilson, "First Translations of the Qur'an," pp. 419–28; Saeed, *Qur'an*, chap. 7. Although doubts about the permissibility of translating the Quran extend to the Prophet's lifetime, renowned Islamic jurists authorized several translations into Persian around the 800s (Yahagi, "Introduction to Early Persian Qur'anic Translations").
67 Rahman, "Translating the Qur'an."
68 Ridge, "Effect of Religious Legislation on Religious Behavior."
69 For a survey of the main studies, see Kuran, "Islam and Economic Performance," pp. 1298–99; and Husain, Zafar, and Ullah, "Ramadan and Public Health." On mental disabilities specifically, see Almond, Mazumder, and van Ewijk, "*In Utero* Ramadan Exposure." Leiper, Molla, and Molla, "Effects on Health," survey the fast's health effects generally. They also identify associations with reduced drug compliance, increased irritability, more headaches, and lower cognitive function. Dehydration is a problem that healthy people can avoid through common-sense precautions. Pakkir Maideen, Jumale, and Balasubramaniam, "Adverse Health Effects," reports that health hazards are minor for fasters without preexisting conditions provided they have a balanced diet.
70 Zoethout, "Ritual Slaughter," pp. 652–63. Zuolo, "Equality among Animals," makes a case for giving equal protections to animals raised for ritual and nonritual slaughter.
71 Abdul Rahman, "Religion and Animal Welfare."
72 Öztaş, Hasanoğlu, Buzgan, Taşyaran, and Koçak Tufan, "Eid al-Adha Associated Infections."
73 This is the main theme of Kuru, *Islam, Authoritarianism, and Underdevelopment*, chap. 6; and Platteau, *Islam Instrumentalized*, chap. 6.
74 Hallaq, *Impossible State*, chap. 3.
75 Kutscher, "Politics of Virtual Fatwa Counseling," p. 34.
76 Human Rights Watch, *"They Are Not Our Brothers,"* pp. 29–33; Nielsen, *Deadly Clerics*, p. 109. Leaders of the Islamic Republic of Iran have issued analogous fatwas targeting non-Shiis (Mozafferi, *Fatwa*, chaps. 2, 4, 6).
77 Arora, "Egypt Bans Resurrection Ertugrul."
78 Agrama, "Ethics, Tradition, Authority," p. 5; Ramstedt, "Fatwa against Yoga"; Phillip, "Frosty Fatwa"; Tawfeek, "Egypt's Dar al-Iftaa"; Al-Kandari and Dashti, "Fatwa and the Internet," p. 137; Shabaan, "Is Keeping Dogs Allowed in Islam"; Blaydes, *State of Repression*, p. 240; Wilks, "Turkey's Religious Authority"; Akhter, "4 Reasons Why Muslims Should Not Celebrate the New Year."
79 Helfont, *Compulsion in Religion*, p. 43; Amanat, *Iran*, pp. 835–44.
80 O'Connor, "Will Facebook Survive?" On digital repression in Iran, see Yalcintas and Alizadeh, "Digital Protectionism."
81 Nielsen, "Changing Face of Islamic Authority," pp. 3–4; Bano, "Protector of the 'al-Wasatiyya' Islam," pp. 87–88; Öztürk, "Turkey's Diyanet," pp. 624–28.
82 Kutscher, "Politics of Virtual Fatwa Counseling"; Chawki, "Islam in the Digital Age"; Mohamed and Abdalla, "What Jihad Questions Do Muslims Ask?"; Marcotte, "Fatwa Online"; Bunt, *Hashtag Islam*, chap. 4. Online fatwa services include FatwaIslam.com (accessed 20 December 2021), islamonline.net (accessed 20 December 2021), islamway.net (accessed 20 December 2021), fetvameclisi.com (accessed 18 September 2020), askimam.org (accessed 20 December 2021),

Notes to pages 188–94   323

Fatwa-Online.com (accessed 30 November 2020), islamweb.net (accessed 9 December 2020), and muslimvillage.com (accessed 9 January 2021).
83 Nielsen, "Changing Face of Islamic Authority," pp. 5–7.
84 Kassem, "Social Media in Egypt"; Pan and Siegel, "How Saudi Crackdowns Fail to Silence Online Dissent"; Michaelsen, "Transforming Threats to Power"; Yeşil and Sözeri, "Online Surveillance in Turkey"; Fatafta, "Transnational Digital Repression."
85 Nielsen, "Changing Face of Islamic Authority," p. 5.
86 Nielsen, "Changing Face of Islamic Authority," p. 5. As of 20 December 2021, three of the seven most widely viewed fatwas on islamway.net concerned "watching pornographic films," "cleansing after masturbation," and "satisfying the desire of women." Jointly, these had been viewed 14.1 million times.
87 About 2.5 percent of all muftis on the Islamic internet are female (Nielsen, "Women's Authority," pp. 52–53).
88 Marcotte, "Fatwa Online," p. 238.
89 Caeiro, "Making of the Fatwa," pp. 85–89.
90 Organization of Islamic Cooperation, "Resolutions on Muslim Communities," p. 5.
91 Wani, "China's Xinjiang Policy," pp. 11–16.
92 Deference to political leaders is a justification ordinarily expressed in private by parties aghast at China's policies. On maintaining good relations with China, see Al-Sudairi, "China," pp. 18–19.
93 Deane, *History of Medieval Heresy*; Greengrass, *Christendom Destroyed*, chaps. 11–15.

CHAPTER 11

1 Computed from Pew Research Center, "Mapping the Global Muslim Population."
2 Frampton, *Muslim Brotherhood and the West*, pp. 11–34.
3 Gerges, *ISIS*, chap. 1.
4 Monahan, "Church Work"; Davidson, Schlangen, and D'Antonio, "Protestant and Catholic Perceptions."
5 Smith, *Wealth of Nations*, pp. 740–50. For elaborations, see McCleary and Barro, *Wealth of Religions*, chap. 2; and Iannaccone, "Consequences of Religious Market Structure."
6 Lupovitch, *Jews and Judaism*, pp. 138–69. Even during the emancipation of European Jews between 1750 and 1880, they faced discrimination in many domains.
7 Momen, *Shi'i Islam*, chaps. 8–9; Amir-Moezzi and Jambet, *What Is Shi'i Islam*, p. 36; Pew Research Center, "Mapping the Global Muslim Population."
8 Khomeini, *Islam and Revolution*, pp. 25–166.
9 Khalaji, "Iran's Regime of Religion," pp. 131–35; Amanat, *Iran*, pp. 781–89.
10 Khalaji, "Iran's Regime of Religion," pp. 133–34, 136–41; Amanat, "From *Ijtihad* to *Wilayat-i Faqih*," p. 187; Mohammadi, *Longevity of Clerical Business as Usual*, pp. 255–56.
11 Algar, *Imam Khomeini*, pp. 7–9.
12 Khalaji, "Iran's Regime of Religion," p. 132; Amanat, "From *Ijtihad* to *Wilayat-i Faqih*," p. 181.

13 Amanat, "From *Ijtihad* to *Wilayat-i Faqih*," pp. 180–87; Moaddel, "Shi'i Ulama and the State," pp. 533–39.
14 Arjomand, *After Khomeini*, chaps. 2–5, 8–9.
15 Arjomand, "Shari'a and Constitution"; Amanat, "From *Ijtihad* to *Wilayat-i Faqih*," pp. 193–96.
16 Modern Shiism has had no schism of comparable global impact. But the 1900s saw the emergence of many sects and subsects of Twelver Shiism, often around a sheikh's teachings. Iran-based Sufi sects have also fractured. See Bos, *Mystic Regimes*, chaps. 2–3.
17 Apolitical Jordanian Salafism: Wagemakers, *Salafism in Jordan*, chaps. 2–4. Evolution of Ennahda's politics: Wolf, *Political Islam in Tunisia*, chap. 6. Categorizations of Salafism: Voll, "Fundamentalism in the Sunni Arab World"; Haykel, "On the Nature of Salafi Thought and Action."
18 Lacroix, "Between Revolution and Apoliticism"; Lauzière, *Making of Salafism*, pp. 1–94; Algar, *Wahhabism*; Kamolnick, "Egyptian Islamic Group"; Nielsen, *Deadly Clerics*, chaps. 4–6.
19 Phillips, *Battle for Syria*, chaps. 5–9; Hughes, "Syria and the Perils of Proxy Warfare"; Cragin, "Tactical Partnerships"; Burweila and Nomikos. "Libya and the New Axis."
20 Wickham, *Muslim Brotherhood*, chaps. 2, 5; Zahid, *Muslim Brotherhood*, chaps. 3–5.
21 Al-Anani, "Rethinking the Repression–Dissent Nexus," pp. 1333–36.
22 Commins, *Wahhabi Mission*; DeLong-Bas, *Wahhabi Islam*, chaps. 1, 6.
23 Kurzman, *Liberal Islam*, compiles the most influential writings of these and other liberal modernists. For critical surveys, see also Kersten, *Contemporary Thought*, chaps. 5–7. Abir, *Saudi Arabia*, pp. 186–89, explores liberal trends in Saudi Arabia.
24 Abu Zayd, *Critique of Religious Discourse*, chaps. 2–3. For accounts of Abu Zayd's goals and methods, see Kersten, "Nasr Hamid Abu Zayd," pp. 4–21; and Tamer, "Nasr Hamid Abu Zayd."
25 Bacık, *Contemporary Rationalist Islam in Turkey*, chaps. 1–3. All but one of the writers whose works Bacık surveys remain active. They are Hüseyin Atay, Yaşar Nuri Öztürk (1951–2016), Ömer Özsoy, Mehmet Hayri Kırbaşoğlu, İlhami Güler, Recep İhsan Eliaçık, Mustafa Öztürk, İsrafil Balcı, and Mehmet Azimli.
26 Abbas, "Between Western Academia and Pakistan," pp. 748–68.
27 Wild, "Sadik Jalal Al-Azm," p. 4. Al-Azm's essay collections include *Is Islam Secularizable?* and *On Fundamentalisms*.
28 Dahlén, *Islamic Law and Modernity*, chaps. 6–7; Ghamari-Tabrizi, "Abdolkarim Soroush."
29 On the two figures, see Cammett, Diwan, Richards, and Waterbury, *Political Economy of the Middle East*, chap. 2; and Kuran, "Islam and Economic Performance," table 1. The nonagricultural share of the labor force was less than 20 percent as late as World War I (Issawi, *Economic History*, p. 118) and the urbanization rate was below 10 percent in 1800 (Bosker, Buringh, and van Zanden, "From Baghdad to London," fig. 3). World Bank data for 2019 yield the corresponding shares as 79.8 percent and 63.7 percent, respectively.
30 Saeed, "Trends in Contemporary Islam," subdivides liberal Muslims into four groups: "secular liberals," "cultural nominalists," "classical modernists," and "progressive ijtihadis."

31 Machlis, "Reevaluating Sectarianism," gives examples of Iraqi and Syrian blends. They include composites of spiritualism and orthodoxy, ecumenism and exclusivism, and doctrinal rigidity and practical permissiveness.
32 On this poem's origins, see Şafak, "Mevlânâ'ya Atfedilen 'Yine Gel...' Rubâîsine Dair." On the teachings of Rumi and the Sufi branch he founded, see Lewis, *Rumi*, chaps. 9–10.
33 Karamustafa, *Sufism*, chaps. 1, 6; Trimingham, *Sufi Orders*, chaps. 1, 8.
34 Fakhry, *History of Islamic Philosophy*, p. 40.
35 Muedini, *Sponsoring Sufism*, chaps. 1–3; Ladjal and Bensaid, "Sufism and Politics"; Bos, *Mystic Regimes*, chap. 4. Saudi Arabia is among the places where Sufis have faced the harshest persecution (Algar, *Wahhabism*, pp. 36–37, 54–56). The state condemns them as apostates, and it has allowed the destruction of their lodges. Even there, though, they are permitted to congregate in private houses (Sedgwick, "Saudi Sufis"). Sirriyeh, *Sufis and Anti-Sufis*, chap. 6, surveys pro- and anti-Sufi political movements.
36 Cesari, *Why the West Fears Islam*; Duderija and Rane, *Islam and Muslims in the West*, chap. 3. On Muslims in the United States specifically, see Corbett, *Making Moderate Islam*; Ba-Yunus and Kone, *Muslims in the United States*, chaps. 4–5; and Hammer, *American Muslim Women*, chaps. 2–6. On Muslims of Western Europe, see Göle, *Daily Lives of Muslims*; Hellyer, *Muslims of Europe*; Maréchal, "Mosques, Organisations and Leadership"; Allievi, "Relations and Negotiations"; and Adraoui, "Salafism in France."
37 Duderija, "Critical-Progressive Muslim Thought," pp. 76–78; Allievi, "Relations and Negotiations," pp. 334–38.
38 Geaves, "Sufism in the UK," pp. 457–58; Sedgwick, *Western Sufism*, pp. 222, 230–33; www.zaytuna.edu; www.minaret.org; Klausen, *Islamic Challenge*, p. 187.
39 Aritonang and Steenbrink, *History of Christianity in Indonesia*, pp. 141–45, 639–43, 711–24.
40 Menchik, *Islam and Democracy in Indonesia*, pp. 36–38, 48–51, 57–58.
41 Bush, *Nahdlatul Ulama*, chap. 3.
42 Bush, *Nahdlatul Ulama*, pp. 118–25.
43 Menchik, *Islam and Democracy in Indonesia*, pp. 73–79, 86.
44 Menchik, *Islam and Democracy in Indonesia*, pp. 116–21; Fealy and McGregor, "Nahdlatul Ulama and Killings." Estimates of the victim count run to 3 million.
45 Mietzner and Muhtadi, "Myth of Pluralism," pp. 66–78; Kayane, "Understanding Sunni–Shi'a Sectarianism"; Menchik, *Islam and Democracy in Indonesia*, pp. 121–22.
46 Gerges, *ISIS*; Ali, "Rise and Fall of Islamic State."
47 Rahman, "Principle of *Shura*"; Shafiq, "Role and Place of Shura"; Shavit, "Is Shura a Muslim Form of Democracy."
48 Lewis, "Some Observations," pp. 53–54.
49 Stroumsa, *Freethinkers in Medieval Islam*, presents the views of two Abbasid polymaths, Ibn al-Rawandi (815–60) and Abu Bakr al-Razi (865–925). For broader surveys of unorthodox views in premodern Islam, see Al-Azmeh, "Abbasid Culture," pp. 76–88; and Kuru, *Islam, Authoritarianism, and Underdevelopment*, pp. 75–80, 134–38, 147–49.
50 Hallaq, *Sharī'a*, pp. 49–51, 110–13; Weiss, "Interpretation in Islamic Law."
51 Strauss, *Persecution and the Art of Writing*; Kuran, *Private Truths, Public Lies*, pp. 337–39.

52 Saeed and Saeed, *Freedom of Religion*, pp. 44–48.
53 Saeed and Saeed, *Freedom of Religion*, chap. 1.
54 Zuckerman, "Gender Regulation"; Campbell-Reed, *Anatomy of a Schism*; Byrne, *Other Catholics*.
55 Arendt, *Origins of Totalitarianism*, chaps. 2–4; Volkov, *Germans, Jews*, chaps. 4–7.
56 Kuru, *Islam, Authoritarianism, and Development*, pp. 3–6, 9–12, 93–101.
57 On the challenges of field work in the Middle East, see Clark, "Field Research Methods." The problems that Clark discusses are common to all authoritarian settings. Gervais and Najle, "How Many Atheists," show that stigmatized religious preferences are difficult to measure even in democratic societies.
58 Khatiri, "Iran's Revolution Continues."
59 Bucar, *Pious Fashion*, chap. 1.
60 On campaigns to constrain the clergy, see Sadri, "Sacral Defense of Secularism"; and Abdolmohammadi and Cama, *Contemporary Domestic and Foreign Policies of Iran*, chap. 5.
61 In the World Values Survey (Wave 6, 2010–14), 14.6 percent of the surveyed Middle Eastern population self-identified as nonreligious and 0.6 percent as atheist. Coverage: Bahrain, Algeria, Iraq, Jordan, Kuwait, Lebanon, Libya, Morocco, Qatar, Tunisia, Turkey, and Yemen.
62 Kuran, *Long Divergence*, pp. 161–64, 251–53; Ağır and Artunç, "Set and Forget?" pp. 723–36; Artunç, "Religious Minorities and Firm Ownership."
63 On this process, see Kuran, *Private Truths, Public Lies*, chaps. 15–17.

CHAPTER 12

1 Perry Anderson, *Lineages of Absolutist State*, pp. 361–94, characterizes the "House of Islam" as a despotism whose sultan had unlimited rights to all wealth, except waqfs. Finer, *History of Government*, vol. 2, pp. 688–94 and 718–21, points to the caliph's unchecked personal power and to his subjects' duty to obey him even when they considered him wrong. Lisa Anderson, "State in Middle East," points to the centralized governance of the region's premodern empires. Darling, *History of Social Justice*, observes that Middle Eastern empires legitimized themselves through the "circle of justice," which involved a strong state perceived as just. Focusing on the Ottoman Empire, Heper, "Ottoman Legacy," holds that in the absence of civil society all power coalesced at the center. According to Wilber, *Iran*, pp. 74–75, under Islamic rule Iran's monarchs governed as the shadow of God on earth.
2 Although they all had assemblies that advised the ruler, their members were appointed and dismissed at will. See Peacock, *Great Seljuk Empire*, chap. 5; İnalcık, *Ottoman Empire*, chap. 12; Levanoni, "Mamluk Conception of the Sultanate"; and Savory, "Safavid Administrative System." On the beginnings of representative assemblies, see Yaycıoğlu, *Partners of Empire*, pp. 117–56, 203–47; Shaw, "Central Legislative Councils"; Marsot, *Egypt's Liberal Experiment*, chap. 2; and Afary, "Civil Liberties."
3 General government final consumption expenditure is 14.4 percent in the Middle East, as against 14.2 percent in the world as a whole (population-weighted averages for 2019, based on data at https://data.worldbank.org/indicator/NE.CON.GOVT.ZS
4 Computed from data at https://datacatalog.worldbank.org. The figures are the latest, as of 2018.

5 Kuran and Rubin, "Financial Power of the Powerless"; Kuran and Lustig, "Judicial Biases."
6 Two works challenge this characterization of passivity: Brummett, *Ottoman Seapower*; and Casale, *Ottoman Age of Exploration*. Early in the explorations, it was rational, they say, for Ottoman rulers to refrain from trying to circumnavigate Africa and reach Asia by sailing west. Neither author establishes, though, that the Ottomans benefited from keeping out of the explorations after the discovery of a new world with immense resources. Until the 1730s, Iran's naval power was too weak even for a major presence in the Persian Gulf (Axworthy, "Nader Shah and Persian Naval Expansion").
7 Banani, *Modernization of Iran*, chaps. 5–7; Findley, *Bureaucratic Reform*, chaps. 3–4; Brown, *Tunisia of Ahmad Bey*, chaps. 6–9; Tignor, *Modernization and British Colonial Rule in Egypt*, chaps. 4–7, 10–12; Kuran, *Long Divergence*, pp. 161–64, 251–53, 298–301.
8 The region's pagan, Jewish, and Christian tribes practiced tithing and almsgiving. See Rosenthal, "Sedaka, Charity," pp. 411–14, 423–30; Watt, *Muhammad at Mecca*, pp. 165–69; and Hurgronje, "Zakāt," pp. 152–53.
9 On the Quran's economic vocabulary and comparative counts of specific usages, see Kuran, "Modern Islam and the Economy," pp. 493–94.
10 For example, 2:177, 2:215, 4:8, 9:60, 24:22. "God's servants" is a translation for *fī sabīlilāh*, literally, "in the cause of Allah."
11 Judaism had formalized this process through the forgiveness of debts every fiftieth year (Leviticus 25:10). For a history, see Zuckermann, *Treatise on the Sabbatical Cycle*.
12 Løkkegaard, "Ghanīma." Quran, 8:1 specifies that booty belongs to "Allah and his Apostle," which implies that the state decided its apportionment. In pre-Islamic Arabia, tribes had divided the spoils of war according to rules that allocated at most a quarter to the leader. In line with these rules, during the Islamic wars of conquest Muslim soldiers were allowed to reserve shares for themselves.
13 Cahen, "Bayt al-Māl, History"; Coulson, "Bayt al-Māl"; Belhaj, "Bayt al-Māl."
14 On tradeoffs between financing government and private incentives to produce, see Mirrlees, "Theory of Optimal Taxation"; and Besley and Ghatak, "Property Rights." Olson, "Dictatorship, Democracy, and Development," pp. 568–73, points to the economic advantages of predictable taxation.
15 For a broader list and variations among schools of law, see Zysow, "Zakāt," pp. 410–14. Al-Māwardi, *Ordinances of Government*, pp. 127–39, provides an eleventh-century account.
16 Webber and Wildavsky, *History of Taxation*, pp. 68–73; Wittfogel, *Oriental Despotism*, pp. 67–72.
17 England: Holmes, *Later Middle Ages*, pp. 77–78. Italy: Webber and Wildavsky, *History of Taxation*, pp. 198–200.
18 Wittfogel, *Oriental Despotism*, pp. 39–40; Mendelsohn, "Corvée Labor"; Henkelman and Kleber, "Babylonian Workers," pp. 163–66. Slaves were also used to build such structures.
19 Millar, "Condemnation to Hard Labour," pp. 130–45; Scheidel, "Slavery and Forced Labour."
20 Transactions undertaken specifically to avoid zakat, such as transferring assets to another person right before the tax is due, do not void the legal duty (Askari, Cummings, and Glover, *Taxation and Tax Policies*, p. 81).

21 Crone, *Meccan Trade*; Bonner, "Poverty and Charity," p. 25.
22 Løkkegaard, *Islamic Taxation*; Cahen, "Régime des Impôts"; Sijpesteijn, *Shaping a Muslim State*, pt. 2, texts 2–5, 8, 21–23, 35–36; Burns, *Medieval Colonialism*, chap. 6.
23 Stasavage, *Decline and Rise*, pp. 204–6.
24 Stasavage, *Decline and Rise*, chaps. 3, 5, 7, 9.
25 Illiteracy can pose a complementary problem. Illiterates cannot browse the Quran on their own. Even for literate readers, understanding verses can be challenging without competency in classical Arabic.
26 For instance, Quran 9:34–35, 17:26–29, 102.
27 Quran 2:261, 59:9. Verse 2:261 says that "those who give their wealth for the cause of Allah" will reap rewards; and verse 59:9 that "those who preserve themselves from their own greed shall surely prosper." Neither requires resource sharing.
28 Hurgronje, "Zakāt," pp. 157–60.
29 Olson, *Logic of Collective Action*, chap. 2.
30 See Dawood's introduction to his translation of the Quran, *The Koran*, pp. 9–14; and Pearson, "Al-Ḳurʾān," pp. 414–19.
31 North and Weingast, "Constitutions and Commitment," draw connections between constraints on government takings and government capacity to borrow. Refinements: Cox, "Was the Glorious Revolution a Constitutional Watershed?"; Stasavage, "Credible Commitment."
32 Mattson, "Status-Based Definitions of Need," pp. 33–40.
33 Al-Māwardi, *Ordinances of Government*, pp. 138–39.
34 Duri, *Early Islamic Institutions*, pp. 107–42; Løkkegaard, *Islamic Taxation*, chaps. 3, 7; Dennett, *Conversion*, pp. 12–13, chaps. 2–6.
35 Burns, *Medieval Colonialism*, chap. 6; Zysow, "Zakāt," p. 410.
36 Sabra, *Poverty and Charity*, pp. 39–40. Early in their rule, the Mamluks made two exceptions. They collected zakat from two wealthy communities: the Karimis, who were long-distance traders, and certain pastoralists in Libya.
37 Greif, *Institutions*, chap. 3; Platteau, *Institutions*, chap. 6.
38 Bravmann, "Surplus of Property"; Schacht, "Zakāt," pp. 1202–4. For the logic of redistribution norms in primitive societies and numerous analogous cases, see Posner, *Economics of Justice*, chap. 6; Platteau, *Islam Instrumentalized*, chap. 5; Henrich and Henrich, *Why Humans Cooperate*; and Gaus, "Egalitarian Species."
39 Of the thirty-two Quran verses that mention zakat, twenty warn believers that punishment awaits evaders. Quran chronologists consider sixteen of these to be from the Medina period.
40 Quran 9:34–35. Hoarding is condemned also in chapters that Quran chronologists date to the Meccan period: 70:15–18, 104:1–4.
41 The verse is 9:60. Its usage of sadaqa came to be interpreted as referring to zakat while maintaining the meaning of voluntary almsgiving in other verses. See Benthall, "Financial Worship," pp. 29–31.
42 North, Wallis, and Weingast, *Violence and Social Orders*, pp. 18–21; Finer, *History of Government*, vol. 1, pp. 34–58.
43 Quran: 9:98. All chronologies of the Quran consider chapter 9 to be among the latest. See Pearson, "Al-Ḳurʾān," pp. 414–19.
44 Ibrahim, *Merchant Capital*, p. 140; Shaban, *Islamic History*, vol. 1, pp. 118–19.

Notes to pages 221–24

45 The available historical sources preclude identifying zakat's evolution with confidence. The full range of controversies are unknown. Clearly, though, regimes based outside of Arabia tended to exempt from regular taxation any assets redefined as "hidden." Hence, Uthman may have presided over a radical reinterpretation with the support of political elites.
46 Zysow, "Zakāt," p. 412.
47 Al-Māwardi, *Ordinances of Government*, pp. 128–35, points to many other variations in interpretations of zakat obligations.
48 Zysow, "Zakāt," pp. 406–7, 410.
49 Quran 9:34.
50 On Christian asceticism, see Delumeau, *Sin and Fear*, chap. 16.
51 These include the customs duty (generally *maks*), the market tax (*ḍarībat al-aswāq*), the building tax (*'arṣah*) and agricultural levies (*'ushr* or *kharāj*, depending on the payer's religion), taxes on houses (*hilālī*), and brokerage charges on the sale of sheep (*niṣf al-samsara*). See Björkman, "Maks"; Grohmann, "'Ushr"; Cahen, "Kharādj"; and Duri, *Early Islamic Institutions*, chap. 2.
52 Abu Yusuf, *Taxation in Islam*, pp. 134–40. For supportive evidence, see Sijpesteijn, *Shaping a Muslim State*, pp. 181–99 and pt. 2.
53 Abu Yusuf starts his treatise by urging the caliph to collect and distribute "sadaqa" according to "traditions from the Prophet and his successors." State-administered collection and distribution would not have to be "introduced" if not previously abandoned.
54 Webber and Wildavsky, *History of Taxation*, p. 74.
55 Some examples: Mamluk Cairo, 1315, 12.5 percent (Lapidus, "Grain Economy," p. 8); Mamluk Syria and Upper Egypt, 1250–1517, 20–30 percent (Tsugitaka, "Fiscal Administration in Syria," pp. 23–24); Iran's Qajar period, 1785–1925, 10–35 percent (Floor, *Fiscal History of Iran*, pp. 320–27); Ottoman Empire, 1601–1700, 10–40 percent (Coşgel, "Taxes, Efficiency, and Redistribution," p. 338).
56 Zysow, "Zakāt," p. 413.
57 None of the three major works focused on the post-1800 period lists zakat in its index. See Owen, *Middle East*; Issawi, *Economic History*; and Owen and Pamuk, *History of Middle East Economies*.
58 Zysow, "Zakāt," p. 409.
59 Blaydes, Grimmer, and McQueen, "Mirrors for Princes."
60 A similar point is made by Rahman, "Islam and Problem of Economic Justice," p. 33.
61 The figure is for February 2021. The averaged countries are Egypt, Iran, Turkey, Iraq, and Saudi Arabia.
62 Mattson, "Status-Based Definitions of Need," pp. 32–33.
63 Mattson, "Status-Based Definitions of Need," pp. 41–44.
64 Other beneficiary categories also sowed conflict. Rich "travelers" could make a case for having the community cover their expenses. Building a bridge could be portrayed as being a devout "servant of God." Twelver Shiis hold that zakat revenue can finance any activity in the community's common interest (Tabātabā'i, *Kharāj in Islamic Law*, pp. 25–27).
65 Webber and Wildavsky, *History of Taxation*, pp. 44–45.

66 Zysow, "Zakāt," pp. 406–9.
67 Mattson, "Status-Based Definitions of Need," p. 39. These jurists included Malik ibn Anas (711–96), Abu Ubayd (770–838), and Ahmad ibn Hanbal (780–855).
68 Ekelund, Tollison, Anderson, Hébert, and Davidson, *Sacred Trust*, chap. 2; Constable, *Monastic Tithes*.
69 Oran and Rashid, "Fiscal Policy in Early Islam," pp. 94–96.
70 Azam, *Pakistan and Islamic Economics*, p. 97.
71 In focusing on Iraq's early centuries, Løkkegaard, *Islamic Taxation*, stresses this point. His work mentions zakat just seven times, which accords with its loss of significance. Six of these references define zakat, or report that rulers preferred other taxes, or hint at zakat evasion.
72 Rodinson, *Islam and Capitalism*, pp. 25–26; Hurgronje, "Zakāt," pp. 161–62; Ibrahim, *Merchant Capital*, pp. 145–48.
73 Al-Ghazali, *Revival of the Religious Sciences*, pp. 34–35.
74 Sabra, *Poverty and Charity*, chaps. 3–4; Lev, *Charity, Endowments*, pp. 53–60; Singer, "Giving Practices in Islamic Societies"; Ahmed, *Role of Zakāh and Awqāf*, chaps. 2, 4–5; Abdul Razak, "*Zakat* and *Waqf*."
75 Of Istanbul's waqfs founded between 1453 and 1923, 37.6 percent named a religious service among their primary functions, 8 percent education, and 6.1 percent the poor (Adıgüzel and Kuran, "Inequality-Preserving Benevolence"). For complementary evidence, see Hoexter, "Charity, the Poor," pp. 150–51; and Ginio, "Living on the Margins," pp. 167–71. Ginio shows that of the eighty-nine new waqfs registered in Salonica between 1694 and 1768, fifty-eight delivered resources directly to clerics; the beneficiaries were "the poor" in twenty-three cases, with the category defined expansively to include clerics.
76 Marcus, "Poverty and Poor Relief," p. 171.
77 Marcus, "Poverty and Poor Relief," especially pp. 172, 174.
78 Cohen, "Feeding the Poor"; Sabra, *Poverty and Charity*, chaps. 3, 7; Hoexter, "Charity, the Poor"; Özbek, "'Beggars' and 'Vagrants'"; Cansunar, "Distributional Consequences of Philanthropic Contributions"; Ginio, "Living on the Margins." The patterns in question are observed also in various modern places, for example, Pahlavi Iran (Jabbari, "Economic Factors"), postcolonial Cairo (Sabry, "How Poverty Is Underestimated"), and post-Ottoman Istanbul (Yılmaz, "Entrapped in Multidimensional Exclusion").
79 Cansunar and Kuran, "Economic Harbingers of Political Modernization."
80 Zysow, "Zakāt," p. 418. Sometimes Quran 87:14 is cited in support of the practice.
81 The literature contains a few references to councils used to collect or distribute zakat. They include a "sadaqa council" that operated during the caliphate of Hisham ibn Abd al-Malik (reigned 724–43; see Duri, *Early Islamic Institutions*, pp. 168, 177). The paucity of references to such official agencies point to their rarity and limited economic impact. Works on Islam's initial two centuries also give evidence of instructions to collect sadaqa or zakat. Sijpesteijn, *Shaping a Muslim State*, reproduces an example from Egypt around 730–50 (text 8). She also reports that zakat collectors faced massive resistance (p. 182).
82 Bashear, "On the Origins of Zakāt," pp. 84–85; Rosenthal, "Sedaka, Charity," pp. 421–23; Ibrahim, *Merchant Capital*, pp. 19, 76; Watt, *Muhammad at Mecca*, pp. 165–69; Hurgronje, "Zakāt," pp. 152–53.

83 Benthall, "Financial Worship," pp. 29–30; Hurgronje, "Zakāt," p. 150; Stillman, "Charity," pp. 106–7.
84 Hurgronje, "Zakāt," p. 150. Classical Islamic teachings emphasize that to fulfill one's zakat duty it is not enough to pay dues. To win divine favor, one must donate without expecting a return, solely out of pious generosity. According to a common interpretation of this teaching, paying zakat was its own reward. Provided the donor's intention (*niyya*) was good, the donation's effects were immaterial.
85 Marcus, "Poverty and Poor Relief," pp. 175–77; Ginio, "Living on the Margins," pp. 169–70; Sabra, *Poverty and Charity*, pp. 50–51.
86 Certain early Muslim writers sought to soothe the poor also by proposing that they would be the "first to enter heaven." See Bonner, "Definitions of Poverty," pp. 341–43.
87 Ybarra, "*Zakât* in Muslim Society"; Benthall, "Financial Worship," p. 35; Stillman, "Charity," p. 115.
88 Commins, *Islamic Reform*, pp. 87–88.
89 Quran verses that treat freeing slaves as inherently meritorious: 24:33, 90:13.
90 Slavery appears in twenty-nine verses of the Quran. Some deal with the legal status of slaves, others with master–slave relations: 2:178, 2:221, 4:3, 4:29–30, 12:30, 16:75, 33:50, 33:55.
91 Quran 4:92, 5:89, 58:3.
92 Lewis, *Race and Slavery*; Ennaji, *Slavery, the State, and Islam*. For a comparison between Islam's positions on slavery and those of earlier monotheisms, see Goldenberg, *Curse of Ham*.
93 Muslim-majority states started to outlaw slavery in the late 1800s. The last to do so was the Islamic Republic of Mauritania, in 1981. But slavery lives on in certain areas, including parts of Saudi Arabia, Sudan, and Sub-Saharan Africa. See Clarence-Smith, *Islam and the Abolition of Slavery*.

CHAPTER 13

1 Ashtor, *Social and Economic History of the Near East*, pp. 78–114; Abu-Lughod, *Before European Hegemony*, chaps. 5–10; Chaudhuri, *Trade and Civilization in the Indian Ocean*, chap. 2; Constable, *Trade and Traders in Muslim Spain*; Goitein, *Mediterranean Society*, vol. 1; Kuran, *Long Divergence*, chap. 3; Blaydes and Paik, "Muslim Trade."
2 Puga and Trefler, "International Trade," pp. 759–67.
3 Jha, "Financial Asset Holdings."
4 Olson, *Logic of Collective Action*, chap. 6; North, Wallis, and Weingast, *Violence and Social Orders*, sects. 2.4, 4.9.
5 Westbrook, "Character of Ancient Near Eastern Law." On later developments with a focus on the West, see Fukuyama, *Origins of Political Order*, chaps. 17–21; and Berman, *Law and Revolution*, chaps. 8–14. On legal evolution in the Islamic Middle East, see Hallaq, *Sharī'a*, pp. 36–55; and Brown, *Rule of Law in the Arab World*.
6 North, *Structure and Change*, chaps. 1–4; Scott, *Seeing Like a State*, chaps. 1–5.
7 Kuran, *Long Divergence*, chap. 3. On geographic differences, see Harris, *Going the Distance*, chaps. 3–8.

8 A full-blown corporation has seven attributes, observes Harris, *Going the Distance*, pp. 251–52: "(1) a separate legal personality, which provides longevity and corporate ownership of property; (2) a collective decision-making mechanism which includes delegated centralized management; (3) joint-stock equity finance; (4) lock-in of the investment; (5) transferability of the interest (decision-making and profits) in the corporation; (6) protection from expropriation by the ruler/state; and (7) asset partitioning, which includes two elements – protection of private assets of shareholders from creditors of the corporation and protection of corporate assets from the creditors of shareholders." No European company had the last attribute until at least the 1700s. The term "business corporation" is used here as a shorthand for a range of businesses that have at least the first three attributes.
9 Harris, *Going the Distance*, chaps. 9–12; Lamoreaux and Rosenthal, "Legal Regime," sect. 5.
10 Harris, *Going the Distance*, chap. 10.
11 De Roover, *Rise and Decline of the Medici Bank*; Hunt and Murray, *History of Business in Medieval Europe*, chaps. 5, 8; Padgett, "Emergence of Corporate Merchant-Banks."
12 Kuran, *Long Divergence*, chap. 8; Rubin, "Institutions, the Rise of Commerce"; Rafeq, "Craft Organization"; Jennings, "Loans and Credit"; Alsabagh, "Before Banks," chaps. 2–3.
13 Clay, "Origins of Modern Banking in the Levant"; Gcyikdağı, *Foreign Investment in the Ottoman Empire*, pp. 100–105; Landes, *Bankers and Pashas*, pp. 67–68, 138–43, 250–51.
14 Jones, *Imperial Bank of Iran*.
15 Rubin, "Bills of Exchange."
16 Kindleberger, *Financial History*, pp. 35–41; Munro, "Medieval Origins of the Financial Revolution"; Kohn, "Money, Trade, and Payments."
17 Business empires were known, but they did not survive the founder's death. Hanna, *Making Big Money in 1600*, provides an example. See also Boogert, "Provocative Wealth," p. 235. Studies on premodern Middle Eastern merchants give no evidence of enterprise continuity across generations (Khoury, "Merchants and Trade"; Abdullah, *Merchants, Mamluks*, chap. 4; Gedikli, *Osmanlı Şirket Kültürü*, chaps. 3, 5). Most of the business families that retained prominence for several generations had European connections (Onley, "Transnational Merchant Families"). The main exception consists of state-connected families that traded across the Indian Ocean before the arrival of the Portuguese. But not even they formed perpetual commercial organizations (Um, *Merchant Houses of Mocha*, pp. 28–35, 78–95; Ashtor, "Kārimī Merchants").
18 Inegalitarian inheritance systems such as primogeniture promoted organizational development through one other channel. Disfavored children sought business opportunities outside the family, which generated trust-building interactions with strangers. Generalized trust rose over time, facilitating both economic modernization and political liberalization (Broms and Kokkonen, "Inheritance Regimes").
19 Kuran, *Long Divergence*, chaps. 2–13.
20 Adıgüzel and Kuran, "Inequality-Preserving Benevolence."
21 On entity shielding and its critical role in economic modernization, see Hansmann, Kraakman, and Squire, "Law and the Rise of the Firm," pp. 1337–43.

22 Executed: Osman II (1622). Deposed: Mehmet IV (1687), Mustafa II (1703), Ahmet III (1730), Selim III (1807).
23 Mandaville, "Usurious Piety"; Kuran, *Long Divergence*, pp. 158–64; Adıgüzel and Kuran, "Inequality-Preserving Benevolence."
24 Cansunar and Kuran, "Economic Harbingers of Political Modernization."
25 Gelderblom, *Cities of Commerce*, chap. 3; Michie, *London Stock Exchange*.
26 London: Todd, "Some Aspects of Joint Stock Companies," sect. 5; Maltby, "UK Joint Stock Companies." Amsterdam: Gelderblom, De Jong, and Jonker, "Formative Years of the Modern Corporation," pp. 1069–70; Zeff, van der Wel, and Camfferman, *Company Financial Reporting*, chap. 2.
27 The earliest was the stock exchange of Istanbul, founded in 1866 (Al and Akar, *Galata Borsası*). It was followed by Alexandria in 1899 and Cairo in 1903 (Raafat, *Egyptian Bourse*, pp. 6–12). Other Arab exchanges came later: Saudi Arabia, 1935 (Azzam, *Emerging Arab Capital Markets*, chap. 6), Beirut, 1945 (Pringuey, *Bourse de Beyrouth*, pp. 11–61), Tehran, 1968 (Dadkhah, "Iran and the Global Finance Markets"), Tunis, 1969 (Calamanti, "Tunis Stock Exchange," sect. 2), Baghdad, 1992 (Kaehler, Weber, and Aref, "Iraqi Stock Market," p. 152).
28 Kuran, *Long Divergence*, chap. 10; Artunç, "Price of Legal Institutions"; Artunç, "Religious Minorities and Firm Ownership"; Alff, "Levantine Joint-Stock Companies"; Boogert, "Ottoman Brokers"; Issawi, "Transformation of the Economic Position of *Millets*"; Turgay, "Trade and Merchants in Trabzon"; Rejwan, *Last Jews of Baghdad*, chap. 1; Der Matossian, "Armenian Commercial Houses"; Moutafidou, "Greek Merchant Families"; Abdulhaq, *Jewish and Greek Communities*, chaps. 2–4. Intercommunal differences were not uniform across space. Moreover, mass poverty existed in all sectarian groups until the early 1900s, even as many non-Muslim communities pulled ahead of Muslims generally.
29 Findley, "Acid Test of Ottomanism"; Kırmızı, "Osmanlı Bürokrasisinde Gayrimüslim İstihdamı," sect. 5; Ortaylı, "Greeks and Ottoman Administration." Between 1939 and 1909, 7 of the 282 Ottoman officials who held the empire's highest non-royal honorific title, pasha, were non-Muslim (Bouquet, *Pachas du Sultan*, pp. 471–91). Late and post-Ottoman Iraq: Simon, "Iraq," pp. 352–55. Nineteenth-century Egypt: Toledano, "Social and Economic Change," pp. 264, 267. Nineteenth-century Iran, Algar, "Religious Forces," p. 730. Nineteenth-century Tunisia: Brown, *Tunisia of Ahmad Bey*, p. 92.
30 Of the 139 deputies in the Ottoman parliament of 1876, 48 were non-Muslim (Devereux, *First Ottoman Constitutional Period*, p. 144), as were 40 of the 281 deputies in that of 1908 (Kansu, *Politics in Post-Revolutionary Turkey*, pp. 443–97). The 120 deputies in Iran's second parliament of 1909–11 included four non-Muslims (Oberling, "Role of Religious Minorities in the Persian Revolution," p. 5). Egypt's parliament of 1924 had 16 Coptic deputies out of a total of 214. Copts had served in every Egyptian representative body from the time its first consultative council was established in 1866 (Carter, *Copts in Egyptian Politics*, pp. 9–15, 143).
31 Hanioğlu, *Brief History of the Late Ottoman Empire*, p. 76; Çadırcı, *Tanzimat Döneminde Anadolu Kentleri*, pp. 212–13; Massot, "Ottoman Damascus during the Tanzimat," pp. 157–59; Maoz, "Syrian Urban Politics," pp. 291–92; Hamilton, *Copts and the West*, pp. 276–78; Rejwan, *Jews of Iraq*, chap. 22; Ceylan, *Ottoman*

Origins of Modern Iraq, chap. 3; Akarlı, *Long Peace*, chaps. 4–7; Saraçoğlu, *Nineteenth-Century Local Governance in Ottoman Bulgaria*, chaps. 3–4.
32 Cohen, "Economic Background"; Goitein, "Rise of the Near-Eastern Bourgeoisie"; Bessard, *Caliphs and Merchants*, pp. 242–45.
33 Bessard, *Caliphs and Merchants*, p. 258.
34 Bessard, *Caliphs and Merchants*, pp. 199, 204–8, 261–62.
35 On state–guild relationships in the Middle East, see Baer, "Guilds"; and Yi, *Guild Dynamics*, chap. 4. On the functions of guilds generally, see Ogilvie, "Economics of Guilds," pp. 173–86.
36 Çizakça, *Comparative Evolution of Business Partnerships*, pp. 184–86.
37 Balla and Johnson, "Fiscal Crisis," pp. 826–41; Salzmann, "Ancien Régime," p. 402; Kiyotaki, *Ottoman Land Reform*, pp. 108–13.
38 Hourani, "Ottoman Reform," pp. 46–64; Yaycioglu, *Partners of the Empire*, chaps. 4–5; Barkey, *Empire of Difference*, pp. 218–25, 252–56.
39 Van Zanden, Buringh, and Bosker, "Rise and Decline of European Parliaments"; Jha, "Financial Asset Holdings," pp. 1495–96; Puga and Trefler, "International Trade," p. 788; Root, *Fountain of Privilege*, chaps. 2–3.
40 Armstrong, "Introduction to Archival Research"; Hives, "History, Business Records."
41 The first chamber of commerce was established in Marseille. Across Europe, chambers started becoming common in the 1760s. See Sack, "European Chambers of Commerce"; and Bennett, *Local Business Voice*, chaps. 1–4.
42 Istanbul's chamber of commerce opened in 1882 (Memiş, *Türkiye'de Ticaretin Öncü Kuruluşu*, pp. 39–59). For other early chambers, see İzmir Ticaret Odası, *19. Yüzyıldan 21. Yüzyıla İzmir Ticaret Odası*, pp. 18–32; Glass and Kark, "Jerusalem Chamber of Commerce"; Gilbar, "Qajar Dynasty viii," sect. 3; Fahmy, *Politics of Egypt*, p. 165. By 1908, the Ottoman Empire had a chamber in 158 locations (Toprak, *Türkiye'de Milli İktisat*, pp. 616–17).
43 Çağatay, "Ribā and Interest," pp. 66–68.
44 Among the enabling conditions was that clerics had lost political power.
45 Kuran and Lustig, "Judicial Biases"; Kuran and Rubin, "Financial Power of the Powerless."
46 Izmirlioglu, "Ottoman Commercial Tribunals"; Ekinci, *Tanzimat*, pp. 97–124; Hoyle, "Structure and Laws of the Mixed Courts of Egypt"; Goldberg, "On the Origins of *Majālis Al-Tujjār*," pp. 193–202.
47 Perkin, *Rise of Professional Society*.
48 Page, Seawright, and Lacombe, *Billionaires and Stealth Politics*.
49 Acemoglu, Johnson, and Robinson, "Rise of Europe"; North and Thomas, *Rise of the Western World*, chaps. 11–12.
50 Cantoni, Dittmar, and Yuchtman, "Religious Competition"; Johnson and Koyama, *Persecution and Toleration*, chaps. 11–14.
51 This point is inspired by Zhang and Morley, "Modern State and the Rise of the Business Corporation," who show that in Western Europe both "demand-side" and "supply-side" developments were essential to the emergence of the business corporation. Zhang, *Ideological Foundations of Qing Taxation*, sect. 2A, uses analogous logic to explain low tax revenue in Qing China, adding that incentive misalignments among state actors can hinder reforms.

52 Der Matossian, "Armenian Commercial Houses"; Moutafidou, "Greek Merchant Families"; Kabadayı, "Mkrdich Cezayirliyan," pp. 283–86; Traboulsi, *History of Modern Lebanon*, pp. 58–59. Ottoman Jews modernized their commercial operations with a delay. When they began the process, it involved developing European-inspired organizational forms (Danon, *Jews of Ottoman Izmir*, pp. 85–90). European expatriates had been forming merchant houses since the 1600s (Davis, *Aleppo*, chap. 13). Boogert, "Ottoman Brokers," documents that in the 1700s the region's European merchant houses almost always worked with non-Muslim local brokers. Non-Muslims thus gained experience with organizations earlier than Muslims.
53 Masters, "Sultan's Entrepreneurs"; Kuran, *Long Divergence*, chap. 10.
54 Toksöz, *Nomads, Migrants and Cotton*, pp. 106–34; Derri, "Imperial Creditors"; Laskier and Simon, "Economic Life," pp. 41–44; Simon, "Iraq," pp. 359–63.
55 Kechriotis, "Educating the Nation," pp. 140–47; Strauss, "Greek Connection"; Zachs, *Making of a Syrian Identity*, pp. 45–85; Ayalon, "Private Publishing in Naḥḍa"; Kasaba, "Economic Foundations of a Civil Society"; Traboulsi, *History of Modern Lebanon*, chap. 4; Baykal, *Ottoman Press*, pp. 14–30; Snir, "Arabic Journalism"; Firro, "Lebanese Nationalism."
56 Jamgocyan, *Banquiers des Sultans*; Kazgan, *Galata Bankerleri*. On professional money-lenders in other Ottoman centers, see Mazower, *Salonica*, pp. 145–49; and Pierret, "Farhi Family," pp. 38–45. On Iran, see Floor, "Bankers (*ṣarrāf*) in Qājār Iran," p. 268.
57 Minoglou, "Ethnic Minority Groups in International Banking"; Landes, *Bankers and Pashas*, pp. 61–62; Floor, "Bankers (*ṣarrāf*) in Qājār Iran," pp. 276–81; Safieddine, *Banking on the State*, pp. 1–2, 15–20.
58 Deeb, "Socioeconomic Role of the Local Foreign Minorities," pp. 16–18.
59 Göçek, *Rise of the Bourgeoisie*, pp. 92–116; Krämer, "Moving Out of Place," pp. 214–18; Fawaz, *Merchants and Migrants*, pp. 101–2.
60 Roudometof, "Rum Millet"; Pizanias, "Reaya to Greek Citizen," especially pp. 17–26, 29–33, 39–45. The movement for Greek independence drew strength also from European scholarship rooting Western civilization in ancient Greece and the revolutionary fervor gripping Europe in the aftermath of the French Revolution.
61 Pizanias, "Reaya to Greek Citizen," pp. 42–43.
62 Turnaoğlu, *Formation of Turkish Republicanism*, pp. 45–49; Küçük, "Osmanlı İmparatorluğu'nda 'Millet Sistemi'"; Erdem, "Greek Revolution."
63 Among the unintended effects of the secularization drives was the boosting of nationalist feelings among non-Muslim minorities (Abu-Manneh, "Christians between Ottomanism and Nationalism"). In turn, separatist movements stimulated further reforms by the Muslim majority.
64 Turkey: Koraltürk, *Erken Cumhuriyet*, pp. 95–202; Toprak, *Türkiye'de Milli İktisat*, chap. 6; Akyıldız, *Anka'nın Sonbaharı*, chaps. 6–8; Egypt: Deeb, "Bank Mısr"; Davis, *Challenging Colonialism*, chap. 5. Iran, where the emphasis was more on gaining ground against foreigners than against the relatively small non-Muslim communities: Gilbar, "Qajar Dynasy viii," sect. 2.
65 Kuran and Rubin, "Financial Power of the Powerless," p. 793; Hansen, "Interest Rates and Foreign Capital in Egypt"; Jones, "Imperial Bank of Iran," p. 76.
66 For examples, see Fattah, "Politics of the Grain Trade in Iraq"; Cora, "Muslim Great Merchant [*Tüccar*] Family"; and Abdulhaq, *Jewish and Greek Communities*, chap. 5.

67 Ağır and Artunç, "Wealth Tax of 1942." On the sectarian biases of the Turkish Republic's economic policies generally, see Koraltürk, *Erken Cumhuriyet*, pp. 121–41.
68 Farha and Mousa, "Secular Autocracy," pp. 181–83, 187–88; Van Gorder, *Christianity in Persia*, p. 75.
69 Matthiesen, *Other Saudis*, pp. 112–13.
70 Elling, *Minorities in Iran*, pp. 51–56, 79–81.
71 Fortune 500 companies: Saudi Aramco (no. 6) and Turkey's Koç Holding (no. 471). Locations of Forbes Global 2000 companies: Saudi Arabia (14), United Arab Emirates (9), Turkey (8), Qatar (6), Kuwait (3), Morocco (2), Lebanon (2), Bahrain, Egypt, Jordan, and Oman.
72 Turkey: Buğra and Savaşkan, "Politics and Class," pp. 41–51. Iran: Jafari, "Ambiguous Role of Entrepreneurs in Iran," pp. 106–13. Turkey–Iran comparison: Shambayati, "Rentier State." Egypt: Fahmy, *Politics of Egypt*, chaps. 5–6. Syria: Haddad, "Business Associations." Morocco and Tunisia: Cammett, "Business–Government Relations."
73 For country cases on Egypt, Jordan, Saudi Arabia, Palestine, Lebanon, Kuwait, Qatar, and the United Arab Emirates, see Ibrahim and Sherif, *From Charity to Social Change*. Iran: Abdolalizadeh and Beygi, "Corporate and Social Responsibility in Iran." Turkey: Arzova, "Turkey: CSR in Practice."
74 Egypt: Blaydes, *Elections and Distributive Politics*, pp. 35–43, 52–58, 125–30, 138–41. Morocco and Tunisia: Cammett, *Globalization and Business Politics*, chaps. 4–6. Turkey: Buğra, *State and Business*, chap. 3; Öniş and Türem, "Entrepreneurs, Democracy." Iran: Harris, "Rise of the Subcontractor State." Region-wide: Diwan, Malik, and Atiyas, *Crony Capitalism*.
75 Adıgüzel, "Non-Media Favors"; Webb, *Media in Egypt and Tunisia*; Guaaybess, "Media Ownership in Egypt."
76 For accounts of Kavala's civic work and legal troubles, see https://osmankavala.org/en.
77 Hoşgör, "Islamic Capital"; Buğra, "Labour, Capital, and Religion."
78 *Ilımlı laikler* and *otoriter laikler*, respectively. This pair is often used interchangeably with *ılımlı Kemalistler* and *otoriter Kemalistler*. On the split, see Ciddi, *Kemalism in Turkish Politics*, pp. 93–100, 106–7, 137–45; and Akkır, *CHP'nin Din Politikaları*, chaps. 3–5. Çarkoğlu, "Religiosity, Support for Şeriat," provides survey evidence of divisions within the left-leaning base.

CHAPTER 14

1 Ágoston, *Guns for the Sultan*, chaps. 1–2.
2 On the transformations that unfolded in an atmosphere of existential crisis, see Kuran, *Long Divergence*, chaps. 9–14; Toledano, "Social and Economic Change"; Fahmy, *All the Pasha's Men*, chaps. 3, 4, 6; and Berkes, *Development of Secularism*, chaps. 3, 10.
3 Lewis, *Muslim Discovery of Europe*; Shaw and Shaw, *History of the Ottoman Empire*, vol. 2, chaps. 1–3; Hourani, *History of the Arab Peoples*, chaps. 16–18.
4 Evidence is present in the author's private collection of Ottoman economic documents of the 1800s. In Istanbul, the early electricity contracts were written only in French, a language unfamiliar to most Islamic judges.

5 This company was chartered in Brussels. On foreign capital in the Ottoman coal industry, see Tak, "Osmanlı Döneminde Ereğli Kömür Madenleri."
6 Kuhnke, *Lives at Risk*; Yavuz, "Batılılaşma Döneminde Osmanlı Sağlık Kuruluşları," pp. 125–41; Abugideiri, *Gender and the Making of Modern Medicine in Egypt*, chaps. 2, 4, 6; Şehsuvaroğlu, Erdemir Demirhan, and Güreşsever, *Türk Tıp Tarihi*, chaps. 8, 17.
7 Lewis, *Middle East and the West*, pp. 37–46; Arkoun, *Islam*, introduction and chap. 7; Baer, "Social Change in Egypt."
8 Davison, *Reform in the Ottoman Empire*, chaps. 1–2, 4; Kuran and Rubin, "Financial Power of the Powerless," sect. 8; Cansunar and Kuran, "Economic Harbingers of Political Modernization."
9 Anderson, "Law Reform in Egypt"; Marsot, *Egypt in the Reign of Muhammad Ali*, pp. 73, 161.
10 Abu-Manneh, *Studies on Islam and the Ottoman Empire*, chap. 5; GhaneaBassiri, "Structuring Sovereignty"; Gammer, "Imam and the Pasha."
11 Among narratives of the Middle East's 1839–1914 reforms known to this author, only those involving Arabia mention zakat.
12 Onar, "İslâm Hukuku ve Mecelle"; Davison, *Reform in the Ottoman Empire*, pp. 253–55.
13 Vassiliev, *History of Saudi Arabia*, pp. 227–32, 620–25; Helms, *Cohesion of Saudi Arabia*, pp. 152–59.
14 Vassiliev, *History of Saudi Arabia*, p. 232; Toth, "Control and Allegiance," pp. 62–66, 70–74; Helms, *Cohesion of Saudi Arabia*, pp. 159–71.
15 See text in Priestland, *Buraimi Dispute*, pp. 168–69.
16 Ayubi, *Political Islam*; Roy, *Globalized Islam*; Mandaville, *Islam and Politics*.
17 Mawdudi, *Let Us Be Muslims*, chaps. 19–23, especially p. 220.
18 Qutb, *Social Justice in Islam*, pp. 133–38, 267–70.
19 Quazi, "Economic Morality in Islam," p. 93.
20 Yousri, "Sustainable Development," quote at p. 43.
21 Chapra, *Islam and Economic Challenge*, pp. 225–26, 270–75.
22 Al-Shiekh, "Zakāt," p. 368.
23 Al Qardawi, *Fiqh al Zakah*, vol. 1, pt. 3; Ahmad, *Economics of Islam*, chap. 4; Mannan, *Islamic Economics*, pp. 284–302; Rahman, *Economic Doctrines of Islam*, vol. 3, chaps. 14–18; Shad, *Zakat and 'Ushr*.
24 Ahmad, *Economics of Islam*, p. 89; Rahman, *Economic Doctrines of Islam*, vol. 3, pp. 225–26.
25 Polemical writings in Islamic economics routinely cite Kahf's works. Among the leading Islamic economists, his scholarly standing places him within the top three according to Google Scholar citation counts in May 2021.
26 Kahf and Al Yafai, "Social Security and Zakāh," p. 190.
27 Kahf and Al Yafai, "Social Security and Zakāh," p. 206.
28 See Chapter 12 for references to the pertinent verses.
29 Kuran, *Islam and Mammon*, chap. 4.
30 Kuran, *Islam and Mammon*, pp. 7–19; Kuran, "Islam and Economic Performance," pp. 1307–11.
31 El-Gamal, *Islamic Finance*, chaps. 1–2.
32 Çokgezen and Kuran, "Between Markets and Islamic Law."

33 Islamic economics has its own niche journals. With rare exceptions, the contributions lack academic rigor.
34 Kuran, *Islam and Mammon*, pp. 28–34.
35 Evidence based on the World Values Survey is in Figure 3.1. Using an earlier wave of the same survey, Guiso, Sapienza, and Zingales, "People's Opium?," show that a Muslim religious upbringing lowers generalized trust but raises trust in government and the courts. Through experiments in Arab countries, others find evidence of a low-trust equilibrium that inhibits profitable exchanges (Bohnet, Herrmann, and Zeckhauser, "Trust and Reference Points for Trustworthiness"; Binzel and Fehr, "Social Distance and Trust"). Synchronizing forty-seven surveys from fifteen Middle Eastern countries, Spierings, "Social Trust," identifies various causal effects of religiosity on trust, some positive and others negative.
36 Hoşgör, "Islamic Capital/Anatolian Tigers," pp. 348–51; Siddiqui, *Economic Enterprise in Islam*; Naqvi, *Ethics and Economics*.
37 Schäublin, "Zakat Practice in the Islamic Tradition," pp. 22–24; Shahid, "Muslim Brotherhood Movement", p. 667; Royle, *Islamic Development in Palestine*, chap. 7. Along with the last work, Benthall, "Islamic Charities," documents that zakat revenue has gone partly to charities, but also to Palestinian universities, unions, militia, and parties.
38 http://misrelkheir.org/en/; www.egyptianfoodbank.com/en; www.khcc.jo/. Each site displays a link for donating zakat. On Rabaa al-Adawiya, see Atia, *Building a House in Heaven*, p. 23.
39 Egypt: Ismail, *Political Life in Cairo*, pp. 75–78. Jordan: Wiktorowicz, *Management of Islamic Activism*, pp. 65–70. Syria: Pierret and Selvik, "Limits of 'Authoritarian Upgrading'," pp. 597–98.
40 Hegghammer, *Jihad in Saudi Arabia*, p. 20
41 Burr and Collins, *Alms for Jihad*, pp. 16–17; Benthall and Bellion-Jourdan, *Charitable Crescent*, p. 72; Mellor, *Voice of the Muslim Brotherhood*, p. 207.
42 Davidson, *Shadow Wars*, pp. 449–50.
43 Countries with mandatory zakat systems: Libya, Malaysia, Pakistan, Saudi Arabia, Sudan, Yemen. Countries with facilitating agencies: Bahrain, Bangladesh, Brunei, Egypt, Indonesia, Iran, Jordan, Kuwait, Lebanon, Oman, United Arab Emirates. Based on Powell, "Zakat," pp. 58–73; and Hasan, "Muslim Philanthropy," table 5.1.
44 Kuran, *Islam and Mammon*, pp. 19–27, where additional details may be found.
45 S&P Global, *Islamic Finance Outlook*, p. 7; Boston Consulting Group, "When the Clients Take the Lead."
46 Based on World Bank, "World Development Indicators Database" for 2020. GDP is measured at purchasing power parity.
47 Beck, Demirgüç-Kunt, and Merrouche, "Islamic vs. Conventional Banking."
48 Ben Naceur, Barajas, and Massara, "Can Islamic Banking Increase Financial Inclusion?" p. 222.
49 Ben Naceur, Barajas, and Massara, "Can Islamic Banking Increase Financial Inclusion?" pp. 222–26.
50 Romano, "Kurds in the Middle East"; Abu-Rabia-Queder, "Bedouin in the Middle East," pp. 302–5; Maddy-Weitzman, "Berbers (Amazigh)"; King, "Black Arabs."
51 In the Middle East, the rate was 18.5 percent. Computed from Harvard Business School, "Adult Literacy Rates"; and United Nations, *World Population Prospects*.

52 On uses of the Islamic partnership, see Kuran, *Long Divergence*, chap. 4.
53 Kuran, *Islam and Mammon*, pp. 7–15.

CHAPTER 15

1 Tocqueville, *Democracy in America*, vol. 1, chaps. 9–12.
2 Greif, *Institutions*, sect. 7.5.
3 In Ottoman realms, the earliest workers' association emerged in 1894, and the first strike wave occurred in 1908 (Karakışla, "Emergence of the Ottoman Industrial Working Class"). In Egypt, the first recorded strike broke out in 1882, and workers' associations began forming around 1899 (Beinin, "Formation of the Egyptian Working Class"). Country-specific accounts focused on later periods: Nichols and Sugur, *Global Management, Local Labour*, chap. 7; Abbas, "Labour Movement in Egypt"; Ladjevardi, *Labor Unions and Autocracy in Iran*; Farouk-Sluglett and Sluglett, "Labor and National Liberation"; Allouini, "Labor Movement in Syria"; Bishara, "Legacy Trade Unions"; Menoret, "Repression and Protest in Saudi Arabia." Comparative accounts of work conditions and labor power: Cammett and Posusney, "Labor Standards."
4 Makdisi, *Rise of Colleges*, pp. 24–25, covers the early history.
5 Quran 2:282.
6 Cansunar and Kuran, "Economic Harbingers of Political Modernization."
7 Cagaptay, *New Sultan*, chaps. 8–10.
8 Koblentz, "Chemical-Weapon Use."
9 Examples of statements from non-Islamists: Zakaria, *Future of Freedom*, chap. 4; Gutkowski, *Secular War*.
10 Kivimäki, "Democracy, Autocrats"; Gause, "Can Democracy Stop Terrorism?"
11 Influential variants: Shuster, *Strangling of Persia*; Makdisi, *Faith Misplaced*, chap. 4; Rodinson, *Islam and Capitalism*, chap. 5; Fattah and Fierke, "Clash of Emotions"; Fromkin, *Peace*, chaps. 57–61.
12 Osman, "Why Border Lines."
13 O'Rourke, *Representing Jihad*.
14 Indonesia and Tanzania are examples. Although most studies relating forms of fractionalization to either civil liberties or political rights find a negative relationship, many find no association or even a positive association (Gerring, Hoffman, and Zarecki, "Diverse Effects of Diversity," table 1).
15 See, generally, Woodberry, "Missionary Roots." On the Middle East specifically, see Anderson, *American University of Beirut*; Freely, *History of Robert College*; and Murphy, *American University in Cairo*.
16 Bertelsen, "Private Foreign-Affiliated Universities"; Erken, "Making of Politics"; Lorentz, "Educational Development in Iran."
17 Pamuk, "Political Power and Institutional Change."

Bibliography

Abbas, Megan Brankley. "Between Western Academia and Pakistan: Fazlur Rahman and the Fight for Fusionism." *Modern Asian Studies*, 51 (2017): 736–68.
Abbas, Raouf. "Labour Movement in Egypt." *Developing Economies*, 11 (1973): 62–75.
Abdelrahman, Maha M. *Civil Society Exposed: The Politics of NGOs in Egypt*. Cairo: American University in Cairo Press, 2004.
Abdolalizadeh, Zoha, and Elham Beygi. "Corporate and Social Responsibility in Iran." In *Sovereign Wealth Funds, Local Content Policies and CSR*, edited by Eduardo G. Pereira, Rochelle Spencer, and Jonathon W. Moses, pp. 511–25. Cham: Springer International, 2021.
Abdolmohammadi, Pejman, and Giampiero Cama. *Contemporary Domestic and Foreign Policies of Iran*. Cham: Palgrave Macmillan, 2020.
Abdou, Ehaab, Mona Atia, Noha Hussein, Homi Kharas, and Amira Maaty. "How Can the U.S. and International Finance Institutions Best Engage Egypt's Civil Society?" Brookings Institution Policy Paper, June 2011.
Abdulhaq, Najat. *Jewish and Greek Communities in Egypt: Entrepreneurship and Business before Nasser*. London: I. B. Tauris, 2016.
Abdullah, Thabit A. J. *Merchants, Mamluks, and Murder: The Political Economy of Trade in Eighteenth-Century Basra*. Albany: State University of New York Press, 2001.
Abdul Rahman, Sira. "Religion and Animal Welfare – An Islamic Perspective." *Animals*, 7 (2017): 1–6.
Abdul Razak, Hamzah. "*Zakat* and *Waqf* as Instrument of Islamic Wealth in Poverty Alleviation and Redistribution." *International Journal of Sociology and Social Policy*, 40 (2020): 249–66.
Abi-Mershed, Osama W. *Apostles of Modernity: Saint-Simonians and the Civilizing Mission in Algeria*. Stanford: Stanford University Press, 2010.
Abir, Mordechai. *Saudi Arabia: Government, Society and the Gulf Crisis*. London: Routledge, 1993.

Abisaab, Rula Jurdi. *Converting Persia: Religion and Power in the Safavid Empire.* London: I. B. Tauris, 2004.
Abou-El-Haj, Rifaʿat ʿAli. *The 1703 Rebellion and the Structures of Ottoman Politics.* Istanbul: Nederlands Historisch-Archaeologisch Institut, 1984.
Abrahamian, Ervand. *A History of Modern Iran.* Cambridge: Cambridge University Press, 2008.
Abugidieri, Hibba. *Gender and the Making of Modern Medicine in Colonial Egypt.* Farnham: Ashgate, 2010.
Abu-Lughod, Janet L. *Before European Hegemony: The World System A.D. 1250–1350.* New York: Oxford University Press, 1989.
Abu-Manneh, Butrus. "The Christians between Ottomanism and Syrian Nationalism: The Ideas of Butrus Al-Bustani." *International Journal of Middle East Studies*, 11 (1980): 287–304.
  Studies on Islam and the Ottoman Empire in the 19th Century (1826–1876). Istanbul: ISIS Press, 2001.
Abun-Nasr, Jamil M. *A History of the Maghrib in the Islamic Period.* Cambridge: Cambridge University Press, 1987.
Abu-Odeh, Lama. "Modernizing Muslim Family Law: The Case of Egypt." *Vanderbilt Journal of Transnational Law*, 37 (204): 1043–146.
Abu-Rabia-Queder, Sarab. "The Bedouin in the Middle East." In *Routledge Handbook of Minorities in the Middle East*, edited by Paul S. Rowe, pp. 301–12. London: Routledge, 2019.
Abu Yusuf. *Taxation in Islam*, translated by A. Ben Shemesh from the Arabic original of 790. Leiden: E. J. Brill, 1969.
Abu Zayd, Nasr Hamid. *Critique of Religious Discourse*, translated by Jonathan Wright from the Arabic original of 1990. New Haven, CT: Yale University Press, 2018.
Acemoglu, Daron, Tarek A. Hassan, and Ahmed Tahoun. "The Power of the Street: Evidence from Egypt's Arab Spring." *Review of Financial Studies*, 31 (2018): 1–42.
Acemoglu, Daron, Simon Johnson, and James A. Robinson. "The Colonial Origins of Comparative Development: An Empirical Investigation." *American Economic Review*, 91 (2001): 1369–401.
  "The Rise of Europe: Atlantic Trade, Institutional Change, and Economic Growth." *American Economic Review*, 95 (2005): 546–79.
Acemoglu, Daron, and James A. Robinson. *Economic Origins of Dictatorship and Democracy.* Cambridge: Cambridge University Press, 2006.
  Why Nations Fail: The Origins of Power, Prosperity, and Poverty. New York: Crown Business, 2012.
  The Narrow Corridor: States, Societies, and the Fate of Liberty. New York: Penguin Press, 2019.
Adar, Sinem. "Religious Difference, Nationhood and Citizenship in Turkey: Public Reactions to an Interreligious Marriage in 1962." *History of the Family*, 24 (2019): 520–38.
Adıgüzel, Serkant. "Non-Media Favors and Pro-Government Media Bias: Evidence from Turkey." Working paper, Duke University, 2022.
Adıgüzel, Serkant, and Timur Kuran. "Inequality-Preserving Benevolence: Wealth Sheltering through the Islamic Waqf." Working paper, Duke University, 2023.
Adraoui, Mohamed-Ali. "Salafism in France: Ideology, Practices, and Contradictions." In *Global Salafism: Islam's New Religious Movement*, edited by Roel Meijer, pp. 364–84. Oxford: Oxford University Press, 2014.

Bibliography

Afary, Janet. "Civil Liberties and the Making of Iran's First Constitution." *Comparative Studies of South Asia, Africa and the Middle East*, 25 (2005): 341–59.
Ağır, Seven. "The Rise and Demise of *Gedik* Markets in Istanbul, 1750–1860." *Economic History Review*, 71 (2018): 133–56.
Ağır, Seven, and Cihan Artunç. "The Wealth Tax of 1942 and the Disappearance of Non-Muslim Enterprises in Turkey." *Journal of Economic History*, 79 (2019): 201–43.
  "Set and Forget? The Evolution of Business Law in the Ottoman Empire and Turkey." *Business History Review*, 95 (2021): 703–38.
Ágoston, Gábor. *Guns for the Sultan: Military Power and the Weapons Industry in the Ottoman Empire*. Cambridge: Cambridge University Press, 2005.
Agrama, Hussein Ali. "Ethics, Tradition, Authority: Toward an Anthropology of the Fatwa." *American Ethnologist*, 37 (2010): 2–18.
Agrast, Mark David, Juan Carlos Botero, Alejandro Ponce-Rodríguez, and Claudia Dumas. *The World Justice Project Rule of Law Index: Measuring Adherence to the Rule of Law around the World*. Chicago, IL: American Bar Association, 2008.
Ahmad, Feroz. *The Making of Modern Turkey*. London: Routledge, 1993.
Ahmad, Sheikh Mahmud. *Economics of Islam*, 2nd ed. Lahore: Sh. Muhammad Ashraf, 1952.
Ahmed, Habib. *Role of* Zakāh *and* Awqāf *in Poverty Alleviation*. Jeddah: Islamic Development Bank, 2004.
Ahmed, Leila. *Women and Gender in Islam*. New Haven, CT: Yale University Press, 1992.
Ahmed, Shahab. *What Is Islam? The Importance of Being Islamic*. Princeton, NJ: Princeton University Press, 2016.
Akarlı, Engin Deniz. *The Long Peace: Ottoman Lebanon, 1861–1920*. London: I. B. Tauris, 1993.
Akbari, Mahsa, Duman Bahrami-Rad, and Erik O. Kimbrough. "Kinship, Fractionalization and Corruption." *Journal of Economic Behavior and Organization*, 166 (2019): 493–528.
Akçam, Taner. *From Empire to Republic: Turkish Nationalism and the Armenian Genocide*. London: Zed Books, 2004.
Akhter, Muhammad Wajid. "4 Reasons Why Muslims Should Not Celebrate the New Year." *Muslim Matters*, 28 December 2012.
Akkır, Ramazan. *CHP'nin Din Politikaları*. Istanbul: Pınar Yayınları, 2019.
Akrami, Seyed Mohammad, Vahideh Montazeri, Somaieh Rashid Shomali, Ramin Heshmat, and Bagher Larijani. "Is There a Significant Trend in Prevalence of Consanguineous Marriage in Tehran? A Review of Three Generations." *Journal of Genetic Counseling*, 18 (2009): 82–86.
Aksan, Virginia H. *Ottoman Wars, 1700–1870: An Empire Besieged*. Harlow: Pearson, 2007.
AKSAV. *Antalya Altın Portakal Kültür ve Sanat Vakfı Resmi Senedi*. Antalya: AKSAV, 1995.
Akşit, Bahattin, Recep Şentürk, Önder Küçükural, and Kurtuluş Cengiz. *Türkiye'de Dindarlık: Muhafazakârlık ve Laiklik Ekseninde İnanma Biçimleri ve Yaşam Deneyimleri*. Istanbul: İletişim, 2012.
Aktar, Ayhan. *Varlık Vergisi ve 'Türkleştirme' Politikaları*. Istanbul: İletişim, 2000.
Akyıldız, Ali. *Anka'nın Sonbaharı: Osmanlı'da İktisadî Modernleşme ve Uluslararası Sermaye*. Istanbul: İletişim, 2005.

Akyol, Mustafa. *Islam without Extremes: A Muslim Case for Liberty*. New York: W. W. Norton, 2011.
  Reopening Muslim Minds: A Return to Reason, Freedom, and Tolerance. New York: St. Martin's, 2021.
Al, Hüseyin, and Şevket Kamil Akar. *Galata Borsası (1830–1873)*. Istanbul: Borsa İstanbul, 2013.
Alam, Muzaffar. "Competition and Co-existence: Indo-Islamic Interaction in Medieval North India." *Itinerario*, 13 (1989): 37–60.
Al-Anani, Khalil. "Rethinking the Repression–Dissent Nexus: Assessing Egypt's Muslim Brotherhood's Response to Repression since the Coup of 2013." *Democratization*, 26 (2019): 1329–41.
Al-Azm, Sadik J. *Is Islam Secularizable? Challenging Political and Religious Taboos*. Berlin: Gerlach Press, 2014.
  On Fundamentalisms. Berlin: Gerlach Press, 2014.
Al-Azmeh, Aziz. *Secularism in the Arab World: Contexts, Ideas and Consequences*, translated by David Bond from the Arabic original of 2008. Edinburgh: Edinburgh University Press, 2019.
  "Abbasid Culture and Universal History of Freethinking Humanism." *Critical Muslim*, 12 (2014): 73–88.
Albouy, David Y. "The Colonial Origins of Development: An Empirical Investigation." *American Economic Review*, 102 (2012): 3059–76.
Alff, Kristen. "Levantine Joint-Stock Companies, Trans-Mediterranean Partnerships, and Nineteenth-Century Capitalist Development." *Comparative Studies in Society and History*, 60 (2018): 150–77.
Algar, Hamid. *Religion and State in Iran 1785–1906*. Berkeley: University of California Press, 1969.
  "Religious Forces in Eighteenth- and Nineteenth-Century Iran." In *The Cambridge History of Iran*, vol. 7, edited by Peter Avery, Gavin Hambly, and Charles Melville, pp. 705–31. Cambridge: Cambridge University Press, 1991.
  Imam Khomeini: A Short Biography. Tehran: Institute for the Compilation and Publication of the Works of Imam Khomeini, 1999.
  Wahhabism: A Critical Essay. Oneanta, NY: Islamic Publications International, 2002.
Al-Ghazali, Abu Hamid. *Revival of the Religious Sciences*, issued as *Imam Ghazali's Ihya Ulum-id-Din*, vol. 1, translated by Fazul-ul-Karim. Lahore: Sind Sagar Academy, 1978; original Arabic edition around 1100.
Al Hariri, Youssef, Walid Magdy, and Maria Wolters. "Arabs and Atheism: Religious Discussions in the Arab Twittersphere." *Social Informatics*, (2019): 18–34.
Ali, Hassanein. "The Rise and Fall of Islamic State: Current Challenges and Future Prospects." *Asian Affairs*, 51 (2020): 71–94.
Ali, Souad Tagelsir. *A Religion, Not a State: Ali 'Abd al-Raziq's Islamic Justification of Political Secularism*. Salt Lake City: University of Utah Press, 2009.
Aliyu, Shehu Usman Rano. "A Treatise on the Socioeconomic Roles of Waqf." Munich Personal RePEc Archive, 2018.
Alkadry, Mohamed G. "Reciting Colonial Scripts: Colonialism, Globalization and Democracy in the Decolonized Middle East." *Administrative Theory & Praxis*, 24 (2002): 739–62.

Alkan, Necati. "Fighting for the Nuṣayrī Soul: State, Protestant Missionaries and the 'Alawīs in the Late Ottoman Empire." *Die Welt des Islams*, 52 (2012): 23–50.

Al-Kandari, Ali A., and Ali A. Dashti. "Fatwa and the Internet: A Study of the Influence of Muslim Religious Scholars on Internet Diffusion in Saudi Arabia." *Prometheus: Critical Studies in Innovation*, 32 (2015): 127–44.

Al-Khalidi, Ashraf, and Victor Tanner. "Sectarian Violence: Radical Groups Drive Internal Displacement of Iraq." Washington, DC: Brookings Institution-University of Bern occasional paper, 2006.

Allani, Alaya. "The Islamists in Tunisia between Confrontation and Participation: 1980–2008." *Journal of North African Studies*, 14 (2009): 257–72.

Allievi, Stefano. "Relations and Negotiations: Issues and Debates on Islam." In *Muslims in the Enlarged Europe: Religion and Society*, edited by Brigitte Maréchal, Stefano Allievi, Felice Dassetto, and Jørgen Nielsen, pp. 331–68. Leiden: Brill, 2003.

Allouini, A. Aziz. "The Labor Movement in Syria." *Middle East Journal*, 13 (1959): 64–76.

Al-Māwardī. *The Ordinances of Government: Al-Aḥkām al-Sulṭaniyya w'al-Wilāyāt al-Dīniyya*, translated by Wafaa H. Wahba from the Arabic original of around 1050. Reading: Garnet, 1996.

Almond, Douglas, Bhashkar Mazumder, and Reyn van Ewijk. 2015. "*In Utero* Ramadan Exposure and Children's Academic Performance." *Economic Journal*, 125 (2015): 1501–33.

Almond, Gabriel A., and Sidney Verba. *The Civic Culture: Political Attitudes and Democracy in Five Nations*. Princeton, NJ: Princeton University Press, 1963.

Al-Mutairi, Saad, Ian Connerton, and Robert Dingwall. "Understanding 'Corruption' in Regulatory Agencies: The Case of Food Inspection in Saudi Arabia." *Regulation and Governance*, 13 (2019): 507–19.

Al Qaradawi, Yusuf. *Fiqh Al Zakah: A Comparative Study of Zakah Regulations and Philosphy in the Light of Qur'an and Sunnah*, 2 vols., translated by Monzer Kahf from the Arabic original of 1973. Jeddah: King Abdulaziz University, 1999.

Al-Rasheed, Madawi. "Women Are Still Not in the Driving Seat in Saudi Arabia." *Guardian*, 27 September 2017.

Al-Raysuni, Ahmad. *Al-Shūrā: The Qur'anic Principle of Consultation*, translated by Nancy Roberts from the Arabic original of 2007. London: International Institute of Islamic Thought, 2011.

Alsabagh, Munther H. "Before Banks: Credit, Society, and Law in Sixteenth-Century Palestine and Syria." PhD dissertation, University of California at Santa Barbara, 2018.

Al-Sayyid, Mustapha K. "A Civil Society in Egypt?" *Middle East Journal* 47 (1993): 228–42.

Al-Shiekh, Abdallah. "Zakāt." *Oxford Encyclopedia of the Modern Islamic World*, vol. 4, pp. 366–70. New York: Oxford University Press, 1995.

Al-Soukkary, Wael Ossama. "Becoming and Being: Atheism as a Social Experience in Egypt." MA thesis, American University in Cairo, 2015.

Al-Sudairi, Mohammed Turki. "China in the Eyes of the Saudi Media." Gulf Research Center paper, February 2013.

Altınyıldız, Nur. "The Architectural Heritage of Istanbul and the Ideology of Preservation." *Muqarnas*, 24 (2007): 281–306.

Amanat, Abbas. "From *Ijtihad* to *Wilayat-i Faqih*: The Evolving of Shi'i Legal Authority into Political Power." In *Apolcalyptic Islam and Iranian Shi'ism*, edited by Abbas Amanat, pp. 179–96, 273–76. London: I. B. Tauris, 2009.
  Iran: A Modern History. New Haven, CT: Yale University Press, 2017.
Ames, Christine Caldwell. *Righteous Persecution: Inquisition, Dominicans, and Christianity in the Middle Ages*. Philadelphia: University of Pennsylvania Press, 2009.
Amir-Moezzi, Mohammad Ali, and Christian Jambet. *What Is Shi'i Islam? An Introduction*, translated by Kenneth Casler and Eric Ormsby from the French original of 2004. London: Routledge, 2018.
Anand, Vikas, Blake E. Ashforth, and Mahendra Joshi. "Business as Usual: The Acceptance and Perpetuation of Corruption in Organizations." *Academy of Management Executive*, 18 (2004): 39–55.
Anderson, Betty S. *The American University of Beirut: Arab Nationalism and Liberal Education*. Austin: University of Texas Press, 2011.
Anderson, J. Norman D. "A Law of Personal Status for Iraq." *International and Comparative Law Quarterly*, 9 (1960): 542–63.
  "Law Reform in Egypt: 1850–1950." In *Political and Social Change in Modern Egypt*, edited by Peter M. Holt, pp. 209–30. London: Oxford University Press, 1968.
Anderson, Lisa. "The State in the Middle East and North Africa." *Comparative Politics*, 20 (1987): 1–18.
Anderson, Perry. *Lineages of the Absolutist State*. London: Verso, 1974.
Anheier, Helmut K., Markus Lang, and Stefan Toepler. "Comparative Nonprofit Sector Research: A Critical Assessment." In *The Nonprofit Sector: A Research Handbook*, 3rd ed., edited by Walter W. Powell and Patricia Bromley, pp. 648–76, 699–701. Stanford: Stanford University Press, 2020.
An-Na'im, Abdullahi A., ed. *Islamic Family Law in a Changing World: A Global Resource Book*. London: Zed Books, 2002.
  Islam and the Secular State: Negotiating the Future of the Shari'a. Cambridge, MA: Harvard University Press, 2008.
Appignanesi, Lisa, and Sara Maitland, eds. *The Rushdie File*. London: Fourth Estate, 1989.
Arab Barometer Wave 5, 2018–2019. www.arabbarometer.org/survey-data/data-analy sis-tool/ (accessed 1 February 2023).
Arab, Pooyan Tamimi. "'A Minaret of Light': Transducing the Islamic Call to Prayer?" *Material Religion*, 11 (2015): 136–63.
Arafat, Alaa Al-Din. *The Rise of Islamism in Egypt*. Cham: Palgrave Macmillan, 2017.
Arat, Yeşim. "Women's Rights and Islam in Turkish Politics: The Civil Code Amendment." *Middle East Journal*, 64 (2010): 235–51.
Arendt, Hannah. *The Origins of Totalitarianism*, new ed. Orlando, FL: Harcourt Brace, 1979.
Aritonang, Jan Sihar, and Karel Steenbrink. *A History of Christianity in Indonesia*. Leiden: Brill, 2008.
Arjomand, Said Amir. "Religious Extremism (*Ghuluww*), Ṣūfism and Sunnism in Safavid Iran: 1501–1722." *Journal of Asian History*, 15 (1981): 1–35.
  The Shadow of God and the Hidden Imam: Religion, Political Order, and Societal Change in Shi'ite Iran from the Beginning to 1890. Chicago, IL: University of Chicago Press, 1984.

"Philanthropy, the Law, and Public Policy in the Islamic World before the Modern Era." In *Philanthropy in the World's Traditions*, edited by Warren F. Ilchman, Stanley N. Katz, and Edward L. Queen II, pp. 109–32. Bloomington: Indiana University Press, 1998.
"Shari'a and Constitution in Iran: A Historical Perspective." In *Shari'a: Islamic Law in the Contemporary Context*, edited by Abbas Amanat and Frank Griffel, pp. 156–64, 229–31. Stanford: Stanford University Press, 2007.
After Khomeini: Iran under His Successors. Oxford: Oxford University Press, 2009.
Arkoun, Mohammed. *Islam: To Reform or to Subvert?* 2nd ed. London: Saqi Books, 2006.
Armstrong, John. "An Introduction to Archival Research in Business History." *Business History*, 33 (1991): 7–34.
Arnaud, Jean-Luc. "Modernization of the Cities of the Ottoman Empire (1800–1920)." In *The City in the Islamic World*, edited by Raymond André, Petruccioli Attilio, and Holod Renat, pp. 953–76, 1399–408. Leiden: Brill, 2008.
Arom, Eitan. "Members as Monitors: In Search of the Ideal Nonprofit Principal." *Columbia Law Review*, 120 (2020): 265–98.
Arora, Jayant. "Egypt Bans Resurrection Ertugrul Turkish TV Series." *Laffaz*, 7 April 2020.
Artunç, Cihan. "The Price of Legal Institutions: The *Beratlı* Merchants in the Eighteenth-Century Ottoman Empire." *Journal of Economic History*, 75 (2015): 720–48.
"Religious Minorities and Firm Ownership in Early Twentieth-Century Egypt." *Economic History Review*, 72 (2019): 979–1007.
Arzova, S. Burak. "Turkey: CSR in Practice." In *Global Practices of Corporate Social Responsibility*, edited by Samuel O. Idowu and Walter Leal Filho, pp. 373–91. Berlin: Springer-Verlag, 2009.
Asad, Talal. *Formations of the Secular: Christianity, Islam, Modernity*. Stanford: Stanford University Press, 2003.
Ashraf, Assef. "The Politics of Gift Exchange in Early Qajar Iran, 1785–1834." *Comparative Studies in Society and History*, 58 (2016): 550–76.
Ashtor, Eliyahu. "The Kārimī Merchants." *Journal of the Royal Asiatic Society*, 88 (1956): 45–56.
A Social and Economic History of the Near East in the Middle Ages. Berkeley: University of California Press, 1976.
Askari, Hossein, John Thomas Cummings, and Michael Glover. *Taxation and Tax Policies in the Middle East*. London: Butterworth Scientific, 1982.
Assad, Soraya W. "The Rise of Consumerism in Saudi Arabian Society." *International Journal of Commerce and Management*, 17 (2007): 73–104.
Atay, Hüseyin. "Fatih-Süleymaniye Medreseleri Ders Programları ve İcazet-Nâmeler." *Vakıflar Dergisi*, 13 (1981): 172–234.
Atçıl, Abdurrahman. "The Safavid Threat and Juristic Authority in the Ottoman Empire during the 16th Century." *International Journal of Middle East Studies*, 49 (2017): 295–314.
Atia, Mona. *Building a House in Heaven: Pious Neoliberalism and Islamic Charity in Egypt*. Minneapolis: University of Minnesota Press, 2013.
Axiarlis, Evangelia. *Political Islam and the Secular State in Turkey: Democracy, Reform and the Justice and Development Party*. London: I. B. Tauris, 2014.

Axworthy, Michael. "Nader Shah and Persian Naval Expansion in the Persian Gulf, 1700–1747." *Journal of the Royal Asiatic Society*, 21 (2011): 31–39.
Ayalon, Ami. "Private Publishing in the *Nahḍa*." *International Journal of Middle East Studies*, 40 (2008): 561–77.
Aydar, Hidayet, and Mehmet Atalay. "The Issue of Chanting the *Adhan* in Languages other than Arabic and Related Social Reactions against It in Turkey." *İstanbul Üniversitesi İlahiyat Fakültesi Dergisi*, 13 (2006): 45–63.
Aygül, Hasan Hüseyin, and Özgür Öztürk. "Dini Çoğulculuk ve Kamusal Alanda Dindar Tüketim Kültürü." *Moment Dergi*, 3 (2016): 190–206.
Ayubi, Nazih N. *Political Islam: Religion and Politics in the Arab World*. New York: Routledge, 1991.
Azak, Umut. *Islam and Secularism in Turkey: Kemalism, Religion and the Nation State*. London: I. B. Tauris, 2010.
Azam, Ikram. *Pakistan and Islamic Economics*. Lahore: Amir Publications, 1978.
Azzam, Henry T. *The Emerging Arab Capital Markets: Investment Opportunities in Relatively Underplayed Markets*. London: Kegan Paul International, 1997.
Babayan, Kathryn. "The Safavid Synthesis: From Qizilbash Islam to Imamate Shi'ism." *Iranian Studies*, 27 (1994): 135–61.
  Mystics, Monarchs, and Messiahs: Cultural Landscapes of Early Modern Iran. Cambridge, MA: Center for Middle Eastern Studies of Harvard University, 2002.
Bacık, Gökhan. *Islam and Muslim Resistance to Modernity in Turkey*. Cham: Palgrave Macmillan, 2020.
  Contemporary Rationalist Islam in Turkey: The Religious Opposition to Sunni Revival. London: I. B. Tauris, 2021.
Baer, Gabriel. *A History of Landownership in Modern Egypt, 1800–1950*. London: Oxford University Press, 1962.
  "Social Change in Egypt: 1800–1914." In *Political and Social Change in Modern Egypt*, edited by P. M. Holt, pp. 135–61. London: Oxford University Press, 1968.
  Studies in the Social History of Modern Egypt. Chicago, IL: University of Chicago Press, 1969.
  "Guilds in Middle Eastern History." In *Studies in the Economic History of the Middle East from the Rise of Islam to the Present Day*, edited by Michael A. Cook, pp. 11–30. London: Oxford University Press, 1970.
Bakhash, Shaul. "The Evolution of Qajar Bureaucracy: 1779–1879." *Middle Eastern Studies*, 7 (1971): 139–68.
Balch, Thomas Willing. "French Colonization in North Africa." *American Political Science Review*, 3 (1909): 539–51.
Bali, Rıfat N. *The "Varlık Vergisi" Affair: A Study on Its Legacy*. Istanbul: ISIS Press, 2005.
  Gayrimüslim Mehmetçikler: Hatıralar, Tanıklıklar. Istanbul: Libra, 2011.
Balla, Eliana, and Noel D. Johnson. "Fiscal Crisis and Institutional Change in the Ottoman Empire and France." *Journal of Economic History*, 69 (2009): 809–45.
Baltacıoğlu-Brammer, Ayşe. "The Formation of Kızılbaş Communities in Anatolia and Ottoman Responses, 1540s–1630s." *International Journal of Turkish Studies*, 20 (2014): 21–48.

"'Those Heretics Gathering Secretly ...': Qizilbash Rituals and Practices in the Ottoman Empire according to Early Modern Sources." *Journal of the Ottoman and Turkish Studies Association*, 6 (2019): 39–60.
Banai, Hussein. *Hidden Liberalism: Burdened Visions of Progress in Modern Iran*. Cambridge: Cambridge University Press, 2021.
Banani, Amin. *The Modernization of Iran, 1921–1941*. Stanford: Stanford University Press, 1961.
Bano, Masooda. "Protector of the 'al-Wasatiyya' Islam: Cairo's al-Azhar University." In *Shaping Global Islamic Discourses: The Role of al-Azhar, al-Medina and al-Mustafa*, edited by Masooda Bano and Keiko Sakurai, pp. 73–88. Edinburgh: Edinburgh University Press, 2015.
  "At the Tipping Point? Al-Azhar's Growing Crisis of Moral Authority." *International Journal of Middle East Studies*, 50 (2018): 715–34.
  The Revival of Islamic Rationalism: Logic, Metaphysics, and Mysticism in Modern Muslim Societies. Cambridge: Cambridge University Press, 2020.
Bano, Masooda, and Hanane Benadi. "Regulating Religious Authority for Political Gains: Al-Sisi's Manipulation of Al-Azhar in Egypt." *Third World Quarterly*, 39 (2018): 1604–21.
Baqutayan, Shadiya Mohamed S., Aini Suzana Ariffin, Magda Ismail A. Mohsin, and Akbariah Mohd Mahdzir. "Waqf between the Past and Present." *Mediterranean Journal of Social Sciences*, 9 (2018): 149–55.
Baram, Amatzia. *Saddam Husayn and Islam, 1968–2003: Ba'thi Iraq from Secularism to Faith*. Baltimore, MD: Johns Hopkins University Press, 2014.
Bardakci, Mehmet, Annette Freyberg-Inan, Christoph Giesel, and Olaf Leisse. *Religious Minorities in Turkey: Alevi, Armenians, and Syriacs and the Struggle to Desecuritize Religious Freedom*. London: Palgrave Macmillan, 2017.
Barkan, Ömer Lütfi, and Ekrem Hakkı Ayverdi. *İstanbul Vakıfları Tahrir Defteri 953 (1546) Tarihli*. Istanbul: Fetih Cemiyeti, 1970.
Barkey, Karen. *Bandits and Bureaucrats: The Ottoman Route to State Centralization*. Ithaca, NY: Cornell University Press, 1994.
  Empire of Difference: The Ottomans in Comparative Perspective. Cambridge: Cambridge University Press, 2008.
Baron, Beth. "Islam, Philanthropy, and Political Culture in Interwar Egypt: The Activism of Labiba Ahmed." In *Poverty and Charity in Middle Eastern Contexts*, edited by Michael Bonner, Mine Ener, and Amy Singer, pp. 239–54. Albany: State University of New York Press, 2003.
Barnes, John Robert. *An Introduction to Religious Foundations in the Ottoman Empire*. Leiden: E. J. Brill, 1986.
Bartolucci, Valentina. "The Perils and Prospects of the French Approach to Counterterrorism." In *The Palgrave Handbook of Global Counterterrorism Policy*, edited by Scott Nicholas Romaniuk, Francis Grice, Daniela Irrera, and Stewart Webb, pp. 437–58. London: Palgrave Macmillan, 2017.
Bashear, Suliman. "On the Origins and Development of the Meaning of Zakāt in Early Islam." *Arabica*, 40 (1993): 84–113.
Baskin, Jonathan Barron, and Paul J. Miranti, Jr. *A History of Corporate Finance*. Cambridge: Cambridge University Press, 1997.

Bassiouni, M. Cherif. *Chronicles of the Egyptian Revolution and Its Aftermath: 2011–2016*. New York: Cambridge University Press, 2017.
Baş, Mustafa. *Türk Ortodoks Patrikhanesi*. Ankara: Aziz Andaç Yayınları, 2006.
Bateson, Mary Catherine. "'This Figure of Tinsel': A Study of Themes of Hypocrisy and Pessimism in Iranian Culture." *Daedalus*, 108 (1979): 125–34.
Baumgartner, Frank R., Jeffrey M. Berry, Marie Hojnaki, David C. Kimball, and Beth L. Leech. *Lobbying and Policy Change: Who Wins, Who Loses, and Why*. Chicago, IL: University of Chicago Press, 2009.
Bayat, Asef. "Activism and Social Development in the Middle East." *International Journal of Middle East Studies*, 34 (2002): 1–28.
Baykal, Erol A. F. *The Ottoman Press (1908–1923)*. Leiden: Brill, 2019.
Baykan, Toygar Sinan. *The Justice and Development Party in Turkey: Populism, Personalism, Organization*. Cambridge: Cambridge University Press, 2018.
Baytal, Yaşar. *Atatürk Döneminde Sosyal Yardım Faaliyetleri (1923–1938)*. Ankara: Atatürk Araştırma Merkezi, 2012.
Ba-Yunus, Ilyas, and Kassim Kone. *Muslims in the United States*. Westport, CT: Greenwood Press, 2006.
Beard, T. Randolph, Robert B. Ekelund, Jr., George S. Ford, and Robert D. Tollison. "The Economics of Religious Schism and Switching." In *The Oxford Handbook of Christianity and Economics*, edited by Paul Oslington, pp. 438–62. Oxford: Oxford University Press, 2014.
Beck, Thorsten, Asli Demirgüç-Kunt, and Ouarda Merrouche. "Islamic vs. Conventional Banking: Business Model, Efficiency and Stability." *Journal of Banking and Finance*, 37 (2013): 433–47.
Becker, Sascha O., Steven Pfaff, and Jared Rubin. "Causes and Consequences of the Protestant Reformation." *Explorations in Economic History*, 62 (2016): 1–25.
Bednar, Jenna, Yan Chen, Tracy Xiao Liu, and Scott Page. "Behavioral Spillovers and Cognitive Load in Multiple Games: An Experimental Study." *Games and Economic Behavior*, 74 (2012): 12–31.
Behar, Cem. *A Neighborhood in Ottoman Istanbul: Fruit Vendors and Civil Servants in the Kasap İlyas Mahalle*. Albany: State University of New York Press, 2003.
Behravesh, Maysam. "Corruption Is a Job Qualification in Today's Iran." *Foreign Policy*, 26 June 2020.
Behrens-Abouseif, Doris. *Egypt's Adjustment to Ottoman Rule: Institutions, Waqf and Architecture in Cairo, 16th and 17th Centuries*. Leiden: Brill, 1994.
"The Waqf of a Cairene Notable in Early Ottoman Cairo." In *Le Waqf dans L'Espace Islamique: Outil de Pouvoir Socio-Politique*, edited by Randi Deguilhem, pp. 123–32. Damascus: Institut Français de Damas, 1995.
"Waqf, in Egypt." *Encyclopaedia of Islam*, 2nd ed., vol. 11, pp. 63–69. Leiden: Brill, 2002.
Bein, Amit. *Ottoman Ulema, Turkish Republic: Agents of Change and Guardians of Tradition*. Stanford: Stanford University Press, 2011.
Beinin, Joel. "Formation of the Egyptian Working Class." *MERIP Reports*, 94 (1981): 14–23.
Beldiceanu, Nicoară. "Recherches sur la Réforme Foncière de Mehmed II." *Acta Historica*, 4 (1965): 27–39.

Belhaj, Abdessamad. "Bayt al-Māl." *Oxford Encyclopedia of Islam and Politics: Oxford Islamic Studies Online.* www.oxfordislamicstudies.com/article/opr/t342/e0116 (accessed 2 February 2023).
Bellin, Eva. "The Robustness of Authoritarianism in the Middle East: Exceptionalism in Comparative Perspective." *Comparative Politics*, 36 (2004): 139–57.
Bengio, Ofra. *Saddam's Word: Political Discourse in Iraq.* New York: Oxford University Press, 1998.
Ben Naceur, Sami, Adolfo Barajas, and Alexander Massara. "Can Islamic Banking Increase Financial Inclusion?" In *Handbook of Empirical Research on Islam and Economic Life*, edited by M. Kabir Hassan, pp. 213–52. Cheltenham: Edward Elgar, 2017.
Bennett, Robert J. *Local Business Voice: The History of Chambers of Commerce in Britain, Ireland, and Revolutionary America, 1760–2011.* Oxford: Oxford University Press, 2011.
Bensoussan, Georges. *Jews in Arab Countries: The Great Uprooting*, translated by Andrew Halper from the French original of 2012. Bloomington: University of Indiana Press, 2019.
Benthall, Jonathan. "Financial Worship: The Quranic Injunction to Almsgiving." *Journal of the Royal Anthropological Institute*, n.s., 5 (1999): 27–42.
  Islamic Charities and Islamic Humanism in Troubled Times. Manchester: Manchester University Press, 2016.
Benthall, Jonathan, and Jérôme Bellion-Jourdan. *The Charitable Crescent: Politics of Aid in the Muslim World.* London: I. B. Tauris, 2003.
Berger, Maurits S. "The Legal System of Family Law in Syria." *Bulletin d'Études Orientales*, 49 (1997): 115–27.
Berkel, Maaike van. "Waqf Documents on the Provision of Water in Medieval Egypt." In *Legal Documents as Sources for the History of Muslim Societies*, edited by Maaike van Berkel, Léon Buskens, and Petra Sijpesteijn, pp. 231–44. Leiden: Brill, 2017.
Berkes, Niyazi. *The Development of Secularism in Turkey.* New York: Routledge, 1998; original edition 1964.
Berkey, Jonathan P. *The Formation of Islam: Religion and Society in the Near East, 600–1800.* New York: Cambridge University Press, 2003.
Berman, Harold J. *Law and Revolution: The Formation of the Western Legal Tradition.* Cambridge, MA: Harvard University Press, 1983.
Bermek, Sevinç. *The Rise of Hybrid Political Islam in Turkey: Origins and Consolidation of the JDP.* London: Palgrave Macmillan, 2019.
Bermeo, Nancy. "On Democratic Backsliding." *Journal of Democracy*, 27 (2016): 5–19.
Berque, Jacques. *Maghreb: Histoire et Sociétés.* Algiers: SNED, 1974.
Bertelsen, Rasmus G. "Private Foreign-Affiliated Universities, the State, and Soft Power: The American University of Beirut and the American University of Cairo." *Foreign Policy Analysis*, 8 (2012): 293–311.
Besley, Timothy, and Maitreesh Ghatak. "Property Rights and Economic Development." In *Handbook of Development Economics*, vol. 5, edited by Dani Rodrik and Mark R. Rosenzweig, pp. 4525–95. Amsterdam: North-Holland, 2010.
Bessard, Fanny. *Caliphs and Merchants: Cities and Economies of Power in the Near East (700–950).* Oxford: Oxford University Press, 2020.

Bharier, Julian. "A Note on the Population of Iran, 1900–1966." *Population Studies*, 22 (1968): 273–79.

Bikmen, Filiz. *The Landscape of Philanthropy and Civil Society in Turkey.* Istanbul: Third Sector Foundation of Turkey, 2006.

Binzel, Christine, and Dietmar Fehr. "Social Distance and Trust: Experimental Evidence from a Slum in Cairo." *Journal of Development Economics*, 103 (2013): 99–106.

Birdal, Murat. *The Political Economy of Ottoman Public Debt: Insolvency and European Financial Control in the Late Nineteenth Century.* New York: I. B. Tauris, 2010.

Bishara, Dina. "Legacy Trade Unions as Brokers of Democratization? Lessons from Tunisia." *Comparative Politics*, 52 (2020): 173–95.

Bittles, Alan H., and Michael L. Black. "Consanguinity, Human Evolution, and Complex Diseases." *PNAS*, 107 (2010): 1779–86.

Björkman, W. "Maks." *Encyclopaedia of Islam*, 2nd ed., vol. 6, pp. 194–95. Leiden: Brill, 1991.

Blackman, Alexandra. "Ideological Responses to Settler Colonialism: Political Identities in Post-Independence Tunisia." PhD dissertation, Stanford University, 2019.

Blaydes, Lisa. *Elections and Distributive Politics in Mubarak's Egypt.* Cambridge: Cambridge University Press, 2011.

"Comment on Eric Chaney's 'Democratic Change in the Arab World: Past and Present'." *Brookings Papers in Economic Activity*, 42 (2012): 404–10.

"State Building in the Middle East." *Annual Review of Political Science*, 20 (2017): 487–504.

State of Repression: Iraq under Saddam Hussein. Princeton, NJ: Princeton University Press, 2018.

"Mamluks, Property Rights, and Economic Development: Lessons from Medieval Egypt." *Politics and Society*, 47 (2019): 395–424.

Blaydes, Lisa, and Eric Chaney. "The Feudal Revolution and Europe's Rise: Political Divergence of the Christian and Muslim Worlds before 1500 CE." *American Political Science Review*, 107 (2013): 16–34.

Blaydes, Lisa, Justin Grimmer, and Alison McQueen. "Mirrors for Princes and Sultans: Advice on the Art of Governance in the Medieval Christian and Islamic Worlds." *Journal of Politics*, 80 (2018): 1150–67.

Blaydes, Lisa, and Christopher Paik. "Muslim Trade and City Growth before the Nineteenth Century: Comparative Urbanization in Europe, the Middle East and Central Asia." *British Journal of Political Science*, 51 (2021): 845–68.

Bligh, Alexander. "The Saudi Religious Elite (Ulama) as Participant in the Political System of the Kingdom." *International Journal of Middle East Studies*, 17 (1985): 37–50.

Bodinier, Bernard and Eric Teyssier, with François Antoine. *L'Événement le Plus Important de la Révolution: La Vente des Biens Nationaux.* Paris: Éditions du CTHS, 2000.

Boduszyński, Mieczysław, Kristin Fabbe, and Chritopher Lamont, "After the Arab Spring: Are Secular Parties the Answer?" *Journal of Democracy*, 26 (2015): 125–39.

Boettke, Peter J. *F. A. Hayek: Economics, Political Economy and Social Philosophy.* London: Palgrave Macmillan, 2018.

Boettke, Peter J., and Rosolino A. Candela. "The Liberty of Progress: Increasing Returns, Institutions, and Entrepreneurship." *Social Philosophy and Policy*, 34 (2017): 136–63.
Boghani, Priyanka. "The Paradox of Saudi Arabia's Reforms." *Frontline*, 1 October 2018.
Bohdanowicz, M. Arsalan. "The Truth about the Armenian Question during the First World War." *Journal of the Pakistan Historical Society*, 1 (1953): 184–204.
Bohnet, Iris, Benedikt Hermann, and Richard Zeckhauser. "Trust and Reference Points for Trustworthiness in Gulf and Western Countries." *Quarterly Journal of Economics* 125 (2010): 811–28.
Bonine, Michael E. "Islam and Commerce: Waqf and the Bazaar of Yazd, Iran." *Erdkunde*, 41 (1987): 182–96.
Bonner, Michael. "Definitions of Poverty and the Rise of the Muslim Urban Poor." *Journal of the Royal Asiatic Society*, 6 (1996): 335–44.
 "Poverty and Charity in the Rise of Islam." In *Poverty and Charity in Middle Eastern Contexts*, edited by Michael Bonner, Mine Ener, and Amy Singer, pp. 13–30. Albany: State University of New York Press, 2003.
Boogert, Maurits H. van den. "Provocative Wealth: Non-Muslim Elites in Eighteenth-Century Aleppo." *Journal of Early Modern History*, 14 (2010): 219–37.
 "Ottoman Brokers in the 18th-Century Levant Trade." In *Ottoman War and Peace*, edited by Frank Castiglione, Ethan Menchinger, and Veysel Şimşek, pp. 368–85. Leiden: Brill, 2020.
Bora, Tanıl. *Cereyanlar: Türkiye'de Siyasî İdeolojiler*. Istanbul: İletişim, 2017.
Bormans, Maurice. "Le 'Ministère de l'Enseignement Originel et des Affaires Religieuses,' en Algérie, et Son Activité Culturelle." *Oriento Moderno*, 52 (1972): 467–81.
Bos, Matthijs van den. *Mystic Regimes: Sufism and the State in Iran, from the Late Qajar Era to the Islamic Republic*. Leiden: Brill, 2002.
Bosker, Maarten, Eltjo Buringh, and Jan Luiten van Zanden. "From Baghdad to London: Unraveling Urban Development in Europe, the Middle East, and North Africa, 800–1800." *Review of Economics and Statistics* 95 (2013): 1418–37.
Boston Consulting Group. "When the Clients Take the Lead: Global Wealth 2021." BCG press release, June 2021. https://web-assets.bcg.com/d4/47/64895c544486a7411b06ba4099f2/bcg-global-wealth-2021-jun-2021.pdf (accessed 2 February 2023).
Böttcher, Annabelle. "Le Ministère des *Waqfs*." *Maghreb, Machrek, Monde Arabe*, 158 (1997) 18–31.
Bottoni, Rossella. "The Headscarf Issue at State Institutions in Turkey: From the Kemalist Age to Recent Developments." In *Freedom of Religion and Belief in Turkey*, edited by Özgür Heval Çınar and Mine Yıldırım, pp. 116–38. Newcastle upon Tyne: Cambridge Scholars Publishing, 2014.
Boulby, Marion. "The Islamic Challenge: Tunisia since Independence." *Third World Quarterly*, 10 (1988): 590–614.
Bouquet, Olivier. *Les Pachas du Sultan: Essai sur les Agents Supérieurs de l'État Ottoman (1839–1909)*. Paris: Petters, 2007.
Bowler, Shaun, and Stephen P. Nicholson. "Information Cues and Rational Ignorance." In *The Oxford Handbook of Public Choice*, vol. 1, edited by Roger D. Congleton,

Bernard N. Grofman, and Stefan Voigt, pp. 381–94. New York: Oxford University Press, 2019.
Boyar, Ebru. "Medicine in Practice: European Influences on the Ottoman Medical Habitat." *Turkish Historical Review*, 9 (2018): 213–41.
Boyle, Kevin, and Juliet Sheen, eds. *Freedom of Religion and Belief: A World Report*. London: Routledge, 1997.
Bozarslan, Hamit. *Histoire de la Turquie: De L'Empire à Nos Jours*. Paris: Tallandier, 2013.
Bras, Jean Philippe. "L'Islam Administré: Illustrations Tunisiennes." In *Public et Privé en Islam: Espaces, Autorités et Libertés*, edited by Mohamed Kerrou, pp. 225–44. Tunis: Institut de Recherche sur le Maghreb Contemporain, 2014.
Bravmann, Meïr. "Surplus of Property: An Early Arab Social Concept," *Der Islam*, 38 (1963): 28–50.
Brentjes, Sonja. *Travellers from Europe in the Ottoman and Safavid Empires, 16th–17th Centuries: Seeking, Transforming, Discarding Knowledge*. Burlington, VT: Ashgate, 2010.
Bright Line Watch. "Tempered Expectations and Hardened Divisions a Year into the Biden Presidency." November 2021 surveys. https://archive.is/NgDZj (accessed 2 February 2023)
Bromley, Patricia. "The Organizational Transformation of Civil Society." In *The Nonprofit Sector: A Research Handbook*, 3rd ed., edited by Walter W. Powell and Patricia Bromley, pp. 123–43. Stanford: Stanford University Press, 2020.
Broms, Rasmus, and Andrej Kokkonen. "Inheritance Regimes: Medieval Family Structures and Current Institutional Quality." *Governance*, 32 (2019): 619–37.
Browers, Michaelle L. *Democracy and Civil Society in Arab Political Thought: Transcultural Possibilities*. Syracuse, NY: Syracuse University Press, 2006.
Brown, Jonathan A. C. "Even If It's Not True It's True: Using Unreliable Ḥadīths in Sunni Islam." *Islamic Law and Society*, 18 (2011): 1–52.
Brown, Leon Carl. "The Role of Islam in Modern North Africa." In *State and Society in Independent North Africa*, edited by Leon Carl Brown, pp. 97–122. Washington, DC: Middle East Institute, 1966.
  The Tunisia of Ahmad Bey, 1837–1855. Princeton, NJ: Princeton University Press, 1974.
Brown, Nathan J. *The Rule of Law in the Arab World: Courts in Egypt and the Gulf*. Cambridge: Cambridge University Press, 1997.
  "Constitutional Revolutions and the Public Sphere." In *The Arab Uprisings Explained: New Contentious Politics in the Middle East*, edited by Marc Lynch, pp. 296–312. New York: Columbia University Press, 2014.
  "The Transition: From Mubarak's Fall to the 2014 Presidential Election." *Adelphi Series*, 55 (2015): 15–32.
  "Citizenship, Religious Rights, and State Identity in Arab Constitutions: Who Is Free and What Are They Free to Do?" In *Freedom of Religion, Secularism, and Human Rights*, edited by Nehal Bhuta, pp. 53–68. Oxford: Oxford University Press, 2019.
Bruce, Benjamin. *Governing Islam Abroad: Turkish and Moroccan Muslims in Western Europe*. Cham: Palgrave Macmillan, 2019.
Bruinessen, Martin van. *Agha, Shaikh and State: The Social and Political Structures of Kurdistan*. London: Zed Books, 1992.

Brummett, Palmira. *Ottoman Seapower and Levantine Diplomacy in the Age of Discovery*. Albany: State University of New York Press, 1994.
Bucar, Elizabeth. *Pious Fashion: How Muslim Women Dress*. Cambridge, MA: Harvard University Press, 2017.
Buchanan, James M., and Gordon Tullock. *The Calculus of Consent: Logical Foundations of Constitutional Democracy*. Ann Arbor: University of Michigan Press, 1962.
Buğra, Ayşe. *State and Business in Modern Turkey: A Comparative Study*. Albany: State University of New York Press, 1994.
  "Labour, Capital, and Religion: Harmony and Conflict among the Constituency of Political Islam in Turkey." *Middle Eastern Studies*, 38 (2002): 187–204.
Buğra, Ayşe, and Osman Savaşkan. "Politics and Class: The Turkish Business Environment in the Neoliberal Age." *New Perspectives on Turkey*, 46 (2012): 27–63.
Bunt, Gary R. *Hashtag Islam: How Cyber-Islamic Environments Are Transforming Religious Authority*. Chapel Hill: University of North Carolina Press, 2018.
Burns, Robert Ignatius, SJ. *Medieval Colonialism: Postcrusade Exploitation of Islamic Valencia*. Princeton, NJ: Princeton University Press, 1975.
Burr, J. Millard, and Robert O. Collins. *Alms for Jihad: Charity and Terrorism in the Islamic World*. Cambridge: Cambridge University Press, 2006.
Burton, John. *The Sources of Islamic Law: Islamic Theories of Abrogation*. Edinburgh: Edinburgh University Press, 1990.
Burweila, Aya, and John M. Nomikos. "Libya and the New Axis of Terror: Reshaping the Security Theater in MENA and Europe." *International Journal of Intelligence and Counterintelligence*, 32 (2019): 54–81.
Bush, Robin. *Nahdlatul Ulama and the Struggle for Power within Islam and Politics in Indonesia*. Singapore: Institute of Southeast Asian Studies, 2009.
Byman, Daniel. "Understanding the Islamic State – A Review Essay." *International Security*, 40 (2016): 127–65.
Byrne, Julie. *The Other Catholics: Remaking America's Largest Religion*. New York: Columbia University Press, 2016.
Çadırcı, Musa. *Tanzimat Döneminde Anadolu Kentleri'nin Sosyal ve Ekonomik Yapıları*. Ankara: Türk Tarih Kurumu, 1991.
Caeiro, Alexandre. "The Making of the Fatwa: The Production of Islamic Legal Expertise in Europe." *Archives de Sciences Sociales des Religions*, 155 (2011): 81–100.
Cagaptay, Soner. *The New Sultan: Erdogan and the Crisis of Modern Turkey*. London: I. B. Tauris, 2017.
  Erdogan's Empire: Turkey and the Politics of the Middle East. London: I. B. Tauris, 2020.
Cagaptay, Soner, and Oya Rose Aktas. "How Erdoganism Is Killing Turkish Democracy: The End of Political Opposition." *Foreign Affairs* online, 7 July 2017. www.foreignaffairs.com/articles/turkey/2017-07-07/how-erdoganism-killing-turkish-democracy (accessed 6 February 2023).
Çağatay, Neşet. "Ribā and İnterest Concept and Banking in the Ottoman Empire." *Studia Islamica*, 32 (1970): 53–68.
Cahen, Claude. "La Régime des Impôts dans le Fayyūm Ayyūbide." *Arabica*, 3 (1956): 8–30.

"Kharādj, in the Central and Western Islamic Lands." *Encyclopaedia of Islam*, 2nd ed., vol. 4, pp. 1030–34 (Leiden: E. J. Brill, 1978).
"Bayt al-Māl, History." *Encyclopaedia of Islam*, 2nd ed., vol. 1 (Leiden: E. J. Brill, 1986), pp. 1143–47.
Çakır, Coşkun. "Türk Aydınının Tanzimat'la İmtihanı: Tanzimat ve Tanzimat Dönemi Siyasî Tarihi Üzerine Yapılan Çalışmalar." *Türkiye Araştırmaları Literatür Dergisi*, 2 (2004): 9–69.
Çakmak, Yalçın. "Richard Leonhard'ın 'Galatya'da Kızılbaşlar' Başlıklı Gözlem-Değerlendirmelerinin Analizi ve Osmanlıca Transkripsiyonu." *Kebikeç*, 48 (2019): 57–81.
Calamanti, Andrea. "The Tunis Stock Exchange." *Savings and Development*, 3 (1979): 157–84.
Cameron, Euan. *The European Reformation*. Oxford: Clarendon Press, 1991.
Cameron, Lisa, Ananish Chaudhuri, Nisvan Erkal, and Lata Gangadharan. "Propensities to Engage in and Punish Corrupt Behavior: Experimental Evidence from Australia, India, Indonesia, and Singapore." *Journal of Public Economics*, 93 (2009): 843–51.
Cammett, Melani. "Business–Government Relations and Industrial Change: The Politics of Upgrading in Morocco and Tunisia." *World Development*, 35 (2007): 1889–903.
  Globalization and Business Politics in Arab North Africa: A Comparative Perspective. Cambridge: Cambridge University Press, 2007.
Cammett, Melani, Ishac Diwan, Alan Richards, and John Waterbury. *A Political Economy of the Middle East*, 4th ed. Boulder, CO: Westview Press, 2015.
Cammett, Melani, and Marsha Pripstein Posusney. "Labor Standards and Labor Market Flexibility in the Middle East: Free Trade and Freer Unions?" *Studies in Comparative International Development*, 45 (2010): 250–79.
Campbell, John. *Travels through Egypt, Turkey, Syria and the Holy Land*. London: W. Reeve, 1758.
Campbell-Reed, Eileen R. *Anatomy of a Schism: How Clergywomen's Narratives Reinterpret the Fracturing of the Southern Baptist Convention*. Knoxville: University of Tennessee Press, 2016.
Cansunar, Asli. "Distributional Consequences of Philanthropic Contributions to Public Goods: Self-Serving Elites in Ottoman Istanbul." *Journal of Politics*, 84 (2022): 889–907.
Cansunar, Asli, and Timur Kuran. "Economic Harbingers of Political Modernization: Peaceful Explosion of Rights in Ottoman Istanbul." SSRN working paper, 2023.
Cantoni, Davide, Jeremiah Dittmar, and Noam Yuchtman. "Religious Competition and Reallocation: The Political Economy of Secularization in the Protestant Reformation." *Quarterly Journal of Economics*, 133 (2018): 2037–96.
Çapa, Mesut. *Kızılay (Hilâl-i Ahmer) Cemiyeti (1914–1925)*. Ankara: Türk Kızılayı, 2009.
Caplan, Bryan. *The Myth of the Rational Voter: Why Democracies Choose Bad Policies*. Princeton, NJ: Princeton University Press, 2007.
Carapico, Sheila. "Egypt's Civic Revolution Turns 'Democracy Promotion' on Its Head." In *Arab Spring in Egypt: Revolution and Beyond*, edited by Bahgat Korany and Rabab El-Mahdi, pp. 199–222. Cairo: University of Cairo Press, 2012.

Çarkoğlu, Ali. "Religiosity, Support for *Şeriat* and Evaluations of Secularist Public Policies in Turkey." *Middle Eastern Studies*, 40 (2004): 111–36.

"Trends in Individual Giving and Foundation Practices." In *Philanthropy in Turkey: Citizens, Foundations and the Pursuit of Social Justice*, edited by Filiz Bikmen and Rana Zincir, pp. 95–142. Istanbul: Third Sector Foundation of Turkey, 2006.

Carter, Barbara L. *The Copts in Egyptian Politics, 1918–1952*. London: Croom Helm, 1986.

Carvalho, Jean-Paul. "Veiling." *Quarterly Journal of Economics* 128 (2013): 337–70.

Carvalho, Jean-Paul, and Mark Koyama. "Jewish Emancipation and Schism: Economic Development and Religious Change." *Journal of Comparative Economics*, 44 (2016): 562–84.

Casale, Giancarlo. *The Ottoman Age of Exploration*. Oxford: Oxford University Press, 2010.

Cason, Timothy, and Lada Gangadharan. "Cooperation Spillovers and Price Competition in Experimental Markets." *Economic Inquiry*, 51 (2013): 1715–30.

Çelik, Gözlem Akarsu. "'Dini Oluşumlar' Raporu'nu Diyanet, Kime Yazdı?" *Gazete Duvar*, 31 May 2019. www.gazeteduvar.com.tr/yazarlar/2019/05/31/dini-olusum lar-raporunu-diyanet-kime-yazdi/ (accessed 3 February 2023).

Celso, Anthony N. "Al Qaeda in the Maghreb: The 'Newest' Front in the War on Terror." *Mediterranean Quarterly*, 19 (2008): 80–96.

Cengiz, Zerrin, Pelin Yenigün Dilek, Ezgican Özdemir, Hande Özhabeş, R. Bülent Tarhan, Ayşe Üstünel Yırcalı, and Ceren Zeytinoğlu. *Yolsuzluk ve Yolsuzlukla Mücadele Türkiye Değerlendirme Raporu*. Istanbul: TESEV, 2014.

Ceron, Andrea. "The Politics of Fission: An Analysis of Faction Breakaways among Italian Parties (1946–2011)." *British Journal of Political Science*, 45 (2013): 121–39.

Cesari, Jocelyne. *Why the West Fears Islam: An Exploration of Muslims in Liberal Democracies*. New York: Palgrave Macmillan, 2013.

Çetinsaya, Gökhan. *Ottoman Administration of Iraq, 1890–1908*. London: Routledge, 2006.

Ceylan, Ebubekir. *The Ottoman Origins of Modern Iraq: Political Reform, Modernization and Development in the Nineteenth-Century Middle East*. London: I. B. Tauris, 2011.

Chadwick, Henry. *East and West: The Making of a Rift in the Church*. Oxford: Oxford University Press, 2003.

Chalcraft, John T. *The Striking Cabbies of Cairo and Other Stories: Crafts and Guilds in Egypt, 1863–1914*. Albany: State University of New York Press, 2005.

Chaney, Eric. "Democratic Change in the Arab World, Past and Present." *Brookings Papers in Economic Activity*, 42 (2012): 363–414.

Chapra, M. Umer. *Islam and the Economic Challenge*. Leicester: Islamic Foundation, 1992.

Charrad, Mounira M. *The State and Women's Rights: The Making of Postcolonial Tunisia, Algeria, and Morocco*. Berkeley: University of California Press, 2001.

Chaudhuri, K. N. *Trade and Civilization in the Indian Ocean: An Economic History from the Rise of Islam to 1750*. Cambridge: Cambridge University Press, 1985.

Chaumont, Eric. "Al-Shāfiʿī." *Encyclopaedia of Islam*, 2nd ed., vol. 9, pp. 185–89. Leiden: E. J. Brill, 2003.

Chavoshian, Sana. "Secular Atmospheres: Unveiling and Urban Space in Early 20th Century Iran." *Historical Social Research*, 44 (2019): 180–205.
Chawki, Mohamed. "Islam in the Digital Age: Counselling and Fatwas at the Click of a Mouse." *Journal of International Commercial Law and Technology*, 5 (2010): 165–80.
Chekir, Hamouda, and Ishac Diwan. "Crony Capitalism in Egypt." *Journal of Globalization and Development*, 5 (2014): 177–211.
Choi, Sung-Eun. *Decolonization and the French of Algeria: Bringing the Settler Colony Home*. Houndmills: Palgrave Macmillan, 2016.
Çiçek, Kemal. *Ermenilerin Zorunlu Göçü 1915–1917*. Ankara: Türk Tarih Kurumu, 2005.
Ciddi, Sinan. *Kemalism in Turkish Politics: The Republican People's Party, Secularism and Nationalism*. London: Routledge, 2009.
CIVICUS. "Enabling Environment Index 2013." http://civicus.org/eei (accessed 2 February 2023).
Çizakça, Murat. *A Comparative Evolution of Business Partnerships: The Islamic World and Europe, with Special Reference to the Ottoman Archives*. Leiden: E. J. Brill, 1996.
  A History of Philanthropic Foundations: The Islamic World from the Seventh Century to the Present. Istanbul: Boğaziçi University Press, 2000.
  "From Destruction to Restoration – Islamic Waqfs in Modern Turkey and Malaysia." *Endowment Studies*, 2 (2018): 83–106.
Clarence-Smith, William Gervase. *Islam and the Abolition of Slavery*. Oxford: Oxford University Press, 2006.
Clark, Janine A. "Field Research Methods in the Middle East." *PS: Political Science & Politics*, 39 (2006): 417–23.
Clarke, John I. "Population Policies and Dynamics in Tunisia." *Journal of Developing Areas*, 4 (1969): 45–58.
Clay, Christopher. "The Origins of Modern Banking in the Levant: The Branch Network of the Imperial Ottoman Bank, 1890–1914." *International Journal of Middle East Studies*, 26 (1994): 589–614.
Clayer, Nathalie. "An Imposed or a Negotiated *Laiklik*? The Administration of the Teaching of Islam in Single-Party Turkey." In *Order and Compromise: Government Practices in Turkey from the Late Ottoman Empire to the Early 21st Century*, edited by Marc Aymes, Benjamin Gourisse, and Élise Massicard, pp. 97–120. Leiden: Brill, 2015.
Cleveland, William L. "The Municipal Council of Tunis, 1858–1870: A Study in Urban Institutional Change." *International Journal of Middle East Studies*, 9 (1978): 33–61.
Cline, Lawrence E. "The Prospects of the Shia Insurgency Movement in Iraq." *Journal of Conflict Studies*, 20 (2000): 44–67.
Cohen, Hayyim J. "The Economic Background and the Secular Occupations of Muslim Jurisprudents and Traditionists in the Classical Period of Islam (until the Middle of the Eleventh Century)." *Journal of the Economic and Social History of the Orient*, 13 (1970): 16–61.
Cohen, Mark R. "What Was the Pact of 'Umar? A Literary-Historical Survey." *Jerusalem Studies in Arabic and Islam*," 23 (1999): 100–157.

"Feeding the Poor and Clothing the Naked: The Cairo Geniza." *Journal of Interdisciplinary History*, 35 (2005): 407–21.
Çokgezen, Murat. "Can the State Make You More Religious? Evidence from Turkish Experience." *Journal for the Scientific Study of Religion*, 61 (2022): 349–73.
Çokgezen, Murat, and Timur Kuran. "Between Markets and Islamic Law: The Evolution of Islamic Credit Cards in Turkey." *Journal of Comparative Economics*, 43 (2015): 862–83.
Cole, Juan. "Al-Tahtawi on Poverty and Welfare." In *Poverty and Charity in Middle Eastern Contexts*, edited by Michael Bonner, Mine Ener, and Amy Singer, pp. 223–38. Albany: State University of New York Press, 2003.
  "Why I Left the Far-Right: Joram van Klaveren's Journey to Islam." Informed Comment, 30 August 2019: www.juancole.com/2019/08/joram-klaverens-journey.html (accessed 2 February 2023).
Coleman, James S. *Foundations of Social Theory*. Cambridge, MA: Harvard University Press, 1990.
Collinson, Patrick. "The Late Medieval Church and Its Reformation, 1400–1600." In *The Oxford History of Christianity*, edited by John McManners, pp. 243–76. Oxford: Oxford University Press, 1993.
Commins, David. *Islamic Reform: Politics and Social Change in Late Ottoman Syria*. New York: Oxford University Press, 1990.
  The Wahhabi Mission and Saudi Arabia. New York: I. B. Tauris, 2006.
Constable, Giles. *Monastic Tithes: From Their Origins to the Twelfth Century*. Cambridge: Cambridge University Press, 1964.
Constable, Olivia Remie. *Trade and Traders in Muslim Spain: The Commercial Realignment of the Iberian Peninsula, 900–1500*. New York: Cambridge University Press, 1994.
Cook, David. *Understanding Jihad*. Berkeley: University of California Press, 2005.
Cook, Michael. *Commanding Right and Forbidding Wrong in Islamic Thought*. Cambridge: Cambridge University Press, 2000.
Cook, Steven A. *False Dawn: Protest, Democracy, and Violence in the New Middle East*. Oxford: Oxford University Press, 2017.
Cooray, Arusha, and Niklas Potrafke. "Gender Inequality in Education: Political Institutions or Culture and Religion?" *European Journal of Political Economy*, 27 (2011): 268–80.
Cora, Yaşar Tolga. "A Muslim Great Merchant [*Tüccar*] Family in the Late Ottoman Empire: A Case Study of the Nemlizades, 1860–1930." *International Journal of Turkish Studies*, 19 (2013): 1–29.
Corbett, Rosemary R. *Making Moderate Islam: Sufism, Service, and the "Ground Zero Mosque" Controversy*. Stanford: Stanford University Press, 2017.
Coşgel, Metin. "Taxes, Efficiency, and Redistribution: Discriminatory Taxation of Villages in Ottoman Palestine, Southern Syria, and Transjordan in the Sixteenth Century." *Explorations in Economic History*, 43 (2006): 332–56.
Coşkun, Ali. *Sosyal Değişme ve Dini Normlar*. Istanbul: Dem, 2005.
Cougar, Yves. *After Nine Hundred Years: The Background of the Schism between the Eastern and Western Churches*. New York: Fordham University Press, 1959.
Coulson, Noel J. "Bayt al-Māl." *Encyclopaedia of Islam*, 2nd ed., vol. 1, pp. 1141–43. Leiden: E. J. Brill, 1986.

Courbage, Youssef, and Philippe Fargues. *Christians and Jews under Islam*, translated by Judy Mabro from the French original of 1992. London: I. B. Tauris, 1997.
Cox, Gary W. "Was the Glorious Revolution a Constitutional Watershed?" *Journal of Economic History*, 72 (2012): 567–600.
  Marketing Sovereign Promises: Monopoly Brokerage and the Growth of the English State. Cambridge: Cambridge University Press, 2016.
Cragin, R. Kim. "Tactical Partnerships for Strategic Effects: Recent Experiences of US Forces Working by, with, and through Surrogates in Syria and Libya." *Defence Studies*, 20 (2020): 318–35.
Cromer, Evelyn Baring. *Modern Egypt*, 2 vols. New York: Macmillan, 1909.
Crone, Patricia. *Meccan Trade and the Rise of Islam*. Princeton, NJ: Princeton University Press, 1987.
  God's Rule: Government and Islam. New York: Columbia University Press, 2004.
Crone, Patricia, and Martin Hinds. *God's Caliph: Religious Authority in the First Centuries of Islam*. Cambridge: Cambridge University Press, 1986.
Cronin, Stephanie. "Importing Modernity: European Military Missions to Qajar Iran." *Comparative Studies in Society and History*, 50 (2008): 197–226.
Cunningham, Robert B., and Yasin K. Sarayrah. *Wasta: The Hidden Force in Middle Eastern Society*. Westport, CT: Praeger, 1993.
Dabashi, Hamid. *Authority in Islam: From the Rise of Muhammad to the Establishment of the Umayyads*. New Brunswick, NJ: Transaction Publishers, 1989.
  "Mīr Dāmād and the Founding of the 'School of Iṣfahān'." In *History of Islamic Philosophy*, edited by Seyyed Hossein Nasr and Oliver Leaman, pp. 1061–124. London: Routledge, 1996.
Dadkhah, Kamran M. "Iran and the Global Finance Markets." In *Iran Encountering Globalization: Problems and Prospects*, edited by Ali Mohammadi, pp. 86–106. London: RoutledgeCurzon, 2003.
Dahl, Robert A. *Democracy and Its Critics*. New Haven, CT: Yale University Press, 1989.
Dahlén, Ashk P. *Islamic Law, Epistemology and Modernity: Legal Philosophy in Contemporary Iran*. New York: Routledge, 2003.
Dallal, Ahmad. "The Islamic Institution of Waqf: A Historical Overview." In *Islam and Social Policy*, edited by Stephen P. Heyneman, pp. 13–43. Nashville, TN: Vanderbilt University Press, 2004.
Danon, Dina. *The Jews of Ottoman Izmir: A Modern History*. Stanford: Stanford University Press, 2020.
Darling, Linda T. *Revenue-Raising and Legitimacy: Tax Collection and Finance Administration in the Ottoman Empire, 1560–1660*. Leiden: E. J. Brill, 1996.
  A History of Social Justice and Political Power in the Middle East: The Circle of Justice from Mesopotamia to Globalization. London: Routledge, 2013.
  "Ottoman Customs Registers (*Gümrük Defterleri*) as Sources for Global Exchange and Interaction." *Review of Middle East Studies*, 49 (2015): 3–22.
Davidson, Christopher. *Shadow Wars: The Secret Struggle for the Middle East*. London: Oneworld, 2016.
Davidson, James D., Joseph A. Schlangen, and William V. D'Antonio. "Protestant and Catholic Perceptions of Church Structure." *Social Forces*, 47 (1969): 314–22.

Davis, Eric. *Challenging Colonialism: Bank Mişr and Egyptian Industrialization, 1920–1941.* Princeton, NJ: Princeton University Press, 1983.

Davis, Ralph. *Aleppo and Devonshire Square: English Traders in the Levant in the Eighteenth Century.* London: Macmillan, 1967.

Davison, Roderic H. *Reform in the Ottoman Empire, 1856–1876.* Princeton, NJ: Princeton University Press, 1963.

Dawson, Lorne. "Church–Sect–Cult: Constructing Typologies of Religious Groups." In *The Oxford Handbook of the Sociology of Religion* (2018 online ed.), edited by Peter B. Clarke, pp. 1–20.

Deane, Jennifer Kolpacoff. *A History of Medieval Heresy and Inquisition.* Lanham, MD: Rowman & Littlefield, 2011.

Deeb, Marius. "Bank Misr and the Emergence of the Local Bourgeoisie in Egypt." *Middle Eastern Studies*, 12 (1976): 69–86.

"The Socioeconomic Role of the Local Foreign Minorities in Modern Egypt, 1805–1961." *International Journal of Middle East Studies*, 9 (1978): 11–22.

Deffains, Bruno, Romain Espinosa, and Christian Thöni. "Political Self-Serving Bias and Redistribution." *Journal of Public Economics*, 134 (2016): 67–74.

Deguilhem, Randi. "On the Nature of Waqf: Pious Foundations in Contemporary Syria." In *Les Fondations Pieuses (Waqf) en Méditerranée: Enjeux de Société, Enjeux de Pouvoir*, pp. 395–430. Kuwait: Kuwait Awqaf Public Foundation, 2004.

"The Waqf in the City." In *The City in the Islamic World*, vol. 2, edited by Salma Khadra Jayyusi, Renata Holod, Antillio Petruccioli, and André Raymond, pp. 929–56. Leiden: Brill, 2008.

Deguilhem-Schoem, Randi. "The Loan of Mursad on Waqf Properties." In *A Way Prepared: Essays on Islamic Culture in Honor of Richard Bayly Winder*, edited by Farhad Kazemi and Robert D. McChesney, pp. 68–79. New York: New York University Press, 1988.

De Jong, Fred. "The Şūfī Orders in Egypt during the 'Urābī Insurrection and the British Occupation (1882–1914): Some Societal Factors Generating Aloofness, Support, and Opposition." *Journal of the American Research Center in Egypt*, 21 (1984): 131–39.

Deligöz, Halil. "The Legacy of Vakıf Institutions and the Management of Social Policy in Turkey." *Administrative Culture*, 15 (2014): 179–203.

DellaPergola, Sergio. *World Jewish Population, 2010.* Storrs: Mandell L. Berman Institute, 2010.

DeLong-Bas, Natana J. *Wahhabi Islam: From Revival and Reform to Global Jihad.* Oxford: Oxford University Press, 2004.

Delumeau, Jean. *Sin and Fear: The Emergence of a Western Guilt Culture, 13th–18th Centuries*, translated by Eric Nicholson from the French original of 1983. New York: St. Martin's Press, 1990.

Demir, İlhan. *Yeni Vakıfların Temel Kitabı.* Ankara: Hu-Der, 1998.

Demirel, Ömer. *Sivas Şehir Hayatında Vakıfların Rolü.* Ankara: Türk Tarih Kurumu, 2000.

Demirezen, İsmail. *Tüketim Toplumu ve Din.* Istanbul: Değerler Eğitim Merkezi, 2015.

Dennett, Daniel Clement, Jr. *Conversion and the Poll Tax in Early Islam.* Cambridge, MA: Harvard University Press, 1950.

Denoeux, Guilain. *Urban Unrest in the Middle East: A Comparative Study of Informal Networks in Egypt, Iran, and Lebanon*. New York: State University of New York Press, 1993.
Deringil, Selim. "'There Is No Compulsion in Religion': On Conversion and Apostasy in the Late Ottoman Empire: 1839-1856." *Comparative Studies in Society and History*, 42 (2000): 547-75.
Conversion and Apostasy in the Late Ottoman Empire. Cambridge: Cambridge University Press, 2012.
Der Matossian, Bedross. "The Armenian Commercial Houses and Merchant Networks in the 19th Century Ottoman Empire." *Turcica*, 39 (2007): 147-74.
De Roover, Raymond. *The Rise and Decline of the Medici Bank, 1397-1494*. Cambridge, MA: Harvard University Press, 1963.
Derri, Aviv. "Imperial Creditors, 'Doubtful' Nationalities and Financial Obligations in Late Ottoman Syria: Rethinking Ottoman Subjecthood and Consular Protection." *International History Review*, 43 (2021): 1060-79.
Devereux, Robert. *The First Ottoman Constitutional Period: A Study of the Midhat Constitution and Parliament*. Baltimore, MD: Johns Hopkins University Press, 1963.
Dinçkal, Noyan. "Reluctant Modernization: The Cultural Dynamics of Water Supply in Istanbul, 1885-1950." *Technology and Culture*, 49 (2008): 675-700.
Dirusso, Alyssa A. "American Nonprofit Law in Comparative Perspective." *Washington University Global Studies Law Review*, 10 (2011): 39-86.
Dittmar, Jeremiah E., and Ralf R. Meisenzahl. "Public Goods Institutions, Human Capital, and Growth: Evidence from German History." *Review of Economic Studies*, 87 (2020): 959-96.
Diwan, Ishac, Adeel Malik, and Izak Atiyas, eds. *Crony Capitalism in the Middle East: Business and Politics from Liberalization to the Arab Spring*. Oxford: Oxford University Press, 2019.
[Diyanet İşleri Başkanlığı]. *Dinî-Sosyal Teşekküller, Geleneksel Dinî-Kültürel Oluşumlar ve Yeni Dinî Yönelişler*. Istanbul: Aydınlık, 2019; leaked classified report.
Do, Quy-Doan, Sriya Iyer, and Shareen Joshi. "The Economics of Consanguineous Marriages." *Review of Economics and Statistics*, 95 (2013): 904-18.
Dogan, Recep. *Political Islamists in Turkey and the Gülen Movement*. Cham: Palgrave Macmillan, 2020.
Doja, Albert. "A Political History of Bektashism from Ottoman Anatolia to Contemporary Turkey." *Journal of Church and State*, 48 (2006): 434-50.
Dolan, Paul, and Matteo M. Galizzi. "Like Ripples on a Pond: Behavioral Spillovers and Their Implications for Research and Policy." *Journal of Economic Psychology*, 47 (2015): 1-16.
Doniger, Wendy. *On Hinduism*. Oxford: Oxford University Press, 2014.
Dönmez, Ali Rıza. "Cumhuriyet Devrinde Vakıflar." PhD dissertation, Ankara University, 1991.
Donner, Fred M. *Muhammad and the Believers: At the Origins of Islam*. Cambridge, MA: Harvard University Press, 2010.
Dorman, W. Judson. "Informal Cairo: Between Islamist Insurgency and the Neglectful State?" *Security Dialogue*, 40 (2009): 419-41.

Doumani, Beshara B. "Endowing Family: *Waqf*, Property Devolution, and Gender in Greater Syria, 1800 to 1860." *Comparative Studies in Society and History*, 40 (1998): 3–41.
  Family Life in the Ottoman Mediterranean: A Social History. Cambridge: Cambridge University Press, 2017.
Doyle, Jessica Leigh. "State Control of Civil Society Organizations: The Case of Turkey." *Democratization*, 24 (2017): 244–64.
Dressler, Markus. "Inventing Orthodoxy: Competing Claims for Authority and Legitimacy in the Ottoman-Safavid Conflict." In *Legitimizing the Order: The Ottoman Rhetoric of State Power*, edited by Hakan T. Karateke and Maurus Reinkowski, pp. 151–73. Leiden: Brill, 2005.
Duderija, Adis. "Critical-Progressive Muslim Thought: Reflections on Its Political Ramifications." *Review of Faith and International Affairs*, 11 (2013): 69–79.
Duderija, Adis, and Halim Rane. *Islam and Muslims in the West: Major Issues and Debates*. Cham: Palgrave, 2019.
Dündar, Sibel, and Ömer Taylan. "İki Laiklik Modeli ve Cumhuriyet Halk Partisi (CHP)." *Dicle Üniversitesi İktisadi ve İdari Bilimler Fakültesi Dergisi*, 7 (2017): 236–45.
Durac, Vincent, and Francesco Cavatorta. *Politics and Governance in the Middle East*. London: Palgrave, 2015.
Duri, Abd al-Aziz. *Early Islamic Institutions: Administration and Taxation from the Caliphate to the Umayyads and 'Abbāsids*, translated by Razia Ali from the Arabic original of 1988. New York: I. B. Tauris, 2011.
Duwaji, Ghazi. "Land Ownership in Tunisia: An Obstacle to Agricultural Development." *Land Economics*, 44 (1968): 129–32.
Düzbakar, Ömer. "Bribery in Islam: Ottoman Penal Codes and Examples from the Bursa Shari'a Court Records of 18th Century." *Bilig*, 51 (2009): 55–84.
Düzdağ, M. Ertuğrul. *Şeyhülislâm Ebussuûd Efendi Fetvaları Işığında 16. Asır Türk Hayatı*. Istanbul: Enderun Kitabevi, 1983.
Easterlin, Richard A. *Growth Triumphant: The Twenty-First Century in Historical Perspective*. Ann Arbor: University of Michigan Press, 1996.
Easterly, William, and Ross Levine. "Tropics, Germs, and Crops: How Endowments Influence Economic Development." *Journal of Monetary Economics*, 50 (2003): 3–39.
Ebrahimnejad, Hormoz. *Medicine, Public Health and the Qājār State: Patterns of Medical Modernization in Nineteenth-Century Iran*. Leiden: Brill, 2004.
Eccel, A. Chris. *Egypt, Islam and Social Change: Al-Azhar in Conflict and Accommodation*. Berlin: Klaus Schwarz Verlag, 1984.
Economist Intelligence Unit. *Democracy Index 2020: In Sickness and Health?* London: Economist Intelligence Unit, 2021.
Efrati, Noga. "Negotiating Rights in Iraq: Women and the Personal Status Law." *Middle East Journal*, 59 (2005): 577–95.
Edlund, Lena. "Cousin Marriage Is Not Choice: Muslim Marriage and Underdevelopment." *American Economic Review*, 108 (2018): 353–57.
Egypt Today staff. "Egypt's Solidarity Ministry Puts Hand on 413 NGOs due to Affiliation to Terror Organizations." *Egypt Today*, article 96579, 10 January 2021.
Ekelund, Robert B., Robert D. Tollison, Gary M. Anderson, Robert F. Hébert, and Audrey B. Davidson. *Sacred Trust: The Medieval Church as an Economic Firm*. New York: Oxford University Press, 1994.

Ekelund, Robert B., Jr., Robert F. Hébert, and Robert D. Tollison. "An Economic Analysis of the Protestant Reformation." *Journal of Political Economy*, 110 (2002): 646–71.
Ekinci, Ekrem Buğra. *Tanzimat ve Sonrası Osmanlı Mahkemeleri*. Istanbul: Arı Sanat, 2004.
Ekins, Emily. "Poll: 62% of Americans Say They Have Political Views They're Afraid to Share." www.cato.org/survey-reports/poll-62-americans-say-they-have-political-views-theyre-afraid-share (accessed 2 February 2023).
El Daly, Marwa. *Philanthropy in Egypt*. Cairo: Center for Development Services, 2007.
Eldem, Edhem. "L'Édit des *Tanzimat* (1839): Une Relecture." *Turcica*, 52 (2021): 201–307.
"Amerika'yı Keşfetme(me)nin Yolları." *Tarih ve Toplum: Yeni Yaklaşımlar*, 18 (Spring 2021): 151–76.
Eleftheriadou, Marina. "Christian Militias in Syria and Iraq: Beyond the Neutrality/Passivity Debate." *Middle East Bulletin*, 28 (July 2015): 13–19.
El Fegiery, Momtaz. "Guarding the Mainstream: Blasphemy and Apostasy in Egypt." In *Freedom of Expression in Islam*, edited by Muhammad Khalid Masud, Kari Vogt, Lena Larsen, and Christian Moe, pp. 111–29. London: I. B. Tauris, 2021.
El-Gamal, Mahmoud A. *Islamic Finance: Law, Economics, and Practice*. New York: Cambridge University Press, 2006.
Elling, Rasmus Christian. *Minorities in Iran: Nationalism and Ethnicity after Khomeini*. New York: Palgrave Macmillan, 2013.
Elsammak, M. Y., A. A. Alwosaibi, A. Al-Howeish, and J. Alsaeed. "Vitamin D Deficiency in Saudi Arabs." *Hormone and Metabolic Research*, 42 (2010): 364–68.
Encarnación, Omar G. *The Myth of Civil Society: Social Capital and Democratic Consolidation in Spain and Brazil*. New York: Palgrave Macmillan, 2003.
Ener, Mine. *Managing Egypt's Poor and the Politics of Benevolence, 1800–1952*. Princeton, NJ: Princeton University Press, 2003.
Engels, Frederick. *Anti-Dühring*, translated by Emile Burns from the German original of 1878. Moscow: Progress Publishers, 1947.
Ennaji, Mohammed. *Slavery, the State, and Islam*, translated by Teresa Lavender Fagan from the French original of 2007. Cambridge: Cambridge University Press, 2013.
Epstein, M. *The Statesman's Year-Book: Statistical and Historical Annual of the States of the World for the Year 1931*. London: Macmillan, 1931.
Erdem, Yusuf Hakan. "The Greek Revolution and the End of the Old Ottoman Order." In *The Greek Revolution of 1821: A European Event*, edited by Petros Pizanias, pp. 257–64. Istanbul: ISIS Press, 2011.
"Erdoğan, Albayrak'ı Halefi Olarak Hazırlıyor." www.cumhuriyet.com.tr, 1028188 (accessed 2 February 2023).
Eren, Muhammet Emin. "İslam Toplumunda Ayrıştırıcı/Ötekileştirici Söylemin Oluşumunda İftirâk (73 Fırka) Hadisinin Rolü." In *Kur'an ve Toplumsal Bütünleşme (Mezhepler ve Dinî Gruplar Arası İlişkiler)*, edited by Hayati Hökelekli and Vejdi Bilgin, pp. 19–34. Bursa: Bursa Büyükşehir Belediyesi Yayınları, 2015.
Erken, Ali. "The Making of Politics and Trained Intelligence in the Near East: Robert College of Istanbul." *European Review of History*, 23 (2016): 554–71.

Erkilet-Başer, Alev. "Sağ Siyasetin Payandası: Araçsalcı Dinsellik." *İslâmiyât*, 3 (2000): 69–78.
Eroler, Elif Gençkal. *"Dindar Nesil Yetiştirmek": Türkiye'nin Eğitim Politikalarında Ulus ve Vatandaş İnşası (2002–2016)*. Istanbul: İletişim, 2019.
Ertem, Adnan. "Osmanlıdan Günümüze Vakıflar." *Vakıflar Dergisi*, 36 (2011): 25–65.
Ertit, Volkan. "God Is Dying in Turkey as Well: Application of Secularization Theory to a Non-Christian Society." *Open Theology*, 4 (2018): 192–211.
Esack, Farid. *The Qur'an: A User's Guide*. Oxford: Oneworld, 2005.
Europa World Year Book 2003, The, vol. 1. London: Europa Publications, 2003.
Evans-Pritchard, Edward E. "Arab Status in Cyrenaica under the Italians." *Sociological Review*, 36 (1944): 1–17.
Eyuboğlu, İsmet Zeki. *Günün Işığında Tasavvuf: Tarikatlar, Mezhepler Tarihi*. Istanbul: Geçit Kitabevi, 1987.
Fahmy, Dalia F., and Daanish Faruqi, eds. *Egypt and the Contradictions of Liberalism: Illiberal Intelligentsia and the Future of Egyptian Democracy*. London: Oneworld, 2017.
Fahmy, Khaled. *All the Pasha's Men: Mehmed Ali, His Army and the Making of Modern Egypt*. Cairo: American University in Cairo Press, 1997.
Fahmy, Ninette S. *The Politics of Egypt: State–Society Relationship*. London: Routledge, 2002.
Fakhry, Majid. *Averroes (Ibn Rushd): His Life, Works and Influence*. Oxford: Oneworld, 2001.
   A History of Islamic Philosophy, 3rd ed. New York: Columbia University Press, 2004.
Farha, Mark, and Salma Mousa. "Secular Autocracy vs. Sectarian Democracy? Weighing Reasons for Christian Support for Regime Transition in Syria and Egypt." *Mediterranean Politics*, 20 (2015): 178–97.
Faroqhi, Suraiya. *Anadolu'da Bektaşilik*, translated by Nasuh Barın from the German original of 1981. Istanbul: Simurg, 2003.
   Artisans of Empire: Crafts and Craftspeople under the Ottomans. London: I. B. Tauris, 2009.
Farouk-Sluglett, Marion, and Peter Sluglett. "Labor and National Liberation: The Trade Union Movement in Iraq, 1920–1958." *Arab Studies Quarterly*, 5 (1983): 139–54.
Fatafta, Marwa. "Transnational Digital Repression in the MENA Region." *POMEPS Studies*, 43 (August 2021): 41–47.
Fattah, Hala. "The Politics of the Grain Trade in Iraq c. 1840–1917." *New Perspectives on Turkey*, 5–6 (1991): 151–65.
Fattah, Khaled, and K. M. Fierke. "A Clash of Emotions: The Politics of Humiliation and Political Violence in the Middle East." *European Journal of International Relations*, 15 (2009): 67–93.
Faust, Aaron M. *The Ba'thification of Iraq: Saddam Hussein's Totalitarianism*. Austin: University of Texas Press, 2015.
Fayed, Ahmed Alaa. "The Current Status of Corruption in Egypt." *Contemporary Arab Affairs*, 10 (2017): 510–21.
Fawaz, Leila Tarazi. *Merchants and Migrants in Nineteenth-Century Beirut*. Cambridge, MA: Harvard University Press, 1983.

An Occasion for War: Civil Conflict in Lebanon and Damascus in 1860. Berkeley: University of California Press, 1995.
Fealy, Greg, and Katharine McGregor. "Nahdlatul Ulama and the Killings of 1965–66: Religion, Politics, and Remembrance." *Indonesia*, 89 (2010): 37–60.
Feldman, Noah. *The Fall and Rise of the Islamic State*. Princeton, NJ: Princeton University Press, 2008.
"Fezzan." *Encylopaedia Britannica*, 11th ed., vol. 10, pp. 307–9. New York: Encyclopeadia Britannnica, 1910–11.
Fildis, Ayse Tekdal. "Roots of Alawite–Sunni Rivalry in Syria." *Middle East Policy*, 19 (2012): 148–56.
Findley, Carter V. *Bureaucratic Reform in the Ottoman Empire: The Sublime Porte, 1789–1922*. Princeton, NJ: Princeton University Press, 1980.
  "The Acid Test of Ottomanism: The Acceptance of Non-Muslims in the Late Ottoman Bureaucracy." In *Christians and Jews in the Ottoman Empire*, vol. 1, edited by Benjamin Braude and Bernard Lewis, pp. 339–68. New York: Holmes and Meier, 1982.
  Ottoman Civil Officialdom: A Social History. Princeton, NJ: Princeton University Press, 1989.
Finer, S. E. *The History of Government*, 3 vols. Oxford: Oxford University Press, 1997.
Fiori, Stefano. "Adam Smith and the Unintended Consequences of History." *History of Economic Ideas*, 22 (2014): 55–74.
Firro, Kais. M. "Lebanese Nationalism versus Arabism: From Bulus Nujaym to Michel Chiha." *Middle Eastern Studies*, 40 (2004): 1–27.
Fischbach, Michael R. *Jewish Property Claims against Arab Countries*. New York: Columbia University Press, 2008.
Fischer, Michael M. J. *Iran: From Religious Dispute to Revolution*. Madison: University of Wisconsin Press, 2003.
Fishman, James J. *The Faithless Fiduciary and the Quest for Charitable Accountability, 1200–2005*. Durham, NC: Carolina Academic Press, 2006.
Floor, Willem M. "The Bankers (ṣarrāf) in Qājār Iran." *Zeitschrift der Deutschen Morgenländischen Gesellschaft*, 129 (1979): 263–81.
Floor, Willem. *A Fiscal History of Iran in the Safavid and Qajar Periods, 1500–1925*. New York: Bibliotheca Persica Press, 1998.
Foa, Roberto Stefan, and Yascha Mounk. "The Signs of Deconsolidation." *Journal of Democracy*, 28 (2017): 5–15.
Fowler, Megan. "Why Congregations Aren't Waiting to Leave the United Methodist Church." *Christianity Today*, 16 July 2021.
Fox, Jonathan. "Religion and State Constitutions Dataset." www.religionandstate.org (accessed 2 February 2023).
Frampton, Martyn. *The Muslim Brotherhood and the West: A History of Enmity and Engagement*. Cambridge, MA: Harvard University Press.
Fredriksen, Paula. *When Christians Were Jews: The First Generation*. New Haven, CT: Yale University Press, 2018.
Freedom House. *Freedom in the World 2012: The Arab Uprisings and Their Global Repercussions*. Washington, DC: Freedom House, 2012.
  Freedom in the World 2020. Washington, DC: Freedom House, 2020.

Freedom in the World 2021. https://freedomhouse.org/report/freedom-world/2021/democracy-under-siege (accessed 2 February 2023).

Freedom on the Net 2019: The Crisis of Social Media. https://freedomhouse.org/report/freedom-net/2019/crisis-social-media (accessed 2 February 2023).

Freely, John. *A History of Robert College*, 2 vols. Istanbul: Yapı-Kredi Yayınları, 2000.

Frend, William H. C. *The Rise of the Monophysite Movement: Chapters in the History of the Church in the Fifth and Sixth Centuries*. Cambridge: Cambridge University Press, 1972.

Friedman, Yaron. "Ibn Taymiyya's Fatāwā against the Nuṣayri-ʿAlawī Sect." *Der Islam*, 82 (2005): 349–63.

Friedmann, Yohanan. *Prophecy Continuous: Aspects of Ahmadī Religious Thought and Its Medieval Background*. Berkeley: University of California Press, 1989.

Fromkin, David. *A Peace to End All Peace: The Fall of the Ottoman Empire and the Creation of the Modern Middle East*, expanded 2nd ed. New York: Henry Holt, 2009.

Fukuyama, Francis. *Trust: The Social Virtues and the Creation of Prosperity*. New York: Free Press, 1995.

The Origins of Political Order: From Prehuman Times to the French Revolution. New York: Farrar, Straus and Giroux, 2011.

Fung, Archon. "Associations and Democracy: Between Theories, Hopes, and Realities." *Annual Review of Sociology*, 29 (2003): 515–39.

Gaborieau, Marc, Alexandre Popovic, and Thierry Zarkone, eds. *Naqshbandis*. Istanbul: ISIS Press, 1990.

Gadelrab, Sherry Sayed. "Medical Healers in Ottoman Egypt, 1517–1805." *Medical History*, 54 (2010): 365–86.

Gaffney, Patrick D. "The Changing Voices of Islam: The Emergence of Professional Preachers in Contemporary Egypt." *Muslim World*, 81 (1991): 27–47.

Gallagher, Nancy Elizabeth. *Medicine and Power in Tunisia, 1780–1900*. Cambridge: Cambridge University Press, 1983.

Gammer, Moshe. "The Imam and the Pasha: A Note on Shamil and Muhammad Ali." *Middle Eastern Studies*, 32 (1996): 336–42.

Gardet, Louis. "Dīn."*Encyclopaedia of Islam*, 2nd ed., vol. 2, pp. 293–96. Leiden: E. J. Brill, 1991.

Gasiorowski, Mark J. "The Failure of Reform in Tunisia." *Journal of Democracy*, 3 (1992): 85–97.

Gaus, Gerald. "The Egalitarian Species." *Social Philosophy and Policy*, 31 (2015): 1–27.

Gause, F. Gregory III. "Can Democracy Stop Terrorism?" *Foreign Affairs*, 84 (2005): 62–76.

Geaves, Ron. "Sufism in the UK." In *Routledge Handbook on Sufism*, edited by Lloyd Ridgeon, pp. 449–60. New York: Routledge, 2021.

Gedikli, Fethi. *Osmanlı Şirket Kültürü: XVI.–XVII. Yüzyıllarda Mudârebe Uygulaması*. Istanbul: İz Yayıncılık, 1998.

Gelderblom, Oscar. *Cities of Commerce: The Institutional Foundations of International Trade in the Low Countries, 1250–1650*. Princeton, NJ: Princeton University Press, 2013.

Gelderblom, Oscar, Abe De Jong, and Joost Jonker. "The Formative Years of the Modern Corporation: The Dutch East India Company VOC, 1602–1623." *Journal of Economic History*, 73 (2013): 1050–76.

Gellately, Robert. *Backing Hitler: Consent and Coercion in Nazi Germany.* Oxford: Oxford University Press, 2001.
Genç, Mehmet. *Osmanlı İmparatorluğunda Devlet ve Ekonomi.* Istanbul: Ötüken, 2000.
Gerber, Haim. *Economy and Society in an Ottoman City: Bursa, 1600–1700.* Jerusalem: Hebrew University, 1988.
  State, Society, and Law in Islam: Ottoman Law in Comparative Perspective. Albany: State University of New York Press, 1994.
  Islamic Law and Culture, 1600–1840. Leiden: Brill, 1999.
  "The Public Sphere and Civil Society in the Ottoman Empire." In *The Public Sphere in Muslim Societies*, edited by Miriam Hoexter, Shmuel N. Eisenstadt, and Nehemia Levtzion, pp. 65–82. New York: State University of New York Press, 2002.
Gerges, Fawaz A. *The Far Enemy: Why Jihad Went Global*, 2nd ed. Cambridge: Cambridge University Press, 2009.
  The Rise and Fall of Al-Qaeda. Oxford: Oxford University Press, 2011.
  ISIS: A History. Princeton, NJ: Princeton University Press, 2016.
Gerring, John, Michael Hoffman, and Dominic Zarecki. "The Diverse Effects of Diversity on Democracy." *British Journal of Political Science*, 48 (2018): 283–314.
Gervais, Will M., and Maxine B. Najle. "How Many Atheists Are There?" *Social Psychological and Personality Science*, 9 (2018): 3–10.
Geyikdağı, V. Necla. *Foreign Investment in the Ottoman Empire: International Trade and Relations 1854–1914.* London: I. B. Tauris, 2011.
Ghabra, Shafeeq. "The Egyptian Revolution: Causes and Dynamics." In *Routledge Handbook of the Arab Spring: Rethinking Democratization*, edited by Larbi Sadiki, pp. 199–214. New York: Routledge, 2015.
Ghamari-Tabrizi, Behrooz. "Abdolkarim Soroush." In *Key Islamic Political Thinkers*, edited by John L. Esposito and Emad El-Din Shahin, pp. 219–44. Oxford: Oxford University Press, 2018.
GhaneaBassiri, Kambiz. "Structuring Sovereignty: Islam and Modernity in the Mosque of Muhammad 'Ali Pasha." *Material Religion*, 16 (2020): 317–44.
Giannakopoulos, Angelos. "Yunanistan ve Türkiye'deki Yolsuzluk Algıları ve Bu Algıların Yolsuzlukla Mücadele Politikaları Üzerindeki Etkisi." *Turkish Journal of Business Ethics*, 3 (2010): 35–45.
Gibb, H. A. R., and Harold Bowen. *Islamic Society and the West: A Study of the Impact of Western Civilisation on Moslem Culture in the Near East*, vol. 1, 2 parts. London: Oxford University Press, 1950.
Gil, Moshe. "The Earliest *Waqf* Foundations." *Journal of Near Eastern Studies*, 57 (1998): 125–40.
Gilbar, Gad. "Qajar Dynasty viii. 'Big Merchants' in the Late Qajar Period." *Encyclopædia Iranica*, online edition, 2015. www.iranicaonline.org/articles/qajar-big-merchants (accessed 2 February 2023).
Gill, Anthony, and John M. Owen IV. "Religious Liberty and Economic Prosperity: Four Lessons from the Past." *Cato Journal*, 37 (2017): 115–34.
Gillespie, Kate, and Gwenn Okruhlik. "Cleaning up Corruption in the Middle East." *Middle East Journal*, 42 (1988): 59–82.
Ginio, Eyal. "Living on the Margins of Charity: Coping with Poverty in an Ottoman Provincial City." In *Poverty and Charity in Middle Eastern Contexts*, edited by

Michael Bonner, Mine Ener, and Amy Singer, pp. 165–84. Albany: State University of New York Press, 2003.
Glaeser, Edward. *Triumph of the City: How Our Greatest Invention Makes Us Richer, Smarter, Greener, Healthier, and Happier*. New York: Penguin Press, 2011.
Glass, Joseph B., and Ruth Kark. "The Jerusalem Chamber of Commerce, Industry, and Agriculture, 1909–1910: An Early Attempt at Inter-Communal Cooperation." *British Journal of Middle Eastern Studies*, 45 (2018): 269–89.
"Global Prevalence of Consanguinity." https://web.archive.org/web/20180303194244/http://www.consang.net/index.php/Global_prevalence (accessed 2 February 2023).
Göçek, Fatma Müge. *Rise of the Bourgeoisie, Demise of Empire: Ottoman Westernization and Social Change*. New York: Oxford University Press, 1996.
Goitein, Shelomo D. "The Rise of the Near-Eastern Bourgeoisie in Early Islamic Times." *Cahiers d'Histoire Mondiale*, 3 (1956): 593–604.
  A Mediterranean Society, 1: Economic Foundations. Berkeley: University of California Press, 1967.
Gökalp, Ziya. *Yeni Hayat, Doğru Yol*, edited by Müjgan Cunbur. Ankara: Kültür Bakanlığı, 1976.
Goldberg, Jan. "On the Origins of *Majālis Al-Tujjār* in Mid-Nineteenth Century Egypt." *Islamic Law and Society*, 6 (1999): 193–223.
Goldenberg, David M. *The Curse of Ham: Race and Slavery in Early Judaism, Christianity, and Islam*. Princeton, NJ: Princeton University Press, 2003.
Goldin, Claudia, Lawrence F. Katz, and Ilyana Kuziemko. "The Homecoming of American College Women: The Reversal of the College Gender Gap." *Journal of Economic Perspectives*, 20 (2006): 133–56.
Goldsmith, Leon T. "Alawi Diversity and Solidarity: From the Coast to the Interior." In *The Alawis of Syria: War, Faith and Politics in the Levant*, edited by Michael Kerr and Craig Larkin, pp. 141–58. Oxford: Oxford University Press, 2015.
Goldziher, Ignáz. "Le Dénombrement des Sectes Mohamétanes." *Revue de l'Histoire des Religions*, 26 (1892): 129–37.
Göle, Nilüfer. *The Forbidden Modern: Civilization and Veiling*. Ann Arbor: University of Michigan Press, 1996.
  The Daily Lives of Muslims: Islam and Public Confrontation in Contemporary Europe, translated by Jacqueline Lerescu from the French original of 2015. London: Zed Books, 2017.
Goody, Jack. *The Development of the Family and Marriage in Europe*. Cambridge: Cambridge University Press, 1983.
Goodwin, Godfrey. *The Janissaries*. Northampton, MA: Interlink, 1994.
Gözaydın, İştar. *Diyanet: Türkiye Cumhuriyeti'nde Dinin Tanzimi*, 2nd ed. Istanbul: İletişim, 2020.
Greatrex, Joan. "The Scope of Learning within the Cloisters of the English Cathedral Priories in the later Middle Ages." In *Medieval Monastic Education*, edited by George Ferzoco and Carolyn Muessig, pp. 41–55. London: Leicester University Press, 2000.
Greengrass, Mark. *Christendom Destroyed: Europe 1517–1648*. New York: Penguin, 2014.
Greif, Avner. *Institutions and the Path to the Modern Economy: Lessons from Medieval Trade*. New York: Cambridge University Press, 2006.

"Family Structure, Institutions, and Growth: The Origins and Implications of Western Corporations." *American Economic Review*, 96 (2006): 308–12.
Greif, Avner, and Guido Tabellini. "The Clan and the Corporation: Sustaining Cooperation in China and Europe." *Journal of Comparative Economics*, 45 (2017): 1–35.
Griffel, Frank. "Toleration and Exclusion: Al-Shāfiʿī and al-Ghazālī on the Treatment of Apostates." *Bulletin of the School of Oriental and African Studies*, 44 (2001): 339–54.
Al-Ghazālī's Philosophical Theology. Oxford: Oxford University Press, 2009.
Grigor, Talinn. "Tehran: A Revolution in Making." In *Political Landscapes of Capital Cities*, edited by Jessica Joyce Christie, Jelena Bogdanović, and Eulogio Guzmán, pp. 347–76. Louisville: University Press of Colorado, 2016.
Grohmann, A. "'Ushr." *Encyclopaedia of Islam*, 1st ed., vol. 4, pp. 1050–52. Leiden: E. J. Brill, 1936.
Grunebaum, Gustave E. von. *Medieval Islam: A Study in Cultural Orientation*, 2nd ed. Chicago, IL: University of Chicago Press, 1953.
Guaaybess, Tourya. "Media Ownership in Egypt (2000–2020): Categories and Configurations." In *Routledge Handbook on Contemporary Egypt*, edited by Robert Springborg, Amr Adly, Anthony Gorman, Tamir Moustafa, Aisha Saad, Naomi Sakr, and Sarah Smierciak, pp. 412–23. London: Routledge, 2021.
Guiso, Luigi, Paola Sapienza, and Luigi Zingales. "People's Opium? Religion and Economic Attitudes." *Journal of Monetary Economics*, 50 (2003): 225–82.
"Social Capital as Good Culture." *Journal of the European Economic Association*, 6 (2008): 295–320.
Gül, Murat. *The Emergence of Modern Istanbul: Transformation and Modernisation of a City*. London: I. B. Tauris, 2009.
Gülalp, Haldun. "Religion, Law and Politics: The 'Trickle-Down' Effects of ECtHR Judgments on Turkey's Headscarf Battles." *Religion and Human Rights*, 14 (2019): 135–68.
Gulf Labour Markets and Migration: https://gulfmigration.grc.net/glmm-database/ (accessed 6 February 2023).
Günaydın, Mehmet. "Din Hizmetlerinde Teknolojinin Kullanılması: Hoparlörle Ezan Okuma Meselesi." In *I. Din Hizmetleri Sempozyumu*, vol. 2, edited by Mehmet Bulut, pp. 31–44. Ankara: Diyanet İşleri Başkanlığı Yayınları, 2008.
Gürakar, Esra Çeviker. *Politics of Favoritism in Public Procurement in Turkey: Reconfigurations of Dependency Networks in the AKP Era*. New York: Palgrave Macmillan, 2016.
Gürbüzel, Aslıhan. "Citizens of Piety: Networks of Piety and the Public Sphere in Early Modern Ottoman Cities." *Journal for Early Modern Cultural Studies*, 18 (2018): 66–95.
Güreh, Sarkis. "Karma Evliliğe Takdis Yok." *Agos*, 6 October 2010.
Gutkowski, Stacey. *Secular War: Myths of Religion, Politics and Violence*. London: I. B. Tauris, 2014.
Haarmann, Ulrich. "Joseph's Law: The Careers and Activities of Mamluk Descendants before the Ottoman Conquest of Egypt." In *Mamluks in Egyptian Politics and Society*, edited by Thomas Philipp and Ulrich Haarmann, pp. 55–84. New York: Cambridge University Press, 1998.

Haberkern, Phillip N. *Patron Saint and Prophet: Jan Hus in the Bohemian and German Reformations.* Oxford: Oxford University Press, 2016.

Habermas, Jürgen. *Between Facts and Norms: Contributions to a Discourse Theory of Law and Democracy*, translated by William Rehg from the German original of 1992. Cambridge, MA: MIT Press, 1996.

Hacker, Jacob S. "Policy Drift: The Hidden Politics of US Welfare State Retrenchment." In *Beyond Continuity: Institutional Change in Advanced Political Economies*, edited by Wolfgang Streeck and Kathleen Thelen, pp. 40–82. New York: Oxford University Press, 2005.

Hackett, Conrad, and Brian Grim. "Global Christianity: A Report on the Size and Distribution of the World's Christian Population." Pew Research Center, December 2011.

Haddad, Bassam. "Business Associations and the New Nexus of Power in Syria." In *Civil Society in Syria and Iran: Activism in Authoritarian Contexts*, edited by Paul Aaarts and Francesco Cavatorta, pp. 69–91. Boulder, CO: Lynne Rienner, 2013.

Hagen, Gottfried. "Kātib Çelebī." At www.ottomanhistorians.uchicago.edu, edited by Cemal Kafadar, Hakan Karateke, and Cornell Fleischer (accessed 2 February 2023).

Haider, Huma. *The Persecution of Christians in the Middle East.* K4D Helpdesk Report. Brighton: Institute of Development Studies, 2017.

Haider, Najam. *Shī'ī Islam: An Introduction.* Cambridge: Cambridge University Press, 2014.

Hallaq, Wael B. "From Fatwās to Furū': Growth and Change in Islamic Substantive Law." *Islamic Law and Society*, 1 (1994): 29–65.

  The Origins and Evolution of Islamic Law. Cambridge: Cambridge University Press, 2005.

  Sharī'a: Theory, Practice, Transformations. Cambridge: Cambridge University Press, 2009.

  The Impossible State: Islam, Politics, and Modernity's Moral Predicament. New York: Columbia University Press, 2013.

Hamburger, Philip. *Separation of Church and State.* Cambridge. MA: Harvard University Press, 2002.

Hamdi, Tahrir Khalil. "Edward Said and Recent Orientalist Critiques." *Arab Studies Quarterly*, 35 (2013): 130–48.

Hamid, Shadi. *Temptations of Power: Islamists and Illiberal Democracy in a New Middle East.* Oxford: Oxford University Press, 2014.

Hamilton, Alastair. *The Copts and the West, 1439–1822: The European Discovery of the Egyptian Church.* Oxford: Oxford University Press, 2006.

Hamilton, Alexander, James Madison, and John Jay. *The Federalist Papers.* New Haven, CT: Yale University Press, 2009; original letters 1787–88.

Hammer, Juliane. *American Muslim Women, Religious Authority, and Activism: More than a Prayer.* Austin: University of Texas Press, 2012.

Hanafi, Sari, and Azzam Tomeh. "Gender Equality in the Inheritance Debate in Tunisia and the Formation of Non-Authoritarian Reasoning." *Journal of Islamic Ethics*, 3 (2019): 207–32.

Hanioğlu, M. Şükrü. *The Young Turks in Opposition.* New York: Oxford University Press, 1995.

"Garbcılar: Their Attitudes toward Religion and their Impact on the Official Ideology of the Turkish Republic." *Studia Islamica*, 86 (1997): 133–58.

"Blueprints for a Future Society: Late Ottoman Materialists on Science, Religion, and Art." In *Late Ottoman Society: The Intellectual Legacy*, edited by Elisabeth Özdalga, pp. 27–116. London: RoutledgeCurzon, 2005.

A Brief History of the Late Ottoman Empire. Princeton, NJ: Princeton University Press, 2008.

Hanna, Nelly. *Making Big Money in 1600: The Life and Times of Isma'il Abu Taqiyya, Egyptian Merchant*. Syracuse, NY: Syracuse University Press, 1998.

Hansen, Bent. "Interest Rates and Foreign Capital in Egypt under British Occupation." *Journal of Economic History*, 43 (1983): 867–84.

Hansmann, Henry. "Reforming Nonprofit Corporation Law." *University of Pennsylvania Law Review*, 129 (1981): 497–623.

Hansmann, Henry, Reinier Kraakman, and Richard Squire. "Law and the Rise of the Firm." *Harvard Law Review*, 119 (2006): 1335–403.

Hanssen, Jens. *Fin de Siècle Beirut: The Making of an Ottoman Provincial Capital*. Oxford: Clarendon Press, 2005.

Harris, Jaime, Robert R. Martin, and Roger Finke. *International Religious Freedom Data, 2008* (10 February 2019 version, www.thearda.com/Archive/Files/Descriptions/IRF2008.asp, accessed 2 February 2023).

Harris, Kevan. "The Rise of the Subcontractor State: Politics of Pseudo-Privatization in the Islamic Republic of Iran." *International Journal of Middle East Studies*, 45 (2013): 45–70.

Harris, Ron. *Going the Distance: Eurasian Trade and the Rise of the Business Corporation, 1400–1700*. Princeton, NJ: Princeton University Press, 2020.

Harrison, Robert S. "Migrants in the City of Tripoli, Libya." *Geographical Review*, 57 (1967): 397–423.

Harvard Business School. "Adult Literacy Rates, 1870–2010." www.hbs.edu/businesshistory/courses/resources/historical-data-visualization/Pages/details.aspx?data_id=31 (accessed 2 February 2023).

Hasan, Samiul. "Muslim Philanthropy: Praxis and Human Security across Muslim Majority Countries." In *Human Security and Philanthropy: Islamic Perspectives and Muslim Majority Country Practices*, edited by Samiul Hasan, pp. 117–44. New York: Springer, 2015.

Hâtemî, Hüseyin. *Önceki ve Bugünkü Türk Hukuku'nda Vakıf Kurma Muamelesi*. Istanbul: İstanbul Üniversitesi Hukuk Fakültesi, 1969.

Medenî Hukuk Tüzelkişileri, vol. 1. Istanbul: İstanbul Üniversitesi Hukuk Fakültesi, 1979.

"Vakıf Kurumuna Hukuk Tarihi Açısından Genel Bir Bakış." *İstanbul Üniversitesi Hukuk Fakültesi Mecmuası*, 55 (1997): 111–28.

Hatina, Meir. *'Ulama', Politics, and the Public Sphere: An Egyptian Perspective*. Salt Lake City: University of Utah Press, 2010.

Hayek, Friedrich A. *Law, Legislation and Liberty*, 3 vols. Chicago, IL: University of Chicago Press, 1973–79.

The Road to Serfdom, edited by Bruce Caldwell based on the original edition of 1944. Chicago, IL: University of Chicago Press, 2007.

Haykel, Bernard. "On the Nature of Salafi Thought and Action." In *Global Salafism: Islam's New Religious Movement*, edited by Roel Meijer, pp. 33–57. Oxford: Oxford University Press, 2014.
Hegazi, Farah F. "Authoritarian Governance and the Provision of Public Goods: Water and Wastewater Services in Egypt." PhD dissertation, Duke University, 2019.
Hegghammer, Thomas. *Jihad in Saudi Arabia: Violence and Pan-Islamism since 1979*. Cambridge: Cambridge University Press, 2010.
Helfont, Samuel. *Compulsion in Religion: Saddam Hussein, Islam, and the Roots of Insurgencies in Iraq*. New York: Oxford University Press, 2017.
Hellyer, Hisham A. *Muslims of Europe: The "Other" Europeans*. Edinburgh: Edinburgh University Press, 2009.
Helms, Christine Moss. *The Cohesion of Saudi Arabia: Evolution of Political Identity*. Baltimore, MD: Johns Hopkins University Press, 1981.
Henkelman, Wouter F. M., and Kristin Kleber. "Babylonian Workers in the Persian Heartland: Palace Building at Matannan during the Reign of Cambyses." In *Persian Responses: Political and Cultural Interaction with(in) the Achaemenid Empire*, edited by Chrristopher Tuplin, pp. 163–76. Oxford: Classical Press of Wales, 2007.
Henrich, Joseph. *The Weirdest People in the World: How the West Became Psychologically Peculiar and Particularly Prosperous*. New York: Farrar, Straus and Giroux, 2020.
Henrich, Natalie, and Joseph Henrich. *Why Humans Cooperate: A Cultural and Evolutionary Explanation*. Oxford: Oxford University Press, 2007.
Heper, Metin. "The Ottoman Legacy and Turkish Politics." *Journal of International Affairs*, 54 (2000): 63–82.
Heper, Metin, and Şule Toktaş. "Islam, Modernity, and Democracy in Contemporary Turkey: The Case of Recep Tayyip Erdoğan." *Muslim World*, 93 (2003): 157–85.
Herrold, Catherine E. *Delta Democracy: Pathways to Incremental Civic Revolution in Egypt and Beyond*. Oxford: Oxford University Press, 2020.
Herrold, Catherine E., and Mona Atia. "Competing rather than Collaborating: Egyptian Nongovernmental Organizations in Turbulence." *Nonprofit Policy Forum*, 7 (2016): 389–407.
Hertog, Steffen. "Shaping the Saudi State: Human Agency's Shifting Role in Rentier-State Formation." *International Journal of Middle East Studies*, 39 (2007): 539–63.
Herzog, Christoph. "Corruption and Limits of the State in the Ottoman Province of Baghdad during the Tanzimat." *MIT Electronic Journal of Middle East Studies*, 3 (2003): 35–42.
Hilbink, Elisabeth. "Review of Encarnación, *Myth of Civil Society*." *Latin American Politics and Society*, 47 (2005): 171–75.
Hinnebusch, Raymond. *Syria: Revolution from Above*. New York: Routledge, 2001.
"Toward a Historical Sociology of State Formation in the Middle East." *Middle East Critique*, 19 (2010): 201–16.
Hiro, Dilip. *Cold War in the Islamic World: Saudi Arabia, Iran and the Struggle for Supremacy*. Oxford: Oxford University Press, 2018.
Hirschman, Albert O. *Exit, Voice, and Loyalty: Responses to Decline in Firms, Organizations, and States*. Cambridge, MA: Harvard University Press, 1970.

Hives, Christopher L. "History, Business Records, and Corporate Archives in North America." *Archivaria*, 22 (1986): 40–57.
Hodgson, Marshall, G. S. *The Venture of Islam: Conscience and History in a World Civilization*, vol. 1. Chicago, IL: University of Chicago Press, 1974.
Hoexter, Miriam. *Endowments, Rulers and Community: Waqf Al-Haramayn in Ottoman Algiers*. Leiden: Brill, 1998.
  "The Waqf and the Public Sphere." In *The Public Sphere in Muslim Societies*, edited by Miriam Hoexter, Shmuel N. Eisenstadt, and Nehemia Levtzion, pp. 119–38. New York: State University of New York Press, 2002.
  "Charity, the Poor, and Distribution of Alms in Ottoman Algiers." In *Poverty and Charity in Middle Eastern Contexts*, edited by Michael Bonner, Mine Ener, and Amy Singer, pp. 145–62. Albany: State University of New York Press, 2003.
Hoffman, Philip T. *Why Did Europe Conquer the World?* Princeton, NJ: Princeton University Press, 2015.
Hoffman, Valerie J. *The Essentials of Ibāḍī Islam*. Syracuse, NY: Syracuse University Press, 2012.
Hogarth, David G. *Wandering Scholar in the Levant*. London: John Murray, 1896.
Holmes, George. *The Later Middle Ages, 1272–1485*. Edinburgh: Thomas Nelson and Sons, 1962.
Hoşgör, Evren. "Islamic Capital/Anatolian Tigers: Past and Present." *Middle Eastern Studies*, 47 (2011): 343–60.
Hourani, Albert H. "Ottoman Reform and the Politics of Notables." In *Beginnings of Modernization in the Middle East*, edited by William R. Polk and Richard L. Chambers, pp. 41–68. Chicago, IL: University of Chicago Press, 1968.
  Arabic Thought in the Liberal Age, 1798–1939, rev. ed. Cambridge: Cambridge University Press, 1983.
  A History of the Arab Peoples. Cambridge, MA: Harvard University Press, 1991.
Hoyle, Mark S. W. "The Structure and Laws of the Mixed Courts of Egypt." *Arab Law Quarterly*, 1 (1986): 327–45.
Huff, Toby E. *The Rise of Early Modern Science: Islam, China and the West*, 3rd ed. Cambridge: Cambridge University Press, 2017.
Hughes, Geraint Alun. "Syria and the Perils of Proxy Warfare." *Small Wars and Insurgencies*, 25 (2014): 522–38.
Human Rights Watch. "Egypt: 3-Year Sentence for Atheist." www.hrw.org/news/2015/01/13/egypt-3-year-sentence-atheist (accessed 2 February 2023).
  "They Are Not Our Brothers": Hate Speech by Saudi Officials. Amsterdam: Human Rights Watch, 2017.
Hume, David. *Enquiries Concerning the Human Understanding and Concerning the Principles of Morals*, 2nd ed. Oxford: Clarendon Press, 1902; original edition 1777.
Hunt, Edwin S., and James M. Murray. *A History of Business in Medieval Europe, 1200–1550*. Cambridge: Cambridge University Press, 1999.
Hunter, F. Robert. *Egypt under the Khedives, 1805–1879*. Pittsburgh, PA: University of Pittsburgh Press, 1984.
Hurgronje, C. Snouck. "La *Zakāt*" (original Dutch edition 1882). In *Œuvres Choisies*, edited by G.-H. Bousquet and J. Schacht, pp. 150–70. Leiden: E. J. Brill, 1957).
Husain, Shehriar, Muhammad Zafar, and Rizwan Ullah. "Ramadan and Public Health: A Bibliometric Analysis of Top Cited Articles from 2004 to 2019." *Journal of Infection and Public Health*, 13 (2020): 275–80.

Hussein, Ebtisam, and Claudia De Martino. "Egypt's Military Post-2011: Playing Politics without Internal Cracks." *Contemporary Arab Affairs*, 12 (2019): 55–74.
Iannaccone, Laurence R. "A Formal Model of Church and Sect." *American Journal of Sociology*, 94 (1988): S241–68.
"The Consequences of Religious Market Structure: Adam Smith and the Economics of Religion." *Rationality and Religion*, 3 (1991): 156–77.
"Sacrifice and Stigma: Reducing Free-Riding in Cults, Communes, and Other Collectives." *Journal of Political Economy*, 100 (1992): 271–91.
Ibn Khaldun. *The Muqaddimah: An Introduction to History*, 3 vols., translated by Franz Rosenthal from the Arabic original of 1379. New York: Pantheon, 1958.
Ibrahim, Barbara, and Dina H. Sherif, eds. *From Charity to Social Change: Trends in Arab Philanthropy*. Cairo: American University in Cairo Press, 2008.
Ibrahim, Mahmood. "Social and Economic Conditions in Pre-Islamic Mecca." *International Journal of Middle East Studies*, 14 (1982): 343–58.
Merchant Capital and Islam. Austin: University of Texas Press, 1990.
İltaş, Davut. "Kur'an Araştırmalarında Önemli Bir Kırılma: Nesih Meselesi." In *Modernleşme, Protestanlaşma ve Selefileşme: Modern İslam Düşüncesinde Nassın Araçsallaştırılması*, edited by Mürteza Bedir, Necmettin Kızılkaya, and Merve Özaykal, pp. 379–430. Istanbul: İSAR, 2019.
Immigration and Refugee Board of Canada. *Egypt: In the Case of a Coptic Christian Married Couple, Possibility of a Court Forcing the Husband to Divorce His Wife if She Converts to Islam; whether the Muslim Religion Obliges a Woman to Divorce Her Husband Because of Her Conversion*, 26 February 2007, EGY102325.E. www.unhcr.org/refworld/docid/469cd6b614.html (accessed 2 February 2023).
İKDAM Eğitim Derneği ve Uluslararası Öncü Eğitimciler Derneği. "'Gençlik ve İnanç' Çalıştayı Sonuç Bildirgesi." *İktibas*, 3 April 2018. http://iktibasdergisi.com/2018/04/03/genclik-ve-inanc-calistayi-sonuc-bildirgesi/ (accessed 2 February 2023).
İnalcık, Halil. *The Ottoman Empire: The Classical Age 1300–1600*, translated by Norman Itzkowitz and Colin Imber. London: Weidenfeld and Nicolson, 1973.
Inglehart, Ronald, Christian Haerpfer, Alejandro Moreno, Christian Welzel, Kseniya Kizilova, Juan Diez-Medrano, Marta Lagos, Pippa Norris, Eduard Ponarin, and Bi Puranen, eds. *World Values Survey, Round Six: Country-Pooled Datafile*. Madrid: JD Systems Institute, 2014. www.worldvaluessurvey.org/WVSDocumentationWV6.jsp (accessed 2 February 2023).
Irwin, Robert. *The Middle East in the Middle Ages: The Early Mamluk Sultanate, 1250–1382*. Carbondale: Southern Illinois University Press, 1986.
Ismail, Salwa. *Political Life in Cairo's New Quarters: Encountering the Everyday State*. Minneapolis: University of Minnesota Press, 2006.
Issawi, Charles. "Egypt since 1800: A Study in Lop-sided Development." *International Journal of Middle East Studies*, 21 (1961): 1–25.
An Economic History of the Middle East and North Africa. New York: Columbia University Press, 1982.
"The Transformation of the Economic Position of the *Millets* in the Nineteenth Century." In *Christians and Jews in the Ottoman Empire*, vol. 1, edited by Benjamin Braude and Bernard Lewis, pp. 261–85. New York: Holmes and Meier, 1982.
Iversen, Torben. "The Logics of Electoral Politics: Spatial, Directional, and Mobilizational Effects." *Comparative Political Studies*, 27 (1994): 155–89.

Iyigun, Murat. *War, Peace, and Prosperity in the Name of God: The Ottoman Role in Europe's Socioeconomic Evolution*. Chicago, IL: University of Chicago Press, 2015.
İzgi, Cevat. *Osmanlı Medreselerinde İlim*, 2 vols. Istanbul: İz Yayınları, 1997.
İzmir Ticaret Odası. *19. Yüzyıldan 21. Yüzyıla İzmir Ticaret Odası Tarihi*. Izmir: İzmir Ticaret Odası, 2002.
Izmirlioglu, Ahmet. "Ottoman Commercial Tribunals: Closer than Enemies, Farther than Friends." *British Journal of Middle East History*, 45 (2018): 776–95.
Jabbari, Ahmad. "Economic Factors in Iran's Revolution: Poverty, Inequality, and Inflation." In *Iran: Essays on a Revolution in the Making*, edited by Ahmad Jabbari and Robert Olson, pp. 163–214. Lexington, KY: Mazda Publishers, 1981.
Jackson, Derrick, and Steven V. Manderscheid. "A Phenomenological Study of Western Expatriates' Adjustment to Saudi Arabia." *Human Resource Development International*, 18 (2015): 131–52.
Jackson, Peter. *The Mongols and the Islamic World: From Conquest to Conversion*. New Haven, CT: Yale University Press, 2017.
Jackson, Sherman A. *On the Boundaries of Theological Tolerance in Islam: Abū Ḥāmid Al-Ghāzalī's Fayṣal al-Tafriqa Bayna al-Islām wa al-Zandaqa*. Oxford: Oxford University Press, 2002.
Jafari, Peyman. "The Ambiguous Role of Entrepreneurs in Iran." In *Civil Society in Syria and Iran: Activism in Authoritarian Contexts*, edited by Paul Aaarts and Francesco Cavatorta, pp. 93–118. Boulder, CO: Lynne Rienncr, 2013.
Jamal, Amaney A. *Barriers to Democracy: The Other Side of Social Capital in Palestine and the Arab World*. Princeton, NJ: Princeton University Press, 2007.
  Of Empires and Citizens: Pro-American Democracy or No Democracy at All? Princeton, NJ: Princeton University Press, 2012.
Jamgocyan, Onnik. *Les Banquiers des Sultans: Juifs, Grecs, Français et Arméniens de la Haute Finance*. Paris: Editions du Bosphore, 2013.
Jenkins, William Bullock. "*Bonyads* as Agents and Vehicles of the Islamic Republic's Soft Power." In *Iran in the World: President Rouhani's Foreign Policy*, edited by Shahram Akbarzadeh and Dara Conduit, pp. 155–75. New York: Palgrave Macmillan, 2016.
Jennings, Ronald C. "Loans and Credit in Early 17th Century Ottoman Judicial Records: The Sharia Court of Anatolian Kayseri." *Journal of the Economic and Social History of the Orient*, 16 (1973): 168–216.
  "Pious Foundations in the Society and Economy of Ottoman Trabzon, 1565–1640: A Study Based on the Judicial Registers (*Şer'i Mahkeme Sicilleri*) of Trabzon." *Journal of the Economic and Social History of the Orient*, 33 (1990): 271–336.
Jha, Saumitra. "Trade, Institutions and Ethnic Tolerance: Evidence from South Asia." *American Political Science Review*, 107 (2013): 806–32.
  "Financial Asset Holdings and Political Attitudes: Evidence from Revolutionary England." *Quarterly Journal of Economics*, 130 (2015): 1485–545.
Johnson, Noel D., and Mark Koyama. *Persecution and Toleration: The Long Road to Religious Freedom*. Cambridge: Cambridge University Press, 2019.
Johnson, Noel D., and Alexandra Mislin. "How Much Should We Trust the World Values Survey Trust Question?" *Economics Letters*, 116 (2012): 210–12.
Johnson, Paul. *A History of Christianity*. New York: Atheneum, 1985.

Bibliography

Johnson, Rosemary Stanfield. "Sunni Survival in Safavid Iran: Anti-Sunni Activities during the Reign of Tahmasp I." *Iranian Studies*, 27 (1994): 123–33.
Jones, Geoffrey. "The Imperial Bank of Iran and Iranian Economic Development, 1890–1952." *Business and Economic History*, 16 (1987): 69–80.
Josua, Maria. "Co-optation Reconsidered: Authoritarian Regime Legitimation Strategies in the Jordanian 'Arab Spring'." *Middle East Law and Governance*, 8 (2016): 32–56.
Kabadayı, Mustafa Erdem. "Mkrdich Cezayirliyan or the Sharp Rise and Sudden Fall of an Ottoman Entrepreneur." In *Merchants in the Ottoman Empire*, edited by Suraiya Faroqhi and Gilles Veinstein, pp. 281–99. Paris: Peeters, 2008.
Kadivar, Mohsen. "Toward Removing the Punishment of Apostasy in Islam." In *Freedom of Expression in Islam: Challenging Apostasy and Blasphemy Laws*, edited by Muhammad Khalid Masud, Kari Vogt, Lena Larsen, and Christian Moe, pp. 207–36. London: I. B. Tauris, 2021.
Kaehler, Juergen, Christoph S. Weber, and Haider Salahal-Din Aref. "The Iraqi Stock Market: Development and Determinants." *Review of Middle East Economics and Finance*, 10 (2014): 151–75.
Kafadar, Cemal. *Between Two Worlds: The Construction of the Ottoman State*. Berkeley: University of California Press, 1995.
Kagel, John H. "Auctions: A Survey of Experimental Research." In *The Handbook of Experimental Economics*, edited by John H. Kagel and Alvin E. Roth, pp. 501–86. Princeton, NJ: Princeton University Press, 1995.
Kahf, Monzer, and Samira Al Yafai. "Social Security and Zakāh in Theory and Practice." *International Journal of Economics, Management and Accounting*, 23 (2015): 189–215.
Kala, Eyüp Sabri. "Mazbut Vakıfların Günümüz Hayır Hizmetleri." *Vakıflar Dergisi*, 54 (2020): 161–84.
Kamali, Mohammad Hashim. *A Textbook of Hadīth Studies: Authenticity, Compilation, Classification, and Criticism of Hadīth*. Markfield: Islamic Foundation, 2005.
Kamen, Henry. *The Spanish Inquisition: A Historical Revision*, 4th ed. New Haven, CT: Yale University Press, 2014.
Kaminski, Matthew. "The Arab Spring Is Still Alive." *Wall Street Journal*, 26 July 2011, p. A17.
Kamolnick, Paul. "The Egyptian Islamic Group's Critique of Al-Qaeda's Interpretation of Jihad." *Perspectives on Terrorism*, 7 (2013): 93–110.
Kansu, Aykut. *Politics in Post-Revolutionary Turkey, 1908–1913*. Leiden: Brill, 1999.
Kaplan, Sena, Gül Pınar, Bekir Kaplan, Filiz Aslantekin, Erdem Karabulut, Banu Ayar, and Uğur Dilmen. "Consanguineous Marriages in Turkey," *Journal of Biosocial Science*, 48 (2016): 616–30.
Kara, İsmail. *Cumhuriyet Türkiyesi'nde Bir Mesele Olarak İslâm*, 2 vols. Istanbul: Dergâh Yayınları, 2008 and 2016.
Karaca, Zafer. *İstanbul'da Osmanlı Dönemi Rum Kiliseleri*. Istanbul: Yapı Kredi Yayınları, 1995.
Karakışla, Yavuz Selim. "The Emergence of the Ottoman Industrial Working Class, 1839–1923." In *Workers and Working Class in the Ottoman Empire and the*

Turkish Republic, 1839–1950, edited by Donald Quataert and Erik Jan Zürcher, pp. 19–34. London: I. B. Tauris, 1995.

Karaman, K. Kıvanç, and Şevket Pamuk. "Ottoman State Finances in European Perspective, 1500–1914." *Journal of Economic History*, 70 (2010): 593–629.

Karamustafa, Ahmet T. "*Kalenders, Abdâls, Hayderîs*: The Formation of the *Bektâşîye* in the Sixteenth Century." In *Süleymân the Second and His Time*, edited by Halil İnalcık and Cemal Kafadar, pp. 121–29. Istanbul: ISIS Press, 1993.

God's Unruly Friends: Dervish Groups in the Islamic Later Middle Period 1200–1550. London: Oneworld, 1994.

Sufism: The Formative Period. Edinburgh: Edinburgh University Press, 2007.

Karpat, Kemal H. *The Gecekondu: Rural Migration and Urbanization*. Cambridge: Cambridge University Press, 1976.

Ottoman Population, 1830–1914: Demographic and Social Characteristics. Madison: University of Wisconsin Press, 1985.

Kasaba, Reşat. "Economic Foundations of a Civil Society: Greeks in the Trade of Western Anatolia, 1840–1876." In *Ottoman Greeks in the Age of Nationalism: Politics, Economy, and Society in the Nineteenth Century*, edited by Dimitri Gondicas and Charles Issawi, pp. 77–87. Princeton, NJ: Darwin Press, 1999.

Kassem, Nermeen. "Social Media in Egypt: The Debate Continues." In *Routledge Handbook on Arab Media*, edited by Noureddine Miladi and Noha Mellor, pp. 74–87. London: Routledge, 2021.

Kassis, Hanna E. *Concordance of the Qur'an*. Oxford: Oxford University Press, 1983.

Kayane, Yuka. "Understanding Sunni-Shi'a Sectarianism in Contemporary Indonesia: A Different Voice from Nahdlatul Ulama under Pluralist Leadership." *Indonesia and the Malay World*, 140 (2020): 78–96.

Kazemipour, Abdulmohammad, and Ali Rezaie. "Religious Life under Theocracy: The Case of Iran." *Journal for the Scientific Study of Religion*, 42 (2003): 347–61.

Kazgan, Haydar. *Galata Bankerleri*. Istanbul: Türk Ekonomi Bankası, 1991.

Kechriotis, Vangelis. "Educating the Nation: Migration and Acculturation on the Two Shores of the Aegean at the Turn of the Twentieth Century." In *Cities of the Mediterranean from the Ottomans to the Present Day*, edited by Biray Kolluoğlu and Meltem Toksöz, pp. 139–56. London: I. B. Tauris, 2010.

Keddie, Nikki R. "The Roots of the Ulama's Power in Modern Iran." *Studia Islamica*, 29 (1969): 31–53.

Kelidar, Abbas R. "Religion and State in Syria." *Asian Affairs*, 5 (1974): 16–22.

Kenan, Seyfi. "III. Selim Dönemi Eğitim Anlayışında Arayışlar." In *Nizâm-ı Kādîm'den Nizâm-ı Cedîd'e III. Selim ve Dönemi*, edited by Seyfi Kenan, pp. 129–63. Istanbul: İSAM, 2010.

Kenny, Lorne M. "The Khedive Isma'il's Dream of Civilization and Progress." *Muslim World*, 55 (1965): 142–55, 211–21.

Kepel, Gilles. *Muslim Extremism in Egypt: The Prophet and Pharaoh*, translated by Jon Rothschild from the original French edition of 1984. Berkeley: University of California Press, 1985.

Kersten, Carool. "Nasr Hamid Abu Zayd: An Introduction to His Life and Work." In *Critique of Religious Discourse*, by Nasr Hamid Abu Zayd, pp. 1–18. New Haven, CT: Yale University Press, 2018.

Contemporary Thought in the Muslim World: Trends, Themes and Issues. London: Routledge, 2019.

Ketchley, Neil. *Egypt in a Time of Revolution: Contentious Politics and the Arab Spring.* New York: Cambridge University Press, 2017.

Khadri, Sabah Anbareen. "Highly-Skilled Professionals in the GCC: Migration Policies and Government Outlook." In *Migration to the Gulf: Policies in Sending and Receiving Countries,* edited by Philippe Fargues and Nasra M. Shah, pp. 81–103. Cambridge: Gulf Research Centre, 2018.

Khalaily, Mohammed, and Doran Navot. "Hamulas and Structural Corruption in the Middle East." In *Corruption and Informal Practices in the Middle East and North Africa,* edited by Ina Kubbe and Aiysha Varraich, pp. 43–64. London: Routledge, 2020.

Khalaji, Mehdi. "Iran's Regime of Religion." *Journal of International Affairs,* 65 (2011): 131–47.

Khalfoune, Tahar. "Le *Habous*, le Domaine Public et le *Trust.*" *Revue Internationale de Droit Comparé,* 2 (2005): 441–70.

Khallaf, Mani. "Community Foundations as a Vehicle for Institutionalizing Corporate Philanthropy in Egypt's New Cities: A Case Study of 10th of Ramadan City." In *Takaful 2011,* pp. 112–42. Cairo: John D. Gerhart Center for Philanthropy and Engagement, 2011.

Khatab, Sayed, and Gary D. Bouma. *Democracy in Islam.* New York: Routledge, 2007.

Khatib, Line. *Islamic Revivalism in Syria: The Rise and Fall of Ba'thist Secularism.* New York: Routledge, 2011.

"Islamic Revival and the Promotion of Moderate Islam from Above." *Syria Studies,* 4 (2012): 29–57.

"Syria's Civil Society as a Tool for Regime Legitimacy." In *Civil Society in Syria and Iran: Activism in Authoritarian Contexts,* edited by Paul Aarts and Francesco Cavatorta, pp. 19–38. Boulder, CO: Lynne Rienner, 2013.

"More Religious, Yet Still Secular? The Shifting Boundaries between the Secular and the Religious in Syria." *Syria Studies,* 8 (2016): 40–65.

Khatiri, Shay. "Iran's Revolution Continues." *National Review,* 6 February 2023, pp. 24–27.

Khomeini, Imam. *Islam and Revolution: Writings and Declarations,* translated from the Persian originals and annotated by Hamid Algar. London: KPI, 1985.

Khoury, Dina Rizk. "Merchants and Trade in Early Modern Iraq." *New Perspectives on Turkey,* 6 (1991): 53–86.

Khuri, Fuad I. *Imams and Emirs: State, Religion, and Sects in Islam.* London: Saqi Books, 1990.

Kienle, Eberhard. *Ba'th v Ba'th: The Conflict Between Syria and Iraq, 1968–1989.* London: I. B. Tauris, 1991.

Kilani, Sa'eda, and Basem, Sakija. *Wasta: The Declared Secret.* Amman: Arab Archives Institute, 2002.

Kılıç, Murat. "Cumhuriyetin İlk Yıllarında Devlet İle Vatandaş Arasında Bir İletişim Aracı Olarak Hutbeler." *Çağdaş Türkiye Tarihi Araştırmaları Dergisi,* 35 (2017): 137–66.

Kimya, Fırat. "Political Economy of Corruption in Turkey: Declining Petty Corruption, Rise of Cronyism." *Turkish Studies,* 20 (2019): 351–76.

Kindleberger, Charles P. *A Financial History of Western Europe.* London: George Allen & Unwin, 1984.

King, Stephen J. "Black Arabs and African Migrants: Between Slavery and Racism in North Africa." *Journal of North African Studies*, 26 (2021): 8–50.
Kinsey, David C. "Education in the Shadow of the State: Private Elementary Schools in Tunisia." *Africa Today*, 14 (1967): 22–24.
Kırlı, Cengiz. "Yolsuzluğun İcadı: 1840 Ceza Kanunu, İktidar ve Bürokrasi." *Tarih ve Toplum, Yeni Yaklaşımlar*, 4 (2006): 45–119.
Kırmızı, Abdülhamit. "Osmanlı Bürokrasisinde Gayrimüslim İstihdamı." *Dîvân İlmî Araştırmalar*, 13 (2002): 295–306.
Kivimäki, Timo. "Democracy, Autocrats and U.S. Policies in the Middle East." *Middle East Policy*, 19 (2012): 64–71.
Kiyotaki, Keiko. *Ottoman Land Reform in the Province of Baghdad*. Leiden: Brill, 2019.
Klausen, Jytte. *The Islamic Challenge: Politics and Religion in Western Europe*. Oxford: Oxford University Press, 2005.
Klesment, Martin, and Jan Van Bavel. "The Reversal of the Gender Gap in Education, Motherhood, and Women as Main Earners in Europe." *European Sociological Review*, 33 (2017): 465–81.
Klüver, Heike, Christine Mahoney, and Marc Opper. "Framing in Context: How Interest Groups Employ Framing to Lobby the European Commission." *Journal of European Public Policy*, 22 (2015): 481–98.
Knysh, Alexander. *Sufism: A New History of Mysticism*. Princeton, NJ: Princeton University Press, 2017.
Koblentz, Gregory. "Chemical-Weapon Use in Syria: Atrocities, Attribution, and Accountability." *Nonproliferation Review*, 26 (2019): 575–98.
Kocamaner, Hikmet. "Regulating the Family through Religion: Secularism, Islam, and the Politics of the Family in Contemporary Turkey." *American Ethnologist*, 46 (2019): 495–508.
Kogelmann, Franz. "Legal Regulation of Moroccan Habous under French Rule: Local Legal Practice vs. Islamic Law?" In *Shattering Tradition: Custom, Law and the Individual in the Muslim Mediterranean*, edited by Walter Dostal and Wolfgang Kraus, pp. 208–32. London: I. B. Tauris, 2005.
Kohlberg, Etan. "Taqiyya in Shī'ī Theology and Religion." In *Secrecy and Concealment: Studies in the History of Mediterranean and Near Eastern Religions*, edited by Hans G. Kippenberg and Guy G. Stroumsa, pp. 345–80. Leiden: E. J. Brill, 1995.
Kohn, Meir. "Money, Trade, and Payments in Preindustrial Europe." In *Handbook of the History of Money and Currency*, edited by Stefano Battilossi, Youssef Cassis, and Kazuhiko Yago, pp. 223–44. Singapore: Springer, 2020.
Konda Araştırma. "Diyanet İşleri Başkanlığı Araştırması: Algılar, Memnuniyet, Beklentiler." In *Sosyo-Ekonomik Politikalar Bağlamında Diyanet İşleri Başkanlığı: Kamuoyunun Diyanet'e Bakışı, Tartışmalar ve Öneriler*, edited by Sevgi Özçelik, pp. 73–139. Istanbul: Helsinki Yurttaşlar Derneği, 2014.
Konda Araştırma. "10 Yılda Gençlerde Ne Değişti." https://interaktif.konda.com.tr/gencler-2018 (accessed 2 February 2023).
Köprülü, Fuad. "Bizans Müesseselerinin Osmanlı Müesseselerine Tesiri." *Türk Hukuk ve İktisat Tarihi Mecmuası*, 1 (1931): 165–313.
Koraltürk, Murat. *Erken Cumhuriyet Döneminde Ekonominin Türkleştirilmesi*. Istanbul: İletişim, 2011.

Bibliography

Koran, The. Translated with notes by N. J. Dawood, 4th rev. ed. Harmondsworth: Penguin Classics, 1974.
Korteweg, Anna C., and Gökçe Yurdakul. *The Headscarf Debates: Conflicts of National Belonging*. Stanford: Stanford University Press, 2014.
Koyuncu, Büke. "*Benim Milletim* ..." *AK Parti İktidarı, Din ve Ulusal Kimlik*. Istanbul: İletişim, 2014.
Krämer, Gudrun. *Hasan al-Banna*. London: Oneworld, 2010.
Krämer, Gudrun. "Moving Out of Place: Minorities in Middle Eastern Urban Societies, 1800–1914." In *The Urban Social History of the Middle East, 1750–1950*, edited by Peter Sluglett, pp. 182–223. Syracuse, NY: Syracuse University Press, 2008.
Küçük, Cevdet. "Osmanlı İmparatorluğu'nda 'Millet Sistemi' ve Tanzimat." In *Mustafa Reşid Paşa ve Dönemi Semineri: Bildiriler*, pp. 13–23. Ankara: Türk Tarih Kurumu, 1985.
Küçük, Harun. *Science without Leisure: Practical Naturalism in Istanbul, 1660–1732*. Pittsburgh, PA: University of Pittsburgh Press, 2020.
Kuhn, Thomas S. *The Structure of Scientific Revolutions*, 2nd ed. Chicago, IL: University of Chicago Press, 1970.
Kuhnke, LaVerne. *Lives at Risk: Public Health in Nineteenth-Century Egypt*. Berkeley: University of California Press, 1990.
Kulat, Mehmet Ali. *Türkiye'de Toplumun Dine ve Dini Değerlere Bakışı*. Ankara: MAK Danışmanlık, 2017.
Kuran, Ercümend. *Avrupa'da Osmanlı İkamet Elçiliklerinin Kuruluşu ve İlk Elçilerin Siyasi Faâliyetleri, 1793–1821*. Ankara: Türk Kültürünü Araştırma Enstitüsü, 1968.
Kuran, Timur. *Private Truths, Public Lies: The Social Consequences of Preference Falsification*. Cambridge, MA: Harvard University Press, 1995.
  "The Provision of Public Goods under Islamic Law: Origins, Impact, and Limitations of the Waqf System." *Law and Society Review*, 35 (2001): 841–97.
  Islam and Mammon: The Economic Predicaments of Islamism. Princeton, NJ: Princeton University Press, 2004.
  "Modern Islam and the Economy." In *The New Cambridge History of Islam: Volume 6, Muslims and Modernity, Culture and Society since 800*, edited by Robert W. Hefner, pp. 473–94. Cambridge: Cambridge University Press, 2010.
  The Long Divergence: How Islamic Law Held Back the Middle East. Princeton, NJ: Princeton University Press, 2011.
  "The Weak Foundations of Arab Democracy." *New York Times*, 28 May 2011.
  "Islam and Economic Performance: Historical and Contemporary Links." *Journal of Economic Literature*, 56 (2018): 1292–359.
  "Zakat: Islam's Missed Opportunity to Limit Predatory Taxation." *Public Choice*, 182 (2020): 395–416.
Kuran, Timur, ed. *Social and Economic Life in Seventeenth-Century Istanbul: Glimpses from Court Records*, vols. 5–8. Istanbul: İş Bank Cultural Publications, 2010–13.
Kuran, Timur, and Scott Lustig. "Judicial Biases in Ottoman Istanbul: Islamic Justice and Its Compatibility with Modern Economic Life." *Journal of Law and Economics*, 55 (2012): 631–66.
Kuran, Timur, and Jared Rubin. "The Financial Power of the Powerless: Socio-Economic Status and Interest Rates under Partial Rule of Law." *Economic Journal*, 128 (2018): 758–96.

Kuru, Ahmet T. "Passive and Assertive Secularism: Historical Conditions, Ideological Struggles, and State Policies toward Religion." *World Politics*, 59 (2007): 568–94.
   Islam, Authoritarianism, and Underdevelopment: A Global and Historical Comparison. Cambridge: Cambridge University Press, 2019.
Kurzman, Charles, ed. *Liberal Islam: A Sourcebook*. Oxford: Oxford University Press, 1998.
Kutscher, Jens. "The Politics of Virtual Fatwa Counseling in the 21st Century." *Masaryk University Journal of Law and Technology*, 3 (2009): 33–49.
Kütükoğlu, Mübahat S. "Osmanlılar'da Gümrük." *Türkiye Diyanet Vakfı İslâm Ansiklopedisi*, 14 (1996): 263–68.
   XX. Asra Erişen Osmanlı Medreseleri. Ankara: Türk Tarih Kurumu, 2000.
Lacroix, Stéphane. *Awakening Islam: The Politics of Religious Dissent in Contemporary Saudi Arabia*, translated by George Holoch from the French original of 2010. Cambridge, MA: Harvard University Press, 2011.
   "Between Revolution and Apoliticism: Nasir al-Din al-Albani and His Impact on the Shaping of Contemporary Salafism." In *Global Salafism: Islam's New Religious Movement*, edited by Roel Meijer, pp. 58–80. Oxford: Oxford University Press, 2014.
Ladjal, Tarek, and Benaouda Bensaid. "Sufism and Politics in Contemporary Egypt: A Study of Sufi Political Engagement in the Pre- and Post-Revolutionary Reality of January 2011." *Journal of Asian and African Studies*, 50 (2015): 468–85.
Ladjevardi, Habib. *Labor Unions and Autocracy in Iran*. Syracuse, NY: Syracuse University Press, 1985.
Laluddin, Hayatullah, Sikandar Shah Haneef, Mohammad Tahir Sabit, and Maya Puspa Rahman. "Revisiting the Concept of *Waqf*: Its Maintenance, Issues and Challenges." *International Journal of Islamic Thought*, 20 (2021): 53–64.
Lamoreaux, Naomi R., and Jean-Laurent Rosenthal. "Legal Regime and Contractual Flexibility: A Comparison of Business's Organizational Choices in France and the United States during the Era of Industrialization." *American Law and Economics Review*, 7 (2005): 28–61.
Landes, David S. *Bankers and Pashas: International Finance and Economic Imperialism in Egypt*. Cambridge, MA: Harvard University Press, 1958.
Langohr, Vickie. "Too Much Civil Society, Too Little Politics: Egypt and Liberalizing Arab Regimes." *Comparative Politics*, 36 (2004): 181–204.
Laoust, Henri. *Essai sur les Doctrines Sociales et Politiques de Taḳī-d-dīn Aḥmad b. Taimīya*. Cairo: Institut Français d'Archéologie Orientale, 1939.
   "Aḥmad b. Hanbal." *Encyclopaedia of Islam*, 2nd ed., vol. 1, pp. 272–77. Leiden: E. J. Brill, 1960.
Lapidus, Ira M. "The Grain Economy of Mamluk Egypt." *Journal of the Economic and Social History of the Orient*, 12 (1969): 1–15.
   A History of Islamic Societies. Cambridge: Cambridge University Press, 1988.
Laskier, Michael Menachem, and Reeva Spector Simon. "Economic Life." In *The Jews of the Middle East and North Africa in Modern Times*, edited by Reeva Spector Simon, Michael Menachem Laskier, and Sara Leguer, pp. 29–48. New York: Columbia University Press, 2002.
Lauzière, Henri. *The Making of Salafism: Islamic Reform in the Twentieth Century*. New York: Columbia University Press, 2016.

Lee, Melissa M., and Nan Zhang. "Legibility and the Informational Foundations of State Capacity." *Journal of Politics*, 79 (2016): 118–32.
Lee, Robert D. "Tunisian Intellectuals: Responses to Islamism." *Journal of North African Studies*, 13 (2008): 157–73.
Leeuwen, Richard van. *Waqfs and Urban Structures: The Case of Ottoman Damascus*. Leiden: Brill, 1999.
Lefèvre, Raphaël. *Ashes of Hama: The Muslim Brotherhood of Syria*. Oxford: Oxford University Press, 2013.
Leiper, J. B., A. M. Molla, and A. M. Molla. "Effects on Health of Fluid Restriction during Fasting in Ramadan." *European Journal of Clinical Nutrition*, 57 (2003): S30–38.
Lerner, Daniel. *The Passing of Traditional Society: Modernizing the Middle East*. Glencoe, IL: Free Press, 1958.
Lev, Yaacov. *Charity, Endowments, and Charitable Institutions in Medieval Islam*. Gainesville: University Press of Florida, 2005.
Levanoni, Amalia. "The Mamluk Conception of the Sultanate." *International Journal of Middle East Studies*, 26 (1994): 373–92.
Levi, Margaret. *Of Rule and Revenue*. Berkeley: University of California Press, 1988.
Lewis, Bernard. "Some Observations on the Significance of Heresy in the History of Islam." *Studia Islamica*, 1 (1953): 43–63.
  The Middle East and the West. Bloomington: Indiana University Press, 1964.
  The Muslim Discovery of Europe. New York: Norton, 1982.
  The Jews of Islam. Princeton, NJ: Princeton University Press, 1984.
  "Ibn Khaldūn in Turkey." In *Studies in Islamic History and Civilization in Honour of Professor David Ayalon*, edited by Moshe Sharon, pp. 527–30. Jerusalem: Cana, 1986.
  Race and Slavery in the Middle East: An Historical Enquiry. New York: Oxford University Press, 1990.
  What Went Wrong? Western Impact and Middle Eastern Response. Oxford: Oxford University Press, 2002.
Lewis, Franklin. *Rumi: Past and Present, East and West*. London: Oneworld, 2000.
Liebesny, Herbert J. "The Development of Western Judicial Privileges." In *Law in the Middle East*, vol. 1, edited by Majid Khadduri and Herbert J. Liebesny, pp. 309–33. Washington, DC: Middle East Institute, 1955.
  The Law of the Near and Middle East: Readings, Cases, and Materials. Albany: State University of New York Press, 1975.
Lieu, Judith. "Self-Definition vis-à-vis the Jewish Matrix." In *The Cambridge History of Christianity*, vol. 1, edited by Margaret M. Mitchell and Frances M. Young, pp. 214–29. Cambridge: Cambridge University Press, 2006.
Livny, Avital. *Trust and the Islamic Advantage: Religious-Based Movements in Turkey and the Muslim World*. Cambridge: Cambridge University Press, 2020.
Løkkegaard, Frede. *Islamic Taxation in the Classic Period, with Special Reference to Circumstances in Iraq*. Copenhagen: Branner and Korch, 1950.
  "Ghanīma." *Encyclopaedia of Islam*, 2nd ed., vol. 2, pp. 1143–47. Leiden: E. J. Brill, 1965.
Lord, Ceren. *Religious Politics in Turkey: From the Birth of the Republic to the AKP*. Cambridge: Cambridge University Press, 2018.

Lorentz, John H. "Educational Development in Iran: The Pivotal Role of the Mission Schools and Alborz College." *Iranian Studies*, 44 (2011): 647–55.
Luebke, Fred C. "The Origins of Thomas Jefferson's Anti-Clericalism." *Church History*, 32 (1963): 344–56.
Lukianoff, Greg, and Jonathan Haidt. *The Coddling of the American Mind: How Good Intentions and Bad Ideas Are Setting Up a Generation for Failure.* New York: Penguin Press, 2018.
Lupovitch, Howard N. "Between Orthodox Judaism and Neology: The Origins of the Status Quo Movement." *Jewish Social Studies*, 9 (2003): 123–53.
Jews and Judaism in World History. London: Routledge, 2010.
MacCulloch, Diarmaid. *The Reformation: A History.* New York: Viking Penguin, 2004.
Macdonald, Duncan Black. *The Religious Attitude and Life in Islam.* New York: AMS Press, 1970; original edition 1909.
Macfarlane, Charles. *Constantinople in 1828: A Residence of Sixteen Months in the Turkish Capital and Provinces*, 2 vols. London: Saunders and Otley, 1829.
Machlis, Elisheva. "Reevaluating Sectarianism in Light of Sufi Islam: The Case-Studies of the Naqshbandiyya and Qadiriyya in Syria and Iraq." *Sociology of Islam*, 7 (2019): 1–21.
MacLean, Gerald M. *The Rise of Oriental Travel: English Visitors to the Ottoman Empire, 1580–1720.* New York: Palgrave, 2004.
Macleod, Arlene Lowe. *Accommodating Protest: Working Women, the New Veiling, and Change in Cairo.* New York: Columbia University Press, 1991.
Maddy-Weitzman, Bruce. "The Berbers (Amazigh)." In *Routledge Handbook of Minorities in the Middle East*, edited by Paul S. Rowe, pp. 313–25. London: Routledge, 2019.
Mahler, Gregory S. *Politics and Government in Israel: The Maturation of a Modern State*, 3rd ed. Lanham, MD: Rowman & Littlefield, 2016.
Mahmood, Saba. "Sectarian Conflict and Family Law in Contemporary Egypt." *American Ethnologist*, 39 (2012): 54–62.
Majlisi, Muhammad Baqir. *Haqqul Yaqeen: A Compendium of Twelver Shia Religious Beliefs*, translated by Athar Husain S. H. Rizvi from the Persian original of 1889. Qum: Ansariyan, 2012.
Makdisi, George. *The Rise of Colleges: Institutions of Learning in Islam and the West.* Edinburgh: Edinburgh University Press, 1981.
Makdisi, Ussama. *Faith Misplaced: The Broken Promise of U.S.–Arab Relations.* Philadelphia, PA: PublicAffairs, 2010.
Malik, Kenan. *From Fatwa to Jihad: The Rushdie Affair and Its Aftermath.* New York: Melville House, 2009.
Malik, Shiv, Jack Shenker, and Adam Gabbatt. "Arab Spring Anniversary: How a Lost Generation Found Its Voice." *Guardian*, 16 December 2011.
Malkoç, M. Numan. *İstanbul'daki Protestan Kiliseler.* Istanbul: Kaya Basımevi, 1999.
Maloney, Michael T., Abdülkadir Civan, and Mary Frances Maloney. "Model of Religious Schism with Application to Islam." *Public Choice*, 142 (2010): 441–60.
Maloney, Suzanne. "Agents or Obstacles? Parastatal Foundations and Challenges for Iranian Development." In *The Economy of Iran: Dilemmas of an Islamic State*, edited by Parvin Alizadeh, pp. 145–76. London: I. B. Tauris, 2000.

"Islamism and Iran's Postrevolutionary Economy: The Case of the *Bonyad*s." In *Gods, Guns, and Globalization: Religious Radicalism and International Political Economy*, edited by Mary Ann Tétreault and Robert A. Denemark, pp. 191–217. Boulder, CO: Lynne Rienner, 2004.

Maltby, Josephine. "UK Joint Stock Companies Legislation 1844–1900: Accounting Publicity and 'Mercantile Caution'." *Accounting History*, 3 (1998): 10–32.

Mandaville, Jon E. "Usurious Piety: The Cash Waqf Controversy in the Ottoman Empire." *International Journal of Middle East Studies*, 10 (1979): 298–308.

Mandaville, Peter. *Islam and Politics*, 2nd ed. New York: Routledge, 2014.

Mango, Andrew. *Atatürk: The Biography of the Founder of Modern Turkey*. Woodstock: Overlook Press, 2000.

Mannan, Mohammad Abdul. *Islamic Economics: Theory and Practice*. Lahore: Sh. Muhammad Ashraf, 1970.

Mantsinen, Teemu T., and Kati Tervo-Niemelä. "Leaving Christianity." In *Handbook of Leaving Religion*, edited by Daniel Enstedt, Göran Larsson, and Teemu T. Mantsinen, pp. 67–80. Leiden: Brill, 2020.

Maoz, Moshe. "Syrian Urban Politics in the Tanzimat Period between 1840 and 1861." *Bulletin of the School of Oriental and African Studies*, 29 (1966): 277–301.

Marashi, Afshin. *Nationalizing Iran: Culture, Power, and the State, 1870–1940*. Seattle: University of Washington Press, 2008.

Marcotte, Roxanne. "Fatwa Online: Novel Patterns of Production and Consumption." In *Political Islam and Global Media: The Boundaries of Religious Identity*, edited by Mellor Noha and Rinnawi Khalil, pp. 231–45. London: Routledge, 2016.

"Suhrawardi." *Stanford Encyclopedia of Philosophy*. Stanford: Center for the Study of Language and Information, Stanford University, 2019.

Marcus, Abraham. *The Middle East on the Eve of Modernity: Aleppo in the Eighteenth Century*. New York: Columbia University Press, 1989.

"Poverty and Poor Relief in Eighteenth-Century Aleppo." *Révue du Monde Musulman et de la Méditerranée*, 55–56 (1990): 171–79.

Marcus, Joel. "Jewish Christianity." In *The Cambridge History of Christianity*, vol. 1, edited by Margaret M. Mitchell and Frances M. Young, pp. 87–102. Cambridge: Cambridge University Press, 2006.

Mardin, Şerif. *The Genesis of Young Ottoman Thought: A Study in the Modernization of Turkish Political Ideas*. Princeton, NJ: Princeton University Press, 1962.

Religion and Social Change in Modern Turkey: The Case of Bediüzzaman Said Nursi. Albany: State University of New York Press, 1989.

Maréchal, Brigitte. "Mosques, Organisations and Leadership." In *Muslims in the Enlarged Europe: Religion and Society*, edited by Brigitte Maréchal, Stefano Allievi, Felice Dassetto, and Jørgen Nielsen, pp. 79–150. Leiden: Brill, 2003.

Mariuma, Yarden. "Taqiyya as Polemic, Law and Knowledge: Following an Islamic Legal Term through the Worlds of Islamic Scholars, Ethnographers, Polemicists and Military Men." *Muslim World*, 104 (2014): 89–108.

Marsot, Afaf Lutfi al-Sayyid. *Egypt's Liberal Experiment: 1922–1936*. Berkeley: University of California Press, 1977.

Egypt in the Reign of Muhammad Ali. Cambridge: Cambridge University Press, 1984.

A History of Egypt: From the Arab Conquest to the Present, 2nd ed. Cambridge: Cambridge University Press, 2007.

Marx, Karl. "Contribution to the Critique of Hegel's *Philosophy of Right*: Introduction" (original German edition 1844). In *The Marx–Engels Reader*, 2nd ed., edited by Robert C. Tucker, pp. 53–65. New York: W. W. Norton, 1978.
Masri, Safwan M. *Tunisia: An Arab Anomaly*. New York: Columbia University Press, 2017.
Massot, Anais. "Ottoman Damascus during the Tanzimat: The New Visibility of Religious Distinctions." In *Modernity, Minority, and the Public Sphere: Jews and Christians in the Middle East*, edited by Sasha R. Goldstein-Sabbah and Heleen L. Murre-van den Berg, pp. 155–84. Leiden: Brill, 2016.
Masters, Bruce. "The Sultan's Entrepreneurs: The *Avrupa Tüccarıs* and the *Hayriye Tüccarıs* in Syria." *International Journal of Middle East Studies*, 24 (1992): 579–97.
Masud, Muhammad Khalid. "Reading Ibn Taymiyya's *al-Ṣārim*: Hermeneutic Shifts in the Definition of Blasphemy." In *Freedom of Expression in Islam: Challenging Apostasy and Blasphemy Laws*, edited by Muhammad Khalid Masud, Kari Vogt, Lena Larsen, and Christian Moe, pp. 75–98. London: I. B. Tauris, 2021.
Mathews, Donald G. *Slavery and Methodism: A Chapter in American Morality, 1780–1845*. Princeton, NJ: Princeton University Press, 1965.
Matic, Natasha M., and Banderi A. R. AlFaisal. "Empowering the Saudi Social Development Sector." *Fletcher Forum of World Affairs*, 36 (2012): 11–18.
Matthiesen, Toby. *The Other Saudis: Shiism, Dissent and Sectarianism*. Cambridge: Cambridge University Press, 2015.
Mattson, Ingrid. "Status-Based Definitions of Need in Early Islamic Zakat and Maintenance Laws." In *Poverty and Charity in Middle Eastern Contexts*, edited by Michael Bonner, Mine Ener, and Amy Singer, pp. 31–51. Albany: State University of New York Press, 2003.
Mawdudi, Abul-Ala. *Islamic Way of Life*, translated from the Urdu original of 1948. Lahore: Islamic Publications, 1950.
  Let Us Be Muslims, translated from the Urdu original of 1940. Kuala Lumpur: Noordeen, 1990.
Mazlumder. *Türkiye'de Dini Ayrımcılık Raporu*. Ankara: İnsan Hakları ve Mazlumlar İçin Dayanışma Derneği, 2010.
Mazower, Mark. *Salonica, City of Ghosts: Christians, Muslims and Jews, 1430–1950*. New York: Alfred A. Knopf, 2005.
McCarthy, Justin. *Muslims and Minorities: The Population of Ottoman Anatolia and the End of Empire*. New York: New York University Press, 1983.
McCarthy, Rory. "Re-thinking Secularism in Post-Independence Tunisia." *Journal of North African Studies*, 19 (2014): 733–50.
McCleary, Rachel M., and Robert J. Barro. *The Wealth of Religions: The Political Economy of Believing and Belonging*. Princeton, NJ: Princeton University Press, 2019.
McClendon, David, Conrad Hackett, Michaela Potančoková, Marcin Stonawski, and Vegard Skirbekk. "Women's Education in the Muslim World." *Population Development Review*, 44 (2018): 311–42.
Médecins Sans Frontières. *International Activity Report 2021*. Lausanne: MSF International, 2022.
Meeker, Michael E. *A Nation of Empire: The Ottoman Legacy of Turkish Modernity*. Berkeley: University of California Press, 2002.

Meier, Astrid. "*Waqf* Only in Name, Not in Essence: Early Tanẓīmāt Reforms in the Province of Damascus." In *The Empire in the City: Arab Provincial Capitals in the Late Ottoman Empire*, edited by Jens Hanssen, Thomas Philipp, and Stefan Weber, pp. 201–18. Würzburg: Ergon-Verlag, 2002.

Melčák, Miroslav. "The Development of *Dīwān al-awqāf* in Egypt in the 19th Century: Regulations of 1837 and 1851." *Oriental Archive*, 78 (2010): 1–34.

Melchert, Christopher. *The Formation of the Sunni Schools of Law: 9th–10th Centuries C.E.* Leiden: Brill, 1997.

Mellor, Noha. *Voice of the Muslim Brotherhood: Daʿwa, Discourse, and Political Communication.* London: Routledge, 2018.

Memiş, Mehmet. "Osmanlı Dönemi Urfa Vakıflarının Eğitim-Öğretim Alanındaki Hizmetleri." In *Osmanlı Medreseleri: Eğitim, Yönetim ve Finans*, edited by Fuat Aydın, Mahmut Zengin, Kübra Cevherli, and Yunus Kaymaz, pp. 503–32. Istanbul: Mahya, 2016.

Memiş, Şefik. *Türkiye'de Ticaretin Öncü Kuruluşu: Dersaadet Ticaret Odası 1882–1923.* Istanbul: İstanbul Ticaret Odası, 2009.

Menchik, Jeremy. *Islam and Democracy in Indonesia: Tolerance without Liberalism.* Cambridge: Cambridge University Press, 2016.

Menchinger, Ethan L. *The First of the Modern Ottomans: The Intellectual History of Ahmed Vasıf.* Cambridge: Cambridge University Press, 2017.

Mendelsohn, I. "On Corvée Labor in Ancient Canaan and Israel." *Bulletin of the American Schools of Oriental Research*, 167 (1962): 31–35.

Menoret, Pascal. "Repression and Protest in Saudi Arabia." *Middle East Brief* (Crown Center for Middle East Studies), 101 (2016): 1–9.

Meral, Yasin. "Osmanlı İstanbul'unda Yahudi Matbaası ve Basılan Bazı Önemli Eserler." In *Osmanlı İstanbulu II*, edited by Feridun M. Emecen, Ali Akyıldız, and Emrah Safa Gürkan, pp. 455–69. Istanbul: 29 Mayıs Üniversitesi, 2014.

Meriwether, Margaret L. *The Kin Who Count: Family and Society in Ottoman Aleppo, 1770–1840.* Austin: University of Texas Press, 1999.

Mernissi, Fatima. *Beyond the Veil: Male–Female Dynamics in Modern Muslim Society*, rev. ed. Bloomington: Indiana University Press, 1987.

Mestyan, Adam. *Arab Patriotism: The Ideology and Culture of Power in Late Ottoman Egypt.* Princeton, NJ: Princeton University Press, 2017.

Metinsoy, Murat. *The Power of the People: Everyday Resistance and Dissent in the Making of Modern Turkey, 1923–38.* Cambridge: Cambridge University Press, 2021.

Mezulis, Amy H., Lyn Y. Abramson, Janet S. Hyde, and Benjamin L. Hankin. "Is There a Universal Positivity Bias in Attributions? A Meta-Analytic Review of Individual, Developmental, and Cultural Differences in the Self-Serving Attributional Bias." *Psychological Bulletin*, 130 (2004): 711–47.

Michaelsen, Marcus. "Transforming Threats to Power: The International Politics of Authoritarian Internet Control in Iran." *International Journal of Communication*, 12 (2018): 3856–76.

Michalopoulos, Stelios, and Elias Papaioannou. "Pre-Colonial Ethnic Institutions and Contemporary African Development." *Econometrica*, 81 (2013): 113–52.

Michie, Ranald C. *The London Stock Exchange: A History.* Oxford: Oxford University Press, 1999.

Mietzner, Marcus, and Burhanuddin Muhtadi. "The Myth of Pluralism." *Contemporary Southeast Asia*, 42 (2020): 58–84.
Millar, Fergus. "Condemnation to Hard Labour in the Roman Empire, from the Julio-Claudians to Constantine." *Papers in the British School at Rome*, 52 (1984): 124–47.
Minoglou, Ioanna Pepelasis. "Ethnic Minority Groups in International Banking: Greek Diaspora Bankers of Constantinople and Ottoman State Finances, c. 1840–81." *Financial History Review*, 9 (2002): 125–46.
Mir, Salam. "Colonialism, Postcolonialism, Globalization, and Arab Culture." *Arab Studies Quarterly*, 41 (2019): 33–58.
Mirrlees, James A. "The Optimal Structure of Incentives and Authority within an Organization." *Bell Journal of Economics* 7 (1976): 105–31.
  "The Theory of Optimal Taxation." In *Handbook of Mathematical Economics*, vol. 3, edited by Kenneth J. Arrow and Michael D. Intriligator, pp. 1197–249. Amsterdam: North-Holland, 1986.
Miura, Toru. *Dynamism in the Urban Society of Damascus: The Ṣāliḥiyya Quarter from the Twelfth to the Twentieth Centuries*. Leiden: Brill, 2015.
Moaddel, Mansoor. "The Shi'i Ulama and the State in Iran." *Theory and Society*, 15 (1986): 519–56.
Moaddel, Mansour. "The Saudi Public Speaks: Religion, Gender, and Politics." *International Journal of Middle East Studies*, 38 (2006): 79–108.
Moazzen, Maryam. *Formation of a Religious Landscape: Shi'i Higher Learning in Safavid Iran*. Leiden: Brill, 2018.
  "The Leading Religious College in Early Modern Iran: Madrasa-yi Sultani and Its Endowment." In *The Empires of the Near East and India: Source Studies of the Safavid, Ottoman, and Mughal Literate Communities*, edited by Hani Khafipour, pp. 482–92. New York: Columbia University Press, 2019.
Moghadam, Vaentine M. *Modernizing Women: Gender and Social Change in the Middle East*, 3rd ed. Boulder, CO: Lynne Rienner, 2013.
Mohamadi, Mehdi, Hassan Rafiey, Mir Taher Mousavi, and Samaneh Hosseinzadeh. "Which Institutions Are Most Corrupt? Prevalence and Social Determinants of Bribery in Tehran." *Crime, Law and Social Change*, 74 (2020): 175–91.
Mohamed, Emad, and Bakinaz Abdalla. "What Jihad Questions Do Muslims Ask?" *Journal of Islamic and Muslim Studies*, 2 (2017): 56–79.
Mohammadi, Majid. *The Longevity of Clerical Business as Usual: A Socio-Political History of Iranian Twelver Shi'i Clergy*. Los Angeles, CA: Dan & Mo Publishers, 2019.
Mohseni-Cheraghlou, Amin, Ramezan Ali Marvi, and Amir Kazemzadeh. "Waqf in Iran: An Overview of Historical Roots and Current Trends." In *Waqf Development and Innovation: Socio-Economic and Legal Perspectives*, pp. 192–206. London: Routledge, 2021.
Mokyr, Joel. *A Culture of Growth: The Origins of the Modern Economy*. Princeton, NJ: Princeton University Press, 2017.
Momen, Moojan. *Shi'i Islam: A Beginner's Guide*. London: Oneworld, 2016.
Monahan, Susanne C. "Who Controls Church Work? Organizational Effects on Jurisdictional Boundaries and Disputes in Churches." *Journal for the Scientific Study of Religion*, 38 (1999): 370–85.
Monshipouri, Mahmood. *Middle East Politics: Changing Dynamics*. London: Routledge, 2019.

Moor, Tine de. "The Silent Revolution: A New Perspective on the Emergence of Commons, Guilds, and other Forms of Collective Action in Western Europe." *International Review of Social History*, 53 (2008): 179–212.
Moore, Barrington, Jr. *Social Origins of Dictatorship and Democracy: Lord and Peasant in the Making of the Modern World*. Boston, MA: Beacon Press, 1966.
Moreen, Vera B. "The Status of Religious Minorities in Safavid Iran 1617–61." *Journal of Near Eastern Studies*, 40 (1981): 119–34.
Mostafaei, Mohammad. "The Crimes of Blasphemy and Apostasy in Iran." In *Freedom of Expression in Islam*, edited by Muhammad Khalid Masud, Kari Vogt, Lena Larsen, and Christian Moe, pp. 101–10. London: I. B. Tauris, 2021.
Motzki, Harald, ed. *Ḥadīth: Origins and Developments*. London: Routledge, 2016.
Moulin, Anne-Marie. "Révolutions Médicales et Révolutions Politiques en Egypte (1865–1917)." *Revue du Monde Musulman et de la Méditerranée*, 52–53 (1989): 111–23.
Moustafa, Tamir. "Conflict and Cooperation between the State and Religious Institutions in Contemporary Egypt." *International Journal of Middle East Studies*, 32 (2000): 3–22.
Moutafidou, Ariadni. "Greek Merchant Families Perceiving the World: The Case of Demetrius Vikelas." *Mediterranean Historical Review*, 23 (2008): 143–64.
Mozafferi, Mehdi. *Fatwa: Violence and Discourtesy*. Aarhus: Aaarhus University Press, 1998.
Muedini, Fait. *Sponsoring Sufism: How Governments Promote "Mystical Islam" in Their Domestic and Foreign Policies*. New York: Palgrave Macmillan, 2015.
Mumcu, Ahmet. *Osmanlı Devletinde Rüşvet (Özellikle Adlî Rüşvet)*, 2nd ed. Istanbul: İnkilâp Kitabevi, 1985.
Mungiu-Pippidi, Alina. "Controlling Corruption through Collective Action." *Journal of Democracy*, 24 (2013): 101–15.
Munro, John H. "The Medieval Origins of the Financial Revolution: Usury, *Rentes*, and Negotiability." *International History Review*, 25 (2003): 505–62.
Murphy, Lawrence R. *The American University in Cairo: 1919–1987*. Cairo: American University in Cairo Press, 1987.
Musallam, Adnan A. *From Secularism to Jihad: Sayyid Qutb and the Foundations of Radical Islamism*. Westport, CT: Praeger, 2005.
Nader, Emir. "Egyptian Court Sentences Man to 3 Years in Prison Following Declaration of Atheism," *Daily News Egypt*, 11 January 2015.
Nagata, Yuzo. *Tarihte Âyânlar: Karaosmanoğulları Üzerinde Bir İnceleme*. Ankara: Türk Tarih Kurumu, 1997.
Nakissa, Aria. "An Epistemic Shift in Islamic Law: Educational Reform at al-Azhar and Dār al-ʿUlūm." *Islamic Law and Society*, 21 (2014): 209–51.
Naqvi, Syed Nawab Haider. *Ethics and Economics: An Islamic Synthesis*. Leicester: Islamic Foundation, 1981.
Neal, Andrew W. *Exceptionalism and the Politics of Counter-Terrorism: Liberty, Security and the War on Terror*. London: Routledge, 2010.
Netanyahu, B. *The Origins of the Inquisition in Fifteenth Century Spain*. New York: Random House, 1995.
Neumann, Christoph K. *Araç Tarih, Amaç Tanzimat: Tarih-i Cevdet'in Siyasi Anlamı*, translated by Meltem Arun from the original German edition of 1992. Istanbul: Tarih Vakfı, 1999.

Nevo, Joseph. "Religion and National Identity in Saudi Arabia." *Middle Eastern Studies*, 34 (1998): 34–53.
Nichols, Theo, and Nadir Sugur. *Global Management, Local Labour: Turkish Workers and Modern Industry*. New York: Palgrave Macmillan, 2004.
Niekerk, Jana van, and Maykel Verkuyten. "Interfaith Marriage Attitudes in Muslim Majority Countries: A Multilevel Approach." *International Journal for the Psychology of Religion*, 28 (2018): 257–70.
Nielsen, Richard A. "The Changing Face of Islamic Authority in the Middle East." *Middle East Brief (Crown Center for Middle East Studies)*, 99 (2016): 1–9.
  Deadly Clerics: Blocked Ambition and the Paths to Jihad. Cambridge: Cambridge University Press, 2017.
  "Women's Authority in Patriarchal Social Movements: The Case of Female Salafi Preachers." *American Journal of Political Science*, 64 (2020): 52–66.
Nissimi, Hilda. *The Crypto-Jewish Mashhadis: The Shaping of Religious and Communal Identity in Their Journey from Iran to New York*. Eastbourne: Sussex Academic Press, 2007.
Nobuaki, Kondo. "The Waqf of Ustad 'Abbas: Rewrites of the Deeds in Qajar Tehran." In *Persian Documents: Social History of Iran and Turan in the Fifteenth-Nineteenth Centuries*, edited by Nobuaki Kondo, pp. 106–28. London: Routledge, 2003.
North, Douglass C. *Structure and Change in Economic History*. New York: W. W. Norton, 1981.
North, Douglass C., and Robert Paul Thomas. *The Rise of the Western World: A New Economic History*. Cambridge: Cambridge University Press, 1973.
North, Douglass C., and Barry R. Weingast. "Constitutions and Commitment: The Evolution of Institutions Governing Public Choice in 17th-Century England." *Journal of Economic History*, 49 (1989): 803–32.
North, Douglass C., John Joseph Wallis, and Barry R. Weingast. *Violence and Social Orders: A Conceptual Framework for Interpreting Recorded History*. Cambridge: Cambridge University Press, 2009.
Oberauer, Norbert. "Early Doctrines on *Waqf* Revisited: The Evolution of Islamic Endowment Law in the 2nd Century AD." *Islamic Law and Society*, 20 (2013): 1–47.
Oberling, Pierre. "The Role of Religious Minorities in the Persian Revolution, 1906–1912." *Journal of Asian History*, 12 (1978): 1–29.
Öcalan, Hasan Basri, Sezai Sevim, and Doğan Yavaş, eds. *Bursa Vakfiyeleri – 1*. Bursa: Bursa Büyükşehir Belediyesi, 2013.
Ochsenwald, William. *Religion, Society, and the State in Arabia: The Hijaz under Ottoman Control, 1840–1908*. Columbus: Ohio State University Press, 1984.
O'Connor, Tom. "Will Facebook Survive? Iran Declares Fatwa against Social Media over Privacy Invasion Claims." *Newsweek*, 12 April 2018.
Ogilvie, Sheilagh. *State Corporatism and Proto-Industry: The Württemberg Black Forest, 1580–1797*. Cambridge: Cambridge University Press, 1997.
  "Guilds, Efficiency, and Social Capital: Evidence from German Proto-Industry." *Economic History Review*, 57 (2004): 286–333.
  "The Economics of Guilds." *Journal of Economic Perspectives*, 28 (2014): 169–92.
Oğuzoğlu, Yusuf. *Osmanlı Devlet Anlayışı*. Istanbul: Eren, 2000.

Olsen, Donald J. *The City as a Work of Art: London, Paris, Vienna.* New Haven, CT: Yale University Press, 1986.
Olson, Mancur. *The Logic of Collective Action: Public Goods and the Theory of Groups*, rev. ed. Cambridge, MA: Harvard University Press, 1971.
  "Dictatorship, Democracy, and Development." *American Political Science Review*, 87 (1993): 567–76.
Onar, Sıddık Sami. "İslâm Hukuku ve Mecelle." In *Tanzimat'tan Cumhuriyet'e Türkiye Ansiklopedisi*, vol. 3, pp. 580–87. Istanbul: İletişim Yayınları, 1985.
Onaran, Nevzat. *Cumhuriyet'te Ermeni ve Rum Mallarının Türkleştirilmesi (1920–1930)*. Istanbul: Evrensel, 2013.
Onay, Ahmet. "Osmanlı'dan Cumhuriyet'e Camilerin Finansmanı." *Değerler Eğitimi Dergisi*, 7 (2009): 43–80.
Ongur, Hakan Övünç. "Performing through Friday *Khutbas*: Reinstrumentalization of Religion in the New Turkey." *Third World Quarterly*, 41 (2020): 434–52.
Öniş, Ziya, and Umut Türem. "Entrepreneurs, Democracy, and Citizenship in Turkey." *Comparative Politics*, 34 (2002): 439–56.
Onley, James. "Transnational Merchant Families in the Nineteenth- and Twentieth-Century Gulf." In *The Gulf Family: Kinship Policies and Modernity*, edited by Alanoud Alsharekh, pp. 37–56. London: Saqi, 2007.
Oppenheim, Samson D. *American Jewish Year Book (1918–19)*. Philadelphia, PA: Jewish Publication Society of America, 1918.
Oran, Ahmad, and Salim Rashid. "Fiscal Policy in Early Islam." *Public Finance*, 44 (1989): 75–101.
Orbay, Kayhan. "Imperial Waqfs within the Ottoman Waqf System." *Endowment Studies*, 1 (2017): 135–53.
Organization of Islamic Cooperation. "Resolutions on Muslim Communities and Muslim Minorities in the Non-OIC Member States." 1–2 March 2019.
O'Rourke, Jacqueline. *Representing Jihad: The Appearing and Disappearing Radical*. London: Zed Books, 2012.
Ortaylı, İlber. "The Greeks and Ottoman Administration during the Tanzimat Period." In *Ottoman Greeks in the Age of Nationalism: Politics, Economy, and Society in the Nineteenth Century*, edited by Dimitri Gondicas and Charles Issawi, pp. 161–67. Princeton, NJ: Darwin Press, 1999.
Osman, Tarek. *Egypt on the Brink: From Nasser to the Egyptian Brotherhood*, rev. and updated ed. New Haven, CT: Yale University Press, 2013.
  "Why Border Lines Drawn with a Ruler in WW1 Still Rock the Middle East." 14 December 2013. www.bbc.com/news/world-middle-east-25299553 (accessed 2 February 2023).
Otterbeck, Jonas. "Battling over the Public Sphere: Islamic Reactions to the Music of Today." *Contemporary Islam*, 2 (2008): 211–28.
Overfield, James H. *Humanism and Scholasticism in Late Medieval Germany*. Princeton, NJ: Princeton University Press, 1984.
Owen, John M., IV, and J. Judd Owen. "Concluding Thoughts." In *Religion, the Enlightenment, and the New Global Order*, edited by John M. Owen IV and J. Judd Owen, pp. 265–73. New York: Columbia University Press, 2010.
Owen, Roger. *The Middle East in the World Economy, 1800–1914*, rev. ed. London: I. B. Tauris, 1993.

Owen, Roger, and Şevket Pamuk. *A History of Middle East Economies in the Twentieth Century*. Cambridge, MA: Harvard University Press, 1999.

Özbek, Nadir. *Osmanlı İmparatorluğu'nda Sosyal Devlet: Siyaset, İktidar ve Meşruiyet (1876–1914)*. Istanbul: İletişim, 2002.

"'Beggars' and 'Vagrants' in Ottoman State Policy and Public Discourse." *Middle Eastern Studies*, 45 (2009): 783–801.

Özcan, Esra. *Mainstreaming the Headscarf: Islamist Politics and Women in the Turkish Media*. London: I. B. Tauris, 2019.

Özsaraç, Yakup. "Vakıflarda Anakronizm: Para Vakıfları Üzerinden Bir Değerlendirme." *Süleyman Demirel Üniversitesi İktisadi ve İdari Bilimler Fakültesi Dergisi*, 26 (2021): 209–23.

Öztaş, Dilek, İmran Hasanoğlu, Turan Buzgan, Mehmet Akın Taşyaran, and Zeliha Koçak Tufan. "Eid al-Adha Associated Infections: Three Case Reports." *Van Veterinary Journal*, 28 (2017): 165–68.

Öztürk, Ahmet Erdi. "Turkey's Diyanet under AKP Rule: From Protector to Imposer of State Ideology." *Southeast European and Black Sea Studies*, 16 (2016): 619–35.

Religion, Identity and Power: Turkey and the Balkans in the Twenty-first Century. Edinburgh: Edinburgh University Press, 2021.

Öztürk, Ahmet Erdi, and Semiha Sözeri. "Diyanet as a Turkish Foreign Policy Tool: Evidence from the Netherlands and Bulgaria." *Politics and Religion*, 11 (2018): 624–48.

Öztürk, Fundanur. "Diyanet Fetvaları ve Açıklamaları: Son 10 Yılda Hangileri Tartışma Yarattı?" www.bbc.com/turkce/haberler-turkiye-42552621 (accessed 2 February 2023).

Öztürk, Mustafa. "Toplumsal Cinsiyet Meselesine Kur'an Zaviyesinden Genel Bir Bakış." In *Dinî ve Toplumsal Boyutlarıyla Cinsiyet*, edited by Üsküdar Belediyesi Çamlıca Sabahattin Zaim Eğitim ve Kültür Merkezi, pp. 165–91. Istanbul: Ensar Neşriyat, 2012.

Öztürk, Nazif. *Menşe'i ve Tarihi Gelişimi Açısından Vakıflar*. Ankara: Vakıflar Genel Müdürlüğü, 1983.

Türk Yenileşme Tarihi Çerçevesinde Vakıf Müessesesi. Ankara: Türkiye Diyanet Vakfı, 1995.

Öztürk, Yaşar Nuri. *Surelerin İniş Sırasına Göre Kur'an-ı Kerim Meali*. Istanbul: Yeni Boyut, 2016.

Paçacı, Mehmet, and Yasin Aktay. "75 Years of Higher Religious Education in Modern Turkey." *Muslim World*, 89 (1999): 389–413.

Padgett, John F. "The Emergence of Corporate Merchant-Banks in Dugento Tuscany." In *The Emergence of Organizations and Markets*, edited by John F. Padgett and Walter W. Powell, pp. 121–67. Princeton, NJ: Princeton University Press, 2012.

Page, Benjamin I., Jason Seawright, and Matthew J. Lacombe. *Billionaires and Stealth Politics*. Chicago, IL: University of Chicago Press, 2019.

Pakkir, Maideen, Naina Mohamed, Abdurazak Jumale, and Rajkapoor Balasubramaniam. "Adverse Health Effects Associated with Islamic Fasting: A Literature Review." *Journal of Fasting and Health*, 5 (2017): 113–18.

Pallis, Alexandros A. "The Population of Turkey in 1935." *Geographical Journal*, 91 (1938): 439–45.

Pamuk, Şevket. "Political Power and Institutional Change: Lessons from the Middle East." *Economic History of Developing Regions*, 27 (2012): S41–46.
Pan, Jennifer, and Alexandra A. Siegel. "How Saudi Crackdowns Fail to Silence Online Dissent." *American Political Science Review*, 114 (2020): 109–25.
Pascual, Jean-Paul. *Damas à la Fin du XVIe Siècle d'Après Trois Actes de Waqf Ottomans*, vol. 1. Damascus: Institut Français de Damas, 1983.
Peacock, Andrew C. S. *The Great Seljuk Empire*. Edinburgh: Edinburgh University Press, 2015.
Pearson, James Douglas. "Al-Ḳurʾān." *Encyclopaedia of Islam*, 2nd ed., vol. 5, pp. 400–432. Leiden: Brill, 1986.
Perkin, Harold. *The Rise of Professional Society: England since 1880*. London: Routledge, 2002.
Peri, Oded. "Waqf and Ottoman Welfare Policy: The Poor Kitchen of Haseki Sultan in Eighteenth-Century Jerusalem." *Journal of the Economic and Social History of the Orient*, 35 (1992): 167–86.
Persson, Anna, Bo Rothstein, and Jan Teorell. "Why Anticorruption Reforms Fail – Systemic Corruption as a Collective Action Problem." *Governance*, 26 (2013): 449–71.
Persson, Torsten, Gérard Roland, and Guido Tabellini. "Separation of Powers and Political Accountability." *Quarterly Journal of Economics* 112 (1997): 1163–202.
Peters, Rudolph, and Gert J. J. De Vries. "Apostasy in Islam." *Die Welt des Islams*, 17 (1976): 1–25.
Petry, Carl F. "Waqf as an Instrument of Investment in the Mamluk Sultanate: Security vs. Profit?" In *Slave Elites in the Middle East and Africa: A Comparative Study*, edited by Miura Toru and Edward Philips, pp. 99–115. London: Kegan Paul International, 2000.
Pew Research Center. "Mapping the Global Muslim Population." Washington, DC: Pew Research Center, 2009.
  "Government Restrictions Index, Appendix E: Results by Country." www.pewresearch.org/wp-content/uploads/sites/7/2016/06/Restrictions2016appendixE.pdf (accessed 2 February 2023).
  "Religious Beliefs and National Belonging in Central and Eastern Europe." Washington, DC: Pew Research Center, 2017.
Phillip, Abby. "Frosty Fatwa: Saudi Cleric Bans Snowmen." *Washington Post*, 13 January 2015.
Phillips, Christopher. "Sectarianism and Conflict in Syria." *Third World Quarterly*, 36 (2015): 357–76.
  The Battle for Syria: International Rivalry in the New Middle East. New Haven, CT: Yale University Press, 2016.
Philpott, Daniel. *Religious Freedom in Islam: The Fate of a Universal Human Right in the Muslim World Today*. Oxford: Oxford University Press, 2019.
Pierret, Thomas. "The Farhi Family and the Changing Position of the Jews in Syria, 1750–1860." *Middle Eastern Studies*, 20 (1984): 37–52.
  Religion and State in Syria: The Sunni Ulama from Coup to Revolution. Cambridge: Cambridge University Press, 2013; original French edition 2011.
  "The Syrian Baath Party and Sunni Islam: Conflicts and Connivance." *Middle East Brief (Crown Center for Middle East Studies)*, 77 (2014): 1–7.

Pierret, Thomas, and Kjetil Selvik. "Limits of 'Authoritarian Upgrading' in Syria: Private Welfare, Islamic Charities, and the Rise of the Zayd Movement." *International Journal of Middle East Studies*, 41 (2009): 595–614.

Pinker, Steven. *The Blank Slate: The Modern Denial of Human Nature*. New York: Viking Penguin, 2002.

Pioppi, Daniela. "Privatization of Social Services as a Regime Strategy: The Revival of Islamic Endowments (*Awkaf*) in Egypt." In *Debating Arab Authoritarianism: Dynamics and Durability in Nondemocratic Regimes*, edited by Oliver Schlumberger, pp. 129–42. Stanford: Stanford University Press, 2007.

Pipes, Daniel. *Slave Soldiers and Islam: The Genesis of a Military System*. New Haven, CT: Yale University Press, 1981.

   The Rushdie Affair: The Novel, the Ayatollah, and the West, 2nd ed. Piscataway, NJ: Transaction Publishers, 2003.

Pizanias, Petros. "From Reaya to Greek Citizen: Enlightenment and Revolution, 1750–1832." In *The Greek Revolution of 1821: A European Event*, edited by Petros Pizanias, pp. 11–81. Istanbul: ISIS Press, 2011.

Platteau, Jean-Philippe. *Institutions, Social Norms, and Economic Development*. Amsterdam: Harwood, 2001.

   Islam Instrumentalized: Religion and Politics in Historical Perspective. New York: Cambridge University Press, 2017.

Popper, Karl R. *The Open Society and Its Enemies*, 2 vols., 5th ed. Princeton, NJ: Princeton University Press, 1966.

Porter, Dorothy. *Health, Civilization, and the State: A History of Public Health from Ancient to Modern Times*. London: Routledge, 1999.

Posner, Richard A. *The Economics of Justice*. Cambridge, MA: Harvard University Press, 1981.

   Sex and Reason. Cambridge, MA: Harvard University Press, 1992.

Powell, Russell. "Zakat: Drawing Insights for Legal Theory and Economic Policy from Islamic Jurisprudence." *University of Pittsburgh Tax Review*, 7 (2009): 43–101.

Powers, David S. "On the Abrogation of the Bequest Verses." *Arabica*, 29 (1982): 246–95.

   "Orientalism, Colonialism, and Legal History: The Attack on Muslim Family Endowments in Algeria and India." *Comparative Studies in Society and History*, 31 (1989): 535–71.

Prak, Maarten. "Corporate Politics in the Low Countries: Guilds as Institutions, 14th to 18th Centuries." In *Craft Guilds in the Early Modern Low Countries: Work, Power, and Representation*, edited by Maarten Prak, Catharina Lis, Jan Lucassen, and Hugo Soly, pp. 74–106. Farnham: Ashgate, 2006.

Priestland, Jane, ed. *The Buraimi Dispute 1950–1961: Contemporary Documents*, vol. 1. Cambridge: Cambridge Archive Editions, 1992.

Pringuey, Roland. *La Bourse de Beyrouth*. Paris: Librairie Générale de Droit et de Jurisprudence, 1959.

"Prohibition of Interfaith Marriage." Law Library of Congress, Washington, DC: US Congress, September 2015.

Prothero, George Walter. *Arabia*. London: HM Stationery Office, 1920.

   French Morocco. London: HM Stationery Office, 1920.

Puga, Diego, and Daniel Trefler. "International Trade and Institutional Change: Medieval Venice's Response to Globalization." *Quarterly Journal of Economics*, 129 (2014): 753–821.
Putnam, Robert D. *Making Democracy Work: Civic Traditions in Modern Italy*. Princeton, NJ: Princeton University Press, 1993.
  Bowling Alone: The Collapse and Revival of American Community. New York: Simon & Schuster, 2000.
Qanuni Madani 1928. www.refworld.org/docid/49997adb27.html (accessed 2 February 2023).
Quazi, Naseem. "Economic Morality in Islam." *Hamdard Islamicus*, 16/4 (1993): 89–102.
Qutb, Sayyid. *Social Justice in Islam*, translated by John D. Hardie from the Arabic original of 1948. New York: American Council of Learned Societies, 1970.
  Milestones, translated from the Arabic original of 1964. New Delhi: Islamic Book Service, 2002.
Raafat, Samir. *The Egyptian Bourse*. Cairo: American University of Cairo Press, 2020.
Radio France International. "Deflection of Religious Debate in French Classrooms on the Rise following Paty Beheading." 6 January 2021. www.rfi.fr/en/france/20210106 (accessed 2 February 2023).
Radsch, Courtney. "First Egyptian Blogger Imprisoned for Writings Is Released." *Huffpost*, 11 May 2011.
Rafeq, Abdul-Karim. "Craft Organization, Work Ethics, and the Strains of Change in Ottoman Syria." *Journal of the American Oriental Society*, 111 (1991): 495–511.
Rahman, Afzalur. *Economic Doctrines of Islam*, vol. 3. Lahore: Islamic Publications, 1976.
Rahman, Fazlur. "Islam and Problem of Economic Justice." *Pakistan Economist* (24 August 1974): 14–39.
  "The Principle of *Shura* and the Role of the Umma in Islam." *American Journal of Islamic Social Sciences*, 1 (1984): 1–9.
  "Translating the Qur'an." *Religion and Literature*, 20 (1988): 23–30.
Rahman, Kaunain. *An Overview of Corruption and Anti-Corruption in Saudi Arabia*. Berlin: Transparency International, 2020.
Raissouni, Ahmed. *Islamic "Waqf Endowment": Scope and Limitations*, translated from the Arabic original by Abderrafi Benhallam. Rabat: ISESCO, 2001.
Rakel, Eva Patricia. *Power, Islam, and Political Elite in Iran: A Study on the Iranian Political Elite from Khomeini to Ahmedinejad*. Leiden: Brill, 2008.
Ramstedt, Martin. "A Fatwa against Yoga: Mitigating Conflict in the Face of Increasing Fundamentalism in Indonesia." *Interreligious Dialogue*, 5 (2011): 1–11.
Rashid, Ahmed. *Taliban: The Power of Militant Islam in Afghanistan and Beyond*, rev. ed. London: I. B. Tauris, 2010.
Rawlings, Helen. *The Spanish Inquisition*. Malden, MA: Blackwell, 2006.
Razek, Ali Abdel. *Islam and the Foundations of Political Power*, translated by Maryam Loutfi from the original Arabic edition of 1925. Edinburgh: Edinburgh University Press, 2012.
Reimer, Michael J. "Urban Government and Administration in Egypt, 1805–1914." *Die Welt des Islams*, 39 (1999): 289–318.

Reinkowski, Maurus. "Hidden Believers, Hidden Apostates: The Phenomenon of Crypto-Jews and Crypto-Christians in the Middle East." In *Converting Cultures: Religion, Ideology and Transformations of Modernity*, edited by Dennis Washburn and A. Kevin Reinhart, pp. 409–33. Leiden: Brill, 2007.

Rejwan, Nissim. *The Jews of Iraq: 3000 Years of History and Culture*. Boulder, CO: Westview Press, 1985.

The Last Jews of Baghdad: Remembering a Lost Homeland. Austin: University of Texas Press, 2004.

Renan, Ernest. *L'Islamisme et la Science*. Paris: Calman Lévy, 1883.

Reynolds, Susan. *Kingdoms and Communities in Western Europe 900–1300*, 2nd ed. Oxford: Oxford University Press, 1997.

Reza, Sadiq. "Endless Emergency: The Case of Egypt." *New Criminal Law Review*, 10 (2007): 532–53.

Ridge, Hannah. "Effect of Religious Legislation on Religious Behavior: The Ramadan Fast." *Interdisciplinary Journal of Research on Religion*, 15 (2019): article 8.

Rijpma, Auke. "Funding Public Services through Religious and Charitable Foundations in the Late-Medieval Low Countries." PhD dissertation, Utrecht University, 2012.

Ringer, Monica M. *Education, Religion, and the Discourse of Cultural Reform in Qajar Iran*. Costa Mesa, CA: Mazda Publishers, 2001.

Rivetti, Paola. "Co-opting Civil Society Activism in Iran." In *Civil Society in Syria and Iran: Activism in Authoritarian Contexts*, edited by Paul Aarts and Francesco Cavatorta, pp. 187–206. Boulder, CO: Lynne Rienner, 2013.

Rivlin, Paul. *Arab Economies in the Twenty-First Century*. Cambridge: Cambridge University Press, 2009.

Roberts, Keith A., and David Yamane. *Religion in Sociological Perspective*, 6th ed. Thousand Oaks, CA: Sage, 2016.

Rodinson, Maxime. *Islam and Capitalism*, translated by Brian Pearce from the original French edition of 1966. New York: Pantheon, 1972.

Muḥammad, translated by Anne Carter from the original French edition of 1961. New York: Pantheon, 1980.

Roland, Gérard. "Understanding Institutional Change: Fast-Moving and Slow-Moving Institutions." *Studies in Comparative International Development*, 38 (2004): 109–31.

Romano, David. "The Kurds in the Middle East." In *Routledge Handbook of Minorities in the Middle East*, edited by Paul S. Rowe, pp. 255–71. London: Routledge, 2019.

Root, Hilton L. *The Fountain of Privilege: Political Foundations of Markets in Old Regime France and England*. Berkeley: University of California Press, 1994.

Root, Jay. "Salman Rushdie Is Attacked Onstage in New York." *New York Times*, 12 August 2022. www.nytimes.com/2022/08/12/nyregion/salman-rushdie-attacked .html (accessed 2 February 2023).

Rosenblatt, Helena. *The Lost History of Liberalism: From Ancient Rome to the Twenty-First Century*. Princeton, NJ: Princeton University Press, 2018.

Rosenthal, Franz. "Sedaka, Charity." *Hebrew Union College Annual*, 23 (1950–51): 411–30.

"Gifts and Bribes: The Muslim View." *Proceedings of the American Philosophical Society*, 108 (1964): 135–44.

Rosenthal, Steven. "Foreigners and Municipal Reform in Istanbul: 1855–1865." *International Journal of Middle East Studies*, 11 (1980): 227–45.

Roudometof, Victor. "From Rum Millet to Greek Nation: Enlightenment, Secularization, and National Identity in Ottoman Balkan Society, 1453–1821." *Journal of Modern Greek Studies*, 16 (1998): 11–48.

Rowe, Paul S. "Christian–Muslim Relations in Egypt in the Wake of the Arab Spring." *Domes*, 22 (2013): 262–75.

Roy, Olivier. *Globalized Islam: The Search for a New Ummah*. New York: Columbia University Press, 2006.

The Politics of Chaos in the Middle East, translated by Ros Schwartz from the original French edition of 2007. New York: Columbia University Press, 2008.

Royle, Stephen. *Islamic Development in Palestine: A Comparative Study*. New York: Routledge, 2017.

Rubin, Jared. "Bills of Exchange, Interest Bans, and Impersonal Exchange in Islam and Christianity." *Explorations in Economic History*, 47 (2010): 213–27.

"Institutions, the Rise of Commerce, and the Persistence of Laws: Interest Restrictions in Islam and Christianity." *Economic Journal*, 121 (2011): 1310–39.

Rulers, Religion, and Riches: Why the West Got Rich and the Middle East Did Not. Cambridge: Cambridge University Press, 2017.

Rugh, William A. "Emergence of a New Middle Class in Saudi Arabia." *Middle East Journal*, 27 (1973): 7–20.

"Education in Saudi Arabia: Choices and Constraints." *Middle East Policy*, 9 (2002): 40–55.

Rustow, Dankwart A. "Transitions to Democracy: Toward a Dynamic Model." *Comparative Politics*, 3 (1970): 337–63.

Saab, Bilal Y. "Can Mohamed bin Salman Reshape Saudi Arabia? The Treacherous Path to Reform." *Foreign Affairs online*, 5 January 2017.

Sabev, Orlin (Salih, Orhan). *İbrahim Müteferrika ya da İlk Osmanlı Matbaa Serüveni (1726-1746): Yeniden Değerlendirme*. Istanbul: Yeditepe, 2006.

Sabra, Adam. *Poverty and Charity in Medieval Islam: Mamluk Egypt, 1250–1517*. Cambridge: Cambridge University Press, 2000.

Sabry, Sarah. "How Poverty Is Underestimated in Greater Cairo, Egypt". *Environment and Urbanization*, 22 (2010): 523–41.

Sack, Detlef. "European Chambers of Commerce in Comparison." In *Chambers of Commerce in Europe: Self-Governance and Institutional Change*, edited by Detlef Sack, pp. 1–24. Cham: Palgrave Macmillan, 2021.

Sadri, Mahmoud. "Sacral Defense of Secularism: The Political Theologies of Soroush, Shabestari, and Kadivar." *International Journal of Politics, Culture, and Society*, 15 (2001): 257–70.

Saeed, Abdullah. "Trends in Contemporary Islam: A Preliminary Attempt at a Classification." *Muslim World*, 97 (2007): 395–404.

The Qur'an: An Introduction. London: Routledge, 2008.

"Blasphemy Laws in Islam: Towards a Rethinking?" In *Freedom of Expression in Islam: Challenging Apostasy and Blasphemy Laws*, edited by Muhammad Khalid Masud, Kari Vogt, Lena Larsen, and Christian Moe, pp. 207–36. London: I. B. Tauris, 2021.

Saeed, Abdullah, and Hassan Saeed. *Freedom of Religion, Apostasy and Islam.* Aldershot: Ashgate, 2004.
Saeidi, Ali A. "The Accountability of Para-Governmental Organizations (*bonyads*): The Case of Iranian Foundations." *Iranian Studies*, 37 (2004): 479–98.
Şafak, Yakup. "Mevlânâ'ya Atfedilen 'Yine Gel...' Rubâîsine Dair." *Tasavvuf*, 24 (2009): 75–80.
Safieddine, Hicham. *Banking on the State: The Financial Foundations of Lebanon.* Stanford: Stanford University Press, 2019.
Saghafi, Morad. "Crossing the Desert: Iranian Intellectuals after the Islamic Revolution." *Middle East Critique*, 10 (2001): 15–45.
Said, Edward W. *Orientalism.* New York: Random House, 1978.
Şakul, Kahraman. "Nizâm-ı Cedid Düşüncesinde Batılılaşma ve İslami Modernleşme." *Dîvân İlmî Araştırmalar*, 19 (2005): 117–50.
Salihu, Habeeb Abdulrauf, and Amin Jafari. "Corruption and Anti-Corruption Strategies in Iran: An Overview of the Preventive, Detective and Punitive Measures." *Journal of Money Laundering Control*, 23 (2020): 77–89.
Salzmann, Ariel. "An Ancien Régime Revisited: 'Privatization' and Political Economy in the Eighteenth-Century Ottoman Empire." *Politics and Society*, 21 (1993): 393–423.
Samuels, David. "Separation of Powers." *The Oxford Handbook of Comparative Politics*, edited by Carles Boix and Susan C. Stokes. https://doi.org/10.1093/oxfordhb/9780199566020.003.0029 (accessed 2 February 2023).
Sanders, Paula. *Creating Medieval Cairo: Empire, Religion, and Architectural Preservation in Nineteenth-Century Egypt.* Cairo: American University in Cairo Press, 2008.
Sapsford, Roger, Gerasimos Tsourapas, Pamela Abbott, and Andrea Teti. "Corruption, Trust, Inclusion and Cohesion in North Africa and the Middle East." *Applied Research in Quality of Life*, 14 (2019): 1–21.
Saraçoğlu, M. Safa. *Nineteenth-Century Local Governance in Ottoman Bulgaria: Politics in Provincial Councils.* Edinburgh: Edinburgh University Press, 2019.
Sarıkaya, Makbule. *Türkiye Himaye-i Etfal Cemiyeti, 1921–1935.* Ankara: Atatürk Araştırma Merkezi, 2011.
Sassoon, Joseph. *Saddam Hussein's Ba'th Party: Inside an Authoritarian Regime.* Cambridge: Cambridge University Press, 2012.
Satyanath, Shanker, Nico Voigtländer, and Hans-Joachim Voth. "Bowling for Fascism: Social Capital and the Rise of the Nazi Party." *Journal of Political Economy*, 125 (2017): 478–526.
Saudi Gazette. "Over 174,000 Women Driving Licenses Issued in 19 Months." Article 590574, 8 March 2020.
Savory, Roger M. "The Consolidation of Safavid Power in Persia." *Der Islam*, 41 (1965): 71–94.
"The Safavid Administrative System." In *The Cambridge History of Iran*, vol. 6, edited by Peter Jackson and Laurence Lockhart, pp. 351–72. Cambridge: Cambridge University Press, 1986.
Schacht, Joseph. "Zakāt." *Encyclopaedia of Islam*, vol. 3, pp. 1202–4. Leiden: E. J. Brill, 1934.
An Introduction to Islamic Law. Oxford: Clarendon Press, 1964.

Schanzer, Carlo. "Italian Colonial Policy in Northern Africa." *Foreign Affairs*, 2 (1924): 446–56.
Schäublin, Emanuel. "*Zakat* Practice in the Islamic Tradition and Its Recent History in the Context of Palestine." In *Histories of Humanitarian Action in the Middle East and North Africa*, edited by Eleanor Davey and Eva Svoboda, pp. 19–26. London: Humanitarian Policy Group, 2014.
Scheidel, Walter. "Slavery and Forced Labour in Early China and the Roman World." In *Eurasian Empires in Antiquity and the Early Middle Ages: Contacts and Exchange between the Graeco-Roman World, Inner Asia and China*, edited by Hyun Jin Kim, Juliaan Vervaet, and Selim Ferruh Adalı, pp. 133–50. Cambridge: Cambridge University Press, 2017.
Schirrmacher, Christine. "Leaving Islam." In *Handbook of Leaving Religion*, edited by Daniel Enstedt, Göran Larsson, and Teemu T. Mantsinen, pp. 81–94. Leiden: Brill, 2020.
Schizer, David M. "Enhancing Efficiency at Nonprofits with Analysis and Disclosure." *Columbia Journal of Tax Law*, 11 (2020): 76–134.
Schoenblum, Jeffrey A. "The Role of Legal Doctrine in the Decline of the Islamic Waqf: A Comparison with the Trust." *Vanderbilt Journal of Transnational Law*, 32 (1999):1191–227.
Schumpeter, Joseph A. *Capitalism, Socialism, and Democracy*, 3rd ed. New York: Harper & Row, 1950.
Scott, James. C. *Seeing Like a State: How Certain Schemes to Improve the Human Condition Have Failed*. New Haven, CT: Yale University Press, 1998.
 The Art of Not Being Governed: An Anarchist History of Upland Southeast Asia. New Haven, CT: Yale University Press, 2009.
Sedgwick, Mark. "Saudi Sufis: Compromise in the Hijaz, 1925–40." *Die Welt des Islams*, 37 (1997): 349–68.
 "Sects in the Islamic World." *Nova Religio*, 3 (2000): 195–240.
 Western Sufism: From the Abbasids to the New Age. Oxford: Oxford University Press, 2017.
Seghal, Neha, and Brian Grim. "Egypt's Restrictions on Religion Coincide with Lack of Religious Tolerance." *Fact Tank*, 2 July 2013.
Şehsuvaroğlu, Bedi N., Ayşegül Erdemir Demirhan, and Gönül Cantay Güreşsever. *Türk Tıp Tarihi*. Bursa: Taş Kitabevi, 1984.
Sékaly, Achille. *Le Problème des Wakfs en Égypte*. Paris: Librairie Orientaliste Paul Geuthner, 1929.
Şen, Ayşe Fulya, and Şule Yenigün Altın. "Sosyal Demokrasiden Yeni Sağa CHP'nin Söylemsel Dönüşümü: Bir Siyasal Söylem Çözümlemesi Denemesi." *Ankara Hacı Bayram Veli Üniversitesi İktisadi ve İdari Bilimler Fakültesi Dergisi*, 21 (2019): 434–61.
Shabaan, Ahmed. "Is Keeping Dogs Allowed in Islam or Not?" *Khalej Times*, 1 August 2016.
Shaban, Muhammad A. *Islamic History: A New Interpretation*, vol. 1. Cambridge: Cambridge University Press, 1971.
Shad, Abdur Rahman. *Zakat and 'Ushr*. Lahore: Kazi Publications, 1986.
Shafiq, Muhammad. "The Role and Place of Shura in the Islamic Polity." *Islamic Studies*, 23 (1984): 419–41.

Shafir, Nir. "Moral Revolutions: The Politics of Piety in the Ottoman Empire Reimagined." *Comparative Studies in Society and History*, 61 (2019): 595–623.
Shah, Timothy Samuel. "The Roots of Religious Freedom in Early Christian Thought." In *Christianity and Freedom: Historical Perspectives*, vol. 1, edited by Timothy Samuel Shah and Allen D. Hertzke, pp. 33–61. Cambridge: Cambridge University Press, 2016.
Shahid, Mohammed K. "The Muslim Brotherhood Movement in the West Bank and Gaza." *Third World Quarterly*, 10 (1988): 658–82.
Shahin, Emad Eldin. *Political Ascent: Contemporary Islamic Movements in North Africa*. Boulder: Westview Press, 1997.
Shambayati, Hootan. "The Rentier State, Interest Groups, and the Paradox of Autonomy: State and Business in Turkey and Iran." *Comparative Politics*, 26 (1994): 307–31.
Shankland, David. "Maps and the Alevis: On the Ethnography of Heterodox Islamic Groups." *British Journal of Middle East Studies*, 37 (2010): 227–39.
Shavit, Uriya. "Is Shura a Muslim Form of Democracy? Roots and Systematization of a Polemic." *Middle Eastern Studies*, 46 (2010): 349–74.
Shaw, Stanford J. "The Origins of Ottoman Military Reform: The Nizam-i Cedid Army of Sultan Selim III." *Journal of Modern History*, 37 (1965): 291–305.
  "The Central Legislative Councils in the Nineteenth Century Ottoman Reform Movement before 1876." *International Journal of Middle East Studies*, 1 (1970): 51–84.
  History of the Ottoman Empire and Modern Turkey, vol. 1. New York: Cambridge University Press, 1976.
  The Jews of the Ottoman Empire and the Turkish Republic. London: Macmillan, 1991.
Shaw, Stanford J., and Ezel Kural Shaw. *History of the Ottoman Empire and Modern Turkey*, vol. 2. New York: Cambridge University Press, 1977.
Shechter, Relli. "Market Welfare in the Early-Modern Ottoman Economy: A Historiographic Overview with Many Questions." *Journal of the Economic and Social History of the Orient*, 48 (2005): 253–76.
Shefer-Mossensohn, Miri. *Ottoman Medicine: Healing and Medical Institutions, 1500–1700*. New York: SUNY Press, 2009.
Shiloah, Amnon. "Music and Religion in Islam." *Acta Musicologica*, 69 (1997): 143–55.
Shipps, Jan. *Mormonism: The Story of a New Religious Tradition*. Urbana: University of Illinois Press, 1985.
Shirazi, Faegheh. *The Veil Unveiled: The Hijab in Modern Culture*. Gainesville: University Press of Florida, 2003.
Shleifer, Andrei, and Robert W. Vishny. *The Grabbing Hand: Government Pathologies and Their Cures*. Cambridge, MA: Harvard University Press, 1998.
Shuster, W. Morgan. *The Strangling of Persia: A Personal Narrative*. New York: Century, 1912.
Sidani, Yusuf M., and Jon Thornberry. "Nepotism in the Arab World: An Institutional Theory Perspective." *Business Ethics Quarterly*, 23 (2013): 69–96.
Siddiqui, Mohammad N. *The Economic Enterprise in Islam*, 2nd ed. Lahore: Islamic Publications, 1979.

Siecienski, A. Edward. *The Filioque: History of a Doctrinal Controversy*. Oxford: Oxford University Press, 2010.
Sijpesteijn, Petra M. *Shaping a Muslim State: The World of a Mid-Eighth-Century Egyptian Official*. Oxford: Oxford University Press, 2013.
Silber, Norman I. *A Corporate Form of Freedom: The Emergence of the Nonprofit Sector*. Boulder, CO: Westview Press, 2001.
Silver, Laura, Moira Fagan, Aidan Connaughton, and Mara Mordecai. "Political Correctness and Offensive Speech." Pew Research Center Report, 2021. www.pewresearch.org/global/2021/05/05/4-political-correctness-and-offensive-speech/ (accessed 2 February 2023).
Simon, Reeva Spector. "Iraq." In *The Jews of the Middle East and North Africa in Modern Times*, edited by Reeva Spector Simon, Michael Menachem Laskier, and Sara Leguer, pp. 347–66. New York: Columbia University Press, 2002.
Singer, Amy. *Constructing Ottoman Beneficence: An Imperial Soup Kitchen in Jerusalem*. Albany: State University of New York Press, 2002.
"Giving Practices in Islamic Societies." *Social Research*, 80 (2013): 341–58.
Sirriyeh, Elizabeth. *Sufis and Anti-Sufis: The Defence, Rethinking and Rejection of Sufism in the Modern World*. London: Curzon, 1999.
Skovgaard-Petersen, Jakob. *Defining Islam for the Egyptian State: Muftis and Fatwas of the Dār al-Iftā*. Leiden: Brill, 1997.
Slackman, Michael, and Mona El-Naggar. "A Radical Revolution." *New York Times*, Opinion section, 8 September 2011.
Smith, Adam. *The Wealth of Nations*. New York: Modern Library, 1937; original edition 1776.
Smooha, Sammy. "Is Israel Western?" In *Comparing Modernities: Pluralism versus Homogenity*, edited by Eliezer Ben-Rafael and Yitzhak Sternberg, pp. 413–42. Leiden: Brill, 2005.
Snir, Reuven. "Arabic Journalism as a Vehicle for Enlightenment," *Journal of Modern Jewish Studies*, 6 (2007): 219–37.
Sobhy, Hania. "Secular Façade, Neoliberal Islamisation: Textbook Nationalism from Mubarak to Sisi." *Nations and Nationalism*, 21 (2015): 805–24.
Sohrabi, Nader. *Revolution and Constitutionalism in the Ottoman Empire and Iran*. Cambridge: Cambridge University Press, 2011.
Soskis, Benjamin. In "A History of Associational Life and the Nonprofit Sector in the United States." In *The Nonprofit Sector: A Research Handbook*, 3rd ed., edited by Walter W. Powell and Patricia Bromley, pp. 23–80. Stanford: Stanford University Press, 2020.
Spannaus, Nathan. "History and Continuity: Al-Azhar and Egypt." In *Modern Islamic Authority and Social Change*, vol. 1, edited by Masooda Bano, pp. 79–101. Edinburgh: Edinburgh University Press, 2018.
Spierings, Niels. "Social Trust in the Middle East and North Africa: The Context-Dependent Impact of Citizens' Socio-economic and Religious Characteristics." *European Sociological Review*, 35 (2019): 894–911.
Srougo, Shai. "Professional Characteristics of the Jewish Guild in the Muslim World: Thessaloniki Dockers at the End of the Ottoman Era." *Mediterranean Historical Review*, 26 (2011): 115–33.

Stark, Rodney, and William Sims Bainbridge. "Of Churches, Sects, and Cults: Preliminary Concepts for a Theory of Religious Movements." *Journal for the Scientific Study of Religion*, 18 (1979): 117–31.
Stasavage, David. "Credible Commitment in Early Modern Europe: North and Weingast Revisited." *Journal of Law, Economics, and Organization*, 18 (2002): 155–86.
  "Was Weber Right? The Role of Urban Autonomy in Europe's Rise." *American Political Science Review*, 108 (2014): 337–54.
  The Decline and Rise of Democracy: A Global History from Antiquity to Today. Princeton, NJ: Princeton University Press, 2020.
Steinberg, Stephen. "Reform Judaism: The Origin and Evolution of a 'Church Movement'." *Journal for the Scientific Study of Religion*, 5 (1965): 117–29.
Stewart, Devin J. *Islamic Legal Orthodoxy: Twelver Shiite Responses to the Sunni Legal System.* Salt Lake City: University of Utah Press, 1998.
Stillman, Norman, A. "Charity and Social Service in Medieval Islam." *Societas*, 5 (1975): 105–15.
Stowasser, Barbara Freyer. *Women in the Qur'an, Traditions, and Interpretation.* Oxford: Oxford University Press, 1994.
Strauss, Johann. "The Greek Connection in Nineteenth-Century Ottoman Intellectual History." In *Greece and the Balkans: Identities, Perceptions and Cultural Encounters since the Enlightenment*, 2nd ed., edited by Dimitris Tziovas, pp. 47–67. London: Routledge, 2017.
Strauss, Leo. *Persecution and the Art of Writing.* Glencoe, IL: Free Press, 1952.
Stroumsa, Sarah. *Freethinkers in Medieval Islam: Ibn al-Rāwandī, Abū Bakr al-Rāzī, and Their Impact on Islamic Thought.* Leiden: Brill, 1999.
Stolle, Dietlind. "Trusting Strangers – The Concept of Generalized Trust in Perspective." ÖZP, 31 (2002): 397–412.
Stormon, E. J., ed. *Towards the Healing of Schism: The Sees of Rome and Constantinople.* Mahwah, NJ: Paulist Press, 1987.
Suárez-Collado, Ángela, and Sergio García-Rendón. "Sweeping under the Rug: The Limitations and Failure of the Formal Fight against Corruption in Morocco." In *Corruption and Informal Practices in the Middle East and North Africa*, edited by Ina Kubbe and Aiysha Varraich, pp. 103–17. London: Routledge, 2020.
Sullivan, Denis J. *Private Voluntary Organizations in Egypt: Islamic Development, Private Initiative, and State Control.* Gainesville: University of Florida Press, 1994.
Sullivan, Zohreh T. "Eluding the Feminist, Overthrowing the Modern? Transformations in Twentieth-Century Iran." In *Remaking Women: Feminism and Modernity in the Middle East*, edited by Lila Abu-Lughod, pp. 215–42. Princeton, NJ: Princeton University Press, 1998.
S&P Global, *Islamic Finance Outlook*, 2022 edition. S&P Global Ratings. www.spglobal.com/ratings/en/research/pdf-articles/islamic-finance-outlook-2022-28102022v1.pdf) (accessed 2 February 2023).
Tabari, Azar. "The Enigma of Veiled Iranian Women." *Feminist Review*, 5 (1980): 19–31.
Tabātabā'i, Hossein Modaressi. *Kharāj in Islamic Law.* London: Anchor Press, 1983.
Tadmouri, Ghazi O., Pradibha Nair, Tasneem Obeid, Mahmoud T. Al Ali, Najib Al Khaja, and Hanan A. Hamamy. "Consanguinity and Reproductive Health among Arabs." *Reproductive Health*, 6 (2009): article 17.

Tadros, Mariz. *Copts at the Crossroads: The Challenges of Building Inclusive Democracy in Egypt*. Cairo: American University in Cairo Press, 2013.
Tak, İsa. "Osmanlı Döneminde Ereğli Kömür Madenleri'nde Faaliyet Gösteren Şirketler." *Atatürk Üniversitesi Türkiyat Araştırmaları Dergisi*, 18 (2001): 253–57.
Talhami, Ghada, and Sadik Al-Azm. "An Interview with Sadik Al-Azm." *Arab Studies Quarterly*, 19 (1997): 113–26.
Talhamy, Yvette. "The *Fatwa*s and the Nusayri/Alawis of Syria." *Middle Eastern Studies*, 46 (2010): 175–94.
Tamer, Georges. "Nasr Hamid Abu Zayd." *International Journal of Middle East Studies*, 43 (2011): 193–95.
Tanyeri-Erdemir, Tuğba, Zana Çıtak, Theresa Weitzhofer, and Muharrem Erdem. "Religion and Discrimination in the Workplace in Turkey: Old and Contemporary Challenges." *International Journal of Discrimination and the Law*, 13 (2013): 214–39.
Tarhan, R. Bülent, Ömer Faruk Gençkaya, Ergin Ergül, Kemal Özsemerci, and Hakan Özbaran. *Bir Olgu Olarak Yolsuzluk: Nedenler, Etkiler ve Çözüm Önerileri*. Ankara: TEPAV, 2005.
Tawfeek, Farah. "Egypt's Dar al-Iftaa Deems Bitcoin Currency as Forbidden in Islam." *Egypt Independent*, 1 January 2018.
Taylor, Charles. "How to Define Secularism." In *Boundaries of Toleration*, edited by Alfred Stepan and Charles Taylor, pp. 59–78. New York: Columbia University Press, 2014.
Terzioğlu, Derin. "How to Conceptualize Ottoman Sunnitization: A Historiographical Discussion." *Turcica*, 44 (2012–13): 301–38.
Teorell, Jan, Aksel Sundström, Sören Holmberg, Bo Rothstein, Natalia Alvarado Pachon, and Cem Mert Dallı. "The Quality of Government Standard Dataset, version Jan22." University of Gothenburg: Quality of Government Institute, 2022. www.gu.se/en/quality-government (accessed 2 February 2023).
Tessler, Mark A. "Political Change and the Islamic Revival in Tunisia." *Maghreb Review*, 5 (1980): 8–19.
Tezcan, Baki. *The Second Ottoman Empire: Politics and Transformation in the Early Modern World*. Cambridge: Cambridge University Press, 2010.
Tezcür, Güneş Murat, and Taghi Azadarmaki. "Religiosity and Islamic Rule in Iran." *Journal for the Scientific Study of Religion*, 47 (2008): 211–24.
Thomas, John Philip. *Private Religious Foundations in the Byzantine Empire*. Washington, DC: Dumbarton Oaks, 1987.
Thomas, Marie-Claude. *Women in Lebanon: Living with Christianity, Islam, and Multiculturalism*. New York: Palgrave Macmillan, 2013.
Thompson, Elizabeth E. *How the West Stole Democracy from the Arabs: The Syrian Arab Congress of 1920 and the Destruction of Its Historic Liberal-Islamic Alliance*. New York: Atlantic Monthly Press, 2020.
Thurston, Alexander. *Boko Haram: The History of an African Jihadist Movement*. Princeton, NJ: Princeton University Press, 2018.
Tignor, Robert. *Modernization and British Colonial Rule in Egypt, 1852–1914*. Princeton, NJ: Princeton University Press, 1966.
  "The Economic Activities of Foreigners in Egypt, 1920–1950: From Millet to Haute Bourgeoisie." *Comparative Studies in Society and History*, 22 (1980): 416–49.

Tilly, Charles. *Contention and Democracy in Europe, 1650–2000*. Cambridge: Cambridge University Press, 2005.
Tiltay, Muhammet Ali, and Ömer Torlak. "Similarities and Differences of Motivations of Giving Time and Money: Giving to Individuals versus Humanitarian Organizations in an Emerging Market." *International Journal of Nonprofit and Voluntary Sector Marketing*, 25 (2020): e1649.
Tlaiss, Hayfaa, and Saleema Kauser. "The Importance of Wasta in the Career Success of Middle Eastern Managers." *Journal of European Industrial Training*, 35 (2011): 467–86.
Tocqueville, Alexis de. *Democracy in America*, translated by Harvey C. Mansfield and Delba Winthrop from the French original of 1835–40. Chicago, IL: University of Chicago Press, 2000.
Todd, Geoffrey. "Some Aspects of Joint Stock Companies, 1844–1900." *Economic History Review*, 4 (1932): 46–71.
Toksöz, Meltem. *Nomads, Migrants and Cotton in the Eastern Mediterranean: The Making of the Adana-Mersin Region 1850–1908*. Leiden: Brill, 2010.
Toledano, Ehud. "Social and Economic Change in the 'Long Nineteenth Century'." In *The Cambridge History of Egypt*, vol. 2, edited by M. W. Daly, pp. 252–84. Cambridge: Cambridge University Press, 1998.
Tooley, Mark. *Taking Back the United Methodist Church*, updated ed. Fort Valley, GA: Bristol House, 2010.
Toprak, Zafer. *Türkiye'de Milli İktisat 1908–1918*. Istanbul: İş Bankası Kültür Yayınları, 2019.
Torrey, Gordon H. "The Ba'th: Ideology and Practice." *Middle East Journal*, 23 (1969): 445–70.
Toth, Anthony B. "Control and Allegiance at the Dawn of the Oil Age: Bedouin, *Zakat* and Struggles for Sovereignty in Arabia, 1916–1955." *Middle East Critique*, 21 (2012): 57–79.
Traboulsi, Fawwaz. *A History of Modern Lebanon*, 2nd ed. London: Pluto Press, 2012.
Transparency International. *Corruption Perceptions Index 2020*. www.transparency.org/en/cpi/2020 (accessed 2 February 2023).
Trial, George T., and R. Bayly Winder. "Modern Education in Saudi Arabia." *History of Education Journal*, 1 (1950): 121–33.
Trimingham, J. Spencer. *The Sufi Orders in Islam*. Oxford: Clarendon Press, 1971.
Tsugitaka, Sato. "Fiscal Administration in Syria during the Reign of Sultan al-Nāsir Muhammad." *Mamluk Studies Review*, 11 (2007): 19–37.
Turgay, A. Üner. "Trade and Merchants in Nineteenth-Century Trabzon: Elements of Ethnic Conflict." In *Christians and Jews in the Ottoman Empire*, vol. 1, edited by Benjamin Braude and Bernard Lewis, pp. 287–318. New York: Holmes & Meier, 1982.
Turnaoğlu, Banu. *The Formation of Turkish Republicanism*. Princeton, NJ: Princeton University Press, 2017.
Türkiye Büyük Millet Meclisi. "On Yedinci İn'ikat." *T.B.M.M. Zabıt Ceridesi*, 24 (1931).
Türkiye Cumhuriyeti Cumhurbaşkanlığı. *2020 Yılı Merkezi Yönetim Bütçe Kanun Teklifi ve Bağlı Cetveller*. Ankara: Cumhurbaşkanlığı, 2020.
Ubicini, M. A. *Lettres sur la Turquie*, 2nd ed. Paris: Librairie Militaire de J. Dumaine, 1853.

Üçer, Cenksu. "Geleneksel Alevîlikte İbadet Hayatı ve Alevîlerin Temel İslâmî İbadetlere Yaklaşımları." *Dinbilimleri Akademik Araştırma Dergisi*, 5 (2005): 161–89.
Uddin, Asma T. "Blaphemy Laws in Muslim-Majority Countries." *Review of Faith and International Affairs*, 9 (2011): 47–55.
Udovitch, Abraham L. "Islamic Law and the Social Context of Exchange in the Medieval Middle East." *History and Anthropology*, 1 (1985): 445–65.
Um, Nancy. *The Merchant Houses of Mocha: Trade and Architecture in an Indian Ocean Port*. Seattle: University of Washington Press, 2009.
Üngör, Uğur Ümit, and Mehmet Polatel. *Confiscation and Destruction: The Young Turk Seizure of Armenian Property*. London: Continuum, 2011.
United Nations High Commissioner for Refugees (UNHCR) Population Statistics Database. http://popstats.unhcr.org (accessed 2 February 2023)
United Nations, Department of Economic and Social Affairs, Population Division. *World Population Prospects 2019*, online ed. Rev. 1. https://population.un.org/wpp/Download/Standard/Population/ (accessed 2 February 2023).
United States Embassy in Egypt. "Egypt 2017 International Religious Freedom Report." https://eg.usembassy.gov/egypt-2017-international-religious-freedom-report/ (accessed 2 February 2023).
Ünlü, Barış. *Türklük Sözleşmesi: Oluşumu, İşleyişi ve Krizi*. Ankara: Dipnot Yayınları, 2018.
Uzunçarşılı, İsmail Hakkı. *Osmanlı Devleti Teşkilâtından Kapıkulu Ocakları*, vol. 1. Ankara: Türk Tarih Kurumu, 1943.
Vahman, Fereydun. *175 Years of Persecution: A History of the Babis and Baha'is of Iran*. London: Oneworld, 2019.
Valentine, Simon Ross. *Islam and the Ahmadiyya Jama'at: History, Belief, Practice*. New York: Columbia University Press, 2008.
Van Gorder, A. Christian. *Christianity in Persia and the Status of Non-Muslims in Iran*. Lanham, MD: Lexington Books, 2010.
Van Nieuwkerk, Karin. "Religious Skepticism and Nonbelieving in Egypt." In *Moving In and Out of Islam*, edited by Karin van Nieuwkerk, pp. 306–32. Austin: Texas University Press, 2018.
  "The Atheist Spring? Emerging Non-Belief in the Islamic World." In *The Cambridge History of Atheism*, edited by Stephen Bullivant and Michael Ruse, pp. 1040–58. Cambridge: Cambridge University Press, 2021.
Van Zanden, Jan Luiten. *The Long Road to the Industrial Revolution: The European Economy in a Global Perspective, 1000–1800*. Leiden: Brill, 2009.
Van Zanden, Jan Luiten, Eltjo Buringh, and Maarten Bosker. "The Rise and Decline of European Parliaments, 1188–1789." *Economic History Review*, 65 (2012): 835–61.
Varol, Muharrem. *Islahat Siyaset Tarikat: Bektaşîliğin İlgası Sonrasında Osmanlı Devleti'nin Tarikat Politikaları (1826–1866)*. Istanbul: Dergâh Yayınları, 2013.
Vassiliev, Alexei. *A History of Saudi Arabia*. London, Saqi Books, 2000.
Vauchez, Stéphanie Hennette. "Is French *Laïcité* Still Liberal? The Republican Project under Pressure (2004–15)." *Human Rights Law Review*, 17 (2017): 285–312.
Verbit, Gilbert Paul, transl. and ed. *A Ninth Century Treatise on the Law of Trusts (Being a Translation of Al-Khassâf, Ahkām al-Waqūf)*. Philadelphia, PA: Xlibris, 2008.

Vesterlund, Lise. "Using Experimental Methods to Understand Why and How We Give to Charity." In *The Handbook of Experimental Economics*, vol. 2, edited by John H. Kagel and Alvin E. Roth, pp. 91–152. Princeton, NJ: Princeton University Press, 2015.
Volkov, Shulamit. *Germans, Jews, and Antisemites: Trials in Emancipation*. Cambridge: Cambridge University Press, 2006.
Voll, John O. "Fundamentalism in the Sunni Arab World: Egypt and the Sudan." In *Fundamentalisms Observed*, edited by Martin E. Marty and R. Scott Appleby, pp. 345–402. Chicago, IL: University of Chicago Press, 1991.
Wani, Ayjaz. "China's Xinjiang Policy and the Silence of Islamic States." *Observer Research Foundation Occasional Paper*, 328 (2021).
Wagemakers, Joas. *Salafism in Jordan: Political Islam in a Quietist Community*. Cambridge: Cambridge University Press, 2016.
Wahl, Fabian. "Political Participation and Economic Development: Evidence from the Rise of Participative Political Institutions in the Late Medieval German Lands." *European Review of Economic History*, 23 (2019): 193–213.
Warburg, Gabriel R. "Islam and Politics in Egypt: 1952–80." *Middle Eastern Studies*, 18 (1982): 131–57.
Warburton, Eliot. *The Crescent and the Cross: Romance and Realities of Eastern Travel*. London: MacLaren, 1849.
Ward, Robert E. "Political Modernization and Political Culture in Japan." *World Politics*, 15 (1963): 569–96.
Watson, Kevin. "Methodism Dividing." *First Things*, March 2020, pp. 21–25.
Watt, W. Montgomery. *Muhammad at Mecca*. Oxford: Oxford University Press, 1953.
Bell's Introduction to the Qur'ān. Edinburgh: University of Edinburgh Press, 1970.
Webb, Edward. *Media in Egypt and Tunisia: From Control to Transition?* New York: Palgrave Macmillan, 2014.
Webber, Carolyn, and Aaron Wildavsky. *A History of Taxation and Expenditure in the Western World*. New York: Simon and Schuster, 1986.
Weismann, Itzchak. *The Naqshbandiyya: Orthodoxy and Activism in a Worldwide Sufi Tradition*. London: Routledge, 2007.
Weiss, Bernard. "Interpretation in Islamic Law: The Theory of Ijtihād." *American Journal of Comparative Law*, 26 (1978): 199–212.
Werner, Christoph. *Vaqf en Iran: Aspects Culturels, Religieux et Sociaux*. Paris: Association pour l'Avancement des Études Iraniennes, 2015.
Westbrook, Raymond. "The Character of Ancient Near Eastern Law." In *A History of Ancient Near Eastern Law*, vol. 1, edited by Raymond Westbrook, pp. 1–90. Leiden: Brill, 2003.
White, Andrew D. *A History of the Warfare of Science with Theology in Christendom*, 2 vols. New York: D. Appleton, 1913.
White, Jenny B. *Islamist Mobilization in Turkey: A Study in Vernacular Politics*. Seattle: University of Washington Press, 2002.
"State Feminism, Modernization, and the Turkish Republican Woman." *NWSA Journal*, 15 (2003): 145–59.
Muslim Nationalism and the New Turks, new ed. Princeton, NJ: Princeton University Press, 2014.

Wickham, Carrie Rosefsky. *The Muslim Brotherhood: Evolution of an Islamist Movement*. Princeton, NJ: Princeton University Press, 2013.
Wiktorowicz, Quintan. "Civil Society as Social Control." *Comparative Politics*, 33 (2000): 43–61.
  The Management of Islamic Activism: Salafis, the Muslim Brotherhood, and State Power in Jordan. Albany: State University of New York Press, 2001.
Wilber, Donald N. *Iran, Past and Present: From Monarchy to Islamic Republic*, 9th ed. Princeton, NJ: Princeton University Press, 1981.
Wild, Stefan. "Sadik Jalal Al-Azm: November 7, 1934 (Damascus) – December 11, 2016 (Berlin)." *Die Welt des Islams*, 57 (2017): 3–6.
Wilks, Andrew. "Turkey's Religious Authority Denounces 'Evil-Eye' Charms." Aljazeera.com, 23 January 2021.
Wilson, M. Brett. "The First Translations of the Qur'an in Modern Turkey (1924–38)." *International Journal of Middle East Studies*, 41 (2009): 419–35.
Wilson, Peter H. *Europe's Tragedy: A History of the Thirty Years War*. London: Penguin Books, 2009.
Winter, Michael. *Egyptian Society under Ottoman Rule, 1517–1798*. London: Routledge, 1992.
Winter, Stefan. *The Shiites of Lebanon under Ottoman Rule, 1516–1788*. Cambridge: Cambridge University Press, 2010.
Wittfogel, Karl A. *Oriental Despotism: A Comparative Study of Total Power*. New Haven, CT: Yale University Press, 1957.
Wolf, Anne. *Political Islam in Tunisia: The History of Ennahda*. Oxford: Oxford University Press, 2017.
Woodberry, Robert D. "The Missionary Roots of Liberal Democracy." *American Political Science Review*, 106 (2012): 244–74.
World Bank. "International Tourism, Number of Arrivals." 2018. https://data.worldbank.org/indicator/ST.INT.ARVL? (accessed 2 February 2023).
  "World Development Indicators Database." https://data.worldbank.org/indicator/NY.GDP.MKTP.PP.CD (accessed 2 February 2023).
  "Worldwide Governance Indicators, 2019." https://info.worldbank.org/governance/wgi/Home/Documents (accessed 2 February 2023).
World Economic Forum. *The Global Gender Gap Report 2020*. Geneva: World Economic Forum, 2019.
Yahagi, Mohammad Jafar. "An Introduction to Early Persian Qur'anic Translations." *Journal of Qur'anic Studies*, 4 (2002): 105–9.
Yalansız, Nedim. "İzmir'de 1989 Yerel Seçimleri." *Tarih Okulu Dergisi*, 7 (2014): 571–97.
Yalcintas, Altug, and Naseraddin Alizadeh. "Digital Protectionism and National Planning in the Age of the Internet: The Case of Iran." *Journal of Institutional Economics*, 16 (2020): 519–36.
Yamani, Mai. "The Two Faces of Saudi Arabia." *Survival*, 50 (2008): 143–56.
Yapp, Malcolm E. "The Modernization of Middle Eastern Armies in the Nineteenth Century: A Comparative View." In *War, Technology and Society in the Middle East*, edited by Malcolm. E. Yapp and Vernon J. Parry, pp. 330–66. London: Oxford University Press, 1975.

Ya-sin, Muhammad Naim. *The Book of Eemaan: The Basis, Reality and Invalidation of Eemaan.* London: Al-Firdous, n.d.

Yavuz, M. Hakan. *Islamic Political Identity in Turkey.* Oxford: Oxford University Press, 2003.

Yavuz, Yıldırım. "Batılılaşma Döneminde Osmanlı Sağlık Kuruluşları." *ODTÜ Mimarlık Fakültesi Dergisi,* 8 (1988): 123–42.

Yaycioglu, Ali. *Partners of the Empire: The Crisis of the Ottoman Order in the Age of Revolutions.* Stanford: Stanford University Press, 2016.

Ybarra, Josep-Antoni. "The *Zaqât* in Muslim Society: An Analysis of Islamic Economic Policy." *Social Science Information,* 35 (1996): 643–56.

Yediyıldız, Bahaeddin. "Vakıf." *İslâm Ansiklopedisi* 137 (1982): 153–72.

Institution du Vaqf au XVIIIe Siècle en Turquie: Étude Socio-Historique. Ankara: Éditions Ministère de la Culture, 1990.

Yener, Serhat. *Dernekler ve Vakıflar Kanunu.* Ankara: Seçkin Yayınevi, 1998.

Yeşil, Bilge, and Efe Kerem Sözeri. "Online Surveillance in Turkey: Legislation, Technology and Citizen Involvement." *Surveillance & Society,* 15 (2017): 543–49.

Yi, Eunjeong. *Guild Dynamics in Seventeenth-Century Istanbul: Fluidity and Leverage.* Leiden: Brill, 2004.

Yıldırım, Ali. *Osmanlı Engizisyonu.* Ankara: Öteki Yayınevi, 1996.

Yıldırım, Onur. "Pious Foundations in the Byzantine and Seljuk States: A Comparative Study of Philanthropy in the Mediterranean World during the Late Medieval Era." *Rivista Degli Studi Orientali,* 73 (1999): 27–52.

Diplomacy and Displacement: Reconsidering the Turco-Greek Exchange of Populations, 1922–1934. New York: Routledge, 2006.

Yıldırım, Rıza. *Aleviliğin Doğuşu: Kızılbaş Sufiliğinin Toplumsal ve Siyasal Temelleri (1300–1501).* Istanbul: İletişim, 2017.

Yıldız, Aysel. *Crisis and Rebellion in the Ottoman Empire: The Downfall of a Sultan in the Age of Revolution.* London: I. B. Tauris, 2017.

Yıldız, Gültekin. *Neferin Adı Yok: Zorunlu Askerliğe Geçiş Sürecinde Osmanlı Devleti'nde Siyaset, Ordu ve Toplum (1826–1839).* Istanbul: Kitabevi, 2009.

Yılmaz, Altuğ, ed. *2012 Declaration: The Seized Properties of Armenian Foundations in Istanbul.* Istanbul: Hrant Dink Foundation, 2012.

Yılmaz, Bediz. "Entrapped in Multidimensional Exclusion: The Perpetuation of Poverty among Conflict-Induced Migrants in an İstanbul Neighborhood." *New Perspectives on Turkey,* 38 (2008): 205–34.

Yom, Sean L. 2005. "Civil Society and Democratization in the Arab World." *Middle East Review of International Affairs* 9: 14–33.

Yousri, Abd al-Rahman. "Sustainable Development: An Evaluation of Conventional and Islamic Perspectives." In *Islamic Perspectives on Sustainable Development,* edited by Munawar Iqbal, pp. 22–57. New York: Palgrave Macmillan, 2005.

Yücekök, Ahmet N. *Türkiye'de Örgütlenmiş Dinin Sosyo-Ekonomik Tabanı (1946–1968).* Ankara: Ankara Üniversitesi Siyasal Bilgiler Fakültesi Yayınları, 1971.

Zachs, Fruma. *The Making of a Syrian Identity: Intellectuals and Merchants in Nineteenth Century Beirut.* Leiden: Brill, 2005.

Zad, Vahid Vahdat. "Spatial Discrimination in Tehran's Modern Urban Planning 1906–1979." *Journal of Planning History,* 12 (2012): 49–62.

Zagorin, Perez. *How the Idea of Religious Toleration Came to the West*. Princeton, NJ: Princeton University Press, 2003.

Zahid, Mohammed. *The Muslim Brotherhood and Egypt's Succession Crisis: The Politics of Liberalisation and Reform in the Middle East*. London: I. B. Tauris, 2010.

Zak, Paul J., and Stephen Knack. "Trust and Growth." *Economic Journal*, 111 (2001): 295–321.

Zakaria, Fareed. *The Future of Freedom: Illiberal Democracy at Home and Abroad*. New York: W. W. Norton, 2003.

Zaller, John. *The Nature and Origins of Mass Opinion*. Cambridge: Cambridge University Press, 1992.

Zarinebaf-Shahr, Fariba. "Qizilbash 'Heresy' and Rebellion in Ottoman Anatolia during the Sixteenth Century." *Anatolia Moderna*, 7 (1997): 1–15.

Zeff, Stephen A., Frans van der Wel, and Kees Camfferman. *Company Financial Reporting: A Historical and Comparative Study of the Dutch Regulatory Process*. London: Routledge, 2016.

Zeghal, Malika. "Religion and Politics in Egypt: The Ulema of Al-Azhar, Radical Islam, and the State (1952–94)." *International Journal of Middle East Studies*, 31 (1999): 371–99.

Zencirci, Gizem. "Civil Society's History: New Constructions of Ottoman Heritage by the Justice and Development Party in Turkey." *European Journal of Turkish Studies*, 19 (2014): 1–20.

Zhang, Taisu. *The Ideological Foundations of Qing Taxation: Belief Systems, Politics, and Institutions*. Cambridge: Cambridge University Press, 2022.

Zhang, Taisu, and John D. Morley. "The Modern State and the Rise of the Business Corporation." *Yale Law Journal*, 132 (2023): 3000–77.

Ziblatt, Daniel. "How Did Europe Democratize?" *World Politics*, 58 (2006): 311–38.

Zilfi, Madeline C. *The Politics of Piety: The Ottoman Ulema in the Postclassical Age (1600–1800)*. Minneapolis, MN: Bibliotheca Islamica, 1988.

Zoethout, Carla M. "Ritual Slaughter and the Freedom of Religion: Some Reflections on a Stunning Matter." *Human Rights Quarterly*, 35 (2013): 651–72.

Zohar, Zvi. "Religion: Rabbinic Tradition and the Response to Modernity." In *The Jews of the Middle East and North Africa in Modern Times*, edited by Reeva Spector Simon, Michael Menachem Laskier, and Sara Reguer, pp. 65–84. New York: Columbia University Press, 2002.

Zonis, Marvin. *The Political Elite of Iran*. Princeton, NJ: Princeton University Press, 1971.

Zorlu, Tuncay. "Süleymaniye Tıp Medresesi – II." *Osmanlı Bilimi Araştırmaları*, 4 (2002): 65–98.

"Klasik Osmanlı Eğitim Sisteminin İki Büyük Temsilcisi: Fatih ve Süleymaniye Medreseleri." *Türkiye Araştırmaları Literatür Dergisi*, 6 (2008): 611–28.

Zuckerman, Phil. "Gender Regulation as a Source of Religious Schism." *Sociology of Religion*, 58 (1997): 353–73.

Zuckermann, B. *A Treatise on the Sabbatical Cycle and the Jubilee*, translated by A. Löwy from the original German edition of 1866. New York: Hermon Press, 1974.

Zuijderduijn, Jaco. "Grave Concerns: Entailment and Intergenerational Agency in Amsterdam (1600–1800)." *History of the Family*, 16 (2011): 343–53.

Zuolo, Federico. "Equality among Animals and Religious Slaughter." *Historical Social Research*, 40 (2015): 110–27.
Zürcher, Eric J. *Turkey: A Modern History*, 4th ed. London: I. B. Tauris, 2017.
Zysow, Aron. "Zakāt." *Encyclopaedia of Islam*, 2nd ed., vol. 11, pp. 406–22. Leiden: E. J. Brill, 2002.

Index

Abbas I, 127
Abbasid Caliphate, 54, 121, 213, 218–19, 222, 225, 242
Abd Al-Raziq, Ali, 138
Abdals, 126
Abdülmecid I, 136
Abu Bakr, caliph, 18, 116–18, 120, 162, 217, 221, 225
Abu Nuwas, 143
Abu Ubayd, 219
Abu Yusuf, 222
Abu Zayd, Nasr Hamid, 197
accounting, standardized, 91
Acemoglu, Daron, 27, 30, 106
Africa, 8
Ahmadism, 172, 203
Ahmed, Shahab, 173
AKP, 153–54, 280
Akşit, Bahattin, 185
Akyol, Mustafa, 197–98, 208
Al Fangary, Mohamed, 96
al-Assad, Bashar, 280
al-Assad, Hafez, 156
Alawism, 125, 134, 171, 193
Al-Azhar, 17, 90, 142, 160, 163, 180, 187
al-Azm, Sadiq, 197–99
al-Baghdadi, Abu Bakr, 199
al-Banna, Hassan, 149, 199
al-Banna, Karim, 155
Albayrak, Berat, 105
Aleppo, 81, 125, 177, 227–28
Alevism, 158, 162, 171, 185, 193

Alexandria, 239
Algeria, 31, 93, 134, 168
Algiers, 227
Ali, caliph, 104, 224
Al-Ihsan Charitable Society, 262
'ālim. See cleric, Islamic
al-Khassaf, 55
Alliance Israélite Universelle, 177
Almond, Gabriel, 100
almsgiving, 214
Al-Qaeda, 174, 195
al-Qasimi, Jamal al-Din, 229
al-Rashid, Harun, 222
al-Sisi, Abdel Fattah. See Sisi, Abdel Fattah
al-Tahtawi, Rifaah, 73
Amsterdam, 239
An-Na'im, Abdullahi, 197–98, 208
Antalya Culture and Art Vakıf, 95
anti-clericalism, 141
Antiquity, 33, 223–24
apostasy
    as instrument of illiberal Islam, 114, 190, 204–6, 272–73
    jailing in Egypt for, 155
    as obstacle to liberal schisms, 19
    as political treason, 119
    precedent for ban on, 116
    as source of intellectual stagnation, 17
Apostasy Wars, 18, 116–18, 120, 131, 221
apparent wealth, 221
Arab Barometer, 163
Arab Gulf, 9

Arab kingdoms, 139
Arab League, 6, 104. *See also* Arab world, member countries
Arab socialism, 139
Arab Spring, xiii, 3–4, 13, 16, 23, 66, 101, 152, 169
Arab world. *See also* Arab League, individual countries
  civic life, 48, 103
  Jewish departures, 159
  liberalization, 107
  sectarian discrimination, 251
  secularist repression, 280
  weakening of Islam, 139
Arabia. *See also* Saudi Arabia
  early Islam, 14, 21, 28, 121–23
  gender customs, 182
  pre-Islamic, 119, 185
  premodern commerce, 217
  Sufism, 134
  Sunnitization, 134
  zakat collection under Ayyubids, 219
Arkoun, Mohamed, 197–98
Armenian Patriarchate, Turkey, 160
Armenians, Turkey, 159
Asia, Central, 8
Assad Quran, 156
assertive Islamic secularism
  authoritarian rule, 280–81
  discontents generated by, 147, 255
  features, 140–41
  homogenization of religious symbols, 161
  logic of, 145–46
  origins, 250
  removal of religious symbols, 142
  resistance to, 147–49
  retreat of, 153–57
  support in 21st century, 209
  as transitional policy, 146
  unveiling campaigns, 142
assertive Islamism, 147–70
Atatürk, Kemal. *See also* Kemalism
  abrogation of Islamic law, 6
  ideology, 139
  opponents of, 161
  reforming Sunni liturgy, 185
  repressiveness, 280
  role model for modernists, 142
  secularization drive, 18, 144
atheism, 155, 209
Austria, 133
autocracy, 16

avârız, 52
Averroes. *See* Ibn Rushd
âyan. *See* Ottoman Empire: provincial notables
Ayyubid Sultanate, 219
Azerbaijan, 193

Babais, 126
Babism, 134
bad hijab, 208
Baghdad, 28, 125, 143, 177, 219
Bahrain, 168, 193
Balkans, 8
Bandits and Bureaucrats, 68
banking
  arrival in Middle East, 249
  conventional, 261
  Islamic. *See* Islamic banking
Barkey, Karen, 68
Barquq, Complex of Sultan, 55
Basra, 219
bāṭin. *See* hidden wealth
Batinism, 125
Bayat, Asef, 97, 99
bayt al-māl. *See* Islam, early: treasury
Beard, Randolph, 178
Bedreddinis, 126
BEFT, 178, 181
Bektashis, 128–29, 150, 170
Ben Achour, Yadh, 142, 197
Ben Ali, Zine El Abidine, 139, 156, 280
Bender-Ereğli United Coal Corporation, 255
Berlin Wall, 169
Bible, 119
bid'a. *See* Islam: heresy
blasphemy
  cases in Egyptian courts, 163
  as evidence of apostasy, 125
  as instrument of illiberal Islam, 114, 190, 204, 273
  as source of intellectual stagnation, 17
Blaydes, Lisa, 58
Boko Haram, 174
bonyad, 48, 96–97
Bonyad for the Oppressed and Wounded Veterans, 96
Bonyad-e Resalat, 96
Book of Mormon, 177
Bouazizi, Mohamed, 3
Bourguiba, Habib, 18, 139, 142–43, 150, 155–56, 161. *See also* Tunisia.
bribery, 106
business association, 20

Index

business corporation. *See* corporation, business
business dynasty, 237

Cairo, 3, 55, 61, 93, 96, 125, 144, 158, 227, 239
caliph, selection, 14
Canadian Council of Muslim Women, 202
capital accumulation, 22, 37
capitulations, 238, 279
Carvalho, Jean-Paul, 176
cash waqf. *See* waqf, Islamic: cash
Catholicism, 114, 175, 178, 189
Catholic-Orthodox split. *See* Christianity: Great Schism
Cengiz, Kurtuluş, 185
Cevdet Pasha, 257
Cevdet, Abdullah, 138
chamber of commerce, 244
Chaney, Eric, 58
charitable corporation. *See* corporation, charitable
checks and balances
  as fount of freedoms, 5
  Middle East, 47, 107, 145, 213, 218
  as protector of liberal order, 24
  Turkey, 5
  Western Europe, 15, 218
Chelbi, Hind, 150
Children's Protection Society, Turkey, 100, 262
China, 188, 216
choice of law for non-Muslims. *See* Islam: choice of law for non-Muslims
Christianity
  apostasy, 38, 119
  asceticism, 222
  birth of, 175
  blasphemy, 38
  corruption in tithing, 225
  during rise of Islam, 175
  Great Schism, 175, 178–79
  heresy, 38
  inquisition, 38, 119
  interest ban, 82
  liberalization, 38
  marriage, 105
  Medieval theological controversies, 158
  out-conversion, 38
  reinterpretation, 272
  religion–church–sect–cult hierarchy, 179
  religious repression, 18, 113, 181
  schism, 181

church
  congregational, 181
  episcopal, 181
  legally recognized in Cairo, 158
  legally recognized in Istanbul, 158
city
  corporate status, 69
  Ottoman policies toward, 41
  premodern Middle East, 74, 77
  roles in political development, 16, 41
  social services, 89
  source of innovation, 68
  Western Europe, 72
Civic Culture, 100
civic education, 17, 100
civic life. *See* civil society
civic skills, 100, 284
CIVICUS, 101
civil law waqf. *See* waqf, modern
Civil Liberties Index, 9, 12
civil society
  composition, 24
  contributions of zakat, 226
  harms, 49
  Middle East
    institutional infrastructure, 22, 285
    modern NGOs, 16
    roles of firms and business associations, 252
    roles of NGOs, 89–108
    roles of waqfs, 43, 66, 84–85, 107
    weakness, 16, 19, 157, 190
  political roles, 49, 106–8
  roles of merchants, 246–48
  transmittor of opinions, 66
  United States, 270
  Western Europe, 100, 275
cleric, Islamic
  attitudes toward economic reforms, 250–51
  corruption, 79
  definition, 16, 112
  economic base, 241, 277, 280
  legitimation of status quo, 137, 186
  participation in corruption, 244
  political influence, 133, 188, 246
  rents from waqfs, 55, 82–83, 91
  roles, 41, 67
  state financing of, 164
clerical governance doctrine, 193
closed society, 24
collective action, 54, 74–75, 84–85

colonization, European
  contibutions to liberalization, 282
  contributions to economic development, 29–31, 88, 281–82
  contributions to modernization, 282
  effects on capacity for collective action, 29
  effects on civil liberties, 30
  effects on democratization, 29
  effects on education, 29
  legal reforms, 31
  repression of Islam, 161
commanding right and forbidding wrong, 111
commerce, Middle East, 20–21
commercial enterprise, 20, 40
confiscation. *See* expropriation
conformism, religious, 37
consanguineous marriage, Middle East, 104–5
constitution, 4, 24–25
consuls, Western, 242
contract enforcement, 233
Copts, 17, 160
Cordoba, 125
corporation
  adoption in Middle East, 19, 21, 90–91, 120, 150, 209, 283
  corruption, 85–87
  as vehicle for collective action, 43
  exclusion from Islamic law, 20–21, 73, 103, 120, 234
  flexibility, 86
  role in Christianity's liberalization, 38
  self-regulation, 69
  spread in Western Europe, 15, 105, 242
corporation, business, 21, 42, 237–38, 332
corporation, charitable, 16, 21, 50
  decision making, 69
  definition, 68
  management, 86
  Middle East, 87
  Ottoman Empire, 94
  separation of beneficiaries and management, 71
  structural variability, 87
  United States, 87
  Western Europe, 70
corporation, nonprofit. *See* corporation, charitable
Corrective Movement, Syria, 156
corruption
  Middle East, 13, 78, 106
  petty, 106
  waqf vs. corporation, 85–87
  Western Europe, 79

Corruption Perceptions Index. *See* Government Cleanliness Index
corvée, 216
Council of Constance, 181
Council of Senior Scholars, Saudi Arabia, 187
cousin marriage, Middle East, 104–5
Critique of Religious Thought, 199
Crusaders, 125
crypto-conversion, 130
cultural isolationism, 19
cyber-mufti, 188
Cyprus, 6

Damascus, 61, 125, 137, 219
dancing, 112
Darwin, Charles, 179
Declaration of Religious Liberty, 114
Deed of Alliance, 243
de-liberalization, 27
democracy, 5, 27
democratic backsliding, 27
democratization
  Middle East, 90
  roles of secularization, 114
  Western Europe, 15, 68
denomination, religious, 174, 180
Deringil, Selim, 137
dīn, 115
Diyanet. *See* Religious Affairs Directorate, Turkey
Doctors Without Borders, 71, 298
documentation in commerce, 279
domino effect, 169
Doomsday. *See* Judgment Day
Druze, 125, 193
Dutch East India Company, 234

East European revolutions, 23, 169
Ebussuûd, 126
education
  Islamic, 17, 36
  modernization of, 29
Egypt
  Al-Azhar's fatwas, 187
  apostasy, 155
  atheism, 155, 163
  blasphemy charges, 17
  Bureau of Statistics, 136
  civil society, 152
  conglomerates, 253
  democratic governance, 49
  Department of Public Works, 136

Index

emergency rule, 144
European immigrants, 136
Europeanization, 136
execution of Sayyid Qutb, 151
falling religiosity, 162
Fatimid, 219
fatwas, 187
foreign settlers, 31
foundation, 95
Islamization, 155
mass finance, 249
military defeats, 133
Mixed Courts, 136
modernization, 136
mosques, 142
nationalist policies toward Islam, 200
NGOs, 96, 100–1
Office of European Affairs, 136
Ottoman period, 52
persecution of atheists, 163
persecution of Islamists, 18, 139, 280
philanthropy, 73
Ptolemaic, 216
pyramids, 216
Railway Administration, 136
regulation of Islam, 134
relations with Saudi Arabia, 172
religious conversion, 9, 164
religious regulation, 142
revolution of 2011, 4, 152
rise of Islamism, 152
surveys on religiosity, 168
waqfs, 95–96
zakat collection under Ayyubids, 219
Egyptian Food Bank, 262
Ekelund, Robert, 178
El-Gamal, Mahmoud, 261
emigration desire, 9
Encyclopedia of Islam, 221
Engels, Friedrich, 146
England, 113, 183, 216, 218, 232, 243
Enlightenment, European, 36, 197
Ennahda, 150, 195
Ennaifer, Hmida, 142, 197
entail, 70–71
enterprise
    giant, 252–53
    longevity, 233, 251
    Middle East
        creativity, 237, 274
        evolution, 278–80
        lack of legal personhood, 239

longevity, 237, 243
perpetual, 237
scale, 237, 243
securitization, 239
simplicity, 21
political influence, 21
scale, 233, 251
entity shielding, 238
entrepreneurship, Middle East, 232–53
equilibrium
    self-enforcing, 34, 37–39, 60, 137, 160, 273
    self-undermining, 34, 37–39, 137
Erbakan, Necmettin, 152, 154
Erdoğan, Recep Tayyip, 96, 101, 105, 153, 162, 164, 208, 280
essentialism, Islamic. *See* Islamic essentialism
European Human Rights Court, 158
European Union, 195
exchange
    impersonal, 103, 237, 284
    personal, 115, 118
excommunication, 175
expropriation, 19

Faith Campaign, Iraq, 156
family, 67
Farabi Bonyad, 96
fasting. *See* Ramadan
Fatih Youth Vakıf, 95
fatwa
    on building a snowman, 187
    on cryptocurrency, 187
    on cyberbanking, 188
    on evil-eye amulets, 187
    on Facebook and Twitter, 187
    on feeding a dog at home, 187
    by Ghazali, 125
    on Gregorian new year, 187
    on hymenoplasty, 188
    by Ibn Taymiyya, 125
    on imported medicine capsules, 187
    issuers, 129–30, 188
    on Netflix, 187
    online services, 188
    by Religious Affairs Directorate, Turkey, 155
    on rival leaders, 187
    on satellite TV, 187
    on sex, 188
    uses by secularists, 187
    uses for legitimation, 187
    on women judges, 194
    on yoga, 187

fictitious person. *See* legal personhood
financialization, 264
firqa, 180
Florence, 234
Forbes Global 2000, 252
Ford, George, 178
Fortune 500, 252
fractionalization, 282
France
　colonialism, 281
　female education, 183
　illiberalism of, 27
　parliament, 243
　protector of Catholics, 91
　religious freedoms, 113
　tax farming, 243
free riding, 25, 88, 118
Freedom House, 9
freedom of association, 24
Freedom Party, Netherlands, 116
freedoms, interactions among, 40–41
Freemasons, 128
French Revolution, 141
fuqarā. *See* poverty: Islamic definition

Gaddafi, Muammar, 280
Gates, Bill, 246
gedik, 239–40, 248
Germany, 49, 106, 176
Ghazali, 36, 125, 195, 226
Global Explorations, 39, 42
God's sovereignty, 187
Gökalp, Ziya, 92–93, 277
GONGO, 100–3
Google sheik, 188
Government Cleanliness Index, 12
government-organized nongovernmental organization. *See* GONGO
Great Britain, 91, 281
Great Schism. *See* Christianity: Great Schism
Greece, 159, 250
guild
　Middle East, 67, 239, 242, 277
　Western Europe, 16, 69
Gülen, Fethullah, 153
Gülenism, 153
Gülhane Edict, 4, 92, 136–37, 241, 246

habous, 48
hajj, 143
halal certificate, 263
halalization, 261

Hallaq, Wael, 186
Hama massacre, 143
Hanafi school of law, 124, 221
Hanbali school of law, 124, 221
Haydaris, 126
Hayek, Friedrich, 40, 207
Hebron, 262
heresy, 17–18, 91, 114, 204
hidden wealth, 221
Hinduism, 124, 183
ḥiyal. *See* Islamic law: ruses
Hizb ut-Tahrir, 144
Hungary, 177
Hus, Jan, 181
Hussein, Saddam, 156
Hussites, 181

Ibadism, 172
Iberia, 8
Ibn Abd al-Wahhab, Muhammad, 196
Ibn Hanbal, 124–25
Ibn Khaldun, 36–37
Ibn Rushd, 125
Ibn Saud, Muhammad, 196
Ibn Taymiyya, 36, 125, 195
icâreteyn. *See* waqf, Islamic: long-term lease
identity, 8, 22, 155, 260
ideology, 25, 134–35
ijtihād, 197
illiberal Islamic schism, 190
illiberal order, 24, 75
inaction, consequences, 39–40
independent Islamic reasoning, 197
India, 8, 27, 173, 272
Indonesia, 191, 202–3
Industrial Revolution, 20–21, 39, 42, 81, 89, 234, 236–37
in-group bias, 245
inheritance system, Islamic. *See* Islamic inheritance system
İnönü, İsmet, 18, 280
institution
　complementarity, 23, 40–41
　evolution, 21, 34, 281
　extractive, 30
　inclusive, 30–31
　Islamic, 34–35
　modernization, 87–88
　origins, 75
　stability, 32
institutional creativity, 39
intellectual creativity, 17, 36, 41, 80

Index

interest ban
  circumvention of, 82, 112
  effect on cash waqfs, 239
  effect on credit relations, 235
  ineffectiveness, 260–61
  measure to reduce enslavement, 22, 275
  Middle East, 245, 255, 261
  morality of, 264
  Western Europe, 245
interest ceiling, 245
Introduction to History, 36
iqta', 55
Iran
  Assembly of Experts, 193
  civic life, 48
  clerical hierarchy, 194
  crypto-Sunnism, 131
  Islamic Republic
    blasphemy charges, 17
    clerical resistance to Khomeini, 194
    constituency for liberalization, 209
    constitution, 193–94
    Council of Guardians, 193–94
    elections, 208
    hijab, 208
    Islamization, 193
    Islamization of knowledge project, 199
    regulation of Shiism, 194
    religiosity, 162
    secular institutions, 6, 120, 252
    Shii privileges, 194
    Shii seminaries, 193
    size of clergy, 193
    Supreme Leader, 193–94
    waqf, modern, 94, 96–97, 193
  Islamic Revolution, 4
  liberalization, 107
  Mongol invasion, 28
  out-marriage rate, 104
  Pahlavi dynasty
    autonomy of clergy, 194
    downfall, 4, 96, 149, 169
    exiling of Ruhollah Khomeini, 151
    opposition to, 29
    policies toward Islam, 18, 134, 200
    repression, 280
    sectarian discrimination, 251
    Westernization, 139
  pro-Shii discrimination, 252
  Qajar dynasty
    emulation of Europeans, 135
    European-style education, 135
    heterodox Islam, 134
    permanent embassies, 135
    waqf nationalizations, 93
    weakness of civil society, 66
  relations with Saudi Arabia, 172
  rights of non-Muslims, 158
  Safavid dynasty
    autocratic rule, 213
    Kizilbashs, 127
    rivalry with Ottoman Empire, 127
    state building, 186, 194
    tolerance of Hindus, 173
  secularization, 193
  Shii legal thought, 194
  Shii population, 191, 193
  Shiitization, 129, 194
  Sufism, 134
  Sunnism, 129
Iraq
  Baath rule
    addition of "God is Great" to flag, 156
    assertive secularism, 139, 143, 156
    policies toward Islam, 134, 200
  Mongol invasion, 28
  Ottoman resistance to Shiism, 134
  political parties, 173
  relations with Syria, 172
  Shii population, 193
  tax rates, Abbasid Caliphate, 218
irtidād. *See* apostasy
Isfahan, 61
Isfahan School, 80
Ishiks, 126
ISIS. *See* Islamic State of Iraq and the Levant
Islam. *See also* Islam, early
  alienation from, 208
  animal rights, 186
  apostasy, 114, 119, 124–28, 272
  attitudes toward Christianity, 39
  Australia, 174
  blasphemy, 114, 125
  boundedness of regulation, 115
  call to prayer, 185
  choice of law for non-Muslims, 141, 159, 240
  commercial institutions, 233–36
  compatibility with modernity, 138
  conservative, 115–16, 141
  constraints on government, 230
  crypto-conversion, 130
  dancing, 112
  declaration of faith, 116

Islam (cont.)
  disestablishment of, 134–35, 138–40
  diversity, 146, 172–74
  divisive issues, 182–89
  during modernization, 255
  entrepreneurship, 232–53
  Europe, 174
  extent of regulation, 115
  fallacies of political irrelevance, 280–83
  financial institutions, 233–36
  forced conversion, 130
  Friday service, 144
  gender norms, 182–84
  halal slaughter, 186
  heresy, 114, 125
  hidden, 146, 149
  in-conversion, 37, 116, 234
  institutional creativity, 33, 282–83
  institutional efficiency, 282–83
  instrument of state building, 186–87
  liberal
    activism, 199–203
    aversion to using force, 204, 273
    constraints on state, 207
    ideological handicaps, 204–6
    leading advocates, 196–99
    organizational capacity, 19, 191–210
    organizational handicaps, 208
    political handicaps, 206–8
    reaching audiences, 205
    religious tolerance, 134
  liberalization of, 283–84
  literalist, 125
  marginalization of, 133–46, 256–58
  marriage rules, 143
  Middle Eastern non-Muslims on, 157
  music, 112
  New Zealand, 174
  North America, 174
  obstacles to religious freedoms, 121–24
  out-conversion, 18, 37, 116–19, 207, 272
  pilgrimage to Mecca, 143
  pillars of, 19, 22, 138, 215
  polygyny, 150
  prayers, 185
  prayer-time alerts, 185
  pre-Islamic influences on, 28
  prohibitions, 260–62
  property rights, 218, 230
  puritanical, 125, 139–40, 195, 262
  reinterpretation of, 115, 119–21, 272
  ritual slaughter, 186
  sects, 146
  shallow governance, 213–31
  sincere practices of, 197
  size of state, 230
  source of legitimacy, 147
  South and Southeast Asia, 174
  spread of, 217
  stance on slavery, 229
  state building, 187
  state–clergy alliance, 207–8
  tolerance, 208
  traditional, 134
  way of life, 115, 269
  weaponization of, 187
  women's rights, 182–84
Islam and Modernity, 197
Islam and the Secular State, 197
Islam without Extremes, 197
Islam, early
  absence of secular sphere, 115
  booty, 215
  communal identity, 175
  composition of army, 122
  emergence, 123, 175
  equalization campaigns, 226
  erosion of fiscal constraints, 219
  establishment of Islamic state, 220
  Golden Age, 23, 119, 121, 195
  internal divisions, 225
  meaning of zakat, 222
  military recruitment, 58
  move from Mecca to Medina, 215
  openness to outside innovations, 255
  as paragon of brotherhood, 225
  poverty alleviation, 225–26
  pre-Islamic customs, 220
  religious freedoms, 36
  religious tolerance, 117
  slavery, 22
  social contract, 217
  social transformation, 220
  as syncretic Abrahamic sect, 175
  taxation, 118, 222
  time span, 8
  treasury, 215
  tribalism, 225
  universalism, 197
Islamic banking, 22
Islamic behavioral norms, 262
Islamic college. *See* madrasa
Islamic courts, 33, 245, 254, 277
Islamic credit card, 261, 271

Index

Islamic Dawa Party, Iraq, 143
Islamic economics, 258
Islamic education, 22, 29, 39, 62–63, 164
Islamic essentialism, 31
Islamic finance, 22, 131, 261, 263–65
Islamic freethinkers, 204
Islamic historicism, 197
Islamic inheritance system, 35, 37, 104, 144, 182, 184, 236–37, 279
Islamic institutional complex, 14, 22, 75, 218, 237, 250, 269, 276
Islamic Jihad, 195
Islamic law
  centrality, 31–32
  circumvention through ruses, 81–82, 244
  development, 8, 28
  economic limitations, 238
  exposure of Middle East to, 6
  incompatibility with separation of powers, 187
  in-marriage, 104
  innovations, 239
  interpretation, 205
  of sale, 115
  Persian influences, 27, 51–52, 54
  Roman influences, 27, 51–52, 54
  schools of, 171
  selective obedience to, 128
  of transactions, 271
Islamic rationalism, 197
Islamic reconstructionism, 197–98
Islamic resurgence, 170
Islamic revival, 170
Islamic State of Iraq and the Levant, 174, 180, 192, 195, 199, 204, 263
Islamic Studies, 63, 180
Islamic trust. *See* waqf
Islamism
  accommodation of modernity, 170, 255
  apolitical, 195
  as reaction to assertive secularism, 19
  assertive, 148
  business organizations, 253
  child marriage, 150
  cross-national demonstration effects, 154
  definition, 8
  economic agenda, 21–22, 253
  entry into formal politics, 151
  gender relations, 150
  hostility to secular Muslims, 151
  illiberalism, 265
  jihadi, 195

liberalization opportunities, 254–65
militant, 151
nihilistic, 148
origins of, 8, 27, 250, 258
passive, 148
prohibitions, 260–62
promotion of zakat, 231, 275
religious freedoms, 256
restoration of Islamic law, 150
rise to power, 148
selective Islamization, 255
spread, 151
Ismail I, 127
Ismail, Khedive, 136
Ismailism, 125, 193
Israel, 6, 159
Istanbul, 31, 37, 55, 57, 61, 93, 96, 135, 227, 239
istibdāl. *See* waqf: asset swap
Izmir, 96

Janissary Corps, 128
Jasmine Revolution, 195
Jerusalem, 83, 123, 175
Jesus, 122, 175, 203
jihad, 123
jihadism, 123, 195
Johnson, Noel, 42, 113
Johnson, Simon, 30
Joint Catholic–Orthodox Declaration, 178
joint-stock company, 238
Jordan, 168, 195
Judaism
  crypto-, 119
  during rise of Islam, 175
  East European schisms, 178
  kosher slaughter, 186
  Middle Eastern, 177
  modern schisms, 176–77
  Orthodox, 176, 178, 181, 189
  out-conversion, 38
  Reform, 19, 176, 178, 180–81, 189, 207
  schisms, 189
  separation from Christianity, 175
  Sephardi, 177
  traditional, 176
judge, Islamic, 50
Judgment Day, 121, 203, 229
Justice and Development Party. *See* AKP

Kaaba, 121, 123
ḳāḍī, 50

Kadızadeli repression, 37
Kahf, Monzer, 259
Kalendaris, 126
Karmatism, 125
Kasımpaşa, 73–74
Kâtip Çelebi, 80
Kavala, Osman, 253
Kemalism, 4, 200. *See also* Atatürk, Kemal
Khalvatis, 129
Khamenei, Ali, 193
Khan, Ayoub, 199
Khomeini, Ruhollah, 17, 149, 151, 193
Khuri, Fuad, 180
King Hussein Cancer Foundation, 262
Kitāb Aḥkām al-Awqāf, 55
Kizilbashs, 126–28
Klaveren, Joram van, 116
knowledge falsification, 36
knowledge, revealed, 69, 79
Koch, Charles and David, 246
Koyama, Mark, 42, 113, 176
Küçük, Harun, 62
Küçükural, Önder, 185
kufr. See Islam:blasphemy
Kuru, Ahmet, 207–8
Kuwait, 94, 168

law breaking, tolerated, 84
laws of association, Middle East, 99
Lebanon, 143, 157, 160, 199
legal personhood, 19, 65, 91, 94, 119, 239, 242, 271
Levant Company, 278
Lewis, Bernard, 158
liberal order
  in Arab world, 3
  definition, 23–27
  economic rights, 19
  in France, 2020s, 27
  Islam's compatibility with, 22
  pathways to, 42–43, 47–48, 275
  political participation, 64
  in Quran, 26
  roles of Islamic institutions in delaying, 22
  roles of nongovernmental organizations, 17
  separation of state and religion, 113
  skills for sustaining, 75
  taxation, 19, 220
  transparency, 64
  in United States, 27
  in Western Europe, 27
liberal state, 24, 26

liberalism, 25–26
liberalization
  absence in Middle East, 5
  effects of educational modernization, 29
  missed opportunities for, 35
  open dialogue, 190
  possibility in Islam, 187
  possibility in Middle East, 22–23, 168–70
  preemptive, 43
  roles of civil society, 49
  roles of corporation, 68
  roles of entrepreneurs, 233
  roles of middle class, 35
  roles of nongovernmental organizations, 75
  roles of secularization, 114
  roles of urbanization, 35
  spearheading by elites, 43
  through a cascade, 209
  Western Europe, 15, 68
Libya, 31, 280
limited-access order, 24
literacy rate, 264
Livny, Avital, 47, 98–99
London, 239
Long Divergence, 233, 237, 284
Luther, Martin, 114, 176, 191

madhab. See Islamic law: schools
madrasa
  curriculum, 69–70, 79–80, 276
  degrading by European colonizers, 63
  emergence of alternatives to, 277
  governance through waqf, 15, 70
  hindrance to creativity, 17
  inflexibility of, 70
  instructional shortcomings, 62–63, 133
  teaching of Americas, 79
  teaching of heliocentric theory, 79
Madrasa-yi Sultani, 70
Maliki school of law, 124–25, 221
Mamluk Sultanate, 52, 55, 119, 219, 227
Marcus, Abraham, 227–28
Maronites, 143
marriage, 104–5
mass production, 237
Mawardi, 219
Mawdudi, Abul-Ala, 258–59
Mecca, 117, 121, 123, 175
Mecelle, 257
media clerics, 188
medical school, 86
Medici family, 235

Index

Medina, 122
Mehmed Ali (Egypt), 256
Mehmet II, 52
Menemen incident, 144
merchant house, 249
merchants, Middle East
   contributions to civil society, 246–48
   handicaps vis-à-vis foreign competitors, 242
   lack of common forum, 244
   lack of organization, 242
   Muslims during modernization, 250–52
   paucity of historical records on, 244
   political weakness of, 42, 240–43
   prominence among jurists of early Islam, 241, 278
   reactions to Western innovations, 278
   roles in dismantling of waqfs, 279
Mesopotamian kingdoms, 216
Methodism, United States, 181–82
Middle East
   anti-secularism, 153
   atheism, 209
   banking, 235
   bill of trade, 235
   censorship, 166–67
   civic life, 33
   commerce, 232, 250–52
   conversion rights, 164
   cooptation of private enterprises, 252
   credit markets, 235–36
   crypto-conversions, 130
   definition, 5
   de-Islamization, 163
   discrimination against non-Muslims, 158
   economic reforms, 21
   entrepreneurship, 252–53
   existential crisis, 21, 35, 133, 214, 238, 241
   expressive freedoms, 166
   fatwa production, 130
   female political empowerment, 182
   freedom of the press, 166
   gender norms, 182–84
   government impartiality toward religion, 165
   government insolvency, 133
   government size, 213
   hidden irreligiosity, 167–68
   hidden religious dissent, 169
   institutional constraints, 201
   institutional stagnation, 236–40
   institutional transplant, 20
   interest, 245
   internal public borrowing, 218
   internet, 166, 188
   legal reforms, 42
   liberalization, 131, 283–84
   lifespans, 200
   literacy, 200
   marginalization of Islam, 133–46
   modernization, 133, 135, 200, 219, 256
   municipalities, 249
   Muslim minorities, 163
   nepotism, 47
   non-Muslims, 131
      conformist pressures within own communities, 157–60
      contributions to secularization, 248–50
      economic ascent of, 133, 135, 159, 240–41
      formal rights, 163
      perspectives on religious freedoms, 157–60
      political gains, 248
      subordinate status, 157
   organizational capacity, 40, 233, 236
   parliaments, 243
   partiality of states to Islam, 164
   political opportunism, 129–30
   political underdevelopment, 33–34
   refugees from Europe, 158
   religious discrimination, 241
   religious diversity, 128
   religious heterogeneity, 130
   religious homogenization, 162–63
   religious intolerance, modern, 166
   religious liberalization, 168–70
   religious preference falsification, 160–62
   rural–urban migration, 157
   secular commercial courts, 246
   secularization, 21, 52, 134, 141, 249
   social regulation of religion, 166
   state
      alliance with clergy, 134, 207–9
      capacity, 129, 224
      economic governance, 213
      religious biases, 207
   stock markets, 239
   urbanization, 200
   weakness of entrepreneurs, 208
   weakness of property rights, 51
   women's rights, 182–84
migration, 9
Military Academy attack, Egypt, 144
Minaret of Freedom Institute, 202
Ministry of Waqfs, Egypt, 93
Ministry of Waqfs, Ottoman, 93
Mir Damad, 80

Mirza Ghulam Ahmad, 172
Misr El-Kheir, 262
modern economic growth, 81
modernist orthodoxy, 134
Modernity Period, Middle East, 8
modernization, 86, 88, 247
Modernization Period, Middle East, 8
modernization, Middle East
  educational reforms, 254
  reinterpretation of Islam, 133
  revival of Muslim commerce, 250
  roles of state, 248
  time span, 8
  transplant of Western institutions, 39, 214, 254–55
moneylender, 249
Mongol invasion, 28–29
Mongols, 125
Monophysites, 122
Moor, Tine de, 43
Mormonism, 177
Morocco, 135
Morsi, Mohamed, 49, 196
mosque, 192, 242
mu'amalat, 115
mu'assasat, 96
Muawiya I, 121
Mubarak, Gamal, 105
Mubarak, Hosni, 4, 66, 101, 105, 152, 155, 280
Muhammad
  capital punishment under, 120
  in Christian sources, 123
  death, 18
  death of, 116
  descendants of, 127
  divisions among Muslims, 180
  governance style, 204
  as Islam's first interpreter, 198
  in Jewish sources, 123
  marriage of, 104
  Mecca period, 117
  Medina period, 117
  as peace maker, 224
  political mission, 121
  practices, 125
  profession, 232
  relations with Christians and Jews, 175
  successors of, 14
  words and deeds, 6
  youth, 28
mujtahid, 193, 205
Mulla Sadra, 80

mu'minūn, 122
municipality, 16, 31, 89–90, 249
Murat III, 79
music, 112
Muslim Brotherhood, Egypt
  during Arab Spring, 4
  branch of Islam, 180
  destruction of, 155
  emergence of, 192, 195–96, 199
  expansionist agenda, 196
  government formed by, 49, 153
  ideology, 149
  ouster from power, 155, 180
  political participation, 154
  resistance to monarchy, 152
  violence, 196
  zakat committees, 263
Muslim Brotherhood, Syria, 143
muslimūn, 122
Muslims. *See also* Sunnism, Shiism, other branches
  American, 198
  Arabic speakers, 185
  classification of, 179–80
  European, 198
  heterodox, 125, 273
  mental disabilities among, 186
  nonpracticing, 19, 198, 201, 273
  of diaspora, 201
mutawalli. *See* waqf: caretaker

Nablus Zakat Committee, 262
Nahdlatul Ulama
  civic activism, 202
  intolerance of Islamic heterodoxies, 203
  tolerance toward Christians, 202
  withdrawal from formal politics, 202
Napoleon I, 133
Naqshbandism, 129, 153
Narrow Corridor, 106
Nasser, Gamal Abdel
  assassination attempts on, 161
  control of Islam, 142
  dissolution of Muslim Brotherhood, 152
  expulsion of foreigners, 31
  illiberal opponents, 161
  persecution of Islamists, 18, 139, 151
  political enemies, 172
  subjugation of NGOs, 100
nepotism, 47, 50, 105
Netherlands, 116
New Testament, 114, 122

Index

new waqf. *See* waqf, modern
NGO. *See* nongovernmental organization
Nimatullahis, 129
Ninety-Five Theses, 176
nisāb. *See* zakat: exemptions
noblesse oblige, 229
nongovernmental organization
   Middle East, 16, 48, 97
   role in liberalization, 75
   under Islamic law, 15
   waqf as, 58–59, 74
North Africa, 6
North, Douglass, 23
Nurju movement, 153
Nursi, Said, 149, 151
Nusayrism. *See* Alawism

obscurantism, 18, 145, 170, 186, 264
observatory, Istanbul, 79
OIC. *See* Organization of Islamic Cooperation
oil, 9
Oman, 172
open society, 23
Open Society Foundation, 162
open-access order, 23
Oran, Ahmad, 225
order, 24
Organization of Islamic Cooperation, 6, 9, 120, 164, 171–72, 188, 195
Orthodoxy, Christian, 175, 178
Ottoman Empire
   apostasy, 126
   Armenians, 249–50
   autocratic rule, 213
   Bulgarians, 250
   Catholics, 91
   Christians, 91–92, 250
   courts, 119
   edicts against religious deviance, 126
   engineering school, 135
   fatwas against religious deviance, 126
   Freemasons, 128
   Grand Mufti, 126
   Greeks, 249–50
   heterodox Muslims, 126
   Islamization, 128
   Janissary Corps, 128
   Jews, 249
   Kizilbashs, 127
   legal pragmatism, 245
   Levantines, 249
   permanent embassies, 135
   privileges of foreign merchants, 119
   Protestants, 91
   provincial notables, 243
   reforms, 238
   religious equality before the law, 136
   religious homogenization, 126
   religious tolerance, 126
   rivalry with Safavid Iran, 127
   Serbs, 250
   Shiism, 126
   state building, 186
   Sunnitization, 127, 131
   tax farming, 242–43
   Turkification, 128
   urban reforms, 94
   waqfs, 52
Ottoman Public Debt Administration, 31
out-marriage rates, 104
overseas trade companies, 234

Pact of Umar, 159
Pahlavi, Mohammad Reza, 280
Pahlavi, Reza, 93, 142
Pakistan, 8, 198–99
Palestine, 6, 122, 216
Palestinian Territories, 262
partnership, Islamic
   early Islam, 232
   enforcement through courts, 234
   features, 57, 236–38
   longevity, 20, 236
   political weakness, 242
   premature dissolution, 20
   size, 20
   termination at will, 274
Peace of Westphalia, 189
People of the Book, 122
periodizations, 8
Persepolis, 216
piety signaling, 149
pilgrimage to Mecca, 215
pious endowment. *See* waqf, Islamic
political decentralization, 22
political liberalization, 13
political participation, 98
politics, participatory, 67
polygyny, 125, 143, 150, 237
polytheism, 123, 272
Popper, Karl, 23
poverty
   elimination campaigns, 228
   Islamic definition, 226, 228

poverty (cont.)
  policies to limit, 22, 229
  unalterability, 227
  visibility, 228
preference falsification
  diffusion across contexts, 36
  on Islamic finance, 264
  political, 99
  religious
    in both directions, 156
    commonness, 160–62
    definition, 130
    effects on private religious preferences, 170
    evidence from World Values Survey, 167–68
    induced by assertive secularists, 151
    induced by obscurantists, 145
    reversal of direction, 147–48, 154
Premodernity Period, Middle East, 8
printing press, 135, 176
professional organizations, 242, 246, 252
property rights
  indigenous roots in Middle East, 214
  of Middle Eastern non-Muslims, 248
  strengthening of, 22, 31, 33, 91
  waqf's effects on, 227
  weakness of, 51, 55
Protestant Reformation, 39, 114, 141, 175–76, 178, 191
Protestantism, 181
Protocol of Reconciliation and Grace through Separation, 182
public goods, 22

Qatar, 168, 172
Qom, 194
Quran
  ambiguities on zakat duty, 221–22, 224
  as constitution, 6
  atheism, 121
  Believers, 122
  canonical compilation, 117, 218
  chapters from Muhammad's Medina years, 220
  chronology, 117
  constraints on predation, 218
  emergence of chapters, 123
  fiscal nomenclature, 222
  fiscal requirements, 218
  freedom of conscience, 123
  gender differences in rights, 182
  government predation, 230
  inconsistencies, 218

  individual rights, 120, 183
  inheritance, 182
  interpretation, 18, 111–13, 197
  liberalism in, 26, 114
  limited government, 230
  marriage, 104
  mentions of zakat, 215
  Muslims, 122
  mutual consent, 14
  out-conversion, 117, 123
  paganism, 124
  polytheism, 121
  punishments, 121
  recitation language, 185
  religious freedoms, 204
  riba ban, 235
  role in state building, 34
  slavery, 124, 229
  subcommunities, 120
  taxation, 19, 217, 220
  terminological ambiguities, 220
  tribalism, 119
  unbelievers, 117
  verses considered obsolete, 119
  wealth accumulation, 222
  wine, 173
Quran school, 148
Qutb, Sayyid, 151, 258

Rabaa al-Adawiya Medical Center, 262
Rafizis, 126
Rahman, Fazlur, 197–99
Ramadan
  Alevi rejection of fasting requirement, 185
  effects of fasting on happiness, 185
  exposure of children to, 215
  fasting during pregnancy, 185
  health effects of fasting, 140, 185, 206
  poor relief during, 227
  restaurant hours in, 149
  rise in Islam's salience, 143
  secularist disapproval of fasting, 154
  share of Turks fasting during, 162
  social regulation of fasting, 166
Rashid, Salim, 225
Rastakhiz, 93, 138
Red Crescent, Ottoman Empire, 94
Red Crescent, Turkey, 100, 262
redistribution in large societies, 225
reform cascade, 23
Reform Edict, Ottoman Empire, 4
refugee, 9

Index

religion
  classification, 174, 179
  definition, 174, 179–80
  exit from, 26
  legitimator of inequalities, 33
  role in establishing rule of law, 33
Religious Affairs Directorate, Turkey
  as instrument of assertive secularism, 155
  as instrument of Islamism, 161
  as voice of Turkish Sunnism, 180, 188
  beginnings, 161
  budget, 164
  religious discrimination against Alevis, 158
religious community, 180
religious compulsion, 26
religious diversification, 171–89
religious freedom. *See also* religious repression
  definitions, 206
  for nonpracticing Muslims, 157
  in early Islam, 36
  instrumentalized, 128–31
  modern Middle East, 156, 163–67, 256
  pathways to, 114, 131
  premodern Middle East, 111–32
  role in liberal order, 36
  transformation under Islamists, 148
  Western Europe, 113
religious opinion. *See* fatwa
religious order, Western Europe, 16
religious preference falsification. *See* preference falsification:religious
religious regulation, 164
religious repression. *See also* religious freedom
  comparative history, 113–16
  international comparisons, 148
  by Islamists, 148
  justifications for, 145
  persistence in Middle East, 271–74
  by secularists, 272
  as source of institutional persistence, 278
  as source of self-censorship, 36
religious sciences, 70
religious toleration, 34, 42
remembrances of Muhammad's words and deeds. *See* Sunna
Reopening Muslim Minds, 197
return of Islam, 170
riba, 112, 235, 264, 275
ridda. *See* apostasy
riot, 66
Robinson, James, 27, 30, 106
Roman Empire, 216

Rubin, Jared, 68
rule of law, 33, 218
Rulers, Religion, and Riches, 68
Rumi, 201
Rumi's Circle, 202
Rushdie, Salman, 17
Russia, 133, 195, 240

sadaqa, 220, 222
Sadat, Anwar, 144, 152, 155
Saddam Institute for the Study of the Holy Quran, 156
Saeed, Abdullah, 121
Saeed, Hassan, 121
Salafism, 196
Salonica, 227
sarraf, 249
Satanic Verses, 17
Saudi Arabia. *See also* Arabia
  apostasy, 206
  constitution, 6
  economic secularization, 252
  falling religiosity, 162
  fatwas, 187
  founding of, 196
  House of Saud's alliance with Wahhabis, 196
  legitimation through Wahhabism, 139
  pro-Sunni discrimination, 252
  relations with Egypt, 172
  relations with Iran, 172
  religious instruction in, 139
  religious police in, 160
  secularization of daily life, 140
  treatment of foreign Muslims, 120
  virginity restoration, 188
  women's rights, 9
  zakat collection, 257
Saudi Supreme Council of the Judiciary, 187
scaling up, organizational, 35
schism
  Abrahamic religions, 174–78, 207
  cost of founding new community, 181
  definition, 19, 174–75, 177–78
  division of assets, 181
  duration, 178
  Islam
    division of assets, 192
    illiberal, 190, 195–96, 204
    liberal, 191–210, 273
    possibilities, 17–19, 189, 194–95
  liberal, 19
  organizational determinants, 180–82

schism (cont.)
  political economy of, 178–79
  Sunni Islam, 192
sect, 174, 180
secularism
  assertive, 140–41
  authoritarian, 253
  libertarian, 141
  mild, 253
  nihilistic, 140
  passive, 140
  resistance to, 148–53
  Western variants, 140
secularization, 18–19, 41, 114
self-enforcing equilibrium. *See* equilibrium, self-enforcing
self-serving bias, 26
self-undermining equilibrium. *See* equilibrium, self-undermining
Selim I, 126–27
Sened-i İttifak, 243
Şentürk, Recep, 185
Şeyh Said rebellion, 161
şeyhülislam. *See* Ottoman Empire: Grand Mufti
Shafii, 124–25, 224
Shafii school of law, 124, 221
shahada, 116
Sharia. *See* Islamic law
Shiism
  apostasy, 124
  centralization, 191
  conduciveness to splintering, 191
  disapproval of first three caliphs, 126
  Ismaili, 125
  legal thought, 194
  number of adherents, 171
  organization of, 193–94
  theocracy as innovation, 194
  Twelver, 127, 163, 193, 221
shirk. *See* polytheism, blasphemy
shura, 14, 28, 112
Sisi, Abdel Fattah, 153, 155, 163
Sivas, 66
slavery, 229, 235
slutty hijab, 208
Smith, Adam, 37, 192
social capital, 75, 100
social desirability bias, 98
social solidarity, 96
Soros, George, 246
Soroush, Abdul-Karim, 197, 199
Spain, Umayyad, 219

Spanish Inquisition, 119
Stasavage, David, 217
state
  building, 186–87
  capacity, 42
  contributions to modernization, 251
  despotic, 24
  legitimation, 209
  shackled, 22
  shallow, 213–31
  unshackled, 230–31
stock market, 91–92, 239
Suez Canal, 136
Sufi Order International, 202
Sufism, 70, 112, 129, 134, 171, 200–1, 272
suftaja, 235
Suharto, 203
Suhrawardi, 125
Suleiman, Abdel Karim, 17
Süleyman II, 56, 79, 127
Süleymaniye Complex, 55
Sunna, 6, 55, 70, 112, 204
Sunni–Shii schism, 14, 19, 171, 273
Sunnism
  apostasy, 124
  Egyptian, 180
  formal religious diversity, 192
  impoverished religious life, 192
  lack of autonomy, 191
  liturgy reforms, 185
  number of adherents, 171
  organization of, 191–93
  orthodoxy, 125, 163
  regulation of mosques, 192
  schism, 192
  state regulation, 192
  Turkish, 180
  violent sects, 196
super-companies, 234
Sykes–Picot agreement, 281
Syria, 199
  Baath rule
    assertive secularism, 139, 143, 156
    policies toward Islam, 134, 200
  early Islam, 122
  military defeats, 133
  Mongol invasion, 28
  Ottoman period, 52, 134
  policies toward Islam, 164
  power sharing following Ottoman rule, 29
  relations with Iraq, 172
  zakat collection under Ayyubids, 219

Index

takāful, 96
Talbi, Mohamed, 141, 197
Taliban, 174
Tanzimat, 136–37, 256
tax evasion, 129
tax farming, 79, 242–43
taxation
   arbitrary, 19–20, 215, 217–18, 231
   formal, 117
   limited, 20
   modernization of, 31
   new forms, 217, 257
   optimal, 216
   predictable, 20, 31, 214
   pre-Islamic, 219
Thirty Years' War (Europe), 178
Tocqueville, Alexis De, 270
tolerance, religious, 38
Tollison, Robert, 178
Torah, 114, 122
Transparency International, 12
Trinity, 122
Trust and the Islamic Advantage, 98
trust in strangers
   Middle East
      determinants of, 47
      effects of civil society on, 47–48, 103
      effects of Islamic finance on, 264
      as reflected in in-marriage, 103–5
trust, European, 70
trust, Islamic. *See* waqf, Islamic
Tunis, 3, 142, 177
Tunisia. *See also* Bourguiba, Habib
   assertive secularism, 18, 134, 139, 155–56, 164, 200
   belief in God, 168
   Chelbi incident, 150
   democratization, 4
   European settlers, 31
   Islamist violence, 161
   persecution of Islamists, 280
   piety signaling, 156
   political parties, 172
   religious preference falsification, 156
   rise of Islamism, 195
   separation of mosque and state, 141, 156
   Western influences on, 139
Turkey
   abrogation of Caliphate, 139, 142, 191
   Alevis, 158, 171
   assertive secularism, 134, 139, 143, 154–55, 164

atheism, 162
banishment of Said Nursi, 151
brotherhoods, 152, 154
charitable organizations, 100
civic life, 48, 101, 162
conglomerates, 253
conservative electoral successes, 154
deism, 162
democracy, 5, 153–54
expansion of Islam's role, 153
falling religiosity, 208
fatwas, 155
headscarf ban, 154
inclusion in Middle East, 6
individual-to-individual giving, 103
Islamic reconstructionists, 198
Islamists, 253
Islamization of daily life, 154
liberalization, 107
modern waqf, 94
modernization, 6
Mongol invasion, 28
mosque attendance, 162
multiparty competition, 152
NGOs, 152
non-Muslims, 31, 251
one-man rule, 9
opinions on Islamic rituals, 185
organized philanthropy, 101
out-marriage rate, 104
persecution of Islamists, 280
piety signaling, 154
political participation, 101
political parties, 172
political rights of non-Muslims, 158
population exchange with Greece, 159
Quran schools, 148
religious associations, 152
religious preference falsification, 154
sectarian cleansing of Christians, 159
secularism, 200
share of population fasting, 162
show trials of AKP years, 153
Sunni Islamic liturgy, 185
teaching of Islam, 142
trust, 47
veiling, 154
War of Independence, 29
wealth tax, 159–60, 251
Westernization, 139
witch hunt against Gülenists, 153

428   *Index*

Turkish Aviation Society, 100, 262
Twelver Shiism. *See* Shiism: Twelver

'ulamā'. *See* cleric, Islamic
Umar I, caliph, 14, 28, 116
Umayyad Caliphate, 14, 28, 54, 121, 123, 213, 219, 222
umma, 21
unintended consequence, 36–37
Union of Utrecht, 114
unions, 277
United Arab Emirates, 94
United Nations Convention Against Torture and Other Cruel, Inhuman, and Degrading Treatment or Punishment, 194
United Nations Covenant on Civil and Political Rights, 206
United States
  charitable corporation sector, 87
  checks and balances, 40
  colonial religious freedoms, 113–14
  Declaration of Independence, 114
  division of powers, 281
  impact on Middle East, 30, 281
  meaning of liberalism, 26
  schisms, 207
  secularism, 140
  support for censorship, 27
  war on jihadism, 195
United Way, 87
university
  corporate status, 69
  curriculum, 69–70
  flexibility, 70
  governance, 70
  medieval, 15
  role in European liberalization, 16
University of Tunis, 142
Unveiling Decree, 142, 148
urbanization, 69
USSR, 195
Uthman, caliph, 14, 221, 224, 226
Uyghurs, 188

veiling, 149, 170, 184, 208
Venice, 232, 243
Verba, Sidney, 100

Wahhabism, 139–40, 171, 180, 195–96
Wallis, John, 23
waqf, Islamic
  asset swap, 81, 83
  as apolitical organization, 72

autonomy, 33
beneficiaries, 63, 66–68
benefits to clerics, 226
benefits to poor, 226
caretaker, 15, 51, 54, 58, 64–66, 73–74
cash, 56, 238–39, 245, 248
charitable, 58, 67
circumvention of legal requirements, 81–84
classic, 56
coalition, 71–74
as constraint on state, 15
corruption, 65, 77–88, 244
court supervision, 78
deed, 50–51, 64–65, 72, 74, 83
definition, 15, 50
demise, 83–84
economic significance, 52–54, 68
educational, 17
effects on civic life, 15–16, 50, 66, 84–85, 89–108
effects on state's fiscal capacity, 60
emergence, 20
employees, 59
expropriation of, 15, 31, 51
family, 58
founder, 56–58, 74, 248
functions, 51, 59
harms to commerce, 237, 279
hospitals founded as, 85–86
immovability of assets, 56, 239
inalienability, 51
inefficiency, 63, 75–77
inflexibility, 16, 35, 57, 61–64, 70, 77, 79–81, 240
instrument of illiberalism, 75
lack of managerial transparency, 64
long-run effects, 41, 89–108
long-term lease, 82–84
managerial discretion, 62, 64
merger, 72–73
modification, 63, 81–84
motives for founding, 41
nationalizations, 52, 84, 90, 93, 133, 135
obstacle to civic engagement, 60
obstacle to liberalization, 35
origins of political features, 54–58
perpetuity, 50, 66
Persian and Roman origins, 54
political community, 65, 85
political identity, 74
political legacies, 270–71
political participation, 15, 50, 64–67
political weakness, 60–76

precursors, 75
privatizations, 52, 83–84, 133, 135, 280
promoter of nepotism, 50
reform of, 85, 90–93
regular, 55, 78, 83
repairs, 74, 82
resource use, 72
sacredness of assets, 15, 51–52, 90
as social contract, 226
as source of political stability, 67–68, 73
as substitute for zakat, 226–27
source of ruler's legitimacy, 84
speed of decision making, 71
state, 55, 63, 78
suppression of social capital, 75–76
trend of new foundings, 91–92
typology, 55–56
unmentioned in Quran, 54, 93
as vehicle for circumventing inheritance rules, 237
as wealth shelter, 20, 51, 55, 58, 67, 227, 237, 275
waqf, modern
accountability, 97
as charitable corporation, 50, 56
board of trustees, 94
charter, 95
contributions to civil society, 15–17, 271
emergence, 94–97, 107
flexibility, 95
founders, 94
funding, 94
legal personhood, 94
organizational features, 16
participation in politics, 94
Waqfeyat Al-Maadi Community Foundation, 96
waqfiyya. *See* waqf: deed
Wars of Religion, Europe, 158
Wealth of Nations, 37
Weingast, Barry, 23
What Is Islam?, 173
wilayat-i faqih, 193
wine, 173
witch hunt, 125
World Alliance for Citizen Participation, 101
World Bank Rule of Law Index, 12
World Council of Churches, 171
World Economic Forum, 182
World Values Survey
data on mosque attendance in Turkey, 162
question on belief in God, 167
question on religiosity, 167
question on trust in strangers, 47

World War I, 99
writing between the lines, 205

Yemen, 168
YouTube scholar, 188

ẓāhir, 221
Zaidism, 193
zakat
as alternative to waqf, 226–27
ambiguities in meaning, 220
as annual tax, 117, 218
beneficiaries, 20, 218
benefits to poor, 20
as charity, 117, 214, 217, 222
conflicts over rules, 224
as constraint on government, 216
core principles, 223
corruption, 225, 263
decentralized transfers, 228
disappearance from policy discussions, 223
disbursements, 220, 223–25
dismantling of, 20, 217, 221–23
dues, 20, 215, 221, 262
enforcement in Saudi Arabia, 257
evasion, 217, 219, 226
as evidence of religious loyalty, 18
evolution of meaning, 222
exemptions, 215–17, 259
financing of state, 118
functions, 19–20, 215, 275
as income tax, 221
instrument of freeing slaves, 229
as instrument of status protection, 224
interpretations, 218
invisibility to historians, 223
as key economic element of Islamic law, 219
lack of intertemporal concerns, 224
as legitimation instrument, 229
loss of significance, 17–19, 35, 38, 219, 223, 231, 275
as means of consumption smoothing, 224
mentions in Quran, 215
modern practices, 262–63
modern scholarship on, 221
monitoring effects of, 228
obligatory, 218, 220–21
organized challenges to, 220
as a pillar of Islam, 215, 230
pre-Islamic origins, 215, 228
progressivity, 216–17, 225
purification instrument, 227–29
rates, 216, 222, 259

zakat (cont.)
　as redistribution instrument, 224, 258–59
　relation to sadaqa, 220
　relations to sadaqa, 222
　relevance to Middle East's reforms, 257
　relevance to modern economic life, 22
　resentment among payers, 220
　revival of, 255, 258–60
　sacredness of revised rules, 217, 222
　as social contract, 216, 229
　source of predictable taxation, 214
　source of property rights, 33
　as source of Muslim identity, 260
　state capacity, 216
　as symbol of Islamic revival, 260
　support for Palestinians, 263
　as vehicle for overcoming envy, 229
　virtues claimed by Islamists, 258
　visibility of beneficiaries, 228
　voluntary, 218, 258
　as wealth tax, 221
zakat al-fitr, 227
zakūt, 228
zandaqa, 125
Zaytouna Madrasa, 142
Zaytuna College, 202